EUROPE AFTER THE CONGRESS OF VIENNA
Boundary of the German Confederation
0
400
Miles
Bergen
Edinburgh
UNITED KINGDOM
OF GREAT BRITAIN AND IRELAND
Dublin
North Sea
London
Thames R.
Amsterdam
K. OF THE UNITED
NETHERLANDS
K.
Brussels
Cologne
Rhine
Frankfort
ATLANTIC
OCEAN
Paris
Seine R.
Strasbourg
Orleans
KINGDOM OF
FRANCE
Loire R.
Saône R.
Berne
SWITZ.
Geneva
Lyon
Bordeaux
Rhône R.
Milan
Turin
Po
Toulouse
Avignon
Marseilles
Oporto
Douro R.
KINGDOM
Ebro R.
K. OF PORTUGAL
Madrid
OF
Lisbon
Tagus R.
Barcelona
KINGDOM OF
SARDINIA
CORSICA
SPAIN
Valencia
Seville
Guadalquivir R.
BALEARIC IS.
Granada

Gulf of Bothnia
FINLAND
(To Russia)
L. Ladoga
St. Petersburg
Gulf of Finland
Volga R.
KINGDOM OF NORWAY AND SWEDEN
Stockholm
Moscow
Riga
W. Dvina R.
RUSSIAN
EMPIRE
Baltic Sea
HLESWIG
Copenhagen
ENMARK
Vilna
Königsberg
Danzig
OLSTEIN
Hamburg
ANOVER
PRUSSIA
Berlin
Posen
Vistula R.
Warsaw
KINGDOM OF POLAND
(To Russia)
Kharkov
Kiev
Elbe R.
Leipzig
SAXONY
UKRAINE
Dnieper R.
CRACOW
GALICIA
Prague
BOHEMIA
EMPIRE
BAVARIA
AUSTRIA
Danube R.
BESSARABIA
Munich
Vienna
Budapest
OF THE
Theise R.
MOLDAVIA
Odessa
CRIMEA
Salzburg
HUNGARY
HAPSBURGS
TYROL
Drave R.
Save R.
LOMBARDY-VENETIA
Trieste
SLAVONIA
BANAT
WALLACHIA
Bucharest
Venice
CROATIA
Black Sea
Ferrara
Belgrade
Danube R.
MODENA
BOSNIA
SERBIA
LUCCA
Florence
Sofia
USCANY
PAPAL STATES
MONTENEGRO
OTTOMAN
Adrianople
Constantinople
Düna
Rome
Salonika
Naples
EMPIRE
KINGDOM OF THE TWO SICILIES
IONIAN IS.
(To Britain)
Athens
Palermo
CRETE
MALTA
(To Britain)
Mediterranean Sea

SECOND EDITION

THE EUROPEAN WORLD SINCE 1815

TRIUMPH AND TRANSITION

SECOND EDITION

THE EUROPEAN WORLD SINCE 1815

TRIUMPH AND TRANSITION

JEROME BLUM *Princeton University*
RONDO CAMERON *Emory University*
THOMAS G. BARNES *University of California, Berkeley*

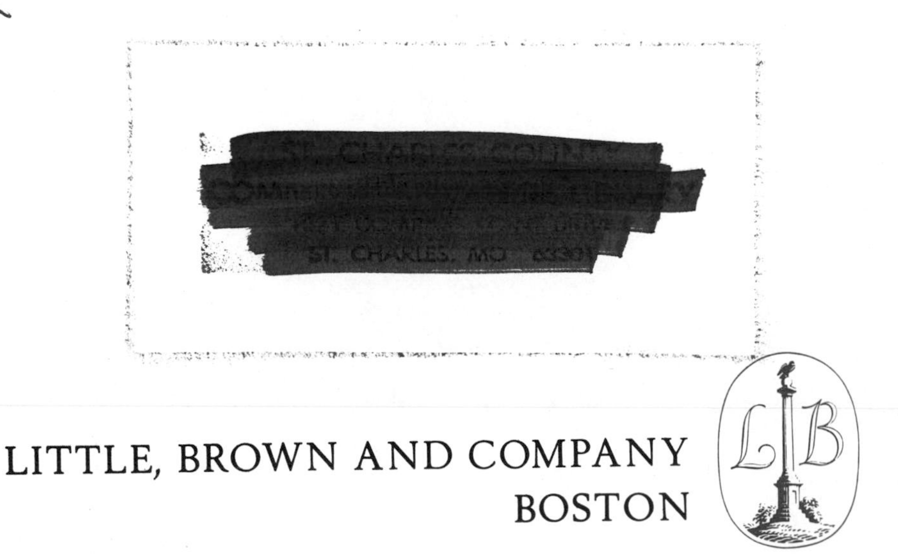

LITTLE, BROWN AND COMPANY
BOSTON

For Alan and Cindia

Maps by Robert C. Forget

LIBRARY OF CONGRESS CATALOG CARD NUMBER 73-81162

A

Published simultaneously in Canada by Little, Brown & Company (Canada) Limited

PRINTED IN THE UNITED STATES OF AMERICA

PREFACE

This book traces the history of the European world since the early nineteenth century, when Europe had just emerged from a period of war and revolution that challenged and transformed many of the traditional values and institutions of European society and civilization. It tells of the ascendancy held by Europe in nearly every sphere of human activity, of how Europeans used and misused that ascendancy, of how they came to share it with non-Europeans, and of how the intermixture in our own time of European, or Western, civilization with non-Western civilizations and cultures is producing a new, global civilization.

We owe many acknowledgments for help that we have received in the writing of this book; so many, indeed, that we cannot name them all. A complete listing would have to begin with the teachers who introduced us to the study of history, would include the many historians whose works we have used, and would end with the students in the classes that we ourselves have taught and who did much to shape our conception of the kind of book we wanted to write. The first edition benefitted from the comments and suggestions of Professors William J. Bouwsma, University of California, Berkeley; Roderic H. Davison, George Washington University; Charles F. Delzell, Vanderbilt University; the late Klaus Epstein, Brown University; Franklin L. Ford, Harvard University; Leonard Krieger, University of Chicago; George L. Mosse, the late Robert L. Reynolds, and Philip D. Curtin, all of the University of Wisconsin; Herbert H. Rowen, Rutgers University; Robert Lindsay, Ohio University; James Sturm, Richmond College of the City University of New York; and Reese Jenkins, Case Western Reserve University.

In this revised edition we have been able to incorporate numerous suggestions made by users of the first edition. We are particularly grateful to the scores of anonymous (to us) college and university professors who filled out a long questionnaire based on their experience with the first edition; we only hope the improvements they suggested will merit their continued use of the new edition. Finally, we wish express again our indebtedness to the editorial staff of the publisher, and especially to Charles Christensen and Miss Lynne S. Marcus.

J.B.
R.C.
T.G.B.

CONTENTS

List of Maps and Charts

List of Illustrations

THE ORIGINS OF THE EUROPEAN WORLD
INTRODUCTION

Europe is the smallest of the five major continents, contains less than 10 per cent of the world's land area and about 20 per cent of the world's population. In quantitative terms Europe may appear of slight importance in our global age.

The "European world," however, is more than a matter of numbers and geography. It is a concept of civilization. It includes European culture in the Western Hemisphere and also outposts of European culture in Asia, Africa, and Australasia. The history of the European world, in short, is the history of Western civilization.

As a distinctly human attribute culture is as old as man himself, but the earliest civilizations for which we have evidence apparently originated in the fourth or fifth millennium before Christ, in association with the development of settled agriculture and the domestication of animals. This occurred first in western Asia, perhaps along the "fertile crescent," the semicircle stretching from Egypt to the Anatolian highlands and down the Tigris and Euphrates valleys to the Persian Gulf. The early civilizations of Babylonia, Egypt, and probably that of the Indus valley in India, were offshoots of this "cradle of civilization." The only other known civilizations with definitely independent origins were those of the pre-Columbian inhabitants of America that evolved in the first millennium after Christ, although the origins of Chinese civilization (second or third millennium B.C.) may have been mostly independent of the original center in western Asia. All other civilizations were, in some measure, derived from these first civilizations.

As a social phenomenon, civilization grows and is transmitted by means of social processes. The growth of civilization is essentially the proliferation and elaboration of all the elements of which civilization is composed. New elements enter the stream by means of chance discovery, and even more by novel combinations of existing elements. These discoveries or new combinations are usually the result of social interaction, as is the transmission of civilization from one generation to another.

The diffusion of civilization is also the result of social interaction, especially through trade, conquest, and mass migration. The confrontation of a relatively primitive society by an advanced or "civilized" society usually results in at least a partial adoption by the former of the civilization of the latter. If, however, the civilized society is feeble it may succumb and its civilization may expire. A civilization is seldom completely obliterated; some of its elements are incorporated into the culture of the more primitive society and help bring about the evolution of a new civilization.

In a very real sense all civilization is a single entity, the civilization of man. But civilization is in a constant state of change and is never quite the same from place to place or at successive points in time, so that it is customary to speak of "civilizations" as well as "civilization." European, or Western, civilization originated from the fusion of German ("Barbarian") culture and Roman civilization during the so-called Dark Ages from the fifth to the tenth century A.D. Roman civilization, in turn, was descended from the earliest civilizations of western Asia and Egypt by way of the Greeks. Since the process of civilization is cumulative, each of these predecessors contributed important elements to the European heritage. Greece and Rome provided the European world with its richest patrimonies. The philosophies and the literature of ancient Greece established a hold on European man's sensibilities unmatched by any other cultural influence save the Christian religious tradition, itself born in the Greco-Roman world. From Rome there descended to the European world the material vestiges of Roman technological skill in roads, aqueducts, and buildings, the pervasive Latin of medieval western Europe, and the legacy of Roman law and the imperial ideal.

From the beginning of their civilization Europeans have been aggressive and expansionist, conquering, colonizing, trading, proselytizing, and ultimately spreading their culture to every part of the world. Initially this cultural expansion owed much to the vigorous propagation of the Christian faith. Christianization gave to the European world a unity and cultural cohesiveness that was the ideological foundation of its civilization. The first phase of expansion reached its apogee in the period from the beginning of the tenth to the beginning of the fourteenth century. During those centuries European culture spread from its initial centers between the Loire and the Rhine rivers in present-day northern France, Belgium, and western Germany throughout the continent, from Spain to Scandinavia, from Iceland to southern Italy, from England to Russia, and even briefly, during the Crusades, to Palestine. The central political fact of European expansion in this early phase was the system of interdependence called feudalism, which knitted diverse and often discordant petty political entities into a defensive posture sufficiently strong to preserve internal order and to withstand threats from without. Economic growth was part of the expansion, and the twelfth and thirteenth centuries witnessed the crest of a wave of material prosperity of the European world with burgeoning towns and cities as the centers of trade.

THE EXPANSION OF THE EUROPEAN WORLD, 1350–1660

In the fourteenth century Europe entered an era of crisis and contraction that lasted more than a hundred years. Recurrent epidemics decimated the population, and the economy of much of Europe declined. Civil wars among ruling cliques of feudal lords and petty princes proved the beginning of the end of the old political structure; feudalism, which in preceding centuries had been the bulwark of internal order, had become the greatest threat to order. Mass insurrections of discontented peasants and urban workers broke out in every part of Europe. Civil commotion was joined by a grass-roots protest against the increasing materialism and decreasing spirituality of the Roman Catholic Church. The papacy, at the pinnacle of its power in the twelfth and thirteenth centuries, now reached the low ebb of its fortunes, and the pope himself for a time became a tool of the French king.

Revival was stimulated by emerging national monarchies, by a new wave of economic expansion, including overseas expansion and colonization, and by a revitalization of European intellectual life. At the expense of the political power of the old aristocracy, kings succeeded in the fifteenth and sixteenth centuries in fashioning nation-states, challenging the interference of both church and local lords in internal affairs and each other in state rivalries that produced wars. The emergent nation-states of Spain, France, and England dominated the international scene of sixteenth- and seventeenth-century Europe. Economic revival, accompanied by increasing population, began in the latter part of the fifteenth century. Commerce and industry expanded as gold and silver poured into Europe from the mines of the Spanish New World, and a worldwide pattern of trade with Europe as its center began to emerge. Starting in the fourteenth century in the Italian city-states, the intellectual and artistic revival of the Renaissance spread to northwestern Europe in the fifteenth and sixteenth centuries and touched every institution and facet of contemporary Europe. It was much more than a new conception of man, a revival of classical learning, and an artistic flowering without parallel in history; it was the expression of a confident civilization prepared for change and demanding expansion.

The confidence of the European world as it broadened its horizons found new outlets beyond the frontiers of Europe. Bold and skillful navigators journeyed to distant, uncharted seas. Their discoveries, followed by colonization and exploitation in the Americas, India, and the East Indies, gave a stake in the greater, once unknown, world to the maritime states of the Atlantic seaboard of Europe and confirmed the shift in the focal point of the European world from the Mediterranean to western Europe.

The unified Christian faith of western Europe raised on the rock of St. Peter, the papacy, fell victim to the new confidence. Beginning with Martin Luther's challenge in 1517 to abuses long evident in the Roman Catholic Church, the Protestant Reformation soon became a revolt against ecclesiastical authority, producing theological variety and denominational atomism and ultimately assuring the triumph of secularism. The key to the success of the Protestant reformers lay in the leverage that their revolt presented to secular rulers for aggrandizement of their power and property. The net gain of the age of the Reformation went to the rulers of the emerging nation-states, whether Protestant or Catholic, who were already fashioning the absolutism that would dominate the European world from the mid-seventeenth to the end of the eighteenth century.

In perhaps the supreme achievement of the epoch, European man evolved a new way of looking at himself, the world, and the universe. Secularism and individualism produced new patterns of thought that made possible new approaches to old problems. Above all, a great outburst of scientific speculation in the sixteenth and early seventeenth centuries heralded the beginning of the revolution in science that is still not ended.

The attainments of the European world during this great age of expansion have about them the aura of modernity. So, too, has the sense of crisis that dominated the first six decades of the seventeenth century. A series of destructive wars, compounded of religious motives and dynastic ambitions, filled most of that period and brought in its wake civil commotion and revolution. The Thirty Years' War, that raged over most of central Europe between 1618 and 1648, involved directly or tangentially all of the principal European powers and most of the lesser states; it also played a part in stirring revolts against monarchic authority in Spain, France, Portugal, the Netherlands, and Naples, and coincided with rebellions in England, Scotland, and Russia. The simple confidence of the Renaissance and the spiritual exhilaration of the Reformation evaporated. The beneficiaries were the new absolutist monarchs under whose rule order was once more regained.

ABSOLUTISM AND ENLIGHTENMENT, 1660–1815

The period from the mid-seventeenth to the early nineteenth century was one of the great transitional epochs in human history. Scientific breakthroughs made by men of immense creativity in the later seventeenth century established firmly the mechanistic interpretation of the physical universe. They also provided a foundation for the Enlightenment of the eighteenth century with its belief in the power of reason to uncover universal natural laws that govern social behavior, just as the great natural scientists had found out the laws that govern physical matter. Transformations in economic life increased man's efficiency in the production of goods, manufactured and grown, launching the European world on industrial and agricultural expansion that soon took on revolutionary proportions. During this epoch the political framework of our own times was established by the final triumph of the secular nation-state. The religious struggle that had kept Europe in turmoil for more than a century ended with the Peace of Westphalia (1648), which terminated the Thirty Years' War, and with it went the last hopes for a united Western Christendom. Religious disputes continued to disturb the internal peace of some countries and to affect relationships between nations, but religion no longer exercised the influence it once had in European affairs.

By 1660 the absolutist solution to the problem of government had largely triumphed in continental Europe. The personal rule of Louis XIV of France (1643–1715) brought absolutism in that country to its pinnacle, provided it with enough momentum to last three-quarters of a cenutry after his death, and spawned imitators all over Europe. Russia emerged as a European power under the rule of Peter the Great (1689–1725), whose conscious imitation of the practices of Western absolutist monarchs was a kind of technological borrowing no less important than the technicians and artisans he imported into Russia in his program of "europeanization." In the eighteenth century a new brand of absolutism known as "enlightened despotism" evolved. It used the doctrines of the Enlightenment to justify absolutism, as theorists had justified it by divine right in the sixteenth and seventeenth centuries. In three states absolutism was successfully resisted by oligarchies that won out over princely pretensions: England, the Duch Republic and Poland. Of these three, Poland did not survive the eighteenth century, the Dutch Republic declined economically and militarily, and England alone emerged as a first-rank power able to seize an empire and retain and strengthen its representative institutions.

Absolutism, though it differed from state to state, invariably comprised governmental centralization, both legal and administrative, and a consequent growth of a bureaucracy dependent upon the absolute monarch; subjugation of the church within the monarch's domain and enforcement of religious uniformity as a facet of political loyalty; a standing army subject to the monarch's discipline; and an amalgam of economic policies (sometimes lumped together under the name mercantilism) aimed at building a strong national economy to make the state as self-sufficient as possible and thereby increase its capacity to wage successful wars. The prime victim of absolutism was everywhere the nobility. In the absolutisms of western Europe the nobility's power was eroded by the loss of its traditional representative institutions, the process of centralization, and the rise through service to the monarch of a new nobility dependent upon the ruler's favor. In central and eastern Europe the absolutist monarch subjugated the nobility to his will by drawing them into state service and by allowing them greater privileges over their peasants. The object of absolutism everywhere was not domestic order and public welfare so much as the aggrandizement of the territory, the power, and the glory of the monarch and of his dynasty. Marriage alliances contracted between royal dynasties as well as wars were the accepted means to these ends. With the added dimension of the colonial dependencies of the powers, dynastic wars became in fact world wars.

In the last quarter of the eighteenth century the American and French revolutions, the most spectacular outbursts of an upsurge of democratic sentiment, heralded the end of traditional absolutism and made all future generations their heirs. The United Nations declaration on the rights of man is largely an echo and amplification of the French declaration and of the "Bill of Rights" of the United States Constitution. The Russian Revolution of 1917 paid homage to the revolution inaugurated at the Place de la Bastille on July 14, 1789. Hungarians sang the "Marseillaise" in the streets of Budapest in 1848, 1918, and 1956, and the Vietnamese declaration of independence of September 2, 1945, quoted Jefferson's immortal "All men are created equal." But democracy was neither immediately nor everywhere triumphant. The French Revolution also produced Napoleon Bonaparte, the first modern dictator, who showed the facility with which a democratic ideology could be turned to serve the aims of domestic despotism and foreign conquest. Moreover, Napoleon's defeat temporarily restored the power and authority of the proponents of the Old Regime. Liberty and justice still had many battles to fight.

SECOND EDITION

THE EUROPEAN WORLD SINCE 1815

TRIUMPH AND TRANSITION

THE NINETEENTH CENTURY: THE GOLDEN AGE OF THE EUROPEAN WORLD
PART ONE

INTRODUCTION: SOCIAL FORCES AND SOCIAL CHANGE

In spite of its recent revolutionary upheavals, the Europe of 1815 more nearly resembled the Europe of 1715 at the death of Louis XIV than it did the Europe of 1914 on the eve of the First World War. In 1815, as in the previous century, more than three-fourths of all Europeans lived in rural villages or isolated homesteads and gained their living directly from the soil. In 1914, on the other hand, the majority in western Europe lived in towns and cities and worked in factories, shops, and offices. In 1815 the average life expectancy at birth was no more than 25 or 30 years, little higher than a century before; in 1914 it exceeded 50 years in most of western Europe and was increasing rapidly. In 1815 only the children of the well-to-do obtained the privilege of a formal education; the majority could neither read nor write. By 1914 almost all European children could attend publicly supported elementary schools and acquire the elements of literacy. In 1815, as before the French Revolution, most governments of Europe were more or less absolutist and aristocratic; participation in the process of government by means of elections was a privilege conferred only on wealthy landowners in a few countries bordering the western seas. By 1914 almost all European countries had some form of representative, if not wholly democratic, government, and in most countries the suffrage extended to all adult males.

These are but a few of the more obvious differences that marked the beginning and the end of Europe's greatest century. How did the changes come about? A few of the broader, more pervasive social forces that provided the dynamics are briefly discussed below.

SCIENCE AND TECHNOLOGY

Among the most fundamental of all sources of social change is new knowledge. Two closely related areas in which new knowledge had a profound impact on Western society in the nineteenth century were the study of the physical universe, or science, and the study of the means of manipulating nature for the production of goods and services, or technology. Important developments in scientific knowledge laid the basis for an increasingly fruitful collaboration between scientists, on the one hand, and industrialists and agriculturists, on the other. Although the full fruits of their collaboration did not appear until the second half of the nineteenth century and later, when scientific theories provided the foundation for new industries and new processes, by the beginning of the century the methods of science were already being applied in technology with gratifying results.

The application of scientific methods to practical problems led to an increasing mastery of nature, but practical results were by no means the only objectives spurring scientific progress. What motivated most scientists was simple curiosity – the desire for a better understanding of nature. Many advances in pure science, such as the discovery of electromagnetism, had far-reaching practical consequences, but scientists frequently left the development and application of their discoveries to other men. Certain findings of science that did not have immediate practical application, such as the doctrine of organic evolution, affected society even more profoundly by questioning old beliefs and raising new philosophic problems.

DEMOGRAPHIC GROWTH AND MATERIAL PROGRESS

Another factor responsible for important social changes was essentially biological. Just as the growth of a single individual from infancy to maturity produces changes in behavior and outlook, the growth of a population alters social institutions and attitudes. At the fall of Napoleon Europe contained approximately 200 million inhabitants, with another 20 or 25 million people of European stock overseas, out of a total world population of almost one billion. At the outbreak of World War I Europeans numbered more than 450 million, or about one-fourth of the world total, with an additional 150 million persons of European ancestry overseas. Peoples of European stock still formed a minority of the world's population, but possessed of a vastly superior technology for both production and destruction, the carriers of Western civilization at the beginning of the twentieth century enjoyed a preponderance of power on the world scene that had never before been witnessed.

The immense population increase could not have taken place without a proportionate increase in the production of the basic necessities of human existence – food, clothing, and shelter. This increase in production, together with the proliferation of commodities and services that were not necessities, actually surpassed the rate of growth of population. Therefore the standard of living rose simultaneously with the increase in population.

A part of the increase in production resulted from the opening of new lands and the tapping of new resources, but most of it resulted from the advance of technology. The increase in agricultural productivity lessened the need for peasants and farmers to be self-sufficient, and made them more able to exchange their surplus for cheaper machine- or factory-made goods. The increased supply of foodstuffs and raw materials also made it possible for a larger proportion of the laboring population to engage in nonagricultural production. Improvements in the technology of manufacturing and transportation were even more spectacular than those in agriculture. The invention of specialized, labor-saving machinery and the development of new forms of power, such as the steam engine, the electric dynamo, and the internal combustion engine, speeded up manufacture and transportation, lowered costs of production, and made possible new products and processes.

CLASS STRUCTURE AND CLASS STRUGGLES

The shift away from agriculture to the new forms of industry by the majority of Europeans led to the growth of cities, the rise of new social classes, the preponderance of new values and attitudes, and brought a host of new problems. It is readily apparent that an individual's place in the social hierarchy depends in part upon the way in which he gains a living, and that individuals in the same occupation are likely to share common values and a common outlook, different from and perhaps conflicting with the values and outlooks of those engaged in other occupations. During the nineteenth century bitter struggles between rival groups for social and political recognition or dominance sometimes occurred.

A close examination of nineteenth-century Europe reveals literally hundreds of identifiable social groups based upon differences in occupation and income, each with its own distinctive values and attitudes, yet each shading imperceptibly into the next along the social spectrum. It is possible to distinguish a few broad groups to which the more formal designation social class may be applied. The most commonly accepted classification distinguishes the landed aristocracy; a middle class of business and professional men (frequently subdivided into an upper middle class or *haute bourgeoisie,* including wealthy merchants, bankers, master manufacturers, and lawyers, and a lower middle class or *petite bourgeoi-*

sie, including retail tradesmen and handicraftsmen); an urban proletariat or working class; and the tillers of the soil or peasants.

At the beginning of the century the peasants formed by far the most numerous class. At the end of the century they still constituted a majority in Europe as a whole, but in the more industrialized areas their relative numbers had drastically decreased. They stood near the bottom of the social scale and rarely exercised effective political power. Isolated by poor communications and bound by a traditionalist mentality, their greatest desire was to obtain land. Their participation in broad social movements was generally sporadic and limited to their immediate economic interests.

In the years immediately after Waterloo the landed aristocracy continued to enjoy a preponderance of social prestige and political power in spite of the effects of the French Revolution. Its position of leadership was sharply challenged, however, by the rapidly growing middle classes. By the middle of the century the latter had succeeded in establishing themselves in the seats of power in most of western Europe, and during the second half of the century they made deep inroads into the exclusive position of the aristocracy in central Europe.

At the beginning of the century the urban workers neither participated in political life nor expected to participate in it. As their numbers grew and the outlines of the new industrial system became clear, they gradually developed a rudimentary class consciousness. At first their demands were moderate, pertaining to improvements in material circumstances and a more equitable distribution of income and wealth. Only later did they seek a voice in government when they discovered the connection between political power and economic reform. On the whole their attempts to gain power by both peaceful and revolutionary means met with little success until late in the nineteenth century, when the suffrage was gradually extended in western Europe and trade unions secured legal recognition.

NEW IDEOLOGIES

In the process of social change the aims of the various competing groups became crystallized in doctrines that are sometimes called ideologies. The very word ideology is a creation of the early nineteenth century. It may be defined as a system of ideas concerned with a particular social or political goal. Closely related to it is the suffix "-ism," whose connection with specific doctrines or ideologies, as liberalism or socialism, also dates from this period. The first half of the nineteenth century witnessed the introduction into our language of almost all the important and highly charged "isms" of today, including both capitalism and communism. At that time, however, the most important were liberalism, nationalism, and socialism.

An individual's social class did not always dictate his ideological convictions. Titled aristocrats sometimes took pride in calling themselves liberals or even socialists, and the majority of socialist leaders and intellectuals had middle-class backgrounds. On the other hand, many members of the lower and middle classes adhered to conservative views. Nevertheless, as a general rule individuals in the same social class tended to subscribe to the same ideology if they took any interest at all in political affairs. Liberalism was the credo of the middle classes, whereas socialism expressed the aspirations of the workers. Conservatism, though not always dignified (or derided) by the designation ideology, enshrined the ideals of those who wished to preserve the status quo; that is, the aristocracy. Nationalism did not belong to any social class as such. It was principally espoused by members of the educated middle classes, but it also reflected the aspirations of the divided peoples of Italy and Germany for a unified nation, and the aspirations of the subject nationalities in the Austrian, Russian, and Ottoman empires, the Belgian Netherlands, Norway, and Ireland for autonomy and freedom. Even the citizens of countries such as Britain, France, and Spain adopted fiercely patriotic attitudes when they thought that their nation's interests were threatened by a foreign power. The proponents of nationalism did not perceive its latent conflict with liberalism and socialism until the revolutions of 1848.

EAST AND WEST: THE WIDENING GAP

A complicating element in the study of the social changes of the nineteenth century is that economic and political developments proceeded at different rates in different parts of Europe. At the beginning of the century there was already a marked difference in the level of development between east and west in Europe, and the gap grew wider with each passing decade. In general, the development of commerce and industry and the ensuing social changes varied inversely with the distance from London, the focal point of capitalist economy. Thus, in the great revolutionary outbursts of 1848, the new middle class rulers of western Europe dealt with the demands of an urban proletariat, whereas the middle classes of central Europe struggled against the entrenched power of the aristocracy. The revolutions of 1848 caused hardly a ripple in Russia. More than half a century later middle classes and workers alike fought for elementary civil and political liberties in Russia, long after France had enacted universal manhood suffrage and at a time when German workers paid allegiance to the largest socialist party in existence.

ROMANTICISM AND REACTION
CHAPTER ONE

The great social changes of the nineteenth century did not sweep Europe all at once in 1815. Even after the cataclysm of the Revolution and the Napoleonic wars the vested interests of the Old Regime exhibited remarkable powers of revival and tenacity. In fact, during the decade following the Congress of Vienna the European scene was dominated by a twofold reaction to those driving forces of change. One was political, the other intellectual. The political reaction had for its aim the restoration of the Old Regime, and thus depended heavily on the doctrines of conservatism. The intellectual reaction, known as romanticism, is more difficult to categorize. Though in some areas, such as poetry and music, it seemed to follow an autonomous pattern of development, completely divorced from broader historical movements, in reality it did not.

So similar were the two reactions immediately after the Congress of Vienna that romanticism appeared to many to be no more than the literary adjunct of conservatism. The romantic temper could not be tied for long to a single political dogma, however. After 1820 a new generation of romantic writers and artists began to flout convention. Liberal and nationalist ideals permeated romantic art and literature, which in turn helped to shape the goals and content of the developing liberal and nationalist movements.

THE VIENNA SETTLEMENT AND THE CONCERT OF EUROPE

Even before the defeat and abdication of Napoleon in 1814 the allies had begun making plans for the reconstitution of Europe. The first Treaty of Paris between the allies and the government of the restored Bourbon Louis XVIII settled the status of France provisionally, but the problems of a general European settlement presented so many complexities and conflicting interests that the victors decided to convene a diplomatic congress of all recognized European powers.

THE CONGRESS OF VIENNA

The Congress of Vienna, which gathered in September, 1814, and did not complete its work until June, 1815, was one of the notable international assemblages of all times. It had a dual character, at once a lavish, extravagant social spectacle of the crowned heads and highest aristocracy of all Europe, and a serious meeting of statesmen and diplomats who were to shape the political destiny of the Continent for more than a generation. Actually, the full congress never assembled officially; the important decisions were all made in secret session by representatives of the great powers. The key personages in the drama were Prince Clemens von Metternich, Austrian chancellor and foreign minister and archetype of the conservative principle; the unpredictable Alexander I, tsar of Russia; Lord Castlereagh, British foreign minister; and Prince Karl von Hardenberg, representative of the king of Prussia. Before the congress was over the French foreign minister Talleyrand, a born aristocrat and consecrated bishop, who served with equal effectiveness the French Republic, Napoleon, and the restored Bourbons, had insinuated himself into the councils of the great powers at Vienna.

These men sought not merely to recreate a Europe congenial to the interests of their own classes and countries, but also to quell forever the manifestations of revolutionary and Bonapartist sentiment and to restore respect for the hierarchy and authority of the established order. In spite of their common aims, they were not at all unanimous on the means of accomplishing them. Divergences of interest arose to thwart their deliberations and delay decisions. By the beginning of 1815 Austria and Britain were on the verge of war against Russia and Prussia as a result of the latter's claims on Poland and Saxony, but Napoleon's return from Elba persuaded them to overcome their differences and close ranks against the common foe. While the armies of the allies gathered once more, the diplomats brought their negotiations to a hurried conclusion and signed the final act of the congress on June 8, 1815, ten days before the fateful battle of Waterloo.

In the first Treaty of Paris the allies had willingly distinguished between France and its former ruler, but treated both with surprising leniency. Napoleon was obliged to renounce the throne of France for himself and his descendants, but in compensation he retained the title of emperor, obtained the island of Elba as a sovereign principality, and received a guaranteed annual income for life. His wife, Marie Louise, obtained the duchies of Parma, Piacenza, and Guastalla, which were to pass on to their son at her death. France retained its boundaries of 1792, larger than those of 1789, and regained its former colonies with the exception of a few strategic islands held by the British.

After the Hundred Days the allies could not overlook the enthusiasm with which the French people had responded to Napoleon; the terms imposed on France were accordingly harsher. The second Treaty of Paris (November 20, 1815) reduced France to its borders of 1790, exacted an indemnity of 700 million francs, required France to support an army of occupation for five years, and forced it to return the art treasures that the Revolutionary and Napoleonic armies had looted from all of Europe. Napoleon, banished to the island of St. Helena in the South Atlantic, died in 1821.

THE NEW MAP OF EUROPE

In redrawing the map of Europe, the diplomats at Vienna paid lip service to the principle of legitimacy, or the reestablishment of the prerevolutionary situation, but in fact the settlement reflected expediency and compromise of the conflicting claims of the victors. The chief point of agreement was the desire to preserve peace through a balance of power. Specifically this meant holding France in check, although Britain and Austria also feared the expansion of Russian influence in Europe, and Austria kept a watchful eye on Prussian ambitions in Germany as well. (See map on p. 25.)

Russia had already acquired Finland from Sweden and Bessarabia from the Ottoman Empire, both of which it retained. Alexander asserted a claim to nearly the whole of Poland, but in the end he compromised by taking most of the former Grand Duchy of Warsaw, or about three-fifths of the Polish-speaking territory, on which he erected the Kingdom of Poland (the so-called Congress Poland) with himself as king. Austria obtained Polish Galicia, Prussia obtained Posen and Danzig, and Cracow became a free city under the joint protection of Austria, Prussia, and Russia. Prussia hoped to absorb all of Saxony, whose king had remained loyal to Napoleon, but this ambition ran counter to the interests of Austria. Although Prussia had to be content with receiving the northern two-fifths of Saxony, it accepted compensation (another catchword of the congress) in the form of a large extension of its prerevolutionary holdings in western Germany, including almost the entire German Rhineland, which provided a convenient bulwark against a renewal of French expansion.

At British urging the congress created another apparent bulwark in the same general area with the Kingdom of the United Netherlands. It was composed of the former Dutch Republic and Austrian Netherlands (modern-day Belgium) under the head of the House of Orange, King William I. The Kingdom of Sardinia (Piedmont) on the southeastern border of France was strengthened by the acquisition of the former republic of Genoa. Austria was "compensated" for giving up its outpost in the Netherlands by the creation of a Lombardo-Venetian kingdom, including the former duchy of Milan and Venetian republic, with the Austrian emperor as king. Austria further strengthened its hegemony in Italy with the restoration of the other petty states to their former rulers, including the States of the Church to the pope, under Austrian protection. Murat was allowed to retain the throne of Naples as the price for his desertion of Napoleon; but after rallying again to Bonaparte during the Hundred Days he was shot as a traitor, and Naples and Sicily were reunited as the Kingdom of the Two Sicilies under the restored Bourbon, Ferdinand I. Another Bourbon, the archreactionary Ferdinand VII, likewise returned to his throne in Spain. In the north Sweden received compensation for the loss of Finland by being allowed to retain Norway, which it had previously won from Denmark, another late deserter of Napoleonic France.

One of the most difficult problems faced by the congress was the reorganization of Germany, complicated by the rivalry of Austria and Prussia. Resurrection of the old Holy Roman Empire with its three hundred petty states was unthinkable. Metternich blocked proposals for a strong federal or unitary state for fear that Austria would lose its influence in south Germany. The solution finally adopted was to create the Germanic Confederation, a loose union of thirty-four sovereign states and four free cities. The Diet, or parliament of the Confederation, which met in the free city of Frankfurt, was in reality an assembly of ambassadors resembling the present General Assembly of the United Nations. Since it had no effective executive authority and since the Diet was under the permanent presidency of the Austrian delegate, the Confederation served Austrian interests by blocking political and social reform. By postponing the creation of a unified German state, however, it built up a store of further difficulties.

Among the worthier and more lasting achievements of the congress was the reestablishment of Switzerland as an independent confederation of twenty-two cantons with an international guarantee of neutrality. The congress inserted a provision for the international regulation of international waterways — the Rhine and Danube in particular. It also made a pronouncement in favor of abolishing the slave trade but took no positive action.

Britain, ultimately responsible for the final defeat of Napoleon, sought no territorial gains on the Continent, although it retained control of the Ionian Islands off Greece, Helgoland in the North Sea, and Malta in the Mediterranean. Britain's main concern was to preserve the balance of power on the Continent, which could be done more effectually without territorial possessions there and by means of its position as the leading, almost the only, seapower. During the wars the British navy had controlled the oceans and therefore the colonial empires of the other European nations. After 1815 the empires were either returned or allowed to go their own course, except that Britain retained the Cape of Good Hope, Singapore, and Ceylon, taken from the Dutch, and several strategic islands in the Indian Ocean taken from France.

THE HOLY ALLIANCE

With the signing of the final act on June 8, 1815, the work of the congress was concluded, although the final settlement had to wait the outcome of the battle of Waterloo. In the fall of 1815 the leading sovereigns and diplomats transferred their activity to Paris to draw up a new treaty for the defeated French.

Meanwhile Alexander of Russia, who was given to mystical flights of imagination, had fallen under the influence of a female religious fanatic, Baroness von Krüdener, who persuaded him of the desirability of establishing the peace on a religious foundation. Accordingly, Alexander proposed to his fellow sovereigns a Holy Alliance, by which they were to regard one another as brothers and govern their conduct by the principles of the Christian religion. Such sentiments were by no means novel, but the document in which they were embodied was so full of empty rhetoric that it soon became a laughingstock. Nevertheless, to avoid offending Alexander, both Francis of Austria and Frederick William of Prussia signed. All the sovereigns of Europe followed suit, except the pope and the sultan – neither of whom had been invited – and the prince regent of Great Britain, whose foreign minister replied disingenuously that the British constitution prohibited him from acting upon "abstract and speculative principles." Although the Holy Alliance lacked operational effect it was regarded by liberals as a sanctimonious cloak to conceal a conspiracy of the signatories against all popular movements for liberalism and reform.

THE QUADRUPLE ALLIANCE AND THE CONGRESS SYSTEM

Of more immediate practical significance was the Quadruple Alliance, to which Great Britain did adhere, along with Austria, Russia, and Prussia. Concluded on the same day as the second Treaty of Paris, it was mainly intended to protect the Vienna settlement and to ensure that France would not again disturb the peace of Europe. Of particular significance was the clause by which the contracting parties agreed "to renew their meetings at fixed periods . . . for the purpose of consulting upon their common interests, and for the consideration of those measures which at each of those periods shall be considered the most salutary for the repose and prosperity of nations, and for the maintenance of the peace of Europe." This clause inaugurated the congress system and the concert of Europe.

The first of the congresses held under the new system took place at Aix-la-Chapelle (Aachen) in 1818. Its principal business was to arrange for the liquidation of the French indemnity and the withdrawal of the army of occupation from French soil. In the three years that had elapsed since Waterloo the restored Bourbon dynasty had apparently entrenched itself in French political life, and France seemed truly reconciled to its new position. The business of the congress was conducted without disagreement. Not only was France relieved of the onus and embarrassment of the army of occupation, but it was admitted to the European concert on an equal footing by means of the new Quintuple Alliance. At the same time the other four took the precaution of renewing in secret the principal provisions of the older alliance to protect themselves against possible French aggression. The congress system thus got off to an apparently brilliant beginning – a success that was matched and complemented by contemporary intellectual developments.

ROMANTICISM IN LITERATURE AND THE ARTS

Romanticism is the word commonly applied to the characteristic intellectual and artistic values and attitudes of the first half of the nineteenth century. Like all such comprehensive terms it covers many diverse and even contradictory currents; it must therefore be used in an approximate rather than a precise sense. It is easier to describe what it was not, or what it was against, than its positive features. It was primarily a reaction against the formalism, mechanism, and rationalism of the Enlightenment. It was also a reaction to the French Revolution, especially to the Republic of Virtue of Robespierre and the tyranny of Napoleon. On its positive side it was essentially a mood, an attitude, a way of looking at and thinking about the world. It manifested itself in many areas – music, art, literature, religion, philosophy, and politics. It emphasized the emotional side of human nature and regarded the spiritual qualities of man as superior to his purely rational faculties. It stressed the unique, the individual, among men and nations instead of their common characteristics. It glorified nature and viewed the physical universe not as a mechanical system or a great cosmic machine but as a living, growing organism. Because it laid great stress on faith and tradition as determinants of and guides for human behavior and social policy, it reinforced the elements of mysticism and pietism in religion. Romanticism achieved its greatest successes in literature and the arts, with which it is most closely identified. Its emphasis on tradition and the glories of the past contributed to the study of history and jurisprudence. Its glorification of nature and opposition to mechanism created a favorable intellectual environment for the biological sciences and prepared the way for acceptance of the theory of organic evolution.

ORIGINS

Although romanticism came into its own in the first or second decades of the nineteenth century, it had its origins in the mid-eighteenth century during the very Age of Reason to which it was a reaction. Among the most important forerunners was Jean-Jacques Rousseau (1712–1778), whose writings contrasted the natural goodness of primitive man, or man in a state of nature, with the artificiality and acquired wickedness of civilized man. His *Confessions,* published in 1783 after his death, set the style for an introspective, intensely personal literature in which all the emotions of the author are bared to public view.

Johann Wolfgang von Goethe (1749–1832), regarded by many as the greatest of German writers, was another forerunner of romanticism, though he later turned against it. With Friedrich von Schiller (1759–1805) he led the *Sturm und Drang* (storm and stress) movement in German literature. The movement, which flourished in the 1780's, emphasized the turbulence of the human spirit – an emphasis that later became a hallmark of romantic literature. Goethe's *Faust,* a long dramatic poem, is one of the literary masterpieces of all time. It is in essence the spiritual autobiography of the author. Based on the old legend of the man who sold his soul to the devil, it portrays the futility of both the life of the mind and the experience of the flesh unless they are fused and ennobled by a generous spiritual compassion for the sufferings of humanity.

A major figure in the romantic movement – indeed, the one who christened it – was a woman, the Baroness de Staël-Holstein (1766–1817). Known to history as Madame de Staël, she was the archetype of the romantic heroine. Born Germaine Necker, daughter of the Swiss financier who became the principal minister of Louis XVI, she was raised in the fashionable Paris salon of her mother. There she was exposed to the wit and elegance of the most celebrated figures of the age. At the age of nineteen she married an obscure Swedish diplomat for whom she had no affection. Although she retained his name throughout her life she rarely lived with him and had several lovers, among them some of the most distinguished literary and political figures of the time, such as Talleyrand and Benjamin Constant. One year before her death she married a man twenty-two years her junior to whom she had already borne a child.

For the three decades from the eve of the French Revolution until her death Madame de Staël was the most talked about and probably the most talkative woman in Europe. She embodied all the diverse, contradictory elements of romantic literature. As a person she was strong-willed, passionate, and uninhibited. As a political figure she was a child of the Old Regime who first embraced the Revolution's program of constitutional monarchy, then turned against the Revolution and fled during the Reign of Terror. She spent much of the remainder of her life traveling in exile, both from the Revolution and from Napoleon, of whom she was an outspoken critic. As a literary figure she was a prolific if mediocre writer (her books are rarely read today), but the facility of her ideas, the force of her personality, and above all the range of her literary acquaintance enabled her to give a certain unity and focus to the romantic movement. In *De l'Allemagne* (On Germany) Madame de Staël first applied the name "romantic" to the new poetic literature of Germany, which was based on the chants of the troubadours and the legends of medieval chivalry that had been discovered by German folklorists. She contrasted this "modern" literature with the cold and formal "ancient" literature of the French classical writers of the seventeenth and eighteenth centuries. The distinguishing feature of romantic literature, she wrote, was "enthusiasm," which she defined as "the love of the beautiful, the elevation of the soul, the enjoyment of devotion, gathered together in the same sentiment which has both grandeur and calm. The meaning of the word according to the Greeks is its most noble definition: enthusiasm signifies *God in us.*"

ROMANTIC POETRY

The romantic era was an age of poetry. Whatever else they wrote, most romantic writers also wrote poetry. Romantic poetry was distinguished by its lyrical qualities. In form it abandoned the stiff formalism of classical or Augustan poetry, and in content it expressed the personality of the poet. William Wordsworth (1770–1850), one of the foremost poets of the English language, exemplified one strand of romanticism. His poetry exudes a love of nature, simplicity, and the idyllic life.

> Therefore am I still
> A lover of the meadows and the woods,
> And mountains; and of all that we behold
> From this green earth;
> well pleased to recognize
> In nature and the language of the sense,
> The author of my purest thoughts, the nurse,
> The guide, the guardian of my heart, and soul
> Of all my moral being.

Samuel Taylor Coleridge (1772–1834), Wordsworth's close friend, exhibited another tendency of romanticism in his fanciful poetic works "The Rime of the Ancient Mariner" and "Kubla Khan." In them he expressed a fascination with faraway places and exotic things. Three other English poets were romantics in their lives (and deaths) as well as in their literature. John Keats (1795–1821), whose father owned a livery stable, died of tuberculosis in Rome at the age of twenty-five. His friend Percy Bysshe Shelley (1792–1822) drowned the following year in a storm in the Mediterranean. Lord Byron (1788–1824) died two years later in Greece while fighting the Turks for Greek independence.

Outstanding among French romantic poets were Victor Hugo (1802–1885), a genius in every branch of literature; Alphonse de Lamartine (1790–1869), a sentimentalist; Alfred de Vigny (1797–1863), a philosopher in verse; and Alfred de Musset (1810–1857), a pessimistic, emotional egoist. The greatest German poet of the romantic era after Goethe was Heinrich Heine (1797–1856), a supreme lyricist. In northern Germany and the Scandinavian countries romantic poetry became fused with folklore, epic sagas, and fairy tales as in the poetry of Adam Oehlenschlager (1779–1850), Denmark's greatest poet, and even more in the works of Hans Christian Andersen (1805–1875) and the German brothers Wilhelm and Jacob Grimm (1786–1859, 1785–1863). German poets wrote many romantic *lieder* or tender lyrics, which were set to music by composers such as Franz Schubert (1797–1828) and Robert Schumann (1810–1856).

ROMANTIC FICTION

Novels were almost as popular as poetry as a literary form during the romantic period. In the early years of the movement novels stressed fantasy and imagination at the expense of verisimilitude. François René de Chateaubriand (1768–1848), accounted by some as the dominant figure in French literary history between Rousseau and Hugo, wrote voluptuous prose describing incredible events and sensations. Several of his novels were set in the wilds of North America and peopled with Indians or Eskimos. This device gave full scope to his ability to depict the savage beauty of nature, the primitive goodness of man, and the all-seeing benevolence of God. A vivid imagination, together with a cavalier disregard for ordinary fact and logic, frequently led him into hyperboles of fanciful exaggeration, such as this description of life among the Eskimos: "the iceberg balances on the waves, its peaks shining, its hollows ordered with snow; the sea wolves give themselves to the passion of love in its valleys. The whales follow its path over the ocean. The hardy savage in the shelter of his floating iceberg presses to his heart the woman whom God has given him and with her finds undreamt joys in this mixture of danger and passion."

Sir Walter Scott (1771–1832) was one of the most successful authors of historical romances. He thrilled readers throughout Europe and America with his stirring tales of medieval chivalry. The genre was continued with great success by the elder Alexandre Dumas (1802–1870). During the later years of the romantic era novelists created more plausible characters and dealt in believable fashion with real social or personal problems, whether they used historical or contemporary settings. The leading practitioners of the school of romantic realism were Stendhal (Henri Beyle, 1783–1842), Hugo, Charles Dickens (1812–1870), and above all Honoré de Balzac (1799–1850).

Across the Atlantic romanticism exercised a sway no less strong than in

Europe. The picturesque tales of James Fenimore Cooper, Washington Irving, and Nathaniel Hawthorne had an avid readership, not only in America but also in Europe. In poetry William Cullen Bryant's reverence for nature, Edgar Allan Poe's lyrical if undisciplined lines, and Walt Whitman's unique paeans of praise to individualism all mark them as true romantics. Henry David Thoreau, even more than Whitman, was a living romantic, intensely individualistic, seeking to live the life of man in the state of nature. Ralph Waldo Emerson's transcendentalism fully matched the idealism of German philosophy. In the United States romantic literature had an even longer vogue than in Europe, as may be seen in the poetry and tales of Henry Wadsworth Longfellow and James Russell Lowell.

HISTORY

History attained popularity as a literary form in the romantic era. In part its vogue resulted from the veneration for the past that was characteristic of the times; in part it arose because historians wrote for the literate general public, not just for other historians. History also had political uses, which helped it to popularity. Thomas Macaulay (1800–1859) wrote Whig history, glorifying England's progress and attributing it to the revolution of 1689; Thomas Carlyle (1795–1881) wrote Tory history, deploring the advance of industrialism and democracy. In France Adolphe Thiers (1797–1877) and François Guizot (1787–1874), both of whom were politicians as well as historians, wrote what might be called the Whig history of the French. Somewhat more radical, the popular historian Jules Michelet (1798–1874) wrote stirring imaginative history aimed at keeping alive the spirit and traditions of the revolution of 1789.

This same period witnessed the beginning of the movement for scientific history. In 1824 the young German historian Leopold von Ranke (1795–1886) published *Zur Kritik neuerer Geschichtschreiber,* which laid the basis for modern historical criticism. Ranke's aim was to write history "as it really happened," although he also professed to see "the hand of God" in history. Friedrich von Savigny (1778–1861), professor of law at the University of Berlin, established the discipline of historical jurisprudence, which maintained that the legal as well as the other institutions of each nation depended upon their own historical development. He opposed the so-called school of natural law, which held that deductive legal principles could be established for all times and places. Shortly afterward another group of German professors inaugurated the historical school of political economy in opposition to the classical or deductive school that flourished in England. The aspect of romanticism that extolled tradition and looked to the past thus proved to have a seminal influence in many areas of intellectual endeavor.

ART

The romantic mood affected the arts quite as much as literature and philosophy. Although sculpture did not flourish during the period, painting was quite distinctive. Artists were much more interested in a lavish use of color and in subject matter and imaginative elements than in the classical concerns of form and precision. As in literature, there were two distinctive tendencies in romantic art. One group of artists glorified the exotic and the heroic. They painted wild landscapes, exaggerated figures, and subjects that appealed to the imagination. Eugene Delacroix's (1798–1863) scenes of the Greek Revolution (although he had never set foot in Greece) are good examples. The other group of artists sought a return to simple, everyday, commonplace things. In the eighteenth century artists who had painted landscapes were regarded as second-rate, but English painters like John Constable (1776–1836) and J. M. W. Turner (1775–1851) restored the art of landscape paintings to its earlier prominence. Constable, for example, painted simple, idyllic rustic scenes that matched in spirit the poetry of Wordsworth. At the same time both groups had many things in common. Delacroix, who was perhaps the most famous of the romantic painters, freely acknowledged his indebtedness to Constable. What they had most in common was a revolt against the prevailing style and traditions of the classicists.

The transition from classical to romantic as the prevailing mode in painting came rather suddenly in the 1820's. During the first two decades of the century painting in Europe, especially in France, had been dominated by Jacques-Louis David (1748–1825), the great painter of the French Revolution and the Napoleonic era, and a confirmed classicist. The latent conflict between the old established doctrines and the new tendencies became public in 1819 with the exhibition of the "Raft of the Medusa" by Théodore Géricault (1791–1824). Classical critics accused romantic painters of "painting with a drunken broom." In reply, the more flamboyant romantic artists disdainfully turned up their coat collars whenever they stood in front of a classical painting "in order not to catch cold." By 1830 romanticism had won the struggle. It fitted better with the temper of the times, and it had greater appeal for the less cultivated artistic tastes of the new middle classes; classicism appealed principally to the older aristocratic values. Although some classical painters continued to work, romantic painting dominated the artistic scene until the advent of realism in the second half of the nineteenth century.

ARCHITECTURE

The romantic invasion of architecture, hinted at in a few buildings of the late eighteenth century, was delayed because of a classical revival stimulated by Thomas Jefferson in America and by Napoleon's admiration for the institutions of the Roman Republic and Empire. Outstanding examples of the classical revival in architecture are the rotunda of the University of Virginia, designed by Jefferson, and the Church of the Madeleine in Paris, which was begun in 1806 at the height of the Napoleonic Empire. Although the classical style continued in widespread use until the middle of the nineteenth century, by the 1830's and 1840's the romantic invasion had begun in earnest. It took the form of a so-called Gothic revival, which exemplified the romantic concern for the historic past – the Middle Ages in particular. It began with the restoration of many medieval castles and fortresses. In France, Viollet-le-Duc (1814–1879) restored the medieval walled city of Carcassonne and the beautiful and elegant Sainte Chapelle in Paris. During this period embellishments were added to a number of very old buildings. The cathedrals of Cologne and of Notre Dame in Paris, for example, had been built over several hundred years in the later Middle Ages, so that it was not too great a stretch of the romantic imagination for the architect to say, when he added a spire to Notre Dame in 1852, that he was "completing" the cathedral.

The rapid growth of cities in the nineteenth century and the no less rapid increase in wealth created a demand for many new buildings, public as well as private. Churches, schools, government buildings, and even railroad stations, gymnasiums, factories, and warehouses employed the Gothic revival style. In a few instances the results were strikingly beautiful and effective, as in the Houses of Parliament in London. Far more frequently, however, the Gothic revival structures were unsuited to the purpose for which they were built, were poorly proportioned and located, lacked adequate lighting and ventilation, and were encumbered by a superabundance of cheap ornamentation that detracted from their aesthetic effect. Much of the responsibility for this so-called Victorian Gothic can be attributed to the influence of the English author and art critic John Ruskin (1819–1900). Ruskin was in many ways a typical romantic, who sought to escape from the hated industrial system of the nineteenth century by encasing it in a medieval shell.

MUSIC

Romanticism registered some of its greatest creative achievements in music. Romantic music appealed to the emotions. Unlike the pure, almost mathematical forms of eighteenth-century music, much of romantic music was programmatic. Symphonies and concertos, as well as operas and songs, tried to tell a story or create a mood. Composers made a greater use of experimentation, innovation, and imagination; they felt less bound by formal rules. They used new instruments and larger orchestras to achieve effects. They drew their themes from ancient folk tales and sagas, as in the operas of Carl Maria von Weber (1786–1826), from nature, as in the great *Pastoral Symphony* of Beethoven, and from tales of heroism and love.

The transition from classicism to romanticism in music and the evolution of the latter is most evident in the works of the great German and Austrian composers from Haydn to Wagner. Ludwig van Beethoven (1770–1827) was the key figure. In the works of Haydn and Mozart the classical music of the eighteenth century had reached its highest peak. Although in the later works of Mozart and the first two symphonies of Beethoven innovations were made that indicated the future directions of music, the innovations remained within the traditions of eighteenth-century music. Not until the third symphony of Beethoven, appropriately called *Eroica* (Heroic), was there a definite break with tradition. Beethoven in music, like Goethe in literature, belonged to both the classic and the romantic periods and exemplified the best of both. Weber, Schubert, Schumann, and Brahms further developed the romantic style, which reached its ultimate development in the spectacular operas of Wagner.

In France the *Symphonie Fantastique* of Hector Berlioz (1803–1869), first performed in 1830, could be called a musical manifesto of the romantic movement. Berlioz acknowledged his indebtedness to Beethoven and asserted that he would realize through conscious discipleship the potentialities inherent in the innovations of Beethoven. In music, as in architecture, romanticism lingered on into the second half of the nineteenth and even into the twentieth century, strongly influencing composers of such widely differing temperaments as Tchaikovsky, Bizet, Dvořák, Grieg, and Sibelius.

ROMANTICISM IN PHILOSOPHY, POLITICS, AND RELIGION

Idealism in philosophy, closely related to romanticism, also flourished in the first half of the nineteenth century. Its most important forerunner was a German, Immanuel Kant (1724–1804). In *The Critique of Pure Reason* he reacted against the excessive rationalism of eighteenth-century philosophers and stressed spiritual qualities and phenomena that could not be grasped by human reason alone. In this respect his thinking accorded well with the temper of romanticism. Kantian idealism was further developed by Johann Fichte (1762–1814) and F. W. Schelling (1775–1854), but the outstanding figure in nineteenth-century idealism was Georg Wilhelm Friedrich Hegel (1770–1831), professor of philosophy at the University of Berlin.

HEGEL AND DIALECTICAL IDEALISM

For Hegel ideas were reality. Material objects and the events of history were mere reflections of ideas. Moreover, specific ideas were only imperfect pieces of a larger whole, an Absolute Idea. The one great reality was the Absolute Idea – "the Idea which thinks itself." One of Hegel's most important contributions to philosophy was the development of the dialectical method of reasoning. Dialectic was by no means new – it had been used at least as early as the time of Socrates – but Hegel made it into a formal logical method. According to the dialectical process, an idea, theme, or "thesis" is opposed by or gives rise to its opposite or contradiction, called the "antithesis." Out of the conflict of the thesis and the antithesis results a new idea or "synthesis," which is not a mere compromise of the old but is new and superior to both. The synthesis, in turn, becomes the new thesis, giving rise to its opposite and resulting in a new and higher synthesis. The process is never-ending. This was an accepted method of argument or reasoning in philosophy and science, but Hegel thought that the process could also be observed in the movement of history. According to him, history proceeds through the conflict of forces or, more precisely, through the conflict of ideas, since historical forces are merely manifestations of pure ideas.

One idea of great importance in Hegelian philosophy was the idea of the state. For Hegel the state was not simply a collection of individuals organized under a government. As an idea, the state was something antecedent to and superior to individuals. The state did not exist for the citizens; the citizens existed for the state. Hegel wrote in his *Philosophy of History,* "The State is the externally existing, genuinely moral life. . . . Truth is the unity of the universal and particular Will, and the universal is to be found in the State, in its laws, its universal and rational arrangements. The State is the Divine Idea as it exists on earth. . . . The State is the Idea of Spirit in the external manifestation of human Will and its Freedom." Such notions, drilled into generations of German schoolboys, had a profound effect on subsequent German history. Filtered through the philosophy of one of Hegel's self-proclaimed disciples, Karl Marx, they have exercised a great influence on the entire world.

According to Hegel, the Prussian state of the restoration period embodied the highest development that mankind had yet reached. He foresaw the further development of Prussia into a greater German nation; that is, the German nation would arise out of a dialectical process of struggle between the thesis of the Prussian state and various antithetical ideas. It would represent the *Volkgeist* or spirit of the German people. His philosophy struck a sympathetic note with the tendency in romanticism that exalted collective ideas and historical tradition, and it gave a profound impetus to nationalist movements, especially the pan-German movement.

Hegel's emphasis on the omnipotence of the state and on the element of conflict in the dialectical process had strong political overtones. As far as he was concerned, war served a moral purpose and was superior to peace, for it kept a people from becoming decadent and weak. The rules of private morality did not apply to states, which were laws unto themselves. Hegel even went so far as to suggest that there might be a few "world-historical" individuals who fitted into the same lawless category as the state.

Romanticism found another philosophical ally in Arthur Schopenhauer (1788–1860), a slightly younger contemporary of Hegel. Hegel's "world spirit" was rational, although it had certain affinities with the mystical anti-rationalism of some of the more extreme romantics. Schopenhauer replaced the spirit by the "will," which was expressly antirational. His influential and profoundly pessimistic book *The World as Will and Idea* prepared the way intellectually for the complete nihilism of certain late nineteenth-century philosophers, especially Friedrich Nietzsche. (See p. 290.)

ROMANTICISM AND RELIGION

Christianity appeared to be a dying force in Europe in the last years of the Old Regime. Under the influence of the Enlightenment even prelates of the Church expressed their skepticism openly, and during the French Revolution the adherents of the cult of reason made a frontal attack on traditional religion. But a religious revival had been foreshadowed in the eighteenth century by Pietism in Germany and Methodism in England. Romanticism greatly strengthened this development. Madame de Staël declared, "I do not know exactly what we must believe, but I believe that we must believe! The eighteenth century did nothing but deny. The human spirit lives by its beliefs. Acquire faith through Christianity, or through German philosophy, or merely through enthusiasm, but believe in something!"

Emotion, sentimentality, and enthusiasm – the hallmarks of romanticism and frequent components of religion – became the ties that bound the two together. Chateaubriand sought to justify Christianity on purely emotional and aesthetic grounds in his widely popular *Genius of Christianity, or Beauties of the Christian Religion* (1802). Fleeing from the "babble of science and reason," he claimed that the sheer beauty of Christianity is sufficient proof of its truth. The similarity between his sentiment and that expressed by Keats in the famous lines

> "Beauty is truth, truth beauty" – that is all
> Ye know on earth, and all ye need to know.

is indicative of the strong affinity between romanticism and the religious revival.

The emotionalism of evangelical preachers and reformers easily gave way to mysticism and fanaticism. In 1814 a Methodist prophetess in London promised to give birth to a Son of God at the age of sixty-five; she was no doubt mentally deranged, but many more or less normal individuals thought they saw visions, heard voices from the tomb, and could communicate with the spiritual world. The Baroness von Krüdener, whose eloquence reduced the Emperor of All the Russias to tears and persuaded him to undertake the Holy Alliance, held daily séances in her apartment in Paris in the fall of 1815. These bizarre gatherings, at which the hostess pretended to receive divine revelations, were attended by the tsar and other monarchs, as well as leaders of Parisian society. For most believers such frenzied experiences served as an emotional release from the cares and frustrations of the everyday world, but among the leaders of religious thought the "religion of the heart" reflected disillusionment with what they considered the "dry rot of rationalism" and the inability of human reason to solve the riddles of the universe. The influential German Protestant theologian Friedrich Schleiermacher (1768–1834) sought to reconcile science and religion by putting them on different planes. In *Addresses on Religion to the Educated Who Despise It* (1799) he explained that religion is not a system of thought but a mystical inner experience that places the individual in direct communion with God. Schleiermacher helped restore religion to respectability among the intellectuals, but many of his followers dropped his tolerance of science and the scientific spirit and went over wholeheartedly to mysticism and obscurantism.

The nineteenth-century religious revival occurred first among the Protestant sects, but it soon spread to Roman Catholicism, where it eventually had its greatest impact. In the 1830's the Oxford Movement tried to reintroduce Catholic doctrine and liturgy into the Church of England. Its leader, John Henry Newman, eventually left the Church of England for that of Rome, in which he became a cardinal. Many leaders of German romanticism became converts to Catholicism. Although this development was at first a personal and emotional reaction, it could not fail to have strong political overtones. With few exceptions its influence was heavily on the side of conservatism. Even the Methodists, most radical of the Protestant sects in religious doctrine, demanded loyalty and obedience to all established authorities. The Protestant state churches of northern Europe held the same view. The most striking religious development of the restoration period was the marked revival of the papacy's influence. Pope Pius VII (1800–1823) gained much sympathy – even in Protestant countries – as a result of Napoleon's persecution. In 1814 he regained temporal control of Rome and the States of the Church.

Most of the statesmen of the restoration regarded religion as a potential ally of great value in their attempt to restore the Old Regime and worked actively for the "union of throne and altar." Every European state had an established church that was supported financially by the state or by its own endowment of lands. Although disputes occasionally arose between the pope and the rulers of Roman Catholic countries over the appointment of bishops and similar matters, the normal situation was one of cooperation to preserve respect for traditional religious and political forms. Pius VII and his energetic secretary of state Cardinal Consalvi negotiated concordats with almost all of the Catholic countries and even made an agreement with Prussia for the regulation of Catholic matters in that Protestant country. The clergy organized societies of laymen, such as the Congregation of the Virgin in France, the San Fedists in Italy, and the Society of the Exterminating Angel in Spain, which were frequently used by aristocratic leaders as instruments for the persecution of liberals.

The belief in the absolute supremacy of the pope, known as ultramontanism, received strong intellectual support in the restoration period. Its greatest theorist was Count Joseph de Maistre, a nobleman who was expropriated by the French Revolution and returned to France in 1815 after many years of exile. In 1817 he published *Du pape* (Of the Pope), in which he argued that in questions of faith and morals the pope was infallible and that all Christian nations should recognize his supremacy as a cure for lawlessness, disorder, and revolution. Maistre did not, however, depend on moral authority alone as a correction for the ills of society: "All greatness, all power, all order," he wrote, "depend upon the executioner. He is the tie that binds society together. Take away this incomprehensible force and at that very moment order is suspended by chaos, thrones fall, and states disappear."

ROMANTICISM AND POLITICS

In politics romanticism is sometimes identified with conservatism because of their common opposition to the principles of the Enlightenment and the French Revolution. The close connection between romanticism and religion, especially the espousal of ultramontane doctrines by many romantic writers, also had much to do with its conservative tendencies. Chateaubriand served the restoration government of France as foreign minister, and many other leaders of romantic thought either took an active part in restoration politics or supported the principles of conservatism in their writings. Sir Walter Scott was an outspoken Tory. The Lake poets – Wordsworth, Coleridge, and Robert Southey (who became poet laureate in 1813) – had been favorable to the French Revolution in their youth, but by 1815 they had gone over to conservatism. The reaction went to even greater lengths among the German romantics.

At the same time, romanticism had no specific political content. It was not an ideology but a mood. If some romantics were conservative or even reactionary in their politics, at least as large a number went to the opposite extreme. The poets Byron and Shelley were flaming liberals, even radicals, in their day. Nor should it be forgotten that although romanticism stressed tradition and the glories of the past, it also gloried in the individual and in his right – indeed, his duty – to develop himself in his own way, according to his own unique experience and the dictates of his "inner voice" or conscience. After about 1820 many of the younger romantics who had not directly experienced the trauma of the French Revolution grew increasingly restive with the stodginess and restrictions of the restoration governments. In France Victor Hugo, who defined romanticism simply as "liberalism in literature," and the poet-politician Alphonse de Lamartine spread the doctrine of romanticism as a liberating force; Heinrich Heine did the same in Germany. Even Chateaubriand became disillusioned with the absolutist tendencies of his new sovereign, Charles X, and supported the Revolution of 1830. In addition, the force of nationalism, which in the first half of the nineteenth century was anything but conservative, drew heavily on the emotional reserves and historical penchant of romanticism.

RESTORATION POLITICS

METTERNICH AND THE CONSERVATIVE REACTION IN GERMANY

The overarching purpose of the deliberations at Vienna and subsequently the congress system was the resurrection and preservation of the old established social order and the exorcism of the demons unleashed by the French Revolution – the demons of liberalism and nationalism in particular. No one could have been better fitted to supervise the task than Metternich. A West German (Rhineland) aristocrat by birth, whose ancestral domains had been swallowed by revolutionary land reform, he became foreign minister and eventually chancellor of the polyglot, multinational Austrian Empire. As Metternich saw it, the problem of Austria was the problem of Europe in microcosm: to preserve the vested interests of the antinational, antiliberal monarchy and aristocracy against the aspirations and encroachments of self-conscious nationalities and a rising middle class. The solution for both was identical, according to Metternich: divide and rule. The peace of Europe and the integrity of the Austrian Empire both demanded that all liberal and nationalist movements be squelched at their source. No means to this end were too reprehensible, nor did Metternich make a distinction between foreign and domestic policy except that of expediency. He suppressed the revolts in Italy and Germany with the same ruthlessness as he did those in Galicia and Lombardy; he intercepted the correspondence of and spied on the rulers of sovereign states as frequently as he did on the leaders of local secret societies. For Metternich, what was good for Austria was good for

EUROPE AFTER THE CONGRESS OF VIENNA
Boundary of the German Confederation
0 300
Miles
FINLAND (To Russia)
St. Petersburg
Volga R.
Moscow
KINGDOM OF NORWAY AND SWEDEN
Stockholm
Baltic Sea
Dvina R.
RUSSIAN EMPIRE
Don R.
North Sea
Copenhagen
DENMARK
UNITED KINGDOM OF GREAT BRITAIN AND IRELAND
Dublin
London
Hamburg
HANOVER
KINGDOM OF PRUSSIA
Vistula R.
Warsaw
KINGDOM OF POLAND (To Russia)
Berlin
Elbe
KINGDOM OF THE UNITED NETHERLANDS
SAXONY
Dnieper R.
Cracow
Frankfort
Rhine
R.
Prague
GALICIA
BOHEMIA
HAPSBURG EMPIRE
ATLANTIC OCEAN
Paris
WURTTEMBURG
BAVARIA
Seine R.
BADEN
Munich
Vienna
Budapest
MOLDAVIA
CRIMEA
KINGDOM OF FRANCE
SWITZ.
TYROL
HUNGARY
WALLACHIA
Black Sea
LOMBARDY-VENETIA
Bucharest
Garonne R.
Turin
Milan
Rhone R.
PARMA
MODENA
Danube R.
BOSNIA
Genoa
LUCCA
Florence
Ebro R.
Marseille
TUSCANY
PAPAL STATES
Adriatic Sea
MONTENEGRO
Constantinople
OTTOMAN EMPIRE
KINGDOM OF PORTUGAL
Douro R.
Tagus R.
Madrid
Lisbon
KINGDOM OF SPAIN
Guadalquivir R.
KINGDOM OF SARDINIA
CORSICA (To France)
Rome
Naples
KINGDOM OF THE TWO SICILIES
IONIAN IS. (To Britain)
GREECE
BALEARIC IS.
Mediterranean Sea
MALTA (To Britain)
CYPRUS
CRETE

Ewing Galloway

Clemens von Metternich, by Sir Thomas Lawrence

"It is necessary to point out in a more particular manner the evil which threatens to deprive [society], at one blow, of the real blessings, the fruits of genuine civilization. . . . This evil may be described in one word—presumption. . . . It is principally the middle classes of society which this moral gangrene has affected. . . . We see this intermediary class abandon itself with a blind fury and animosity . . . to all the means which seem proper to assuage its thirst for power, applying itself to the task of persuading kings that their rights are confined to sitting upon a throne, while those of the people are to govern, and to attack all that centuries have bequeathed as holy and worthy of man's respect." Secret Memorandum of Metternich to Emperor Alexander of Russia, December 15, 1820, reprinted in MEMOIRS OF PRINCE METTERNICH (New York, 1880–1882).

Europe; more pointedly, what threatened Europe in the form of revolution, wherever it took place and whatever its inspiration, threatened disaster for Austria.

In the wake of the Napoleonic wars liberal and nationalist aspirations were present throughout Europe, but especially in Metternich's own backyard, Germany. Both the French Revolution and the Napoleonic wars made a profound imprint upon Germany. The wars not only destroyed the antique Holy Roman Empire, the political framework of pre-Napoleonic Germany, but they also kindled a flame of patriotism for a German fatherland that had never been. The revolutionary reforms of the political, social, and economic orders in France led German liberals to believe that such reforms might equally well serve Germany. The Vienna settlement, as applied to Germany, failed to satisfy either the liberals or the nationalists. The weak Germanic Confederation disappointed the hopes of the latter for a unified German state, and the reactionary domestic policies of the rulers who were influenced by Metternich disappointed the liberal reformers. Prussia, in particular, disappointed both nationalists and liberals, who in 1815 had expected it to take the lead in creating a progressive German nation. Instead, reactionary elements in Prussia curbed the reforming zeal of Chancellor Hardenberg, while the king, Frederick William III, fell increasingly under the influence of Metternich and the Austrian emperor. In default of other leadership, university students strongly influenced by romanticism took over the liberal and nationalist movements. They organized student groups called *Burschenschaften* (the forerunners of American college fraternities) to agitate for liberal and patriotic goals. On the whole their methods were innocuous as their aims were idealistic, but occasionally the exuberance of youth led them into riotous demonstrations. For example, the Wartburg Festival of October, 1817, organized to celebrate two great patriotic events, the tercentenary of Luther's revolt from the Church and the fourth anniversary of the battle of Leipzig, climaxed in a bonfire episode in which various symbols of the old order were consigned to the flames. Metternich, whether personally alarmed or not, took advantage of such demonstrations to frighten the German rulers with specters of revolutionary conspiracy.

In 1819 the assassination of the reactionary journalist August von Kotzebue by a *Burschenschafter* from Jena gave Metternich the opportunity he needed to clamp controls on the universities and other centers of liberal ferment. He called representatives of the eight largest German states to Carlsbad in the summer of 1819 and persuaded them to adopt the Carlsbad Decrees, which he had ratified by the Federal Diet in Frankfurt the following September. The decrees contained three major provisions: (1) the appointment of political commissioners for all German universities, with powers of summary dismissal of both students and

Courtesy of the British Museum

"Colour Structure, Moon Burst," by J. M. W. Turner

"So great was Turner's output — his bequest to the nation comprised some two hundred and eighty pictures and between nineteen and twenty thousand water-colours and drawings — so vast his range and creative genius that one can say little more than this: what Michelangelo is in figure painting Turner is in landscape and seascape. Beginning as the assistant of Thomas Malton he advanced irresistibly, engulfing or comprehending all that had gone before him in landscape. . . . Having disposed of them he went his way, until he had created a new heaven of vision." C. H. Collins Baker, BRITISH PAINTING (London, 1933).

---

professors; (2) strict censorship of the press; (3) the creation of a special commission of inquiry — a sort of secular inquisition — to investigate and prosecute secret societies and others suspected of harboring subversive ideas. Although the rulers of some of the smaller states resented this interference with their internal affairs, Metternich's system prevailed, reinforced by a network of police spies and international agents. Except for a few brief and ineffectual episodes of agitation in the wake of the revolutions of 1830, his repression effectively stifled all manifestations of liberalism and nationalism in Germany until 1848.

THE BOURBON RESTORATION IN FRANCE

The government of the Bourbon Restoration in France rested on an uneasy compromise between the bourgeois liberalism surviving from the Revolution and the absolutist, so-called legitimist, aspirations of the monarchy and returned émigré nobility. This compromise, embodied in the Charter of 1814 and amended somewhat in 1830, served France as a constitution until 1848. The Charter, which Louis XVIII professed to grant voluntarily to his people, opened with a long preamble invoking Divine Providence and recalling the glories of the ancient monarchy, just barely omitting the phrase "divine right of kings." It continued with a series of twelve articles devoted to the "public rights of the French," a slightly modified restatement of the Declaration of the Rights of Man, and concluded with a brief and rather vague stipulation concerning the form of the government.

Executive power was vested in the king, to be exercised through his ministers. The Charter also provided for a bicameral legislature on the British model, with a Chamber of Peers appointed by the king — some hereditary, some for life — and a Chamber of Deputies indirectly elected by a franchise that was sharply restricted by age and property qualifications. In effect, the vote was restricted to approximately one of every hundred adult males — that is, those who belonged to the landed aristocracy and the upper bourgeoisie. They were considered the legal nation or *pays légal*. Two provisions of the Charter – one deliberately vague, the other quite explicit – are especially notable because of their subsequent history. One stated tersely that the "King's ministers are responsible," without stating to whom – the king or the chambers. The other permitted the king to issue ordinances "necessary for the . . . safety of the State."

Hastily composed though it was, the Charter might have become the basis for an evolving constitutional monarchy of the British type if it had not been for the men who manipulated it. Although the compromise could not prevent the White Terror of 1815 and 1816, in which royalists wreaked vengeance on former revolutionaries and Bonapartists, the worldly, cynical Louis for a time succeeded in placating most segments of the French population. But in 1820 the assassination of the king's nephew, the duke de Berri, forced the king to countenance a reactionary policy inspired by the Ultras – the extreme rightists – surrounding his brother, the future Charles X. Charles succeeded to the throne in 1824. With the Villèle ministry, which lasted from 1821 to 1827, the Ultras made a determined attempt to restore as far as possible the position that they had held under the Old Regime.

TORY RULE IN BRITAIN

Great Britain emerged from the Napoleonic wars as the most powerful and resplendent nation of the time. Alone among the victorious allies, Britain had opposed France continuously since the outbreak of war in 1792 (except for the brief truce of Amiens, when all of Europe was at peace). British money financed the triumphant coalition, British industry supplied it, and at Waterloo British troops under the duke of Wellington led it to the final victory. The British navy ruled the seas, protecting an enlarged empire; it was the only remaining empire of any significance. At home the changes in agriculture and industry that were to revolutionize economic and social life in the course of the nineteenth century were already under way, creating new wealth and affluence.

Nevertheless, the victory was not achieved without sacrifice. Under the pressure of war many of the traditional liberties of Englishmen had been suspended or restricted, as in the hated Combination Acts of 1799 and 1800. The very changes in agriculture and industry that produced riches and victory also produced dislocation and distress. War-induced inflation redistributed income at the expense of the least well-to-do, and a long postwar depression, accompanied by unemployment and falling wages, created popular discontent and reinforced demands for political, social, and economic reform. These movements were led by men such as the radical journalist William Cobbett (1763–1835), the humanitarian philanthropist Robert Owen (1771–1858), the egotistical demagogue Henry

"Orator" Hunt (1773–1835), and the utilitarian philosopher Jeremy Bentham (1748–1832). The governing Tory party responded to them with a reactionary policy as severely repressive as that inspired on the Continent by Metternich.

The Tories had been in power almost continuously since 1783. Although generally their leaders came from the same social class as the Whigs – that is, the aristocracy – and did not differ greatly in matters of principle, they clung resolutely to their positions for reasons of personal interest. Lord Liverpool, prime minister from 1812 to 1827, was a man of upright character though mediocre intelligence, but many of his supporters were venal, corrupt, and reactionary. Their policies were facilitated by their victory over Napoleon and also by the upper-class fear of social revolution and by the weakened authority of the crown. The dissolute and unpopular Prince of Wales (who later became George IV) reigned as regent for his father George III, permanently insane from 1811 to his death in 1820.

The Tory response to the postwar depression took the form of the new Corn Law of 1815, which almost totally excluded imported grain, thereby raising prices and keeping up rents on the estates of the wealthy. The government abolished the income tax and imposed new excise taxes on commodities consumed by the populace. In answer to the demands for reform expressed in petitions, public meetings, demonstrations, and occasional riots, the government adopted the infamous Coercion Acts of 1817, which suspended the right of habeas corpus, extended the meaning of the expression "seditious and treasonable activities," and increased the severity of punishment for violations.

In 1819 in the midst of the postwar depression a crowd assembled on St. Peter's Field in Manchester to listen to "Orator" Hunt demand parliamentary reform and repeal of the Corn Laws. Although the gathering was peaceable in itself, the authorities took fright and ordered soldiers to arrest the speaker and disperse the mob. The ensuing melee, in which eleven persons were killed and more than four hundred injured, was dubbed the Peterloo Massacre. In addition to the use of force, the government resorted to stringent new legislation. The Six Acts of 1819 went further than the Coercion Acts, imposing restrictions on the press, the right of assembly, and the right to bear arms. In 1820 the government was further convinced that these measures were amply justified when it discovered and frustrated the Cato Street conspiracy, an extremist plot to assassinate the cabinet in one blow.

OTHER REACTIONARY REGIMES

Elsewhere the prospects for liberalism and reform fared no better. In Sweden the French marshal Bernadotte, who had been elected crown prince in 1810, succeeded to the throne as Charles XIV in 1818. He followed a sternly reactionary and absolutist policy in Sweden and also in Norway, which had been joined to the Swedish crown against the wishes of the Norwegians. The newly created Kingdom of the Netherlands had a moderately liberal constitution on the model of the French Charter, but the arbitrary and stubborn King William I, former Prince of Orange, frequently over-stepped his prerogatives and aroused the antagonism of his subjects. The Belgians in particular, who had not been consulted on the decision to unite them with the Dutch, resented the inferior position that they occupied in the union.

The situation was worse to the south. The Bourbon Ferdinand VII, restored to the throne of Spain in 1814, promised to retain the liberal constitution adopted by the Cortes in 1812 at the height of the Spanish opposition to Napoleon. He soon defaulted on his promise and unleashed an orgy of reaction, misrule, and persecution that alienated even the army, one of the pillars of his regime. Under the surveillance of Austria the petty despots of Italy willingly danced to the tune of Metternich. In Piedmont the restored Victor Emmanuel I hated the principles of the French Revolution so much that he abolished the French legal codes and other reforms and restored almost intact the old semifeudal regime. He even uprooted the French plants in his botanical garden. At Rome Pius VII reestablished the Jesuits on a worldwide basis; the order had been widely regarded as a friend of absolutism and had been officially dissolved in 1776. The pope also reinstituted both the Inquisition and the Index and created a wholly clerical government for the States of the Church. Even in decentralized, republican Switzerland most of the cantons followed a reactionary policy and, under pressure from the great powers, persecuted political refugees from neighboring countries. In eastern Europe Tsar Alexander I of Russia, regarded as somewhat liberal in his youth, became increasingly reactionary.

By the beginning of 1820 the revolutionary ardor that had disturbed the tranquillity of Europe for more than three decades seemed to have been quelled at last. Yet the appearance was deceiving. In the overseas outposts of Western civilization the fires of revolution burned brightly, and in Europe itself the embers smoldered beneath the ashes of reaction.

THE RISING TIDE OF REVOLUTION
CHAPTER TWO

The antagonisms engendered by the oppressive policies of the restoration governments, together with powerful economic and social forces, gradually eroded and eventually overthrew the political and social system of the Vienna settlement. Revolutionary outbursts, at first weak and sporadic, grew in frequency and power throughout the first half of the century to culminate in the widespread and nearly simultaneous disorders of 1848. The revolutionists sought intellectual justification for their activities in the ideologies of liberalism and nationalism, sometimes strongly tinged with romanticism and occasionally with socialism. As long as both liberals and nationalists struggled against the same reactionary governments, it was easy for them to believe that they also struggled for the same objectives: liberty and self-determination. Not until 1848 did they discover the possibility of inherent conflict between the two.

REVOLUTIONARY CURRENTS: LIBERALISM AND NATIONALISM

LIBERALISM

Liberalism has many definitions, but classical or nineteenth-century liberalism embodied a belief that human progress could best be achieved by means of individual liberty and free institutions. Liberals advocated constitutional government, freedom of the press and religion, free speech, and freedom for individuals to pursue their own economic interests. Liberalism did not, however, involve the idea of democracy in the first half of the nineteenth century, for democracy meant the rule of the people. Liberalism was the creed of the growing middle classes, who wished to curb the arbitrary power of absolute monarchs and the special privileges of the landed aristocracy but did not want rule by the unpropertied masses. With the passage of time the basic ideas of liberalism proved capable of great extension, and in some cases liberalism gradually blended into republicanism, socialism, or a faith in democracy.

The first use of the word liberal in a political sense occurred in the 1820's, and was intended as an epithet, in much the same way that a demagogue today might label his domestic political opponent a Socialist or Communist. The Spanish revolutionaries of 1820 called themselves *liberales.* Supporters of the conservative or reactionary governing parties in France and Britain promptly applied the label to their opponents, where it stuck, eventually to be worn with pride. English liberals liked to trace their origins back at least to Magna Carta. Whether or not that claim was legitimate, it is clear that the political experiences of the seventeenth century had much to do with shaping English liberalism. In particular, Locke's treatises on civil government served as a foundation for much of the best liberal theory in England as well as on the Continent and in North America. The outstanding contemporary philosopher of English liberalism was Jeremy Bentham (1748–1832).

BENTHAM AND UTILITARIANISM

Bentham, scion of generations of successful London lawyers, trained for the legal profession himself. From the outset of his career he took an interest in legal reform. In his first published work, *A Fragment on Government* (1776), the young radical attacked the great jurist Blackstone for the latter's praises of the British constitution, which Bentham believed to be exaggerated and unjustified. In 1789 he published his most influential book, *An Introduction to the Principles of Morals and Legislation.* He continued to agitate for reform and to write throughout his long life (his collected works fill more than a dozen large volumes), and he inspired a whole school of philosophers and reformers whose influence in the world today is very strong.

Unlike other liberal philosophers in the tradition of Locke and the Enlightenment (including the American and French revolutionaries), Bentham rejected the doctrine of natural rights as a basis of political philosophy, calling it in effect metaphysical nonsense. Bentham adopted what he thought was a more practical, realistic approach and attempted to root his philosophy in human nature and psychology. "Nature has placed mankind under the governance of two sovereign masters, *pain* and *pleasure*. . . . They govern us in all we do, in all we say, in all we think: every effort we can make to throw off our subjection, will serve but to demonstrate and confirm it." Human happiness, according to Bentham, consisted in the attainment of pleasure and the avoidance of pain. The quality or property of conferring happiness Bentham called "utility"; hence his philosophy is called utilitarianism. "By the principle of utility is meant that principle which approves or disapproves of every action whatsoever, according to the tendency which it appears to have

The Mansell Collection

Jeremy Bentham

"Bentham has been in this age and century the great questioner of things established. It is by the influence of the modes of thought with which his writings innoculated a considerable number of thinking men, that the yoke of authority has been broken, and innumerable opinions, formerly received upon tradition as incontestable, are put upon their defence and required to give an account of themselves. Who, before Bentham . . . dared to speak disrespectfully . . . of the British Constitution, or the English Law? He did so; and his arguments and his example together encouraged others. . . . Until he spoke out, those who found our institutions unsuited to them did not dare to say so, did not dare consciously to think so. Bentham broke the spell." John Stuart Mill, ESSAYS ON POLITICS AND CULTURE, ed. Gertrude Himmelfarb (Garden City, N.Y., 1962).

to augment or diminish the happiness of the party whose interest is in question." The object of government was to promote human happiness, which had been stated in the formula "the greatest good of the greatest number" by Beccaria, Bentham's Italian predecessor. Bentham and his followers, therefore, judged governments according to the manner in which their policies conformed to the principle of utility.

Bentham's followers included many distinguished intellects of the first half of the nineteenth century, including James Mill and his famous son, John Stuart Mill. The latter was a notable example of utilitarian education: he learned Greek at the age of three, digested David Ricardo's *Principles of Political Economy and Taxation* at thirteen, and had a nervous breakdown at twenty; but he recovered and went on to become one of England's foremost philosophers. The utilitarians were not overtly revolutionary; in their personal lives most of them were eminently respectable, even staid. Nevertheless, their ceaseless questioning and agitation for reform and a philosophy that was congenial to the British middle classes enabled them to carry out a series of silent revolutions, which were the more effectual in that they did not arouse undying, unregenerate opposition. In the words of John Stuart Mill, written in 1838, six years after Bentham's death, "The father of English innovation, both in doctrines and in institutions, is Bentham: he is the great *subversive,* or in the language of continental philosophers, the great *critical* thinker of his age and country."

CONTINENTAL LIBERALISM

French liberalism drew heavily on the writers of the Enlightenment and the ideals of the Revolution, but at the same time French liberals sought to dissociate themselves from Jacobinism and the excesses of the Revolution. As a result, whereas English liberalism was pragmatic, flexible, and evolutionary, French liberalism approached dogmatism. Indeed, one group of French liberals called themselves *doctrinaires.* They regarded the Charter of 1814 as a satisfactory instrument of government and were well content, on the whole, with the restoration government until it began to swing back toward royal absolutism under Charles X. Slightly to the left of the doctrinaires was a group that played a leading role in the revolution of 1830. It included the philosopher Benjamin Constant, the aging Marquis de Lafayette, and the fiery young journalist Adolphe Thiers. The greatest of the French liberal philosophers, Alexis de Tocqueville, belonged to no one school or party. Although he was an aristocrat, he foresaw the advent of democracy and sought to warn his countrymen and all mankind to make the most of its virtues without letting it result in mediocrity and mass tyranny. In his view the spirit of government was far more important than its outward forms.

Elsewhere on the Continent liberalism had few followers and fewer spokesmen, except in Belgium and Germany. Liberalism appealed especially to the middle classes of business and professional men. It flourished where they were most numerous and influential. In southern and eastern Europe liberalism became the creed of a few disaffected intellectuals who had little popular support. The smaller their prospects for success, the shriller became their pronouncements and the more violent their actions. Liberals in these areas of retarded economic and social development were eventually absorbed by the prevailing conservatism, or attracted to more radical ideologies.

NATIONALISM

The word nationalism refers to the awareness, sometimes reaching the intensity of a religious belief, of belonging to a distinct nationality. Although nation-states such as the Spanish, French, and English monarchies had arisen in the late Middle Ages, nationalism as a mass phenomenon developed only at the end of the eighteenth century. The first French Republic contributed to the development of popular nationalism with its patriotic symbols and *levée en masse* (military conscription). The revolutionary and Napoleonic wars helped spread it to much of the rest of Europe through emulation of or opposition to the conquering French. The Germans, who were divided and subject to foreign rule and oppression, were perhaps the foremost spokesmen of nationalist sentiments. Johann Gottfried Herder (1744–1803), a German clergyman and a forerunner of romanticism, first advanced a systematic theory of nationalism. His was a cultural nationalism, but under the impact of the Napoleonic wars nationalism became far more political. In "Addresses to the German Nation" Johann Fichte declared in 1808 that "to have character and to be German undoubtedly mean one and the same thing." When the War of Liberation began in 1813, he sent his students to fight against the French.

Nationalism continued to flourish and spread after the fall of Napoleon. National minorities in the polyglot Hapsburg and Russian empires and oppressed nationalities in Norway, Ireland, and the Belgian Netherlands sought to throw off alien rule. Politically divided nationalities — the Germans and Italians in particular — began to dream of unified national states. The current of nationalism even stirred the subject principalities of the Ottoman Empire in the Balkan peninsula. Romanticism played a part in this phase of the movement. The collectors of folk tales and folk songs, the philologists who sought to revive medieval Gaelic, Norwegian, or Slavonic languages, the poets and novelists who wrote of the heroic past, even the artists and musicians contributed to the development of national identities and patriotic sentiments. After 1815 the restoration governments pursued essentially cosmopolitan, antinational policies under the influence of Metternich, but they actually stimulated the growth of nationalism through their crude, inefficient attempts to repress it. Most of the youth groups and revolutionary secret societies that sprang up after 1815 — the *Burschenschaften* in Germany, the *Carbonari* in Italy, the *Hetairia Philike* in Greece, and others — were strongly nationalistic, as were the leaders of the revolutions in the New World.

REVOLUTION AND SELF-GOVERNMENT IN THE AMERICAS

The ideals of self-determination and self-government quickly took root in the Western Hemisphere after the successful revolt of Britain's American colonies. Not all who fought for American independence did so in the name of democracy, but the Declaration of Independence planted democratic seeds in virgin soil and the war itself fertilized them with the blood of patriots. Thereafter the growth of democracy could not be restrained. The example of the United States as a free, independent, and self-governing republic gave inspiration and courage to those both north and south of its borders who opposed the ineptitude and exploitation of their European rulers. After a series of constitutional struggles the inhabitants of Canada gained limited self-government within the framework of the British Empire. The colonies of Spain and Portugal achieved full independence, although difficulties of communication and the pronounced regionalism of some of the leaders of the former Spanish colonies resulted in the formation of many quarrelsome and unstable republics instead of one or a few large nations.

THE UNITED STATES: TERRITORIAL EXPANSION AND THE RISE OF THE COMMON MAN, 1815–1850

At the time of adoption of the Constitution of 1789 electoral procedures in the United States were by no means democratic. The Constitution provided for indirect election of the President, the Vice President, and the Senate, and allowed each state to determine the manner of choosing its members of the House of Representatives. Most states had substantial property and other qualifications for the suffrage, which sharply limited the number of voters. As a result, for the first decade under the Constitution most state governments and the national government had a marked aristocratic character. The first notable change occurred with the election of Thomas Jefferson in 1800, sometimes called the Jeffersonian revolution because of Jefferson's forthright democratic philosophy. Thereafter the democratic tide rose rapidly, and by 1830 nearly all states had adopted white manhood suffrage. The new states west of the Alleghenies played a prominent part in the process of democratization. Their constitutions manifested the spirit of independence and egalitarianism of their inhabitants, who were mainly frontiersmen and small farmers. The triumph of democratic sentiment was symbolized by the presidential election of 1828, when Andrew Jackson of Tennessee became the first president from a state west of the Alleghenies.

The Constitution strengthened the central government at the expense of the states, but it did not reduce the latter to insignificance. Alexander Hamilton, Washington's principal adviser, sought to make the national government a more vigorous agency for the promotion of commerce and industry, but the Jeffersonians reversed the tendency. Although the exigencies of war in Europe and eventually in the United States required Jefferson and Madison temporarily to exert greater authority as presidents, with the end of the war they returned to their earlier doctrine of state sovereignty. In his last official act as president in 1817, Madison vetoed a bill that would have permitted the national government to undertake a substantial program of internal improvements (mainly road and canal construction). Until the Civil War his successors generally followed his precedent.

The limited powers exercised by the national government in the realm of internal affairs did not imply a negative role for government in general. State and local governments took an active part in promoting economic development and social welfare legislation in the first half of the nineteenth century. Their role differed from the role of governments in seventeenth- and eighteenth-century Europe, for instead of being imposed from above, their participation in the economic and social life of the citizenry sprang from the interests and wishes of the people themselves.

As a consequence of its rapid expansion the United States came into conflict with its neighbors, especially those to the south and west. In 1819 Spain ceded Florida to the United States after a series of border disturbances. Shortly afterward westward-bound Americans began to move into Texas, which had been part of Mexico since Mexico's successful revolt from Spain in 1821. By the 1830's Texas's population of Anglo-American stock surpassed that of Mexican ancestry. Texas declared and won its independence from Mexico in a brief war in 1836 and in 1845 the Republic of Texas petitioned for annexation to the United States. This action and other difficulties between the United States and Mexico led to war in 1846. By the Treaty of Guadalupe Hidalgo in 1848 Mexico gave up its claims to Texas, recognized the Rio Grande as the boundary between Mexico and the United States, and ceded the territories of New Mexico and California to the United States for the sum of $15,000,000. In 1846 the United States settled its dispute with Great Britain over the boundaries of the Oregon territory. These settlements, together with the Gadsden Purchase of land from Mexico in 1853, rounded out the limits of the continental United States.

BRITISH NORTH AMERICA: LIMITED SELF-GOVERNMENT AND REBELLION

After the American Revolution thousands of British loyalists migrated from the United States to New Brunswick and the region north of lakes Erie and Ontario. To prevent difficulties with the French-speaking population, the British government in 1791 divided its territory into Upper Canada (later called Ontario and chiefly English) and Lower Canada (later Quebec, largely French). Each division had a royal governor, an appointed legislative council, and an elective assembly. These organs were given limited self-government, although Parliament retained the right to veto colonial legislation.

During the War of 1812 the United States attempted to conquer and annex Canada, but the Canadians remained loyal to the British crown and repulsed the invasion. Shortly after the war, however, trouble arose between the popularly elected assemblies and the imperial authority represented by the royal governors and legislative councils. After negotiations failed to solve the problems, the popular party led by William Lyon Mackenzie rose in an unsuccessful rebellion in 1837. Lord Durham, the new governor-general for all of British North America, treated the rebels with leniency and submitted a now famous report to London calling for colonial self-government. In 1840 Parliament passed the Union Act, which abolished the division between Upper and Lower Canada and introduced a number of administrative reforms. It did not fully meet the issue of responsible government, however, and the problem continued to plague British-Canadian relations until after the American Civil War.

REVOLT AND DISUNION IN LATIN AMERICA

During the Napoleonic wars, when the French drove Ferdinand VII of Spain from his throne and made Spain a French satellite, Spain's American colonies refused to acknowledge French sovereignty and began to experiment with self-government. The American and French revolutions had already implanted the idea of independence. When in 1814 Ferdinand indicated his intention to restore the old colonial system intact, the movement for independence gathered speed.

The Spanish colonies had ample cause for rebellion. Except for the ineffectual reforms of Charles III in the eighteenth century, the oppressive character of Spanish rule had changed little in almost three hundred years. The colonies enjoyed not the slightest measure of self-government. The viceroys and other high officials of both state and church came directly from Spain. The native-born inhabitants of Spanish ancestry, who were called creoles and controlled most of the domestic wealth, shared with the mestizos, those of mixed Spanish and Indian ancestry, a common hatred of their overlords. As for the Indians, they lived either in a tribal

state or in a condition bordering on slavery. There was also a small number of Negro slaves.

The independence movement was hindered at first by the confused state of affairs in the mother country, the attitude of the local aristocrats, and poor communications. Only the United Provinces of La Plata (Argentina) and Paraguay had succeeded in establishing independence by 1816. Thereafter the movement developed rapidly. José de San Martín, one of the leaders of the Argentinian revolt, joined forces with Bernardo O'Higgins to liberate Chile in 1818. With the assistance of a British naval officer, Lord Cochrane, he then moved by sea against Peru, the center of Spanish power in South America, and proclaimed its independence in 1821. Simón Bolívar, another popular hero, led the independence movement in northern South America and created the state of Gran Colombia (comprising Colombia, Venezuela, Ecuador, and Panama). In Mexico the movement for liberation developed into a revolt of the lower classes against the native aristocracy, but when independence came in 1821, it took the form of a reactionary government dominated by aristocratic elements. Stimulated by the revolt in Mexico, the Central American provinces rebelled and in 1823 established the United Provinces of Central America. By 1825 Spain had been excluded from the Western Hemisphere except for the islands of Cuba and Puerto Rico.

Brazil arrived at the same point as the former Spanish colonies by a different route. The Portuguese king moved his seat of government to Brazil in 1808 when he was threatened by Napoleon, and he continued to reside there until 1821. During this period Brazil came to regard itself as an independent nation. When the king returned to Portugal he left his son, Dom Pedro, as regent in Brazil. The Brazilians declared their independence and persuaded Dom Pedro to remain at the head of the government as constitutional monarch of the Empire of Brazil.

Domestic revolutions in Spain and Portugal in 1820 and the favorable attitudes of Great Britain and the United States toward independence for the colonies materially assisted the movement. At the Congress of Aix-la-Chapelle in 1818 and again at Verona in 1822, Tsar Alexander of Russia proposed concerted intervention by European powers to restore Spain's colonial empire, but the British had developed strong commercial interests in Latin America and had no desire to see the colonies again placed under Spain's restrictive colonial regime. Inasmuch as Britain maintained undisputed mastery of the seas, the tsar's proposal came to naught. In 1823 George Canning, the British foreign minister, suggested that the United States and Great Britain issue a joint declaration warning other European powers not to interfere with Spain's former colonies, but John Quincy Adams, the American secretary of state, felt that the United States should not "come in as a cockboat in the wake of the British man-of-war." He preferred unilateral action. American officials were also concerned about the activities of Russian explorers and trappers along the Pacific coast. In December, 1823, President James Monroe stated the Monroe Doctrine in a message to Congress. Principally drafted by Adams, it declared "that the American Continents, by the free and independent condition which they have assumed and maintain, are henceforth not to be considered as subjects for future colonization by any European power."

The new nations of Latin America soon discovered that independence alone did not bring tranquility. A few idealists like Bolívar dreamed of a unified nation of all Spanish-speaking peoples in South America, and Mexico at one time attempted to incorporate all the states of Central America. Yet the sources of discord were too many and too great. The administrative divisions and isolation of the colonial period left a legacy of separatism and rudimentary nationalism that the ephemeral cooperation of the revolutionary period could not overcome. Poor communications and geographic and climatic differences also hindered attempts at permanent union and played into the hands of ambitious political leaders, each of whom wished to carve out his own personal domain. At the end of the wars of independence ten new nations emerged from the remnants of the old Spanish and Portuguese empires. Less than a generation later the number had grown to eighteen by a process of division and separation. Throughout the century border disputes and other conflicts proved to be the chronic state of affairs among these new nations.

Their domestic affairs were no more peaceful or happy than their interstate relations. Revolution, civil war, political instability, and other ailments of the body politic remained endemic. One of the most important difficulties was the fact that since most Latin Americans were illiterate, poverty-stricken, and completely inexperienced in managing their own affairs, they were unprepared for self-government. In addition, except for Brazil they all chose the most difficult form of government – the republican form. Because of the strong vested interests of the church and the resident aristocracy their history has been punctuated by revolution, palace revolt, and dictatorship. Liberals opposed conservatives, federalists fought centralists, anticlericals struggled against the clergy, and ambitious, scheming individuals sought positions of power, prestige, and wealth. The history of Latin America in the nineteenth century proved to be a dismally accurate preview of developments in the nations of Asia and Africa in the twentieth century when they were liberated from colonial rule.

ROMANTIC REVOLUTION, 1820–1829

Metternich's system survived its first test in Germany, but it soon faced greater strains elsewhere, leading to the ultimate disruption of the concert of Europe. The oppressive policies of restoration rulers in the Iberian and Italian peninsulas provoked popular uprisings which, although easily repressed by armed intervention of the great powers, caused a split between Great Britain and its continental allies. An eventually successful nationalist revolt in Greece produced a chain of repercussions that fur-

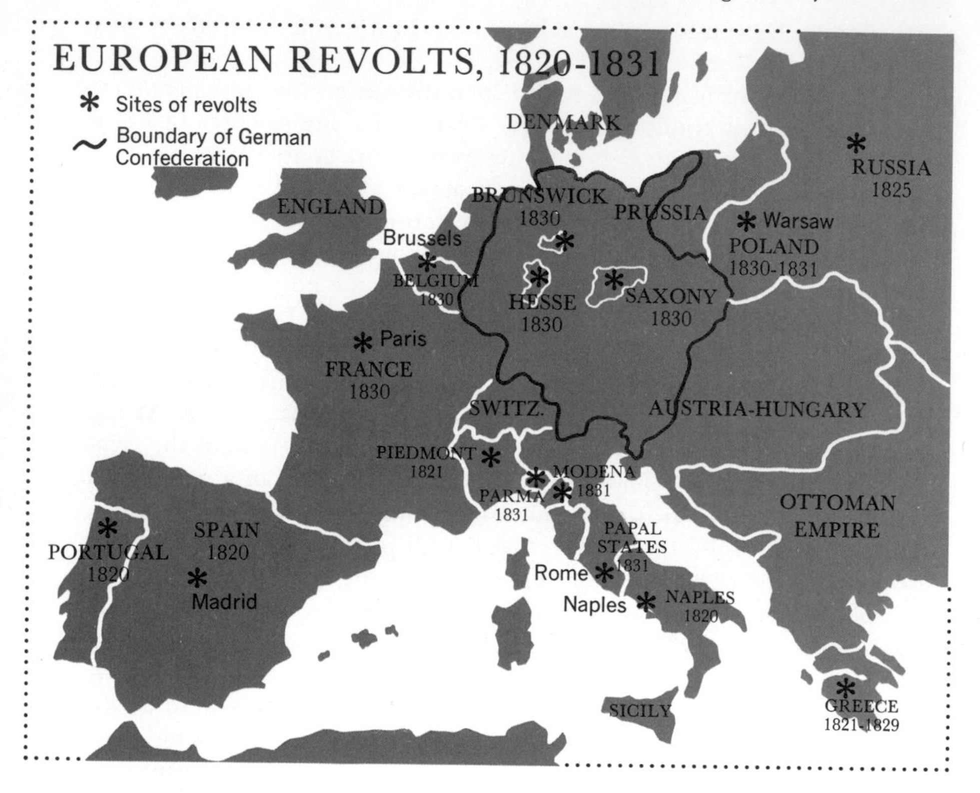

ther weakened international cooperation. Finally, a liberal revolution in France broke the conservative monopoly of the reins of government and inaugurated a series of defections from the conservative camp.

SPAIN, 1820

The witless reaction of Ferdinand VII in Spain (see p. 32) led his government into increasing difficulties. In an effort to regain the American colonies, which had been a major source of government income, Ferdinand gathered a large army at Cadiz in preparation for embarkation. Demoralized by the incompetence of the government, the army mutinied and began to march on the capital. Spontaneous riots and demonstrations in support of the army broke out in Madrid, Barcelona, and other major urban centers, forcing Ferdinand to restore the liberal constitution of 1812.

At the first news of the revolt Alexander of Russia called for a congress to take concerted action to crush it. The British foreign minister, Castlereagh, responded that the Spanish revolution was a domestic affair; Britain was committed by treaty only to preventing the return of Napoleon and guaranteeing the territorial arrangements agreed upon at

Vienna. Castlereagh and Alexander had differed before on the question of the Spanish colonies at the Congress of Aix-la-Chapelle. Not only did Britain, as the world's greatest trading and industrial nation, stand to gain by the collapse of Spain's restrictive colonial system, but its interest in preserving a balance of power also required opposition to Russian intervention in the affairs of western Europe. Metternich, who also suspected Alexander's belated but overenthusiastic support for absolutism, had stood with Castlereagh in 1818 and was inclined to do so again, when events took an unexpected turn.

PORTUGAL AND ITALY, 1820

The revolution in Spain proved contagious. Within the year similar revolutions took place in Naples and Portugal, and during the following year in Piedmont and Greece. Metternich could ill afford to ignore the revolutions in Italy. In fact, Austria had a treaty with Naples prohibiting constitutional changes that had not also been agreed upon for the Austrian possessions in Italy. Alarmed by the outbursts, the great powers held a congress at Troppau, Austria. Russia, Austria, and Prussia signed an agreement, called the Troppau Protocol, providing for intervention by the powers to suppress domestic revolutions, which they labeled "a threat to the peace of Europe." Britain abstained but did not seek to prevent Austria from sending an expeditionary force to put down the risings in Italy. By the late spring of 1821 Austrian troops occupied Italy from tip to toe and the absolutist sovereigns had been restored in both Naples and Piedmont.

No decision concerning the revolution in Spain was reached at Troppau or at Laibach, to which the congress adjourned at the beginning of 1821. A new congress took place in Verona in 1822. Louis XVIII of France, seeking to bolster French prestige within the concert of Europe and to prevent Russian soldiers from crossing French soil on their way to Spain, applied to the congress for approval of his plan to restore Ferdinand and abolish the Spanish constitution. Britain opposed any joint action in Spain but could not prevent the French expedition, which after a brief campaign in the summer of 1823 defeated the revolutionary army and restored Ferdinand once again.

The revolution in Portugal contained elements of nationalism as well as liberalism, adding substance to its pronounced romantic coloring. During the Napoleonic wars the Portuguese king, John VI, had retired to Brazil, leaving the government of Portugal to a regency dominated by the British. After 1815 the anomalous situation continued until insurgents overthrew the regency, adopted a liberal constitution on the model of the Spanish constitution, and demanded that John return as constitutional monarch. Rather than lose his Portuguese throne altogether, John came back in 1822, but he soon began to intrigue against his liberal supporters. A civil war was in progress when John died in 1826. The country became further divided between the supporters of John's eldest son and heir, Dom Pedro, to whom he had earlier left the government of Brazil, and his younger son Dom Miguel, who was supported by the most reactionary factions. Dom Pedro complicated the situation by refusing to leave Brazil, whose independence from Portugal he had already declared. He abdicated the Portuguese throne in favor of his seven-year-old daughter Maria da Gloria, with the understanding that she would marry her uncle, Dom Miguel. Miguel, a personal friend and great admirer of Metternich, assented to this solution and even agreed to respect the constitution; but as soon as he arrived in Lisbon he deposed his young bride-to-be, abrogated the constitution, and ruled alone as absolute monarch.

GREECE, 1821–1829

The revolution in Greece had an even greater element of nationalism, strongly tinged with the romanticism of the Philhellenes, Western Europeans who regarded the modern Greeks as the direct descendants of the ancient Athenian democracy. After more than three hundred years of Turkish rule the Greeks had experienced a cultural and economic revival in the second half of the eighteenth century. Although the French Revolution did not affect Greece directly, it had contributed to the revival of Greek nationalism. Encouraged by the revolts in Spain and Italy, the Greeks finally rose against their Turkish masters in 1821. The revolt posed a delicate question for the diplomats of the great powers. On the one hand, the Greeks were Christian and European; the Turks were not. On the other hand, a revolution was still a revolution, regardless of the parties. Metternich's preferred solution was to let it burn itself out "beyond the pale of civilization," but it refused to do so. Paradoxically, Alexander wished to intervene on behalf of the revolutionaries, hoping to expand Russian influence in the Balkans at the expense of the Turks, long an aim of the Russians. Britain thereupon felt obliged to intervene in order to prevent Russian expansion.

While the great powers, including France, sparred with one another, the Greeks kept up the struggle against the Turks and even found time and energy to fight among themselves. The Turks, meanwhile, had been joined by the sultan's vassal, Mohammed Ali of Egypt. Eventually the Russians, British, and French, each with one eye upon the others, undertook semiconcerted action, with the Russians going so far as a formal declaration of war and an invasion of Turkey in 1828. The Treaty of Adrianople on September 14, 1829, ended the war and provided for an independent Greece. The Russians strengthened their protectorate over the principalities of Moldavia and Wallachia, still nominally within the Ottoman Empire, while those provinces gained greater autonomy for domestic affairs. Serbia, which had also been the scene of nationalist agitation, likewise obtained autonomy from Turkey.

THE DECEMBRIST REVOLT IN RUSSIA, 1825

Even Russia experienced a brief attempt at revolution. Until 1820 the changeable Alexander I had toyed with reform and plans for a constitution. When Russia acquired Finland from Sweden in 1809, Alexander organized that country as an autonomous grand duchy with himself as duke and allowed the Finns constitutional government. The Polish kingdom created at Vienna was also given a parliament and other constitutional forms, although Alexander as king frequently frustrated their operation and after 1820 increasingly opposed the aspirations of the nationalist Poles. Meanwhile, as Alexander's plans for reform in Russia never seemed to materialize and as he became more frankly reactionary and autocratic, army officers who had been infected with liberalism by contact with the West began to form secret societies to propagate their ideas.

When Alexander died on December 13, 1825, a brief interregnum resulted from his failure to stipulate clearly the line of succession. Since Alexander had no children, his brother Constantine would normally have succeeded him, but Constantine had renounced the succession in favor of his younger brother Nicholas – without informing Nicholas of the fact. For nearly three weeks Russia had no emperor. The leaders of one of the army's secret societies tried to take advantage of the situation by staging an ill-planned, half-hearted coup d'état. Nicholas immediately took charge, suppressed the uprising, summarily executed or exiled its leaders, and inaugurated a thirty-year reign of autocracy and repression. The ill-fated Decembrist Revolt became one of the legends of revolutionary liberalism, but Russia, like Spain and Portugal, did not in fact possess the social basis for a truly liberal movement.

LIBERAL REVOLUTION, 1830–1834

A dozen years after the Congress of Vienna the system it established had been tested in almost every spot. Liberal and nationalist demonstrations and revolts had been quelled in Germany, Italy, Spain, Portugal, and Russia. Reactionary domestic policies had hardly been challenged in the Austrian Empire and France. Only in Greece had a revolution succeeded, and that after several years of bitter struggle and with the support of some of the great powers. It seemed that Metternich's system of divide and conquer, repress and rule, had stood up well. Yet it was clear that a rift had taken place on the international scene and was growing wider, threatening to extend to domestic affairs as well. Although Britain was governed by a conservative majority, the Tories, its interests differed sharply from those of the landowning aristocracies and absolutist monarchies of central and eastern Europe. The growth of commercial and industrial middle classes, in France and the Low Countries as well as in Britain, strengthened the growing liberal movement and accentuated the differences between the constitutional governments of the west and the absolutist governments of the rest of Europe. The breakdown of the concert of Europe, presaged by the differences between Alexander and Britain on the question of the Spanish colonies as early as 1818, was accomplished by 1823. In the words of George Canning, who succeeded Castlereagh as British foreign minister in 1822, it was "every nation for itself and God for us all." Metternich's system had survived the first wave of revolutionary assaults but, weakened by the withdrawal of the British, it would be rudely shaken by the second.

THE REVOLUTION OF 1830 IN FRANCE

After the assassination of the duke de Berri in 1820 the French government became increasingly reactionary. It forced a new electoral law favorable to the old aristocracy at the expense of the middle class; enacted a stringent press law; turned education over even more completely to the church and in other ways facilitated the "union of throne and altar"; dissolved the National Guard, a stronghold of the middle class; and indemnified the nobility for their losses during the revolution at the expense of the bourgeois holders of government bonds.

These measures aroused opposition and resentment among the very people whose good will and cooperation was most necessary to the existence of the regime: the upper bourgeoisie and their journalistic and political henchmen. They included such men as banker Jacques Laffitte, industrialist Casimir Périer, journalist Adolphe Thiers, and wily, aging Talleyrand, who even in semiretirement could not break his lifelong habit of plotting against the regimes he had helped create. These men were liberals in politics, skeptics in religious matters, and ambitious in all things. Under the restricted franchise of the restoration monarchy they alone shared effective political power with the aristocracy; they were the cutting edge of the new social classes created by the revolutionary economic changes. Louis XVIII, for all his faults, had recognized the necessity of cultivating them and very nearly succeeded in attaching them permanently to the regime, at least as a "loyal opposition." To Charles X and his advisers, however, the wealth, ideas, and above all the social and political pretensions of these men were anathema.

Oblivious of the resentment his policies aroused, Charles in 1827 called for a new election to strengthen his majority in the Chamber of Deputies. Greatly to his chagrin the election returned a liberal majority. He was obliged to appoint a moderate ministry and rescind the most stringent provisions of the press and censorship law. In 1830 Charles again tired of the fetters of constitutionalism, dissolved the chamber, and called for

The Bettmann Archive

At the Barricades, July, 1830, by Georges Cain

"People of Paris, Charles X has ceased to reign over France! Unable to forget the origin of his authority, he has always considered himself as the enemy of our country and of its liberties which he was unable to comprehend. After attacking our institutions in an underhand manner by every means that hypocrisy and fraud offered him, when he felt himself strong enough to destroy them openly, he resolved to drown them in the blood of the French. Thanks to your heroism, an end has been put to the crimes of his power." Proclamation of the Municipal Commission of Paris, July 31, 1830, reprinted in J. B. Duvergier, COLLECTION COMPLÈTE DES LOIS, DÉCRETS, etc. (Paris, 1838), Vol. XXX.

---

a new election. Instead of giving him a majority, the election strengthened the opposition. Without convening the new chamber, Charles and his ministers began preparing a group of ordinances that had the effect of a royal coup d'état: they dissolved the chamber before it met, called for yet another election, amended the electoral law to reduce the electorate by three-fourths, and provided for strict censorship of the press.

These ordinances were published on July 25, 1830. Two days later Thiers and other journalists who had financial backing from the liberals defied the ordinances and distributed circulars calling on the people of

Paris to resist the king's violation of the Charter. Once again the French bourgeoisie asked the mobs of Paris to fight their revolution, and once again the barricades appeared. Revolutionary committees were quickly formed, arms appeared and were distributed to the street fighters, and elements of the disbanded National Guard redonned their uniforms. On July 28 the mobs seized the Hôtel de Ville (city hall) and raised the triumphant tricolor. After a dispirited attack on the crowds the regular troops revolted and fraternized with the people. Once again Paris had made a revolution – but this time with negligible bloodletting and almost before the provinces knew about it.

The revolution succeeded, but who was the victor? Two distinct elements participated in the victory: the liberal journalists and politicians who had fomented it, and the mobs of Paris, "the people," who had executed it. The former wanted a strictly limited constitutional monarchy dominated by the men of wealth, such as the one which had issued from the English revolution of 1689 and which the Charter had failed to give them. The Parisian street fighters were vaguely republican in sentiment but were less organized. On the morning of July 30 Paris awoke to find the city placarded with posters calling for Louis Philippe, duke of Orleans, to take the throne. He was a relative of the Bourbons but was well known for his bourgeois sentiments and interests. He had participated in the early stages of the great revolution of 1789, and his father, called Philippe Égalité because of his extreme devotion to the revolutionary cause, had even voted for the execution of Louis XVI. The next day, July 31, Louis Philippe traveled to the Hôtel de Ville where, draped in the tricolor, Lafayette presented him to the crowd and called for "a throne surrounded by republican institutions." Thus began the July Monarchy, so-called because of the date of its inauguration. After swearing to uphold the Charter, which had been amended by omission of both the monarchic preamble and provision for government by ordinance, Louis Philippe on August 9 was proclaimed "King of the French, by the grace of God and the will of the nation."

BELGIAN INDEPENDENCE

News of the revolution in France traveled fast. Within a month it triggered an uprising in Brussels, which, however, had more nationalist and fewer class characteristics. The Belgians had no voice at Vienna in the decision to place them under the rule of the Dutch king, who differed in language and religion (the Belgians spoke Flemish or French and were Catholic). The more numerous Belgians had a just pride in their own history and traditions and resented domination from The Hague. At first the revolutionaries demanded only a separate legislature and administration under a common king, but in the face of King William's stubborn opposition they soon declared for complete independence.

A number of international factors favored Belgian independence. The French, who were mindful of their own revolution and anxious for a revision of the Vienna settlement, were favorably disposed. Austria and Russia, who would have intervened by force, found themselves unable to do so because of similar nationalist uprisings in their own multinational empires. Most important, in Great Britain a new Whig ministry, with Viscount Palmerston as foreign secretary, had just taken over the reins of government. Britain had already split with the other great powers on the question of internal revolutions, and Palmerston in particular was favorable to national self-determination. He persuaded representatives of the other powers to accept Belgian independence and, when William attempted to regain his provinces by force, sanctioned British and French military and naval support to repel the Dutch invaders. William was forced to agree to an armistice but rejected a permanent peace settlement. Finally in 1838, under pressure from his own subjects as well as the great powers, he signed the treaty recognizing Belgium as an "independent and perpetually neutral state," whose neutrality was collectively guaranteed by all the great powers.

Meanwhile, under the benevolent protection of both France and Great Britain the Belgians had already created a national state – the first in Belgian history. As in France, the mobs in the streets were responsible for the success of the revolution, but middle-class business and professional men soon took over leadership of the movement. Of the various alternative forms of government they clearly preferred a strictly limited constitutional monarchy like that of France or England. Although the constitution they adopted was the most liberal in Europe at the time, it granted the right to vote to less than fifty thousand in a country with a total population of four million. Their first choice for a king was the duke de Nemours, second son of Louis Philippe; but the displeasure of Palmerston, who had no intention of seeing Belgium exchange a Dutch for a French king, persuaded Louis Philippe to veto the selection. The Belgians eventually settled on Prince Leopold of Saxe-Coburg-Gotha, a younger son of one of the oldest and most respected ruling houses of Germany. For the Belgians he had the additional advantage of having been "domesticated" by long residence and close connections in Britain, since he was the widower of Princess Charlotte of England and the uncle and trusted adviser of the future Queen Victoria. To enhance further his own prestige and that of Belgium, he shortly married the daughter of Louis Philippe.

REVOLUTION AND ANARCHY IN THE IBERIAN PENINSULA

In Spain and Portugal the civil wars of the 1820's continued into the following decade. The coup d'état of 1828 by Dom Miguel of Portugal signaled a renewal of the struggle between absolutism and constitutionalism in that country. In 1832, with the assistance of Britain and France Maria da Gloria was restored to the Portuguese throne, and in 1836 she married Duke Ferdinand of Saxe-Coburg. The next quarter century was characterized by continued financial and political instability. Lacking fundamental legal reforms and the growth of a vigorous middle class, parliamentary liberalism maintained a precarious existence in Portugal, eventually to succumb to revolution and dictatorship.

After his second restoration to the throne of Spain in 1823, Ferdinand VII demonstrated his complete incapacity for learning from experience by resorting again to reaction and repression. After his death in 1833 his brother Don Carlos contested for the throne with the supporters of Ferdinand's infant daughter Isabella. Isabella's mother turned to the constitutionalists for support and, through them, to France and Britain. In 1834 Britain, France, Spain, and Portugal formed a Quadruple Alliance designed to protect the constitutional monarchs of the two latter countries. Although the alliance defeated the Carlists, the social and economic basis for enlightened self-government did not exist in Spain any more than in Portugal and the countries of eastern Europe. Corruption, instability, and civil war continued to characterize the government of Spain.

OTHER REVOLUTIONARY MOVEMENTS

The July Revolution in France had repercussions in other lands, but with few exceptions they accomplished little. In Italy secret revolutionary societies were formed by young liberals whose patriotism had been aroused during the Napoleonic era. Chief among them was the *Carbonari* (charcoal burners), which sought eventual unification in a single national Italian state. Early in 1831, encouraged by the success of the revolutions in France and Belgium and hoping for French intervention against the Austrians, they staged risings in Modena, Parma, and the States of the Church. Temporarily successful, the revolutionists were soon disappointed by the response of France, whose bourgeois government had no desire to jeopardize its own position by antagonizing the other great powers. The Italian revolts quickly succumbed to Austrian force.

Poland was another area in which patriotic and nationalist sentiments had been stirred by the Napoleonic reorganization and then left unrealized by the settlement at Vienna. In 1830 the Poles also revolted against their foreign overlord, the tsar. Led by secret societies of intellectuals, students, and aristocrats, the revolution at first scored a surprisingly quick success, but torn by factional disputes among their leaders and lacking the hoped-for assistance from the west, the revolutionaries fell in 1831 before the ferocious reprisals of the Russian army. Tsar Nicholas abolished the Polish constitution, closed the University of Warsaw, and initiated an intensive policy of russification of the Polish people. Most of the active revolutionists who escaped death, including the composer Chopin, fled to western European capitals, especially Paris, where they kept alive the hope of a Polish nation and contributed to the intellectual and cultural life of the West.

In central Europe the revolutions of 1830 had fewer repercussions. The subjects of the duke of Brunswick expelled their ruler, and the governments of some of the other smaller states made temporary liberal concessions, but Austria and Prussia stood firm. In 1832 Metternich persuaded the Diet of the Germanic Confederation to adopt the oppressive Six Acts, which renewed and extended the earlier Carlsbad Decrees. In 1833 the rulers of Austria, Prussia, and Russia signed a secret treaty in which each reaffirmed its absolutist policies and promised to aid the other in the event of revolution.

PARLIAMENTARY REFORM IN GREAT BRITAIN

Seasoned by centuries of evolving constitutional government, Great Britain narrowly avoided the kind of revolutionary upheaval that infected the Continent by a prudent if reluctant compromise on the part of the aristocracy with the new middle classes. In England the landowning aristocracy already had connections with the growing commercial and industrial movement. Nevertheless, in the immediate post-Napoleonic years the governing Tory party, frightened by demands for political, social, and economic reforms, pursued a reactionary domestic policy scarcely different from those on the Continent.

ORIGINS OF THE REFORM MOVEMENT

No sooner had the reactionary policies triumphed in England than a reaction to them developed. The government suffered a serious decline in prestige because of its unsuccessful attempt to force through a bill permitting the scandalous and dissolute George IV to divorce his wife, Caroline of Brunswick. The return of economic prosperity after 1821 caused a decline in radical demonstrations by the working classes, but at the same time it strengthened the self-confidence and ambition of the ever-growing middle classes.

In 1822 a series of cabinet changes following the suicide of Castlereagh introduced a number of younger men who, though they called themselves Tories, were more in step with the times than their predecessors. Until then the Whigs and Tories had not been political parties in the modern sense. The designations applied only to members of Parliament and their friends and supporters, all of whom in both parties belonged to the ruling elite. A man's allegiance within these loose alliances depended as much on personal ties and family tradition as on political principles. Party organization outside of Parliament was nonexistent, and party discipline within Parliament was lax. The reforms of the 1820's and 1830's did a great deal to bring the modern two-party system into being.

Among the outstanding new figures in the cabinet after 1822 was George Canning (1770–1827), who as head of the foreign office carried forward the independent, liberal-leaning foreign policies inaugurated by Castlereagh. William Huskisson (1770–1830), an economic and financial expert, simplified and reduced the maze of taxes and restrictions hampering the development of commerce and industry. Robert Peel (1788–1850), son of a wealthy manufacturer, became home secretary and revised the criminal and penal laws in a humanitarian direction. He obtained legislation reducing the number of capital offenses from over two hundred to about one hundred and created the Metropolitan Police Force, whose members were called bobbies or peelers, in derision at first, in affection later. In 1824 Parliament repealed the hated Combination Acts, which had been used to prevent the formation of trade unions. In all these reforms the influence of Jeremy Bentham and the utilitarians was very strong.

The next phase of the reform movement primarily concerned religious questions. The Test and Corporation acts, relics of the religious struggles of the seventeenth century, barred both Catholics and Nonconforming Protestants (dissenters from the established state church of England) from holding political office. Earlier attempts to repeal these obnoxious laws had been frustrated by the stubborn opposition of the Ultras, as the reactionary wing of the Tory party came to be called in the 1820's because of its similarity to the reactionary French aristocracy. In 1828 Lord John Russell, a Whig, introduced a bill exempting Nonconformists from the provisions of the acts. The duke of Wellington, who was himself an Ultra and who had just become prime minister, at first opposed the bill but then agreed to compromise in the hope of strengthening his support among the more liberal Tories and the Whigs. The bill passed with minor amendments. Immediately the reformers introduced a bill for Catholic emancipation. It passed the House of Commons by a narrow margin in spite of Wellington's opposition but was defeated in the House of Lords. In the following year Wellington, fearing a civil war in predominantly Catholic Ireland, reversed his stand and forced an emancipation bill through Parliament.

This action alienated Wellington's strongest supporters and weakened the Tory party, preparing the way for the first Whig government in almost half a century. In the summer of 1830, at nearly the same time as the July Revolution in France, George IV died and was succeeded by his brother, William IV. According to ancient custom, the change of monarchs required a new general election. The Whigs made a vigorous campaign in favor of reforming the House of Commons. Small groups of reformers had called for revision of the electoral system for many years, but reform had never before been a major issue in a general election. That the Whigs made it one in 1830 reflected as much their hunger for office and their desire to capitalize on the opportunities of the moment as it did their genuine interest in political and social change. The limited nature of the reforms that they proposed clearly indicated this fact.

THE STRUGGLE FOR REFORM

Without doubt, great need for reform existed. Apart from the high property and similar qualifications that limited the franchise to a small fraction of the population, the distribution of seats in Commons in no way reflected the true balance of either population or interests. Although boroughs (incorporated towns) and counties had representatives in Commons, the allocation of seats had been made centuries earlier, before the population shifts connected with the growth of manufacturing had occurred. Some boroughs were entirely under the control of one great landlord; they were called pocket boroughs. Others, the rotten boroughs, had such a small population that the voters could easily be bribed or intimidated. Many of the new manufacturing cities in the north had no representatives at all. In general, the older agricultural areas, dominated by the great aristocratic families, were greatly overrepresented at the expense of London and the new industrial areas.

The results of the election gave the Whigs a small majority, and the Wellington cabinet gave way to one headed by Earl Grey, the leader of the Whigs. His was a strange cabinet to bring about a popular reform, for it was composed almost entirely of aristocrats, a majority of whom were titled peers. But the Whigs had no intention of putting across a democratic reform. They differed from the aristocratic Tories only in that the latter felt that any "tampering" with the existing constitution would result in a national catastrophe, whereas the equally aristocratic Whigs believed that only a timely and judicious revision of the electoral system could prevent catastrophe. A radical journalist put the matter bluntly when he wrote, "The promoters of the Reform Bill projected it, not with a view to subvert, or even remodel our aristocratic institutions, but to consolidate them by a reinforcement of sub-aristocracy from the middle classes."

In spite of the moderate nature of the proposed reform and the electoral mandate in its favor, the Tories fought strenuously to prevent it. The First Reform Bill was introduced by Lord John Russell in March, 1831, and passed Commons with a majority of one in the largest vote ever recorded in Parliament, but it was thrown out on a technicality. Grey dissolved Parliament at once and called for a new election that became almost a referendum, since the Whigs campaigned for "the Bill, the whole Bill, and nothing but the Bill." Oddly enough, the electorate comprising the privileged few returned a majority favorable to the bill.

Culver Pictures, Inc.

The Reform Bill of 1832 Receiving the Royal Assent
in the House of Lords

"The whole measure will add to the constituency of the Commons House of Parliament about half a million persons, and these all connected with the property of the country, having a valuable stake amongst us, and deeply interested in our institutions. . . . I think that those measures will produce a farther benefit to the people, by the great incitement which it will occasion to industry and good conduct. For when a man finds, that by industrious exertion, and by punctuality, he will entitle himself to a place in the list of voters, he will have an additional motive to improve his circumstances, and to preserve his character among his neighbors. I think, therefore, that in adding to the constituency, we are providing for the moral as well as for the political improvement of the country." From Lord John Russell's speech introducing the Parliamentary Reform Bill, March 1, 1831, HANSARD'S PARLIAMENTARY DEBATES, 3rd ser. (London, 1831), Vol. II.

The new Commons then passed the bill with more than one hundred votes to spare, but the House of Lords defeated it by a small majority.

By this time agitation throughout the country had reached a fever pitch. "Political unions" in the larger cities, especially Birmingham, held mass meetings and hinted at dire consequences if the House of Lords did not reconsider. Lawless mobs, composed of propertyless individuals who stood to gain nothing directly, rioted, rampaged, and even held the city of Bristol for two days. The reforming government put down the outbreaks and punished the offenders as severely as the Tories would have. At the same time the government threatened to force the king to create enough new peers to reverse the vote in the House of Lords if the latter did not accept the bill. In June, 1832, the House of Lords finally acquiesced and, with many abstentions by unrepentant Tories, passed a slightly amended bill.

THE NATURE AND SIGNIFICANCE OF THE REFORM

The immediate outcome little merited the tumult and excitement. Although the suffrage was extended by about 50 per cent, it was still restricted by formidable property qualifications. Less than 20 per cent of the adult male population (or approximately 750,000 in 1832) could vote after the reform. Only 143 seats of a total of more than 650 in the House of Commons were redistributed, with the counties and manufacturing cities of the north gaining slightly at the expense of the smaller towns. Pocket boroughs did not altogether disappear, for more than sixty members were still directly dependent on large landowners (mainly peers) for their seats. As before, the agricultural south remained overrepresented in comparison with the industrial north and, especially, London. Since the act contained no provision for a secret ballot, the voters in the smaller districts continued to be subject to bribery, influence, and coercion.

Nevertheless, the reform of 1832 did grant recognition to the growing middle classes and made them allies, not opponents, of the established order, as Grey intended. The mere fact of its passage marked a turning point in English constitutional history. The method of its passage – that is, appeal to the electorate, pressure on the king, and threatening the House of Lords – set precedents that were even more important than the reform itself. Although its immediate effects disappointed its more radical supporters, notably the working men who had demonstrated in its favor, it probably forestalled a violent political change and paved the way for eventual democratic evolution.

THE BALANCE SHEET OF REVOLUTION

The post-Napoleonic conservative reaction attained its apogee by 1820. Within a dozen years thereafter it had suffered severe setbacks throughout western Europe. The main challenge to the conservatism of crown, church, and aristocracy came from the liberalism of the growing middle classes. The latter groups achieved their greatest strength where the progress of commerce and industry was greatest; that is, in Britain, France, and Belgium. In central Europe the appeal of liberalism united with that of nationalism in the struggle against aristocratic, absolutist, antinational regimes, but they made little headway as long as commerce and industry remained small-scale and backward. In eastern Europe both liberalism and nationalism – faint breaths at best – were stifled beneath the heavy hand of absolutism. Thus, the ideological gap between east and west grew wider as the gap in material progress increased.

THE REVOLUTION IN ECONOMIC LIFE
CHAPTER THREE

The revolutionary political changes of the first half of the nineteenth century cannot be fully understood without reference to the revolution in economic life. Indeed, the whole history of the European world in the nineteenth century and afterward may be seen as the story of the unfolding consequences and interconnections of two great revolutions that took place at the end of the eighteenth century: the political revolution in France and the revolution of agriculture and industry in Britain.

Some historians consider that revolution is a misnomer when applied to the changes in technology and business organization that constituted the core of the transformation of economic life. They point out that such changes had been taking place more or less continuously over many centuries — in fact, since paleolithic times — and that to call such a long drawn-out process a revolution is misleading. On the other hand, if we look at the consequences of those changes in the nineteenth century, the word revolution is appropriate. Until the end of the eighteenth century economic changes took place almost imperceptibly, too slowly to attract much attention or to modify significantly the traditional agrarian basis of society. Beginning in the 1780's, however, technical innovation in British industry remarkably stepped up the whole process of social change and by the middle of the nineteenth century had converted Great Britain into the first industrial society.

The diffusion of the new technology led other nations into industrialism: Belgium and France first, partly because of their proximity to Great Britain; then the United States, bound to Britain by cultural and economic ties. By the end of the nineteenth century Germany after an extremely rapid rise joined the others in the forefront of industrial nations. By that time other nations had begun industrial revolutions of their own: among them the Netherlands, Switzerland, the Scandinavian countries, northern Italy, Russia, and Japan. The twentieth century has seen the extension of industrial technology, sometimes with great political and social turmoil, to Latin America, Asia, and Africa, with almost every nation in the world attempting to acquire for itself the essentials of modern industry. The beginnings of the movement extended roughly from 1780 to about 1850 or 1860.

THE RISE OF MODERN INDUSTRY

The words industrialism and modern industry refer to the mode of production characterized by extensive use of mechanical power, heavy machinery, and other forms of expensive capital equipment. The most significant improvements in technology therefore involved the use of machinery and mechanical power to perform tasks that had been done far more slowly and laboriously by human and animal power, or that had not been done at all. To be sure, elementary machines like the wheel, the pulley, and the lever had been used from antiquity, and for centuries mankind had used a fraction of the inanimate powers of nature to propel sailing ships and actuate windmills and water wheels for rudimentary industrial processes. During the eighteenth century a notable increase in the use of water power occurred in such industries as grain milling, textiles, and metallurgy; and in recent times we have witnessed the proliferation of a wide variety of prime movers, from small electric motors operated on household current to huge nuclear reactors; but the most important developments in the application of power in the early stages of industrialization were those associated with the introduction of the steam engine and the spread of its use in both industry and transportation.

THE NATURE OF EARLY INDUSTRIALISM

Under the domestic system of manufacture the labor force had been dispersed throughout the countryside in close proximity to supplies of food, and although each worker was financially dependent upon his merchant employer, he was to some extent his own boss. On the other hand, water wheels and then steam engines required the concentration of operations and therefore of operatives at a single location. Buildings were needed to house both machinery and workers. Thus evolved the factory system. Originally factory meant an establishment for traders or their agents, called factors, carrying on business in a foreign country. It acquired its current meaning at the end of the eighteenth century, although before that time isolated examples of factories in the modern sense, with or without power machinery, could be found.

The use of mechanical power, especially steam engines, to drive machinery raised the further possibility of almost continuous and more or less automatic operation. The factory system thus revolutionized the

Radio Times Hulton Picture Library

Women Engaged in Power Loom Weaving,
from an engraving by Allom, c. 1840

"The industrial revolution is to be thought of as a movement, not as a period of time. . . . Its character and effects are fundamentally the same. Everywhere it is associated with a growth of population, with the application of science to industry, and with a more intensive and extensive use of capital. Everywhere there is a conversion of rural into urban communities and a rise of new social classes. But in each case the course of the movement has been affected by circumstances of time and place. Many of the social discomforts that have been attributed to the industrial revolution in Britain were, in fact, the result of forces which (for all we know) would still have operated if manufacture had remained undeveloped and there had been no change of economic form."
T. S. Ashton, THE INDUSTRIAL REVOLUTION; 1760–1830 (London, 1948).

---

habits and conditions as well as the results of human labor. The pace of industry, no longer governed by the rhythm of the seasons and frailties of the flesh, had to adjust to the throbbing pulse of engines and the tireless arms of iron. Before the development of more humane standards and the passage of protective labor legislation, the competition of unscrupulous or hard-pressed employers, struggling to pay the high fixed costs of the new equipment, stretched the length of the working day to twelve, fourteen, and even sixteen hours, with few if any breaks for meals or rest. Such hours, of course, were not unknown in the earlier domestic system or in agriculture, but those workers could set their own pace. Some factory owners failed to provide adequate health and safety facilities and paid their workers in truck (merchandise) instead of money.

Many laborers resented the new machinery, which they blamed for the loss of their skills, and objected to the monotonous routine of the factory. Labor discipline became a major concern. Employers frequently resorted to large-scale employment of women and children where it was made possible by automatic or semiautomatic machines, because they formed a more docile as well as a cheaper labor force. Another factor widening the gulf between employer and employee was the increasing size of enterprise. Under the handicraft system of production a master craftsman might employ a few apprentices, and perhaps a journeyman or two, all of whom might live under his roof. A merchant manufacturer might distribute his materials to a dozen domestic workers, or even as many as fifty, if his was a very large undertaking. The new factories employed hundreds, sometimes thousands, of workers. With such a labor force it became less and less usual for the employer to be personally acquainted with his workers or interested in them individually. The immediate adverse consequences of the technological and organizational changes, however, should not obscure the truly epoch-making benefits that resulted in the long run: the lighter burden and greatly increased productivity of human labor brought about by human ingenuity.

PREREQUISITES AND CONCOMITANTS OF INDUSTRIALISM

Before the factories, the machinery, and the new forms of power could take full effect, certain other changes had to take place. Among the most important were increased commercialization of economic life, the growth of banks and other financial institutions, and the improvement of transportation and communication facilities. Agrarian reform, although not a prerequisite in the strict sense, was an almost universal concomitant of industrialism.

Commerce — the exchange of one commodity or service for another, either directly in the form of barter or indirectly by means of money — is to be found in almost all forms of human society, from the most primitive to the most socialistic. In traditional agrarian societies such exchanges are restricted both geographically and in the volume and variety of goods and services exchanged. In modern industrial societies specialization and division of labor require a highly developed commercial or market system to facilitate exchange. There must be individuals who do not grow or otherwise produce goods directly but who make their living by serving as intermediaries or middlemen in the process of exchange.

Such a class of individuals had existed in western Europe for many centuries. They generally lived in the towns and were known as burghers or bourgeoisie. The geographical discoveries of the fifteenth and sixteenth centuries, which greatly extended the market area and the volume and variety of exchangeable goods, as well as stimulated the money economy by the influx of precious metals, caused their wealth to grow and strengthened their position in society. In the seventeenth and eighteenth centuries they were frequently able to influence the councils of state to adopt policies favorable to their mercantile interests, especially in the Dutch Netherlands and Britain. By the end of the eighteenth century organized commerce, domestic as well as international, occupied a significant segment of the population of western Europe and indirectly affected a far larger proportion.

As the commercialization of economic life increased, special institutions arose to provide credit and to finance trade and industry. The great public banks, such as the Bank of Amsterdam and the Bank of England, catered mainly to large-scale international commerce and the financial needs of governments. By the early nineteenth century most important financial centers had such public banks, which in time became central banks or bankers' banks, controlling the flow of credit throughout their national economies. For the smaller merchants and manufacturers numerous private bankers supplied the need for short-term credit to finance the turnover of trade and industry.

The movement of large quantities of bulky, low-value goods, such as grain from the fields to the growing urban markets, timber for building, coal and ores, required cheap dependable transportation. Prior to the railroad era water routes provided the most economical and efficient arteries of transport. Britain owed much of its early prosperity and its head start in modern industry to its island position. The long coastline, excellent natural harbors, and many navigable streams eliminated much of the need for overland transportation that hindered the growth of commerce and industry on the Continent. In the latter half of the eighteenth century the British extended their natural transport routes with hundreds of miles of canals and improved turnpikes. The greatest improvements in transportation and communication, however, such as railroads, steamships, the telegraph, and eventually automobiles, airplanes, and the wireless radio, developed out of the process of industrialization itself.

AGRARIAN CHANGE

Agrarian reform had several facets. The question of land tenure, how the land was owned or held, was perhaps the most fundamental. Feudal tenure did not recognize private property as such. Rights to the use of land were extremely diffuse, extending from the highest nobleman to the lowliest serf. The trend toward private ownership of property and individual responsibility worked itself out over a period of centuries and took various forms. The process of consolidation and enclosure in England eventually resulted in the creation of huge estates, sometimes of several thousand acres each, in the hands of a relatively small number of wealthy landlords. By the 1870's fewer than seven thousand individuals owned four-fifths of the land in the United Kingdom. The great estates were not generally cultivated as single units. Usually they were rented to capitalistic tenant farmers in farms of about one hundred acres.

In France the lands of the church (the largest landholder before the French Revolution) and the feudal aristocracy were expropriated during the revolution. In some instances peasants obtained legal title to the land that they cultivated, but much was taken by the government and sold to bourgeois speculators, who subsequently resold it to land-hungry peasants or returning aristocrats. In the end France became a nation of small peasant proprietors. In 1882, with over half the population engaged in agriculture, the average size of French farms was less than twenty-five acres. More than three-quarters of the peasant proprietors owned farms smaller than five hectares (12.5 acres), and two-thirds of these tiny farms were actually less than one hectare (2.5 acres) in size. These petty proprietors had to take jobs, frequently as hired hands on larger farms, to support themselves and their families.

The edict of emancipation of 1807 laid the basis for the liberation of the serfs in Prussia, the largest state in Germany. It was long believed that the Prussian reform resulted in the monopolization of most of the land by the aristocratic landowners (the Junkers), and that most of the peasants lost their holdings and were forced to become laborers on the farms of the Junkers, or, especially after 1850, moved to the burgeoning industrial areas to become factory workers. This view has been challenged by a modern German scholar who made a careful statistical analysis of the land records. He found that the number of large landowners did increase after the emancipation and that these men did dominate commercial production; but he also found that the number of small landowners increased as well, and at a much more rapid rate than the large landowners. These small proprietors acquired their land through the operations of the emancipation legislation, through the division of common pasture land and its conversion into plowland, and through the conversion into plowland of forests and of so-called wastelands that had hitherto been untilled. Some of these peasant proprietors had sizable and prosperous farms. By far the largest number, however, had holdings so small that, like their French counterparts, they had to find other employment, often as hired hands on the farms of the Junkers and the wealthier peasants, to make ends meet. In 1907, of the 2.6 million individual farms in the Prussian provinces, 63 per cent had only 5 acres or less.

Elsewhere in western and central Europe land reform followed either the French or the Prussian model. In much of eastern and southern Europe no effective reform took place until after the revolutionary upheavals in the twentieth century. Wherever it did occur, the usual consequence was increased productivity and the commercialization of agriculture.

The progress of agricultural technology was no less important than the reforms in land tenure. The latter were in part a means of achieving the former. So long as the land was cultivated in common, it was impossible for a single individual to introduce new crops and new methods of cultivation or to improve his livestock by selective breeding, and obedience to traditional routine prevented radical changes in technology by a whole village. When the consolidated and enclosed lands came into private hands, especially the hands of improving landlords or commercially-minded tenant farmers who had the wealth and the interest to experiment with new techniques, it became possible to discover and apply new and better methods.

THE INDUSTRIAL REVOLUTION IN BRITAIN

The expression industrial revolution has a long and controversial history. First used by Frenchmen in the 1820's to compare the economic changes with the great French Revolution of 1789, it gained currency at the end of the nineteenth century when it was used by British social reformers in interpreting the origins of contemporary social problems. The conventional dates assigned to the revolution were 1760 to 1830, although some scholars favored a longer period, such as 1750 to 1850, and others argued that the beginning date should be 1780 or 1785, with no fixed terminal date for the completion of the revolution. Still other authorities, stressing the continuity of industrial change, sought to prove that there was no such thing as an industrial revolution, or that at best it was but a special case of a more general process. Serious students of the subject have long since given up the cataclysmic interpretation, and most agree that the expression itself is meaningless except as a stylized, shorthand designation for a highly significant period in British economic and social history.

Whatever the dispute regarding the utility of the name, there is no doubt as to the importance of the process it describes. The two generations of Britons on either side of the year 1800 witnessed changes that have profoundly influenced the subsequent history not only of their island but of the entire world. But why Great Britain? Might not the industrial revolution have occurred elsewhere than in Britain? There is general agreement that the economic expansion of the second half of the eighteenth century, of which the industrial revolution was the culmination, was a general phenomenon affecting most of western Europe and North America as well. Had the British population been suddenly wiped out in 1750 by some mysterious plague that affected no other area, it is conceivable – even probable – that an industrial revolution would have occurred eventually either in western Europe or the United States. British primacy was due to a fortuitous combination of both dynamic and static factors. One such factor was its insular position at the crossroads of maritime traffic, both east and west and north and south; insularity not only lowered transport costs but also granted costless protection from the destruction and disruption of continental warfare. But insularity alone was not enough.

Commercialization of economic life had proceeded further in Great Britain than in any other nation except possibly the Netherlands. As early as the end of the seventeenth century British foreign trade per capita exceeded that of other nations, and London had developed a surprisingly sophisticated commercial and financial organization. Moreover, after 1689 the financial as well as the commercial policies of the government came into the hands of men experienced in private financial and commercial transactions.

Increased commercialization also interacted in dynamic fashion with that other great sector of economic activity, agriculture. Improvements in agricultural techniques introduced in the seventeenth century spread during the eighteenth century in response to the heightened demand brought on by the great increase in population. The result was a significant rise in agricultural productivity and agricultural income, making British agriculture a lucrative market for industrial products as well as a supplier of foodstuffs and raw materials for British industry.

The process of economic development was an immensely complicated one, involving social, political, and intellectual as well as economic changes. The dynamic central factor in the industrial revolution itself, however, was technical innovation in three strategic areas: cotton textiles, the iron industry, and the perfection of the steam engine.

The manufacture of cotton cloth was a relatively new industry in Great Britain. It grew up early in the eighteenth century after the woolen interests persuaded Parliament to adopt the Calico Acts of 1700 and 1720, prohibiting the importation of cotton goods from India. At first the industry employed the hand processes that were common in the other textile industries and frequently used a mixture of linen and cotton yarn in weaving. Because it was new, cotton manufacture was less subject than other industries to restrictive legislation and gild rules or to traditional practices that obstructed technical change. The popularity of gaily colored or printed cotton goods also led to a rapid increase in demand, which acted as a stimulus to technical innovation. Deliberate efforts to invent labor-saving machinery for spinning and weaving were made at least as early as 1730. The early spinning machines were not successful, but in 1733 a Lancashire mechanic, John Kay, invented the flying shuttle which enabled a single weaver to do the work of two, thereby increasing the pressure of demand for yarn. In 1760 the Society of Arts added to the incentive of the market by offering a prize for a successful spinning machine. Within a few years several devices for mechanical spinning were patented. The first was James Hargreaves's spinning jenny, invented in 1765 but not patented until 1770. The jenny was a relatively simple machine; in fact, it was little more than a spinning wheel with a battery of several spindles instead of one. It did not require mechanical power and could be operated in a spinner's cottage, but it allowed one man to do the work of several.

The water frame, a spinning machine patented by Richard Arkwright in 1769, had more general significance. Arkwright, a barber and wig maker by trade, probably did not invent the water frame himself, and his patent was subsequently voided; but of all the early textile innovators he was the most successful as a businessman. Because the water frame operated with water power and was heavy and expensive, it led directly to the factory system. The factories, however, were built most often by streams in the country or in small villages, so that they did not result in concentrations of workers in the cities.

The most important invention in spinning was Samuel Crompton's mule, so called because it combined elements of the jenny and the frame. Perfected between 1774 and 1779, the mule could spin finer, stronger yarn than any machine or hand spinner, and it could also be adapted for steam power. The steam engine was first applied to spinning in 1785 and soon became the almost inevitable concomitant of cotton manufacture.

The new spinning machines reversed the pressure of demand between spinning and weaving, and led to a more insistent search for a solution to the problems of mechanical weaving. In 1785 Edmund Cartwright took out a patent for a power loom. Cartwright, a clergyman without training or experience in either mechanics or textiles, solved the basic problem of mechanical weaving by the application of sheer intelligence. Many minor difficulties of a practical nature hindered the development of the power loom until the 1820's, however, when an improved version manufactured by the engineering firm of Sharp and Roberts in Manchester was widely adopted throughout the cotton districts.

A rapid increase in cotton consumption followed, creating a new bottleneck in the supply of raw cotton. India had supplied most of the imports of raw cotton, but its production did not expand rapidly enough to fill the growing demand. Cotton production began in the American South, but the high cost of separating seeds by hand from the short-staple American fibers discouraged it until 1793, when Eli Whitney, a New Englander visiting in the South, invented a mechanical gin. This machine answered the need so well that the southern United States quickly became the leading supplier of raw material to what soon became Britain's leading industry.

These inventions were the most important but by no means the only ones affecting the cotton industry. A host of minor improvements took place in all stages of production from the preparation of the fibers for spinning to bleaching, dyeing, and printing. Since Britain did not grow any cotton domestically, the import figures for raw cotton give a good indication of the pace at which the industry developed. From less than a million pounds at the beginning of the century, imports rose to about five million pounds in the 1770's, more than fifty million pounds in 1800, and more than a billion pounds in 1860. A large and growing percentage of the cotton manufacture was exported; by 1803 the value of cotton exports surpassed that of wool, which for centuries had been Britain's leading industry. As the cheap, machine-produced cottons went to markets all over the world, they spread enthusiasm for the new techniques of industry.

The second industry to be revolutionized was, unlike cotton, an ancient one in Britain. Iron had been produced there from the early Middle Ages, but it was primarily a rural occupation. Charcoal was used to smelt the iron ore; consequently, for reasons of economy, production took place on a small scale in forested areas far from the centers of population and industry. In the seventeenth century the increasing demand for iron, together with the high price of charcoal as a result of forest exhaustion, led to a search for a less expensive fuel. Coal, known to be plentiful in Enland, had long been used for some industrial purposes as well as domestic heating, but raw coal contained impurities that were injurious to the quality of iron produced with it. In the first half of the eighteenth century the Darby family, a father-and-son team of Quaker iron founders in the west of England, discovered through patient experiment that good quality iron could be made with coal if the coal were first coked (heated to high temperatures in closed ovens) to drive out the impurities. The process became public knowledge after 1750, and the output of both coal and iron increased rapidly.

The iron industry had not yet solved all of its problems. The product of the blast furnace, in which the ore is smelted, is not only hard but because of its carbon content is also brittle, and cannot be easily shaped or hammered. To remove the carbon and make wrought iron that is soft and pliable enough to be worked into useful shapes, the pig iron had to be refined. The traditional method required alternate heating and hammering of the pigs, or bars, to drive out all the carbon and other impurities. Even when done with the aid of huge trip hammers driven by water power, this was a slow and cumbersome process. Thus the use of coke in the blast furnace created an imbalance in the industry similar to that created in the cotton industry by the spinning machines. The solution was arrived at independently and almost simultaneously by two men, Peter Onions and Henry Cort, in 1783 and 1784. The puddling process of refining iron (so called because the molten iron was stirred in puddles)

Maudslay's Original Screw-Cutting Lathe (1797)

"Modern industry had therefore itself to take in hand the machine, its characteristic instrument of production, and to construct machines by machines. . . . It was necessary to produce the geometrically accurate straight lines, planes, circles, cones, and spheres, required in the detailed parts of machines. This problem Henry Maudslay solved by the invention of the slide rest, a tool that was soon made automatic. . . . This mechanical appliance replaces, not some particular tool, but the hand itself, which produces a given form by holding and guiding the cutting tool along the iron or other material operated upon. Thus it becomes possible to produce the forms of the individual parts of machinery with a degree of ease, accuracy, and speed, that no accumulated experience of the hand of the most skilled workman could give."
Karl Marx, CAPITAL (Chicago, 1906).

---

also used coke as a fuel, which freed the iron industry completely from dependence on charcoal and concentrated it in larger units in the vicinity of the coal fields. These regions became the new homes of the iron-using industries as well. Cort also patented a rolling mill, in which white-hot iron was squeezed between huge rollers to drive out impurities and to impart desired shapes, such as sheets, rods, rails, and beams. Britain soon changed from an iron-importing nation to the world's leading exporter of iron and ironwares.

Without these developments in the iron and cotton industries there would have been no industrial revolution, but the crowning technical achievement of the eighteenth century was the perfection and utilization of the steam engine. Some of the properties of steam had been known in antiquity, but no serious attempts to utilize it for practical purposes occurred until the seventeenth century. At the beginning of the eighteenth century an English mechanic, Thomas Newcomen, built a crude engine capable of actuating a pump. Engines of this type were used for more than a century to pump water from coal mines, but their efficiency was too low to permit widespread application to other industrial processes. Between 1763 and 1782 James Watt, originally a builder of scientific instruments for the University of Glasgow, made a number of improvements that resulted in a far more efficient, economical engine. Watt's engine could convert the reciprocal movement of the piston into rotary motion, which made the engine adaptable for driving industrial machinery. Within a few years it had been applied to industries as diverse as mining, flour milling, pottery, brewing, and distilling, not to mention the two most important users, cotton manufacture and iron working.

In spite of the magnitude of these achievements, no single industry in Britain had completed its technical revolution as early as 1830, though iron and cotton had gone very far. By 1851, however, when Queen Victoria dedicated the Crystal Palace, a huge structure of iron and glass to house the world's first international industrial exhibition, workers in British industry outnumbered those in agriculture and Britain had become the "workshop of the world."

EARLY INDUSTRIALISM IN EUROPE AND AMERICA

Elements of the new technology began to be diffused almost immediately. In 1779, less than five years after completion of Watt's first successful engine in Britain, the Perier brothers set up an engine of the same type in France. In 1782 construction of the first continental blast furnace designed for coke began at Le Creusot in eastern France. French textile manufacturers had been in touch with the British industry even before the great inventions, and by 1790 there were approximately nine hundred spinning jennies in France. In the latter year Samuel Slater, an English mechanic who had worked in Arkwright's mills, emigrated to America, secured financial support from two wealthy merchants in Providence, and established a flourishing cotton industry in Rhode Island.

In spite of these early achievements, industrialism did not make rapid progress in either Europe or America. The manufacturers in Britain jealously guarded the secrets of their new industries. The government prohibited the exportation of machinery or the emigration of skilled artisans, for which it provided stiff penalties, including death. Although such laws were frequently circumvented, their existence discouraged widespread diffusion of the new technology. For example, Slater dared not bring either machines or drawings to America but memorized the designs and traveled incognito. The turmoil and dislocation brought on by the French Revolution and the revolutionary and Napoleonic wars, accentuated by Napoleon's Continental System and the British blockade, also hindered the diffusion of technology and the transition of continental industry to more modern methods. Perhaps most important, the prerequisites of industrialism had not been fully met either on the Continent or in America, much less in other lands, so that demand for the new methods was not as great as in Britain.

Effective industrialization began on the Continent only after 1815. Even then it was confined to a relatively small area and proceeded much more slowly than in Britain. Faced with the competition of their more advanced British counterparts, the new textile industries could not compete in international trade and had to rely on high tariffs to protect the more limited domestic markets. The iron industries of France and Belgium began the shift from charcoal to coke in the 1820's, but the transition was not completed until the 1850's. By the middle of the nineteenth century Belgium, favored by plentiful supplies of coal, an advantageous location, an industrious population, and wise legislation, had advanced further than any other continental nation on the road to industrialism. France ranked second, but it had more difficult problems of location and resources and was already beginning to manifest what became its typical schizophrenic attitude toward modern industry. The new techniques of industry had barely been implanted in western Germany, northern Italy, Bohemia, and in the immediate vicinity of Vienna. Elsewhere Europeans in 1850 were very far from even the beginnings of an industrial revolution.

The situation in the United States was slightly different. European travelers noted early the American passion for high productivity and their ingenuity in inventing labor-saving machinery. Eli Whitney, inventor of the cotton gin, made a still greater fortune by devising a system for the mass production of muskets with standardized, interchangeable parts. Many of the American labor-saving devices could be used on a relatively small scale, such as the mechanical reaper (1834) and the sewing machine (1846). This bent of American industrialism resulted from a number of factors: a chronic shortage of labor, especially labor having the traditional skills; the fluidity of American society; the abundant opportunities for individual advancement; and the wealth of natural resources. Yet in spite of its promising beginnings, America did not create an industrial society during the first half of the nineteenth century. The reasons that contributed to American inventive ingenuity also contributed to delaying the development of large-scale industry, especially abundance of land and resources and opportunities for individual achievement. Prior to the Civil War America was far more concerned with agriculture and the opening of the West than with industrialization.

RAILROADS

Inadequate transportation facilities constituted a major obstacle to industrialization in both continental Europe and the United States. Lacking Britain's endowment of natural waterways and handicapped by greater distances, continental and American industrialists found themselves pent up in local markets that offered little scope for extensive specialization and expensive capital equipment. The railroad and, to a lesser extent, the steamship changed this state of affairs. The railroads offered cheaper, faster, more dependable transportation, and also, during the period of their construction, which lasted roughly from 1830 until the end of the century, their demands for iron, coal, timber, and machinery proved a potent stimulus to the industries that supplied them.

German miners introduced wooden tracks for coal carts in the British coal industry as early as the sixteenth century. By the end of the eighteenth century British coal fields had many miles of railways on which wagons were propelled by gravity, horsepower, and human beings. Richard Trevithick operated the first steam locomotive on one of these tracks in 1804. Trevithick's engine and others like it were at first too heavy and inefficient to be commercially successful. After several improvements on both engines and tracks George Stephenson heralded the railway era in 1825 with a successful run over the tracks of the new Stockton and Darlington railroad, and inaugurated it in 1830 with the opening of the Liverpool and Manchester, the first railroad designed from the beginning for steam locomotion. Thereafter the British railroad network developed rapidly as each new line increased the demand for more. By 1850 Britain had more than a fourth of its eventual network, almost as much as the rest of Europe combined.

France, Austria, and the United States had short, horse-drawn railroads by 1830, but the United States outstripped Britain and rivaled all of Europe in the construction of railroads. It drew upon European capital and suppliers as well as upon the abundant enthusiasm of private promoters and federal, state, and local governments to span the vast distances of the country. Many of the railroads were cheaply constructed, however, and were built to widely varying standards.

Belgium made the best early showing of any continental country in railroad planning and construction. Rejoicing in its newly won independence, the middle-class government resolved to build a comprehensive network at state expense to facilitate the export of Belgian manufactures and win the transit trade of northwestern Europe. The first section, and the first wholly steam operated railroad on the Continent, opened in

1835. Ten years later the basic state-owned network was complete, after which the job of providing branch and secondary lines was turned over to private enterprise.

France and Germany were the only other continental nations to make significant railroad progress by mid-century. Germany achieved the most. Beginning with the Nürnberg-Fürth in 1835, construction took place at varying but generally rapid rates in several of the German states. Some followed a policy of state ownership and operation; others left railroads to private enterprise, usually with subsidies. Still others allowed both state and private enterprise. Although France had a centralized government and by 1842 a comprehensive railroad plan, it built more slowly. Parliamentary wrangling over the question of state or private enterprise and sectional conflicts over the location of the main lines held up the railroad era in France until the coming of the Second Empire. After 1852 railroad construction proceeded rapidly.

Table 1 *Railroad Mileage in Selected Countries, 1840–1870*

	1840	*1850*	*1870*
United States	2,800	9,000	53,000
Great Britain	1,800	6,600	15,600
German states	400	3,500	11,150
France	260	1,800	10,750
Austrian Empire	100	1,000	5,750
Russian Empire	25	400	7,000
Belgium	200	540	1,800
Netherlands	20	100	840
Switzerland	1	15	840
Spain	—	18	3,300
Italian states	12	240	3,700
Scandinavia	—	—	1,600

Table 2 *World Railroad Mileage, 1830–1870*

	1830	*1840*	*1850*	*1870*
Europe	60	2,800	14,000	65,000
North America	—	2,800	9,000	56,000
Asia	—	—	200	5,100
South America	—	—	—	1,800
Africa	—	—	—	1,100
Australia	—	—	—	1,000
World Total	60	5,600	23,200	130,000

STEAMSHIPS

The steamship, although developed earlier than the locomotive, played a less vital role in the expansion of commerce and industry. In fact, for ocean commerce the wooden sailing ship reached its peak development, both technically and in the tonnage of goods carried, after 1850. In the first half of the century steamers made their greatest contribution in the development of inland commerce. Credit for inventing the steamboat is usually given to the American Robert Fulton, whose ship the *Clermont* made its first successful run on the Hudson in 1807, though there are other earlier claimants for this distinction. Within a few years steamers appeared on the Great Lakes and the rivers of the Mississippi system as well as in coastal waters. Prior to 1850 steamboats probably contributed more than railroads to opening the trans-Allegheny West. In Europe they could be seen on such broad rivers as the Rhine, the Danube, the Rhone, and the Seine, as well as on the Mediterranean and Baltic seas and the English Channel. Steam came to the North Atlantic with the voyage of the auxiliary steamer *Savannah* in 1820, but regular transatlantic service began in 1838, when the *Sirius* and *Great Western* made simultaneous voyages from England to New York. Samuel Cunard, an Englishman, inaugurated his famous line in 1840, but soon ran into stiff competition from other companies. Until the end of the American Civil War ocean steamers carried chiefly mail, passengers, and expensive, lightweight cargo. The age of the ocean steamer did not arrive until the development of the compound engine and the opening of the Suez Canal in 1869.

COMMUNICATIONS

Perhaps no single invention of the nineteenth century compared with that of printing in the fifteenth century in its effect on the field of communications. Nevertheless, the cumulative effects of nineteenth-century innovations were comparable. Paper-making machinery, invented about 1800, and the cylindrical printing press, first used by the London *Times* in 1812, greatly reduced the cost of books and newspapers. Together with the reductions in stamp and excise taxes on paper and printing, they brought reading material within reach of the masses and contributed to their increasing literacy. By mid-century the penny press was a reality. The invention of lithography in 1819 and the development of photography after 1827 made possible the cheap reproduction and wide dissemination of visual images, with effects on the spread of culture and enlightenment that have been debated ever since.

One communications invention that won almost universal acclaim was the introduction of the penny post by Britain in 1840. Within a few years most Western countries had adopted a system of flat-rate, prepaid postal charges. Even more significant was the invention of the electric telegraph by the American Samuel Morse in 1832. Practical application of the telegraph did not begin until the 1840's, however, and the world did not feel its full effects until after mid-century.

SOCIAL ASPECTS OF EARLY INDUSTRIALISM

The revolutionary changes in technology and in the character of economic activity that took place with increasing rapidity throughout the nineteenth century cannot be fully appreciated without considering their impact on the people who experienced them. In fact, it is the human consequences that justify the use of the word revolution. These consequences varied widely from individual to individual, and from one social group to another, but there were certain broad social changes that affected the whole of Western civilization.

POPULATION GROWTH

One of the most spectacular results of industrialization was the enormous increase in population. In the middle of the seventeenth century the population of the world has been estimated at slightly more than 500 million people, of which about one-fifth lived in Europe. By the middle of the twentieth century world population approached 2.5 billion people, a five-fold increase in 300 years. All of the increase did not take place in Europe or areas of European settlement, which indicates that industrialization was not the only factor causing the growth; the correlation is close enough, however, to indicate that the two phenomena were associated.

The largest increase of people of European stock during this population explosion took place in the nineteenth century. Britain and Germany, the two most important industrial nations, had rates of growth averaging somewhat more than 1 per cent per year. (A constant rate of 1 per cent per year would result in a doubling of the population in about seventy years.) In the United States, where the growth of population was favored by wide expanses of cheap land, rich resources, free immigration, and a fluid social structure, population grew from about 5 million in 1800 to more than 75 million in 1900, for a growth rate in excess of 3 per cent. (At 3 per cent the population would double in less than twenty-five years.) Russia, which was one of the least industrialized countries in Europe but which possessed vast empty tracts of land, had one of the highest rates of population growth, from about 37 million to more than 100 million. France, which had the largest population in Europe in the early eighteenth century, lagged far behind the others in its rate of growth.

The growth in population was due principally to industrialization and the increase in agricultural productivity. The improvements in transpor-

Table 3 *The Growth of Population (millions)*

	1800	*1850*	*1900*	*1950*
Europe	187.0	266.0	401.0	559.0
United Kingdom	16.1	27.5	41.8	50.6
Germany	24.6	35.9	56.4	69.0
France	27.3	35.8	39.0	41.9
Russia	37.0	60.2	111.0	193.0 (1946)
Spain	10.5	n.a.	16.6	28.3
Italy	18.1	24.3	32.5	46.3
Sweden	2.3	3.5	5.1	7.0
Belgium	n.a.	4.3	6.7	8.6
Netherlands	n.a.	3.1	5.1	10.1
North America	16.0	39.0	106.0	217.0
United States	5.3	23.2	76.0	151.7
South America	9.0	20.0	38.0	111.0
Asia	602.0	749.0	937.0	1,302.0
Africa	90.0	95.0	120.0	198.0
Oceania	2.0	2.0	6.0	13.0
World Total	906.0	1,171.0	1,608.0	2,400.0

n.a.: not available

tation and communication and in medical science and sanitation contributed to the growth of population even in areas that did not experience industrialization directly, sometimes with dire consequences.

URBANIZATION

Another striking characteristic of recent history, closely associated with industrialization and the growth of population, has been the growth of cities. Cities have existed from the beginnings of civilization, but until the industrial revolution the greater part of the population lived in small rural villages or the open countryside. At the beginning of the nineteenth century this proportion was 60 per cent in England and Wales, about 75 per cent in France, the Low Countries, western Germany, and Italy, and 90 per cent or more in most of the rest of the world. By 1850 half the English population lived in towns and cities, and by 1900 most other industrial nations had a simliar proportion of urban dwellers. This trend has continued to the present day.

The population of industrial countries not only lived in cities; it went by preference to the largest cities. For example, in England and Wales the proportion of the population living in small towns (2,000–20,000 inhabitants) has remained roughly constant at about 15 per cent from the beginning of the nineteenth century to the present day, whereas the proportion in large cities (over 20,000 inhabitants) has risen from 27 per cent to more than 70 per cent. In 1800 there were barely twenty cities

Table 4 *The Growth of Large Cities and Metropolitan Areas (thousands)*

	1800	*1850*	*1900*	*1950*[a]
London	959	2,681	6,581	10,200
Manchester	77	303	544	1,965
Liverpool	82	397	685	1,445
Birmingham	71	242	522	2,400
Glasgow	77	329	736	1,600
Paris	600	1,422	3,670	6,350
Marseilles	111	195	491	715
Lyons	90	177	459	740
Berlin	172	500	2,712	3,900
Hamburg	130	132	706	1,800
Cologne	50	97	373	1,125
Frankfurt	48	59	289	850
Essen	5	9	216	3,175
St. Petersburg (Leningrad)	220	485	1,150	3,250
Moscow	250	365	1,000	6,500
Kiev	20	61	275	925
Antwerp	62	88	277	630
Brussels	90	251	604	1,115
Amsterdam	201	224	511	1,125
Zurich	12	42	168	420
Copenhagen	101	130	469	1,215
Stockholm	76	93	301	985
Vienna	247	444	1,675	1,900
Prague	75	206	382	980
Budapest	54	178	732	1,670
Barcelona	115	175	533	1,550
Rome	153	175	463	1,625
Naples	350	449	564	1,230
Milan	134	200	491	1,575
New York	64	696	3,437	13,300
Chicago	0	30	1,699	5,325
Philadelphia	81	409	1,294	3,350
Detroit	1	21	286	3,275
Los Angeles	2	11	102	4,275

[a]Metropolitan area.

in Europe with a population of as much as 100,000, and none in the Western Hemisphere; by 1900 there were more than 150 such cities in Europe and North America, and by 1950 more than 600. In the mid-twentieth century there were more cities and supercities (called metropolitan areas) with a population in excess of 1 million (sometimes greatly in excess) than there were cities with a population of 100,000 in 1800.

There are many social and cultural reasons why people want to live in cities. Historically the chief limitation on the growth of cities has been economic: the impossibility of supplying large urban populations with the necessities of life. With the technological improvements of modern industry not only were these limitations relaxed, but in some cases economic considerations also required the growth of cities. In preindustrial societies even most of the nonagricultural population lived in rural areas. It was cheaper to carry the finished products of industry such as textiles and iron to distant markets than to carry food and raw materials to concentrations of workers. The introduction of steam power and the factory system, the transition from charcoal to coke as fuel for the iron industry, and the improvements in transportation and communication changed this situation. The rise of the factory system necessitated a concentration of the work force. Because of the new importance of coal some of the largest centers of industry arose on or near the sites of coal deposits – the Black Country of England, the Ruhr Valley in Germany, the area around Lille in northern France, and the Pittsburgh area in America.

As commerce expanded, the demand for specialized facilities for the movement and storage of goods and for various other commercial and financial services increased, adding to the importance of port cities and other transportation centers such as New York, Liverpool, Hamburg, Marseilles, and Cologne. Transportation factors also permitted the growth of commerce, industry, and population in the old established political, administrative, and cultural centers, such as London, Paris, and Berlin. As the industrial and commercial centers grew in size and importance, the service trades of butcher, baker, and barber, not to mention doctors, lawyers, firemen, hotel keepers, entertainers, and so on, gathered around to add their numbers.

The growth of cities was not an unmixed blessing. Living and working conditions in the earliest industrial cities were frequently as bad as or worse than anything that could be found in the preindustrial countryside. Cities were filled with huge ramshackle tenements or long rows of miserable cottages in which the families of the working classes crowded four, eight, even twelve or more persons to a room. The buildings were so badly constructed that sometimes whole blocks collapsed, as though struck by an earthquake. Sanitary facilities were generally nonexistent, and refuse of all kinds was disposed of by being thrown into the street. Where drainage facilities existed they usually took the form of open ditches in the middle of the streets, but more often than not rain, waste water, and refuse were left to stand in stagnant pools and rotting piles that filled the air with vile odors and served as breeding areas for cholera and other epidemic diseases. Swine and other animals ranged the streets and courtyards, rooting in the refuse heaps. The streets themselves were mostly narrow, crooked, unlighted, and unpaved. Over all hung a black pall of

Editorial Photocolor Archives, Inc.

The Houses of the Poor Are Not the Palaces of the Rich
engraving by Gustav Doré

"Every great city has one or more slums, where the working class is crowded together. . . . These slums are pretty equally arranged in all the great towns of England, the worst houses in the worst quarters of the towns; usually one or two-storied cottages in long rows, perhaps with cellars used as dwellings, almost always irregularly built. . . . The streets are generally unpaved, rough, dirty, filled with vegetable and animal refuse, without sewers or gutters, but supplied with foul, stagnant pools instead. . . . Further, the streets serve as drying grounds in fine weather; lines are stretched across from house to house, and hung with wet clothing." Friedrich Engels, THE CONDITION OF THE WORKING CLASS IN ENGLAND IN 1844 (London, 1892).

smoke and grit from factory smokestacks and household chimneys. Except for the greater quantities of smoke, conditions in the industrial areas did not differ greatly from those of earlier towns and cities, but their greater size and number made them more pernicious. That people consented to live in such conditions is evidence of the great economic pressures that drew them from the country into the factories.

In part, the deplorable conditions resulted from extremely rapid growth, inadequacy of the administrative machinery, lack of experience by local authorities, and the consequent absence of planning. For example, Manchester, the center of the cotton textile industry in Great Britain, grew from a "mere village" at the beginning of the eighteenth century to a town of 25,000 in 1770 on the eve of the industrial revolution. By 1800 it had a population of almost 100,000, and by 1850 more than 300,000. Yet it did not secure a charter of incorporation until 1838. The growth of other cities was even more rapid. Chicago, first settled in 1816, rose from 30,000 in 1850 to more than 500,000 in 1880 and more than 1 million in 1890.

Although there was a general if gradual improvement in conditions within the purview of public authorities throughout the nineteenth century, many of the worst conditions were beyond their competence until new laws were passed. The public authorities could pave the streets, install sewers and street lights, and issue regulations to provide for proper ventilation, but they could not except in the most general way ensure that buildings were properly designed and erected or prevent four families from living in a dwelling designed for one. The responsibility rested in part upon the greed or indifference of landlords and builders, but also upon the poverty and ignorance of the people themselves.

NEW SOCIAL CLASSES

A third major consequence of industrialization was the growth of new social classes that overshadowed or completely replaced those which had previously existed. The bourgeoisie, or middle class, had existed in limited numbers in preindustrial society in western Europe. As early as the seventeenth century in the more commercially advanced nations, such as Britain and Holland, the gentry and nobility had begun to form a loose, informal alliance with the upper middle classes, frequently by intermarriage. With the continued commercialization of society and the beginning of industrialization, the numbers and wealth of the middle classes grew, leading to an increase in their influence and especially their aspirations. In countries where the political and social structure was sufficiently flexible – Britain is the classic example – their aspirations were gradually translated into political power. The Great Reform of 1832 marked the triumph of this group and ensured middle-class dominance in British social and political life for almost a century. Where social and political institutions were not sufficiently flexible – and here the classic example is

France — the rising aspirations of the middle classes came into direct conflict with the interests of the older aristocracy, resulting in revolution. The great French Revolution of 1789 and the lesser revolution of 1830 were essentially bourgeois or middle-class revolutions.

A new class of industrial workers emerged with the industrial system and began to gain numerical superiority, especially in the cities. But to speak of "the" working class is misleading, for there were many gradations and differences within the laboring population. Factory workers proper (including many women and children), although among the objects of greatest attention for historians of the industrial revolution, were only one element of it. Moreover, within that one element there were many differences in attitude and circumstance, for instance, among textile workers, iron workers, pottery workers, and so on. Miners (also including some women and children in the earliest stages of industrialization), though they resembled factory workers in some respects, differed in many others. Domestic servants, artisans, and handicraftsmen had existed in large numbers before the industrial revolution. Many of the skilled workers sank to the status of the unskilled as machines replaced them in their work. Others, including carpenters, masons, machinists, and typesetters, found the demand for their services increasing with the growth of cities and industry. Casual laborers, such as dockers and porters, constituted another important group, as did transport workers, clerks, and so on. The common characteristic that enables us to treat these various groups as one for some purposes (although even it was not precise or universal) was the fact that the individuals composing them depended for a living upon the sale of their labor for a daily or weekly wage. Since wages were generally quite low, and since there were periodic seasons of slack work and industrial depression, the livelihood thus gained was skimpy and precarious. Bad as they were, the conditions of life and work of the industrial workers probably were better than they had been for the masses of the population before the industrial revolution.

ECONOMIC LIBERALISM, LAISSEZ FAIRE, AND FREE TRADE

The economic aspect of nineteenth-century liberalism was closely associated with the so-called classical school of political economy. The creators and leading spokesmen of this school were a kindly Scots philosopher, a parson of the Church of England, and a converted Jewish stockbroker of London.

CLASSICAL POLITICAL ECONOMY

Adam Smith (1723–1790), professor of moral philosophy in the University of Glasgow, was as much a product of the Enlightenment as was Thomas Jefferson or the Marquis de Condorcet. He was also thoroughly steeped in the British empirical tradition of philosophy (David Hume was a close personal friend), had traveled widely on the Continent, and had gained practical experience in business and government as a commissioner of customs (import taxes). His great work, *An Inquiry into the Nature and Causes of the Wealth of Nations,* was first published in 1776. In it Smith analyzed and vividly described the benefits of specialization and division of labor among individuals and geographical regions. Smith was thoroughly individualistic. Like Bentham and other liberals, he regarded the welfare of individuals as the ultimate goal of all human endeavor, and in common with other philosophers of the Enlightenment he had an optimistic view of the possibilities of human progress. Borrowing the concept of natural law from Newtonian physics, he thought he detected a "natural harmony" in the social universe, according to which an "invisible hand," the force of competition in free markets, led each individual to contribute to the interest of society while pursing his own self-interest. It followed that the government should interfere with individual economic activity as little as possible, apart from maintaining the basic conditions of order and justice: "According to the system of natural liberty, the sovereign has only three duties to attend to: . . . first, the duty of protecting society from the violence and invasion of other independent societies; secondly, the duty of protecting, as far as possible, every member of the society from the injustice or oppression of every other member of it, or the duty of establishing an exact administration of justice; and, thirdly, the duty of erecting and maintaining certain public works and certain public institutions." In short, *The Wealth of Nations* provided powerful arguments in favor of individual economic freedom and free international trade and against the cumbersome governmental restrictions on trade and enterprise that had grown up in preceding centuries.

The Reverend Thomas Robert Malthus (1766–1834) followed Smith on most points but radically reversed his optimistic view of the beneficent results of the economy operating in accordance with natural laws. In *An Essay on the Principle of Population* (1798) Malthus stated his view that population tends to grow more rapidly than food supply, except when it is checked by famine, disease, war, and other forms of misery and vice. Although Malthus later modified his theory to include "moral restraint" (voluntary limitation of births through celibacy and late marriage) as a "preventive check" on population growth, the implications of his theory were clear: the masses of mankind were forever destined to live in misery at a near-subsistence level of income.

When Malthus's gloomy conclusions were combined with the "iron law of wages" popularly associated with the name of David Ricardo, they led Thomas Carlyle to label political economy (or economics) the "dismal science." Ricardo (1772–1823), a stockbroker by profession, developed the "labor theory of value," which was implicit in the work of his predecessors Smith and John Locke and which later formed the basis of Marxian economics. According to Ricardo, the value of any commodity is proportional to the amount of labor necessary to produce it. Since labor itself resembles a commodity insofar as it is bought and sold, its value (the wage rate) varies with the price of food necessary for the subsistence of the laborer and his family. Ricardo argued that actual wages could not rise above a minimum subsistence level for any prolonged period, because the increase in population and in the price of foodstuffs would force them back to the "natural," or customary, level. Although this theory has long since been proven fallacious, it had great influence in the nineteenth century on the thought of orthodox economists and statesmen and of revolutionaries such as Karl Marx. It inspired the new Poor Law of 1834, which greatly simplified the administration of poor relief and contributed to the mobility of labor, but also imposed harsh "means tests" on applicants for relief and forced them into prisonlike workhouses as a condition for obtaining relief.

Classical economics received its ultimate statement from the pen of John Stuart Mill (1806–1873), who published his *Principles of Political Economy* in 1848. Mill added little of novelty but synthesized and systematized the contributions of his predecessors. Mill's authority was rarely questioned for more than a quarter of a century thereafter, and the general policy prescriptions of classical economics that he defined commanded wide adherence until well into the twentieth century. Nevertheless, criticism from without, from socialists and others, and new theoretical developments from within gradually eroded its theoretical basis. Mill himself in his later years began to question some of the principles that he had earlier taken for granted and he began to move in the direction of a vague humanitarian socialism. Meanwhile, the implementation of the classical doctrines in legislation and public policy marked a triumph rarely achieved by purely intellectual ideas. That triumph was best summed up in two phrases: free trade and laissez faire.

CORN LAW REPEAL AND FREE TRADE

The heart of the free trade movement in Great Britain was the drive to repeal the Corn Laws, which placed an almost prohibitive tax on the importation of wheat and other bread grains. Popular sentiment for the repeal resulted in 1839 in the creation of the Anti-Corn Law League under the leadership of Richard Cobden, a Manchester manufacturer and outspoken pacifist, and John Bright, a Quaker industrialist of Rochdale. The league mounted a strong and effective campaign to influence public opinion. It was supported in particular by the so-called Manchester School, which was not a school at all but a loose association of industrialists, humanitarian reformers, middle-class radicals, and intellectuals from London and other provincial cities as well as Manchester. The cir-

The Mansell Collection

John Stuart Mill

"The rapid success of the Political Economy showed that the public wanted, and were prepared for such a book. Published early in 1848, an edition of a thousand copies was sold in less than a year. Another similar edition was published in the spring of 1849; and a third, of 1250 copies, early in 1852. It was, from the first, continually cited and referred to as an authority, because it was not a book merely of abstract science, but also of application, and treated Political Economy, not as a thing by itself, but as a fragment of a greater whole; a branch of Social Philosophy." AUTOBIOGRAPHY OF JOHN STUART MILL (New York, 1924).

cumstance that ensured the success of the movement was the disastrous potato famine of 1845–1846 in Ireland. The final vote in the House of Commons in May, 1846, found the Conservative prime minster, Sir Robert Peel, and about one hundred of his supporters joining with a majority of the Whigs in favor of repeal.

Peel's government had previously simplified customs procedures and had taken a few steps in the direction of freer trade. With the crumbling of the Corn Laws, the principal bastion of the protectionists, other legislative obstacles to complete free trade soon disappeared. In 1849 Parliament repealed the Navigation Acts, the foundation of the old colonial system, and by 1860 virtually complete free trade had been achieved.

LAISSEZ FAIRE

The free trade movement was one of the most conspicuous and successful aspects of a general tendency toward the relaxation of governmental controls over economic activity that characterized the middle decades of the nineteenth century, in Great Britain particularly. It derived its political and economic strength from the increasing power of the middle classes and its intellectual justification from the teachings of the classical economists. The principles underlying the tendency are sometimes referred to collectively by the French phrase *laissez faire,* which first appeared in English usage in 1825. The phrase is literally translated by the imperative "let do." The popular understanding of it was that individuals, especially businessmen, should be left free of all governmental restraint (except criminal laws) to pursue their own selfish interests. Carlyle satirized it as "anarchy plus a constable."

Laissez faire in practice, however, was by no means as heartless, as selfishly motivated, or as inexorable as extremist statements indicated. The main target of the classical economists and the new commercial and industrial classes was the old apparatus of mercantilist economic regulation, which in the name of national interest frequently erected pockets of special privilege and monopoly and in other ways irrationally interfered with individual liberty and the pursuit of wealth. In addition to the Corn Laws and the Navigation Acts, the means of mercantilist control included chartered companies with monopoly privileges, such as the East India Company and the Hudson's Bay Company, prohibitions on the export of machinery and the emigration of skilled artisans, the Combination Acts, the usury laws, and much similar legislation.

At the same time that Parliament was dismantling the old system of regulation and special privilege, however, it was enacting a new series of regulations concerned with the general welfare, especially of those least able to protect themselves. The measures included the Factory Acts, new health and sanitary laws, and the beginnings of public education. These measures were not the work of any one class or segment of the population. Humanitarian reformers of both aristocratic and middle-class backgrounds joined forces with leaders of the working classes to agitate for them, and they were voted for by Whigs and Tories as well as Radicals.

CONTINENTAL AND AMERICAN ECONOMIC POLICIES

Economic liberalism, though not confined to England, found its leading advocates and practitioners there. The French spokesmen of the classical school were J. B. Say, a follower of Adam Smith, and Frédéric Bastiat, who sought to popularize its doctrines in a series of "economic sophisms." While the majority of French businessmen paid lip service to the principles of individualism and laissez faire, at the same time they clamored for protection of their own economic interests. Instead of evolving in the direction of free trade, French commercial policy remained rigidly protectionist until after 1850. Industrialists and agriculturists alike sought subsidies and special favors for their own industries, while insisting on strict atomistic competition within the labor force. The hated *livrets* or workers' passbooks, requiring employer approval for a change of jobs, placed the workers at a great disadvantage in bargaining with their employers. Under the authoritarian regime of the Second Empire (see pp. 147–148), France at last took some hesitating steps in the direction of economic liberalism.

Middle-class rule in Belgium proved somewhat more dynamic and progressive than in France. The new government, favored by the cooperation of French and British capitalists and engineers, set out at once to add the benefits of material prosperity to the achievement of national independence. It established public and private credit on a sound basis and facilitated the formation of new industrial and commercial enterprises. As a result of such measures, its rich coal resources, and its favorable geographical location, Belgium soon became the most highly industrialized and one of the most prosperous nations on the Continent. It produced no great liberal economist of the stature of Adam Smith or J. B. Say, but it followed their teachings in practice with exemplary success.

In the interests of administrative efficiency and fiscal responsibility the government of Prussia reformed its tariff system and in 1834 took the lead in creating the Zollverein, a customs union or free trade area, which eventually included all German states except Austria. This promoted economic development and material prosperity and thereby strengthened the middle classes, but the Zollverein was also a political measure designed to strengthen Prussia at the expense of Austria. Prussia's leaders realized that a customs union from which Austria was excluded could be of great importance in a future struggle for supremacy in central Europe.

In general, in places where the middle classes had not yet succeeded in breaking the grip of aristocratic-autocratic rule, economic liberalism, like political liberalism, made little headway. The situation in Germany, where political liberalism had found an ally in nationalism, produced its own special variant of economic doctrine. Friedrich List (1789–1846), a forerunner of the historical school of political economy, and an ardent advocate of railroads and the Zollverein, published *The National System of Political Economy* in 1841. He argued that the doctrines of the classical economists did not have universal validity, though they were not wholly incorrect. According to him, the appropriate economic policy depended upon the specific conditions of time and place. Free trade and a minimal role for government suited England very well, where commerce and industry were already developed, but in a backward, divided nation like Germany the government should take a much more positive role in the development of the productive forces of the nation. List's argument had widespread influence, not only on Germany in the nineteenth century but also on the nations that tried to achieve national self-sufficiency between the two World Wars and on the former colonial dependencies that tried to develop their own national economies after World War II.

List lived for a number of years in the United States, where he obtained many ideas subsequently elaborated in his book. Americans in the first half of the century differed not so much on the role of the government in the economy as on which level of government should play the most active role. The classical economists had few purist adherents in the United States. Varied as actual economic policies were in the numerous burgeoning states, they achieved a pragmatic and workable compromise between the demands of individual liberty and the requirements of society. Owing to rival sectional interests and the triumph of the Jeffersonian and Jacksonian democrats, the federal government played the minimal role assigned by classical theory and until the Civil War followed a liberal or low tariff commercial policy. State and local governments on the other hand took an active role in promoting economic development and social welfare. The American System, as Henry Clay called it, regarded government as an agency to assist individuals and private enterprise and to hasten the development of the nation's material resources.

THE INDUSTRIAL REVOLUTION IN PERSPECTIVE

The industrial revolution, in the broadest sense of the term, cannot be assigned specific dates, nor was it confined to a single country or geographical area. Under a variety of labels, such as the automation movement in highly industrialized countries and programs of economic development in the poorer nations of the world, it is still going on today. In the long view of history, however, the industrial revolution in Britain appears as one of the great watersheds in the progress of civilization. For the first time in the annals of mankind a society surmounted the niggardliness of nature and broke out of the Malthusian trap. No longer were the masses destined to live out their earthly existence in endless backbreaking toil under the constant threat of death by starvation or disease.

In view of this achievement it is curious that so much of the historical controversy surrounding the industrial revolution has focussed on the question of whether it was good or bad. It is true that it involved displacement and the disruption of traditional behavior, along with much suffering on the part of many of those affected: any process of radical social change, no matter how beneficial in the long run, is bound to create hardship for those with a vested interest in the status quo. In arriving at a final assessment of the consequences of any historical event or movement, however, the historian must ask, What was the alternative? For the industrial revolution in Britain, the answer is provided by contemporaneous events in Ireland. (That the Irish were governed from London, although not unrelated to their fate, does not alter the significance of the example.) The Irish population increased from about 4 million in 1780 to more than 8 million in 1840 without significant industrialization or agrarian reform. The result was the disastrous potato famine of the 1840's, which through starvation and emigration reduced the population by more than 2 million in the space of ten years. Without the continued expansion of industry and the increase in agricultural productivity made possible by the industrial revolution, the whole of Europe might have shared Ireland's fate.

REVOLUTION AT FLOODTIDE
CHAPTER FOUR

Between 1832 and 1848 the middle classes in Great Britain, France, and Belgium, working in cooperation with the few liberal representatives of the old aristocratic elements, sought to consolidate their recently achieved preponderance of political power. Although they continued to make liberal reforms, liberalism in western Europe ceased to be a revolutionary force and became a defender of the new status quo in the face of growing demands by the urban working classes for more far-reaching democratic and social reforms. The rapidity of industrial development and the progress of reform in Britain and Belgium gradually reconciled the workers to liberalism. The slower pace of change in France, together with the narrow, short-sighted selfishness of French liberals, built up a store of tension and resentment in French society that suddenly overflowed in revolution. As on previous occasions, the revolution in France served to trigger a series of revolutionary outbursts throughout Europe, especially in central Europe, where liberal, national, democratic, republican, and socialist sentiments freely mingled in their common antagonism to the old order.

CONTRASTING LIBERALISMS IN THE WEST

THE VICTORIAN ERA IN BRITAIN

Parliamentary reform, in spite of its long-run significance, did not immediately introduce radical changes into the fabric of British life. It did accelerate the course of social and economic reform and inaugurated a gradual realignment of British politics and political parties. In the new alignment, which emerged gradually between 1832 and the second reform bill in 1867, party discipline was strengthened and both parties built extraparliamentary organizations to influence the electorate. The Tories became the Conservative party, representing primarily the landed interests, the established church, and eventually the advocates of imperialism. The Whigs became the Liberal party, spokesmen for the commercial and manufacturing classes and advocates of reform. Paradoxically, Conservative governments carried two of the most important reforms of the century – the repeal of the Corn Laws in 1846 and the second reform bill or Representation of the People Act of 1867, which extended the suffrage to the majority of urban workers. These two reforms split party loyalties and occasioned much delay in the emergence of the new system, but they clarified the principles that divided the parties and laid the foundation for subsequent party cohesion.

In the two preceding centuries the unpopularity, incapacity, and weakness of British monarchs had contributed greatly to strengthening the evolving system of representative, parliamentary government. Under the dissolute George IV (1820–1830) and the petty William IV (1830–1837) the popularity of the monarchy reached a low ebb. When William died, its future was uncertain. His successor on the throne was his niece Victoria, a girl of eighteen, who was scarcely prepared for the role she had to assume. Under other circumstances her youth, inexperience, and sex might have been fatal handicaps. As it happened, they suited almost perfectly the prevailing temper of the ruling bourgeoisie. She was prim, almost prudish. She had a profound respect for the British constitution and for her own place within it. She lacked imagination and a sense of aesthetics, but she had a stern, puritanical devotion to duty and morality. In 1840 she married Albert of Saxe-Coburg-Gotha, a serious, sensible man who was her counterpart in almost every respect; she bore him nine children. Albert's encouragement of scientific, technological, and industrial progress showed that he was in step with the times. Victoria's reign, the longest in British history (1837–1901), coincided almost exactly with the peak of British economic supremacy and political influence. It is hardly to be wondered that her name became the symbol of an age.

THE PROGRESS OF REFORM

The victory of the Whigs in 1832 ensured the continuation of reform. The reforms were of many types. Some of the major ones, such as the electoral reform and the subsequent reorganization of local government, reflected chiefly the interests of the middle classes. Administrative reforms, such as the New Poor Law of 1834 and the introduction of the penny post in 1840, represented a triumph for the rationalism of the exponents of Bentham's utilitarianism. Humanitarian measures such as the abolition of slavery and factory legislation resulted from the reaction of middle-class consciences to the exposure by utilitarian reformers of grave social evils. John Stuart Mill put it well when he wrote in 1838, "The changes which have been made, and the greater changes which will be made, in our institutions, are not the work of philosophers, but of the interests and instincts of large portions of society recently grown into strength. But Bentham gave voice to those interests and instincts."

One of the first acts of the reformed Parliament in 1833 was the abolition of slavery throughout the empire. Trading in slaves had been illegal since 1807, but the institution of slavery itself still existed in the West Indies and other tropical colonies. To abolish slavery without violating the property rights of the slave owners, the British taxed themselves for 20 million pounds sterling to be paid as compensation to the owners.

A new Factory Act was passed in the same year with the aid of the Tories, who hoped to hit back at the newly enfranchised mill owners through their pocketbooks. It extended the scope of earlier laws dating back to 1802, which had prohibited the employment of children under the age of nine in cotton mills and limited the workday of children between nine and thirteen to twelve hours. The earlier legislation had covered only the cotton industry and failed to provide for effective enforcement. The act of 1833 extended the provisions to all textile factories, imposed a maximum eight-hour day on children from nine to thirteen, and a twelve-hour day on those from thirteen to eighteen, provided paid inspectors who were responsible to the Home Office in London, and insisted on two hours daily of compulsory schooling for working children.

The act of 1833 precipitated a campaign for the regulation of adult labor, which eventuated in the Ten Hours Bill of 1847. After shocking revelations of conditions in the mining industry, the Mines Act of 1842 extended regulation and inspection to coal mines and prohibited the employment of women and children underground. Another Factory Act in 1844 required safety devices on industrial machinery and imposed additional safeguards. In the next two decades more and more industries were brought within the scope of the factory acts, and the general principle of state regulation of working conditions was firmly established.

A major step that followed logically from the Reform Bill of 1832 was the Municipal Reform Act of 1835. It provided for town councils elected by the taxpayers and employing paid officials. Subsequent legislation further strengthened local self-government and at the same time provided for greater central coordination. For example, after a recurrence of cholera in 1848 sanitary reformer Edwin Chadwick secured the establishment of a central board of health with powers to create local boards. During the next two decades local authorities were compelled to provide a water supply, sewers, and waste disposal and to appoint professional sanitary inspectors.

THE JULY MONARCHY IN FRANCE

In France the Charter of 1814, as revised in 1830, was essentially a contract between the monarch and the upper bourgeoisie, who were its principal beneficiaries. The revisions abolished hereditary membership in the Chamber of Peers, dropped Catholicism as the state religion, restricted censorship of the press except against "radical agitation," and assured constitutional, parliamentary government. Control remained firmly in the hands of men of property. Amendments to the electoral law enlarged the suffrage from about 90,000 to about 170,000 but retained formidable property qualifications for office-holding and voting. An American, John Jay, had said, "The men who own the country ought to govern it"; no government more clearly exemplified that maxim than the July Monarchy in France.

The true political division of the country was tripartite, but two of the three major groups were excluded from the political process – one by choice, the other by legislation. On the extreme right were the ultramontanists and supporters of the defunct Bourbons, who began to call themselves legitimists. Although they were eligible to vote and hold office, the majority retired to their estates or town houses to await a counterrevolution that never came. On the extreme left were the republicans and socialists, most of whom were excluded from legal participation by the property qualifications. Concentrated in the cities, especially Paris, they agitated and conspired for a revolution, which, when it came, surprised even them. The middle-class parliamentary forces that occupied the center made a show of party politics with various sham divisions such as left center, or right center, but in fact they were firmly united in the belief that no more fundamental alterations in the social and political structure were desirable. Jacques Laffitte and Adolphe Thiers, leaders of the "party of movement," talked vaguely of extending the benefits of the regime to the less favored classes; but they did nothing about it in the few brief periods when they held the reins of government. Casimir Périer, first leader of the "party of resistance," defined his policy as that of the *juste milieu,* that is, the middle way between absolutism and clericalism on the one hand and republicanism and democracy on the other. He demonstrated his meaning in 1831 by suppressing with violence and brutality a rising of workers in Lyons, in which more than six hundred persons died. After his death in the cholera epidemic of 1832, his principal successor, François Guizot, piously proclaimed the government of the revised charter "the most perfect ever devised."

Much of the actual character of the July Monarchy derived from and was symbolized by its only monarch, Louis Philippe. Despite his noble birth, the new king had long associated with the men of wealth who put him on the throne. He shared their tastes and aspirations, their virtues and their vices. He was shrewd, sober, and industrious, prudent in conduct, inherently conservative in outlook. A wealthy man in his own right, he adored wealth for its own sake and admired the men who possessed it. In some respects a sort of male Victoria, he nevertheless harbored a secret desire to wield political power himself. He was able to gratify this desire after 1840 by means of Guizot, his principal minister and the other archetype of the July Monarchy.

Guizot was a Protestant who reflected well the spirit and outlook of the *haute bourgeoisie*. He had written a history of the English revolution of 1689 and found his ideal of society in the government and social order that resulted from that event. When he secured the king's confidence in 1840 after ten years of ministerial instability caused by conflicting personal ambitions of the supporters of the throne, he systematically consolidated support for his own ministry by means of wholesale bribery and corruption. Personally incorruptible, he did not scruple at preying on the moral weaknesses of others. In this way he contrived to impose on French government and society a superficial stability that lasted until 1848.

The notable difference between middle-class government in France and Britain was not the extent of corruption, for Britain had its share of that; it was the almost total absence of reform measures by the French. Not only did French ministers draw the line at further extensions of the suffrage, but they showed no interest in the administrative, judicial, and economic reforms that appealed to middle-class sentiment in Britain. Aside from an insignificant and ineffective child labor law, the one important piece of progressive legislation in the whole of the July Monarchy was Guizot's law of 1833 relating to elementary education. The principal purpose of the law was to establish at least one elementary school in each of France's 38,000 communes as the beginning of an attack on mass illiteracy. Although the objective was laudable, the law fell far short of its goal in execution. Moreover, the clergy received a large measure of control over the schools in order to ensure "safe doctrine" for the children of peasants and workers and to conciliate the Catholic Church, which had formerly been an object of attack by French liberals. All other demands for political, social, and economic reform Guizot countered with the self-satisfied admonition, "Make yourselves rich."

THE GROWTH OF SOCIAL PROTEST

While the middle classes of western Europe struggled to remake society according to their own ideas, the swelling urban working classes began to assert their claims as well. In the beginning their attempts took the form of futile riots and strikes against industrialism. Increasingly, however, the workers turned to the formation of labor or trade unions, which were often bitterly opposed and repressed by middle-class employers and governments. They sent petitions to the government for legislative or administrative remedy, formed friendly societies and cooperatives for mutual self-help, and resorted to outright revolutionary activity. The outbursts increased in intensity and frequency as the workers realized that the middle classes had no intention of sharing the gains that they had won with working-class support during the events of 1830 and 1832.

ROBERT OWEN

The first great spokesman for the workingman was not himself a member of the working classes, although he had risen from their ranks. Robert Owen (1771–1858), son of a Welsh artisan, left school at the age of nine to seek his fortune. After a variety of experiences he became at the age of twenty hired manager of a large Manchester cotton mill. Within a few years he became part owner and general manager of another mill in New Lanark, Scotland, which included a company town with schools, churches, and a hospital. It soon became a model of paternalistic endeavor.

A man of great humanitarian feeling, Owen early came to the conclusion that social environment exercised the greatest influence in the formation of individual character. By paying high wages, providing decent living and working conditions, and strictly limiting child labor, Owen created a contented labor force and also earned substantial profits. Beginning with the publication of *A New View of Society* in 1813, he sought to convince the aristocratic rulers of Europe and America to substitute his new "rational system of society," a system based on cooperation, for the existing organization. He campaigned ceaselessly for several years and built up a small but enthusiastic following among workingmen and a few radical reformers, but he made no lasting impression on the ruling classes. In 1824 he set off with a band of disciples to organize a cooperative commonwealth in the wilderness of America at New Harmony, Indiana. Quarrels and misfortune soon caused dissension, and it collapsed completely after Owen's return to England in 1828.

By then Owen had become the hero of the working classes. Many working-class organizations looked to him for leadership. Until 1832, however, he occupied himself in assisting passage of the Reform Bill, expecting that the reformed Parliament would extend the suffrage to workers. When it became evident that it would not, Owen turned for support to the working-class organizations. A number of trade unions had been formed after the repeal of the Combination Acts in 1824, and at the beginning of 1834 Owen organized most of them into "one big union," the Grand National Consolidated Trades Union, which soon enrolled more than half a million members.

The basic strategy of the organization was the general strike, a "Grand National Holiday," to force the government and employers to agree peaceably to the demands of the workers. The government took fright and in March, 1834, sentenced six Dorsetshire agricultural laborers, the famous Tolpuddle martyrs, to exile in the Australian penal colony for organizing a branch of the union. As a result of this example of government repression, as well as of the dissension among the leaders, the Grand

National broke up as quickly as it had formed. Although Owen continued to write and to agitate until the end of his long life, the leadership of working-class organizations soon passed to other hands.

CHARTISM

With the failure of their direct attempts to obtain redress of economic and social grievances, the leaders of the working classes returned to political action to secure it indirectly. In 1836 a group of politically conscious skilled workers created the London Working Men's Association to agitate for parliamentary reform, and in the following year the Birmingham Political Union, which had played an important role in the passage of the first Reform Bill, was reactivated. In 1838 these two groups, reinforced by delegates from the northern counties, met in Birmingham to adopt the People's Charter, a petition to Parliament for further political reform. The charter contained six points, all of which were related to the organization of Parliament. It called for (1) universal male suffrage, (2) annual parliaments, (3) a secret ballot, (4) equal electoral districts, (5) abolition of the property qualification for members of Parliament, and (6) payment of members.

Motions were introduced in the House of Commons to consider the charter in 1839 and 1842 after active campaigns and agitation throughout the country. On both occasions the motions were defeated by large majorities. Strikes, riots, and other popular disturbances followed, and each time the government took stern repressive measures. In 1840 more than five hundred Chartist leaders were in jail. Several, originally sentenced to death, had their sentences commuted to transportation to the Australian penal colony for life. In the face of such opposition the organization soon melted away. It revived briefly in the wake of the revolutions on the Continent in 1848, but the government took preventive measures, such as the recruiting of special constables from the middle classes, and a great demonstration planned for London broke up without even presenting its petition to Parliament.

In retrospect the demands of the Chartists appear reasonable. Within two generations all but annual parliaments had been achieved without special agitation. In the distressed period of the late 1830's and early 1840's, however, with its bad harvests, industrial depression, and popular unrest, Britain's new middle-class rulers felt too insecure to trust their fate to universal suffrage. A distinguished modern historian has stated that the failure of the Chartists demonstrated "not the weakness of the English working classes . . . but the strength of the middle classes." However that may be, the pace of industrial expansion, more rapid in Britain than in France, drained the pools of social unrest and sapped the basis of revolutionary discontent. As early as 1832 a witness before a parliamentary committee on manufactures was asked, "Do you think the working classes . . . ever show political discontent so long as they are doing well in their particular trade?" "Not at all," he replied.

FRENCH SOCIALISM

In France the number of urban workers rose spectacularly between 1830 and 1848. Paris had the largest concentration of industrial wage earners of any city in Europe (London, the only city with a larger population, had fewer engaged in manufacturing and similar occupations). Not all of them worked in factories; the majority, perhaps, toiled at home or in small shops under less favorable circumstances than those of the factory workers. Nevertheless, they all constituted a propertyless proletariat that proved to be fertile soil for radical reformers.

Paris also had the largest concentration of radical intellectuals of any city in Europe. It served as the great gathering place of the dispossessed, the disenchanted, and the exiled of all countries. Republicanism and socialism flourished in its intellectual climate, nourished by the traditions of the French Revolution – Jacobinism and Babeuvism in particular – as well as by the great and obvious contrast between rich and poor.

One of the first important socialist thinkers of modern times was the quixotic philosopher Henri de Saint-Simon (1760–1825). Although of noble birth, Saint-Simon fought against England during the American Revolution, abdicated his heritage during the French Revolution, and won and lost a fortune by speculation. For the last twenty-five years of his life he settled down to serious study, meditation, and writing, frequently living off the charity of his friends. Saint-Simon criticized the existing inequalities of wealth, but he criticized even more strongly the social system that rewarded the unproductive or "parasitical" elements in society, especially the aristocracy, while oppressing the workers or "industrialists." According to Saint-Simon, an *industriel* was anyone who produced a useful commodity or service; therefore farmers, common laborers, artisans, merchants, engineers, and bankers were all industriels. He projected a hierarchic society governed by "wise men" – philosophers, scientists, and engineers – in which everyone would be obligated to work according to his talents and would be rewarded in proportion to his contribution. Saint-Simon was no democrat, and many of his ideas were wildly impractical, but his numerous writings provided a rich store of inspiration for future reformers of all varieties, and some of the products of his imagination proved strangely prophetic of the organization of later societies, both democratic and totalitarian.

In his last years Saint-Simon attracted a small band of devoted disciples, many of whom were young engineers, financiers, and intellectuals, who created a school to propagate his ideas. They caught from him a vision of the immense possibilities of science applied to industry and preached the virtues of material advance. After the revolution of 1830 they thought the time had come for social reorganization and undertook a vigorous missionary and propaganda campaign. The staid bourgeois monarchy of Louis Philippe had scant use for their bizarre customs and beliefs, especially after one of their leaders, Prosper Enfantin, converted their teachings into a mystical, half-pagan religion. Under legal prosecution the formal organization dissolved itself in 1832, but many of its members became wealthy and respectable businessmen, bankers, and engineers in capitalistic French society.

Some of the many socialists and other radicals who inhabited Paris under the July Monarchy devoted themselves to theorizing and constructing elaborate blueprints of ideal societies, others to organizing secret societies and working actively for the overthrow of the existing government. One of the most colorful of the latter was Auguste Blanqui (1805–1881). The son of a revolutionist of 1789, Blanqui joined the Carbonari at the age of sixteen. He participated in both the revolution of 1830, which inaugurated the July Monarchy, and in that of 1848, which overthrew it. In the intervening years he organized secret societies and participated in numerous plots and uprisings. Surely one of the longest-lived of all professional revolutionaries, he spent thirty-seven of his seventy-six years in prison, survived to take part in the overthrow of the Second Empire, and died while agitating against the Third Republic.

Two theorizers deserve special mention, more for the novelty than for the practical consequences of their ideas. Charles Fourier (1772–1837) devised a scheme whereby all mankind would be divided into groups of 1,620 individuals each, with equal numbers of men and women. They would be settled on great estates called *phalanstères,* where they would engage in both agricultural and industrial activities. Each phalanstery would have common facilities, such as kitchens, dining rooms, and nurseries. Individuals would not necessarily share equally in the produce, however. In fact, Fourier made special provision for capitalistic financing by means of stock issues and advertised in newspapers for backers, but no capitalist stepped forth to finance his socialist project.

Étienne Cabet (1788–1856), like Fourier, envisioned a utopia which he called Icaria, consisting of isolated, more or less self-contained communities; but unlike Fourier, Cabet required complete equality. In 1848 Cabet actually led a band of disciples to America, where they attempted to create such a community. Many similar communities were created in the American wilderness on the basis of Fourier's and Owen's ideas. Among the most famous of these "backwoods utopias" were Brook Farm, Massachusetts, and the Oneida Community in New York. The luster of the former was due chiefly to the literary celebrities who inhabited or patronized it, while the latter gained renown partly as a consequence of its commercially successful silver-plated tableware. The Mormons and other communitarian religious sects also borrowed from the ideas of Owen, Fourier, and Cabet. Sooner or later they all broke up as a result of economic failure or internal dissension, or they adjusted themselves to the society around them. None were ever established in Europe itself.

Neither a system builder nor a conspirator, P. J. Proudhon (1809–1865) gave birth to a new doctrine known as anarchism. Anarchism subsequently became identified with lawlessness, violence, and terrorism as a result of the tactics of late nineteenth-century revolutionists who called themselves anarchists. Such activities, however, had no place in the thoughts or intentions of Proudhon, who was personally gentle and pacifist. Unlike most other radical thinkers, Proudhon was an authentic product of the working classes, and began his career in the printing trades. He read widely, educated himself, and became a prolific writer. He opposed force and coercion in all forms and regarded the modern state as the source of the greatest oppression. He held that state socialism and communism were as antithetical to true liberty as capitalist or feudal society. As the solution to social problems, he called for the voluntary cooperation of free individuals organized in small communities under a loose federalism.

Louis Blanc (1811–1882), one of the most influential of French socialists, played an active role in the provisional government of 1848. A journalist and historian by profession, he published his most famous book, *The Organization of Labor,* in 1838. In it he exposed what he regarded as the evils of free, capitalistic competition, called on the government to guarantee the "right to work," and proposed the creation of "social workshops" operated by the workers themselves. Blanc coined the phrase, "From each according to his abilities, to each according to his needs," in contrast to the Saint-Simonian doctrine, "From each according to his abilities, to each according to his works." Unlike other early socialists who belittled politics and ignored or opposed the role of government, Blanc believed the government should assist in establishing the social or national workshops. He did not regard revolution as inevitable or even desirable; instead, he felt that the workshops, once established, would beat the capitalists at their own game and ultimately drive them out of business. Blanc was one of the most important forerunners of modern democratic state socialism.

THE BIRTH OF MARXISM

Karl Marx (1818–1883), the most famous and influential of all socialist theorists, and Friedrich Engels (1820–1895), his faithful friend and collaborator, were products of German bourgeois radicalism. Marx was sent by his father, a Rhineland attorney, to study law at the University of Bonn. He devoted his first year to romantic poetry and bacchanalian brawls and was expelled for engaging in a duel. The next year he went

The Bettmann Archive

Karl Marx

"Marx was before all else a revolutionist. His real mission in life was to contribute, in one way or another, to the overthrow of capitalistic society and the state institutions which it had brought into being, to contribute to the liberation of the modern proletariat, which he *was the first to make conscious of its own position and its needs, conscious of the contradictions of its emancipation. Fighting was his element. And he fought with a passion, a tenacity and a success such as few could rival."* Friedrich Engels, "Speech at the Graveside of Karl Marx," in Karl Marx and Friedrich Engels, SELECTED WORKS (Moscow, 1955).

to the University of Berlin, where he fell under the spell of Hegelian philosophy and took a degree in philosophy. Prevented from teaching because he was an atheist, Marx edited a liberal bourgeois newspaper in Cologne for a time, but the paper was suppressed by the authorities in 1843 for criticizing the absolutist government of Russia. Marx then went to Paris, where he supported himself by writing while studying political economy and socialism. There he met Engels.

Engels, son of a wealthy Rhineland textile manufacturer, had earlier been sent to England to learn the cotton trade in his father's firm in Manchester. While there he wrote a book vilifying capitalism and describing in a somewhat exaggerated manner the condition of the English laboring classes. Although he charged the English capitalists with driving women and children into "wage slavery" and prostitution and destroying family life, he did not bother to marry the Irish factory girl whom he kept as a mistress for many years. On the other hand, Marx, far from living up to the stereotype of the wild-eyed revolutionary, was a conventional family man and a devoted husband and father.

In 1847 Marx moved to London at the invitation of Engels. They joined a small revolutionary group called the League of the Just, later renamed the Communist League, which Engels described as "not much more than the German branch of the French secret societies." Having been invited by the league to draw up a statement of principles, Marx and Engels published the *Communist Manifesto* in January, 1848, on the eve of the revolutions in Europe. The timing was purely coincidental, for the *Manifesto* had no influence at all in provoking or directing the course of the revolutions. Published in the German language in London, it was for many years known only to a small group of personal friends and acquaintances. Not until Marx had gained notoriety as a socialist with the publication of his *Critique of Political Economy* and above all of *Capital,* the first volume of which appeared in 1867, did the *Manifesto* assume a prominent place in socialist literature.

The *Manifesto* was intended primarily as a propaganda device to convince the workers of their own importance, call them to unity, and stir them to action. It began with a striking and wildly inaccurate introduction: "A spectre is haunting Europe – the spectre of Communism. All the powers of old Europe have entered into a holy alliance to exercise this spectre: Pope and Tsar, Metternich and Guizot, French Radicals and German police-spies." It concluded with an even more stirring call to action: "Let the ruling classes tremble at a Communist revolution. The proletarians have nothing to lose but their chains. They have a world to win. Working men of all countries, unite!"

Between these dramatic passages Marx and Engels set forth in drastically abbreviated form the substance of the historical and economic theory that Marx subsequently developed in his more scholarly publications. They developed the theory that "the history of all hitherto existing society is the history of class struggles." They cited the fact that feudal lords had replaced Roman patricians as the ruling class and serfs had replaced slaves as the exploited class of society. With the development of commerce in the late Middle Ages a new class, the bourgeoisie, developed to dispute control of society with the old feudal nobility. After many struggles the bourgeoisie eventually triumphed in the English revolutions of the seventeenth century and the French Revolution of 1789. Accordingly, the rest of Europe was now ripe for a bourgeois or liberal revolution. Meanwhile, the growth of the bourgeoisie as a social class had given rise to its antithesis, the proletariat. Society was becoming more divided as these two great antagonistic classes swallowed up all other classes. The stage was being set for the final clash of power between the proletariat and the bourgeoisie, in which the former would inevitably triumph in accordance with the laws of history.

The *Manifesto* also set forth the essence of Marxian economic theory, in which it was maintained that under capitalist society the proletarian class was being enlarged by the displacement of petty bourgeois elements and being driven to the margin of subsistence by the operation of capitalist wage slavery. Marx and Engels developed the idea that the Communists were the elite or "advance guard" of the proletarians, who would engineer the revolution against capitalist society. In a very general way they presented a program for the transition from capitalism to communism, involving measures such as the abolition of private property, enactment of a steep progressive income tax, centralization of credit in the hands of the state, and free public education. Finally they criticized the other socialist doctrines and tried to show that their own brand of socialism was the only one capable of resolving the "contradictions" of capitalist society.

It is important for an understanding of Marxism to know its sources, for little in Marxism was completely original. Marx's great contribution lay in his novel combination of a number of elements from various intellectual fields. From German philosophy, especially that of Hegel, Marx took the idea of the dialectical movement of history. Unlike Hegel, who regarded ideas as the dynamic forces, Marx acquired from the materialistic philosophers of the eighteenth century the notion that material conditions are the most important social forces: "What individuals are depends upon the material conditions of production. . . . The mode of production of the material subsistence conditions the social, political, and spiritual life-process in general. It is not the consciousness of men which determines their existence, but on the contrary it is their social existence which determines their consciousness."

English political economy, especially that of Ricardo, gave Marx the labor theory of value, which he carried to its logical conclusion: the goods produced by labor have a value greater than the subsistence wages paid to the workers. The "surplus value" is kept by the capitalist employers. For example, Marx estimated that a laborer working for six hours a day will produce enough to support himself and his family at a bare subsistence standard. The wage that he earns will be the equivalent of the cost of the commodities produced in those six hours. If, however, the laborer works for twelve hours, the employer will capture the surplus value produced by the additional six hours of labor. He will add it to capital in order to hire more labor and produce more commodities. Since the purchasing power of labor is insufficient to purchase all of the commodities created by capitalist production, the process results in overproduction and economic crises, which will become more and more severe until capitalist society itself finally disappears in depression and revolution.

From French socialism Marx acquired the idea of the necessity for common ownership of property or the means of production. After the final overthrow of capitalist society only one class will remain, the proletariat, which will own all property in common. With the abolition of private property no further antagonisms can arise to create a class struggle, and the socialist millennium will be inaugurated.

Marx and Engels had correctly predicted the outbreak of revolution on the Continent. In the spring of 1848 they returned to Germany to attempt to give the revolution a socialist direction, chiefly by publishing a newspaper in which they advocated the cause of the working classes against both the old absolutism and the new bourgeoisie. The revolution failed, partly because of the split between the bourgeoisie and the workers, and in 1849 Marx and Engels returned to England. Engels resumed his business career and used a part of the profits to subsidize his friend, while Marx took up the systematic study and elaboration of his doctrine.

THE REVOLUTION OF 1848 IN FRANCE

For almost twenty years French workers and radicals, who felt cheated by the sudden "change of ministries" of 1830, agitated and conspired for reform or revolution. Their opposition took the form of strikes, riots, urban insurrections and assassination attempts against the king and his ministers. Most of their demonstrations had strong republican or socialist overtones. The authorities managed to keep them under control only by extreme repression. The rigidity and corruption of the regime under Guizot also led to demands for reform by the bourgeois or loyal opposition. Men like Thiers merely wanted a change of ministers that would return them to power. Others, such as the poet Lamartine, went so far as to suggest an abdication. Only a handful, including Louis Blanc and

Alexandre Ledru-Rollin, overtly proclaimed their republicanism, but even they did not openly advocate revolution.

Nevertheless, the course of events drifted steadily toward revolution. Humanitarian novelists like Victor Hugo, Georges Sand, and Eugène Sue depicted the plight of the common man in a form approaching an appeal for democracy and socialism. Jules Michelet, Lamartine, and Louis Blanc wrote histories of the Great Revolution suggesting its unfinished character, and Thiers recalled the glories of Napoleon in contrast to the timid, unglamourous foreign policy of Guizot. Poor harvests and a severe economic crisis in 1846–1847 increased working-class distress and led to a revival of protest meetings. Since the law forbade overt political gatherings, the meetings took the form of popular banquets at which the reformers addressed large assemblies of the lower middle and working classes. By the end of 1847 almost every city and town in France had staged at least one such banquet.

THE FEBRUARY DAYS

The leaders of the opposition planned to culminate their "campaign of banquets" with a huge gathering in Paris, right in the face of the government. First planned for February 20, 1848, it was postponed until February 22, then canceled altogether. The government ordered its cancellation and the moderate leaders willingly acquiesced, for they had become belatedly aware of the revolutionary temper of the common people in Paris and did not wish to give occasion for violence. But the people were not to be denied, and on the appointed day the streets of Paris filled with milling people. Groups of students and some of the more daring leaders resolved to carry out the banquet. The mobs alternately jeered and cheered the army troops and regiments of the National Guard that were called up to preserve order. Some of the guard even joined the people in calling for Guizot's dismissal. Stones were thrown, windows were broken, sporadic fighting broke out, and street barricades were erected in the working-class quarters of the city.

On February 23 Louis Philippe finally dismissed Guizot, but that evening soldiers guarding the ministry panicked and fired into the mob, killing several people. By morning the whole city was in an uproar. The troops were disorganized, and the National Guard refused to fire on the populace, demonstrating with it instead. On February 24 Louis Philippe abdicated in favor of his ten-year-old grandson and departed for England, but the Chamber of Deputies refused to accept his designated successor. While the duchess of Orleans was in the Chamber with her son, pleading with it to accept him as king and her as regent, the mobs invaded the Chamber and under the leadership of republican orators forced the deputies to name a provisional government. That evening at the Hôtel de

Ville the poet Lamartine, who had suddenly become converted to republicanism, announced the fall of the monarchy and proclaimed for the second time in French history a republican government.

THE PROVISIONAL GOVERNMENT

Once again the common people of Paris together with middle-class politicians had made a revolution with a minimum of bloodshed. Yet for a time it was uncertain what the outcome would be — whether the middle classes would reassert their predominance, or whether the workers would achieve their goal of a genuine social revolution. The Provisional Government was an amalgam of two groups: the moderate republicans, named in the chamber by the abdicating deputies (actually the list had been drawn up in the editorial offices of the moderate republican newspaper, the *National*), and the "social" republicans or socialists, named by the mobs at the Hôtel de Ville (their list had been drawn up in the offices of the radical newspaper, the *Réforme*). The outstanding figure was Lamartine, who took over Guizot's former post, the ministry of foreign affairs. The government also included the socialist Louis Blanc, the famous astronomer François Arago, a moderate republican, and a genuine proletarian called Albert (his last name was Martin but no one ever used it). Altogether there were eleven members of widely varying backgrounds, interests, and personalities.

Apart from its hasty formation and varied composition, the atmosphere in Paris made it difficult for the Provisional Government to pursue a straightforward policy. People still roamed the streets in a holiday mood, streaming through palaces and other public buildings and constantly sending delegations to call on the government. In the new democratic spirit of the times the government could not risk antagonizing them by failing to listen to their demands. Among a number of hastily decreed reforms it proclaimed universal suffrage, freedom of the press and of assembly, opening of the National Guard to all citizens, abolition of the death penalty, and many emergency measures to cope with the rapidly deteriorating economic situation.

Among the most famous of its actions was the creation of the National Workshops. Although they were ostensibly inspired by Louis Blanc's proposed "social workshops," they were far from the nationalized industries envisioned by him. The National Workshops were, in fact, mere open-air public works projects, which soon degenerated into simple ditch-digging and eventually into a straight dole for the unemployed workers. Instead of being placed under the supervision of Blanc himself, they were turned over to Alexandre Marie, minister of public works, who had little sympathy for the scheme. As a result of mounting unemployment throughout the country, workers streamed to Paris, where the workshops were concentrated. By June more than 120,000 had been enrolled, but another

Courtesy of Bibliothèque Nationale

The Mob Invades the Throne Room in the Tuileries Palace, February 24, 1848, lithograph by Janet Lange

"The blood of the people has flowed as in July [1830]; but this time this brave people will not be deceived. It has won a national and popular government in accord with the rights, progress and will of this great and noble people. . . . The provisional government wants a republic, subject to the ratification of the people, who will be immediately consulted. The unity of the nation, composed henceforth of all the classes of citizens who compose it; the government of the nation by itself; liberty, equality and fraternity as fundamentals; the people for our emblem and watchword; this is the democratic government which France owes itself and which our efforts will secure for it." Proclamation of the Provisional Government, February 29, 1848, reprinted in J. B. Duvergier, COLLECTION COMPLÈTE DES LOIS, DÉCRETS, etc. (Paris, 1948).

50,000 had been turned away. The presence of these thousands of hungry, idle, sullen men, disquieting middle-class property owners with their talk of the "right to work," was an ominous portent for the future of the revolution.

In foreign affairs the policy of the Provisional Government exhibited the same indecision. News of the February revolution in Paris spread like wildfire throughout Europe, setting off other revolutionary outbursts and striking fear into the hearts of absolutist rulers and middle-class property owners alike. Many Europeans expected revolutionary France to come to the aid of revolutions elsewhere, as in 1792, and many Frenchmen advocated such a policy. But Lamartine, fearing defeat by a hostile coalition and possibly the spread of radical revolution at home, equivocated. In a "Manifesto to Europe," which violated established diplomatic protocol by being addressed to peoples as well as to sovereigns, he declared that France no longer felt bound by the treaties of 1815, but would abide by them in fact; that it would "protect" legitimate national movements abroad, but would not resort to arms. Such contradictory statements made it not at all surprising that neither Frenchmen nor other European governments knew what to expect from France.

THE CONSTITUENT ASSEMBLY

Meanwhile, the people of France prepared to give their answer to the question: whither the revolution? The Provisional Government decreed elections for a Constituent Assembly to be held under universal manhood suffrage – the first time such a bold experiment in democracy had been tried in Europe – although the more radical members of the government wanted to postpone the elections in order to "educate" the rural voters. Many peasants were illiterate; most had given no thought to politics. Some feared expropriation of their property by the socialists. The majority, having no experience in elections or self-government and poorly informed on the issues and the course of events in Paris, simply voted for the local notables – attorneys, businessmen, and large landowners – who had managed affairs under previous regimes. The result was a triumph of the moderates, who gained about 500 of a total of almost 900 seats in the assembly. The radicals and socialists together garnered fewer than 100. It was even more disquieting for the future of the republic that avowed monarchists, legitimists as well as Orleanists (partisans of Louis Philippe), obtained more than a third of the total representation.

The Constituent Assembly had a dual task: to draw up a new constitution for the Second Republic and to govern it in the interim. It began the latter task by dismissing the Provisional Government with a vote of thanks that passed by only twelve votes. To replace it, the assembly elected an executive commission of five men drawn from its own members. All of them had served in the Provisional Government, but none were from the extreme left.

Unfortunately for France, the assembly and the Parisian workers at once conceived an almost instinctive hostility for one another. The workers, most of whom were unemployed and hungry, demanded immediate and far-reaching economic and social reforms, which the parliamentarians, as members of the propertied classes, had no intention of granting. On May 15 a group of workers invaded the assembly, declared it dissolved, and named a new provisional government. This time the National Guard, which had sided with the people against the government in February, came to the aid of the assembly, dispersed the mob, and arrested its leaders.

THE JUNE DAYS

The social cleavage between the moderates and the workers now became more marked. The assembly immediately took steps to dissolve the National Workshops. The following month passed in growing tension as the workers, deprived of their most experienced leaders, retreated sullenly to their own districts in the city, while orators in the assembly demanded "order in ideas" as well as order in the streets. On June 22 Marie announced that the government would use force if necessary to disperse the men of the workshops. By morning of the next day the barricades were rising again in the streets, while the government prepared to carry out its threat.

The line of battle was clearly drawn: the bourgeoisie against the proletariat. The assembly named General Louis Cavaignac as military dictator. His favorite military tactic was to let the enemy dig into fortified positions, then blast it out with artillery. The first shot was fired shortly after noon on Friday, June 23. For three full days the streets of Paris flowed with blood and echoed to the sound of cannon and muskets as Frenchmen fought Frenchmen in the first clear-cut full-fledged class warfare in modern history. Unnumbered thousands of workers with their women and children participated in the defense of the barricades. They fought desperately and, for a time, effectively in the narrow, crooked streets and alleys; but the outcome was never in doubt. When quiet descended on the evening of June 26 (except for the sounds of firing squads summarily executing the leaders), fifteen hundred had been killed and thousands more wounded. Of some fifteen thousand prisoners, about two-thirds were imprisoned without trial for terms of one to ten years; thousands more were transported to Algeria.

Paris remained officially in a "state of siege" until October 19, with fifty thousand soldiers patrolling its streets. In this oppressive atmosphere most of the reforms decreed by the Provisional Government were revoked. Censorship of the press was reimposed and all political clubs forbidden. Imprisonment for debt and the death penalty for a variety of offenses were reintroduced. The assembly even scrapped the "right to work" clause, which had already been written into the first draft of the new constitution. Thus ended the first major attempt of the working classes to take the reorganization of society into their own hands.

OTHER REVOLUTIONARY MOVEMENTS

"When France sneezes, Europe catches cold." Metternich, to whom this witticism is attributed, did not take such a light view of the events that followed the February days in Paris, which drove even him into exile and

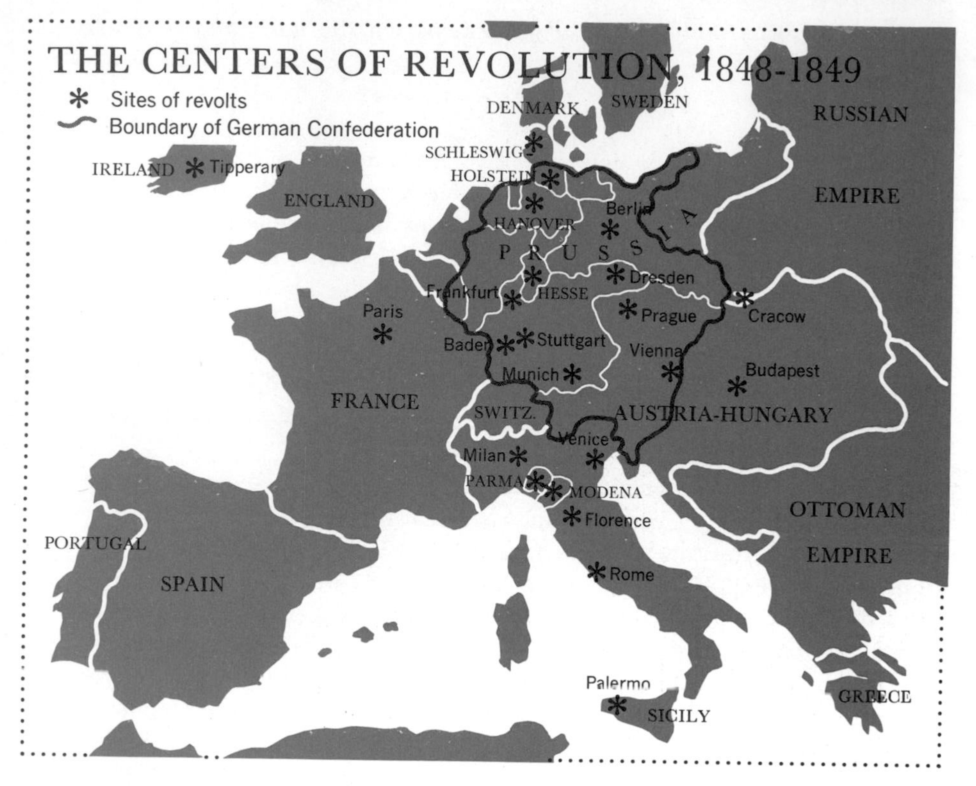

retirement. Revolutionary pressures had been building up in Europe for decades, and the poor harvests and commercial depression of the years immediately preceding 1848 brought them to the bursting point. Minor outbreaks of violence occurred in Switzerland and Italy even before the Paris insurrection. Before the year was over, every nation in Europe except Russia had felt the winds of change if not the full fury of the revolutionary storm.

In Belgium the liberals under Charles Rogier, a leader in the revolution of 1830, offered concessions before a revolution could erupt. A new electoral law doubled the number of eligible voters by lowering property qualifications, thus ensuring the allegiance of the lower middle classes. A public works program and liberalized poor relief sapped the revolutionary inclinations of the workers. Although a few riots and street demonstrations took place in the larger cities in the spring, a new election in June repudiated the radical party and vindicated the government's policy of compromise and reform.

The Netherlands's working class was not as large or important as that of Belgium, but the government was more absolutist. The middle classes pressed the king to accept a constitutional revision that introduced ministerial responsibility and substituted indirect election of members of the upper chamber for appointment by the king. In this way the Dutch avoided the violence that afflicted much of the rest of Europe, and paved the way for further peaceful democratic evolution.

In Denmark, Frederick VII ascended the throne in 1848 and immediately became involved in a war with the German states over the duchies of Schleswig and Holstein. At the conclusion of the war in the summer of 1849 Frederick granted a new constitution that provided for a bicameral legislature, a responsible ministry, and other features of limited monarchy on the British pattern.

Spain and Portugal had exhausted themselves in revolutionary struggles in preceding decades. The impotent middle classes and almost nonexistent industrial working classes offered but a slight base for the type of social revolution that took place elsewhere in western Europe. Attempted risings in Madrid and other cities barely got beyond the riot stage before being squelched by the authorities.

Britain averted class warfare during the revival of Chartist agitation, but in Ireland it faced a nationalist revolt by its Irish subjects. The famine of the "hungry forties" contributed to the growth of radicalism, and the leadership of Irish nationalism passed to the Young Ireland party, founded in 1840 by William S. O'Brien (1803–1864). A series of disturbances in 1847 and 1848 culminated in a full-fledged revolt at Tipperary in July, 1848. O'Brien had hoped for peasant support, but the peasants failed to rise, and the police quickly dispersed the rebels.

Except for the Irish outbreak, the revolutionary movement in western Europe exhibited a clear pattern of developing class consciousness brought about by the growth of modern industry. The propertied middle classes were able to curb the power of the monarchs and the aristocracy in proportion to their strength, while the growing working classes sought to share in the fruits of political reform. Although the possessors of special privileges naturally resisted efforts to dilute or abolish their privileges, the gradual peaceful evolution toward democracy in Britain, the Low Countries, and the Scandinavian nations showed that warfare between different social classes was not inevitable.

In central Europe another factor was added to these same elements of change: the force of nationalism, which was equally powerful and even more explosive. According to the German historian Friedrich Dahlmann, an active participant in the events of 1848, the Germans discovered then that their thirst for freedom was in fact a lust for power. John Stuart Mill commented sadly, "In the backward parts of Europe and even (where better things might have been expected) in Germany, the sentiment of nationality so far outweighs the love of liberty that the people are willing to abet their rulers in crushing the liberty and independence of any people not of their race and language." This powerful ideology, together with the greater economic and social backwardness of central Europe in comparison with the west, explains the greater violence and fewer lasting achievements of the revolutions there, as well as the slower and more difficult evolution of democracy.

THE GERMANIES

Within weeks of the abdication of Louis Philippe in France a series of popular demonstrations and constitutional changes took place throughout southern and western Germany. In Baden, Württemberg, Bavaria, Hesse-Cassel, Nassau, Brunswick, Thuringia, and the free cities of Frankfurt, Bremen, Hamburg, and Lübeck, the rulers bowed to demands for constitutions and responsible ministries where none existed, and liberalized them where they did. Preparations went forward for the convocation of an all-German constituent assembly. For the most part this activity was the work of middle-class liberals – the progressive business leaders and professional men of the thriving commercial centers of western Germany who had grown impatient with the restrictive and stuffy conservatism of existing governments. The nascent industrial working classes participated only slightly, and even then in support of the moderate demands of their employers. Few voices were raised on behalf of complete democracy, and almost none for socialism.

The changes came about peaceably, with few instances of violence. The rulers of the petty German states, along with everyone else, had been taken by surprise by the sudden collapse of the monarchy in France. When they discovered with relief that the reformers in their own bailiwicks would be satisfied with liberal reforms and did not demand republican government, they went along almost gladly.

The keys to the revolutions in central Europe rested in Vienna and Berlin. No one seriously believed that a revolution could succeed so long as Metternich stood firm and Frederick William of Prussia commanded an army. Great was the surprise, therefore, when on March 13, Metternich resigned and fled Austria. Three days later barricades went up in Berlin, mobs besieged the royal palace, and people fought with soldiers in the streets.

Frederick William, an emotional, dreamy, vacillating individual who eventually went insane, lacked all the qualities of greatness that the times required. From the beginning of his reign in 1840 he had made vague promises of reform that never seemed to materialize. As recently as 1847 he had convened a United Diet composed of representatives of the eight provincial diets of the Prussian kingdom, which he peremptorily dissolved when it failed to do his bidding. Now his "beloved Berliners" threatened him with bodily harm if he did not yield to their demands. After much hesitation and wavering the king decided on concessions.

As the crowds gathered on March 18 to hear his proclamation abolish-

Courtesy of Hamburger Kunsthalle

Cortege of the Victims of the March Revolution, 1848,
(detail) by Adolph Menzel

"When the soldiery had marched off something happened that in dramatic force and significance has never been surpassed in the history of revolutions. From all parts of the city solemn and silent processions moved toward the royal palace. They escorted the bodies of those of the people who had been killed in the battle (with the royal troops); the corpses of the slain were carried aloft on litters. . . . So the processions marched into the inner palace court, where the litters were placed in rows in ghastly parade, and around them the multitude of men with pallid faces, begrimed with blood and powder smoke, many of them still carrying the weapons with which they had fought during the night."
Carl Schurz (1829–1906), REMINISCENCES (New York, 1907–08).

---

ing censorship and reconvening the United Diet to prepare a constitution, fighting broke out between the soldiers and the people. For two days the battle raged, until the king, sick at the sight of bloodshed and at the thought of massacring his own people, had the troops withdrawn and exposed himself to the mercies of the mob. His faith was not misplaced. Although he was obliged to salute the corpses of slain rebels and parade through the streets in the newly adopted black, red, and gold tricolor of united Germany, his subjects continued respectful and obedient. A new ministry took office, consisting mostly of middle-class liberals from the Prussian Rhineland, and the new Prussian Diet began to draw up a constitution. All went smoothly for a time. The king's weak behavior and lack of leadership lost him the support of some Germans who had expected him to take the lead in creating a German state, but there appeared no reason to doubt his commitment to reform. Attention shifted to Frankfurt, where delegates were assembled to debate the future of a united Germany.

The German National Assembly (*Nationalversammlung*) met for the first time in St. Paul's Church, Frankfurt, on May 18, 1848. More than two months previously a group of about fifty West German liberals had met in Heidelberg and issued a call for a preliminary parliament, which gathered in Frankfurt on March 31. This *Vorparlment* had no legal standing (only two Austrians attended, while seventy-two came from little Baden), but it took upon itself the task of arranging for the election of delegates to the National Assembly from all the German states. The resulting assembly was nearly six hundred strong. It included men of all ranks, from a Silesian peasant to a sovereign prince, but most came from upper middle-class occupations, and were lawyers, judges, bureaucrats, and professors. To give it a vestige of legality, the frightened Diet of the old Germanic Confederation had approved the elections, and after the Assembly met, the Diet actually dissolved itself.

All delegates agreed that Germany must be united, but the character of the union proved a thorny problem. A republic was out of the question, as well as any form of highly centralized state, because too many vested interests were involved, especially those of the ruling princes. Some sort of federal empire seemed to be indicated, in which the component parts would retain local autonomy. But in that case what states should be included, and who should be emperor? How could Austria, which was already an empire, be included in a larger empire? The *Grossdeutsch* (Great German) party favored including the German-speaking provinces of Austria (together with Bohemia), whereas the *Kleindeutsch* (Little German) group wanted to exclude Austria. While the dispute simmered, the assembly chose to involve itself in a more pressing matter, the war with Denmark.

Although the duchies of Schleswig and Holstein were for the most part German-speaking (in fact, the latter was a member state of the Germanic Confederation), they belonged to the king of Denmark. In the "springtime of nations" that followed the February revolution in Paris the duchies revolted against the new Danish king and declared their sympathy for the German parliament. When the Danish army occupied them, the assembly in Frankfurt commissioned Frederick William to send Prussian troops on its behalf to "liberate" their fellow Germans. Frederick William did so, but in August he succumbed to pressure from Britain and Russia to conclude an armistice and evacuate his troops.

By this time the German people were drunk with nationalism and regarded the armistice as a betrayal. The assembly at first refused to ratify it, but lacking an armed force or executive power, it eventually had to bow to the fait accompli and recognize the armistice. The mob in Frankfurt, harangued by nationalist demagogues, now turned on the delegates to the assembly as traitors and invaded their meeting place. The middle-class parliamentarians, thoroughly frightened by this view of the people, called on Austrian and Prussian soldiers to disperse the mob, which they did with their customary brutality. The results were disastrous for the prestige of the assembly. Alienated from the masses and embarrassed by their dependence on armed force against their own constituents, the delegates were vulnerable to the reaction that soon overtook them and their once-high hopes for a liberal, united Germany.

THE HAPSBURG MONARCHY

In Vienna the news of the revolution in Paris encouraged the opponents of Metternich's regime to press for liberal reforms. The reformers included persons from all social classes: business and professional men who resented economic controls and exclusion from political power, workers, peasants in the countryside, even a few aristocrats who were bored by the stuffiness and restrictions of the government. Students from the university, the sons of aristocracy and the upper middle classes, actually took the initiative in fomenting revolution. They paraded, fraternized with the workers from the factory suburbs, and clashed with soldiers guarding the imperial palace. Faced with the near-certainty of bloody street-fighting and unable to depend upon the loyalty of the troops, the 75-year-old Metternich resigned on March 13. Fully aware of his unpopularity, the champion of autocracy fled the country in disguise under cover of darkness to seek haven in that bastion of constitutionalism, England.

Without Metternich's iron will and wily mind, the government of the feeble-minded Emperor Ferdinand I floundered aimlessly. Within a few days it gave in to demands for the abolition of censorship, promised to convoke a constitutional convention, and permitted the formation of a volunteer National Guard. Flushed with their triumph over the aged chancellor, the students formed an "academic legion" and a "committee of safety" to keep watch on the government and prevent it from backsliding into reaction. In May the government attempted to reassert its authority but backed down when it met determined opposition. The imperial family fled to Innsbruck, leaving the city controlled by the students and middle-class guardsmen.

At the same time national minorities in the polyglot dominions of the emperor were raising the standard of revolt. The Hungarian Diet under the leadership of Louis Kossuth proclaimed a constitution that made Hungary entirely independent of Austria, retaining only the link of a common king-emperor. The Czechs of Bohemia and Moravia convened a Pan-Slavic Congress in Prague and demanded autonomy from Vienna. Lombardy and Venetia revolted, and most of the other subject nationalities — Croats, Slovaks, Serbs, Slovenes, Poles, Ruthenians, and others — demanded either autonomy or extensive reforms. So powerless was the government to resist that it appeared for a time that the ancient Hapsburg monarchy would simply evaporate.

The tide began to turn in June, when imperial armies in Bohemia and Lombardy scored victories over the rebellious subjects. Even more ominous for the national movements were their relations with one another. In spite of common grievances against the ruling German-speaking minority, they could not agree on joint action and mutual support. Although the Magyars of Hungary were insistent on independence for themselves, they tried to magyarize the predominantly Slavic peasant population and turned down requests for autonomy from the Croatians and other minorities within the boundaries of the kingdom of Hungary. The imperial government at last regained some of its customary composure and shrewdly took advantage of these differences by appointing Baron Jellachich, a Croatian, commander-in-chief of the imperial army in Hungary.

The imperial forces gradually regained control of the Austrian provinces of the empire and retook Vienna itself in October, but the battle raged back and forth in Hungary. In April, 1849, the Hungarians formally severed all ties with the old empire, proclaiming a republic with Kossuth as president. For a few months it appeared that they might succeed in winning their independence, but during the summer the Russian tsar, who was untroubled by revolutions of his own, sent his army to the aid of his fellow monarch. Kossuth resigned and fled in August. In the Hapsburg dominions, as in Germany proper, the conflicting objectives of liberalism and nationalism defeated one another.

ITALY

Divided and oppressed, Italy had fallen far from the position of leadership it once held in the arts of civilization and reached its nadir in the first half of the nineteenth century. More than three-fourths of the Italian population eked out a bare subsistence in agriculture. A large, ill-trained, and parasitic clergy, totaling in some areas a tenth of the population, weighed heavily on the country. Poverty, ignorance, and superstition were rife throughout the peninsula, each feeding on the other. Except in Piedmont and the States of the Church, the ruling classes were identified directly or indirectly with a foreign power. As a result, the revolutionary movement in Italy was infected from the beginning with nationalism, and revolutionary outbreaks took on the characteristics of a war of liberation.

In 1846 the college of cardinals elected a liberal pope, Pius IX. For the next two years he dallied with the notion of uniting all Italy under the protective shield of the Holy See. Fearful of the secular and radical nature of Giuseppe Mazzini's "Young Italy" movement (see pp. 151–152), he had naive dreams of restoring the papacy to a primacy in Italy that it had never really had. His hope of influencing Catholic Austria to agree to his ambitions proved futile, for Metternich's opposition to liberalism and nationalism was absolute. Pius built up a modest following of liberals in Italy and persuaded some conservative elements to be receptive to change — though hardly to the changes that caught even Pius by surprise in 1848.

Sicily, long treated as a conquered province by the Bourbon Kingdom of the Two Sicilies with its capital in Naples, rose in revolt in January, 1848. The insurrection soon spread to Naples, where liberals forced the king to grant a constitution. In little more than a month the rulers of Tuscany and Piedmont and Pius himself had given in to similar pressures. In the midst of these developments news of the revolutions in Paris and Vienna reached Italy, bringing new hope and courage to the Italians, who expected assistance from revolutionary France against a weakened Austria.

The inhabitants of Milan revolted on March 18 and in five days of house-to-house combat drove out the Austrian army of General Radetzky. Stimulated by this event, the Venetians under Daniele Manin proclaimed a republic on March 22. On the same day King Charles Albert of Piedmont, under pressure from the liberals and patriots who had earlier compelled him to grant a constitution, declared war against the Austrians in support of the Milanese. In a matter of weeks contingents of soldiers and volunteers from all Italy, including the States of the Church, joined in the attack. Patriotic excitement reached a fever pitch, and for a few days it seemed that Italy would soon be free of foreign domination from the Alps to Sicily.

These bright hopes were doomed to quick extinction. Pius IX, who had earlier given his blessing to the papal volunteers, now disclaimed any intention of making war on Catholic Austria, cutting the ground from beneath those patriots who had looked to him to head an Italian confederation. In May a successful counterrevolution in Naples resulted in the withdrawal of Neapolitan troops. Finally, the Piedmontese failed to follow up their early successes in the field. The Austrian government had ordered Radetzky to seek an armistice and to cede Lombardy to Piedmont if necessary, but Radetzky ignored these orders, launched a counteroffensive, and on July 24 delivered a crushing defeat to Charles Albert at Custozza. Within ten days the Austrians again controlled all of Lombardy and were restrained from an invasion of Piedmont only by warnings from Britain and France.

Defeated and disappointed though they were, Italian patriots did not give up the struggle. The Venetians held out against an Austrian siege, and both Piedmont and Tuscany retained their constitutions and their hopes. In Rome the liberals grew critical of Pius IX for his failure to lead a united Italy, whereupon he became bitter and resentful. After the assassination of his prime minister by a radical democrat, Pius fled in November to the protection of the reactionary king of Naples. The people of the States of the Church reacted by electing a constituent assembly, which on February 9, 1849, proclaimed the Roman Republic and called Mazzini to be its leader. Giuseppe Garibaldi (1807–1882), a colorful patriot and soldier of fortune, now put his legion of volunteers (called Redshirts from the only vestige of uniform they wore) at the service of the Roman Republic. In March Charles Albert once more succumbed to liberal pressures and broke the armistice with Austria; once more the patriots took heart and dreamed of a free, united Italy. Yet in less than two weeks Radetzky delivered another and final humiliating defeat to Charles Albert, who abdicated his throne, went into exile, and shortly died.

THE FAILURE OF '48

The revolutionary wave that broke over Europe in 1848 had been building for many years. After its first major crest in the 1790's it had receded slightly, only to come back with renewed force. By the logic of the situation – a logic perceived by such disparate personalities as Karl Marx and Metternich – it should have overwhelmed all opposition in 1848. But it did not. Why? The answer can be given only tentatively, even after the lapse of more than a century. It would seem to be related to the disparate progress of modern industry, on the one hand, and to the idea of nationalism, on the other. The revolutions of 1848 were at once class struggles, provoked by the rise of industry, and nationalist wars of liberation. The forces of conservatism took advantage of the divided ambitions of their opponents to crush the movements utterly. The high tide of revolution came in the late spring of 1848; thereafter the revolutionists fought defensive, losing battles. After 1848 the worst was still to come. Liberalism and socialism went into eclipse, and although nationalism survived and flourished, it was a nationalism far different from the noble, generous movement of pre-1848. In the reaction of realism – the ebb tide of revolution – all tender ideals had to adjust to the new world of science and power, or perish.

THE REALIST REACTION
CHAPTER FIVE

Europe awoke on the morrow of revolution as a man awakes after an evening of debauchery. Europe was sadder, wiser, less glamorous, less idealistic. A new outlook dominated the scene that, for brevity, may be referred to as realism, though conventional definitions cannot fully convey the realist cast of mind. The word was first employed in 1850 to describe a new style of painting, and it spread rapidly to literature. Soon it became evident that the literary tendencies to which the name referred had earlier roots, and that these, in turn, owed much to the progress of science in the first half of the nineteenth century.

As scientific progress accelerated and as the findings of science became more widely disseminated, the realist point of view permeated every area of life, including politics, where it frequently took the base form of *Realpolitik*. (See p. 144.) In literature and the arts realism was a reaction to the fantasies of the late romantic movement; in philosophy and social thought, to the idealism of Kant and Hegel; in science, to unverifiable speculation; and in politics, to the idealism and romanticism of the revolutionary epoch. Realism pervaded the whole of Western culture from the failure of the revolutions of 1848 to the new outbursts of nationalistic and imperialistic fervor in the 1880's. The manner in which the revolutions were liquidated did much to set the tone of the period.

EBB TIDE OF REVOLUTION, 1848–1851

By the late summer of 1849 the revolutionary movement had been suppressed throughout Europe. Its last vestiges were the ephemeral republics of Venice and Hungary. A period of stark reaction set in everywhere. Apart from the moderate parliamentary and electoral reforms in the smaller states of western Europe and the paper constitutions of Prussia and Austria, the only permanent political achievement of the revolutionary outbursts seemed to be the Second Republic in France. Even there the appearance was deceptive, for the political and social character of the republic was markedly conservative, and the republic itself was destined for a short life.

THE REACTION IN FRANCE

The Provisional Government of February, 1848, had been replaced in May by the executive commission of the Constituent Assembly, which in turn gave way during the June Days to the military dictatorship of General Cavaignac. Under his protection the assembly continued its work of drawing up a new constitution. As approved on November 4, 1848, the document provided for a single-chamber Legislative Assembly and a president to wield executive power. Both the assembly and the president were to be elected by universal male suffrage, the former for three years, the latter for four.

In the presidential election announced for December 10, 1848, five candidates presented themselves. Cavaignac, touted as the "savior of the republic," had the support of the more conservative republicans. The moderate and radical republicans split over three candidates. The fifth contender was a political dark horse with a name known to all, Louis Napoleon Bonaparte.

Louis Napoleon was ostensibly the nephew of the first Napoleon, although his legitimacy was doubtful and there was no positive proof of his paternity. After 1815 he fell under the proscription imposed on all members of the Bonaparte family. Raised by his mother in exile, he set foot in France only twice between 1815 and 1848, both times as a conspirator and outlaw. In 1836 he tried to foment a rebellion in the garrison at Strasbourg but was ignominiously captured and returned to exile. In 1840 he landed at Boulogne with a small band of followers, again was captured, and was imprisoned in the fortress of Ham from which he had escaped as recently as 1846.

Louis Napoleon was an enigmatic mixture of visionary dreamer, romantic adventurer, benevolent despot, and shrewd practical politician. His great rival of later years, Chancellor Bismarck of Prussia, referred to him contemptuously as "a sphinx without a riddle" and "a great unrecognized incapacity," but opinions of later historians remain divided on his motives, his ability, and even his achievements and failures. Nevertheless, in addition to the prestige of his name, it was precisely because he seemed to be all things to all men that he scored his notable electoral triumphs. In the presidential election of 1848 he obtained more than three-fourths of the total vote.

The Second Republic resembled an unwanted child, rejected by its parents almost as soon as it was born. The new president indicated the strength of his republican sentiments by appointing a cabinet composed chiefly of supporters of the ousted regime of Louis Philippe. Elections for the new assembly in the spring of 1849 resulted in a clear majority for the monarchists – legitimists as well as Orleanists. The radical republicans made a slight comeback, but the moderate republicans who had framed the constitution were almost completely eliminated. The spectacle of a republic with a Bonaparte executive and a monarchist legislature was strange indeed. Moreover, the constitution contained a serious defect in that it did not provide a method for settling disputes between the legislature and the executive.

For a time Louis Napoleon cooperated with the conservative and monarchist majority while he consolidated the bases of his own personal power. In order to win favor with Catholics, he dispatched French troops in the spring of 1849 to suppress the Roman Republic and restore the pope. The following year he acquiesced in the Falloux Law on education, which gave the clergy a large measure of control over the educational system. The propertied middle classes in France had a tradition of Voltairean skepticism, but the rise of socialism and the threat of social revolution led them to view the Church as a bulwark of the status quo and a defender of property rights. In this respect the revolutions of 1848 brought about a religious revival among the middle classes in much the same way that the revolution of 1789 did among the aristocracy. Louis Napoleon also signed assembly sponsored bills that deprived the majority of the urban working class, the stronghold of radicalism, of its right to vote, imposed greater censorship of the press, and in other ways restricted political freedom.

At the same time Louis Napoleon built up his own Bonapartist party. As early as October, 1849, he replaced his Orleanist ministry, much of which was drawn from the assembly, with a cabinet of personal admirers from outside the assembly. Increasingly he came into conflict with the monarchist majority in the assembly. The crux of the dispute was the provision of the constitution prohibiting the president from succeeding himself. When his proposal to amend the clause was defeated by more than one hundred votes in July, 1851, Louis Napoleon resolved on other means to obtain his object.

The president made a series of speaking tours of the provinces, gauging the temper of the populace and posing as the champion of the people against the assembly. He also reorganized the higher echelons of the army and the civil administration, replacing officers and officials suspected of either monarchist or republican leanings with those loyal to himself. In great secrecy he and a small group of his closest collaborators, including the count de Morny, his illegitimate half-brother, laid plans for a coup d'état. Early in the morning of December 2, following a magnificent presidential ball on the previous evening, soldiers placarded Paris with the news that the president had dissolved the assembly. Other soldiers arrested a number of deputies, prominent journalists, and other potential opposition leaders in their beds and occupied the meeting hall of the assembly. Thus far the coup had gone without violence or bloodshed. On the following day, however, a group of republican deputies organized a rising in the working-class quarters of Paris. Barricades went up in the streets in the usual manner, but the army moved against them promptly and crushed the rebellion with much bloodshed and thousands of arrests.

The same proclamation that announced the dissolution of the assembly also proclaimed the restoration of universal suffrage and called upon the people to ratify the president's actions and give him authority to draft a new constitution. A plebiscite on December 21 resulted in a majority of 92 per cent in favor of the regime. Although it was a managed election with no alternative provided in the event of a negative vote, it appears that most Frenchmen, weary of both street fighting and parliamentary wrangling, preferred the security of a benevolent dictatorship to the strife and uncertainties of self-government. Thus ended the last act of a drama that had begun with the overthrow of Louis Philippe in February, 1848.

THE REACTION IN THE HAPSBURG DOMINIONS

The reaction began early in the Austrian Empire. In June, 1848, the wife of the military commander in Prague, Prince Windischgrätz, was accidentally killed in the course of a popular demonstration in support of the revolution. For five days Windischgrätz mercilessly bombarded the city with artillery from surrounding fortifications. At the end of that time no sign of resistance remained, and Windischgrätz made himself military dictator of all Bohemia. Simultaneously General Radetzky took the offensive against the Piedmontese in northern Italy and won an overwhelming victory on July 24 at Custozza. To reestablish his control and authority in Lombardy and to revenge himself for Milan's "five glorious days" in March, he subjected Milan to the same treatment as Prague.

Next came the turn of Vienna. In October Windischgrätz and Jellachich, the military commander in Hungary, surrounded the city and subjected it to the same methodical, ruthless bombardment. After the city fell they summarily executed scores of radical leaders. When Windischgrätz marched on Budapest in January, 1849, the city took note of the fate of the others and surrendered without resistance. The proclamation of the Hungarian Republic in the spring of 1849 temporarily gave the revolutionaries new hope, and they drove the Austrians out of all Hungary. Soon afterward, however, Austria accepted the proffered aid of the tsar, and Russian troops in the summer of 1849 joined with those of General Haynau, "the Hyena," to overrun and subjugate the Hungarians. In spite of earlier promises of clemency, General Haynau brutally executed the Hungarian leaders.

Prince Felix Schwarzenberg, brother-in-law of Windischgrätz and political adviser to Radetsky, became Austrian prime minister after the fall of Vienna. In December, 1848, he persuaded both the weak-minded Emperor Ferdinand and his brother, the Archduke Franz Karl, to abdicate in favor of the latter's eighteen-year-old son, Franz Josef. The new monarch followed the counsel of Schwarzenberg and soon proved himself the prince's equal in determination to tolerate no liberal tendencies. In March, 1849, Schwarzenberg dissolved the newly elected Reichstag, discarded its draft constitution providing for a decentralized, federal form of government, and promulgated one of his own that provided for a highly centralized administration. The provisions for a representative diet and a responsible ministry never took effect; in 1851 the constitution itself was "suspended" – permanently.

Schwarzenberg died in 1852, but his policies were carried on by his minister of interior, Alexander Bach. The administrative system of Austria for the decade between the revolution and the War of 1859 became known as the Bach System. In addition to extreme centralization and bureaucratic rule, the system was characterized by a vigorous policy of germanization and the strict repression of all liberal symptoms.

THE REACTION IN ITALY

The reactionary denouement in Italy followed swiftly Radetzky's defeat of Charles Albert in March, 1849. The Austrians mopped up in northern Italy and restored the grand duke of Tuscany, while in the south Neapolitan troops reconquered Sicily. Most disheartening of all, Louis Napoleon Bonaparte, recently elected president of the French Republic, sent a French expeditionary force to put down the Roman Republic and restore Pius IX by force of arms. Garibaldi and the Romans put up an heroic defense, holding out for more than two months, but on July 2 Garibaldi withdrew from the city and led his partisans on an equally heroic but disastrous retreat. On August 28, 1849, when the Venetians, besieged by the Austrians without and by starvation and cholera within, finally capitulated, the last spark of revolutionary nationalism in Italy seemed to expire. Thus ended Italy's attempt to "make itself."

THE REACTION IN GERMANY

In Prussia, King Frederick William, encouraged by the success of the Austrian government in retaking Vienna, dissolved the Prussian Constituent Assembly in December, 1848, and promulgated a constitution on his own authority. The constitution provided for a bicameral legislature, the Diet, with the upper house (*Herrenhaus*) reserved for the privileged orders. The lower house, nominally elected by universal manhood suffrage, actually gave a preponderance of influence to the wealthy by means

Brown Brothers

Giuseppe Garibaldi

"When the people see him they take fire. There is a magic in his look and in his name. It is only Garibaldi they want. . . . Sometimes he seems more than a living being or is he an archangel who spreads his wings and whirls his sword like a sunray?" Entries of May 14 and Aug. 20, 1860, in Giuseppe Cesare Abba, THE DIARY OF ONE OF GARIBALDI'S THOUSAND, tr. E. R. Vincent (London, 1962).

of a complicated system of indirect election based on taxpaying ability. The ministers of the government did not form a cabinet responsible to the Diet but were individually responsible to and directly dependent upon the king. When the Diet was not in session, the king could rule by decree. In spite of some superficial concessions to parliamentarianism, the Prussian state retained its authoritarian and aristocratic character.

With its authority reestablished, the Prussian government undertook a frankly reactionary policy. It repealed earlier liberal legislation, such as that curtailing the privileged position of the nobility, and enacted new and repressive measures directed against freedom of the press, freedom of assembly, and other liberties that peoples with constitutional governments had come to regard as rights. The nobility and the Junker aristocracy of great landowners monopolized the posts of power and prestige in the court, the government, and the army. Not only the radicals but even those who regarded themselves as liberals were hounded out of the government and, in some cases, out of the country. Many chose exile and new careers in the United States.

The triumph of reaction in Austria and Prussia ensured the success of similar movements in other German states, which in some cases called on the larger states for military support in suppressing their still rebellious subjects. The last hope of German liberals rested on the Frankfurt Assembly, but this hope, too, faded. Having been deflected from their original purpose of providing a parliamentary constitution for a unified Germany by the Danish question, then bogged down in the dispute between the *Grossdeutsch* and *Kleindeutsch* parties, the delegates finally agreed on a compromise document in March, 1849. Since the Austrians ruled themselves out of any participation in the proposed federation, the delegates invited Frederick William of Prussia to accept the title "Emperor of the Germans," provided for in the constitution. Frederick William had wavered back and forth on the question of a united Germany, as he had on many other questions. Now he half-assented to the proposal from Frankfurt but insisted that the rulers of the other German states must also agree to have him as their sovereign. Three weeks passed, and a number of the smaller states accepted the new constitution, but at the same time the king's conservative advisers were urging him to resist the temptation of "a crown from the streets" as inconsistent with his "divine right" as king of Prussia. On April 21, he announced that under no circumstances would he accept the crown from an elected assembly.

This announcement shattered the last illusions of the Frankfurt Assembly. Prussia and Austria ordered their delegates to return home, and the delegates from other states soon followed. Only a small band of the most radical deputies remained. When driven from their meeting place by Austrian troops, they tried to continue their sessions in Stuttgart, but again the soldiers dispersed them, imprisoning some and driving others into exile. Thus ended, ingloriously, the convention that had been hailed as "the most distinguished constituent body in history." The liberal parliamentarians in Frankfurt had demonstrated great oratorical ability but little governing ability. Distracted from the pursuit of liberty by the pursuit of power and national glory, they lost all. With their failure Germany lost its opportunity for peaceful unification under a liberal constitution.

REALISM IN LITERATURE AND THE ARTS

The new temper of Europe received its most forceful literary and artistic expression in novels and paintings, but the reaction in the intellectual and artistic spheres was neither as abrupt nor as complete as the political reaction. Although the vogue of realism reached its peak in the 1850's, earlier work had clearly foreshadowed the movement and formed a bridge between the romantic and the realist eras. It is even more important to realize that realist art and literature did not completely dominate the period. In Britain and the United States, art and literature were blander, less critical, and more at peace with the world, except for a few self-conscious social critics. Finally, as a result of increasing wealth, population, and literacy, more and more people from the middle classes became interested in art and literature. Since the newly successful businessmen and their wives were not necessarily sophisticated judges, not all of the vast increase in literary and artistic production was of high quality. Most of it continued to exploit the proven demand for subjects and styles of the romantic.

THE REALIST NOVEL

Realist novels can be distinguished from their romantic predecessors by both subject matter and method of treatment. The typical romantic novel dealt with heroic figures in exotic settings, while the typical realist novel dealt with ordinary people in ordinary pursuits. Instead of employing exaggerated language and emotions, realist novelists devoted themselves to close observation and precise description. Usually they sought to convey an impression of matter-of-fact detachment and absence of sentimentality. They often dealt with social and psychological problems, but in doing so the best of them let the episodes and characters speak for themselves, rather than pontificating on the obvious.

Stendhal (pseudonym of Henri Beyle, 1783–1842), earliest precursor of the new tendency, chose conventional romantic themes for his novels *Le rouge et le noir* (1830) and *La chartreuse de Parme* (1839), but the deft irony with which he treated them set him apart from other romantic writers. Honoré de Balzac (1799–1850) was perhaps the greatest of the romantic realists. His style was still in the romantic tradition of unruly exaggeration, but his subjects were ordinary people and his intention was to portray them clearly as such. The long series entitled *La comédie humaine* (*The Human Comedy*) is an almost documentary account of life in France under the July Monarchy. The style of the English writer Charles Dickens (1812–1870) was similar in many respects to Balzac's. Victor Hugo (1802–1885) – novelist, dramatist, essayist, poet – spanned the romantic and realist eras in the same way that Goethe bridged the romantic era and the Enlightenment. Hugo's *Notre Dame de Paris* (1831) is one of the masterpieces of romantic literature, but in *Les misérables* (1862) and *Les travailleurs de la mer* (1866) he dealt with contemporary social problems in a realistic fashion with only minor lapses into pathos and overt sentimentality.

William Thackeray (1811–1863) wrote what might be called a manifesto of the realist novelist in *Vanity Fair* (1848). It carried the subtitle *A Novel without a Hero,* a contradiction in terms to the romantics. According to Thackeray, a novel should "convey as strongly as possible the sentiment of reality as opposed to a tragedy or poem, which may be heroical." Gustave Flaubert (1821–1880) brought the realist novel to its pinnacle of perfection. His most famous work, *Madame Bovary* (1857), is a candid, penetrating study of the narrow, barren, and sordid life in the provinces. In *L'éducation sentimentale* (1869), the title of which might have belonged to a romantic novel, he portrayed his own youth with graphic, restrained irony in a study in disenchantment. Flaubert's meticulous craftsmanship influenced many younger writers, even those who adopted different literary styles.

Romanticism had a longer vogue in Germany and the United States than in France and England. Not until the last quarter of the century did American writers take up realist themes and styles, as in the novels of Samuel Clemens (Mark Twain), William Dean Howells, and Stephen Crane. Gottfried Keller's *Der grüne Heinrich* (1854–1855, revised 1879) is a landmark in Swiss literature, but it is little known outside German-speaking countries. Russian authors made some of their greatest contributions in this period. Ivan Turgenev (1818–1883), author of *Fathers and Sons* (1862), and Feodor Dostoevski (1821–1881), author of *Crime and Punishment* (1866) and *The Brothers Karamazov* (1880), were masters of the psychological novel, gripping stories of inner conflict with great emotional impact. Leo Tolstoi's *War and Peace* (1865–1869), an epic of the Napoleonic wars, is regarded by some critics as the greatest novel of the nineteenth century, by others as the greatest novel of all time. Although all three authors clearly belonged to the category of realist novelists, they brought new insights and inspiration from their Russian environment.

It should be noted that the realist novelists in no sense formed a school with definite rules or objectives. Nor was realism in literature restricted, even approximately, to the third quarter of the nineteenth century. On

Courtesy of The Metropolitan Museum of Art
Bequest of Mrs. H. O. Havemeyer, 1929. The H. O. Havemeyer Collection

the contrary, realism is a more or less permanent component of literature, now waxing, now waning, but always present in some degree. What the major writers of this period had in common was a tendency to react against the earlier artistic excesses of romanticism. Their reaction was strongly influenced by the political watershed of 1848 and by the growing prestige of science. The influence of science was particularly marked in the major development within realism called naturalism.

Émile Zola (1840–1902), the founder and leading exponent of naturalism, lived until the twentieth century, but his enormous output clearly reflected the formative influences of his youth during the Second French Empire. The most important influences were the literary canons of Flaubert, the reformist zeal of Victor Hugo, and most important, materialistic science. Zola regarded himself as a kind of scientist-artist. Not content merely to describe life as he saw it, like the earlier realists, Zola insisted on dissecting and analyzing it as a biologist would analyze a living organism. He called his twenty-volume series on the Rougon-Macquart family "the natural and social history of a family under the Second Empire." Zola even wrote a treatise on the "experimental novel" in the manner of Claude Bernard's famous treatise on experimental medicine. In it he said: "The experimental novel is a consequence of the scientific evolution of the century; it continues and completes physiology, which itself leans for support on chemistry and medicine; it substitutes for the study of the abstract and metaphysical man the study of natural man, governed by physical and chemical laws, and modified by the influences of his surroundings; it is in one word the literature of our age, as the classical and romantic literature correspond to a scholastic and theological age." Zola's views represented the extreme development of the realist reaction in literature. By no means did all of his contemporaries agree with him; even as he penned his manifesto, *Le roman expéri-*

"The Young Bather," by Gustave Courbet

"In particular, the art of painting can consist only in the representation of objects visible and tangible to the painter. . . . I hold also that painting is an essentially concrete *art, and can consist only of the representation of things both* real *and* existing. *It is an altogether physical language, which, for its words, makes use of all visible objects. An* abstract *object, invisible or nonexistent, does not belong to the domain of painting.*

"Imagination in art consists in finding the most complete expression for an existing thing, but never in imagining or creating this object itself." Open letter from Courbet to a group of prospective students, Paris, 1861, reprinted in R. J. Goldwater and M. Treves, ARTISTS ON ART (New York, 1947).

mental (1880), the pendulum began to swing back in the opposite direction.

REALIST PAINTING

Just as novelists were influenced by science, mid-nineteenth-century painters were influenced by one of science's technical offshoots, the infant art of photography. Although in later years painters regarded the improved camera as an unfair competitor and moved on to different styles, in the 1850's and 1860's they strove to emulate the camera in capturing reality. Realist art, like realist literature, differed from its predecessors in both technique and choice of subjects. Realist paintings contained neither the exaggerated and exotic figures of the romantics nor the stylized and lifeless creatures of the classical school. Instead, painters took scenes from everyday life – peasants, workers, merchants and prostitutes, the ugly as well as the beautiful (with perhaps a slight bias in favor of the former) – and painted them as they saw them. Gustave Courbet (1819–1877), the outstanding artist of the realist school, wrote of one of his earliest and most famous paintings, "The Stonebreakers," "I have invented nothing. I saw the wretched people in this picture every day as I went on my walks."

The word realism was first applied to painting to describe one of Courbet's paintings in 1850. Courbet, an egotistical man, wore the label proudly. His personal stationery carried the heading, "Gustave Courbet, Master Painter, without ideals and without religion." He frequently boasted that he had no use for women (other than his models) except as vehicles for carnal satisfaction, and many of his paintings reflect that attitude. However deplorable his personal morals, his influence on art was great. The critic Sainte-Beuve wrote of Courbet that he looked on "vast railway stations as new churches for painting, to cover the big walls with a thousand subjects . . . picturesque, moral, industrial . . . in other words the saints and miracles of modern society."

In realist art, as in literature, France held unquestioned pre-eminence. Honoré Daumier (1808–1879) was even more famous for his social and political caricatures than for his vivid paintings of ordinary life. The lithographs of Paul Gaverni (1804–1866) captured the grit as well as the glitter of Parisian life. Jean-François Millet (1814–1875) devoted himself to scenes from rural life, though with perhaps a touch of sentimentality that was not characteristic of most realist painters. Théodore Rousseau (1812–1867) and his disciples in the Barbizon School contributed robust landscapes. At the same time, Adolf Menzel (1813–1900) of Germany deserves credit for being the first serious painter to take as a subject the interior of a factory.

Realist painting of the French school had little direct impact on British art. In England a group of painters known as the Pre-Raphaelites formed a "brotherhood" in 1848. They usually chose historical subjects and had close affinities with the romantics, but in one respect at least they resembled the realists. They strove to avoid all "exaggerated action . . . false sentiment, voluptuousness, poverty of invention." For inspiration they looked to the "purity" and "simplicity" of the Italian painters prior to Raphael, from whom they chose their name.

POETRY, DRAMA, AND MUSIC

The lyric and dramatic arts suffered in the era of realism. Railroads, factories, and scientific laboratories did not lend themselves as themes for dramatic or lyric treatment. In "The Song of the Shirt" Thomas Hood tried to make poetry an instrument of social criticism and reform, but he succeeded only in creating bathos. Romanticism continued supreme in all these art forms. Although some outstanding figures emerged, such as Brahms, Liszt, Tchaikovsky, and Wagner in music, for the most part the quality was not high. Tennyson and Browning in England and Longfellow in the United States achieved great popularity, but their work has not stood the test of time as well as that of some of their less well-known contemporaries.

Like realism in the novel and painting, the most significant development in poetry was a reaction to romanticism. It was also a reaction against the bourgeois philistinism that made Tennyson and his followers rich and famous. Théophile Gautier (1811–1872) first announced the doctrine of "Art for Art's Sake" in 1835, but the movement did not reach its peak until the later 1860's. It was called the Parnassian movement from *Le Parnasse contemporain,* the journal of poetry that served as its organ. Its outstanding representatives were Charles Baudelaire (1821–1867), whose *Fleurs du mal* (*Flowers of Evil*), published in 1857, caused a sensation and Baudelaire's conviction on a charge of "corrupting public morals"; Arthur Rimbaud (1854–1891), who gave up poetry in 1873 at the age of nineteen; and Paul Verlaine (1844–1896). The scandalous private lives of the poets, especially Rimbaud and Verlaine, brought the movement into disrepute with the general public. The Parnassians shared with the realists, especially Flaubert, a concern for technical perfection and the precisely correct word, phrase, or intonation. In other respects, such as their colorful evocation of exotic or pagan themes, they were far removed from the main course of life and literature. As precursors of the symbolist movement of the end of the century (see pp. 284–285), they exerted a greater influence on subsequent generations than on their own.

ARCHITECTURE AND SCULPTURE

The realist reaction made no imprint on architecture itself. The few structures that showed new designs and utilized new materials – the

London Crystal Palace of 1851, iron railroad bridges, the first skyscrapers in Chicago and New York, and the Eiffel Tower of 1887 – all were created by civil engineers, not architects. For architecture the nineteenth century, especially its middle decades, was an era of eclecticism. Churches, schools, universities, and even hospitals were made to look like medieval cathedrals or monasteries. Public buildings, banks, and railroad stations adopted the classical, baroque, or renaissance styles. Domestic architecture might have had any or all styles, or no style at all.

It is difficult to account for this "poverty of invention" in architecture unless one considers the tastes – or lack thereof – of the consuming public. Architects, unlike writers and artists, must work to the order of their customers. The successful businessmen on city councils, the boards of directors of banks and railroads, the trustees of schools, colleges, and charitable institutions, had neither the training nor the time to appreciate subtle distinctions of style, much less to assess the significance of possible new developments. If they could distinguish between a classical and a Gothic façade, they had reason for self-congratulation. As a result, they relied on the judgment of such self-appointed arbiters of public taste as John Ruskin, whose popular books of literary and artistic criticism pandered to the lowest common denominator of public taste. "Ornamentation is the principal part of architecture," wrote Ruskin; and Sir George Gilbert Scott (1811–1878), one of the most sought-after Victorian architects, agreed that "the great principle" of architecture is "to decorate construction." Architects became "designers of façades," adding more and more corners, cupolas, gewgaws, and bric-a-brac with no functional significance.

Sculpture suffered a similar fate. The rapid growth of cities and the new wealth that they created brought an unprecedented demand for decorative and monumental statuary. Unfortunately the canons of taste responsible for its selection were no better than those in architecture. Not one sculptor of the period has left his name among those of the great.

THE PROGRESS OF SCIENCE

Modern science influences our lives in a multitude of ways; indeed, its influence is almost omnipresent. Since the eighteenth century there has been an increasing interaction between science and technology, affecting industrial progress and economic organization as well as working conditions and living standards. No less important has been the intellectual influence of science, altering man's conception of himself and his place in the universe. So pervasive has been its influence in modern times that the principal intellectual characteristics of an entire era are sometimes denoted by reference to a single science or scientific genius. In the eighteenth century the Enlightenment or Age of Reason was also called the Age of Newton. Under the intellectual supremacy of physics, physical and mechanical analogies such as natural law, natural rights, separation of powers, checks and balances, and so on, were applied in political and social philosophy, art, literature, and even music.

At the beginning of the nineteenth century the intellectual atmosphere was essentially antiscientific. The anti-intellectualism of the romantic movement and the political and religious reactions did not accord scientists the same high esteem which they had held prior to the French Revolution, and which they were to enjoy again later in the century. Nevertheless, scientific work continued and produced a number of important discoveries. The most momentous advance took place in the science of biology. The theory of organic evolution advanced by Charles Darwin (1809–1882) and several others had no significant applications, such as the new sciences of electricity, organic chemistry, or bacteriology; but in its general intellectual influence it ranked without a doubt as the major scientific theory of the nineteenth century. Evolutionary ideas were in the air even before the publication in 1859 of Darwin's *On the Origin of Species;* afterwards evolutionary thinking permeated every aspect of intellectual life, notably social and political theory and philosophy.

THE METHODS AND INSTRUMENTS OF SCIENCE

Scientific method is sometimes regarded by admiring but innocent laymen as a rigorous, prescribed set of rules governing all research and discovery in the natural sciences, certain to produce the desired results. In fact, very little is known about what goes on in the minds of creative scientists; scientists themselves are frequently unable to give coherent explanations of the manner in which they obtain new theoretical ideas. Nevertheless, certain generally accepted procedures have been followed by most scientists since the time of Bacon, if not that of Aristotle. These procedures include observation, experimentation, and reasoning or logical (including mathematical) analysis, although they do not necessarily occur in that order. Intuition also plays an important role but by its very nature defies any attempt to formulate rules for it.

Within this general framework there is much room for individual variation. Darwin and Louis Pasteur (1822–1895) are examples. Contemporaries of one another and both biologists, they held first rank as scientists by virtue of their contributions; yet their contributions as well as their methods belonged to quite different orders. Pasteur conformed to the popular notion of the scientist as a man who works in a laboratory with test tubes and similar paraphernalia. He made one great theoretical contribution to biology, the germ theory of disease, but he also devised a host of practical applications of this theory, including specific cures for diseases affecting the wine-growing and silkworm industries, an inoculation against hydrophobia or rabies, and the process of sterilization through pasteurization. By contrast, Darwin rarely entered a laboratory. He arrived at his single daring and shocking hypothesis before he was thirty years old, and then spent more than twenty years patiently gathering and marshaling the evidence before he published it.

Most scientists did their work in a laboratory or its equivalent. At the beginning of the nineteenth century the laboratory method and experimental technique were already established as a result of the great prestige of Lavoisier and his followers. Laboratories, however, like professional scientists, were still quite rare. The majority of scientists, especially in Britain, were men of independent means. On the Continent conditions were somewhat better. The great scientific institutions of the French Revolution, the École Polytechnique and the École Normale Supérieure, which combined instruction with research at a very high level, were widely imitated in other countries, especially Germany. The science faculties of the moribund German universities were reorganized in the first half of the century on the lines of the École Polytechnique. In the United States, pure science, as opposed to ingenious tinkering, had few devotees until after the Civil War, when American universities were reorganized on the German pattern, which by that time had become supreme.

In the course of their work scientists found it necessary to devise many new instruments of research. At the beginning of the century laboratory equipment was simple, not to say primitive. It consisted principally of weights and balances, rules and calipers, and a few miscellaneous caldrons and similar containers. During the next fifty years or so scientists added new devices for heating, lighting, and measuring and invented several major instruments of research. The achromatic microscope (*c.* 1830) proved a boon to all branches of biology and medical science and was especially influential in the development of cell theory. The spectroscope, perfected in the 1850's, not only facilitated the detection and identification of elements on earth but also helped to ascertain the composition of the stars and measure their temperatures and motion. The first of the giant modern reflecting telescopes, with a 72-inch metallic mirror, was erected in Ireland in 1845. Before his death in 1867 Michael Faraday had begun to conduct experiments with vacuum tubes, the essential instrument of atomic and radiation physics in the twentieth century.

The use of mathematics and the development of new mathematical methods and theorems became increasingly important for almost all branches of science. Because of Newton, mathematical analysis was already well established in mechanics and optics, and Lavoisier had made limited use of it in chemistry. The development of the laws of probability by Laplace, Gauss, and others at the beginning of the century laid the foundations of mathematical statistics, which were of fundamental importance for research on the kinetic theory of gases and for Mendel's work on genetics and heredity in the 1860's. Mathematics helped to break down the barriers between the various branches of science. At the beginning of the century physics, chemistry, botany, zoology, and so forth were all regarded as independent pursuits. Successive discoveries more and more affirmed the essential unity of nature and hence of science.

FUNDAMENTAL PRINCIPLES AND BASIC SYNTHESES

The belief that atoms are the smallest particles of matter, "the building blocks of nature," may be found among the ancient Greeks and Romans, but atomic theory received its first systematic modern statement from the Englishman John Dalton in 1808. By 1830 the list of common elements was near completion. The Swedish chemist Jöns Berzelius then introduced the notational system of modern chemistry, compiled a table of atomic weights, and derived the formulas of many simple compounds. In the 1860's the Russian Dmitri Mendeleev classified all the elements then known according to their atomic weights and other characteristics, deduced that their properties were functions of their weights, and predicted the existence of other elements that were then unknown. The periodic law that he formulated was verified with striking success within his lifetime: three of the unknown elements were discovered, had the properties he predicted, and fitted into the appropriate gaps in his periodic table. Since then many other elements have been discovered — and some created — all in accordance with the periodic law.

Another puzzling problem for chemists was the nature of organic compounds and their relationship to inorganic ones. According to the vitalists, whose ranks included Pasteur and many other eminent scientists, life processes did not obey the same laws that governed inorganic matter but were directed by some unexplained and perhaps inexplicable "vital principle." The first major blow to this position came in 1828 when the German Friedrich Wöhler synthesized urea, an organic compound, in the laboratory. It was soon discovered that all organic compounds contained the element carbon in combination with a relatively small number of other elements, chiefly oxygen, hydrogen, and nitrogen. They were all among the most common elements to be found on the earth's surface and in the atmosphere. In succeeding years many other organic substances, including some not found in nature, were synthesized in laboratories. The vitalist controversy was finally resolved in the biological sciences. The development of cell theory in the 1830's, the studies of digestion, respiration, and metabolism by the Frenchman Claude Bernard in the 1840's and 1850's, and finally the germ theory of disease itself convinced most scientists that the "vital principle" was an unnecessary postulate.

The new offshoots of biology, such as bacteriology and microbiology, together with organic chemistry had many important applications in medicine and pharmacy as well as agriculture and industry. In 1844 an American dentist, Horace Wells, first used nitrous oxide as an anesthetic; it was followed by ether in 1846 and chloroform in 1847. In 1865 a Scottish physician, Joseph Lister, introduced antiseptic surgery with the liberal use of carbolic acid. The combination of anesthesia and antisepsis effected a revolution in medical technology and greatly reduced the death rate in childbirth and surgery. The revolution was not effected without opposition, however, from both within and without medical circles. Religious leaders objected to the use of anesthesia in childbirth on biblical grounds (Genesis 3:16) until Queen Victoria's doctor administered chloroform to her in 1853.

THERMODYNAMICS AND ELECTROMAGNETISM

Thermodynamics, the science dealing with thermal energy or heat, was in a surprisingly backward state in the first half of the nineteenth century. The steam engine, its foremost practical application, had reached a fairly advanced stage of development on the slenderest of theoretical foundations. Indeed, scientists learned far more from the steam engine than its inventors and perfectors learned from science. A French scientist, Sadi Carnot, published a memoir in 1824 on the pure theory of heat engines, which laid the basis for subsequent research. Further work in the 1840's by J. R. Meyer in Germany and James Joule in England on the energy equivalents of heat in other forms (mechanical, electrical, etc.) led to the statement in 1847 by the German Hermann von Helmholtz of the First Law of Thermodynamics, concerning the conservation of energy. This seemingly simple, even obvious principle had numerous practical applications and immense theoretical significance.

The science of electricity belongs almost wholly to the nineteenth century. Electrical phenomena had been observed in ancient times, but as late as the eighteenth century electricity was regarded simply as a curiosity. Toward the end of that century the researches of Benjamin Franklin in America and of the Italians Luigi Galvani and Alessandro Volta, who invented the voltaic pile or battery, raised it from the status of a parlor trick to a laboratory pursuit. In 1807 Sir Humphry Davy discovered electrolysis, the phenomenon by which an electric current decomposes the chemical elements in certain aqueous solutions, which gave rise to the electroplating industry. The next phase in the study of electricity was dominated by Davy's student Michael Faraday, the Danish physicist Hans Oersted, and the French mathematician André Ampère. In 1820 Oersted observed that an electric current produces a magnetic field around the conductors, which led Ampère to formulate a quantitative relationship between electricity and magnetism. Between 1821 and 1831 Faraday discovered the phenomenon of electromagnetic induction (the generation of an electrical current by revolving a magnet inside a coil of wire) and invented a primitive generator and electric motor.

Building on these discoveries, Samuel Morse developed the electric telegraph in America between 1832 and 1844, although the industrial utilization of electricity was held up until the 1870's by the difficulties involved in devising an economically efficient generator.

Faraday's experiments and discoveries were of fundamental importance, but they lacked a satisfactory theoretical basis. It was supplied in the 1860's by James Clerk Maxwell, who deduced mathematically a theoretical velocity for electromagnetic waves that was equivalent to the velocity of light. In fact, Maxwell regarded light as one of many electromagnetic waves and predicted the existence of still others. His prediction received spectacular confirmation in 1885, when Heinrich Hertz of Germany observed the existence of radio waves, which were developed practically by the Italian physicist Guglielmo Marconi after 1895.

ORGANIC EVOLUTION

The most important scientific event of the nineteenth century in its impact on the world was the publication in 1859 of Darwin's *On the Origin of Species.* The essential message of this book, as it reached the public, was that nature's creatures – including man – had not been created *de novo* by the hand of God, as taught in the Old Testament and generally accepted by Christians and non-Christians alike, but that each had evolved from earlier and simpler forms of life. The reaction to this message in both scientific and nonscientific circles was immediate, far-reaching, and clamorous. Most scientists granted it at least qualified acceptance, and some, such as T. H. Huxley, became enthusiastic Darwinians. Nonscientists, however, especially those in religious groups, greeted it with reactions ranging from stunned disbelief to violent opposition.

In retrospect, the furor occasioned by this careful, modestly written book seems surprising. Evolution was by no means a new idea in 1859. In the previous year both Darwin and Alfred Russell Wallace, another British naturalist who had arrived independently at similar views, had presented their ideas in memoirs to the Linnaean Society in London. Darwin had formulated his basic hypothesis more than twenty years before. As early as 1802 the French paleontologist J. B. Lamarck had advanced a theory of evolution that even included the inheritance of acquired characteristics. Lamarck's arguments were not as solidly based as Darwin's, nor did he reach as wide an audience, but Herbert Spencer and others had already accepted the gist of them and were working along similar lines well before 1859.

Abundant evidence existed in both biological and nonbiological sciences to prove that the earth and its creatures had not subsisted without change from the day of creation. Employing James Hutton's *Theory of the Earth* (1785) and Sir Charles Lyell's monumental three-volume *Principles of Geology* (1830–1833), geologists were busy demonstrating that

Thames & Hudson Archives, London

Cartoon of Charles Darwin, from *The Hornet*, March 22, 1871

"Man is descended from some less highly organized form. . . . The grounds upon which this conclusion rests will never be shaken, for the close similarity between man and the lower animals in embryonic development, as well as in innumerable points of structure and constitution, both of high and the most trifling importance . . . are facts which cannot be disputed. . . . When viewed by the light of our knowledge of the whole organic world, their meaning is unmistakable. The great principle of evolution stands up clear and firm, when these groups of facts are considered in connection with others, such as the mutual affinities of the members of the same group, their geographical distribution in past and present times, and their geological succession. It is incredible that all these facts should speak falsely." Charles Darwin, THE DESCENT OF MAN (New York, 1875).

the age of the earth was far greater than even the most liberal interpretations of the biblical accounts would allow. They also proved that far from remaining in its original state, the earth's surface had undergone tremendous upheavals in the past and was still in a constant process of transformation. Paleontologists pointed to the fossilized remains of creatures that were no longer extant to show that earlier forms of life had existed. For a very long time men had been engaged in the selective breeding of livestock and other animals on an empirical, nonscientific basis. Economists like Friedrich List had emphasized the evolutionary nature of social development through a series of stages. Historians like H. T. Buckle had emphasized the influence of environment on personal and national characters. From many angles – natural science, agricultural technology, social philosophy, and history – influences were converging on the notion of organic evolution. Darwin supplied the missing element: a conception of the mode of operation of the evolutionary process.

The Darwinian theory may be reduced by drastic oversimplification to three major points. The first point Darwin took from the Malthusian theory of population: in every species nature gives birth to more individuals than the means of subsistence will support. Second, this overpopulation results in a competition for survival, a struggle for existence. Finally, and most important, in the process of inheritance chance variations or mutations occur among individuals, making some more suitable and adaptable to the environment than others. Those that are "naturally selected" for survival continue to propagate their own kind. The others, the "unfit," are weeded out and do not propagate. In spite of the title of the book, it was not actually a theory of the origin of species but only of their survival. Darwin slurred over the crucial question of why mutation takes place on the assumption that it was a matter of random variation. For biologists this point proved to be the most controversial, but its subtlety escaped most laymen. For them the controversy lay in other realms.

THE WARFARE OF SCIENCE WITH THEOLOGY

Historically there has been a long conflict between materialistic science and supernatural religion. For most of modern history this conflict seethed below the surface, but in the latter half of the nineteenth century it broke out into full-fledged ideological warfare. In earlier days, when religion was dominant, scientists had tried to disavow the conflict. Galileo and others recanted their scientific beliefs when challenged by the Church. Newton, a pious man, felt that his discoveries about the nature of the universe only established the greater glory of the Creator. Even Darwin, an agnostic, tried to disarm his critics in advance by writing, "I see no good reason why the views given in the volume [*On the Origin of Species*] should shock the religious feelings of anyone. . . . There is grandeur in this view of life, with its several powers, having been originally breathed by the Creator into a few forms or into one; and that, whilst this planet has gone cycling on according to the fixed law of gravity, from so simple a being endless forms most beautiful and most wonderful have been, and are being evolved." Yet this bland reassurance could not calm the troubled spirits within and without the churches.

SCIENCE ON THE OFFENSE

Many elements of conflict existed between the findings of science and the traditional teachings of Christianity. Most fundamental was the fact that scientists disputed the literal interpretation of the Bible, especially biblical chronology and the stories of Genesis. For instance, a seventeenth-century bishop had worked out a systematic but most unscientific chronology that placed the origin of the earth in the year 4004 B.C. In no way could this account be reconciled with geological, paleontological, archaeological, and even historical evidence on the age of the earth. Scientific evidence tended to undermine belief in miracles, such as the virgin birth and bodily resurrection. Defenders of religion asserted that these events could not be understood scientifically because they were supernatural and therefore superscientific, but scientists refused to be convinced.

Religious defenses were further shaken when some biblical scholars adopted the canons of modern historical and literary criticism and subjected the Bible to historical and realistic reinterpretation. Such books as D. F. Strauss's *Das Leben Jesu* (1836) and Ernest Renan's *Vie de Jésus* (1863), which pictured Jesus naturalistically as a mortal, were profoundly disturbing to the faithful. Other scholars sought to strengthen Christian faith by freeing it from a dependence on obviously discredited dogmas, and replacing the literal interpretation of the Bible with an allegorical one, trying to interpret it as a dramatic story that illustrates great moral truths. Even this could not deflect scientists' criticism of the attribution to God of such human traits as benevolence and anger. In such an intellectual environment the arrival of Darwinian biology did not cause the "warfare of science with theology," as the struggle was called by the president of Cornell University, Andrew Dickson White; it merely precipitated the outbreak of overt hostilities.

THE THEOLOGICAL COUNTERATTACK

The various churches reacted to the scientific offensive in different ways. Liberal Protestant and Jewish theologians attempted to redefine religion so as to remove the elements of conflict and make religion compatible with science. Other Protestants adopted a fundamentalist attitude: whenever scientific findings conflicted with the fundamentals of their faith they denounced science as untrue and a work of the devil. Only the Roman Catholic Church returned the challenge with a deliberate and sustained counterattack.

As early as 1832 Pope Gregory XVI in the encyclical *Mirari vos* had condemned liberty of conscience and the press as well as revolts against established government. In 1854 Pope Pius IX promulgated the Dogma of the Immaculate Conception, which held that the Virgin Mary was conceived without the taint of original sin bestowed on all other mortals. The pope hoped to strengthen the Church in its struggle with materialism; instead, he hardened the lines of resistance and made the reconciliation of science and religion even more difficult to achieve. The high point of the Church's counterattack came ten years later in 1864, when Pius IX issued the encyclical *Quanta cura* and its appended *Syllabus of Errors*. By then the papacy had lost all its temporal domain to the new kingdom of Italy with the exception of the city of Rome and its immediate vicinity. (See pp. 155–156.) Not only was it in danger of losing Rome itself, but also its political relations with several other states were in a precarious position. Accordingly, the pope lashed out at science and other aspects of contemporary society that he associated with the Church's troubles.

The *Syllabus of Errors* consisted of eighty propositions which it labeled as contrary to the principles of the Christian religion. They included pantheism, naturalism, "absolute" and "moderate" rationalism, and most other contemporary "isms." The syllabus castigated the notions of religious toleration and freedom of conscience, upheld the necessity of temporal power for the Roman Catholic Church, rejected the separation of Church and state but insisted on the supremacy of the Church over civil law, and claimed for the Church complete control over education, science, philosophy, and intellectual and cultural affairs in general. It concluded with a ringing denunciation of the idea that "the Roman Pontiff can and should reconcile and align himself with progress, liberalism, and modern civilization."

The syllabus brought joy to the hearts of Ultramontane Catholics, but it aroused further the suspicions and hostility of non-Catholics – Protestants, Jews, and freethinkers alike – and cut the ground from under liberal Catholics who had been working to restore Catholic prestige and make their church an instrument of progress.

The final salvo of the Catholic Church's counterattack came from the Vatican Council, the first general council of the church in three centuries, which assembled in Rome in 1869. The original intent of the council was to restate and strengthen the position of the Church on Church-state relations, but the only positive action it took (on a proposition that had not appeared in the original agenda) was to proclaim the Dogma of Papal Infallibility: the dogma that the pope, when speaking *ex cathedra* on a question of faith and morals, speaks with the voice of God.

THE CHURCH ON THE DEFENSIVE

The counterattack failed, at least in its primary objective. Soon after the proclamation of papal infallibility Italian soldiers occupied Rome and Victor Emmanuel proclaimed the Eternal City as capital of the kingdom of Italy. The Vatican Council adjourned *sine die.* The Italian government offered the pope an annuity and guaranteed him the treatment due the head of a sovereign state, but the pope (who had already excommunicated Victor Emmanuel and several Italian statesmen) refused all offers of compromise, placed the ban of the Church on the king and his government, and regarded himself as "the prisoner in the Vatican."

The Roman Catholic Church had its difficulties elsewhere as well. Immediately after the proclamation of papal infallibility Austria annulled its concordat with the Church. Soon afterward the chancellor of the new German Empire inaugurated a policy of persecution of the Church known as the *Kulturkampf,* which led to a long struggle on the question of Church-state relations and alienated many members of the Church. (See p. 217.) Within the Church the victory of the reactionary party led to the excommunication of the liberal Catholics who refused to accept defeat. Dissension among Catholics themselves spread to Germany, Austria, Switzerland, and the Netherlands.

No less disturbing to the Catholic Church was its loosening hold over its rank-and-file members. In this situation it was not alone, for all Western religions experienced the same problem. Basically the decline was brought about by materialism in the broadest sense. Propagation of the discoveries of science together with the spread of education and literacy led to an undermining of faith in religious teachings. Material progress, relaxed political controls, crumbling social distinctions, and the consequent attempt of individuals of all social classes to better themselves economically steadily diverted their attention from religious activities and weakened the church hierarchy's control. The large-scale population shifts induced by industrialization and urbanization also loosened church ties. The slow reaction of all churches to the demoralizing living and working conditions in the large new industrial centers further alienated large masses of erstwhile believers. The opposition of most established churches to trade unions, socialism, and other attempts of the workers to improve their lot gave ample opportunity to the proponents of religious disbelief.

Pius IX died in 1878. His long regime, which had been hailed at its inception in 1846 as inaugurating a new era for the Roman Catholic Church, ended with that Church shaken to its foundations, holding only the shreds of its former power and prestige. The new pope, Leo XIII, was sixty-eight years old and in very frail health. Few people expected him to live longer than two or three years at most. He was regarded as a temporary pope; the Church would regroup its forces and elect a young and vigorous head. Instead, Leo lived for another twenty-five years and brought the papacy to a new peak of prestige.

MATERIALISM AND POSITIVISM

Materialism in the strict sense is the belief that all phenomena of the universe, including man, consist ultimately of matter and energy. It is closely related to realism in modern philosophy, which is defined as the belief that the physical universe has an objective existence independent of the observer. Both conceptions are antithetical not only to the supernatural and metaphysical principles of revealed religion but also to the various idealist philosophies, such as the Hegelian, which hold that ultimate reality consists only of ideas.

Nineteenth-century science gave powerful support to the advocates of realism and materialism. It strengthened the tendency that had been present in political and social philosophy at least from the time of Locke to look at natural science as a model for the analysis of social phenomena. The founders of modern economics, or political economy, borrowed heavily from Newtonian physics for both their concepts and their terminology. Increasingly they referred to their subject as a science. In the nineteenth century the predominant influence on political and social philosophy came from the biological sciences, which affected them in two ways: first, by providing analogies and terminology; second, by providing the principle of evolution.

SOCIAL DARWINISM

The expression Social Darwinism refers to the application of the principle of organic evolution as stated by Darwin to the phenomena of society. The most popular and influential exponent of Social Darwinism was Herbert Spencer (1820–1903), an English engineer and social philosopher, whose prolific but often superficial pen inundated the literate public during the entire second half of the nineteenth century. Spencer, who had already begun his evolutionary thinking before 1859, eagerly seized Darwin's theory and applied it directly if indiscriminately to society, making social change a mere continuation of biological evolution. The doctrine implicit in Darwinian biological theory – that conflict and strife are good and synonymous with progress – became explicit in Spencer's version. According to him, the competition of individuals, business firms, or nations ensures the "survival of the fittest" and the subjugation or elimination of the "unfit," unless it is hindered by "artificial" restraints on the "natural" process of selection. Social Darwinism reinforced the arguments of the classical economists against state interference with the economy, which accounted for Spencer's enormous popularity with successful businessmen. Andrew Carnegie's reaction after reading Darwin and Spencer was, "Not only had I got rid of theology and the supernatural, but I had found the truth of evolution. 'All is well since all grows better' became my motto, my true source of comfort." Paradoxically, the radical intellectual doctrine of evolution had become an argument for maintaining the status quo.

Not all Social Darwinists – the expression is sometimes used rather loosely – derived the same lesson from organic evolution as Spencer and Carnegie. When the liberal English economist and political philosopher Walter Bagehot (1826–1877) applied it by analogy to the study of the British constitution in *Physics and Politics* (which might more aptly have been called "Biology and Social Science"), he argued for a greater degree of political freedom and democracy. On the other hand, the American sociologist Lester Ward denied the direct applicability of Darwinism to society. "The fundamental principle of biology," he wrote, "is natural selection, that of sociology is artificial selection. The survival of the fittest is simply the survival of the strong, which implies and would better be called the destruction of the weak. If nature progresses through the destruction of the weak, man progresses through the protection of the weak." Darwinism also inspired the British Fabian socialists (see p. 197), and exerted a profound influence on the thought of Karl Marx. Marx even wished to dedicate the first volume of *Das Kapital* to Darwin, but the latter circumspectly declined the honor.

Darwinism gave an apparently scientific basis to the fallacious distinction between "superior" and "inferior" races. The invocation of biology in this case served merely as adornment for arguments that sprang from quite different sources. In 1853 J. A. de Gobineau (1816–1882), a French nobleman, laid the basis for much subsequent pseudoscientific writing on the subject of race in an *Essay on the Inequality of Human Races.* Houston Stewart Chamberlain (1855–1927), an Englishman who married Richard Wagner's daughter and became a German citizen, did much through his writings to establish the myth of a uniquely pure and therefore superior "Teutonic race." Malicious journalists published reams of pseudoscientific material intended to convince their readers of the mental or moral deficiencies of the Semitic, Slavic, or Latin "races." One disastrous result of this perversion of Darwinian biology was its application to non-European "races" in the outburst of imperialist sentiment at the end of the century. (See p. 283.)

AUGUSTE COMTE AND MODERN SOCIOLOGY

The most ambitious, systematic, and comprehensive attempt to apply the methods of science to the study of society was made by the French philosopher Auguste Comte (1798–1857). Comte's major work was *La philosophie positive* (*Positive Philosophy*). It was the foundation stone of modern positivism, the system of philosophy that recognizes only observable phenomena and scientifically established fact. Comte interpreted the intellectual history of the world as passing through three great ages: the theological, metaphysical, and scientific. He thought that Europe in the nineteenth century was on the verge of the third and final age.

Comte classified all "positive" (verifiable) knowledge into a series of categories of increasing specificity and complexity, in which the "laws" of the more complex sciences rested upon those of the simpler and more abstract. Mathematics, with its self-evident axioms and abstract theorems, formed the base of his intellectual pyramid, surmounted by the physical sciences, the earth sciences, and the biological sciences. Capping the edifice was sociology, a comprehensive social science including economics, anthropology, history, and psychology. Comte therefore has a claim as the founder of modern sociology as well as positivism.

Comte's writing is sometimes both ponderous and pompous. Apart from his classifications, conceptions, and strictures on scientific and philosophic methods, he contributed little of substance to either sociology or social philosophy. The vogue of positivism lasted only a short time, and sociology did not become a recognized social science until the end of the nineteenth century, when it took a form different from that envisaged by Comte. Nevertheless, Comte was a major figure in the history of thought. His influence, both direct and indirect, was enormous on men of such varied temperaments and accomplishments as John Stuart Mill, Herbert Spencer, Ernest Renan, Hippolyte Taine, and the American pragmatic philosophers of the twentieth century. He was as responsible as any for the general acceptance of science as a special and authoritative branch of knowledge.

REALISM IN RETROSPECT

Realism, the prevailing intellectual temper of the third quarter of the nineteenth century, placed a high value upon action, power, success, material progress, and the exact representation of nature. It glorified struggle and conflict, from which manliness and progress were presumed to result. It cared little for sentimentality, scoffed at romanticism and idealism, and scorned mysticism and the supernatural. The firmness with which the revolutions of 1848 were suppressed, and the success of *Realpolitik* in unifying Italy and Germany, seemed to justify this attitude in practical politics. The achievements of science and the retreat of traditional religion increased its intellectual stature as well as its popularity, especially among the middle classes, who were the chief beneficiaries of the substantial technical and economic progress of the period. Artists and litterateurs as well as social philosophers took natural science as their model and guide. In spite of a certain crassness and callousness, realism was an optimistic outlook. Its legacy to succeeding generations was beneficial, on the whole. Yet it contained certain unresolved – almost undetected – ethical and philosophical problems, which caused immediate anguish and suffering for many and in the long run overwhelmed the optimistic outlook itself.

THE POLITICS OF POWER, 1852–1871
CHAPTER SIX

The two decades from the coup d'état of Louis Napoleon to the proclamation of the German Empire witnessed fundamental changes in the structure of the European state system, in the nature of the political process, and in the character and the behavior of statesmen and politicians. The most striking changes were the unification of Germany and Italy into two powerful nations in central Europe. Yet the method of their unification was itself a manifestation of equally important if more subtle changes in the mentality of political leaders, the essence of which can be stated in a single phrase: the willingness to use force to achieve purely political goals. Although the domestic political struggles of the first half of the nineteenth century frequently erupted in revolution, their objective was an idealistic vision of a more nearly perfect society. After the failure of the revolutions of 1848, idealism was replaced by political realism or *Realpolitik,* in which practical interests and material advantage became the sole consideration of ambitious statesmen and politicians, who felt that any practical means were justified in order to gain their often ignoble ends.

This new outlook operated on the international no less than the national plane. In fact, the growth of constitutional and democratic sentiment forced even dictatorial rulers to cater somewhat to public opinion domestically, or at least to manipulate that opinion behind a façade of constitutionalism, but no similar constitutional check existed in international relations. Astute political leaders could manipulate the passions of inflamed nationalism to support their use of naked force. Between 1815 and 1853 the interests of the great powers and the efforts of statesmen were aimed at avoiding wars among the European states; revolutions there had been, numbers of them, but no major wars. Again from 1871 to 1914, except for peripheral conflicts such as the Balkan wars, no European nation fought another. In the two decades corresponding to the life of the Second French Empire, however, European nations fought five significant wars, involving all the great powers in one or another. They were brief, limited wars, but they were fought for political advantage. With the possible exception of the Crimean War, they were deliberately provoked by some person or persons for a definite political purpose. Although circumstances differed in the United States, there, too, North and South resorted to the use of force in a long and bloody civil war rather than settle their differences by peaceful negotiations.

NAPOLEON III AND THE SECOND FRENCH EMPIRE

The coup d'état of December 2, 1851, ushered in a period of frankly dictatorial government, to which the trappings of constitutionalism were soon added. The plebiscite that confirmed the coup d'état also authorized the prince-president (as he was now called) to draw up a new constitution. One of its provisions extended the term of the presidency to ten years, but no one seriously expected the term to expire in a normal manner. The progress of Louis Napoleon Bonaparte from constitutional official to dictatorial chief of state to emperor paralleled that of the first Napoleon, but it took less time because of the earlier precedent. The Bonapartists prepared an elaborate campaign to organize popular acceptance for a return to the empire. The prince-president made a speaking tour of the provinces, much in the manner of later American presidential campaigns, at which paid demonstrators and soldiers raised cries of "Vive Napoléon" and "Vive l'empire." In November, 1852, a new plebiscite duly ratified a return to the empire, which was proclaimed on December 2, exactly one year after the coup d'état and forty-eight years to the day after the proclamation of the First Empire.

THE "AUTHORITARIAN EMPIRE"

The Second Empire introduced no fundamental changes in the structure of government. With minor changes in wording, the constitution of January 14, 1852, served the empire as well as the dictatorial republic. The empire was simply the frosting on the Napoleonic cake. The new emperor chose the title Napoleon III to indicate that he regarded himself as the successor to the son of Napoleon I, who in fact had never been recognized as emperor. The constitution gave the chief of state almost unlimited authority: he commanded the armed forces, the police, and the civil service; he alone could initiate legislation, declare war, and conclude treaties; and at his will he could rule by decree. To assist him in the task of government, the constitution provided four bodies, two of them actual working groups, the other two chiefly for decoration. In fact, the constitution stated expressly that "the Emperor governs *by means of* the ministers, the Council of State, the Senate, and the Legislative Body."

The ministers had charge of the day-to-day operations of the executive departments but did not form a cabinet in the modern sense. They had no collective responsibility either to the legislature or to the emperor; they were individually appointed by and could be dismissed by the emperor alone. Selected primarily on the basis of personal loyalty and competence, they were simply the chief administrative assistants of the emperor. The Conseil d'État, likewise appointed by the emperor, had as its principal function the drafting of legislation. It was not, however, a legislative body in the ordinary sense. Composed of high-ranking civil servants and other technical experts, it merely ensured that the laws desired by the emperor were given the proper form.

The members of the Senate were appointed for life by the emperor from outstanding persons in all walks of life. They had very little to do other than to perform ceremonial functions and to ratify such changes as Napoleon wished to make in the constitution. The Corps Legislatif preserved a semblance of representative government, but no more than that. Its members, the deputies, were elected by universal male suffrage for six-year terms; but they lacked the power to introduce or amend legislation and could only accept or reject what the emperor proposed. Their debates were not open to the public, nor were any records preserved. Moreover, at election time the government put up a slate of official candidates whose campaign expenses it paid and whom it favored in other ways. Under these circumstances it required a hardy individual to pose as an opposition candidate.

Immediately following the coup d'état the government was a military dictatorship, but within a few months the dictatorship began to take on a more benign aspect. The first eight years are sometimes called the period of personal rule or the "authoritarian empire." The government maintained strict control of the press, suppressed all overt manifestations of political hostility, and mainly followed its own interests. Yet it was not an oppressive dictatorship; it was on the whole a rather benevolent despotism. The government did not lack popular support in the country, and it continually sought to increase the bases of that support by means of individual and group favors and political bribes. The peasants, who were still the most numerous class, provided the government with its largest number of supporters, while the upper middle classes, the bourgeoisie of rich merchants, manufacturers, financiers, and professional men — most of whom had been Orleanist in their sympathies — occupied the highest posts and derived the most benefits from government favors. The aristocracy remained legitimist (pro-Bourbon) in its sympathies for the most part, while the urban workers, despite some weak attempts by the government to gain their favor, remained tinged with republicanism.

THE "LIBERAL EMPIRE"

During the 1860's an evolutionary process gradually modified the political institutions of the empire. The emperor himself had said early in his career, "Liberty will crown the edifice." In the Second Empire liberty was the reward of the people for obedience, and it came after, not before, the establishment of order and the development of the constitutional system. Liberal reforms, aimed chiefly at giving the Legislative Body a greater share in government, took place in 1860, 1862, 1867, and 1869. Finally in 1870 the Senate became the upper house of the legislature, and a responsible cabinet was introduced – that is, a cabinet responsible to the legislature instead of the emperor. Opposition deputies increased from eight in 1852 to more than 150 in 1869, which represented a majority of the Corps Législatif. These developments were clearly in the direction of a constitutional monarchy. The reforms were not entirely voluntary, however. The emperor gave in to public opinion and to political pressures that were exerted upon him chiefly as the result of embarrassments over his foreign policies. Nevertheless, he did so with good grace and appeared to have established a dynasty and a government that might give France political stability.

DOMESTIC POLICY

When setting the stage for the proclamation of the empire in 1852, the prince-president sought to undercut those who insinuated that a return to the empire would involve France in war. On the contrary, he said, "L'empire, c'est la paix" (The empire means peace). What he should have said was, "The empire means prosperity" – within two years France was involved in the Crimean War – for the era of the Second Empire was one of the most prosperous periods in all French history. Favorable international conditions partially accounted for the prosperity, for it was a period of general economic expansion throughout the world; but Napoleonic economic policies were also responsible.

Napoleon III's economic policy contrasted strongly with his political policy. Whereas the latter was one of restraint, control, and supervision, the former encouraged private initiative and enterprise. Stimulated by a lowering of tariffs in the 1850's and a network of trade treaties beginning with the Cobden-Chevalier Treaty of 1860, foreign commerce expanded by more than 5 per cent per year. New business firms multiplied, especially after the passage of laws permitting free incorporation with limited liability in 1863 and 1867. New types of financial institutions were created by private initiative but with government encouragement and support; the Crédit Foncier, a mortgage bank, and the Crédit Mobilier, an industrial credit institution, were both established in 1852. They contributed to prosperity in France and also were widely imitated abroad. Three of the four largest commercial banks in France, nationalized in 1945, date from the era of the Second Empire.

The railroad network was one of the major achievements in the area of economic policy. The Second Empire granted charters for more than one-half the eventual mileage and witnessed the completion of more than a third of it. The telegraph network expanded from two thousand to more than seventy thousand kilometers. In 1855 the Crédit Mobilier created with a government subsidy the steamship company that became the French Line. Stimulated by railroad construction and the general economic expansion, the iron industry completed its transition to coke smelting and adopted new methods for making cheap steel. While transforming and expanding the domestic economy, Frenchmen extended their economic interests abroad. Foreign investments rose from about two billion to more than twelve billion francs, while French businessmen, bankers, and engineers spread through Europe and much of the rest of the world building railroads, digging mines and canals, and creating banks and industrial establishments. The greatest single achievement of French enterprise, and possibly the greatest engineering feat of the nineteenth century, was the digging of the Suez Canal, carried out between 1854 and 1869 by a company headed by Ferdinand de Lesseps.

A project closely related to economic policy (for it was intended in part to give employment to the workers of Paris and wean them from socialism), but which had broader cultural and even political objectives as well, was the reconstruction and beautification of Paris. This work went on for many years and cost many millions of francs. It made Paris one of the most beautiful cities in the world, with wide boulevards, magnificent vistas, beautiful parks, lavish public monuments, and a modern sanitary system. Fortunately for future generations, the city planners of the Second Empire did not neglect aesthetic considerations in their striving for efficiency.

The reconstruction of Paris was only one aspect of a general effort to restore the nation to the position of prestige that it had maintained in times past and to cover the empire with glory. The major part of this effort was expended in the nation's foreign relations, but Napoleon III and his supporters did not neglect the cultivation of artistic, cultural, and scientific triumphs. The emperor set the social tone early in his reign by his marriage to Eugénie de Montijo, the daughter of a minor Spanish nobleman. Having been unsuccessful in his attempts to find a bride from one of the reigning dynasties, he reportedly "married for love" this obscure and impoverished but chaste and dignified young Spanish beauty. The marriage contributed greatly to his popularity in the early years of the empire. In time Eugénie's clerical inclinations and legitimist sympathies created political difficulties for the empire, but as a generous and impulsive sponsor of charities she contributed greatly to making the empire palatable and even popular among workers and peasants alike, and as a leader of fashion she made Paris once more the center of European high society.

Eugénie's devout Catholicism symbolized the regime's dilemma in religious policy, and also contributed to it. The emperor, a free thinker, could not afford to antagonize the large body of French believers. As president of the republic he had made several concessions to the Church. Under the empire he continued this policy, but at the same time certain features of his foreign policy – his encouragement of Italian nationalism, in particular – tended to alienate the clerical party in France.

FOREIGN POLICY: THE CRIMEAN WAR AND THE CONGRESS OF PARIS

The principal objective of Napoleon's foreign policy was to restore France to its position of power, influence, and glory as the arbiter of Europe. The several glaring failures that eventually led to the downfall of his regime sometimes obscure his temporary success. The first major test came in a renewal of what is known as the Eastern question. In 1853 Russia and Turkey went to war, and France and Britain joined Turkey as allies early in the following year. From one point of view the war was only one in a long series of conflicts between Russia and Turkey, but the involvement of the Western powers made it a struggle of more general significance. The apparent cause for French participation was a dispute between France and Russia concerning the custody of Christian shrines in Palestine, which had been growing more intense since 1851. The Ottoman Turks, as nominal rulers, had allowed both governments certain rights of protection for Christian pilgrims. Napoleon inflated this dispute far beyond its true importance, hoping to curry favor with the clerical opposition by posing as protector of the Church, and at the same time hoping to regain for France and the empire some of its lost glory by scoring a diplomatic victory over Russia.

The actual fighting, confined primarily to the Crimean peninsula in the Black Sea, was almost inconsequential. None of the powers involved regarded the issues as important enough to justify a major effort, and commercial relationships through the Baltic Sea were hardly affected. The casualties from disease and inadequate medical care rivaled those resulting from poor planning and logistics and the incompetence of the generals. Florence Nightingale eventually provoked sweeping reforms in army medical care and public health nursing by exposing the atrocious medical and sanitary conditions of the British army. Following the death of the Russian Tsar Nicholas I and the threat of Austrian intervention on the side of the Western allies, Russia agreed to an armistice at the beginning of 1856.

A general settlement of the issues growing out of the war took place at the Paris Peace Congress in the spring of 1856. Although Napoleon III failed to secure a revision of the Vienna settlement, the effect of the war and the congress was to reestablish France as the most powerful nation on the Continent. The birth of an heir to the imperial throne while the congress was in session added to the luster of the occasion and appeared to ensure the success of the dynasty. The congress also produced the germ of Napoleon's next major foreign policy adventure – his participation in the unification of Italy.

THE RISORGIMENTO AND ITALIAN UNITY

Prior to 1860 Italy had never been a unified nation. In ancient times it formed part of the Roman Empire, but not as a nation. After the fall of Rome it broke up into several barbarian kingdoms, and the process of fragmentation continued throughout the early Middle Ages. In the later Middle Ages Italy again became the center of European civilization, but it remained politically divided into numerous small republics and principalities. With the rise of large nation-states in early modern times these tiny city-states became battlegrounds and objects of plunder and oppression by their larger neighbors, a situation that continued until after the middle of the nineteenth century. The word *risorgimento,* therefore, meaning resurrection or resurgence, is not strictly accurate when applied to the political movement for national unity in Italy in the nineteenth century. Nevertheless, it does convey a sense of the patriotic spirit and messianic fervor that characterized the leaders of the movement.

THE RISE OF NATIONAL CONSCIOUSNESS

The first stirrings of national consciousness took place in the eighteenth century, when some educated Italians began to speak of their homeland as Italy rather than Tuscany, Lombardy, or Romagna. The French Revolution and the period of French domination under Napoleon fanned the flames of nationalism in Italy, as elsewhere, but the illusion of unity and nationality that Napoleon created with his sham Kingdom of Italy was short-lived. Italians who had hoped for a unified national state were gravely disappointed with the settlement of the Congress of Vienna, which resurrected the numerous small states, almost all of them under foreign domination.

The 1815 settlement did not reproduce exactly the pre-Napoleonic situation. In the north, Lombardy and Venetia were incorporated directly into the Austrian Empire. Under the protection of Austria, Bourbons or Hapsburgs ruled in the tiny duchies of Modena, Parma, and Lucca, in the slightly larger Grand Duchy of Tuscany, and in the still larger Kingdom of the Two Sicilies, whose capital was Naples. Only the

States of the Church had a genuinely native Italian ruler, and he, too, was under Austrian protection. The Kingdom of Sardinia, the eventual leader of the movement for Italian unification, was a curious mélange, an artificial state composed of four major subdivisions differing in climate, resources, institutions, and even language: the island of Sardinia, whence the union got its name, languishing in the backwaters of feudalism; Savoy, which gave the kingdom and later Italy its ruling dynasty, geographically, economically, and culturally a part of France; Genoa, the former commercial republic added to the kingdom in 1815; and Piedmont, the real head and body of the country, containing not only the capital but about four-fifths of the total population.

In the three decades after the Congress of Vienna the Kingdom of Sardinia showed no sign that it would eventually take the lead in a liberal and national movement; on the contrary, its restored monarch outdid the Austrian rulers of Lombardy and Venetia in the vehemence of his attempts to undo the work of the French Revolution and return to the ancien régime. The oppressive atmosphere of the Metternichean reaction seemed to stifle temporarily all liberal and nationalist sentiment. The most daring and fanatic radicals, mainly young intellectuals and adventurers, formed secret revolutionary societies, such as the Carbonari. These groups instigated the insurrections of 1820 and 1821 and 1830 and 1832, doomed to failure by the ignorance and apathy of the peasants. (See pp. 45, 52.) The early insurrections were aimed simply at the overthrow of existing governments and the attainment of an idealized, romanticized, abstract liberty. Their failure subtly transformed their romantic liberalism into a liberal nationalism with the goal of a united, independent Italy.

ALTERNATIVE APPROACHES TO NATIONAL UNITY

Between the revolutions of 1830 and 1832 and those of 1848 three different approaches to the problem of unity were proposed. Giuseppe Mazzini (1805–1872), a young veteran of the Carbonari, was disappointed but not disillusioned by the failures of 1830 and 1832. He advocated a centralized democratic republic, to be achieved by a simultaneous mass uprising against all the existing governments. To further his ideas he founded a new organization called Young Italy, which was to enroll young patriots and inculcate in them Mazzini's ideas of liberty, democracy, and republicanism. Similar movements in other countries soon imitated Young Italy, and in 1834 Mazzini took the lead in founding a Young Europe. Mazzini was a gifted orator and idealistic writer, but his program had limited appeal for the illiterate masses and the timid middle class. He dissipated his energies and organization in ill-prepared and ineffective risings like those of the Carbonari. Although he played a leading role in the short-lived Roman Republic of 1849 and lived to witness the unification of

Italy in 1870, he died a broken man, his ideal of a democratic republic unfulfilled.

Vincenzo Gioberti (1801–1852), a Catholic priest, advocated a federation of Italian states under the presidency of the pope. The supporters of his proposal, known as the Neo-Guelphs from the name of the medieval papal party, took heart with the elevation to the papacy of Pius IX in 1846. The new pope was regarded as a liberal reformer, and his first actions seemed to support this view, but his experiences in the revolution of 1848 left him an embittered reactionary. Support for the Neo-Guelph position could still be found as late as 1859, but the events of the following year permanently alienated the papacy from the nationalist movement.

The final approach to the achievement of Italian unity, the one that ultimately triumphed, developed slowly and with less precisely defined methods. Championed by middle-class and aristocratic Piedmontese statesmen such as Cesare Balbo, Massimo d'Azeglio, and Camillo di Cavour, it regarded the Kingdom of Sardinia as the only really independent state in Italy and the one that would have to take the lead. For this to come about, several conditions had to be met. First, the government itself had to be turned into a progressive, constitutional monarchy. Second and even more important, Austria had to be expelled from Italy. Both of these conditions seemed to be far in the future until the dramatic changes of 1848.

THE REVOLUTIONS OF 1848

The revolutions of 1848 gave the supporters of all three proposed solutions an opportunity to achieve what they could. For a very brief interval the various partisans actually cooperated with one another. The results, mostly negative, revealed the military weakness and divided councils of the Italian states. The pope's reversion to absolutism and reaction disqualified him as a leader of the nationalist movement. The failure of the Roman and Venetian republics to obtain popular support throughout the country, despite their heroic resistance against overwhelming odds, eliminated republicanism as a catalyst of Italian nationalism. Only one bright spot remained: the almost accidental fashion in which Piedmont retained its liberal constitutional regime. The inexperience of Victor Emmanuel, the new king, together with the firmness of d'Azeglio and the constitutional party, resulted in the retention of the liberal *Statuto* (constitution) of 1848 with its bicameral legislature and responsible cabinet.

CAVOUR AND THE PROGRESS OF PIEDMONT

Of the three possible means to a united and independent Italy, only one remained. Even that one might have amounted to naught if it had not been for the remarkable ability of Camillo di Cavour (1810–1861). A nobleman with the outlook of a progressive bourgeois, Cavour pioneered scientific agriculture in Piedmont, promoted banks and railroads, and in 1847 founded the liberal newspaper *Il Risorgimento.* To practical experience he added years of study in history, politics, and economics. He traveled widely, admired the constitutional regimes of France and England, and was an enthusiastic if undogmatic exponent of the classical school of political economy. Although he remained in the background, he played an important role in projecting and retaining the *Statuto* in 1848 and 1849, and in 1850 he drafted the Siccardi laws, which drastically curbed the powers of the Church. Later in the same year he entered the cabinet as minister of agriculture and commerce, shortly taking on the portfolios of the navy and finance as well. In 1852 he became prime minister, a post that he held almost without interruption until his death in 1861.

From the beginning of his political career Cavour made it clear that he intended to make Piedmont economically progressive and politically liberal. He negotiated trade treaties, built railroads, introduced new industries, and carried out a comprehensive reform of the administrative and legal systems. Although these actions had little apparent connection with the movement for unification, Cavour stressed time and again that financial stability and economic progress were the two "indispensable conditions" if Piedmont was to assume the leadership of the Italian peninsula. To accomplish these goals he warmly welcomed French and British investors, entrepreneurs, and engineers, who contributed greatly to the remarkable economic progress of Piedmont in the 1850's.

Cavour had another reason for cultivating the friendship of France and Britain. He correctly read the lesson of 1848 and 1849, namely that Italy could never "make itself," according to the slogan of those years (*Italia farà da sé*), as long as Austria stood in the way. It is frequently stated that Cavour took Piedmont into the Crimean War in 1855 on the side of France and Britain for the express purpose of embarrassing Austria and raising the Italian question at the peace conference. Whether or not that was true, he certainly made the best of his opportunities, and although he did not succeed in placing Italy on the agenda of the conference itself, he did obtain a favorable hearing for the cause of Italian independence. Cavour would have liked to have had Britain as an ally in a military confrontation with Austria, but he realized that such an alliance was out of the question, not only because of the distance but also because Britain depended upon Austria to maintain the balance of power in central and eastern Europe. The most he could hope for from Britain was benevolent neutrality. For an active ally he had somehow to persuade the quixotic emperor of the French to come to his assistance.

Napoleon III was not adverse in principle to aiding Piedmont. As Corsicans, the Bonapartes had Italian blood in their veins. Napoleon I had catered to Italian nationalism, had created a mock kingdom of Italy, and had called his son the King of Rome. Napoleon III had carefully fostered the legend that his uncle was a champion of oppressed nationalities and, as a romantic revolutionary himself, had even been a Carbonaro and taken part in the Italian revolts of 1830 and 1831. Moreover, he felt that to overturn completely the hated settlement of 1815 he must humiliate Austria as he had already humiliated Russia. On the other hand, Napoleon recognized the risks involved. The French clerical party was certain to oppose any tampering with the temporal rule of the pope. Britain was likely to oppose a disturbance of the status quo. Defeat by Austria was at least a possibility. Prussia might come to the aid of Austria by invading across the Rhine. Finally, a strong, united Italy might not be satisfied with the role of client state to France.

At length, however, Cavour persuaded Napoleon. In July, 1858, the two statesmen met secretly like conspirators in the resort village of Plombières in eastern France. There they agreed provisionally upon the terms under which France would come to the aid of Piedmont. They set up a "defensive" military alliance, which was to drive the Austrians out of Italy if Austria could be provoked into attacking Piedmont. Lombardy and Venetia were to be added to the Kingdom of Sardinia; all the Italian states were to be grouped into a federation under the nominal suzerainty of the pope; and as the price of its participation, France was to receive Savoy and Nice. As a preliminary arrangement, Napoleon's aging, dissipated cousin, Prince Jerome Napoleon, was given the fifteen-year-old daughter of Victor Emmanuel, Clothilde, in marriage.

THE WAR OF 1859 AND THE ACHIEVEMENT OF ITALIAN UNITY

By a combination of intrigues and Austrian blunders Cavour provoked Austria into invading Piedmont on April 29, 1859. The Austrian general delayed so long in pressing his attack that the French army, utilizing the recently completed railroads in France and Piedmont, had time to arrive on the scene. After a series of preliminary skirmishes, two bloody battles were fought at Magenta and Solferino in June and resulted in an Austrian retreat into the Quadrilateral, a group of fortresses in Venetia. At this point, on July 11, 1859, Napoleon III, who had personally led his troops into Italy, suddenly signed an armistice with the Austrian emperor at Villafranca without consulting his Italian allies. The terms of the armistice provided for Austria to cede Lombardy to France, which would then give it to Piedmont; Austria retained Venetia. It has been said that Napoleon negotiated the armistice because the carnage of battle had turned him against war. It is far more likely that his immediate motives were his fear that a prolonged siege of the Austrian forces might tempt Prussia to cause trouble on the Rhine, his increasing difficulties with the French

clerical party, and his fear of the growing force of Italian nationalism. In any event, Victor Emmanuel accepted the terms, but Cavour, who regarded Napoleon's action as a breach of trust, resigned his premiership in a rage.

Meanwhile events in central Italy had taken an unexpected turn beyond the control of the principal actors. Popular revolts broke out in Tuscany, Parma, Modena, and some of the States of the Church, where the insurgents drove out their former rulers and demanded union with Piedmont. In order to take advantage of this new development, Cavour returned as prime minister in January, 1860. In the Treaty of Turin on

March 24, 1860, he negotiated the annexation of the duchies, giving Napoleon Savoy and Nice as provided in the original agreement at Plombières. At this point another flamboyant character re-entered the scene. Garibaldi, who had played a prominent part in the military defense of the Roman Republic in 1849, began organizing his volunteer Red Shirt army in Genoa in order to take Nice, his birthplace, and hold it against the French. While formally denouncing Garibaldi, Cavour secretly persuaded him to move on Sicily instead, hoping to save himself embarrassment with the French and also to cause difficulty for the reactionary Francis II, king of Naples and Sicily.

Garibaldi landed in Sicily in May and succeeded beyond all expectation. Having no more than a thousand untrained volunteers but supported by popular uprisings against the hated Bourbons, he defeated an army of twenty thousand, conquered Sicily in less than three months, and crossed the Straits of Messina to the mainland south of Naples, which he took without a struggle. Garibaldi now planned to march on Rome and perhaps Venetia. At this Cavour became alarmed, fearing French intervention. He acted to head off this possibility by sending his own army across the remaining States of the Church, avoiding Rome itself, and thwarting Garibaldi's further progress. Plebiscites in Naples, Sicily, Umbria, and the Marches favored union with the north. On March 17, 1861, the first Italian parliament in history proclaimed the Kingdom of Italy, with Victor Emmanuel as king and a constitution based upon the Piedmontese *Statuto* of 1848.

Cavour, the architect and first prime minister of a united Italy, did not long enjoy his triumph. In June he died of exhaustion and overwork, leaving to his successors a host of unsolved problems. Prominent among them was the fate of Venetia, still governed by the Austrians, and the province of Rome, still ruled by the pope and occupied by the French. No less important were the financial and political problems of welding into a single nation the disparate parts of the Italian peninsula. Venetia fell to the Italians in 1866 in return for their participation in the Austro-Prussian War of that year. Rome was annexed after the defeat of Napoleon III in the Franco-Prussian War of 1870. The domestic political and financial problems, however, remained to plague succeeding governments in Italy throughout the remainder of the nineteenth and well into the twentieth century.

FOUNDATIONS OF GERMAN UNITY

Germany, like Italy, had not been a unified state in modern times. The Holy Roman Empire had grouped more than three hundred petty principalities into a loose confederation from the time of the Middle Ages, but the empire as such had no effective power. The French under Napoleon

The Italian Army Breaches the Walls of Rome, September 20, 1870
sketch from *The Illustrated London News*

"At 5 o'clock on the morning of the 20th instant, a cannonade was opened, two breaches were effected at half-past 8, and at 10 o'clock the Italian troops entered the city. . . . Those who reflect cannot but foresee that the establishment, in one and the same city, of a constitutional and excommunicated King by the side of an infallible Pope, of a Representative Parliament by the side of an absolute authority, of a liberty of the press and freedom of discussion by the side of the Inquisition . . . is giving a legal sanction to a state of things which can hardly be expected to work harmoniously, or, indeed, without creating very serious embarrassment, confusion, and misunderstandings." The British Representative in Rome to the Foreign Office, September 22, 1870, BRITISH AND FOREIGN STATE PAPERS, Vol. LXII.

---

overthrew the empire in 1806, incorporated the left bank of the Rhine and part of northwestern Germany into the French Empire, organized central Germany from the Baltic to the Alps as the Confederation of the Rhine under Napoleonic domination, pushed Austria to the east almost out of Germany, and left Prussia as a truncated buffer state in the shadow of Russia. Opposition to Napoleon and the French occasioned a national revival in Germany that in time focused on Prussia as the potential liberator of Germany. Many Germans hoped that the Congress of Vienna would create a unified German nation, but this aspiration ran counter to the interests of Austria and of Metternich, who feared a loss of Austrian influence in a unified Germany. Therefore the congress sanctioned the creation of the Germanic Confederation (*Deutscher Bund*) under the permanent presidency of Austria, which was composed of only thirty-eight in place of more than three hundred sovereign states but which in other respects was similar to the old Holy Roman Empire. (See p. 18.) The oppressive Metternichean system appeared to stifle German political development until 1848; but powerful forces were at work behind the drab facade.

INTELLECTUAL AND CULTURAL FOUNDATIONS

Romanticism greatly influenced German nationalism. Romantic poets, novelists, and composers stirred nationalist aspirations by evoking a heroic and largely nonexistent past and extolling the greatness of the German people – the *Volk*. Philosophers and literary critics attempted to show that Germanic culture was superior to others. Hegel sought to show by means of dialectical reasoning how unity might come out of disunity, how strength might result from weakness. Friedrich List emphasized the role of the state in economic affairs and tried to show that a unified nation could be created by appropriate economic policies.

Liberalism also influenced the idea of German nationalism. The west German bourgeoisie wanted both constitutional government and favorable economic policies. Since they had neither under the existing regime, they hoped for a unified national state that would provide both. Liberalism reached its height in the Frankfurt Assembly of 1848. The failure of that body to achieve unification or constitutional government resulted in a revulsion against liberalism, and many liberals turned in disillusion or frustration to the reactionary forces of militarism and power politics to achieve the goal of national unity.

ECONOMIC FOUNDATIONS

The German economy was poor and backward in the first half of the nineteenth century. Primarily agrarian, it had small concentrations of industry in the Rhineland, Saxony, Silesia, and the city of Berlin, but much of the industry was of the handicraft variety. Poor transportation and communications facilities held back economic development. Progress was further retarded by the numerous political divisions with their separate monetary systems, commercial systems, and other obstacles to commercial exchange. The revolutionary reforms introduced by the French under Napoleon, many of which were maintained after 1815, alleviated the situation, but they were insufficient in themselves and did not extend

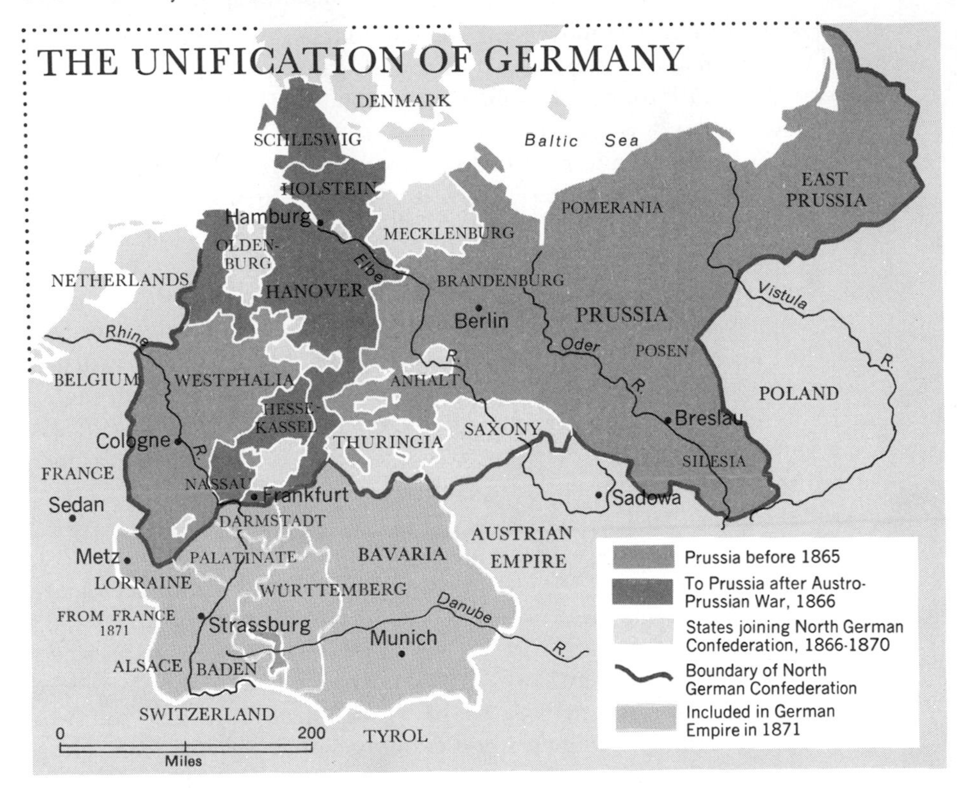

to the whole of Germany. Statesmen like Stein and Hardenberg, who came to power in Prussia after the disastrous defeat at Jena, recognized economic backwardness as one cause of their military and political weakness. They sought to reform Prussia as a means of strengthening the nation to resist the oppressor Napoleon. They abolished serfdom, relaxed restrictions on economic activity (of the Jews in particular), promoted freedom of occupational choice, and created so-called free trade in land by abolishing the distinctions between noble and non-noble land. These and other reforms promoted greater geographical and social mobility and led to a revival of economic activity.

The most important economic reform instigated by Prussian officials was the formation of the *Zollverein* (literally, tariff or customs union). They laid its foundations in 1818 by enacting a common tariff for all of Prussia, which after the Congress of Vienna had more internal tariff barriers than political subdivisions. Several smaller states, some of which were completely surrounded by Prussian territory, joined the Prussian tariff union, and in 1834 the adherence of the larger southern German states resulted in the creation of the Zollverein itself. Abolition of artificial restrictions on the movement of commodities by creation of a common German market, a forerunner of today's European Common Market, increased specialization and exchange and made a German economy possible before there was a German nation.

If the Zollverein made a unified economy possible, the railroads made it a fact. When railroads were introduced in the 1830's all the German states begain building them more or less simultaneously, some by means of private enterprise, others by state initiative. As a result, Germany made relatively rapid progress in railroad building – more so, for example, than France, which had a unified government but was divided over the question of state versus private enterprise. To construct the railroads also required the states to agree upon routes, rates, and other technical matters, resulting in greater interstate cooperation. The linking of east and west by the railroads facilitated an exchange of ideas as well as merchandise and broke down local loyalties in favor of a greater German nationalism.

Taking advantage of the favorable opportunities presented by the Zollverein and the railroads, German businessmen created a number of new banks and industrial enterprises, especially in the 1850's and 1860's. They engaged in Germany-wide as well as international activities. For example, the Darmstädter Bank was founded in 1853 in the sleepy provincial capital of the small state of Hesse-Darmstadt, just south of Frankfurt, because its founders could not secure a charter from either the free city of Frankfurt or the Prussian authorities in Cologne, the two economic centers of western Germany. Nevertheless, it operated on a much wider stage than the petty state from which it had received its charter. It raised money in Paris and promoted industry – iron and steel mills, coal mines, and railroads – throughout Germany. Other banks founded on its model did likewise. Their activities contributed to the establishment of economic unification well in advance of political unity.

PRUSSIAN POLICY AND THE RISE OF BISMARCK

By the middle of the nineteenth century the way had been prepared for the eventual unification of Germany. Two large questions remained: Who would bring it about? What form would it take? The questions were essentially political, and they had several possible solutions. The liberal solution called for a centralized, parliamentary government, which might be either republican or monarchic. It had been attempted by the Frankfurt Assembly of 1848 and 1849 but had been defeated by the resurgence of conservatism.

The Prussian king, who was unwilling to accept the crown from the Frankfurt Assembly, had his own ideas for uniting Germany under Prussian hegemony. His plan, which resembled the *Kleindeutsch* or little Germany proposal, called for a federal union of the German states (except

Austria) under his presidency as king of Prussia. This proposal was put forward in 1849, and a draft constitution was ratified by representatives of a number of the smaller states at Erfurt in March, 1850. Immediately it encountered opposition from Austria, which reconstituted the Diet of the old Germanic Confederation and vied for the adherence of the smaller states. War between Prussia and Austria appeared imminent. Since the south German states favored the looser confederation projected by Austria, and the Russian tsar was threatening to take the side of Austria, the Prussian king sent his principal minister to Olmütz in November, 1850, to negotiate a strategic withdrawal. At the so-called humiliation of Olmütz the Prussians agreed to dissolve the Erfurt Union and recognize the reestablished Germanic Confederation under the presidency of Austria. Thus the situation that had existed before 1848 was substantially reestablished, and the question of further unification seemed to be postponed indefinitely.

The general political reaction that took place throughout Europe after 1848 was particularly marked in Prussia. Although the Prussian king had granted an apparently democratic constitution to his subjects after the revolution of 1848, he continued to exercise a large measure of autocratic authority. Instead of evolving in a liberal sense, as did the authoritarian government of Napoleon III, the Prussian constitutional system actually became more reactionary.

In 1857 Frederick William IV, who had always been mentally unstable, went insane. His brother, Prince William, became regent in 1858 and ascended the throne in 1861. By training a professional soldier, William I had the military man's devotion to duty but also his lack of understanding of and impatience with the intricacies of politics and civilian government. Austria's defeat in the War of 1859 provided Prussia with an opportunity to take a larger role in German affairs, but it was not prepared either diplomatically or militarily to assert itself vigorously. To remedy the latter deficiency, William's newly appointed minister of war, General von Roon, and the chief of the general staff, General von Moltke, undertook to modernize and enlarge the Prussian army. In doing so, they ran into opposition from liberals in the *Landtag* (lower house of Parliament), who feared the army as an instrument of reaction and oppression and who had no desire to pay the increased taxes that the army reforms would require. For more than two years they held the government at an impasse, refusing to vote the needed credits. At length in 1862, when William was on the point of abdication, von Roon persuaded him to bring Otto von Bismarck into the government.

Bismarck was a Junker, one of the aristocratic landowners from the area east of the Elbe River who formed the backbone of the Prussian officer corps and civil service. During the Frankfurt Assembly of 1848 he conceived a strong dislike for the parliamentary maneuvering of the bourgeois liberals. From 1851 to 1859 he served as Prussia's representative at the Diet of the Germanic Confederation, where he took the measure of Austrian diplomacy. In 1859 he went to St. Petersburg as ambassador to the tsar, and in 1862 he served briefly as ambassador to France before being recalled to become minister-president (prime minister) of the Prussian cabinet. An outspoken conservative and a man of indomitable will, Bismarck was also a master practitioner of *Realpolitik,* the politics of realism; indeed, it was he who gave currency to the word. Speaking to a committee of the Prussian Diet, he furnished the key to his personality and policy: "The great questions of the day will not be decided by speeches and majority votes – that was the mistake of 1848 and 1849 – but by blood and iron." When the Diet again refused to vote the necessary taxes, Bismarck simply ignored it and proceeded to collect and spend the money in defiance of the parliamentarians.

Bismarck was not a conventional German nationalist but a Prussian patriot. Far from dreaming of a greater German fatherland, he merely wanted to enhance the prestige and power of Prussia. To do so, he realized that he would have to diminish the influence of Austria and win the support of the smaller German states. He therefore took every opportunity to prick Austrian sensibilities and at the same time shrewdly courted the favor of those (including many liberals) who desired a united Germany. A prize occasion for doing both was the revival of the Danish question, which had so disastrously disrupted the German liberal movement in 1848.

THE DANISH WAR OF 1864

The duchies of Schleswig and Holstein belonged to the king of Denmark as his personal hereditary possessions, although both were populated largely by Germans and Holstein was a member of the Germanic Confederation. An attempt by the Danish king to incorporate Schleswig with Denmark and to impose a new charter on Holstein aroused German nationalists and led to a call for intervention by the federal Diet. Bismarck did not feel strong enough to act alone and persuaded Austria to join Prussia in an invasion of the duchies. The war, which ended quickly in the complete defeat of Denmark, furthered Bismarck's aims in three main ways. First, it gave the reformed Prussian army a baptism of fire, in which it proved itself an efficient fighting force. Second, it enhanced the prestige of Prussia with German nationalists. Third, it provided abundant opportunities for Prussia to pick further quarrels with Austria. In the Treaty of Vienna of 1864 Denmark ceded the disputed duchies to Austria and Prussia jointly. Under the Convention of Gastein in the following year the two powers agreed to maintain joint sovereignty, but Prussia was to occupy and administer Schleswig, whereas Austria was to do the same with Holstein. Thus, Austria-dominated Holstein became virtually an enclave in Prussian territory, with Vienna hundreds of miles away.

Meanwhile, Bismarck had made sure of his international position. He won the friendship of the Russian tsar by supporting the latter's suppression of the Polish rebellion of 1863. In 1865 Bismarck visited Napoleon III and hinted at possible French territorial gains in the Rhineland in the event of a war between Prussia and Austria in which the former was victorious. Finally in April, 1866, Prussia concluded an alliance with Italy, to take effect in case of war with Austria within three months; the prize for Italy was to be the cession of Venetia. The stage was now set. All that remained was to provoke Austria into war.

THE AUSTRO-PRUSSIAN WAR OF 1866

The provocation was easily arranged as a result of the difficulties in Schleswig and Holstein. Bismarck ordered Prussian troops into Holstein, and Austria persuaded the Diet of Confederation to declare Prussia an aggressor. Bismarck thereupon announced that the federal constitution had been violated and declared the Confederation dissolved. Since most of the German states took the side of Austria, the odds appeared heavily weighted against Prussia. But Prussia was prepared, and the others were not. Prussia's modernized army used new breech-loading rifles, called needle guns because the firing pin had a long needlelike point, whereas Austrian troops still relied on old-fashioned muzzle-loading muskets. The German general staff made effective use of railroads and the telegraph for quick deployment of troops. The campaign, known as the Seven Weeks' War, was a forerunner of the German blitzkriegs (lightning wars) of World War II. The federal Diet voted condemnation of Prussia on June 14, 1866. Before the end of June Prussian troops had overrun Hanover, Austria's chief northern ally, and turned against the south German states. The major campaign took place in Bohemia between Austria and Prussia. Using the railroads, three separate Prussian armies converged on the main concentration of Austrian troops, and on July 3 at Königgrätz (Sadowa) they won a crushing victory.

This sudden outcome surprised all Europe. Napoleon, who had expected a long war from which France would benefit, offered his services as mediator, but Bismarck outmaneuvered him. Although William I and the Prussian general staff favored marching to Vienna, Bismarck insisted on a quick armistice and lenient treatment for Austria, both to forestall the possibility of French intervention and to soothe injured Austrian pride. Austria had to give up Venetia to Prussia's ally Italy (which ironically had been defeated on both land and sea) and pay an indemnity to Prussia, but otherwise it suffered no territorial losses. Prussia incorporated Hanover, Hesse-Cassel, Nassau, and Frankfurt in addition to Schleswig and Holstein, and received a free hand to reorganize the remainder of the north German states. These provisions were contained in the Treaty of Prague, August 23, 1866.

Triumph in the field vindicated Bismarck's policy on the domestic front. In a patriotic frenzy the Prussian Diet voted overwhelmingly to legalize the government's past expenditures on the army and to allow increased funds for the future. The action split the Prussian liberals for two generations, with the majority supporting Bismarck in the newly formed National Liberal party and condemning the minority of Progressives to increasingly ineffectual protest. German liberalism, a fragile flower at best, virtually withered on the stem.

THE CLASH OF POWER IN NORTH AMERICA

The willingness to use force in the settlement of disputes did not pertain to Europe alone. The United States had led the way in its war of conquest against Mexico from 1846 to 1848. In 1854 the American ministers to the principal European nations met in Ostend, Belgium, and declared that if Spain refused to sell Cuba, the United States would be justified in taking it by force. The Ostend Manifesto startled Europeans and also many Americans, for slavery was practiced in Cuba as well as in the southern states, and most northerners had no wish to see slavery extended. This fact made the Ostend Manifesto meaningless, and foreshadowed the impending struggle between slave states and free states in the American Civil War.

CIVIL WAR IN THE UNITED STATES

The causes of the Civil War were manifold and complex. They were rooted in the divergent economic and social development of North and South. Slavery was doomed to extinction in the United States until Eli Whitney's invention of the cotton gin and the burgeoning cotton industry in England gave it new life. Southern plantation owners found a buoyant and expanding market for cotton overseas, and the spread of cotton culture in the Gulf coastal plain entailed the spread of slavery. The North, meanwhile, began to develop manufacturing industry based on free labor.

The settlement of the Ohio Valley and the Old Northwest, chiefly by migrants from the Northeast, did not involve the question of slavery. Expansion into the trans-Mississippi West, however, brought the rival social systems into direct competition. In the Missouri Compromise of 1820 Missouri was admitted without restrictions as to slavery, but thereafter all portions of the Louisiana Purchase north of latitude 36°30′ (the southern boundary of Missouri) were to be free of slavery. The acquisition of Texas and the New Mexico territory and the admission of California to the Union in 1850 again raised the question of the extension of slavery. The Kansas-Nebraska Act of 1854, which established the doctrine of popular sovereignty, and the decision of the Supreme Court in the Dred Scott case in 1857, which declared the Missouri Compromise unconstitutional, further inflamed the issue. It came to a head in the presidential election of 1860.

The Republicans nominated Abraham Lincoln and campaigned on a platform opposing the extension of slavery and favoring a homestead law and a protective tariff, all of which were anathema to the South. Lincoln did not obtain a single electoral vote in the slave-holding states; but since the Democratic party split into two factions, North and South, and the border states formed yet another party, the Constitutional Union party, a Republican victory was assured. South Carolina seceded from the Union immediately after the election. By the time Lincoln assumed office, a number of other southern states had also seceded and had joined in the Confederate States of America. When the commander of the federal garrison of Fort Sumter in the Charleston harbor refused to surrender it to South Carolina in April, 1861, a Confederate army bombarded it. The Civil War had begun.

The North had an enormous advantage over the South with more than twice the population, a more highly developed transportation system, flourishing manufacturing industries, organized military forces, and an established civil administration. Nevertheless, Northern expectations of a quick victory were disappointed by inadequate planning, military blunders, and determined Southern resistance. The South was fortunate in obtaining as commander in chief of its forces General Robert E. Lee, a Virginian who resigned his commission in the Union Army to accept the position. The North was plagued by a succession of incompetent or politically minded generals until 1864, when Lincoln selected Ulysses S. Grant as commander in chief on the basis of his brilliant campaigns in the Mississippi Valley. By this time the South was approaching complete exhaustion. The Union blockade cut off its exports of cotton and imports of war supplies, while campaigns in the West split off Texas, Louisiana, and Arkansas and hemmed in the remaining Southern states. Grant finally surrounded the main Confederate army in Virginia, and Lee surrendered at Appomattox Courthouse on April 9, 1865.

The assassination of Lincoln just five days after Lee's surrender and the disputes between Congress and Lincoln's successor, Andrew Johnson, cost the nation the opportunity for a rapid and equitable reconciliation of North and South. Lincoln had proclaimed the emancipation of slaves on January 1, 1863, which was subsequently ratified by the Thirteenth Amendment to the Constitution. Determined to press its advantage in controlling the future development of the nation, the radical Republican majority in Congress imposed harsh measures of reconstruction on the vanquished southern states, which poisoned relations between North and South and retarded the political, social, and economic development of the latter for many years.

Westward expansion continued during and after the war years. The first transcontinental railroad was chartered by Congress with liberal grants of federal land in 1862 and was completed in 1869. The rapid spread of settlement that ensued brought renewed conflicts with the Indians, who were subdued by federal troops and placed on reservations.

INTERVENTION IN MEXICO

Shortly before the American Civil War another civil war, the equivalent of a social revolution, broke out in Mexico. The liberal faction under Benito Juarez (1806–1872) overthrew the dictator Santa Anna and undertook a large program of political, social, and religious reform. Napoleon III, seeking clerical support at home, new glory for the empire, and reconciliation with Austria over its loss of Lombardy, sent a French expeditionary force to aid the conservative opponents of Juarez and induced Maximilian of Austria, former viceroy of the Lombard-Venetian kingdom, to accept the throne of a Mexican empire under French protection. After a prolonged campaign in 1863 French forces occupied Mexico City, where Maximilian took up residence in the following year. Although the French action clearly violated the Monroe Doctrine, the United States's involvement in its own civil war prevented any immediate active response. The United States had earlier recognized the Juarez government, however, and as soon as circumstances permitted, it began to make energetic protests to France. Because of his precarious position in Europe after the Austro-Prussian War, Napoleon decided to withdraw in 1867. Juarez captured and executed Maximilian shortly afterward, thus ending Europe's last serious attempt at armed intervention in the New World.

CONFEDERATION IN CANADA

The Union Act of 1840, which united Upper and Lower Canada (see p. 40), did not fully meet the need for self-government. Difficulties and disputes over border questions continued to flare between the French-speaking and British inhabitants of Canada, between Canada and Britain, between Canada and the United States, and between Britain and the United States. Fortunately they were all settled without recourse to arms. In 1867 the British North American Act gave complete self-government to Canada. It provided for a federation of the provinces of Quebec, Ontario, New Brunswick, and Nova Scotia in the Dominion of Canada. Each province retained its provincial government with certain specified rights. With the example of the United States before it, however, the act provided that all rights not specifically conferred upon the provinces remained with the Dominion government. The latter consisted of a bicameral parliament, a responsible cabinet, and a governor-general with only nominal powers as representative of the British crown. In 1869 the Dominion purchased the Northwest Territories from the Hudson's Bay Company, and in subsequent years it admitted new provinces on a basis of equality with the old. By achieving consolidation and expansion without resorting to force, Canada was an exception to the rule.

THE WATERSHED OF 1867–1871

The changes in the map and temper of Europe after 1848 seemed to have no clearly defined pattern or direction before 1866. Until then they were subject to reversal. The outcome of the Austro-Prussian War, however, had a definitive stamp. In the next four years further major changes fixed the framework of European politics and diplomacy until 1914.

One consequence of the Austro-Prussian War was a fundamental reorganization of the Austrian Empire, known thereafter as the Austro-Hungarian Empire or Dual Monarchy. Another was the creation of the North German Confederation, the forerunner of a larger German Empire, under the domination of Bismarck and Prussia. Italy, enlarged by the addition of Venetia, now needed only Rome to complete its unification. Bismarck's skillful diplomacy and Napoleon's own foreign policy blunders (such as the ill-advised campaign in Mexico) served to isolate France diplomatically. Although Britain held aloof from European affairs, it, too, witnessed important domestic changes in the direction of greater democratization. The smaller states also underwent changes, and some became pawns in the game of great power politics.

THE SPANISH REVOLUTION OF 1868

After the death of Ferdinand VII in 1833 the nominal Spanish ruler was his daughter, Isabella II. (See p. 52.) Actually, control of the government alternated between rival and shifting alliances of ambitious generals and corrupt politicians. Isabella's own behavior contributed to the scandalous reputation of the court and the discredit of the government. Although a few railroads were built after 1848 and commerce and industry picked up somewhat through the initiative of foreign entrepreneurs, the lot of the people remained as miserable as ever. At length, in 1868, a rising of disaffected army officers led by General Juan Prim won the support of the masses, and the queen fled the country. A provisional government established universal manhood suffrage, promulgated a liberal constitution, and began a long and futile search for a suitable constitutional monarch. In the process the Spanish inadvertently provided an incident that served as one of the causes of the Franco-Prussian War. At the end of 1870 the Spanish persuaded Amadeo I, younger son of

Victor Emmanuel of Italy, to accept the throne. After two years of well-intentioned but continually frustrated struggles, Amadeo abdicated in disgust and returned to Italy, leaving the Spanish situation more confused than ever. After a brief attempt at republican government, followed by further civil wars, a conservative coup d'état in 1874 reestablished the Bourbon monarchy in the person of Isabella's son, Alfonso XII.

THE NORTH GERMAN CONFEDERATION

Meanwhile Bismarck undertook his reorganization of northern Germany. Since Prussia had already absorbed the largest of the other north German states except Saxony, the task was relatively simple. The constitution of 1867, which later served as the basis of the constitution of the German Empire, provided that the presidency of the confederation should be hereditary with the king of Prussia. The only other constitutional official was the chancellor (Bismarck), responsible to the king alone. To give the new regime the trappings of democracy Bismarck allowed a legislature, the *Reichstag,* elected by universal suffrage but with strictly limited powers. As a further check on the popular will the constitution provided for a kind of upper chamber, the *Bundesrat,* composed of the personal representatives of the various sovereign princes, but with their representation arranged in such a way that Prussia could always command a majority. The twenty-two component states retained autonomy in domestic matters, but foreign relations and military affairs were the exclusive province of the king acting through his chancellor.

By this time Bismarck was determined to unify Germany completely – excluding Austria – under Prussian auspices. Constitutionally the incorporation of the four states south of the Main River seemed to be an easy matter, since the framework already existed, but politically it was necessary to overcome the antipathy of the Catholic populations of southern Germany to Protestant Prussia, and to balk Napoleon's certain opposition to a strong, united Germany. The Danish War, by putting Prussia in the role of protector of German interests, helped break down southern as well as northern provincialism. This work was continued by the rabidly patriotic *Nationalverein* (National Society). The Austrian War, by excluding Austria from participation in German affairs, forced the southern states into an unwilling alliance with Prussia and left them with no other champion but France. Bismarck realized that the final resolution of the question would depend upon a successful war with France.

BISMARCK AND NAPOLEON

Bismarck had already made use of Napoleon's susceptibility to flattery and vague promises at the time of the Austro-Prussian War, when he dropped hints about allowing France "compensation" in the form of an extension of the French borders in the Rhineland. The sudden conclusion of the war and Bismarck's skillful maneuvering deprived Napoleon of any gain. He subsequently sought to salve his own and France's injured pride by annexing Luxembourg and Belgium. In both cases his diplomatic blunders and Bismarck's skill resulted in further humiliation.

Napoleon no less than Bismarck now regarded war as inevitable. Feverishly he sought to build alliances, but to no avail. Austria was clearly in no position to take the field again so soon; in any case, the Hungarians, who now shared power in the empire, would hear none of it. Italy was equally beholden to France and Prussia for previous gains but the French alone stood in the way of complete unification by their continued occupation of Rome. Bismarck also assured himself of the good will of Russia, and by communicating word of Napoleon's designs on Belgium to Britain, he effectively forestalled any sympathy for France in that quarter.

At this point the vacant Spanish throne played a part in Franco-Prussian relations. Prince Leopold of Hohenzollern-Sigmaringen, a relative of King William of Prussia, had been offered the Spanish crown but refused it on William's advice in deference to the sensibilities of Napoleon. In the spring of 1870 Bismarck engineered a renewal of the offer for the express purpose of embarrassing France. When news of the offer leaked out, the new and inexperienced French cabinet of the parliamentary empire reacted violently and demanded an immediate withdrawal of the prince's candidacy. Not content with obtaining this, the French sought a formal letter of apology from the Prussian king to Napoleon. The French ambassador presented the request to King William at the resort town of Ems. The king refused politely but firmly and sent Bismarck in Berlin a telegram detailing the affair. Eager to provoke France, Bismarck edited the telegram so as to make it appear to be a new insult to France and leaked it to the press.

THE FRANCO-PRUSSIAN WAR

Immediately upon publication of the famous "Ems dispatch," the French government decided upon war. It made a formal declaration on July 19, 1870. Napoleon was beset by doubt and hesitation, but his cabinet and the French populace in general went to war almost joyfully, expecting an easy victory. They did not realize the extent of inefficiency and demoralization in the French high command, nor did they take account of the fact that the Prussian general staff, with the Danish and Austrian experience behind it, had been planning this war for almost three years.

Three German armies invaded France simultaneously over the northeastern frontier and quickly got behind the main French forces, cutting their supply lines. They besieged one large French army in the fortress of Metz and surrounded another at Sedan near the Belgian frontier. Napoleon, physically ill and emotionally disturbed, had nevertheless insisted

Radio Times Hulton Picture Library

The Proclamation of the Kaiser, by Anton von Werner
Versailles, January 18, 1871, after the defeat of France

"I was convinced that the gulf which in the course of history had opened between north and south in our country because of differences in ways of life and dynastic and tribal loyalties could not be more effectively bridged than through a common national war against the traditionally aggressive neighbor."
Bismarck quoted in O. Pflanze, BISMARCK AND THE DEVELOPMENT OF GERMANY (Princeton, 1963).

---

on leading personally the army at Sedan. On September 2, 1870, after two days of merciless bombardment, Napoleon capitulated with 100,000 men.

When news of the event reached Paris, mobs from the streets invaded the legislature and demanded the overthrow of the empire. In accordance with well-established ritual a provisional government was formed. It proclaimed the Third Republic at the Paris city hall on September 4, 1870. Called the "Government of National Defense," it fought valiantly but in a hopeless cause. Most of the standing army surrendered meekly, and the raw recruits and untrained officers who fought on were no match for the Prussian army. Paris itself, which had been besieged by two Prussian armies since mid-September, surrendered on January 28, 1871, by which time resistance in the provinces had also collapsed. The Treaty of Frankfurt of May 10, 1871, required the French to give up Alsace and a part of

Lorraine, pay an indemnity of five billion francs, and maintain a German army of occupation until the indemnity was acquitted.

In the meantime Bismarck had carried out his aim of making the Prussian king ruler of all Germany. The French declaration of war forced the southern German states to fight on the side of Prussia, and the success of German arms in the field stimulated a popular demand for the union of northern and southern Germany. Bismarck negotiated with the German princes for them to proclaim William I emperor of Germany on January 18, 1871. With a keen but ironic sense of history, Bismarck staged this performance in the famous Hall of Mirrors in the palace at Versailles, where in former times other German princes had paid court to Louis XIV of France.

THE TRIUMPH OF REALPOLITIK

In less than two decades the map of central Europe had been redrawn almost completely. In France an empire rose and fell, and as it fell, a new one arose in united Germany. Italy took advantage of the withdrawal of French troops from Rome to replace them with its own and make Rome the capital of united Italy. The Austrians, driven from Germany and forced to share their power with the proud Magyars of Hungary, looked southeastward to the Balkans for further expansion. All these changes had been achieved by Realpolitik and the naked use of force, aided by the inflamed passions of popular nationalism.

In some respects the new balance of power was better than the old. For more than forty years it maintained the peace (except for minor peripheral conflicts), the longest period of general peace in European history. It was a period of unparalleled economic prosperity and apparent social progress. Yet the foundations of the new era contained a fatal defect. It had been created by force, and it had to be maintained by force; it was the era of the "armed peace." Eventually the foundations cracked, and Europe experienced a new and greater holocaust.

THE SPREAD OF MODERN INDUSTRY CHAPTER SEVEN

A quarter century elapsed between the Crystal Palace Exhibition in London in 1851, the first international industrial fair, and the Philadelphia Centennial Exposition in 1876, America's first "world's fair." During that period several nations joined Britain in the ranks of industrial societies. The Philadelphia event constituted a sort of declaration of American industrial independence from Britain a century after political independence, although the United States continued to import British capital. French industrialization, which made slow progress before 1848, speeded up dramatically under the Second Empire. Belgium, which began its rapid industrialization in the 1830's soon after winning political independence, was by 1870 the most highly industrialized nation on the Continent. Germany, Switzerland, and the Netherlands had all begun the process of industrialization and in a few other countries signs of strain in the traditional agrarian framework of society were beginning to show. Nevertheless, Britain remained far and away the world's leading industrial nation.

By the beginning of the twentieth century the picture had changed radically. The United States, Germany, and France had all risen to challenge and in some cases to surpass British supremacy. The smaller nations of western Europe – the Scandinavian countries as well as Switzerland and the Low Countries – had modern progressive industries. In eastern Europe even autocratic Russia entered upon a sort of industrial revolution under tsarist auspices. Everywhere in Europe the old traditional society was giving way to the new social forces unleashed by modern industry.

In most respects the process of industrialization in the second half of the nineteenth century represented an intensification and geographical diffusion of earlier tendencies and produced similar consequences. At the same time it had certain distinctive characteristics that have led some historians to call it the "new industrialism."

TECHNOLOGICAL BASES OF THE NEW INDUSTRIALISM

Industrialization before 1850 was confined chiefly to coal, iron, and textiles, with steam engines supplying the motive power. Factory methods and new technologies gradually penetrated to other industries, but even in Britain much so-called manufacturing still took place under the putting-out (domestic) system or in small workshops with little or no mechanical power. As technology became increasingly scientific in the second half of the century — that is, based upon the findings as well as the methods of science — the flow of technical innovations quickened dramatically. New industries arose, existing industries adopted new techniques, the factory system spread, and an ever-larger proportion of an increasing population became involved in the industrial system.

CHEAP STEEL

Among the most important if not most dramatic technological innovations of the second half of the century were new methods for making steel. Actually a special variety of iron, steel had been made for many centuries but in small quantities at high cost. As a result, its use was limited to such quality products as watch springs, surgical instruments, and fine cutlery. In 1856 Henry Bessemer, an English inventor, announced a new method for producing steel directly from molten iron, eliminating the puddling process and yielding a product harder and more durable than puddled iron. The output of Bessemer steel increased rapidly and soon displaced ordinary iron in a variety of uses. The Bessemer process did not always yield a uniformly high grade of steel, however, and could not be used with phosphorus-bearing iron ores. To remedy the former defect a father-and-son team of French metallurgists, Pierre and Émile Martin, and the Siemens brothers, Ernst in Germany and William in England, developed in the 1860's the "open hearth," or Siemens-Martin, furnace. In 1878 two English cousins, Thomas and Gilchrist, patented a process to permit the use of the plentiful phosphorus-bearing iron ores. As a result of these and other innovations, the annual world production of steel rose from less than half a million tons in 1865 to more than fifty million tons on the eve of World War I.

The expansion of the steel industry had a profound impact on other industries, both those that supplied the steel industry (such as coal) and those that used steel. Steel rails for railroads lasted longer and provided greater safety than iron ones. Steel plates for shipbuilding resulted in

Courtesy of the United States Navy

H.M.S. *Dreadnaught*

"From a very early period I had become deeply impressed with the importance of the application of my new steel to shipbuilding, and my first impulse was naturally to try and force my own conviction on the British Admiralty, and induce them to employ it in the construction of ships of war. But the remembrance of my treatment at Woolich [army arsenal] came upon me as a warning. . . . This experience determined me not to be foiled a second time by attempting to convince the 'How-not-to-do-it' Government official. I therefore preferred to await the more certain and reliable action of mercantile instinct. Private shipbuilders, I had no doubt, would soon find out the merits of steel, and feel a personal interest in its adoption." SIR HENRY BESSEMER, F.R.S. AN AUTOBIOGRAPHY (London, 1905).

---

larger, lighter, faster ships and could also be used as heavy armor for warships. The use of steel beams and girders made it possible to build skyscrapers and a variety of other structures. Steel replaced iron and wood in tools, toys, and hundreds of other products ranging from steam engines to hairpins.

NEW ENERGY SOURCES AND PRIME MOVERS

Steam remained the major source of mechanical energy throughout the nineteenth century, but new forms of power developed to supplement and in some cases to replace it. The steam engine itself underwent further developments, which made it a more powerful and efficient prime mover. In 1884 Charles Parsons, a British engineer, patented the steam turbine, which found its principal uses in driving ocean liners and warships and in generating electricity. The early reciprocating steam engines built by James Watt developed between 10 and 25 horsepower; in the 1860's large compound marine engines produced more than 1,000 horsepower; in the early twentieth century huge steam turbines could generate more than 100,000 horsepower.

The steam turbine applied the expansive powers of steam to the principle of the hydraulic turbine, which had been perfected by French engineers in the 1820's and 1830's. The hydraulic turbine had first been used in various milling operations as a more efficient substitute for its ancestor, the old-fashioned water wheel. It soon came to have a more exalted use in the production of electricity. The possibility of generating electricity mechanically had been known since the decisive experiments of Faraday with electromagnetism in 1831 (see p. 134), but no economically feasible means of generating power in large quantities had been discovered. In 1873 a paper maker in southeastern France attached his turbine, which drew water from the Alps, to a dynamo for the production of electricity. This apparently simple innovation had important long-range consequences, for it enabled regions poor in coal but rich in waterpower to supply their own energy requirements. The invention of the Parsons steam turbine in the following decade freed the generation of electricity from waterpower sites and shifted the energy balance back toward coal and steam, which remain today the most important sources of electrical energy. Nevertheless, the development of hydroelectric power became tremendously important for countries previously in the backwaters of industrial development, such as Norway, Sweden, Switzerland, and Italy.

Contemporaneously a host of practical applications for electricity were developed. Electricity had been used in the new electroplating industry and in telegraphy from the 1840's. Lighthouses began to utilize electric arc lamps in the late 1850's, and by the 1870's they were being used in a number of factories, stores, theaters, and public buildings. The perfection of the incandescent electric lamp between 1878 and 1880 almost simultaneously by Joseph Swan in England and Thomas Edison in the United States made arc lighting obsolete and inaugurated a boom in the electrical industry. For several decades electricity competed hotly with two other recently perfected illuminants, coal gas and kerosene.

Electricity had many uses other than illumination. It is one of the most versatile sources of power available to man. In 1879, the same year that Edison patented his electric lamp, another of the Siemens brothers invented the electric streetcar, which had revolutionary consequences for mass transportation in the burgeoning metropolises of the time. Within a few years electric motors had found dozens of industrial applications, and inventors were even beginning to think of household appliances.

Petroleum is another major energy source that came into prominence in the second half of the nineteenth century. Although it was known and used earlier through accidental discoveries, its commercial exploitation began with the drilling of Drake's well at Titusville, Pennsylvania, in 1859. Like electricity, liquid petroleum and its byproduct, natural gas, were at first used primarily as illuminants. Concurrently with their growth in production, several French and German inventors perfected the internal combustion engine. By 1900 a variety of such engines were available, most of which used as fuel one of the several distillates of liquid petroleum, such as gasoline or diesel oil. By far the most important use for the internal combustion engine was in light transport facilities, such as automobiles, motor trucks, and busses, but it also had industrial applications and made possible the development of the airplane in the twentieth century. Apart from its use in engines, petroleum competed with traditional energy sources in household and industrial heating.

THE APPLICATION OF SCIENCE

All of these developments relied much more than earlier technological innovations on the application of science to industrial processes. The electrical industry in particular required a high degree of scientific knowledge and training. In other industries scientific advance became more and more the prerequisite of technological advance.

The science of chemistry proved especially prolific in giving birth to new products and processes. It had already created artificial soda, sulfuric acid, chlorine, and a number of other heavy chemicals of particular importance in the textile industry. While seeking a synthetic substitute for quinine in 1856, William Perkin, an English chemist, accidentally synthesized mauve, a highly prized purple dye. This was the beginning of the synthetic dyestuffs industry, which within two decades had practically driven natural dyestuffs off the market. Synthetic dyestuffs proved to be the opening wedge of a much larger complex of organic chemical industries, whose output included such diverse products as drugs and pharmaceuticals, explosives, photographic reagents, and synthetic fibers. Coal tar, a byproduct of the coking process previously regarded as a costly nuisance, served as the principal raw material for these industries, thus turning a bane into a blessing.

Chemistry also played a vital role in metallurgy. In the early nineteenth century the only economically important metals were those known from antiquity: iron, copper, lead, zinc, tin, mercury, gold, and silver. After the chemical revolution associated with Antoine Lavoisier, the great French chemist of the eighteenth century, many new metals including aluminum, nickel, magnesium, and chromium were discovered. In addition to discovering them, scientists and industrialists found uses for these new metals and devise economical methods of producing them. One major use was in making alloys, a mixture of two or more metals that has characteristics different from those of its components. Brass and bronze are examples of natural alloys (which occur in nature). Steel itself is actually an alloy of iron with a small amount of carbon and sometimes other metals. In the second half of the nineteenth century metallurgists devised many special "alloy steels" by adding small amounts of manganese, tungsten, vanadium, etc., to impart specially desired qualities to ordinary steel. They also developed a number of nonferrous alloys.

Chemistry likewise came to the aid of such old, established industries as food processing and preservation. Canning and artificial refrigeration produced a revolution in dietary habits and, by permitting the importation of otherwise perishable foodstuffs from the New World and Australia, allowed Europe's population to grow far beyond what its own agricultural resources would support. At the same time the scientific study of the soil that was initiated in Germany in the 1840's led to greatly improved agricultural practices and the introduction of artificial fertilizers. Scientific agriculture developed along with scientific industry.

THE REVOLUTION IN COMMUNICATIONS

The nineteenth century witnessed a marked acceleration in the tempo of human life resulting from major innovations in the field of communications. The railroad and steamship inaugurated the process. Their major contribution was the increased volume and reduced cost of transportation. The most important innovation affecting the speed of communications was the electric telegraph, developed to a practical stage in the 1840's. By 1850 most major cities of Europe had been linked by telegraph wires, and in 1851 the first successful submarine telegraph cable was laid under the English Channel. In 1866, after ten years of trying and several failures, Cyrus W. Field succeeded in laying a telegraph cable under the North Atlantic Ocean, providing nearly instantaneous communication between Europe and North America. The telephone, patented by Alexander Graham Bell in 1876, made distant communication even more personal, but its principal use was in facilitating local communications.

In the area of mass communications improvements in printing and typesetting culminated in the Linotype machine, invented by the German-American Ottmar Mergenthaler in 1885, further extending the influence of the daily newspaper. One of America's great inventive geniuses, Thomas Edison, invented both the phonograph (1877) and the motion picture camera (1887). The Italian inventor Guglielmo Marconi invented wireless telegraphy or radio in 1895. As early as 1901 a wireless message was transmitted across the Atlantic, and by the time of the *Titanic* disaster in 1912 radio had come to play a significant role in ocean navigation. With the exception of mechanical typesetting, however, these innovations did not achieve commercial importance until after World War I. Their true significance was more cultural than economic. In the field of business communications the invention of the typewriter (Sholes patent, 1868; "Model I Remington," 1874) and other rudimentary business machines helped busy executives keep up with and contribute to the increasing flow of information that their large-scale operations and worldwide activities made necessary.

BUSINESS ORGANIZATION AND THE WORLD MARKET SYSTEM

The technological innovations discussed above, in addition to increasing the productivity of human labor and the range of products available to consumers, brought about significant changes in the organization of production and trade and posed important problems of public policy. In order to take advantage of the new methods of steel-making, power production, and other innovations, industrial firms had to operate on a much larger scale. This, in turn, required new legal forms of business organization to attract the necessary capital and technical skills. The new large-scale units undermined the individualistic basis of the economy and threatened to establish a new hierarchic order of society.

At the same time, the search for new sources of raw materials and new outlets for the products of expanding industries brought the whole world into the market system of Western economy. This expansion, together with the nationalist spirit of the times, frequently led Western nations to the brink of conflict with one another and to the extension of direct or indirect political as well as economic control over non-Western areas.

CORPORATIONS, CARTELS, AND TRUSTS

The expression "business organization" is frequently used in two different senses: functional and legal. Manufacturing establishments may be classified functionally according to whether they adopt the domestic (putting-out) system, the handicraft workshop, or the factory system. Although the introduction of the factory system is sometimes regarded as synonymous with the industrial revolution, it by no means immediately displaced the earlier and simpler forms of organization. They continued to exist in many old, established industries, and even some new industries found them suitable. The majority of new industries, however, especially those with large capital requirements or those that catered to mass markets, found it necessary to adopt the factory system. Modern mining operations also resemble the factory system in organization and discipline, even though they are not housed in factories.

Legally, business firms are grouped into single proprietorships, partnerships, and joint-stock companies or corporations. In America the term corporation usually means a business firm in which the owners have the privilege of limited liability; that is, they cannot be sued personally for the debts of the firm. In Europe the word corporation refers most often to political, religious, and fraternal organizations. The English equivalent of the American corporation is a limited company (meaning limitation of liability) or, more generally, a joint-stock company, although the latter may or may not have the privilege of limited liability.

In the early days of the industrial revolution nearly all business firms were proprietorships or partnerships. Charters of incorporation could only be obtained by special acts of king or Parliament, who usually reserved such charters for companies with monopolistic privileges, such as the Bank of England or the East India Company. As long as new firms could begin on a relatively small scale and grow by the reinvestment of profits this was a satisfactory situation, and a strong tradition of individual initiative and responsibility grew up in such British industries as iron and textiles. When it became necessary to make large fixed-capital investments at the beginning of an enterprise on which profits might be realized only over a span of many years, however, the simpler legal forms no longer sufficed. Such conditions were first encountered generally in canal and railroad building. Since such undertakings were in the nature of public utilities, the authorities readily granted charters of incorporation with limited liability, and by the middle of the nineteenth century investors in Britain, France, and Belgium were accustomed to buying and selling railroad shares and bonds on their financial markets.

Legislatures occasionally granted charters of incorporation to new mining, metallurgical, and banking enterprises as well, especially in Belgium and the United States, but to get these charters required special lobbying expenses and provided occasions for corruption and abuse. Continental countries possessed an intermediate form of organization called the *société en commandite* or limited partnership, which provided limitation of liability for some investors without the necessity for a special charter. With the increasing scale of enterprise, demands arose for general or free incorporation laws, that is, laws permitting any group of individuals to obtain a corporate charter by fulfilling certain specified conditions. Because of their egalitarian sentiments and hostile attitudes toward special privilege, the American states were the first to enact such laws in the 1830's and 1840's. Britain enacted a series of laws between 1855 and 1862 granting general limited liability upon simple registration, and most continental countries followed suit in the 1860's and 1870's.

By the 1870's new problems of industrial organization began to emerge. Cost reductions as a result of technical innovations and the widening of markets by improvements in transportation, together with the possibility of free incorporation, greatly increased competition among firms and led to cutthroat price wars and lower profits. To eliminate such ruinous competition, industrialists resorted to various tactics. On the Continent they formed cartels, in which independent firms agreed to divide their markets, limit production, and maintain prices. In Britain and the United States (especially the latter), where the common law doctrine of conspiracy in restraint of trade limited such combinations, legal trusts were formed to bring formerly competing concerns under a single management. A notable example was the Standard Oil Trust, formed by John D. Rockefeller and his associates between 1879 and 1882. A wave of antitrust legislation designed to enforce competition eventually broke up these trusts in the United States, while the temptation to break agreements in order to obtain a larger share of the market made the European and international cartels notoriously unstable.

Industrialists, frequently with the aid of bankers, then undertook to gain direct control of markets by outright consolidation and combination. In several industries, such as transportation, mining, and metallurgy, substantial economies in production could be secured by either horizontal or vertical integration, that is, by combining many units at the same stage in the production process under one management (horizontal integration), or by combining several units in successive stages (vertical integration). A company owning coal and ore mines, blast furnaces, steel mills, and metal fabricating plants is a good example of vertical integration. Such huge aggregations of economic power could easily eliminate smaller competitors, either by buying them out or by driving them into bankruptcy through localized price wars. By monopolizing both production and the demand for particular types of labor, they could also maintain high prices and low wages, thus creating enormous fortunes for those in control. Through bribery and corruption as well as more subtle forms of influence the owners of these large concentrations of wealth could also affect government policy, both foreign and domestic, in ways favorable to themselves.

THE NETWORK OF WORLD TRADE

The unprecedented growth of population and production together with improvements in transportation and communications broke down regional and even natural barriers to the movement of people and commodities. Western European nations, no longer able to supply their burgeoning populations and industries with domestically produced foodstuffs and raw materials, relied increasingly on imports from overseas. To pay for these essential imports, they exported chiefly manufactured goods. The British cotton industry, for example, drew its raw material from the American South, India, Egypt, and Brazil and sold its yarn and cloth in every country of the world. In the late nineteenth century overseas sales accounted for about two-thirds of its total receipts. British industry as a whole exported between 25 and 30 per cent of its entire production.

British dependence on overseas trade was unusually large, just as the cotton industry was exceptional in drawing all of its raw material from abroad. Nevertheless, some of the smaller nations of the Continent depended even more than Britain on foreign trade (chiefly with their neighbors), and all nations participated in the intensification of international commerce. For the world as a whole the role of such commerce became more important than it was at any time prior to 1860 or subsequent to 1914.

Europe had long depended on imports of such exotic commodities as the fabulous spices that lured the early explorers into the search for new routes to the East. In the nineteenth century the range and quantity of these goods increased, their production (usually under European control) became more systematic, and the techniques of their distribution became more complex and more highly refined. Even the lowest paid European factory worker could begin the day with tea from China or Ceylon, coffee from Brazil, or cocoa from Africa. More important than the trade in these amenities, however, was trade in the staples in which Europe had once been self-sufficient.

Wheat from Russia and the United States occasionally came to western Europe in years of poor local harvest and high prices after 1815. The flow increased along with the population. After 1870 it became a torrent, as transcontinental railroads and farm machinery opened new and highly productive wheat regions in America, and improvements in steamships made it possible to transport bulky goods cheaply over long distances. By 1900 western Europe imported more than half of its grain supply. The United States, Canada, Argentina, India, and Australia were the largest overseas suppliers. Southern Russia contributed significantly through its Black Sea ports. Britain became by far the largest importer, but a number of smaller nations also depended heavily on imports. Denmark and the Netherlands gave up wheat growing almost entirely and specialized in livestock production and dairying by feeding their animals on cheap imported grain. France and Germany, with more and better grain land, resorted to tariff protection for agriculture and depended less on imports.

Similar developments took place in other important staples. As early as 1850 Australia supplied the British woolen industry with half its raw material; by 1900 the quantity of wool coming from Australia and New Zealand had increased more than tenfold, completely swamping European production. Germany and Spain, formerly important exporters of high quality wool, became net importers. South Africa, India, and South America also added to the pressure on European wool growers. The opening of China and Japan, both important producers of raw silk, subjected French and Italian silk growers to stiff competition. European livestock producers suffered similar competition after the development of artificial refrigeration in the 1870's. Steamships equipped with refrigeration machinery brought mutton from Australia and beef from Australia,

Argentina, and the United States. This development stimulated a boom in the range cattle industry of the American West and led to the formation of huge meat-packing industries in such cities as Chicago, Omaha, and Kansas City.

The exchange of manufactures for foodstuffs and raw materials characterized the economic relations between western Europe and the remainder of the world. There was also sizable trade among the industrial countries themselves. They were, in fact, one another's best customers. Although in some respects their economies were competitive, in others they were complementary. Each specialized in the production of certain commodities and obtained the others by trade.

FREE TRADE AND THE RETURN TO PROTECTION

Although improvements in transportation and communications eliminated the natural barriers to a freer international exchange of goods, the world trading system that developed in the second half of the nineteenth century would not have been possible without changes in national economic policies to eliminate or reduce the artificial barriers. The early movement for free trade achieved notable success with Corn Law repeal in Great Britain in 1846 and the Anglo-French Cobden-Chevalier trade treaty of 1860. Britain was by then committed to practically complete free trade and negotiated no more important treaties. France became the keystone of a treaty system that brought the world as close to complete free trade as it has ever been. It did so by negotiating a number of trade treaties providing for mutual reduction or elimination of tariff barriers. The treaties usually contained a "most favored nation" clause, by which each signatory promised to extend to the other the lowest tariff rate available to any nation. Since France's trading partners also made treaties with one another, this resulted in an almost automatic general tariff reduction each time a new treaty took effect.

The only important trading nation to hold aloof from the movement was the United States. Before the Civil War the United States had usually followed a low or moderate tariff policy in deference to the cotton-exporting states of the South. The pressures of war finance led the Union to increase tariffs as a means of raising revenue. After the war, with the South reduced to political impotence, Northern manufacturers succeeded in raising tariffs to ever higher levels in order to protect themselves from foreign competition. For the remainder of the century and well into the next, the United States was the outstanding protectionist nation. It did not long stand alone, however.

The flood of agricultural imports into Europe in the 1870's, as well as the increased competition in manufactured goods among the industrial nations, soon led to demands by both farmers and industrialists for protection for their special interests. In 1879 Bismarck gave in to their demands for domestic political reasons, and by 1880 Russia, Germany, and France had begun to denounce their trade treaties and enact higher tariffs. Although Britain and some of the smaller nations remained faithful to free trade principles, the majority joined in a general return to protection. Nevertheless, protectionist measures did not attain the fantastic extremes of earlier centuries, or of the neomercantilism of the 1930's. For the world as a whole the entire period from about 1850 to 1914 appears in retrospect as one of relatively free international trade.

INCREASING COMPLEXITY OF CAPITALIST INSTITUTIONS

One of the distinguishing features of capitalism as an economic system is that decision-making is decentralized. For the system to function it is necessary to coordinate in some fashion the varied activities of the countless individuals who compose it. The most important institution for coordination under capitalism is the market, defined technically as any place in which buyers and sellers may communicate with one another for the purpose of concluding a transaction. (In this sense the market may be a telegraphic wire or even a postal system.) As capitalism expanded geographically and socially, bringing a larger proportion of the population within its ambit, the system of markets necessarily became more ramified and complex. The Australian shepherd, the Scottish sailor, the London dock worker, the German weaver, and the Polish peasant who bought a woolen cloak all belonged to the same chain of production, distribution, and consumption. Similar chains were represented by the American Negro sharecropper, the Liverpool porter, the Manchester cotton spinner, and the Chinese coolie; or the Canadian wheat farmer, the Dutch miller, and the Swiss baker. The connecting links in these chains were supplied by a host of specialized factors and agents: importers and exporters, auctioneers and warehousemen, bankers and brokers, insurance underwriters, and many more. Each contributed in some fashion to the functioning of the worldwide market system.

Organized markets and intricate communications systems flashed the news of shortages and surpluses, as reflected in price fluctuations, to producers and consumers around the world, enabling them to alter their plans accordingly. Commercial banks provided the short-term credit that enabled commodities to move in local as well as international trade, while investment banks, insurance companies, and stock exchanges facilitated the flow of individual savings into long-term investments. Although similar institutions had existed earlier, the first modern stock exchange was founded in London in 1773 and incorporated in 1801. Others soon followed in other financial centers. At first they handled mainly government securities and the shares of the great chartered companies, then with the coming of the railroad age and the growth of joint-stock companies they added other securities as well. It became possible for small investors to purchase stocks or bonds in businesses that they had never seen. Though unscrupulous persons sometimes took advantage of the unwary, and professional speculators occasionally rigged or cornered a market, the overall advantages of the system were many.

By this means it was possible for a capitalist to invest abroad without stirring from his office or home. Such foreign investment not only provided the fixed capital necessary for the development of backward countries, but also served as a vehicle for the diffusion of technology and organizational skills from more advanced nations. In addition to earning profits for the investor, it contributed to the general welfare by opening new sources of supply and providing new markets. Foreign investment had its darker side as well, however. In many instances, especially those involving loans to governments, the capital was not used productively but was spent for armaments, warships, and the support of enlarged armies and corrupt political regimes. Sometimes foreign investments served as the vehicle or the excuse for imperialist control by Western nations over non-Western peoples. Finally, in the political and monetary chaos following wars, such as that after World War I, investors might lose everything, although such risks were not confined to foreign investment but characterized the entire interdependent capitalist economy.

INTERNATIONAL MIGRATION

The free international economy involved the export of people as well as commodities and capital. International travel did not normally require passports or visas until World War I, and change of citizenship was generally a simple matter of declaring one's intentions. Altogether, about 60 million people left Europe between 1815 and 1914. Of these, almost 35 million came to the United States, and an additional 5 million went to Canada. Some 12 or 15 million went to Latin America, chiefly Argentina and Brazil. Australia, New Zealand, and South Africa took most of the rest. The British Isles (including Ireland) supplied the largest number of emigrants – about 18 million. Large numbers also left Germany, the Scandinavian countries, and after about 1890, Italy, Austria-Hungary, and the Russian Empire (including Poland). Migration within Europe was also substantial, although in many cases it was only temporary. Large numbers of Poles and other Slavic and Jewish peoples moved west into Germany, France, and elsewhere. France attracted Italians, Spanish, Swiss, and Belgians, while England obtained immigrants from all of Europe. In the east the tsar settled about 1.5 million peasant families in Siberia between 1861 and 1914, in addition to many criminals and political deportees.

Except for the latter, the migrations were mostly voluntary. In a few cases the migrants fled from political persecution or oppression. The majority moved in response to economic pressure at home and opportunities for a better life abroad. In the eight years following the great famine of 1846, for example, more than 1,200,000 people left Ireland for the United States and many more crossed the Irish Sea to Britain. In spite of occasional hostile reactions in the receiving countries, the immigrants and their children made significant contributions to the economic, cultural, and political life of their adopted countries. New and nearly empty lands overseas, such as Australia and New Zealand, attracted a steady stream of immigrants, most of them from the British Isles. Many Britishers went to Canada, too. Relatively large numbers of Italians and Germans migrated to what became the economically most progressive countries of South America. In the United States the economic, scientific, literary, artistic, and political achievements of immigrants and their descendants are both noteworthy and obvious.

NATIONAL ECONOMIC STYLES

The industrial countries had many characteristics in common that differentiated them from their preindustrial neighbors, but each also developed certain distinctive traits of its own. As a result of differences of physical environment, historical tradition, and the timing of industrialization, each specialized in particular lines of industry and developed its own style of economic institutions and responses to world market conditions. Britain, France, and Belgium, the pioneers of industrial development, served as tutors and suppliers of capital for their less highly developed neighbors. They also paid a penalty for their precocity in the form of overcommitment to lines of industry that were already becoming obsolete by the end of the nineteenth century. The younger and more vigorous industrializing nations profited from the experience and capital of the pioneers and also proved more flexible in adopting new technologies.

BRITAIN, FRANCE, AND BELGIUM: THE DIFFUSION OF TECHNOLOGY AND THE EXPORT OF CAPITAL

British artisans and entrepreneurs helped implant the seeds of modern industry on the Continent and in North America almost as soon as they sprouted in Britain itself. (See pp. 70–74.) Soon after the Napoleonic wars British capitalists began to invest some of the accumulated profits of industry in foreign countries. At first the export of capital took the form of loans to foreign governments, and by the 1840's British railroad contractors using British capital had begun to assist in the construction of railroads all across the Continent. After mid-century the British turned increasingly to overseas investments, especially in the British Empire and the United States. By 1870 British foreign investments approximated 4 billion dollars, of which about 60 per cent was in loans to governments

Table 1 *The Progress of Industrialization, 1870–1913*

	1870	*1913*
United Kingdom		
Coal (millions of long tons)	110.0	287.0
Pig iron (millions of long tons)	6.0	10.3
Steel (millions of long tons)	0.2	7.7
Foreign trade[1] (millions of dollars)	3,186.0	6,837.0
Germany		
Coal and lignite (millions of metric tons)	34.0	277.3
Pig iron (millions of metric tons)	1.3	19.3
Steel (millions of metric tons)	0.17	18.3
Foreign trade[1] (millions of dollars)	1,433.0[2]	4,970.0
France		
Coal (millions of metric tons)	13.1	40.8
Pig iron (millions of metric tons)	1.2	5.2
Steel (millions of metric tons)	0.08	4.7
Foreign trade[1] (millions of dollars)	1,094.0	2,953.0
United States		
Coal (millions of long tons)	29.5	508.9
Pig iron (millions of long tons)	1.7	31.0
Steel (millions of long tons)	0.07	31.3
Foreign trade[1] (millions of dollars)	868.0	4,392.0

(long ton = 2,240 lbs.)
(metric ton = 2,204.6 lbs.)

[1] Imports plus exports; figures for United Kingdom and United States include re-exports.

[2] Figure for 1872.

Sources: E. Varga, *Mirovye Ekonomicheskie Krizisy 1848–1935* (Moscow, 1937), I, part III, app. III, tables 1, 2, 3, 4; foreign trade data from W. S. and E. S. Woytinsky, *World Commerce and Governments* (New York, 1955), pp. 48, 50.

and the remainder in railroads, banks, and other commercial and industrial enterprises.

The resources for these investments came chiefly from the earnings of British shippers, bankers, and insurance underwriters, for Britain had long imported more than it exported. It could do so with ease, and could even increase its foreign investments as a result of income received from earlier investments. By 1914 British foreign investments amounted to 19 billion dollars, or almost 40 per cent of total British wealth excluding land. Most of the investments still represented loans to governments, but they also took the form of sheep ranches in Australia, cattle ranches in the United States and Argentina, wheat farms in Canada, tea plantations in Ceylon, rubber plantations in Malaya, and gold mines in South Africa, as well as railroads, banks, mines, and port and dock facilities distributed throughout every inhabited continent and in almost every country of the world.

As early as the 1830's French engineers, entrepreneurs, and capitalists began to assist the industrial development of France's neighbors, especially Belgium, Germany, and Italy. After 1850 the French took the major role in the construction of railroads throughout southern and eastern Europe, dug canals (of which the most famous is Suez), built port and dock facilities, water and gas works, and so on. The French also invested heavily in government securities, especially those of its Latin neighbors and, after 1890, Russia. By 1914 French foreign investments totaled nearly 10 billion dollars (about 30 per cent of French national wealth excluding land) and, like the British, were distributed throughout the inhabited world. Belgium also invested a large proportion of its national wealth abroad, but because of its much smaller population the total was less impressive. Belgian engineers played a significant role in mining, metallurgy, and railroads in Europe and elsewhere. Toward the end of the century other industrializing nations of Europe, notably Germany, the Netherlands, and Switzerland, repaid their foreign borrowings and became net lenders. Collectively, however, their investments in 1914 amounted to less than those of France alone and only about half those of Britain.

Britain reached its peak of industrial supremacy in relation to other nations in the two decades between 1850 and 1870. In the latter year it accounted for more than 30 per cent of the world output of industrial products. France and Belgium also reached their relative peaks in the same period, although French industrial output accounted for little more than 10 per cent of the world total, and Belgium accounted for only 3 per cent. All three countries continued to make industrial progress thereafter, but at a slower rate than previously and much slower in relation to the progress of other nations. In 1913 the United States produced a staggering 35 per cent of the world's manufacturing output and Germany produced more than 15 per cent, whereas Britain fell to 14 per cent and France fell to less than 7 per cent.

Textiles, coal, iron, and engineering, the bases of Britain's early prosperity, remained its standbys. British industrialists were slow to adopt new technological innovations, even in industries in which they had long maintained superiority. In part, the backwardness of the British educational system may be blamed, for Britain was the last major nation to adopt universal public elementary schooling, and the few great British universities paid slight attention to scientific or engineering training. In part, the relative decline of British, French, and other Belgian industry was the inevitable result of industrialization in other lands. Much of the responsibility, however, belonged to the entrepreneurs. The sons or grandsons of the original founders of British enterprises did not exhibit the dynamism of their forebears. Frequently they adopted the life of leisured gentlemen and left the day-to-day operations of the firms to hired managers. In foreign markets they lost ground to more aggressive trade rivals, such as Germany and the United States, and suffered the humiliation of an invasion of their domestic market by cheaper and better foreign manufactures. In 1914 Britain had the highest standard of living of any European nation, but it had lost its secure position as the world's leading industrial nation.

In France, a land of small peasant proprietors, agriculture continued to occupy a larger proportion of the population than in other advanced industrial nations. French industry, which was more varied and catered especially to limited markets for quality products, developed fewer large-scale, mass-production manufacturing units. The slow growth of French population and the policy of tariff protection for both agriculture and industry, which insulated French entrepreneurs from the stimulus of the world market, also condemned France to slower industrial growth. Nevertheless, on the eve of World War I Frenchmen enjoyed the highest standard of living on the Continent, and in Europe were second only to Britain.

GERMAN INDUSTRY AND ECONOMIC EXPANSION

While the older industrial economies coasted along on their early superiority, German industry grew rapidly. The growth of population alone — from less than 25 million in 1815 (according to the boundaries of 1871) to more than 65 million in 1914 — was sufficient to cause grave concern to Germany's neighbors. Three other outstanding factors also contributed significantly to German industrial progress.

First, Germany possessed unusually large reserves of coal, especially in the famous Ruhr Valley, which supported important metallurgical, engineering, chemical, and electrical industries. Second, the German educational system, from the preprimary grades — *kindergarten* is a German word — through the numerous excellent universities, was not only the most comprehensive in the world but also the best suited to the needs of an industrial state. A series of reforms in Prussia during the Napoleonic wars laid the basis for the modern educational system of Germany and provided for universal and compulsory education of all children from the ages of six through fourteen. Besides the elementary schools, a variety of secondary schools prepared students for the universities or gave them manual or technical training appropriate to their stations. Throughout Germany the old universities were revitalized and several new ones were founded. Scientific training borrowed heavily from the curriculum and methods of the École Polytechnique, the noted French revolutionary school, but was made available to a far larger number of students than in the French system. A number of specialized technical schools, including engineering colleges and business schools at the university level, were founded. Thus, as science became more and more the foundation of industry, Germany stood ready to take advantage of the situation. When American educators in the 1870's began to be concerned with the need for remodeling their system of higher education, they turned to Germany rather than to France or England for a model.

Third, Germany developed a banking system that was uniquely adapted to the need for industrial development. Prior to 1848 German banking, like the German economy as a whole, was backward in comparison with other Western nations. Again Germany borrowed from and improved on French models. In the 1850's and 1860's German financiers founded a number of banks similar to the French Crédit Mobilier (see p. 147), expressly for the purpose of creating and nourishing new large-scale industries. In time most of these banks established networks of branches and affiliates throughout Germany and in foreign countries. In this way they not only economized on capital and catered to the needs of German industry but also facilitated the extension of Germany's foreign commerce by providing credit to exporters and foreign merchants. The consequences were spectacular, and alarming, to industrialists and statesmen of other countries.

German coal production rose more than sixfold between 1870 and 1914, pig iron production rose more than tenfold, and steel, a relatively new industry in 1870, rose almost one hundredfold. By 1895 Germany produced more steel than Britain and by 1914 it produced more than twice as much. During the same period German foreign commerce surpassed that of the United States and France, and though it still lagged slightly behind that of Britain, the gap was closing rapidly.

INDUSTRY IN AMERICA

On the eve of World War I Germany was the most powerful industrial nation in Europe, but the most spectacular example of rapid national growth was the United States. The first federal census of 1790 recorded fewer than 4 million inhabitants. In 1870, after the limits of continental expansion had been reached, the population had risen to almost 40 million, larger than that of any European nation except Russia. In 1915 the population surpassed 100 million. Although the United States received the bulk of emigration from Europe, the largest element of population growth resulted from an extremely high rate of natural increase. At no time did the foreign-born population surpass one-sixth of the total. Nevertheless, the American policy of almost unrestricted immigration until after World War I placed a definite stamp on national life, and America became known as the "melting pot" of Europe.

The numbers of immigrants entering annually rose rapidly though unsteadily from less than ten thousand in the 1820's to more than 1 million in the years immediately prior to the first World War. Until the 1890's by far the majority came from northwestern Europe, including Germany.

Immigrant stock from these countries continued to constitute the largest part of the foreign-born population. By 1900, however, new immigrants from Italy and eastern Europe dominated the listings. In 1910 the foreign-born population numbered 13,500,000, or about 15 per cent of the total population. Of these, about 17 per cent came from Germany; 10 per cent from Ireland; almost as many from Italy and the Austro-Hungarian monarchy; about 9 per cent each from Great Britain, Scandinavia, Canada, and Russia; almost 7 per cent each from Russian, Austrian, and German Poland; and a scattering from other countries.

Income and wealth grew even more rapidly than population. From colonial times the scarcity of labor in relation to land and other resources had meant higher wages and a higher average standard of living than in Europe. This fact, together with the related opportunities for individual achievement and the political liberties enjoyed by American citizens, drew the immigrants from Europe. Between the end of the Civil War and the outbreak of World War I the average income per capita roughly tripled. The primary sources of the enormous increase were the same as those operating in western Europe, the rapid progress of technology and increasing regional specialization. In addition, the continued scarcity and high cost of labor placed a premium on labor-saving machinery. In agriculture, for example, the best European practices yielded consistently higher returns per acre than in the United States, but American farmers using relatively inexpensive machinery (even before the introduction of the tractor) obtained far larger yields per worker. The large internal market, entirely free of artificial trade barriers, permitted an even greater degree of regional specialization than the regime of relatively free trade in Europe.

In spite of the rapid growth of large cities, the United States remained predominantly a rural nation. The urban population did not pull abreast of the rural population until World War I. The westward movement continued after the Civil War, encouraged by the Homestead Act and the opening of the trans-Mississippi West by means of the railroads. Until the 1890's American exports consisted principally of agricultural products. Foundations were being laid, nevertheless, for America's subsequent industrial prowess. The nonagricultural labor force surpassed workers in agriculture as early as 1870. In the 1880's the income from manufacturing exceeded that from agriculture. By 1900 the United States had become the world's foremost industrial nation.

The large domestic market might have meant little for large-scale industry in America had it not been for the relatively open and fluid character of American social classes. In spite of the ethnic and regional diversity of the American people, the absence of rigid class boundaries assured the development of relatively uniform tastes, creating a large homogeneous market for mass-produced manufactures. American industrialists were quick to take advantage of the opportunity. All the features of the new technology that encouraged large-scale industry acted with extra force in the United States, and in one industry after another – iron and steel, petroleum, sugar refining, tobacco processing, meat packing, and many others – huge integrated concerns emerged to serve national and international markets.

The so-called antitrust legislation actually encouraged the concentration of industry, for although it penalized collusion in the form of cartel and trust agreements, it did not penalize bigness as such. As a result, a large merger movement developed in the 1890's. The first billion dollar corporation in the world was the United States Steel Corporation, created in 1901. By 1904 more than 300 large industrial combinations controlled more than 40 per cent of the manufacturing capital of the nation and affected about four-fifths of the major American industries. Of the 92 largest combinations in 1904, 78 produced 50 per cent or more of the output of their industries; 57 produced 60 per cent or more; and 26 produced 80 per cent or more. These figures actually understate the degree of concentration, for by means of interlocking directorates, communities of interest, and the cooperation of important investment banking houses, such as that of J. P. Morgan, a relatively small number of individuals could wield enormous power and influence throughout the whole economy.

American political life in the period after the Civil War reflected the domination of the country by big business. At the beginning of the twentieth century public exposure of a number of flagrant examples of evil and corruption in business and government, as well as in the living and working conditions of the industrial population, stimulated a reform movement. It was dominated by middle-class leaders from the liberal professions. Known as Progressives, these socially conscious citizens gained influence in both political parties and restored a measure of decorum and direction to American life.

INDUSTRIALIZATION IN OTHER LANDS

Industrialism barely affected the smaller nations of northwestern Europe, except Belgium, in the first half of the nineteenth century, but in the second half of the century they all made rapid strides. In spite of important individual differences, the Netherlands, Switzerland, and the Scandinavian countries generally followed the same path of economic progress. This began with legal, commercial, and educational reforms dating from the French Revolution but not carried to completion in every case until after 1848. All developed strong educational systems and a vigorous middle class. They participated in the commercial revival of the 1850's, chartered banks, and began the construction of railroad systems. In the 1860's they joined the free trade movement. Industrialization proper did not get underway in earnest until the 1870's, but then it proceeded apace. Native industrialists developed industries that utilized skilled labor and local resources. Switzerland, Sweden, and Norway, for example, made extensive use of hydroelectricity, whereas Denmark and the Netherlands concentrated chiefly on intensive agriculture and the processing of agricultural products. By the beginning of the twentieth century all could boast of prosperous, progressive industries and a standard of living comparable with any on the Continent.

Northern Italy, lower Austria (the region around Vienna), and Bohemia also began to industrialize. Bohemia in particular developed some mining activity, and they all engaged in the processing of metals; but their mainstays were the relatively low-skilled industries, such as textiles and leather working. Their efforts to industrialize were not notably successful, and they remained predominantly rural and agrarian.

For Russia the Crimean War revealed that numbers and size were no offset to economic backwardness. Immediately after the war the tsar undertook an ambitious program of railroad construction, utilizing foreign capital and technical personnel. After a number of false starts the program finally began to catch on in the 1870's. In 1892 the government began construction of the Trans-Siberian railroad, the first track of which was opened in 1905. In spite of great progress, the vast distances in Russia left many areas completely inaccessible by modern means of transportation. The emancipation of the serfs was carried out by the tsar in 1861 as a deliberate effort to modernize his country, but it did not immediately have the desired effects. In fact, during the generation or so after liberation the agrarian situation deteriorated.

The efforts of successive tsars to make Russia a powerful industrial nation finally began to bear fruit in the 1890's. Massive imports of foreign capital were lured into Russia by political alliances, government guarantees, protective tariffs, and state subsidies. Under the direction of foreign entrepreneurs and engineers, Russia obtained large-scale, relatively modern industries. In the last decade of the century production of coal increased by 131 per cent, petroleum by 132 per cent, and pig iron by 190 per cent. Russia also had a large textile industry, which on the eve of World War I ranked fourth in the world in size. The petroleum industry, which developed rapidly after 1870, accounted for about one-fourth of the world production and vied with that of the United States for first place. Nevertheless, apart from the petroleum industry, which was based on unusually rich deposits, was financed and managed by foreign capitalists and entrepreneurs, and competed in the world market, Russian industries existed only by virtue of state protection and subsidy, islands of modernity in a sea of backwardness. Elsewhere in eastern and southern Europe similar if smaller islands existed, but they were of minor importance, having little influence on the preindustrial economy that characterized the area.

ORGANIZED LABOR AND THE REVIVAL OF SOCIALISM

The history of socialism and of organized efforts to improve the conditions of the urban working classes before 1848 belongs as much to the history of ideas as to the history of social movements. The two decades after 1848 showed this characteristic clearly. In Britain the failure of the Chartist movement temporarily disillusioned the rank-and-file workingmen with grandiose schemes of universal regeneration, while the gradual improvement in wages and working conditions brought about by the advance of industry dulled the edge of criticism of the industrial system. In France, persecution and exile for the popular radical leaders of the 1840's, as well as strict police supervision and repression of any hint of mass action by the mobs of Paris and other industrial cities, effectively squelched incipient labor movements and reduced the urban population to an unusual state of docility. Elsewhere in Europe political oppression was even more severe than in France. Industrial workers were too few in number and too weak in organization to present a serious threat to the existing political and social order.

THE COOPERATIVE MOVEMENT

In localities where industrial workers were sufficiently numerous and inclined to collective action, they resorted to devices that would ameliorate their circumstances without arousing the hostility of the larger community. Britain became the home of the consumer cooperation movement with the formation of the first such cooperative at Rochdale in 1844. By mid-century more than one hundred similar cooperatives had been formed in northern England and Scotland, and by 1863 the movement was strong enough to establish a Cooperative Wholesale Society. In subsequent years the movement extended its activities into production, insurance, and banking. In France and other continental countries small-scale artisans formed producer cooperatives and mutual credit societies in an effort to stave off ruin from the competition of larger, more efficient industrial units, but only in agriculture did producer cooperatives achieve notable success. Denmark is an outstanding example of a nation in which, after the 1870's, agriculture was organized predominantly on cooperative lines. In the twentieth century a strong cooperative movement developed in Sweden, embracing both agricultural and producer cooperatives in the urban areas. Outside of Scandinavia, however, the cooperatives affected only a small fraction of the working population.

THE RISE OF TRADE UNIONS

Another form of working-class self-help, which in the long run amounted to much more than the cooperative movement, was the trade (or labor) union movement. Although trade unions have a long history, running back to the journeymen's associations of the later Middle Ages, the modern movement dates from the rise of modern industry. In the first half of the nineteenth century unions were weak, localized, and usually short-lived in the face of opposition by antagonistic employers and unfavorable or repressive legislation. Most Western nations have passed through at least three phases in their official attitudes toward trade unions. The first phase, that of outright prohibition or suppression, was typified by the Le Chapelier Law of 1791 in France, the Combination Laws of 1799 and 1800 in Britain, and similar legislation in other countries. In the second phase, marked in Britain by the repeal of the Combination Laws in 1824 and 1825, governments granted limited toleration to trade unions, allowing their formation but frequently prosecuting them for engaging in overt action such as strikes. A third phase, not achieved until the twentieth century in some countries and not achieved at all in others, accorded full legal rights to workingmen to organize and engage in collective activities. A fourth phase, resorted to by totalitarian countries after World War I, in effect regimented workers into trade unions that became instruments of the state.

In Britain nationwide trade-union organization fell off between 1834 and 1851. Then the Amalgamated Society of Engineers (machinists and mechanics) was formed, the first of the so-called New Model unions. The distinctive feature of the New Model union was that it organized skilled laborers only and on a craft basis, such as typographers, tailors, stonemasons, shipwrights, and carpenters; it represented the aristocracy of labor. Unskilled workers and workers in the new factory industries remained unorganized until near the end of the century. New Model unions aimed modestly at improving the wages and working conditions of their own members, who were already the best paid in British industry, by peaceful negotiations with employers and mutual self-help. They eschewed political activities and rarely resorted to strikes except in desperation. As a result, they grew in strength but membership remained low. Attempts to organize the large mass of semiskilled and unskilled workers resulted in successful strikes by the "match girls" (young female workers in the match industry) in 1888 and the London dock workers in 1889. By 1900 trade union membership surpassed 2 million, and in 1913 it reached 4 million, or more than one-fifth of the total work force.

On the Continent, trade unions made slower progress. From the beginning French unions were closely associated with socialism and similar political ideologies. The varying and mutually antagonistic forms taken by French socialism badly splintered the union movement, resulted in a fickle and fluctuating membership, and made it nearly impossible to agree on nationwide collective action. In 1895 French unions succeeded in forming a national nonpolitical General Confederation of Labor (C.G.T.), but even it did not include all active unions and frequently had difficulty in commanding local obedience to its directives. Like French political parties, the French labor movement remained decentralized, highly individualistic, and generally ineffective.

The German labor movement dated from the 1860's. Like the French, it was associated from the beginning with political parties and political action; unlike the French, it was more centralized and cohesive. There were three main divisions in the German labor movement: the Hirsch-Dunker or liberal trade unions, appealing mainly to skilled craftsmen; the socialist or free trade unions, having a far larger membership; and somewhat later the Catholic or Christian trade unions, founded with the blessing of the pope in opposition to the "godless" socialist unions. By 1914 the German trade union movement had 3 million members – five-sixths belonged to the socialist unions – and was the second largest in Europe.

In the economically backward countries of southern Europe, and to some extent in Latin America, French influence predominated in working-class organizations. Trade unions were fragmented and ideologically oriented. They were savagely repressed by employers and the state and were mostly without consequence. Trade unions in the Low Countries, Switzerland, and the Austro-Hungarian Empire followed the German model. They achieved moderate success at the local level, but religious and ethnic differences as well as opposition from government hindered their effectiveness as national movements. In the Scandinavian countries the labor movement developed its own distinctive traditions. It allied itself with the cooperative movement as well as with the Social Democratic political parties and by 1914 had done more than any other trade union movement to alleviate the living and working conditions of its membership. In Russia and elsewhere in eastern Europe trade unions remained illegal until after World War I.

Early attempts to form mass working-class organizations in the United States came to naught in the face of governmental and employer opposition and the difficulty in securing cooperation among workingmen of different skills, occupations, religions, and ethnic backgrounds. In the 1880's Samuel Gompers took the lead in organizing closely knit local unions of skilled workers only, and in 1886 he united them into the American Federation of Labor. Like the New Model unions of Britain, the A.F.L. followed "bread and butter" tactics by concentrating on the welfare of its own members, steering clear of ideological entanglements and avoiding overt political action. In consequence, it succeeded in achieving many of its limited goals but left the majority of American industrial workers unorganized. In the British dominions trade unions developed in traditional British form but with a greater commitment to socialist programs. The first Trades Union Congress in Australia took place in 1879, only eleven years after the first of its kind in Britain.

Throughout most of the nineteenth century the Roman Catholic hierarchy regarded with disfavor the formation of exclusively working-class organizations, such as trade unions, and tried to prohibit its members from participating in them. Its opposition contributed to the weakness of the union movement in France and other Catholic countries. Pope Leo XIII (1878–1903) reversed this attitude and encouraged the formation of specifically Christian, or Catholic trade unions as a means of combating the secularism of socialist unions and winning workers back to the Church. Catholic union movements developed in Belgium, Austria, Italy, and Germany, but they remained relatively small and unimportant.

SOCIALIST THOUGHT AND ORGANIZATION

Although the two decades after 1848 were relatively barren of socialist political activity, they witnessed the elaboration by Karl Marx of the foremost of all socialist theories. Marx dabbled briefly in socialist political organization in 1864 when he took the lead in forming the International Workingmen's Association (later called the First International). The association was the creation of political refugees like Marx, and its objective was to foster the spread of socialist doctrine in workers' organizations throughout the world. The delegates to its conferences spent most of their time and energy wrangling with one another over points of doctrine and contributed little to the actual spread of socialism. The bitterest division took place between Marx and Mikhail Bakunin (1814–1876), a Russian anarchist, and eventually led to the disruption of the organization. To prevent the organizational apparatus from falling into Bakunin's hands, Marx contrived in 1872 to move the headquarters to New York, where it became moribund and quietly expired in 1876.

More vigorous social movements were growing up on the Continent. In 1863 Ferdinand Lassalle formed the General German Workingman's Association, partly a trade union and partly a political party. Lassalle accepted much of the Marxian doctrine but believed that socialism could be established by political action without revolution. In 1875, after the death of Lassalle, his followers amalgamated with those of Marx to form the German Social Democratic party. Under the astute leadership of Wilhelm Liebknecht and August Bebel the party achieved such surprising success at the polls that even Bismarck took alarm, and in 1878 he persuaded the Reichstag to outlaw the Social Democrats. (See p. 218.) The antisocialist laws lapsed after Bismarck's retirement, however, and the party, which had gone underground in the interval, bounded back stronger than ever. It obtained one and a half million votes in 1890 and more than four million votes in the elections of 1912. By then it was the largest single party in the German Empire, having almost a third of the members of the Reichstag, but because it steadfastly refused to participate in coalition governments the combined opposition of the other parties sufficed to keep it out of office.

French socialists also made political gains, but their internal divisions prevented them from presenting a united front to the electorate or in the French parliament. Although France had a Marxist party, French workers found the anarchist and syndicalist doctrines more attractive. The outstanding leader of French socialism was Jean Jaurès, an Independent Socialist who looked to the French revolutionary tradition rather than to Marxism or anarchism for the justification of socialism. At the same time he worked unceasingly to achieve cooperation among the various socialist groups. He succeeded for a time after 1905, but the French socialists splintered again in 1910 when one of their number who had joined the government used the army to break a railroad strike. On the eve of World War I the various socialist parties constituted the second largest group in the French Chamber of Deputies.

British socialism developed piecemeal, with little systematic theoretical basis. Curiously, Marx did not attempt to create an organized following in the country of his adoption. The Fabian Society, an organization devoted to peaceful social reform and the gradual socialization of industry, did not engage in political action as such but employed publications and lectures to expose the inadequacies of the existing social system and to propose remedies and reforms. The Fabians owed more to Bentham than to Marx. Their emphasis on gradualism and peaceful evolution was distinctively British. Whereas the Fabians represented a middle-class, intellectual approach to socialism, the followers of J. Keir Hardie, a Scottish coal miner and trade union organizer, represented a working-class, political approach. Hardie took the lead in uniting the various socialist factions and the Trades Union Congress in support of the Labour Representation Committee, which became the Labour party in 1906. Although the Labour party did not commit itself definitely to a program of socialization until 1918, the influence of its socialist components moved it steadily in that direction.

Social Democratic parties on the German model were founded elsewhere in Europe: Belgium (1885), Austria (1889), Hungary (1890), Bulgaria (1891), Poland (1892), Rumania (1893), Holland (1894), Russia (1898), Finland (1903), and Serbia (1903). The anarchist and syndicalist movements dominated socialist action groups in Italy, Spain, and Portugal. Social Democratic parties also developed in Denmark (1878), Norway (1887), and Sweden (1889), but because they were in close alliance with the cooperative and trade union movements, they adopted a more gradual approach to socialism, closer to the British than to the German model. The Christian Socialist movement did not develop an effective political arm.

From its beginnings socialism stressed the common, collective interests of peoples regardless of national frontiers and sought to develop a sense of international solidarity among its adherents. The First International, formed in advance of the national socialist parties, clearly reflected this emphasis. After its demise representatives of the various socialist parties formed the Second International Workingmen's Association in Paris in 1889. Unlike its highly centralized predecessor, the Second International was a loose association of component national groups. It did not establish a permanent secretariat until 1900. The debates at its annual congresses did much to stimulate public awareness of socialism and exposed national differences within socialist groups. One major difference concerned the role of socialist parties in national political life and was closely connected with the doctrinal dispute over "revisionism." (See pp. 221–222.) In general, socialists from countries where more or less democratic political practices prevailed (such as Britain, France, and the Scandinavian countries) favored peaceful cooperation and even collaboration with nonsocialist reformers. Those from countries with less well developed parliamentary forms of government or with none at all advocated nonparticipation in bourgeois politics and continued revolutionary agitation.

An even more important issue concerned the role of socialist parties in wartime, and on this rock the international socialist movement finally shattered. Congresses at Stuttgart (1907) and Copenhagen (1910) passed resolutions demanding joint action by workers to prevent war but provided no effective machinery for it. When war broke out in 1914, minorities in every socialist party adopted a pacifist or neutral stance, but the majority in every case supported their national war effort. This failure of the socialists to abide by their principles not only disrupted socialism as an international movement but also seriously divided and weakened the various national socialist parties.

RADICALISM AND THE WORKERS

Karl Marx had prophesied that with the advance of modern industrialism and capitalism the laboring masses would sink deeper into poverty and destitution as they grew in numbers, until at last they would rise in revolt against their capitalist overlords. One would suppose that in line with this prediction labor organizations would exhibit the greatest radicalism and be most disposed to violence in those nations where capitalism and modern industry had made the greatest strides. In fact, the events of history revealed this prophecy to be the very opposite of the truth. Britain, the first industrial nation in the nineteenth century and the most capitalistic, did indeed have the largest trade union movement, but its workers quickly abandoned the goal of a radical reconstruction of society in favor of a policy of gradual, peaceful reform. In Germany, which was still industrially backward in the 1860's, the early trade union movement adopted a radical ideology, but as German industry progressed and trade unions grew in numbers, trade union tactics followed an increasingly peaceable approach. The divided French union movement, which was given to periodic outbursts of violence, mirrored the small-scale, relatively unprogressive character of French capitalism. Ironically for Marx, who despised the Russians, it was in Russia, the least capitalistic of all major powers and the only one in which trade unions were entirely illegal, that the workers resorted to violence most often and finally achieved a proletarian revolution.

DEMOCRATIC REFORM AND SOCIAL STRIFE, 1871-1914

CHAPTER EIGHT

Paralleling their continued technological and economic progress, the nations of western Europe experienced what may with qualification be called political progress. By the third quarter of the nineteenth century the governments of all western European countries were responsive to, though not necessarily controlled by, the needs and interests of the middle classes. The leaders of the working classes had made their bids for political consideration, as in the Chartist demonstrations in Britain and the revolutions of 1848 on the Continent. That these bids most often took the form of demands for the right to vote testifies to the extraordinary effectiveness of the propagandists of the liberal political theory of representative government. By the end of the nineteenth century most of the demands had been conceded; with minor qualifications universal manhood suffrage was the rule in most western European nations. It did not follow that workers controlled the governments, however.

In spite of the great importance of modern industry, industrial workers rarely constituted an actual majority of the labor force. Peasants with a traditionalist mentality and workers in the various service trades, many of whom shared the outlook of the middle classes, usually outnumbered industrial workers. Moreover, the latter were frequently slow to develop their own political organizations. Many of them demonstrated a marked indifference to or ignorance of the political process, and the politically conscious workers rarely approached unanimity on political goals. The upper and middle classes made use of their greater wealth, superior organization, and the power of government itself to frustrate the intention of working-class political leaders to gain control of the apparatus of government. Continuing social strife resulted in spite of acknowledged progress in the political sphere.

THE TRIUMPH OF DEMOCRACY IN BRITAIN

The British Parliament after 1832 legislated a number of important economic and social reforms, but Parliament itself was far from being a democratic body. Only one adult male in six could vote for members of the House of Commons in the early 1860's. Several proposals for the extension of the franchise had been made, but all had been defeated by the combined opposition of the Whigs and Tories. The aristocratic and upper-middle-class politicians who dominated Parliament had reached what has been called the Victorian Compromise, blurring party lines and delaying the emergence of the modern two-party system. One of the chief architects of the compromise was Lord Palmerston (1784–1865). After Palmerston's death the rivalry between the Liberals and Conservatives, as the parties then came to be known, grew more acute, and the issues that divided them became more sharply defined. In large measure this development resulted from the personal rivalry and political astuteness of two remarkable men.

DISRAELI AND GLADSTONE

Benjamin Disraeli (1804–1881), one of the most colorful personalities in the history of British politics, typified a new breed of man — the professional politician. The son of a Christianized Jew, Disraeli lacked the aristocratic birth, wealth, and family connections that were normally required for political leadership in Britain; but he possessed driving ambition, a gift for oratory, a fertile imagination, and a prolific pen (he supported himself outside of Parliament as a writer of popular novels). By dint of sheer skill and audacity he worked himself into the highest ranks of the Tory (Conservative) party and became the leading spokesman for the landed aristocracy, many of whom were unable to speak coherently for themselves. He first attracted public notice in the 1830's as one of the young Tory Radicals concerned with the plight of the growing urban working classes. In the next decade he split with his party leader, Robert Peel, and spoke for the protectionist interests in the Corn Law debates. He served as chancellor of the exchequer on three occasions after 1852, became leader of the House of Commons in 1867, and prime minister in 1868. Although his party was defeated in the election that year, he remained as leader of the opposition and served again as Conservative prime minister from 1874 until 1880.

William Ewart Gladstone (1809–1898) was Disraeli's counterpart and his great rival as leader and architect of the modern Liberal party. The son of a wealthy Liverpool merchant, Gladstone made his debut in politics with the Tories, but during the Corn Law controversy he seceded with the Peelites and became the financial expert of the Liberal party.

Brown Brothers

Benjamin Disraeli

"In Disraeli's career there was the realisation in fact of the dream which has floated before the eyes of many an ambitious youth. . . . And though it was attained in this case, as in most others, 'by force,' it was in fair and open Parliamentary fight, and, as regards the main struggle, in what looked at first like a hopeless defiance hurled by a pigmy at a giant. . . . Not only was Disraeli's political advantage won in fair fight. It was also uncontaminated by any suspicion that he was in politics for pecuniary gain." George Earle Buckle and W. F. Monypenny, THE LIFE OF BENJAMIN DISRAELI, EARL OF BEACONSFIELD (New York, 1913–20), Vol. VI.

He was twice chancellor of the exchequer between 1852 and 1866 and served as prime minister four times between 1868 and his retirement in 1894.

THE "LEAP IN THE DARK" AND FURTHER POLITICAL REFORMS

The first major issue to face Disraeli and Gladstone after the death of Palmerston found them on the same side, though for different reasons. Gladstone introduced a bill in 1866 for an extension of the electorate, only to have it defeated by defections from his own Liberal party. Although the Conservatives (as well as many Liberals) traditionally had been opposed to extensions of the franchise, it became clear to Disraeli that further electoral reform could not be long postponed. He resolved to capture the credit for his own Conservative party and win the allegiance of the underprivileged classes. He thereupon introduced his own bill for electoral reform, which became law on August 15, 1867.

This "leap in the dark," as the measure was characterized by the Conservative prime minister, Lord Derby, enfranchised the majority of the urban working classes and roughly doubled the electorate, from about 1 million to about 2 million. Thereafter all householders who paid a certain low minimum in direct taxes could vote in elections for members of the Commons. The franchise in the country districts remained restricted to the more substantial proprietors and farmers, however, and in the cities there were many who were unaffected, including women, domestic servants, and the lowest strata of workers. In spite of some redistribution of seats in the Commons, electoral districts were far from equal, and the medieval distinction between borough and shire (roughly, city and country) was maintained. Nevertheless, a significant reform had been achieved. Disraeli crowed that he had "dished the Whigs" and expected the people to be properly grateful. Unhappily for him the new electorate favored the Liberals, and in the next general election in 1868 Gladstone's party swept to an overwhelming triumph.

The next major extension of the franchise took place under the auspices of the Liberals. The Third Reform Act of 1884 removed most of the remaining barriers to universal manhood suffrage by adding some 2 million agricultural laborers and rural artisans to the voting rolls. The companion Redistribution Act of 1885 abolished the distinction between borough and shire and divided the country into single-member parliamentary constituencies of roughly equal size. Two archaic practices did not disappear until 1948: special members for the universities of Oxford and Cambridge, and plural voting for individuals – mostly wealthy businessmen – who lived in one constituency and worked in another. The final steps to complete universal suffrage took place after World War I. An act of 1918 gave the vote to all males over the age of twenty-one and all women over the age of thirty; and in 1928 women were placed on the same basis as men.

Meanwhile a number of other important political reforms had been effected. In 1858 the property qualification for members of Parliament was abolished. In the same year Lionel Rothschild, a well-propertied individual, became the first professing Jew to enter the House of Commons, which had refused him a seat for ten years although he had been repeatedly re-elected by the City of London. The Ballot Act of 1872 introduced the secret ballot, eliminating much bribery and intimidation at the polls and incidentally making it easier for radicals to secure election. One radical was Charles Bradlaugh, an avowed atheist first elected to Parliament in 1880, who refused to take the oath of office because it included the words, "So help me God." The Commons refused to seat him until 1886 when, after several lawsuits and repeated re-election, Bradlaugh took his seat. In 1888 he secured the passage of a bill removing all religious tests for members of Parliament.

A final set of measures democratizing Parliament and the nation became law in 1911. In 1909 the House of Lords defeated the budget bill of David Lloyd George, the Liberals' fiery chancellor of the exchequer. After two general elections in 1910 showed that the mass of the electorate were behind the Liberals, they persuaded the king to threaten to create 250 Liberal peers unless the Lords gave up the right of veto on all money bills and limited themselves to a suspensive veto on other legislation. In the face of this threat — the same weapon used by the Whigs in 1832 — the Lords capitulated in 1911. The bill provided for general elections at least once every five years, and another law passed shortly afterward provided for payment of salaries to members of the House of Commons. Thus, with minor exceptions, all the demands posed by the Chartists and brusquely rejected more than three-quarters of a century earlier (see p. 95) had been enacted into law.

THE RISE OF THE LABOUR PARTY

A major objective of the Chartists had been to secure representation for workers in Parliament and to make the latter body more responsive to the will of the masses. Even before all their demands had been achieved, the workers succeeded in making their voices heard in Parliament. A few trade union officials won election to the House of Commons as early as the 1870's; they usually voted with the Liberals and were known somewhat derisively as Lib-Labs. J. Keir Hardie foreshadowed a new approach when he won election as an independent in 1892 and shocked the Commons by appearing in the House in a tweed jacket and cloth cap, escorted by a trumpeter. In the following year he formed the Independent Labour party. To strengthen the bases of his support, Hardie persuaded the Trades Union Congress, the Fabians, and other democratic groups to join with the I.L.P. in forming the Labour Representation Committee. In the election of 1900 the committee supported fifteen candidates and succeeded in electing two. It was a small beginning, but it laid the basis for labor representation in Parliament. In the next general election in 1906 the committee put up fifty candidates, elected twenty-nine, and promptly transformed itself into the Labour party.

The new party received a severe setback in 1909, when W. V. Osborne, a union member, won a legal decision in the House of Lords (the final court of appeal) invalidating the practice of trade union contributions to political parties. Since most of Labour's representatives were trade union officials and their campaigns were financed in part with trade union funds, this posed a serious and immediate threat to the future of the party. In 1911 the Liberals came to their aid (thereby contributing to their own demise) with a provision for payment of salaries to members of the House of Commons, but the larger issue was left unresolved. The trade unions began to take matters into their own hands. A wave of increasingly bitter strikes in 1911 and 1912 and the invasion of syndicalist ideas from the Continent persuaded the Liberals in 1913 to pass a new Trade Union Act permitting the unions to make political contributions from a special fund, subject to the consent of individual members. Thereafter the strength of the Labour party increased steadily. Although it divided on the issue of supporting the war effort, as did workers' parties in other countries, one of its members served in the coalition War Cabinet, and in 1922 it replaced the Liberals as the official opposition party.

SOCIAL REFORM

Political reform and the rise of the Labour party were closely connected with social reform and governmental reorganization. In spite of its reputation as a bastion of liberty and its remarkable economic progress, British society in the second half of the nineteenth century was in many respects curiously antiquated. Carrying devotion to laissez faire principles to an extreme, the government acknowledged slight responsibility for such matters as public health, welfare, or education. The structure of government itself was a ramshackle conglomerate of diverse administrations with little centralized direction or control. Nepotism and minor forms of corruption flourished in a situation in which government was regarded almost as a family affair, or at best as the concern of the propertied classes.

Overhaul of the administrative machinery of government constituted a major prerequisite for extensive social reform and modernization. Gladstone tackled the problem in his first administration, from 1868 to 1874, with measures making the civil service accessible by competitive examination, reorganizing the army (including abolition of the practice of purchasing commissions), and reforming the judiciary. In his turn Disraeli codified and extended the various measures dealing with public health and sanitation and made an initial though inadequate attack on the disgraceful conditions of urban housing. Another Conservative government in 1888 carried further the reform of local government.

In spite of its head start in modern industry, Great Britain lagged behind the Continent in measures dealing with the specific hazards of industrial society. The Employers' Liability Act of 1880 required employers to grant compensation to workers for injuries received on the job if the worker could prove that the injury did not result from his own or a co-worker's negligence. In 1906 the law was extended and the emphasis was reversed to cover all injuries "except in cases of serious and willful misconduct." In 1909 Lloyd George inaugurated old-age pensions for retired workers whose annual income was less than $150. In 1911 Lloyd George and young Winston Churchill, who was then a Liberal, led the fight for a National Insurance Act, the most important welfare legislation in Britain to that date. Modeled on German precedents, the law codified earlier accident insurance provisions, extended them to other forms of disability such as sickness, and introduced a limited plan for unemployment compensation. Although Great Britain did not measure up to the advanced practices on the Continent, it preceded the United States in these matters by a quarter of a century.

Nowhere did Britain lag further behind other Western nations than in public support of education. Until 1870 the only schools available were those operated by private or religious foundations, most of which charged fees, except for the parish schools in Scotland. As a result, fully half of the population received no formal education at all. Only the well-to-do received more than the rudiments. This factor more than any other served to preserve Britain's archaic class structure in an age of otherwise rapid social change and contributed notably to the relative decline of Britain's industrial leadership. The Education Bill of 1870 provided state support for existing private and church-connected schools that met certain minimum standards. Not until 1891, however, did education become, even in principle, both free and universal up to the age of twelve. As late as the 1920's only one in eight of the eligible population attended a secondary school.

In higher education England also lagged behind the Continent and the United States. Until state scholarships were instituted in the twentieth century, Oxford and Cambridge were open only to the sons of the wealthy, mainly the aristocracy. By contrast, Scotland, with a much smaller population than England, had four ancient and flourishing universities open to all qualified applicants. London's University College, in existence from 1825, became the University of London in 1898 with the addition of more colleges. In 1880 Manchester became the first provincial city to obtain a new university. By the beginning of the twentieth century the movement to establish municipal universities in the larger cities finally got under way, but even after World War I only four persons per thousand in the appropriate age group were enrolled in a university.

Adult education of the self-help variety had long been popular in Britain, partly as an offset to the inadequate provision of formal educational opportunities. With the rise of labor-class consciousness the movement took on a social orientation. In 1899 Ruskin Hall was established at Oxford as a workingman's college. The Workers' Educational Association, formed in 1903 to reach workers without access to other educational facilities, played a prominent role in bringing culture to the masses and preparing them for a more responsible – and occasionally more aggressive – role in society.

THE IRISH QUESTION

One of the most troublesome problems to face successive British governments in the nineteenth century was that of Ireland. The British had traditionally treated the Irish as a conquered people, and the Irish had never made willing subjects. When Gladstone became prime minister for the first time in 1868, he declared it his "mission" to pacify Ireland. Although he sympathized with oppressed nationalities elsewhere, Gladstone regarded religion and land tenure as the main sources of Irish discontent. Most of the Irish, except in the northern province of Ulster, were Roman Catholics, yet they were taxed to support the established Church of Ireland, the Irish branch of the Church of England. One of Gladstone's first measures was a bill to disestablish the Irish church, which became law in 1869. The following year Parliament passed the Irish Land Act, giving some protection to tenants and facilitating peasant proprietorship. These measures did not, however, allay Irish discontent with English rule. One group of Irish nationalists making use of the recent extension of the franchise formed the Home Rule party to agitate in Parliament for a separate Irish legislature. Charles Parnell, paradoxically a Protestant of English descent, took over the leadership of this movement soon after his election to the House of Commons in 1875. Parnell regarded land reform as a mere palliative and promptly initiated a campaign to ostracize any tenants or landlords who took advantage of the new law. A certain Captain Boycott, the first victim of the campaign, thereby acquired the dubious distinction of having his name become a new word in the English language. The government imprisoned Parnell and several of his followers but released them after six months on their agreement to call off the "boycotts" and to cooperate with the Liberals for further reforms.

After the general election of 1885 Parnell's party held the balance of power in the House of Commons. Parnell first allowed a Conservative government to take office, but when it failed to give him satisfaction, he threw his support to the Liberals. Gladstone promptly introduced a bill to grant home rule, but defections within his own party defeated it. After long debates Gladstone's second home rule bill passed Commons with a small majority in 1893, only to go down to overwhelming defeat in the House of Lords. Gladstone wished to call for new elections, but his cabinet refused to support him. He thereupon retired from politics, an old and disillusioned man, his dream of Irish pacification unfulfilled.

For a time the Irish problem subsided. The Conservatives, who ruled from 1895 to 1905, described their policy as "killing home rule with kindness." In 1912 the Liberals introduced a third home rule bill. It aroused great opposition, not only in the Lords, many of whom were landowners in Ireland, but also among the Protestant inhabitants of Northern Ireland or Ulster, who would be submerged in a united Irish parliament. After long and bitter debates the bill reached its third reading in the Commons in May, 1914. Had it become law at once, civil war between volunteer groups of militiamen in Ulster and the south would certainly have taken place. This catastrophe was postponed by the greater catastrophe of World War I, which overshadowed all other political issues. In a hastily reached compromise the bill received royal assent in September, 1914, with a proviso that it would not take effect until the war was over and new amendments were made to deal with the problem of Ulster. In the event, it never took effect, but bequeathed a bitter legacy to the postwar generation.

THE THIRD FRENCH REPUBLIC

The capitulation of Napoleon III to the Germans at Sedan on September 2, 1870, and the quick reaction of the people of Paris in deposing him brought down the curtain on the Second Empire with a sudden thump. No one knew what the title would be when it rose on the next act in the drama of French politics. Even the names of the principal actors could not be foretold with certainty. *Entre acte,* the Government of National Defense provided a thrilling diversion with its heroic but hopeless attempt to continue the war. It even brought forward a new star in Léon Gambetta, a young radical republican who escaped from besieged Paris in a balloon to organize resistance forces in the provinces. By mid-January the futility of further armed resistance became apparent to all but Gambetta and a relatively small number of last-ditch radicals and socialists. When Paris capitulated on January 28, the armistice provided for the election of a representative assembly to determine whether or not the war should be continued and, if not, on what terms the peace should be concluded.

The hastily called election took place on February 8. Under the circumstances elaborate campaigns and even systematic party programs were impossible. The only issue was peace or war. There could be no doubt that most Frenchmen, war-weary, dispirited, and dismayed, favored peace. Since the radical republicans constituted the only important group prominently identified with a desire to continue the war, it was not surprising that the people voted overwhelmingly for conservatives. When the new National Assembly met for the first time in Bordeaux on February 13, it counted among its numbers more than four hundred monarchists and only about two hundred avowed republicans.

The assembly elected Adolphe Thiers, the most prominent remaining Orleanist politician, as chief executive of the provisional government and empowered him to negotiate a peace treaty with Bismarck. The Prussians imposed severe terms: the transfer of Alsace and part of Lorraine to the new German Empire; payment of a war indemnity of five billion francs (about one billion gold dollars); and a Prussian army of occupation until final payment of the indemnity. Over the heated objections of Gambetta and other radicals (including Louis Blanc, a figure out of the past, and Georges Clemenceau, a prefiguration of the future), the assembly unhappily accepted these terms by a majority of more than five to one. In early March it moved to Versailles to decide upon the definitive form of government. Before it could come to grips with this difficult problem, it found itself involved in a brief but bitter civil war.

THE PARIS COMMUNE

The main republican strength lay in the working classes of the large cities, especially Paris. They had held out longest against the besieging armies and regarded the provisional government's capitulation as a form of betrayal. They resented the monarchist domination of the new assembly as well as the latter's decision to make Versailles, reminiscent of the Old Regime, the capital instead of Paris. When Thiers canceled the wartime moratorium on the payment of debts and rents and cut off the dole to members of the National Guard, the resentment of the Parisians mounted; when on March 18 he ordered the seizure of their arms, it overflowed. The regular army at first refused to fire on the people, but angry mobs seized and murdered two of its generals. The government then ordered a new siege of Paris, this time by Frenchmen. These developments, plus the fact that wealthier residents had long since fled the city, gave control of the city to the most radical elements. They proclaimed a self-governing Commune on the model of 1792 and called on other cities to take similar steps and convert France into a decentralized federal republic. Sympathetic rebellions elsewhere in France soon fell before government forces, but the Communards (not to be confused with Communists) of Paris held out for more than two months.

The fighting was the bloodiest of its kind in history. In the final week alone (May 21–28) more than 15,000 died – many more than during the

Bulloz

Execution at the Cemetery of Père Lachaise, May 28, 1871
from the series "Crimes of the Commune"

Sunday, 28 May 1871.
"I rode in a cab along the Champs-Élysées. In the distance legs, legs running in the direction of the great avenue. I leaned out of the cab window. The entire avenue was filled with a confused mob, between two lines of troopers. I got out of the cab and joined the people running to see what was happening. It was the prisoners who had just been taken at Buttes-Chaumont, marching in ranks of five, with a few women in their midst. 'There were six thousand of them,' a trooper in the escort told me. 'Five hundred were shot on the spot.'"
Edmond de Goncourt, JOURNAL (Paris, 1956).

June Days of 1848. The Communards executed many hostages, including the archbishop of Paris, and in their last hours set fire to several public buildings, notably the Tuileries palace and the city hall. The attacking forces shot on sight, and after the final collapse of the Commune they executed thousands.

Such an orgy of blood-letting could not fail to have important long-run consequences. Coming after similar episodes at the beginning of the two previous French republics, it created an almost unbridgeable chasm between the affected social classes. The collective psychological scars that it left have not fully healed after a century. Yet in one sense it worked to the benefit of the Third Republic. After many of the most radical republican leaders had been executed, imprisoned, deported, or exiled, those who remained either stayed in the background or took a more moderate line, thereby giving the moderate and conservative republicans an opportunity to win the majority of the French people away from monarchic leanings. A notable example of the transformation was Léon Gambetta, who in spite of his earlier intransigence took the view that a conservative republic was better than no republic at all.

THE ESTABLISHMENT OF THE REPUBLIC

For most of its first decade the Third Republic threatened to relapse into a monarchy at any moment. That it did not do so at once can be accounted for only by the divisions among the monarchists themselves. In the assembly they were split almost evenly between the supporters of the Legitimist (Bourbon) count of Chambord (Henry V, as he styled himself), grandson of Charles X, and the Orleanist count of Paris, grandson of Louis Philippe. Since Chambord had no direct heirs, the rival monarchist groups agreed that he should first accede to the throne but should name the count of Paris as his successor. Chambord, who had spent forty of his fifty years in exile, returned to France in July, 1871, to announce the terms on which he would accept the throne. They amounted to little less than an integral restoration of the Old Regime, symbolized by his insistence on replacing the French tricolor with the Bourbon fleur-de-lis. Such a restoration was not acceptable to many of Chambord's own supporters, much less acceptable to the Orleanists, whose ideal was a British type of constitutional monarchy, and anathema to the resurgent republicans. In the by-elections held shortly before Chambord's manifesto the republicans gained 99 out of 114 seats in the assembly.

To give themselves time to regroup and reformulate their strategy, the monarchists allowed Thiers to assume the title of president of the Republic in August, 1871. At the same time they declared their intention not to dissolve the assembly until it had given France a new constitution, which they intended should be monarchic. As time went by, the monarchists became increasingly suspicious of Thiers's connivance with the republicans for a maintenance of the status quo. Thiers ultimately declared that "the republic is the form of government which divides us least." In 1873, therefore, as soon as Thiers's government had paid the last installment of the indemnity to Prussia, the monarchist majority in the assembly forced him to resign and replaced him with Marshal MacMahon, an old soldier of monarchist predilections but little experience in politics. At the appropriate moment he was to give way to royalty.

The results of by-elections steadily whittled down the majority of the monarchists, who realized that they would have to act promptly to preserve the framework for a royalist restoration. They obtained the enactment of the so-called organic laws of 1875, which served France as a constitution for the entire life of the Third Republic. It is one of the ironies of French history that the only republican constitution that did not proclaim itself to be based on "eternal and immutable" principles – one, indeed, frankly regarded as provisional – should have given France its longest period of stable government in modern times. The laws provided for a bicameral legislature with an upper house, the Senate, elected indirectly for long and staggered terms; a lower house, the Chamber of Deputies; a cabinet and prime minister responsible to the legislature; and a figurehead president elected by the legislature. Although republican in name, such a constitution could easily be made to serve a constitutional monarchy as well. On the last day of 1875 the National Assembly that had been elected at the beginning of 1871 to decide on the question of peace or war dissolved itself to make way for the new constitutional system that it had designed.

THREATS TO THE REPUBLIC

The new Chamber of Deputies, elected by universal manhood suffrage, had a republican majority of more than two to one. This majority did not mean that the Republic was solidly established, however, for MacMahon's term as president had five years to run, and the new Senate was dominated, as intended, by conservatives inclined toward monarchy. The republicans themselves were divided into three broad groups: conservative republicans, mainly ex-Orleanists like Thiers; moderate or opportunist republicans; and the radicals led by Gambetta, egalitarian in spirit and Jacobin by tradition. In subsequent years this division accounted for the extreme instability of ministries, whose life expectancy averaged less than one year. As long as the monarchist-clerical coalition posed a serious threat to republican institutions, however, the various republican groups banded together in an uneasy alliance to meet the successive crises, of which there were several in the next twenty-five years.

The first overt crisis was the *seize mai* episode. On May 16, 1877, President MacMahon in a moment of impatience provoked the resignation of Jules Simon, the moderate republican prime minister. When the Chamber of Deputies refused to approve the prime minister designated by the president, MacMahon dissolved it and called a new election. Although the republicans lost a few seats, they still commanded a substantial majority and forced the president to accept a ministry in which they had confidence. Thereafter no president or prime minister of the Third Republic forced a dissolution of the Chamber. In January, 1879, partial elections to the Senate resulted in republican control of that body. This surprising outcome demonstrated that republican sentiment had infiltrated and conquered even the small towns and villages, which held the balance of power in indirect elections for the Senate. Faced with hostile majorities in both Chamber and Senate, President MacMahon resigned a year before his term expired.

With the Republic apparently safeguarded, the opportunists, who now occupied the center of the stage, proceeded to carry out their legislative program. Its overriding objective was to instill such strong republican sentiments in Frenchmen that no internal threat to the Republic could ever again arise. In order to win the allegiance of the working classes, the government amnestied the remaining veterans of the Commune and in 1884 legalized trade unions once again. Otherwise the government paid scant heed to the needs and desires of workingmen, with the result that anarchist and socialist doctrines retained a strong hold on French workers, and their loyalty to the bourgeois republic remained suspect.

The government took more positive action in the field of education and religion. In both instances the aim was to restrict the influence of the church and the clerical party, the strongest allies of the monarchists. A law in 1882 introduced compulsory public education between the ages of six and thirteen and ensured that it would be free of all religious training. A generation of dedicated schoolmasters drilled the youth of France with ideals of patriotism, republicanism, and secularism. In the process they reduced illiteracy from a third or more of the adult population to a negligible figure. The government once more legalized divorce (first legalized during the Revolution, then banned in 1816), thus striking another blow at the moral influence of the church.

Before these measures could produce their full effects, new threats to the regime arose. In 1886 General Georges Boulanger became minister of war for a brief period. He was a strikingly handsome and impressive man, given to frequent and elegant public appearances (usually on a white horse), who came to symbolize for many Frenchmen the desire and possibility of revenge against Germany. Although originally sponsored in politics by the radical republicans, he soon began to cultivate friendships on the extreme right as well. In either case he was a danger to the center parties, who quickly dropped him from office. In 1887 the government was weakened by revelations that the president's son-in-law had been peddling political favors and influence, while Boulanger's popularity continued to grow in spite of all the government could do to keep him out of the public view. In January, 1889, after a particularly impressive showing by Boulanger in a Paris by-election, conditions seemed ripe for a coup d'état. Although it probably would have been accepted by a majority of the people, Boulanger lost his nerve at the crucial moment and, instead of marching on the government, sought the solace of his mistress. Soon afterward he fled into exile in Belgium, where he committed suicide in 1891.

The most serious threat, not only to the government but to the whole fabric of French society, arose in the Dreyfus case. Evidence that secret documents of the French army had been transmitted to Germany led in 1894 to the trial and conviction by a court-martial of Captain Alfred Dreyfus, a Jewish officer on the general staff. Dreyfus was sentenced to life imprisonment on Devil's Island. It subsequently developed that he had been convicted on forged evidence and that the real culprit was still on active duty with the army, but the army acquitted the guilty man and refused to reopen the Dreyfus case. In 1898 the affair became a cause célèbre with the dramatic intervention of the novelist Émile Zola, who published an open letter (*J'accuse*) to the president accusing by name the high officers of the army responsible for railroading Dreyfus and shielding the guilty. Individual personalities were soon pushed into the background by the political, social, and religious overtones of the struggle. The Dreyfusards, or defenders of Dreyfus, regarded themselves as defenders of the Republic and of the "ideas of 1789," whereas in the opposite camp were ranged all those who had consistently opposed those ideas in the past—the diehard royalists and ultramontane Catholics, as well as the aristocratic officer corps and professional anti-Semites. All France took sides, sometimes in the form of open clashes in the streets. Even the socialists under the leadership of Jean Jaurès rallied to the defense of Dreyfus and the Republic. At length in 1906 Dreyfus was completely exonerated, decorated, and restored to the army with the rank of major.

For the nation at large the more important consequence of the Dreyfus affair was the victory of the Republic over its enemies, the resulting reform of the army, and the separation of church and state. As early as 1901 the government adopted a set of stringent laws directed principally at the monastic orders whose members had taken an active part in the anti-Dreyfusard agitation. Stronger measures followed, resulting in the suppression of some orders, the closure of Catholic schools, and the secularization of church property. Finally in 1905 France abrogated Napoleon's Concordat with the pope and declared a complete separation of church and state. In subsequent years the restrictions on monastic orders were relaxed, Catholic schools reopened, and the churches returned to the congregations; but separation of church and state remains today as much a principle of French as of American political life.

LA BELLE ÉPOQUE

In spite of the humiliation of 1870–71 and the numerous crises both foreign and domestic in which France was involved before 1914, many Frenchmen after World War I looked back on the prewar years as *la belle époque,* the good old days. Their attitude seems paradoxical, but it had a reasonable basis. The outlook for France had been bleak indeed in the 1870's, but the situation gradually improved until, in the last decade before World War I, Frenchmen not only enjoyed reasonable political stability but also military strength and greater prosperity than ever before. After a long depression from 1882 to 1897 the French economy recovered its vitality and exhibited a growth rate equal to that of any advanced industrial nation. By the early years of the twentieth century the French had forged a strong alliance with Russia and had even brought Great Britain out of its "splendid isolation" into an *entente cordiale.* (See pp. 319–320.) Frenchmen could once more hold up their heads with the proud nations of the world.

After the Dreyfus affair no major political crisis or scandal troubled the domestic scene until World War I. Cabinets continued to rise and fall with alarming frequency, but such ministerial instability was accepted by the French as one of the facts of political life. It was quite consistent with a fundamental political and social stability, for the ministers in successive cabinets usually came from the same coalition of political parties. In many instances an individual minister retained his post even though the cabinet itself changed. The professional and expert civil service provided a fundamental continuity of administration through all the surface changes of ministries. Thus, the fragmentation and apparent disorderliness of French political life with its multiplicity of parties and ever-changing ministries, was superficial and somewhat illusory. Frenchmen themselves, who through sad experience had grown to distrust strong governments, seemed to prefer the situation.

THE SECOND GERMAN REICH

The first Germanic empire, founded by Charlemagne, existed (in form, at least) for a thousand years. The second empire or Reich, founded by Bismarck, lasted only from 1871 to 1918. The immediate cause of its downfall was defeat in World War I, but even if there had been no war, it is unlikely that it would have long endured in its original form. More than any other government in modern times, including even the Napoleonic empire, it was the creation of a single individual. As long as the creator remained in control, he succeeded by devious stratagems and abrupt changes of course in making its complicated machinery function remarkably well. Thereafter, in spite of a superficial semblance of harmonious, almost monolithic operation, the centrifugal tendencies of its parts created strains that sooner or later would have torn it asunder. Accordingly, the history of the Second Reich divides itself for purposes of narrative and analysis into two periods: that of Bismarck (1871–1890) and that of his successors (1890–1918).

THE STRUCTURE OF THE GOVERNMENT

The form of the government was itself a bundle of paradoxes and ambiguities: monarchic, federal, and democratic in appearance, but paternalistic and authoritarian in fact. The constitution, adopted on April 14, 1871, was simply a remodeled version of the constitution of the North German Confederation, which had also been a creation of Bismarck. The empire was composed of twenty-five formerly independent states (four kingdoms; eighteen duchies, grand duchies, and principalities; and three free cities) plus the "imperial territory" of Alsace-Lorraine. The component states conserved much autonomy for strictly local government matters, such as education, although even there they had to fight against the Prussianizing tendencies of the imperial government. The imperial government had principal responsibility for military and foreign affairs but also exerted its authority in economic, social, and religious matters. For the exercise of its functions it possessed a bicameral legislature and an imperial cabinet or chancellery. The office of emperor was hereditary in the person of the king of Prussia.

The Reichstag, the lower house of the Imperial Diet or legislature, gave the regime its semblance of democracy. Representatives were elected from single-member constituencies by universal manhood suffrage. The powers of the body were severely limited, however, especially in the matter of finances, the crucial element in representative government. In certain circumstances the imperial government could dispense with approval of the budget by the Reichstag. All legislation from the Reichstag had to be agreed to by the Bundesrat or federal council, which consisted of the personal representatives of the ruling princes and in which Prussia could always command a majority. The imperial chancellor, appointed by the emperor, served as president of the Bundesrat, but he was responsible neither to it nor to the Reichstag.

Under these conditions the Reichstag functioned mainly as a register of public opinion, which the government might follow or not. Bismarck, as chancellor, did not scruple to override public opinion on occasion, but as a shrewd politician, he sought more often to lead and manipulate it. This he did by working with the principal parties in the Reichstag. The Conservative party represented chiefly the East Elbian Junker aristocracy, Bismarck's own class. The National Liberal party represented the west German bourgeoisie of wealthy merchants, industrialists, and financiers. The Catholic Center party had its main strength in south Germany, but it also had representatives wherever Catholics were numerous, as among Rhenish workers and Silesian peasants. In addition to these major parties there were several minor ones: the Progressives, liberals who had opposed Bismarck in the past; the Social Democrats, representing the workers; and representatives of national minorities such as the Danes, the Poles, and the inhabitants of Alsace-Lorraine.

BISMARCKIAN POLITICS

Bismarck's policies appear at first sight curiously contradictory, as though he did not know what he wanted. First he favored free trade, then he became an ardent protectionist. He opposed colonial expansion, but laid the foundations of the German overseas empire. He persecuted the socialists, but enacted the first state-supported social insurance system in the world. In foreign affairs, he who had earlier deliberately provoked three wars devoted his efforts to preserving the peace. Yet underneath these apparent inconsistencies lay a determined and consistent purpose: to preserve the empire and his own place within it. The empire had been created by force, and it might be destroyed by force; therefore he must prevent war. If the socialists constituted a menace to the internal stability of the government, the workers must be weaned away from socialism. When the National Liberals' enthusiasm for free trade and his own leadership showed signs of slackening because of the industrial depression of the 1870's and increasing foreign competition, he put through the protective tariff law of 1879 in order to placate the manufacturers and also curry favor with the Conservatives. Similarly, his conversion to colonialism was no more than a strategic concession to the force of public opinion.

The first major domestic problem faced — or provoked — by the new government concerned its relations with the Roman Catholic Church. The issue was the supremacy of church or state in the areas where their interests overlapped, especially with respect to authority over the individual. The name given to the issue, *Kulturkampf,* meaning struggle for civilization, signified Bismarck's intention that there should be no divided loyalties within the empire. As recently as 1864 in the *Syllabus of Errors* the Church had declared it an "error" (hence a sin) to believe that the civil authority of the state should be superior to or separated from the Roman Catholic Church, and in 1870 the Church had laid down the doctrine of papal infallibility in questions of faith and morals. It was perhaps even more important from Bismarck's point of view that the traditionally Catholic south German states resented domination by Protestant Prussia, for political and cultural as well as religious reasons, and it was they who provided the strength and leadership of the Center party in opposition to Bismarck.

Between 1871 and 1875 Bismarck undertook a number of measures designed to harass, weaken, and even destroy the Catholic Church in Germany. Most of the measures applied only to Prussia, since the other states retained autonomy in religious, educational, and cultural affairs. Some, however, including the expulsion of the Jesuits, the severance of diplomatic relations with the Vatican, and the law making civil marriage compulsory, affected the entire empire. In spite of intense persecution, the Catholics showed no sign of wavering and in some respects actually throve on it. At length Bismarck realized the futility of his policy; when the more diplomatic and conciliatory Leo XIII succeeded Pius IX in 1878, Bismarck relaxed his campaign and eventually called it off altogether. By 1883 the *Kulturkampf* was at an end.

Some historians have speculated that the religious question was secondary in Bismarck's mind when he undertook the *Kulturkampf* and that what he really wanted was a convenient whipping boy to divert public attention from other problems and to arouse popular sentiment in favor of the empire. This interpretation gains credence from the next episode in Bismarck's domestic policies, the persecution of the socialists. In the elections of 1878 almost all the opposition parties made gains at the expense of the National Liberals. This development prompted Bismarck to "build a bridge" between the agrarian protectionists in the Conservative party and the industrialists in the National Liberal party, who had begun to demand protection for their own products, by effecting the protective tariff law of 1879. Simultaneously he initiated a campaign against the socialists, who were the weakest and most vulnerable of the opposition parties. His justification came from two recent attempts to assassinate the emperor. Although the socialists were in no way involved with either attempt, he used them as a pretext for outlawing the Social Democratic party. Although the Reichstag refused to unseat the socialist members, and several were re-elected as independents with trade union support, the party itself was forced underground, and many of its leaders were imprisoned or sought refuge abroad.

When it appeared likely that this policy, too, might backfire, Bismarck resolved to win the workers away from socialism with a carrot-and-stick technique. In 1883 he sponsored a compulsory sickness insurance plan for workers, followed in 1884 by an accident insurance plan, and in 1889 by a pension plan for the aged and permanently disabled. These measures were consolidated and extended by Bismarck's successors and gave

---

Dropping the Pilot, cartoon from *Punch*
March 29, 1890

"The Emperor related the whole story of his difference with Bismarck. He said that relations had become strained as early as December. The Emperor then desired that something should be done upon the question of the workmen. The Chancellor objected. . . . This friction had considerably disturbed the relations between Bismarck and the Emperor, and these were further strained by the question of the Cabinet Order of 1852. Bismarck had often advised the Emperor to grant the ministers access to himself and this was done. But when communications between the Emperor and his ministers became more frequent, Bismarck took offense, became jealous, and revived the Cabinet Order of 1852 in order to break communications between the Emperor and his ministers. . . . The last three weeks were occupied by unpleasant discussions between the Emperor and Bismarck. It was, as the Emperor expressed it, 'a stormy time,' and the question at issue was, as the Emperor went on to say, whether the Hohenzollern dynasty or the Bismarck dynasty should reign." MEMOIRS OF PRINCE CHLODWIG OF HOHENLOHE-SCHILLINGSFURST (New York, 1906).

Germany the first and most comprehensive system of social insurance and labor protection dealing specifically with the new problems created by modern industrial society.

DROPPING THE PILOT

In 1888 the old emperor, William I, died. Frederick III, his son and successor, survived him by only three months. The new emperor, William II, grandson of Queen Victoria of Britain as well as of William I, was only twenty-nine at the time. Handsome and intelligent, he promised to bring an unaccustomed glamor to the throne. But he was also headstrong

Courtesy of *Punch* Magazine

and unpredictable and lost no time in coming into conflict with the venerable Bismarck, who for so long had had things his own way. The differences between the two were not merely differences of policy, or even of personality, though these counted for much; fundamentally they were differences between the generations. The immediate sources of friction involved both foreign and domestic policy. William objected to Bismarck's conciliatory gestures to Russia. At the same time he favored the conciliation of the working-class population at home and allowed the antisocialist laws to lapse. Even more revealing of their basic differences, William objected to Bismarck's practice of sitting in on interviews between the emperor and his other ministers. At the beginning of 1890 William suggested to Bismarck that he should "ask permission to resign." Bismarck refused, but William persisted and soon drove him from the chancellery. It was an ironic turn of events. Bismarck, who had so carefully insulated the office of chancellor from both popular and parliamentary opinion, now found himself ejected by his own creation, the emperor.

Bismarck's departure had more serious consequences for international affairs than for domestic politics. (See p. 318.) It was in foreign policy that he had achieved his greatest success, and this was precisely the arena in which his successors were least able and successful. In domestic policy he had managed by intricate footwork to hold in check temporarily the centrifugal tendencies of the nation. In the long run, however, his domestic policies contributed to widening and perpetuating the internal divisions of the German people.

BISMARCK'S SUCCESSORS

William's dismissal of Bismarck made it clear that he intended to serve in effect as his own chancellor. To fill the office, he first selected General George von Caprivi, a soldier and administrator without political experience. Caprivi's tenure (1890–1894) was notable chiefly for the negotiation of a number of commercial treaties that aroused the fury of the great landowners, the stalwarts of the Conservative party. Caprivi also managed to antagonize the Catholics, the colonialists, and the militarists. These misfortunes, together with the difficulty of working with the emperor, who was given to making policy pronouncements in public without consulting his ministers, led to Caprivi's resignation.

The chancellorships of Caprivi's successors — Prince Hohenlohe-Schillingsfürst (1894–1900), Count von Bülow (1900–1909), and Theobald von Bethmann-Hollweg (1909–1917) — were increasingly dominated by military and foreign affairs in the march toward World War I. Under Hohenlohe two projects that had been long in preparation reached completion. The opening of the Kiel Canal, joining the Baltic and North seas, capped a period of significant improvement in Germany's internal communications system and symbolized its advent as a sea power. The codification of civil law, which had been in process since 1871, gave the German states a uniform, comprehensive legal system for the first time in their history. The new code went into effect January 1, 1900.

THE "REVISIONIST" CONTROVERSY

The empire experienced its only parliamentary crisis of the Western type in 1906 when the Center party, which had held the balance of power in the Reichstag since 1890 and derived great advantage from it, joined with the Social Democrats and other radical parties to defeat a government bill to strengthen Germany's colonial empire. Bülow dissolved the Reichstag and called on the electorate to repudiate the Catholics and socialists. In the election of 1907 the Center party held its ground, but the Social Democrats lost heavily in their only major setback between 1890 and 1914. This defeat played an important role in the reorientation of Social Democratic policies, which in turn had reverberations in the entire international socialist movement.

At the time of its formation the German Social Democratic party had adopted a party platform that represented a compromise between Marxian revolutionary socialism and Lassallean state socialism. Under Bismarck's persecution the ideology of the party steadily became more revolutionary, until in 1891 it adopted an almost pure Marxian platform, which remained official doctrine until 1918. During the period of persecution some of the party members went into foreign exile. One of the exiles, Eduard Bernstein, spent much time in England, where he observed the operation of the British parliamentary system and became acquainted with several of the Fabian leaders. After his return to Germany in the 1890's he advocated that Social Democratic parties should abandon their revolutionary ideologies and work within the established political order for peaceful social, economic, and political reform. He pointed out that contrary to Marx's prophecy, the masses were not growing poorer; their position was steadily improving. The bourgeois state was not approaching a final crisis; it was gaining in strength as it became more democratic. Hence, instead of trying to overthrow the state, the socialists should try to hasten its evolution in the direction of democracy and socialism. Bernstein's modifications of orthodox Marxist doctrine became known as revisionism and had a powerful impact on the socialist movement both in Germany and abroad.

The German Social Democratic party debated Bernstein's revisionism in party congresses in 1901 and 1903. In formal votes the congresses defeated Bernstein's proposals, but in actual practice the leadership conformed more and more to the tactics of gradualism. Although the party clung to its tradition of nonparticipation in bourgeois governments, it went so far as to help the Progressives organize the Reichstag after the latter obtained a plurality in the election of 1912.

On the eve of World War I Germany appeared to be a powerful, cohesive state. Powerful it was, both militarily and economically, but politically and socially it was a divided nation in spite of its semblance of unity. Apart from its federal structure and the continuing suspicion between Protestant Prussia and the Catholic south, the social divisions between the workers and the middle classes, and between the urban dwellers, the landed aristocracy, and the peasantry, were great and pervasive.

The artificial Bismarckian constitution, despite its increasingly anachronistic character, remained rigid in the mold of its maker. Although the patriotic enthusiasm generated by the outbreak of World War I temporarily submerged the political and social antagonisms, they lay just under the surface and sprang forth in still more virulent form in the wake of the wartime defeat.

THE LESSER STATES OF WESTERN EUROPE

In an era of international rivalries the very fact of great power status introduces a bias into the domestic political history of the great powers, a bias often exaggerated by historians. With the smaller states, on the other hand, we can abstract from the influences of international politics and observe the details of social, political, and economic forces at close range, as though in a laboratory. And, in some cases, we can observe the repercussions of great-power politics on nations whose vital interests may be involved but who, in the nature of the case, cannot take independent action. The results are not without general interest.

ITALY

Italy occupied an ambiguous position in the late nineteenth century. Its population entitled it to rank with the smaller of the great powers, and its political leaders definitely had great power aspirations. They built up an army and navy, entered alliances with the other great powers, and made a bid for colonial empire. Yet basically Italy was a poor country with grave internal problems, quite unsuited for the great power status it tried to maintain.

Italy had few natural resources and no coal at all. The population density was one of the highest in Europe, yet much of the country was mountainous and infertile. Well over half the population derived its meager subsistence from agriculture, conducted under essentially medieval conditions, especially in the south. A few regions in the north, such as Piedmont and Lombardy, had relatively progressive agriculture and even some modern industry, but this only accentuated the great disparity between north and south. The majority of Italians were illiterate in 1860. The state made no provision for public education until 1877, and even then it was largely ineffective, although some gains in literacy were achieved by 1914.

One of the most critical Italian political problems was the relationship of the state and the Catholic Church. The pope refused to accept the law of papal guarantees (see p. 140) and forbade Catholics to participate in national politics or government. For a country with a 99 per cent Catholic population this might have led to a paralysis of all political and governmental affairs except that many Italians, though nominal Catholics, were either nonbelievers or anticlerical. Yet the Church's ban did prevent devout Catholics from contributing constructively to political life. The Church partially relaxed its ban on political participation in 1904 and repealed it in 1919; but it did not come to terms with the Italian government until 1929, when it concluded the Lateran Treaty with Benito Mussolini.

Italian political parties grouped themselves in loose coalitions of Right and Left, although the names themselves were almost meaningless. *Transformismo* (opportunism) is the best description of their policies, the objective of which was to gain and retain office by whatever means they could. In 1876 the Left overthrew the Right, which had governed the country since the death of Cavour; and until after World War I various shifting coalitions of the Left dominated the cabinet. Agostino Depretis, Francesco Crispi, and Giovanni Giolitti were the outstanding names of the period, chiefly for the ingenious forms of corruption and pressure that they invented to remain in power. The parliament served as a bazaar for special interests and a sounding board for demagogic nationalist oratory, while the social and economic welfare of the population went unheeded. Less than 10 per cent of the population had the franchise until 1912, when all males over the age of thirty were permitted to vote. Socialist and anarchist sentiment made rapid headway among the workers after about 1890. In the absence of any machinery for making their grievances known in a legitimate fashion, the workers resorted to strikes, riots, and other forms of lawlessness, which became endemic and provided the seedbed for the rival totalitarian movements that sprouted after World War I.

SPAIN AND PORTUGAL

Spain differed from Italy primarily in its steady retreat from any claim to great power status. The restored Bourbon government of 1874 had the appearance of a constitutional monarchy but the substance of a seventeenth-century absolute monarchy. The king ruled with the assistance of a cabal of ministers, who easily dominated the hand-picked Cortes (parliament). The enactment of universal male suffrage in 1890 failed to change the situation, for the strong clerical influence throughout the country was favorable to the monarchy. Spain remained predominantly rural, and economic and social conditions in the rural areas had changed little since the sixteenth century. In the few large cities where modern industry took root, notably Barcelona, socialists and anarchists made converts among the disaffected workers, but calls to class war in the form of general strikes went unheeded in the country at large. A more serious menace to the government was the pronounced regionalism in some of the provinces, especially in Catalonia and the Basque country, which took the form of demands for local autonomy or even a federal form of government.

Spain lost most of the remnants of its colonial empire in the war with the United States in 1898, although it retained a few toeholds in Africa. The war revealed for both Spaniards and outside observers the full extent of Spanish backwardness and political demoralization. Urgent pleas by patriotic liberals for national regeneration evoked little response. Apathy ruled on the surface, while revolutionary pressures were building up below.

Economic and social conditions in Portugal resembled those in Spain, but the revolutionary ferment formed more quickly. The extravagance and licentiousness of Carlos I (1889–1908) in a country noted for its poverty, together with an extremely repressive and dictatorial regime, provoked the assassination of the king and his eldest son in 1908. Two years later an insurrection overthrew Manuel II, his successor, and a republic was proclaimed. The republican regime had an idealistic program of reform, which it initiated with an attack on the privileged position of the Church, the stronghold of royalism and reaction. The liberal republicans maintained their precarious position for a few years, but they had little chance of success. They were a tiny group surrounded by powerful, reactionary landlords and an illiterate, clerically dominated peasantry on the one side and disaffected, anarchist urban workers on the other. Portugal, like Spain and Italy, lacked both the economic and social prerequisites to make a democracy function effectively.

SWITZERLAND AND THE LOW COUNTRIES

The history of the small nations of northwestern Europe furnishes an illuminating contrast to that of the Mediterranean area. Although the natural endowments of Switzerland and the Low Countries were no greater, and they were plagued with religious and ethnic divisions as well, they all contrived to make democracy work.

The Swiss consist of a German-speaking majority, with four French cantons in the west and two Italian cantons south of the Alps; but at no time has a major political dispute flared along linguistic lines. Although in 1847 the Catholic central cantons leagued against the Protestant cantons in the west and north, since the settlement of 1848 religious strife has been equally absent. This remarkable record was in part the result of a desire to preserve Swiss neutrality and to prevent great power intervention in domestic affairs. The spirit of toleration and willingness to compromise developed into a national tradition. In 1874 the constitution of 1848 was revised to give the federal government still larger powers at the expense of the cantons, but it also contained the novel democratic safeguards of the initiative and referendum. It strengthened the already advanced educational system by requiring universal free elementary schooling under federal supervision. Because of the Swiss system of education and their tradition of fine craftsmanship, modern industry made steady progress. After 1880 hydroelectricity helped to offset the lack of other natural resources. In the 1890's Switzerland adopted a comprehensive program of social welfare legislation on the German model, and in 1898 it began to nationalize the railroads. By 1914 the Swiss enjoyed not only political democracy but also one of the highest standards of living in Europe.

The Belgians are divided between the French-speaking Walloons in the south and east and the Flemish in the north and west. Although the nation is Catholic on the whole, the Walloons had a tradition of anticlericalism which flourished in the Liberal and later the Labor parties, whereas the Catholic party drew its main strength from Flanders. The Liberal-Catholic coalition that ruled the country in the perilous years after the achievement of independence in 1830 broke up in 1847. The Liberals generally controlled the government until 1884. In 1879 they passed a law that prohibited religious education in state-supported schools and withdrew state aid from Church-related schools. That resulted in their defeat at the polls in the next election. The new Catholic government reversed the law of 1879, and in 1895 a new law made instruction in the Catholic religion compulsory, even in public schools.

Property qualifications for voting, even after the liberalization of 1848, limited the electorate to less than 5 per cent of the population. The majority of workingmen were effectively disfranchised. In 1855 trade unionists and socialists formed the Belgian Labor party and began to agitate for electoral reform. Under the threat of a general strike in 1893 the parliament introduced universal manhood suffrage, but modified it with a provision allowing plural voting for those with special property, educational, and other qualifications. Agitation broke out again during the following decade, and in 1913 another general strike resulted in a promise of electoral revision; but before it could be implemented, World War I intervened. Not until 1919 did Belgium achieve the ideal of "one man, one vote."

The Dutch had no significant ethnic problems, though the religious division of the country provided a full measure of political headaches. Under the restricted suffrage that prevailed until 1917 (in spite of minor extensions in 1887 and 1896) the anticlerical Liberal party, which drew its strength from the professional men and merchants of the cities, had the largest representation in parliament. They stood firmly for a system of free secular schools. In 1889, however, a rare Catholic-Calvinist coalition secured financial assistance for the church-related schools. Religious disputes continued to flare up, to which were joined demonstrations by workers in favor of political and social reform. None of these reached revolutionary proportions, and the Netherlands, like Belgium and Switzerland, evolved peacefully if slowly in the direction of full democracy.

SCANDINAVIA

The Scandinavian countries, especially Sweden, present an unusual example of a relatively rapid, complete, and successful transition to modern industrial conditions with a minimum of social friction and dislocation. In 1850 economic conditions had changed little from those that prevailed in the eighteenth century and earlier. In Sweden, 90 per cent of the population lived in rural areas, and 80 per cent gained their living directly from agriculture. As late as 1870 more than 72 per cent of the population still drew their sustenance from agriculture, and the rural population accounted for 87 per cent. During the 1850's and 1860's the first railroads and modern financial institutions made their appearance. Economic thought and policy veered away from the older mercantilist notions toward liberalism and free trade. The rising world demand for iron and timber, especially after the free trade treaties of the 1860's, imparted a new impulse to Swedish industry. The curve of industrial production turned sharply upward in the 1870's and reached peak rates in the 1890's and the first years of the twentieth century, when the value of output in manufacturing, mining, and handicraft industries first exceeded that of agricultural and subsidiary occupations, including forestry. New industries — pulp and paper, mechanical engineering, electrical products and power — swelled the volume of industrial production and created new demands for labor. By 1910 more than half the population and an even larger proportion of the labor force lived and worked in nonagricultural conditions and occupations. Equally rapid and extensive political and social changes accompanied the economic changes with surprising ease. From autocratic-aristocratic rule the government evolved through liberal parliamentary forms toward the social welfare state for which Sweden has subsequently become famous. In 1914 the Social Democratic party, unknown in 1890, won a third of the seats in the lower house of the Riksdag.

Since the Scandinavians were relatively homogeneous in race, religion, and culture, they had no significant religious or ethnic problems. They did, however, have a nationality problem. At the Congress of Vienna Norway had been placed under the Swedish crown, although it had its own Storting (parliament). The Norwegians were never happy over union with the Swedes. In the latter half of the century a strong national revival took place, expressed chiefly in literature and music and producing such eminent figures as Henrik Ibsen, Björnstjerne Björnson, and Edvard Grieg. Political agitation followed, and in 1905 the Storting declared the union with Sweden dissolved. Rather than resort to force (as the Swedish king had done in similar circumstances in 1814), the Swedish Riksdag acquiesced and approved a treaty of separation. Norway elected a Danish prince as king but retained and extended its highly democratic political system, perhaps the most advanced in Europe.

Many factors accounted for the success of the Scandinavian countries in achieving both political and economic progress. Three in particular stood out (shared to some extent by Switzerland and the Low Countries), in sharp contrast to the countries of the Mediterranean. In the first place, all had relatively good educational systems dating from the early nineteenth century. This created a more intelligent, adaptable population and facilitated economic and political change. Second, none of the countries was tempted to play the role of a great power. They not only avoided the economic strain of maintaining large standing armies and engaging in armaments races but were also spared the establishment of military elites, which in almost every other country proved to be fundamentally undemocratic. Third, whether or not this contributed in a positive fashion to political stability, all the countries had multiparty political systems. Anglo-Saxons are accustomed to regard the two-party traditions of the British Parliament and the American Congress as the best guarantee of political stability and orderly government, so that it is worth noting that other, equally democratic countries have managed very well with three or more parties. Perhaps the fundamental reason for success is that the Scandinavians simply wanted democracy.

THREE ARCHAIC EMPIRES
CHAPTER NINE

The optimism, confidence, and increasing rapport between the government and the governed that followed the spread of democratic reform in western Europe was not shared by the peoples who lived in the three great empires that made up eastern Europe. In Russia, the Hapsburg dominions, and the Ottoman Empire the always immense gulf between rulers and ruled widened in the century between 1815 and 1914. The rulers sought to prevent the social and political changes of western Europe from invading their domains. Failing that, they tried to contain the changes within the old order in such a way as to subtract as little as possible from their own power and to keep their people in continued subservience. Their efforts failed, in part because they lacked the vision and the courage to make needed fundamental reforms in the political and social structure, in part because they could not overcome the unsatisfied aspirations of the subject peoples. As a result, their empires lacked the inner strength and cohesion to withstand the catastrophes that rained upon them during World War I.

RUSSIA IN THE NINETEENTH CENTURY

Until 1906 Russia successfully withstood the new liberal and nationalist pressures of the nineteenth century. The tsars were able to retain absolute power because most Russians were peasants who held their ruler in almost religious awe. The urban middle class – the people who in the west took the lead in progressive reform – formed a small minority of Russia's population. Leadership in the movement for reform came from the intellectuals or intelligentsia, as the Russians called them. They were drawn at first almost entirely from the nobility and gentry and only later in the nineteenth century from the educated members of the middle class. They used every device they could think of, from literature to assassination and open revolt, to force change. They met with repeated failures until early in the twentieth century, when changes in the Russian social and economic structure provided the mass following that they needed to compel the government to make concessions.

ALEXANDER I

Much was expected of Alexander I when he succeeded to the throne of Russia in 1801. As a youth, he had been drilled in the ideals of the Enlightenment by his tutor, César La Harpe, a Swiss disciple of the *philosophes*. Alexander liked to talk about the rights of man and the obligations of a monarch to his subjects, but events proved that his liberalism was only a façade. An indecisive man, he was given to paradoxical behavior and sudden enthusiasms, supporting without restraint any idea that attracted him, then tiring of it and devoting himself with equal ardor to some other proposal. Although he ordered a number of minor reforms during his early years on the throne and met frequently with a so-called unofficial committee of liberals to discuss innovations such as emancipation of the peasantry and granting a constitution, Alexander refused to face squarely the central issues of serfdom and autocracy.

With the passing years Alexander increasingly concerned himself with foreign affairs. As he grew older, he also turned toward religious mysticism. The uncertainty and indecision that clouded his reign pursued him even after his death in 1825. For years a fanciful story persisted that he had feigned death and gone to Siberia, where he supposedly lived as a saintly monk until 1864.

THE REIGN OF NICHOLAS I

In contrast to the ambivalence of Alexander, Tsar Nicholas I (1825–1855) knew exactly how he wanted to govern. His philosophy of government found expression in the doctrine called Official Nationality, which was proclaimed in 1833 by his minister of education, Count Uvarov. Its three principles were orthodoxy, autocracy, and nationality; that is, adherence to the state religion, unquestioned supremacy of the tsar, and dedication to the regime. A conscientious, hard-working man, Nicholas loved military life and thought he could run Russia as if it were one vast army that would obey without hesitation his every command. He could not abide opinions that differed from his; and to stamp them out, he gave greater powers to the secret police, allowing it to arrest and deport people and confiscate property without legal process. That organization, reputed to have its agents everywhere, became the hated symbol of Nicholas's regime.

Despised though he was by liberals, Nicholas was not unaware of the need for reform. Continued peasant unrest and a frightening increase in acts of violence by serfs against their masters persuaded Nicholas that unless serfdom was abolished, the security of the state would be in danger. During his reign he appointed ten different secret committees to make recommendations, but he could not bring himself to make changes that would reduce the privileges of the nobles, the bulwark of tsarist autocracy. He did permit Count Paul Kiselev, the minister for state domains, to improve the condition of the state peasantry, who lived on state land and made up over half of Russia's 50 million peasants. He also intervened on the side of the serfs by limiting the authority of serf owners in the Russian-Polish frontier provinces, where the lords were Roman Catholic Poles and the peasants Orthodox Russians. Political and not humanitarian considerations inspired the action: the Polish nobility had risen against Russian rule in 1830–31, and Nicholas wanted to clip its power and win the support of the peasantry for the throne.

The efforts made by Nicholas's government to stifle independent thought and expressions of discontent could not suppress the spectacular intellectual outburst that made his reign and his successor's the golden age of Russian culture. Men of great creative ability appeared in many branches of art and learning, above all in literature. Within a few decades a constellation of geniuses that included the poet Pushkin and the novelists Gogol, Turgenev, Dostoevski, and Tolstoi, to name only those best known to Western readers, created one of the world's great literatures. Nearly all the important writers of the period were members of the nobility and gentry, as were most of their readers. In spite of their high-born origins, they often criticized Russian institutions, especially serfdom, autocracy, and bureaucracy.

In the 1820's groups or circles of young intellectuals began to meet to discuss new Western philosophies, in particular those of Schelling and Hegel. The circles became the centers of intellectual life and therefore of intellectual discontent with and alienation from the Russia of their day. The movement reached its height in the early 1840's, when two opposing schools of thought emerged, the Westernizers and the Slavophiles. Their debate became a central theme of Russian intellectual life, lasting into the twentieth century. The Westernizers maintained that the Slavic world was part of Western culture and that Russia should follow the same pattern of development as the nations of the West. The Slavophiles were romantic nationalists who held that Russian culture was superior to that of the decadent West. Russia, they said, contained within itself the seeds of its own regeneration and need not look abroad for guidance.

Nicholas, who was as determined to prevent change in other lands as he was to maintain the status quo in Russia, saw himself as the champion of legitimacy and the foe of revolution everywhere. In 1830 he was ready to send an army into western Europe to put down the revolutions. When in that same year Polish patriots rebelled against Russia, he moved

Culver Pictures, Inc.

Retreat of the Russians from the South Side of Sevastopol, September 8, 1855

"The army of Sevastopol, like the sea in a gloomy, billowing night, surging and receding, and agitatedly quivering in all its mass, swaying near the bay, on the bridge and on the northern side, moved slowly in the impenetrable darkness, away from the place where it had left so many brave brothers — away from the place which had been watered by its blood — from the place which for eleven months had withstood an enemy twice as numerous, and which now it was to abandon without a battle." From Leo N. Tolstoi, SEVASTOPOL, reprinted in THE COMPLETE WORKS OF COUNT TOLSTOY (Boston, 1904–05), Vol. II.

ruthlessly against them, ended what was left of Polish autonomy, and introduced a vigorous program of russification. In 1848 he sent troops to suppress the Rumanian nationalist movement against Turkey, Russia's old enemy, lent money to Austria to aid in its fight against revolutionaries, and in the summer of 1849 ordered 200,000 troops into Hungary to crush the revolt against the Hapsburgs.

In addition to these defenses of legitimacy, Nicholas's armies won easy victories in short wars against Persia and Turkey. His record of success gave the tsar inflated ideas about Russian military strength that led him into the Crimean War. (See pp. 149–150.) That war not only resulted in a military defeat but also created difficult financial problems for the government and, far more serious, led to a great new wave of peasant unrest and violence. Nicholas died in December, 1855, and his son, Alexander II, quickly agreed to an armistice.

THE TSAR-LIBERATOR

The new tsar was by nature and conviction a conservative who admired his father's methods of government and shared his dread of change. The Crimean fiasco and the rural disorders, however, compelled him to realize that unless fundamental reforms were made the state might collapse, and that the abolition of serfdom was the most urgent reform. Most of the serf owners opposed the measure, warning of dire social and economic consequences, but Alexander made it clear that nothing would deter him. After several years of intensive preparation the law was ready for the tsar's signature in February, 1861. Its provisions fell far short of the hopes of Russia's peasants. It gave the serfs land and freedom, but the conditions worked hardship on them and favored their former masters. The peasants did not get land immediately; many of them had to wait as long as twenty years. The price the peasant paid his former master for the land was set by law at a figure well above the market price. The state paid the nobles for the redeemed land in government bonds bearing 5 per cent interest, and the peasants had to repay the state in annual instalments at 6 per cent interest over a period of forty-nine years. The peasants could get the land at no cost only if they were willing to take an allotment one-fourth the area of a full-sized holding.

The emancipation decree also placed severe restrictions on the peasant's individual freedom. Since the men who drafted the law believed that the freed serfs would not be ready to run their own lives, they put them under the control of the village communes. The commune, not the individual peasant, held title to the redeemed land and periodically redistributed it among the commune members, supervised farming operations, provided village government and police services, and arranged for tax and redemption payments, which were paid communally. A peasant had to get the commune's permission to leave the village, and even if he never returned he remained a member of the commune, responsible for his share of communal taxes and other obligations. The intention of the restrictions was to prepare the peasant for complete personal freedom, but as the years went by, this intention was forgotten. Many Russians, from the reactionary right to the radical agrarian left, acquired a mystical attitude toward the peasantry, holding that it made an irreplaceable moral and spiritual contribution to Russian life and must therefore continue to be given special protection and special treatment and to remain in the communes. Not until the revolution of 1905 did the government abolish most of the restrictions that barred the peasant from the personal freedom enjoyed by other subjects of the tsar.

Brown Brothers

Alexander II of Russia

"Alexander II was by no means insensible to the spirit of the time. He was well aware of the existing abuses, many of which had been partially concealed from his father, and he had seen how fruitless were the attempts to eradicate them by a mere repressive system of administration. . . . He had inherited from his father a strong dislike to sentimentalism and rhetoric of all kinds. This dislike, joined to a goodly portion of sober common sense, a limited confidence in his own judgment, and a consciousness of enormous responsibility, prevented him from being carried away by the prevailing excitement." D. Mackenzie Wallace, RUSSIA (London, 1877).

The shortcomings of the emancipation law laid the foundation for decades of rural poverty, discontent, and radical agitation. The peasants were burdened with heavy redemption payments or allotments of land too small to support them. Their poverty and the system of communal land redistribution discouraged individual initiative in the improvement of farming, so that productivity remained low. The former landowners, who had been heavily in debt before the emancipation (mainly to the government's mortgage banks), used most of the redemption money paid them by the government to settle old debts or spent it foolishly; they invested little in improving the land that they still had. Within two decades of the emancipation many of them were more heavily in debt than ever and had lost all or part of their land through foreclosure.

"THE GREAT REFORMS"

The emancipation decree was the first in the series of reforms carried through by Alexander II. In 1864 local government, which had been in the hands of aristocrats and crown officials, was reorganized with the establishment of district and provincial assemblies or *zemstvos.* The members of each district zemstvo were elected by a system that favored the nobility but gave the peasantry a voice; delegates to the provincial zemstvo were chosen by the district zemstvos of the province. The activities of the zemstvos were limited to such matters as schools, public health and welfare, roads and bridges, and the encouragement of local industry and agriculture. They met only once a year, and they had to depend upon the officials and police of the government to carry out their programs. The reform was introduced initially in only nineteen provinces and spread gradually to others. As the years went by, the increasingly reactionary government imposed additional restrictions on zemstvo activities. Despite these handicaps the zemstvos compiled an outstanding record of achievement, especially in providing schools and medical services for the peasantry. As a first step toward representative government, they whetted the appetites of many Russians for a greater voice in running the country. In 1870 municipal government was reformed by the introduction of arrangements much like those of the zemstvo system.

Shortly after passage of the zemstvo law in 1864 Alexander ordered the reconstruction of the judicial system on the Western model to replace Russia's archaic, corrupt, and unfair system of justice. The reform provided for equality before the law, simplification of the court system with lower and higher courts, public trials, juries for serious criminal cases, uniform judicial procedures, defense lawyers, and judges who were government employees but could not be removed except for misconduct in office. As with the zemstvo system, the judicial reform was introduced gradually and sometimes with important modifications. In Poland and certain other areas, for instance, trial by jury was not allowed and special courts were retained for the peasants and for ecclesiastical matters, including divorce. The government retained its power to punish without trial those whom it felt threatened public order, and it used pressure on judges. Nonetheless, the new system was greatly superior to the old one. Despite government interference the courts maintained a high degree of independence, and the practice of the law attracted many able and courageous men of progressive views who became leaders in movements for greater freedom.

The last of the "great reforms" in 1874 reorganized the army, whose conscripts had come exclusively from the lower classes, especially the peasantry. All males became eligible for the draft at the age of twenty. The term of active service, which had been reduced a few years earlier from twenty-five to fifteen years, was cut to six years, followed by nine years in the reserve and five more in the militia. The conditions of army life were improved somewhat, and elementary education was made available to draftees.

Alexander's reforms swept away antiquated institutions and practices and prepared Russia to take a place among the modern nations of Europe. The transition from old to new, however, was not easy. The reforms themselves, as well as their shortcomings, encouraged demands for more liberalization, while the government, fearing that more concessions would weaken its autocratic power, refused to go any further. Discontent grew, and radicals began to engage in underground activities. In 1863 revolution broke out again in Poland, where only the year before Alexander had restored much autonomy to the Poles. The rising was crushed and a harsh retribution was carried out, including an acceleration of the policy of russification. These developments played into the hands of the reactionary elements in the nobility and bureaucracy who had always opposed reform. When in 1866 a former university student tried to assassinate Alexander, reactionary influence once again became paramount in government. New controls were put on the universities, censorship was tightened, and new regulations began to dilute the impact of the zemstvo and judiciary reforms.

RADICALS AND REVOLUTIONARIES

The reaction strengthened the radical sentiment, especially among intellectuals, who more and more came from non-noble backgrounds; by 1880 over half of Russia's university students were from the middle and lower classes. Many intellectuals were attracted to the doctrines of populism, which maintained that the peasant communes and the artisans' cooperatives (artels), institutions peculiar to Russia, would enable Russia to pass directly into socialism without going through the capitalist stage of development. In the 1870's thousands of youthful populists called *Narodniki* (from *narod,* people) disguised themselves as peasants and in groups of two and three "went to the people," infiltrating the villages to preach their revolutionary creed. The peasants were bewildered and suspicious of the invaders; sometimes they aided the police in apprehending them. Other radicals adopted the extreme cult called nihilism – Turgenev coined the word in the novel *Fathers and Sons* in 1862 – which urged the renunciation of all traditional values and institutions as worthless. Still others were drawn to the revolutionary anarchism taught by Michael Bakunin, which condemned state and society and praised destruction. Nihilism and anarchism merged with terrorism when these idealistic but irresponsible young people began to work off their frustrations against the regime in deeds of senseless violence.

After the collapse of the "to the people" movement some populist leaders decided that if the masses could not be roused, intellectuals acting alone should try to overthrow the government. They became full-time revolutionaries. Police bungling that would be unbelievable if it were not documented enabled these people to move freely around the country, to penetrate the police apparatus with their own agents, to escape from prison, and when jailed to keep in touch with their confederates. Some of them decided that by assassinating government leaders they could produce chaos and revolution or at least frighten the government into making concessions. One group took Alexander II as its special target, and in 1881, after seven attempts, it succeeded at last in killing its quarry. Although the radicals won the sympathy of many people, the number who took an active part in the movement was always small. Their historical importance, however, far outweighed their small number, for they established the organized revolutionary movement that in one of its several forms eventually took over Russia and had an enormous effect on the course of world history.

THE LAST ROMANOV AUTOCRATS

Far from promoting the cause of freedom, the assassination of the tsar and other officials served to deepen the reactionary policies of the government. Alexander III (1881–1894) and Nicholas II (1894–1917), son and grandson of the murdered Alexander, were narrow-minded bigots of limited intelligence who surrounded themselves with extremely reactionary counselors. The government did its best to hobble the reforms of Alexander II, much preferring the despotism of Nicholas I. Under the guidance of Constantine Pobedonostsev, chief lay official of the Russian Orthodox Church, the state instituted a militant religious policy that identified loyalty to the state with loyalty to the church, saw the Orthodox Church as the bulwark protecting Russia from the corruption of Western liberal ideas, and discriminated against other religions.

The Jews, who after centuries of harsh treatment had received some concessions from Alexander II, became the victims of especially cruel persecution. The prominence that they had won in scholarship, business, the professions, and above all in the revolutionary movement persuaded the government to take extreme measures, such as disenfranchisement and restrictions on the number admitted to secondary schools and universities. It also tolerated and sometimes instigated bloody anti-Jewish riots, called pogroms, in cities in southwestern Russia. In its effort to impose uniformity and curb nationalistic sentiment among its other subject peoples, the government put new emphasis on russification, including the compulsory use of Russian as the language of instruction in schools and the abrogation of local privileges. This policy led the government in 1899 to take away the special provincial autonomy of the Finns, thereby transforming them from loyal subjects of the tsar into his bitter enemies.

LIBERALS AND MARXISTS

A liberal movement that favored a constitutional monarchy on the Western model emerged in the 1890's, drawing its chief support from men who were active in the zemstvos and the professions and who were repelled by the extremism of both the revolutionary radicals and the reactionary government. Braving official disapproval, they held conferences, issued resolutions, and published an illegal newspaper to spread their views. In 1905 they formed themselves into the Constitutional Democratic party, called Cadets from the initials (KD) of the party's name in Russian.

Meanwhile, radicalism, continuing to win new adherents from those who saw no hope for Russia save through a violent overturn, consolidated itself around the turn of the century into two main groups. The heirs of the populists called themselves Social Revolutionaries or SR's and continued to place their hopes in mass peasant rebellion and terrorism. Others, disenchanted with populism's reliance on the peasantry, turned to Marxism.

Marxism had first won adherents in Russia during the 1880's, and in 1898 nine representatives of Marxist groups met at Minsk to form the Social Democratic Labor party or SD's, the precursor of the Communist party of Soviet Russia. Subsequent party congresses were held abroad until 1917, since the party itself was proscribed and most of its members were living in exile. It was in London in 1903 that the fateful split occurred between the Bolsheviks (majority), led by Vladimir Ulyanov, better known as Lenin, and the Mensheviks (minority) over the question of party control. The Bolsheviks favored tight central control of the party and insisted that after the revolution a dictatorship of the proletariat must be imposed, in which there would be no collaboration with the liberal bourgeoisie. The Mensheviks looked forward to a transitional period during which liberals and socialists would cooperate and from which the socialist society would evolve. Efforts in later years to reconcile the two groups failed, and in 1912 the Bolsheviks expelled the Mensheviks from the party, and so committed it to rigid central control and noncooperation with other leftist movements.

ECONOMIC CHANGE

Between 1861 and 1914 Russia finally began to modernize its economy. From the 1860's to the mid-1880's the economy moved forward slowly, in part because it was a period of adjustment to the great reforms, in part because the government had long been uninterested in promoting industrialization and in fact had feared it as a disruptive force. In the latter part of the 1880's Russian industrial production began to advance at a startling pace, growing during the 1890's at an estimated average annual rate of 8 per cent.

A change in the government's attitude toward active sponsorship of industrialization played the determining role in bringing about the upsurge. Credit for the reversal of policy mainly belonged to S. Y. Witte, who in 1892 became minister of finance. Witte argued that the tsarist autocracy could not survive and Russia could not remain a great power unless the government sponsored and guided economic growth. He concentrated on railroad construction (between 1890 and 1900 nearly 15,000 miles of track were laid) and on the iron, steel, and machinery industries. Lacking the capital needed for expansion, the government borrowed abroad, especially from France, in order to import the necessary equipment. To pay the interest on its debts, the government imposed heavy indirect taxes, which bore with special weight upon the peasantry. The peasants had to sell more grain to raise the cash for the increased taxes, which provided additional grain for export. In effect, the cost of the forced industrialization of the 1890's was borne mainly by the peasants, as it was again in the era of forced industrialization under Soviet Communism. The boom of the 1890's ended in 1900, and depresssed conditions persisted until 1906, when industrial production again rose sharply. By then an entrepreneurial class had emerged that was able to take over leadership in economic life from the government.

Industrialization brought with it a large increase in the industrial proletariat, although as late as 1914 there were only about 3 million factory workers out of a population of 170 million. Most of the workers were concentrated in a few industrial centers. Russian factories were typically large establishments, since the government was not interested in sponsoring small factories; over half the industrial enterprises had more than five hundred workers each. This concentration made it easier to propagandize and organize the workers. Unrest developed early, strikes became frequent, and the Marxists made many converts among the industrial workers.

The condition of the peasantry continued to deteriorate, aggravated by the burden of taxes and redemption payments and by the great increase in rural population, which produced a steady diminution in the size of the average family's holding. There was no compensating increase in agricultural productivity, for the peasants persisted in their traditional, inefficient farming methods. By 1900 an estimated 52 per cent were unable to support themselves from their shrunken holdings and had to find supplementary employment. Living as they did on the margin of subsistence, they fell easy prey to famine and disease; the death rate in Russia at the beginning of the twentieth century was nearly twice that of England.

THE RUSSO-JAPANESE WAR

The political degeneration of China and the construction by Russia between 1891 and 1903 of the Trans-Siberian railroad linking European Russia with the Pacific stirred Russian ambitions for territorial expansion in the Far East. Russia extended its sphere of influence to Manchuria, obtained a twenty-five year lease on the Liaotung peninsula with the city of Port Arthur, and started a military penetration of Korea under the guise of exploiting timberlands. These advances brought Russia into conflict with Japan, which had its own plans for expansion at China's expense. Like everyone else, the Russians underestimated the strength of the Japanese, who had only recently emerged from centuries of backwardness. In February, 1904, the Japanese attacked the Russian fleet at Port Arthur without warning, as they were to do thirty-seven years later against the American fleet at Pearl Harbor. In the war that followed, Russian forces were handicapped by grotesquely inadequate leadership and matériel and by the difficulties of supplying the war theater. They suffered defeat after defeat, culminating in the destruction in May, 1905, of the Russian Baltic fleet in the Tsushima Straits off Korea after it had sailed halfway around the world. At the peace conference arranged by President Theodore Roosevelt at Portsmouth, New Hampshire, in 1905 the Russians had to give up their recent acquisitions and accept a Japanese protectorate over Korea.

THE REVOLUTION OF 1905

The unrelieved series of military and naval defeats in what had been from the outset an unpopular war inflamed public opinion against the autocracy, and demands for political liberties and other reforms gained a massive following. In St. Petersburg a huge but orderly crowd of workers led by Father Gapon, a priest who was also a police agent, came to the Winter Palace to petition the tsar for reforms. Troops opened fire on the demonstrators, killing well over a hundred and wounding many more. Bloody Sunday, the name that was quickly attached to the massacre, spurred new demands and new unrest. Strikes erupted in many parts of the country; peasant unrest and open outbreaks spread. A council or *soviet* of workers' deputies, dominated by the radicals, was elected in St. Petersburg; soon similar soviets were formed in other cities. Sailors on the battleship *Potemkin* mutinied. The radicals stepped up their propaganda, and some of them renewed the terrorist tactic of assassinating high officials. The revolutionary wave culminated in October, 1905, in a general strike that paralyzed the empire.

The tsar and his advisers finally realized they must yield. Nicholas issued a manifesto providing for freedom of speech, press, and assembly, the election of a Duma or parliament by nearly universal manhood suffrage, and the promise that no law would be promulgated without the Duma's approval. The October Manifesto converted autocratic Russia into a constitutional monarchy. It satisfied the liberals, but not the radicals. Nor did it end worker and peasant unrest; the government had to use military action and arrests before order was restored at the end of 1905.

THE CONSTITUTIONAL MONARCHY

Just before the first Duma convened in 1906, the government, back firmly in control, issued the so-called Fundamental Laws that provided for the retention by the tsar of many of his autocratic powers. Dominated by anti-government parties, the Duma quickly came into conflict with the administration, and Nicholas dissolved it and ordered the election of a new Duma. The second Duma met for only three months before it, too, was dissolved by the tsar. To ensure cooperative Dumas in the future, the government changed the electoral laws to guarantee the domination of the landed gentry. The third and fourth Dumas each lasted the full term of five years.

With the Duma under control, the government under the leadership of Peter Stolypin, the chief minister, set out to eradicate the revolutionary movement. In 1906 and 1907 thirty-five hundred people, mostly government officials but also a significant number of innocent bystanders, had been assassinated by terrorists. Using extralegal means, the government's police agencies rounded up, imprisoned, and executed radicals, and for a while Russia enjoyed relative freedom from revolutionary agitation, although Stolypin himself was assassinated in 1911.

Stolypin did not rely on suppression alone to ward off revolution; he hoped to win mass support for the throne by a program whose central feature was an agrarian reform that abruptly reversed the government's peasant policy. A series of decrees known collectively as the Stolypin Reforms wiped out most of the restrictions on the personal liberty of the peasant, allowed him to sever his connection with the commune and become the owner of his own holding, permitted him to exchange the scattered strips of his communal allotment for a consolidated farm, arranged for the partition of common pastures and meadows among the new individual peasant proprietors, canceled the remaining redemption payments, and established a Peasant Land Bank to lend to peasants who wanted to buy more land. Stolypin called these measures "a wager, not on the wretched and drunken, but on the sound and strong," expecting that the industrious and ambitious peasants would take advantage of the law, prosper, and become the rural bulwarks of the regime. By the end of 1915 between one-quarter and one-half of the peasant households in European Russia had withdrawn from their communes to become private proprietors. Government pressure explained only part of the success of the reform; the peasants welcomed the opportunity to free themselves from communal restraints and at long last became their own masters.

WAR AND REVOLUTION

During the years of constitutional experiment Russia became more deeply involved in international power politics, climaxed by the outbreak of war in August, 1914. Russia's entry into that war at first met with a great patriotic outburst, but defeats in battle and privation at home soon turned the people against the government. In March, 1917, a revolution broke out that forced Nicholas from the throne and opened a new era in Russia's and the world's history. As those events recede into the past, the thesis that imperial Russia would have survived if it had not been for the shock of World War I gains supporters. They argue that the reforms introduced after 1905 gave Russia a viable constitutional form of government, that the economy was advancing, and that the spread of education produced growing numbers of forward-looking men who would have led their nation in continued progress. If fate had only given Russia time — if there had been no First World War — there would have been no Russian Revolution and no Soviet Union. Such is the view of one group of experts. Others believe that military defeat only hastened the decay that had been eating away at Russia for a long time. Had there been no war, revolution would still have come, though perhaps not in the extreme form of communism. According to this view, the war only speeded up the inevitable collapse.

AUSTRIA: THE MULTINATIONAL EMPIRE

The Hapsburg Monarchy was not a state in the modern sense of the word; it was the personal realm of the house of Hapsburg. Elsewhere monarchs dedicated themselves to welding the groups over whom they ruled into a common nationality. In contrast, the Hapsburg emperors rejected the national idea, spurning it so completely that they did not even have an official name for their realm: Austria and the Hapsburg Monarchy served only as names of convenience. The empire was an association of eleven nationalities — German, Magyar, Czech, Pole, Croat, Italian,

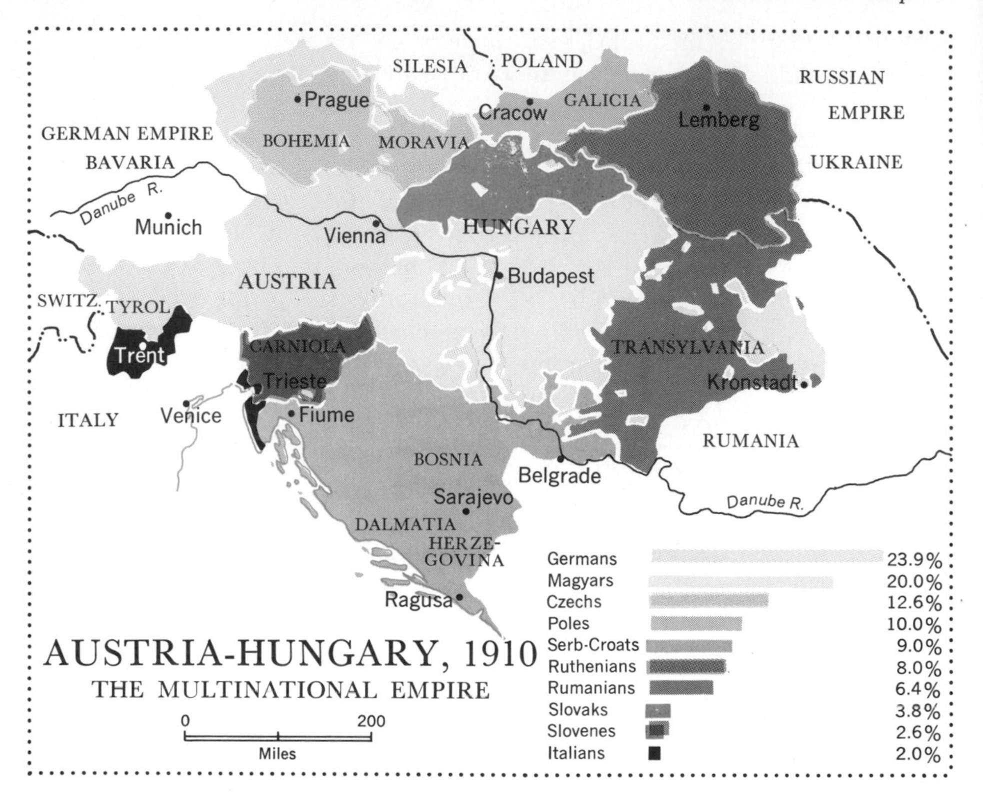

Ruthenian, Rumanian, Slovak, Serb, and Slovene—each with its own language, culture, and traditions. The Germans and the Magyars were the dominant nationalities, forming 23.9 per cent and 20 per cent respectively of the empire's population in 1910. Next came the Czechs with 12.6 per cent and the Poles with 10 per cent. The other ethnic groups ranged from 9 per cent to 2 per cent of the total population. Most of the people of each nationality lived in their historic homelands: the Germans in the western provinces (modern Austria), the Magyars in Hungary, the Czechs in Bohemia and Moravia, the Poles and Ruthenians in Galicia, and so on. There had been much internal migration, however, so that different national groups, especially the Germans, were scattered through the realm.

The single most important reason why this strange empire stayed together was that its peoples shared a common loyalty to the Hapsburg emperor. Although the intensity of the loyalty varied among the nationalities, the dynasty provided the supreme bond of union. The armed forces and the bureaucracy, whose members were drawn from all nationalities, also served as important cohesive forces and symbols of the supranational character of the empire. The throne had close ties with the

Roman Catholic Church, to which three-quarters of the empire's people belonged, and Catholicism acted as another supranational unifying force. Similarly the aristocracy, with its close links to the throne and its monopoly on social, political, and military leadership, helped to hold the empire together. Economic factors had an important cohesive effect, the industrial districts of the German and Bohemian provinces exchanging their manufactured goods for the foodstuffs and raw materials of Hungary and Galicia. Most of the empire was linked by the Danube and eventually by the railroad network that reached out in every direction from Vienna.

These unifying forces created among the peoples of the empire feelings of common interest that were the foundations upon which the empire rested. Until 1916 many among even the most ardent nationalist leaders believed that the empire would survive. They wanted to gain a greater voice for their nationalities within the empire, not to destroy it. Their agitation, however, continually threatened the authority of the government. To deal with the threats, the rulers in Vienna tried a series of solutions, but none could satisfy all the conflicting desires. In the end, unsatisfied nationalist aspirations, aggravated by defeat in World War I, led to the empire's collapse in 1918.

CENTRALIZED ABSOLUTISM: THE BACH SYSTEM

The first attempted solution, a regime of centralization called the Bach System, was adopted after absolutism had re-emerged from the events of 1848 and 1849. Provincial privileges and autonomy were abolished, and an intensive policy of germanization was introduced, with German the only official language and the chief language of instruction in higher education. The government actively promoted economic development. In agrarian matters it provided emancipated serfs with sizable holdings of land at prices averaging one-third of the market value and required the peasants to pay only a third of that, with the central and provincial governments paying the other two-thirds. This policy stimulated farm production and made the peasants a major market for manufactured goods. Austrian industry and commerce also participated in the general prosperity of the 1850's.

Despite prosperity the government had trouble meeting the costs of its expanded program. When depression occurred in 1857, the government's fiscal position became critical. To make matters worse, during the Crimean War Austria had alienated both Russia and the western powers. Nationalist discontent with the policy of centralization reached alarming proportions, especially in Hungary. In 1859 Austria's difficulties persuaded Emperor Napoleon III of France and Prime Minister Camillo Cavour of Sardinia to strike at the Hapsburgs' Italian possessions. Defeat in that war reduced Austria's prestige still further, worsened its financial problems, and stirred up new troubles in Hungary. Emperor Franz Josef, always suspicious of abstract principles and long-range plans, preferred to handle problems as they arose. Deciding that it was time to abandon centralized absolutism for a new policy, he dismissed Bach and other ministers and inaugurated a new policy.

CONSTITUTIONAL ABSOLUTISM

Decrees of 1860 and 1861 established a constitutional system for the monarchy with an imperial diet (Reichsrat) and provincial diets, but the throne still held supreme power. The value of the reform was vitiated by an electoral system that assured German domination of the Reichsrat, by the extreme limitation of the powers of the provincial diets, and by the failure to provide for parliamentary control over legislation and finance.

The reform understandably did not satisfy non-German nationalists. Their passive resistance, including refusal to send representatives to the imperial diet, made it impossible for the government to function effectively. After 1864, with the war with Prussia approaching, the emperor decided to try a new tactic to hold the empire together. His ministers entered into negotiations with the Magyars, who were the second largest ethnic group in the empire and implacable foes of centralization. Francis Deak, leader of the Hungarian nationalists, proposed a compromise that would make the Magyars equal partners with the Germans in dominating the empire. Discussions were in progress when war broke out with Prussia. Austria's quick defeat played into the hands of the Magyars, for more than ever the Hapsburgs needed Hungary to prevent the dissolution of the empire and to regain status as a great power. The emperor agreed to Magyar proposals, and the famed Compromise (*Ausgleich*) of 1867 opened a new era in Hapsburg history that lasted until 1918.

DUALISM

The Ausgleich transformed the unitary Hapsburg empire into a dual monarchy of two equal states with one ruler, who was simultaneously emperor of Austria and king of Hungary, one army, and joint ministries charged with the conduct of foreign affairs, finance, and military matters. All the other nationalities were made subservient to the will and interests of the Germans in the Austrian part of the empire and to the Magyars in the Hungarian part. Each part had its own parliament, ministers responsible to the parliament, and civil service. Each parliament chose sixty-man delegations, who met to decide matters of common interest. Treaties between the two countries, renewable every ten years, regulated tariffs, currency, and similar matters.

Dualism worked well enough to enable the empire to hold together for another fifty years, but throughout that half-century the danger of collapse was never distant. The unsatisfied nationalist ambitions of the subject peoples grew in proportion to the efforts of the dominant Germans and Magyars to suppress them. Cultural and social organizations that emphasized ethnic traditions took on new vitality. Most of the nationalist leaders did not yet want independence, however, demanding instead a federal system in which they would be on an equal footing with the Germans and Magyars. The Magyars, meanwhile, gained an even greater influence in the army and the central administration.

The Czechs, third largest ethnic group in the empire, replaced the Magyars as the most vocal and discontented of the subject nationalities. To placate them, Franz Josef in 1871 offered them autonomy and agreed to be crowned king of Bohemia; but the determined opposition of the Magyars, who feared that concessions to the Czechs would stir up demands from the Slavs in Hungary, persuaded him to withdraw his offer. The disappointed Czechs showed their resentment by boycotting the imperial and provincial parliaments until 1878.

In 1879 the emperor broke with the German bourgeois liberals who dominated the Austrian parliament. The rupture worked to the benefit of the Czechs and other national groups. The German liberals had put through a series of progressive measures that included reform of court procedures, freedom of speech and press, the abolition of church control of the schools, and the establishment of compulsory elementary education. Franz Josef, who had never been happy with the liberals, lost his patience when they opposed Austrian occupation of the Turkish provinces of Bosnia and Herzegovina. He decided to appease the subject nationalities to gain their support against the German liberals. He appointed Count Edward Taafe as the new prime minister to carry out the program. Taafe, a master of political improvisation and compromise, persuaded the representatives of the Czechs and other nationalities to join with the German conservatives and clericals in a parliamentary bloc, known as the Iron Ring, to support the emperor's policies against the liberals. He rewarded them with a series of concessions to their nationalist ambitions. The Czech language was recognized as an official language along with German; changes in the electoral laws enabled the Czechs to win control of their provincial diet; and the University of Prague was split into two sections, one Czech and one German Similar though less extensive concessions were made to the Poles and Slovenes.

NATIONALIST TENSIONS AND CONSTITUTIONAL CRISIS

Taafe's political skill gave the empire more than a decade of relative calm, a luxury it had not enjoyed for thirty years. It did not, however, stifle the nationalist strivings of the subject peoples. After his fall in 1893 nationalist agitation took on still more fervor with new and more aggressive organizations, such as the Young Czechs. The Pan-Slav movement, advocating a union of all Slavic peoples, gained strength, and some of its adherents talked of "liberation" by Russia, greatest of the Slavic states. Nationalist activity also assumed a new vitality among the Yugoslavs (South Slavs), as the Serbs, Croats, and Slovenes were called.

The increase in nationalist activities of the subject peoples stimulated increased opposition by the Magyars and Germans. The Magyars, who formed barely half the population of the Hungarian part of the empire, intensified their policy of holding the other ethnic groups in check. The Croats, who as a reward for loyalty to the Hapsburgs in 1848 had been allowed to retain much autonomy within the Hungarian kingdom, lost many of their privileges. They and other minorities were subjected to an unrelenting program of magyarization.

The Germans, frightened by the threat to their domination of Austria, turned in increasing numbers to new, stridently nationalist movements. A fanatic named Georg von Schönerer preached doctrines of German racial superiority, anti-Semitism, and pan-Germanism, pointing to Hohenzollern Germany as the leader of all Germans. Karl Lueger, mayor of Vienna from 1897 to 1907, formed the Christian Socialist party, whose platform combined clericalism, anticapitalism, and anti-Semitism. He drew wide support from urban shopkeepers and artisans, who felt threatened by the advances of capitalist industry and commerce. Peasants, who suffered from the competition of large estates and mechanized farming, were also attracted by the appeals of Christian Socialism. Such people were traditionally suspicious of the Jews and were easily convinced that the latter, who had become important in Austrian economic life, were responsible for their economic difficulties. Among those who found themselves in sympathy with Lueger's doctrines was a recent arrival in Vienna, a young drifter named Adolph Hitler.

During this period Viktor Adler, a one-time rabid pan-German, organized scattered Austrian Marxian groups into the Social Democratic party. Although the new organization at first accepted Marx's doctrine of inevitable revolution, it soon copied the revisionist outlook of the German Social Democrats, advocating social change by parliamentary means rather than violent overthrow. Reflecting the ethnic diversity of the empire, the socialists split their party and the trade unions they dominated into separate and virtually independent national sections united only in name.

As nationalist passions rose, debates in the Austrian parliament became so heated that physical attacks and raucous disturbances made it impossible for the legislature to carry on business. Since the emperor and his ministers were authorized by law to legislate when the parliament was not in session, they dissolved the parliament and summoned it only when the budget had to be passed. Constitutional parliamentary government broke down, and the empire stood on the verge of dissolution.

Franz Josef once again realized that changes had to be made. In 1907 he introduced universal manhood suffrage in the Austrian part of the empire, taking care to ensure adequate representation for the national minorities. The Social Democrats were the chief beneficiaries of the reform, becoming the largest party in the parliament. Yet the reform did not alter the pattern of the parliament's unruly behavior and ineffectiveness. Most of the ministries from 1907 to 1914 lacked a parliamentary majority, and the government had to resort frequently to its emergency powers. Universal suffrage had not been extended to Hungary, and Franz Josef used the threat of its introduction – and the diminution in Magyar power that it would produce – to beat down Magyar's demands for more independence from imperial control. By not introducing suffrage reform into Hungary, however, Franz Josef stirred up still more resentment among the subject peoples.

The emperor's only son, Rudolf, shot himself and his young mistress at Meyerling in 1889 in a tawdry tragedy that still inspires novelists and playwrights to endless romantic speculations. The Archduke Franz Ferdinand, nephew and now heir apparent of the aged Franz Josef, seems to have favored a vague form of federalism that would have increased the power of the subject nationalities and strengthened the power of the throne at the expense of the dominant Germans and Magyars. The emperor did not care for his nephew, however, and in any case Franz Ferdinand never had the opportunity to demonstrate his intentions.

In the years before 1914 Vienna won universal fame for its beauty, its aristocratic splendors, and the courtliness, gaiety, and sophistication of its people. It was a world center of art, letters, drama, music, education, and science. All the world danced to Viennese waltzes and hummed the melodies of Viennese operettas. Most of its people seemed unaffected by the crisis of the empire. Nevertheless, the crisis grew greater with each passing year. Austria's involvement in the Balkans, always a source of international tension, brought on a new threat of war in 1908 when the empire formally annexed Bosnia and Herzegovina. Relations with Russia and Serbia deteriorated, Slavic nationalist movements in the empire took on new strength, and new enthusiasm appeared for the cause of Pan-Slavism. Other national groups who had been relatively quiescent, such as the Italians in southern Austria, began to make trouble. In Hungary deputies rioted in parliament and at one session fired a shot at the prime minister. Fighting broke out in the streets, and young, rabidly nationalist Serbs and Croats decided to take matters into their own hands by resorting to terrorism and assassination. Such was the situation in June, 1914.

THE OTTOMAN EMPIRE

Like the realm of the Hapsburgs, the Ottoman Empire was torn by the nationalist aspirations of its subject peoples. It suffered other grave disabilities: extreme corruption and inefficiency in government and the constant intervention of the great powers in its affairs. Paradoxically, the latter handicap helped stay the disruptive force of nationalism, for each power was so fearful that a rival might gain from the dissolution of the empire that each thought its own best interest lay in keeping the empire alive.

By the beginning of the nineteenth century the disintegration of the central government proceeded so far that only a few districts remained under the direct control of the sultan. Although the empire stretched from Algeria to Persia and reached up into the Balkan peninsula of Europe, most of the provinces were governed by nominal vassals who paid only ceremonial tribute and allegiance to the sultan. In the course of the century foreign conquest and native rebellions gradually whittled away the provinces until on the eve of World War I the empire included only the region between the Mediterranean and the Tigris-Euphrates rivers and a small strip of Macedonia, in addition to its historic homeland in Anatolia.

In 1830 France began a long-drawn-out conquest of Algeria, and in 1881 it established a protectorate over Tunisia. In 1831 Mohammed Ali, an Albanian adventurer who had entered Ottoman military service and rose to become ruler of Egypt, challenged the sultan's control of Syria. After a decade of strife and confusion the government of the sultan regained Syria with the aid of Great Britain and other European powers, but in return he recognized Mohammed Ali as the hereditary ruler of Egypt. In 1878 Great Britain occupied the island of Cyprus and in 1882 established its control over Egypt. Italy completed the spoliation of the Turks' North African empire with the conquest of Tripoli in 1911–12.

THE "NEW NATIONS" OF THE NINETEENTH CENTURY

The majority of the inhabitants of the Balkan territories of the Ottoman Empire were European in speech and Christian in religion. Increased commercial and intellectual contacts with western Europe introduced men of the middle classes to Western ideas of freedom and secularism, while continued Turkish oppression and corruption stirred up discontent among the peasantry. Inspired by the French Revolution, leaders began to urge rebellion and independence.

In 1804 the Serbs rose against their Turkish overlords. Led by George Petrovich, also known as Kara (black) George, a prosperous pig dealer, the Serbs enjoyed initial success, but by 1813 the Turks had regained control. In 1815 the Serbs rose again, led by Milosh Obrenovich, another pig dealer and a political rival of Kara George. In 1817 the sultan recognized Obrenovich as prince of Serbia, and in 1829 by the Treaty of Adrianople he granted Serbia a large measure of local autonomy, although it remained until 1878 as a province of the Ottoman Empire. The feud between the Obrenoviches and the Karageorgeviches, with the two dynasties alternating on the throne for more than a century, was symptomatic of the internal divisions within the other Balkan nationalities, which hindered their liberation from Turkish rule or condemned them to internal strife and political turmoil after achieving independence.

The initial Serbian risings attracted little international attention, unlike the reaction when the Greeks revolted in 1821. (See pp. 46–47.) When the great powers finally established Greece as an independent kingdom in 1830, they drew frontiers for the new state that left many Greeks outside its borders. That decision caused much trouble in later years.

The Treaty of Adrianople of 1829 granted Russia a protectorate over the principalities of Moldavia and Wallachia, although they remained nominally parts of the Ottoman Empire. After defeat in the Crimean War, Russia had to give up its protectorate, but reestablishment of direct Turkish rule was unthinkable. After several years of dispute among the powers over the disposition of the territories, the native inhabitants took matters into their own hands in 1859 by electing Alexander Cuza, a native landowner, as prince of both. Two years later they merged into a single state called Rumania. Cuza initiated a reform program that included freeing the peasants from forced labor for the landowners, confiscating monastic estates, and providing a constitution and universal manhood suffrage. Such radical reforms in a country that was still under the nominal sovereignty of the sultan alienated the dominant landowning classes. In 1866 they overthrew Alexander and replaced him with a Hohenzollern prince, whose dynasty ruled Rumania until 1944. The other new nations created by the gradual dissolution of the Ottoman Empire – Montenegro, Bulgaria, and Albania – had to await further international developments before achieving independence.

TURKISH ATTEMPTS AT REFORM

The Turkish rulers of the Ottoman Empire strove vainly to prevent the loss of their sovereignty. Internal divisions between those who wished to introduce Western reforms and those who wished to return to old-fashioned centralized despotism, as well as the vested interests of many semi-independent military, political, and religious leaders, repeatedly frustrated their attempts. Sultan Selim III (1789–1807) attempted to remodel the military establishment on European lines and to introduce other Western reforms, but the powerful janissary corps dethroned and murdered him. Mahmud II (1808–1839), his successor, was plagued by the revolts in Serbia and Greece and moved more slowly to consolidate power, but in 1826 he took advantage of a revolt by the janissaries to massacre the entire force and abolish it forever. Mahmud's last years were marred by the success of the revolt in Greece, defeat by Russia in 1829, and the encroachments of his vassal Mohammed Ali of Egypt, with the result that he failed to reestablish authority and power of the central government.

Abdul Mejid (1839–1861), Mahmud's successor, was a mere boy at the time of his accession. Under the influence of his principal minister, the Western-educated Reshid Pasha, he introduced a new era of reform in Turkey called the *Tanzimat*. A series of decrees introduced changes in many aspects of Ottoman administration and legal procedures with the aim of making the empire into a modern nation on the Western model. The alliance of Turkey with the Western powers in the Crimean War further strengthened the hand of the reformers, and in 1856 the sultan promised increased efforts to modernize the empire. The reformers could not, however, overcome the inefficiency and uncooperativeness of the bureaucracy or the opposition of vested interests to changes in the power structure. The reforms also proved costly in a pecuniary sense. The government borrowed in Great Britain and France to finance its role in the Crimean War, and the debt rose rapidly in succeeding years. Unable to meet the interest payments, the government defaulted in 1876 and had to submit to financial control by the great powers on behalf of its European creditors. This development, together with the renewed revolts in the Balkans, led to the overthrow of the reforming party and brought the *Tanzimat* to a close.

THE "SICK MAN OF EUROPE"

The reformers made one last effort to retrieve the situation in 1876 by staging a coup d'état and proclaiming a constitution of the Western type that called for the assembly of the first Turkish parliament. Abdul Hamid II (1876–1909), the new sultan, allowed the regime to function just long enough to prevent further intervention by the Western powers, then he prorogued the parliament, abolished the constitution, and restored the traditional despotism. In spite of the defeat by Russia in the war of 1877–78, which led to complete independence for Rumania, Serbia, and Montenegro, and autonomous status for Bulgaria under Russian protection (see p. 325), the "sick man of Europe," as Turkey became known in the Western press, exhibited remarkable powers of survival and recuperation.

During these years tensions were heightened within the empire and its former provinces by an intensification of Western interest which was part of the new age of imperialism. The major European states used their economic power to extend their political control over the economically backward countries of the Balkans and the Near East, building railroads and public works, organizing banks, and extending loans to governments in return for economic concessions and political alliances. Foreign economic penetration promoted the growth of capitalist techniques and institutions, which increasingly displaced traditional methods of production and exchange and brought more and more people into the market system. Taxes soared as governments tried to get money to repay foreign

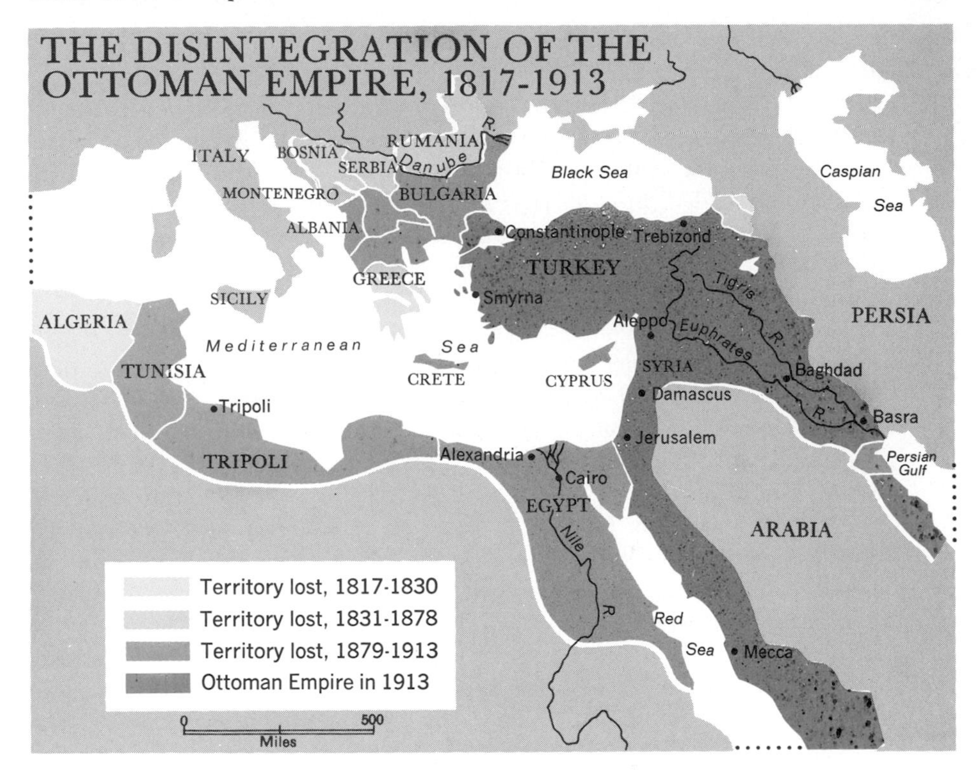

loans, and when not enough money could be raised, the governments had to agree to varying degrees of foreign control over state revenues to ensure repayment. The difficulties of economic life were worsened by a population increase that produced rural overpopulation; many peasants were left landless, and most of the others had plots too small to support a family adequately.

Increasing contacts with the West fostered a discontent with the traditional way of life and the traditional system of values that had earlier made the people accept their lot without complaint. Men of the new generation saw that it was possible to break free from the old restraints and rise to wealth and prominence. The expansion of educational facilities gave ambitious young men the opportunity to prepare themselves for leadership.

THE YOUNG TURK REVOLUTION

The new attitudes found political expression in increased nationalist activity and in the formation of underground revolutionary and terrorist societies with such names as the International Macedonian Revolutionary Organization (usually called IMRO), Union or Death, and the Black

Hand. The first successful revolution engineered by the new generation occurred in Turkey under the leadership of men who called themselves the Young Turks. In 1908 a secret organization of army officers threatened armed revolt unless Abdul Hamid, whose name had become an international byword for cruelty and misrule, restored the constitution of 1876. The sultan yielded, but the next year after an attempted counterrevolution, the Young Turks forced Abdul Hamid to abdicate and changed the constitution to make the cabinet responsible to the parliament rather than to the sultan.

The success of the Young Turk revolution awakened fears in the Balkan states, Austria, and Russia that Turkey might be on the verge of a revival that would lead to efforts to regain lost territory and lost prestige. Austria and Russia decided to move before that could happen. They agreed that Austria would annex Bosnia and Herzegovina and that Russia would have the right to send its warships through the straits of the Bosporus and Dardanelles. Austria quickly announced the annexation, but the Russians discovered that the other powers would not consent to the straits passage. Bitter charges and countercharges were exchanged, and for a time war seemed inevitable. The danger was overcome, but Russia, chagrined and furious with what it considered Austria's duplicity, planned revenge and worked to persuade the Balkan states to league together in defense against further Austrian territorial expansion in the Balkans. The danger of Turkish revival convinced the Balkan leaders that such a confederation was necessary. In 1912 Serbia, Greece, Bulgaria, and Montenegro formed the Balkan League, directed against Turkey. Thus the stage was set for the Balkan wars, which served as a prelude to World War I and the eventual demise of the "sick man of Europe."

THE REVIVAL OF WESTERN IMPERIALISM
CHAPTER TEN

While the great land empires of eastern Europe were undergoing stress and change that eventually led to their downfall, the nations of western Europe embarked upon a disastrous race for overseas empires that held profound implications for the entire world. In fact, the period from 1870 to 1914 is sometimes referred to as the "age of imperialism," but this is misleading if not positively inaccurate. The main scramble of European nations for overseas territories did not get under way in earnest until the 1880's; nor did they begin to relinquish their colonies until forced to do so by circumstances during and after the Second World War. More fundamentally, imperialism was not a new phenomenon in either 1885 or 1870. Imperialism is as old as civilization itself. In the earliest civilizations of which we have any record, those of Egypt and Sumer, native populations were ruled and exploited by alien conquerors. A large part of recorded history deals with the rise and fall of empires. Vast, well-organized empires existed in Asia when half-naked savages still populated most of Europe. Empires existed in Africa and America after a fashion before the voyages of Columbus. Europeans themselves, however, have been among the most expansionist and imperialist of peoples, from the time of their Greek and Roman forebears right down to the twentieth century. In the Middle Ages they expanded throughout continental Europe. Between 1500 and 1800 they spread their civilization to North and South America and established beachheads around Africa and the Indian Ocean.

Imperialism was thus not new, but in spite of the ubiquity of earlier imperialisms, that of the late nineteenth century did have certain distinctive features. In the first place, the expansion was more rapid, better organized, and the penetration into alien societies was deeper than in previous imperialisms. Second, imperialist conquest was directed chiefly toward tropical or semitropical areas. Third, imperialism was not accompanied by large-scale migrations from Europe to the areas of imperial control. Emigration occurred, of course, on the largest scale in history; but the emigrants went chiefly to self-governing nations and territories such as the United States, Latin America, and the British dominions. Finally, the great burst of imperialist expansion after 1885 came after almost a century in which Europeans had generally manifested a striking lack of concern for imperial expansion, amounting in some cases to outright anti-imperialism.

THE SECOND BRITISH EMPIRE

The first or old British Empire attained its greatest extent in the decade following 1763. As a result of the Seven Years' War, Britain gained Canada, islands and trading posts in the West Indies and Africa, and a greatly enlarged sphere of influence in India. The American Revolution reduced substantially the extent of the empire, deprived it of its most flourishing colonies, and led to some fundamental changes in imperial policy. The Napoleonic wars represented the last of the great colonial struggles between France and Britain. The outcome completely eliminated France as a rival in the traditional areas of imperial conflict, brought some more or less fortuitous accretions to the British Empire, and left Britain the undisputed "mistress of the seas." Shortly afterward the revolt of the Spanish colonies in America and the separation of Brazil from Portugal reduced the formal hegemony of European powers in overseas areas to its smallest extent in three hundred years.

For two generations thereafter colonial and imperial questions receded in public interest. Continental countries focused their attention on domestic and European problems: reform and revolutions, national unification, industrialization, and power politics. With but few minor exceptions these left little energy for or interest in the creation of colonial empires. Britain, with its far-flung possessions and mastery of the sea lanes, was in a very different position. It could not afford to ignore questions of imperial policy, and it continued to make minor additions to its empire throughout the century. It has been said that Britain "acquired an empire in a fit of absence of mind." That is not literally true, of course, since each acquisition either had a specific objective or was a reaction to a specific situation; yet the statement does emphasize that there was no comprehensive design for imperial conquest.

AUSTRALIA, NEW ZEALAND, AND THE SOUTH PACIFIC

Europeans first became aware of Australia in the early decades of the seventeenth century as a result of the exploratory activity of the Dutch, who called it New Holland, although it may have been sighted by the

Portuguese a hundred years earlier. Its full extent and its character as an island-continent remained unknown for many years. Its inhospitable western and northern coasts and the lack of any obvious resources of value to Europeans did not encourage settlement. Not until the English explorer Captain James Cook discovered the more fertile east coast on his first Pacific voyage (1768–1771) did the British government take an interest. At first the government contemplated using it for the resettlement of loyalist refugees after the American Revolution but eventually decided on making it a penal colony to relieve the crowded British prisons. In January, 1788, the first convoy of convicts dropped anchor in Botany Bay near the site of the future city of Sydney.

The first years of the colony, named New South Wales, were difficult and turbulent. Convicted criminals did not make ideal settlers in a virgin land, even though many came from debtors' prisons or had been imprisoned for other minor offenses. Not until sheep raising was introduced in 1794 did the colony have the foundations of a viable economy. The first free settlers apart from soldiers arrived in 1793. By 1810 more than 3,000 free settlers had come, attracted by the offer of land grants. In 1816 the British government removed all legal restrictions on free emigration to Australia. Britain continued to use New South Wales as a penal colony until 1840, however, and convicts were sent to some other parts of Australia until 1867. Altogether, approximately 75,000 convicts were transported, but free settlers outnumbered both convicts and emancipists (those who had served their penal terms) long before the practice ceased. In the process of settlement the native inhabitants were almost exterminated before measures were taken to place them on reservations and protect them.

When first settling at Botany Bay, the British claimed only the eastern half of the continent. Until 1803 the belief persisted that New South Wales and New Holland (the western half) were separate islands. In 1829 the government extended its claim to the whole continent, and shortly afterward it founded or allowed settlements at Perth in Western Australia, Adelaide in South Australia, and Melbourne in what eventually became the province of Victoria. Settlements had been established in Tasmania as early as 1803. As penal colonies, the settlements were at first under the direct control of the crown, whose authority was exercised by a royal governor. Elements of representative government were introduced in the 1820's and broadened in subsequent years. In 1850 Parliament passed the Australian Colonies Government Act, which granted the colonies complete self-government for most practical purposes.

The discovery of gold in Victoria in 1851 stimulated the economy and brought an influx of new immigrants from all over the world. Although sheep raising remained the staple industry and the foundation of the Australian economy throughout the nineteenth century, its labor requirements were not large, so that most of the new arrivals settled in the coastal cities. Australia became a predominantly urban society at a relatively early date. In 1866 the parliament of Victoria enacted a protective tariff at the height of the free trade movement in Europe, and most other colonies followed suit. Australia also experienced a precocious development of trade unions, and before the end of the century several of the colonies, with Victoria again leading the way, had adopted remarkably advanced social legislation.

During the nineteenth century each of the colonies more or less went its own way under both royal and self-government. Until the 1880's all attempts to create some sort of federation or national government foundered on the mutual jealousies of the separate colonies. In 1898 agreement was reached on a draft constitution for a federal structure which borrowed many of its elements from the United States but retained the British system of responsible cabinet government. On January 1, 1901, the first day of the twentieth century, the Commonwealth of Australia came into existence.

New Zealand was discovered by the Dutch mariner Abel Tasman in 1642 and rediscovered by Captain Cook in 1769, but Europeans made no effective settlement there until well into the nineteenth century. The native inhabitants, Maoris of Polynesian origin, were far more advanced socially and culturally than the aborigines of Australia and made excellent warriors. In addition, both European missionaries and the British government opposed European settlement. Eventually the political pressure of colonization companies together with the depredations of unprincipled traders and illegal settlers persuaded the British government to proclaim sovereignty in 1840; the first formal settlement took place in the same year. The early years were marked by lawlessness and conflict with the natives, culminating in the first Maori War (1843–1848). The progress of the colony was rapid, however, and by 1852 the British settlers had achieved effective self-government.

As in Australia, pastoralism formed the basis of the New Zealand economy. Sheep raising was supplemented by cattle and dairy farming after the introduction of mechanical refrigeration in 1882. The New Zealanders also developed a strong labor movement and enacted progressive social legislation. In 1907 the British government granted New Zealand dominion status.

In the process of acquiring and settling Australia and New Zealand the British discovered and took possession of a number of islands in the South Pacific. The first British settlement on a Pacific island was strictly illegal: the settlers were mutineers from the famous ship *Bounty,* who landed on Pitcairn Island in 1790 and took wives among the native women. The British government annexed the island in 1838.

British activity in exploration and discovery in the South Pacific was paralleled by that of the Dutch and French. In 1828 the Dutch laid claim to the western half of New Guinea, and in 1842 the French initiated a deliberate policy of annexation in compensation for diplomatic rebuffs in Europe. The main rush to claim Pacific islands came after 1880, however, when France and Britain were joined by Germany and the United States.

SOUTH AFRICA

The British first established themselves in South Africa during the Napoleonic wars in order to prevent the Cape of Good Hope from falling into the hands of the French. Cape Colony had been settled by the Dutch in the mid-seventeenth century as a way station for ships of the Dutch East India Company. Utilizing slave labor, the colonists devoted themselves to agriculture and pastoral pursuits. By the middle of the eighteenth century they had pushed the limits of their settlement north to the Orange River. After the Napoleonic wars the British government encouraged immigrants to settle in Cape Colony, instituted new administrative and judicial systems, and substituted English as the official language. The abolition of slavery throughout the British Empire in 1834 (see p. 91) created labor problems and financial difficulties for the Boers or Afrikaners (as descendants of the Dutch colonists were called), who claimed they received insufficient compensation. The British attempts to ensure more humane treatment for the natives by granting them land and permitting them to move about freely also annoyed the Boers, who had pursued a policy of native repression. To escape this interference, the Boers in 1835 began their Great Trek to the north, creating new settlements in the region between the Orange and Vaal rivers (which became the Orange Free State), north of the Vaal River (the Transvaal, which became the South African Republic in 1856), and on the southeast coast (Natal).

In spite of the Boers' attempts to isolate themselves from the British, conflict continued to mark the history of the colonies throughout the century. In 1843 after a short war with the Boers the British annexed Natal, which contained British settlers. For a few years at mid-century the British claimed sovereignty over the entire area south of the Vaal River, but by a convention of 1854 they agreed to withdraw to the Orange River. In 1877, after a failure of efforts to create a South African federation, the British governor of Cape Colony forcibly annexed Transvaal. A revolt of the Boers in 1880–81 led Gladstone, who had again become prime minister, to recognize the independence of the South African Republic once more. In addition to the conflicts between the British and the Boers, both groups clashed frequently with the African tribes. The encounters ended sooner or later in defeat for the latter. Many of the tribes were practically exterminated as a result, and most of the remainder were reduced to a state of servitude not far from slavery, especially those under Boer rule.

The Boer and British settlements were at first primarily agrarian, but in 1867 the discovery of diamonds in Griqualand, a region formerly set aside for natives, led to a great influx of treasure seekers from all over the world. In 1886 gold was discovered in Transvaal. These events completely altered the economic basis of the colonies and intensified political rivalries. They also brought to the fore one of the most influential persons in African history, Cecil Rhodes (1853–1902).

Rhodes, an Englishman, came to Africa in 1870 at the age of seventeen and quickly made a fortune in the diamond fields. In 1880 he helped found the De Beers Mining Company, which by 1888 had acquired a practical monopoly of diamond mining. He also organized the Consolidated Goldfields Company, which achieved a similar position in the Witwatersrand, or 'Rand. In 1887 he organized the British South Africa Company, and in 1889 he secured a royal charter from the British government granting it extensive rights and governing powers over a vast territory north of Transvaal, subsequently called Rhodesia.

Not content with mere profits, Rhodes took an active role in politics and became an ardent spokesman for imperialist expansion. He entered the Cape Colony legislature in 1880 and became prime minister of the colony ten years later. One of his major ambitions was to build a railroad "from the Cape to Cairo" – and to build it all on British territory. President Kruger of the South African Republic, who not only would not join a South African union but also refused permission for the railroad to cross Transvaal, temporarily blocked his objective. Rhodes determined to squeeze Transvaal into submission between the vise of his South Africa Company in the north and Cape Colony in the south. He also encouraged the *Uitlanders* (Dutch for foreigners, mainly British) within the South African Republic in their plans to revolt against Kruger. The plan called for Dr. L. Starr Jameson, chief administrator of Rhodes's South Africa Company, to lead a force across the border in support of the rebels. Jameson jumped the gun, however, and the Boer government, which had discovered the plot, captured him and his army of five hundred on January 2, 1896, only four days after he had crossed the border.

The repercussions of the Jameson Raid were numerous and far-reaching. The British government denied any knowledge of the conspiracy, sentenced Jameson to prison, and forced Rhodes to resign as prime minister of Cape Colony because of his complicity. It genuinely desired to avoid war with the Boers, but extremists on both sides in South Africa pushed the issue to its fateful conclusion. In October, 1899, the South African or Boer War began. The British, who had only 25,000 soldiers in South Africa against 75,000 Boers, suffered a number of early defeats. With the arrival of reinforcements, numbering 300,000 by the end of the war, the British rallied and in less than a year completely overran both the Orange Free State and Transvaal. The Boers resorted to guerrilla warfare that dragged on for another year and a half before they finally yielded on May 31, 1902.

The British had introduced limited representation in the Cape Colony as early as 1825. In 1853 they introduced a representative assembly, and in 1872 they permitted fully responsible government. The Boer republics had also been self-governing, and soon after the Boer War the British in an extraordinary reversal changed their policy toward the Boers from one of repression to one of conciliation. Transvaal regained responsible government in 1906, and the Orange Free State in 1907. The movement for union with Cape Colony and Natal gathered momentum, and in 1910 the Union of South Africa joined Canada, Australia, and New Zealand as a fully self-governing dominion within the British Empire.

INDIA

Early British conquests in India had been made not by the British government but by the East India Company acting under a royal charter. After the Seven Years' War widespread corruption among company officials and brutal exploitation of the natives led to progressive government intervention. The Regulating Act of 1774 provided for the appointment of a governor-general by the crown and the limitation of the company's privileges. The India Act of 1784 placed the company under the control of the newly created India Office, thus providing a clumsy "dual government." A law in 1813 abolished the company's monopoly of trade between India and Britain, and another law in 1833 abolished its monopoly of trade with China.

The East India Company thus ceased to be a trading company almost completely. It obtained most of its revenue in the form of taxes from the provinces it governed. Some it administered directly, others indirectly by means of native rulers. By 1820 it had brought all of India under its control. Subsequently it added several outlying provinces, such as Kashmir, Punjab, and a part of Baluchistan. In a series of wars between 1825 and 1885, Burma was annexed bit by bit, and eventually was attached to British India. The British became involved in the Malay peninsula during the Napoleonic wars and gradually extended their control over it in the course of the century, and also took Ceylon from the Dutch.

Governing this vast conglomerate was no easy task. A great diversity of languages, religions, customs, and traditions existed side by side. Hindus and Moslems accounted for the major part of the population of some 200 million, but there were many lesser religious cults as well. Each great cultural tradition contained many different races, sects, and social castes. Such diversity and lack of national sentiment had facilitated the original conquest, but it complicated enormously the task of government.

The Mansell Collection

Sepoys Dividing the Spoils

"We are in sad anxiety about India, which engrosses all our attention. Troops cannot be raised fast or largely enough. And the horrors committed on the poor ladies — women and children — are unknown in these ages, and make one's blood run cold. . . . There is not a family hardly who is not in sorrow and anxiety about their children, and in all ranks — India being the place where every one was anxious to place a son." From a letter of Queen Victoria to the king of the Belgians, September 2, 1857, in Arthur Christopher Benson and Viscount Esher, THE LETTERS OF QUEEN VICTORIA (London, 1908), Vol. III.

The company made a few attempts to introduce unified practices on the Western model, such as British courts and law codes, but native susceptibilities were easily offended. On the whole, the company found it easier to leave things as they were.

One example of the difficulties occurred in 1857 and brought about the final extinction of the East India Company. Four-fifths of its army consisted of natives — Moslems, Hindus, and others. A number of actions and rumors of actions by the officials of the company inflamed the religious ardor of the troops and aroused fears of forcible conversion to Christianity. In May three regiments of sepoys (native troops) mutinied and marched on Delhi. The revolt soon spread to other parts of India, and for a time it appeared that the British would be driven out entirely. Eventually they rallied and by July, 1858, had defeated the rebels and restored their power. The reaction in Britain was distinctly unfavorable to the company. In August Parliament passed a new India Act transferring the company's powers directly to the crown, which then introduced a number of reforms in the Indian administration. Although the changes were immediately provoked by the Sepoy Mutiny, they corresponded with a new attitude toward imperial and colonial affairs that had been gaining strength in Britain.

ANTI-IMPERIALISM AND THE REVIVAL OF IMPERIAL SENTIMENT

India and the "settlement colonies" (those with large numbers of British settlers), which eventually became self-governing dominions, were not the only components of the British Empire in the mid-nineteenth century. The empire included a number of minor possessions in and around the Caribbean and trading posts on the West African coast, as well as a number of islands and other fortified strong points on sea lanes throughout the world, held chiefly for strategic reasons: Gibraltar, Malta, Aden, Singapore, the Falkland Islands, and others. The methods by which this disparate assemblage was governed were complex, confusing, and at times even chaotic. No single, simple system of colonial administration existed either in the colonies or in London. Each colony had its own unique legal system, which might include elements of French, Spanish, Dutch, or even Moslem or Hindu law, depending on its prior history. Both crown and Parliament claimed the right to regulate colonial affairs. In practice, Parliament usually left matters to the various government departments, but it never abdicated its right to legislate either for particular colonies or for the empire as a whole. In addition to the India Office, which had its own more or less clearly defined responsibilities, colonial affairs fell under the jurisdiction of the Colonial Office (attached to the War Office until 1854), the Board of Trade, the Treasury, and even the Home Office on occasion. Moreover, military and naval officers, governors-general, high commissioners, and other officials in the field frequently acted quite independently of superior authority, although nominally taking orders from London.

The generation after 1815 witnessed a growing wave of criticism of some of the pillars of the old colonial system: slavery, the penal system, the restriction of colonial trade, and the political restrictions imposed on the colonies by the government in London. Critics accused the colonial administration of extravagance and inefficiency. Political, religious, humanitarian, and economic arguments were advanced to buttress the criticism, which owed much to the growth of Benthamite liberalism. Three schools of thought gradually emerged on the subject of colonial reform. The first, which gained influence in the 1830's, paradoxically sought to cure the evils of the old colonial system by a new and more vigorous wave of colonial expansion – by the emigration of British settlers to unpopulated territories rather than by the conquest of existing societies. Led by Edward Gibbon Wakefield, the founder in 1830 of the Colonization Society, this group influenced settlement policy in Australia and was instrumental in securing the annexation of New Zealand in 1840. At the other extreme were those who wanted to see Britain shed its colonies altogether in the belief that it could gain the commercial advantages of trade without the expense and political risks of administration. They used as their prime example the rapid growth of commerce with the United States after the American Revolution. Called "little Englanders," they achieved their greatest influence, such as it was, in the 1850's and 1860's at the peak of the free trade movement. A third, intermediate, more pragmatic group stressed administrative simplification and efficiency, humanitarian reform, and the gradual extension of self-government. Although they were less vocal than the others, they succeeded in obtaining responsible and strategic positions in the government and in the long run were the most influential.

None of the colonial reformers had his way entirely. No matter how dedicated and hardworking, they were frustrated by the inertia of the political system, stymied by the resistance of vested interests, and overwhelmed by the march of events throughout the vast and far-flung territories that they administered. After 1870 major new developments completely altered the environment in which they labored. In the election of 1874 the Conservatives under Disraeli defeated Gladstone's Liberals on a platform of "giving the country a rest" from domestic reform measures. In 1875 on behalf of the British government Disraeli melodramatically purchased from the bankrupt khedive of Egypt his shares in the Suez Canal Company. In 1876 he bestowed on Queen Victoria the title "Empress of India." In these and other ways he rekindled popular enthusiasm for imperial expansion. No less important was the changing world situation, which brought other nations into the imperial picture. The creation of the German Empire, the Russo-Turkish War, and the depression that began in 1873 set the stage for a competitive scramble for colonies in which Britain, as the leading imperial nation, could hardly avoid involvement.

THE OPENING OF ASIA

Although parts of Asia had been open to European influence and conquest since the beginning of the sixteenth century, much of it remained in isolation. In the first half of the nineteenth century Britain controlled India and some of its surrounding territories, the Dutch held most of the islands of the East Indies, and Spain retained the Philippines. The French and Portuguese maintained small trading settlements on the Indian coasts. The vast and ancient empire of China, however, as well as Japan, Korea, and the principalities of Southeast Asia, attempted to remain aloof from Western civilization, which they regarded as inferior to their own. They refused to accept Western diplomatic representatives, excluded or persecuted Christian missionaries, and allowed only a trickle of commerce with the West.

RUSSIAN EXPANSION IN ASIA

Russian frontiersmen began to explore the vast wilderness of Siberia about the time of the first English settlements in North America. In 1637 they reached the Pacific coast, and by the end of the seventeenth century they were encroaching on the Chinese borders far to the south. Russian expansionism was relatively quiescent in the eighteenth century, although by the end of the century the Russians had established a claim on Alaska and in the early years of the nineteenth century set up trading posts on the coast of northern California. Siberia, a forbidding land at best, remained thinly populated and underdeveloped. The next main thrust of Russian expansion in Asia, which took place in the nineteenth century, was directed toward the warmer lands to the south and was closely connected with the desire to secure ice-free ports.

In a series of wars against the Ottoman Empire and Persia between 1800 and 1830 Russia gained control of the entire north coast of the Black Sea. In succeeding decades it pressed its advance into central Asia, annexing the trans-Caspian area in 1881 and Turkestan in 1884–85. These advances resulted in conflicts with Persia and Afghanistan and in tense diplomatic relations with the British. Britain had earlier fought minor wars with both Persia and Afghanistan to protect its passage to India and the Indian frontiers, and it had established a sort of informal protectorate over both countries. The Anglo-Russian tension in the Middle East continued throughout the final quarter of the nineteenth century, becoming especially acute after 1896. At length the Anglo-Russian Entente of 1907, occasioned by mutual fear of Germany (see p. 322), led to agreement and the relaxation of tension. Afghanistan remained a buffer state between Russian Turkestan and British India, with Russia recognizing predominant British interests in the control of its foreign relations. Without consulting the Persian government, the two great powers divided Persia into spheres of influence, north and south, with a neutral sphere between them. Thus, although both Persia and Afghanistan retained nominal independence, they were in fact narrowly circumscribed.

The Russians pursued aggressive policies in eastern Asia as well. In 1850 they established a settlement on the Amur River on the border of the Chinese Empire. Shortly afterward they extracted from the Chinese two treaties that extended Russian territory to the shores of the Sea of Japan. In 1860 they founded the city of Vladivostok. Toward the end of the century intervention in the Sino-Japanese War and in Korea, the lease of the Port Arthur naval base on the Yellow Sea, and the occupation of Manchuria brought them into conflict with the equally aggressive Japanese. Russian refusal to negotiate differences led directly to the outbreak of a disastrous war in 1904. (See p. 239.)

CHINA, THE PAPER DRAGON

The Chinese Empire in the nineteenth century was ruled by the Manchu dynasty, the last in a long succession of dynasties that had risen and fallen in China for more than three thousand years. The Manchu dynasty was about two hundred years old and had already begun to show signs of decrepitude before the Europeans intervened to hasten its demise.

British commercial interests provided the initial occasion for intervention. Chinese tea and silks found a ready market in Europe, but British traders could offer little in exchange that appealed to the Chinese until they discovered that the Chinese had a marked taste for opium. The Chinese government forbade its importation, but the trade flourished by means of smugglers and corrupt customs officials. When one honest official at Canton seized and burned a large shipment of opium in 1839, the British traders demanded retaliation. Lord Palmerston, the foreign secretary, informed them that the government could not intervene for the purpose of permitting British subjects to violate the laws of the country with which they traded, but the military and diplomatic representatives on the spot disregarded these instructions and took punitive action against the Chinese. Thus began the Opium War (1839–1842), which ended with the dictated Treaty of Nanking. Under it China ceded to Britain the island of Hongkong, agreed to open five more ports to trade under consular supervision, established a uniform 5 per cent import tariff, and paid a substantial indemnity. The opium trade continued.

The ease with which the British prevailed over the Chinese encouraged other nations to seek equally favorable treaties, which were accordingly granted. Such a show of weakness by the Chinese government provoked demonstrations that were both anti-government and anti-foreign and led to the Taiping Rebellion (1850–1864). Government forces eventually defeated the rebels, but in the meantime the general lawlessness gave Western powers another excuse for intervention. In 1857–58 a joint Anglo-French force occupied a number of principal cities and extorted further concessions, in which the United States and Russia also participated.

China's history for the remainder of the nineteenth century followed a depressingly similar pattern. Concessions to foreigners led to fresh outbreaks of anti-foreign violence and lawlessness, leading in turn to further reprisals and concessions. Recognizing the general weakness of China, still other nations joined in the scramble for concessions and special privileges: Germany, Portugal, and even Japan, which had resisted Western pressures while adopting Western ways. Japan went to war against China in 1894–95, forcing the latter to recognize the independence of Korea and to cede Formosa, the Pescadores Islands, and the Liaotung peninsula. Other nations were eager to participate in a general dismemberment of China but could not agree on the division of spoils. In the end, China avoided complete partition by the great powers only by virtue of great power rivalry. Instead of outright partition, Britain, France, Germany, Russia, the United States, and Japan contented themselves with special treaty ports, spheres of influence, and long-term leases of Chinese territory. At the initiative of the American secretary of state, John Hay, the great powers agreed in 1899 to follow an "open door" policy in China by not discriminating against the commerce of other nations in their own spheres of influence.

Continued humiliations resulted in a final desperate outburst of anti-foreign violence known as the Boxer Rebellion (1900–1901). Boxers was the popular name given to the members of a secret society called The Society of Harmonious Fists, whose aim was to drive all foreigners from China. In risings in several parts of the country they attacked Chinese converts to Christianity and murdered hundreds of missionaries, railroad workers, businessmen, and other foreigners, including the German minister to Peking. The first attempts of British and other military forces to occupy Peking were repulsed. A second and larger joint expedition took the capital, meted out severe reprisals, and exacted further indemnities and concessions. Thereafter the Chinese government was in a state of almost visible decay. It succumbed in 1912 to a revolution led by Dr. Sun Yat-sen, a Western-educated physician, whose program was "nationalism, democracy, and socialism." The Western powers did not attempt to interfere in the revolution, but neither were they perturbed. The Republic of China that resulted remained weak and divided, its hopes of reform and regeneration long postponed.

JAPAN REBUFFS THE WEST

In the first half of the nineteenth century Japan maintained its policy against foreign intrusion more effectively than any other Oriental nation. Gradually, under continuous Western pressure for diplomatic representation, missionary activity, and commercial intercourse, the pillars of resistance weakened. In 1853–54 they collapsed in the face of representations made by Commodore Matthew Perry, a United States naval commander, backed by the threat of force. Soon other Western nations obtained trading and diplomatic privileges similar to those gained by the United

States. As in China, anti-foreign rioting broke out, lives were lost, and property was destroyed. The Western navies began to take reprisals. It seemed as if Japan was destined to repeat the experience of the other victims of Western imperialism, perhaps even more rapidly. Then a remarkable change took place.

Prior to 1868 Japan was ruled not by the emperor but by the shogun, a powerful feudal lord; the nominal emperor's functions were chiefly religious. The anti-foreign sentiment provoked by the concessions of the shogun developed into a movement to restore the emperor to his rightful position as head of the government. The movement was fortuitously aided in 1867 by the accession of a vigorous, intelligent young emperor, Mutsuhito, almost simultaneously with the accession to the shogunate of a man who belonged to the emperor's party. In the following year the latter abdicated the shogunate, and the emperor began to rule in fact as well as in name. The event, marking the birth of modern Japan, is called the Meiji Restoration from the name Meiji, meaning Enlightened Government, which Mutsuhito chose to designate his reign, as was the custom in Japan. The Meiji period lasted from 1868 to the death of Mutsuhito in 1912.

Immediately upon coming to power, Mutsuhito changed the tone of the anti-foreign movement. Instead of attempting to expel the foreigners, Japan cooperated with them but kept them at a polite distance. Intelligent young men went abroad to study Western methods in politics and government, military science, industrial technology, trade, and finance, with the aim of adopting the most efficient methods. The old feudal system was abolished, almost in a single stroke, and replaced by a highly centralized bureaucratic administration modeled on the French system, with an army of the Prussian type and a navy of the British type. Industrial and financial methods came from every country, but especially from the United States. The results of this vigorous, forward-looking policy soon became apparent. Foreign commerce made spectacular gains, modern industries arose where none had been before, and Japanese military might soon won the incredulous respect of the Western world. In 1894–95 Japan quickly defeated China, its neighbor and former mentor, and joined the ranks of the imperialist nations by annexing Chinese territory and staking out a sphere of influence in China proper. Even more surprisingly, just ten years later Japan decisively defeated Russia.

The Russo-Japanese War resulted directly from the imperial rivalry of the two nations in China and Korea. Japan attempted to negotiate a settlement of disputed claims on several occasions, but the Russians, who regarded the Japanese as little different from the Chinese and Koreans, treated the proposals with disdain. Provoked by the affront to their national pride, the Japanese in February, 1904, bottled up the Russian Asiatic fleet in Port Arthur and two days later declared war. To Western observers it looked like an Oriental David attacking the Russian Goliath. The Japanese soon showed their mettle by inflicting a series of defeats on Russian armies along the Yalu River and in Manchuria. To regain control of the seas between Japan and the mainland, the Russians sent their Baltic fleet on a seven months' cruise around the tip of Africa, but no sooner had it arrived in Eastern waters in May, 1905, than the Japanese sank almost the entire fleet. This shattering and humiliating loss, together with the outbreak of domestic revolution, persuaded the Russians to accept President Roosevelt's offer of mediation. By the Treaty of Portsmouth in September, 1905, the Russians acknowledged Japanese predominance in Korea, transferred their lease on Port Arthur and the Liaotung peninsula to Japan, and ceded to Japan the southern half of Sakhalin. Thus did the Japanese prove that they could play the white man's game.

KOREA, INDOCHINA, AND THAILAND

Korea in the nineteenth century was a semi-autonomous kingdom under the nominal suzerainty of the Chinese, although the Japanese had long had claims there. Like China and Japan, Korea followed a rigid policy of exclusion. Shipwrecked foreign seamen were not allowed to leave the country, and the few missionaries who entered the country in one way or another, mainly French Catholics, were frequently persecuted. Western "gunboat diplomacy" gradually opened the country to foreign influence and commerce in the second half of the century, but the bitter rivalry of China and Japan for predominance as well as the general poverty of the country discouraged Western diplomats and traders. After increasing tension over a period of twenty years, war finally broke out between China and Japan in 1894. The Japanese won easily. Although Korea had been the principal cause of the war, the Treaty of 1895 ending it did not result in Japanese annexation. Japan remained content with China's recognition of Korean "independence." For the next ten years Russia replaced China as Japan's chief rival for hegemony in Korea, until the outcome of the Russo-Japanese war forced Russia to concede Japan's "preponderant interests." Finally, after a series of rebellions against Japanese-imposed puppets, Japan formally annexed Korea in 1910.

Indochina is the name frequently applied to the vast peninsula of Southeast Asia because the culture of the area is essentially an amalgam of classical Indian and Chinese civilization. Prior to the nineteenth century the rulers of the various principalities and kingdoms recognized a vague allegiance to the Chinese emperor. In the course of the century the British, operating from India, established control over Burma and the Malay States and eventually incorporated them into the empire. The eastern half of the peninsula, including the principalities of Tonkin, Laos, Cambodia, Cochin China, and Annam, was ruled by the emperor of Annam. French missionaries had been active in the region since the seventeenth century, but in the first half of the nineteenth century they were subjected increasingly to persecution, giving the French government an excuse for intervention. In 1858 a French expedition occupied the city of Saigon in Cochin China, and four years later France annexed Cochin China itself. Once established on the peninsula, the French found themselves involved in conflicts with the natives, which obliged them to extend their "protection" over ever larger areas. In the 1880's they organized Cochin China, Cambodia, Annam, and Tonkin into the Union of French Indochina, to which they added Laos in 1893.

Thailand (or Siam, as it was called by Europeans), between Burma on the west and French Indochina on the east, had the good fortune to remain an independent kingdom. It owed its independence to two principal factors: a series of able and enlightened kings, and its position as a buffer between French and British spheres of influence. Although it was opened to Western influence by gunboat treaties, like most of the rest of Asia, its rulers reacted with conciliatory gestures and at the same time strove to learn from the West and to modernize their kingdom. Even this might not have saved it from the fate of Burma and French Indochina had it not been for the Anglo-French rivalry. In 1893 it faced a grave threat from the French, but an Anglo-French agreement of 1896 gave it a joint guarantee of independence. Few other non-Western nations were so fortunate.

THE PARTITION OF AFRICA

Culturally, most of Africa in the nineteenth century was at the opposite extreme from Asia. Asia had very ancient, even decadent civilizations, while Africa south of the Sahara had none, or so it appeared to Europeans of that time, although results of recent research have shown that this view was incorrect. Islamic North Africa, on the other hand, resembled Asia. Asians had highly developed and refined religious traditions; the religions of black Africa were primitive and tribal. The tribe served as the basis of social and political organization, although tribes might occasionally be grouped into something resembling kingdoms and even empires.

Whatever the differences between Asians and Africans, their similarities are more important for an understanding of their vulnerability to Western imperialism. They were alike in three principal ways. In the first place, they were technologically backward. Second, they had weak, unstable governments, shifting political allegiances, and warring internal factions. A third similarity had no functional significance, yet it did have an important bearing on Western attitudes toward Asians and Africans: both had colored skins, in contrast to the predominantly fair-skinned Europeans.

Although the similarities explain much of the vulnerability of Asians and Africans to Western imperialism, they do not explain why Europeans wanted to create colonial empires, or why the revival of imperialism took place when it did. The precise timing of Western imperialism can be understood only in relation to intra-European diplomacy and power politics, inasmuch as imperial rivalries were mostly extensions of European great power rivalries. In the specific case of Africa the timing can be explained partly by the gradual dissolution of the Ottoman Empire in the north and by the mutual antagonism of two ethnic groups of European descent in the south, the Boers and the British.

The continuing conflict between the Boers and the British pushed the limit of European settlement and control north from the southern tip of Africa. In the process native Africans were overrun, outflanked, pushed aside, and sometimes brutally butchered as if they were animals in the path of the two antagonists. They were rarely the direct objects of the imperialist drive; rather they were its incidental victims. The Anglo-Boer conflict resulted in the settlement of Transvaal and the Orange Free State and also brought into the British Empire Basutoland (1868), Bechuanaland (1885), Swaziland (1902), and Rhodesia (1889).

ISLAMIC AFRICA

Prior to 1880 the only European possession in Africa, apart from British South Africa and a few coastal trading posts dating from the eighteenth century or earlier, was French Algeria. Charles X undertook to conquer Algeria in 1830 in a belated attempt to stir up popular support for his regime. The conquest came too late to save his throne and left a legacy of unfinished conquest to his successors. Not until 1879 did civil government replace the military authorities. By then the French had begun to expand from their settlements on the African west coast. By the end of the century they had conquered and annexed a huge, thinly populated territory (including most of the Sahara Desert), which they christened French West Africa. In 1881 they took advantage of border raids on Algeria by tribesmen from Tunisia to invade Tunisia and establish a protectorate. The French rounded out their North African empire in 1912 by establishing a protectorate over the larger part of Morocco (Spain claimed the small northern corner) after lengthy diplomatic struggles, especially with Germany.

More important events were taking place at the eastern end of Islamic Africa. The opening of the Suez Canal by a French company in 1869 revolutionized world commerce. It also endangered the British lifeline to India – or so it seemed to the British. Thereafter it became a cardinal tenet of British foreign policy to exert as much control as possible over the canal area and its approaches and to prevent them from falling into the hands of an unfriendly power at any cost. Their designs were fortuitously favored by the financial difficulties of the khedive (king) of Egypt. Although the khedives were nominally tributary to the sultan in Constantinople, they had long followed an independent policy, at times amounting to outright insubordination. In their effort to build Egypt up to the status of a great power they incurred enormous debts to Europeans (mainly the French and British) for such purposes as an abortive attempt at industrialization, the construction of the Suez Canal, and an attempted conquest of Sudan. This financial stringency enabled Disraeli to purchase the khedive's shares in the canal company. In an effort to bring some order into the finances of the country, the British and French governments appointed financial advisers who soon constituted the effective government. Egyptian resentment at foreign domination resulted in widespread riots in which many Europeans living in Egypt lost their lives. To restore order and protect the canal, the British in 1882 bombarded Alexandria and landed an expeditionary force. The occupation of Egypt had begun.

Gladstone, the British prime minister, assured the Egyptians and the other great powers (who had been invited to participate in the occupation but declined) that the occupation would be temporary, since its only purpose was the restoration of order and the preservation of European lives and property. Once in, however, the British found to their chagrin that they could not get out easily or gracefully. Besides continued nationalist agitation, which necessitated the presence of the army, the British inherited from the government of the khedive the latter's unfinished conquest of Sudan. In pursuing this objective, which seemed to be justified by the importance to the Egyptian economy of controlling the upper Nile, the British ran head-on into conflict with the French, who were expanding eastward from their West African possessions. At Fashoda in 1898 rival French and British forces faced one another with sabers drawn, but hasty negotiations in London and Paris prevented actual hostilities. At length the French withdrew, preparing the way for British rule in what became known as Anglo-Egyptian Sudan.

One by one the Turkish sultan's nominal vassal states along the North African coast had been plucked away until only Tripoli remained, a long stretch of barren coastline backed by an even more barren hinterland. Italy, its nearest European neighbor, was a late-comer both as a nation and as an imperialist. It had managed to pick up only a few narrow strips on the East African coast and had been ignominiously repulsed in an attempted conquest of Ethiopia in 1896. It watched with bitter, impotent envy while other nations picked imperial plums. In 1911, having carefully prepared a series of agreements with the other great powers in order to have a free hand, Italy picked a quarrel with Turkey, delivered an impossible ultimatum, and promptly invaded Tripoli. The war was something of a farce, with neither side vigorous enough to overcome the other. The threat of a new outbreak in the Balkans, however, persuaded the Turks to make peace in 1912. They ceded Tripoli to Italy, and the Italians renamed it Libya.

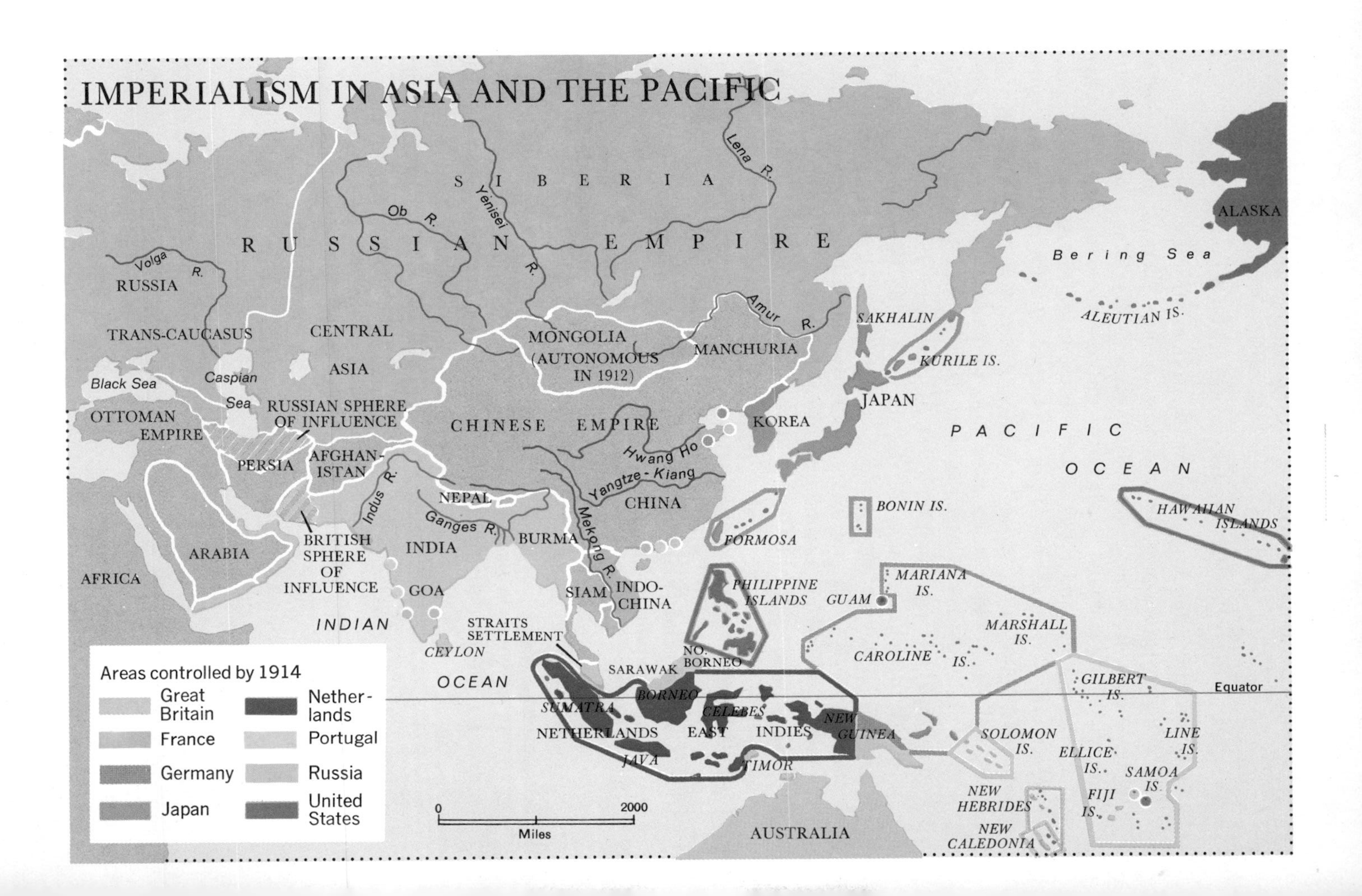

IMPERIALISM IN ASIA AND THE PACIFIC
SIBERIA
RUSSIAN EMPIRE
Ob R.
Yenisei R.
Lena R.
Volga R.
RUSSIA
TRANS-CAUCASUS
CENTRAL ASIA
Black Sea
Caspian Sea
OTTOMAN EMPIRE
RUSSIAN SPHERE OF INFLUENCE
PERSIA
AFGHAN-ISTAN
ARABIA
AFRICA
BRITISH SPHERE OF INFLUENCE
Indus R.
NEPAL
Ganges R.
INDIA
GOA
CEYLON
INDIAN OCEAN
MONGOLIA (AUTONOMOUS IN 1912)
MANCHURIA
Amur R.
CHINESE EMPIRE
Hwang Ho
Yangtze-Kiang
CHINA
KOREA
JAPAN
SAKHALIN
KURILE IS.
Bering Sea
ALEUTIAN IS.
ALASKA
PACIFIC OCEAN
BURMA
Mekong R.
SIAM
INDO-CHINA
STRAITS SETTLEMENT
FORMOSA
BONIN IS.
HAWAIIAN ISLANDS
PHILIPPINE ISLANDS
GUAM
MARIANA IS.
MARSHALL IS.
CAROLINE IS.
NO. BORNEO
SARAWAK
BORNEO
SUMATRA
CELEBES
NEW GUINEA
NETHERLANDS EAST INDIES
JAVA
TIMOR
SOLOMON IS.
GILBERT IS.
ELLICE IS.
LINE IS.
SAMOA IS.
FIJI IS.
NEW HEBRIDES
NEW CALEDONIA
AUSTRALIA
Equator
0
2000
Miles
Areas controlled by 1914
Great Britain
France
Germany
Japan
Nether-lands
Portugal
Russia
United States

THE BERLIN CONFERENCE AND FINAL PARTITIONS

Central Africa, much of it covered with dense tropical jungles and inhabited by Negroes, was the last area in the "dark continent" to be opened to European penetration. Its inaccessability, inhospitable climate, and exotic flora and fauna – all amply embroidered upon in the accounts of early explorers and traders – were responsible for Africa's sobriquet and formidable reputation. Prior to the nineteenth century the only European claims in the region were those of Portugal: Angola on the west coast and Mozambique on the east, both on the southern perimeter. The activities of explorers such as the Scottish missionary David Livingstone and the Anglo-American journalist H. M. Stanley in the 1860's and 1870's did much to arouse popular interest. In 1876 King Leopold of Belgium organized the International Association for the Exploration and Civilization of Central Africa and hired Stanley to establish settlements in the Congo. Agitation for colonial enterprise reached a peak in Germany with the formation of the German African Society in 1878 and the German Colonial Society in 1882. A reluctant Bismarck allowed himself to be converted to the cause of colonialism. The discovery of diamonds in South Africa stimulated exploration in the hope of similar discoveries in central Africa. Finally, the French occupation of Tunis in 1881 and the British occupation of Egypt in 1882 set off a scramble for claims and concessions.

The French, who had earlier staked a claim at the mouth of the Gabun River, hurriedly extended it to a large region north of the Congo and established a further claim to Dahomey. The Germans established a base in southwest Africa in 1883 and claimed protectorates over Togoland and the Cameroons in 1884. In the same year Portugal claimed both sides of the mouth of the Congo, and early in 1885 Spain claimed protectorates over Rio de Oro (Spanish Sahara) and Rio Muni (Spanish Guinea), while Britain did the same in Nigeria.

The sudden rush for territories naturally created frictions that might have led to war. To head off this possibility, and incidentally to balk British and Portuguese claims, Bismarck and Jules Ferry, the French prime minister, called an international conference on African affairs to meet in Berlin in 1884. Fourteen nations including the United States sent representatives. The conferees agreed on a number of pious resolutions, including one calling for the suppression of the slave trade and slavery, which was still a flourishing institution in Africa. More important, they recognized the Congo Free State headed by Leopold of the Belgians, an outgrowth of his International Association, and laid the ground rules for further annexations. The most important rule provided that a nation must effectively occupy a territory in order to have its claim recognized.

On the east coast of Africa much the same process of occupation took place. In 1882 the Italians occupied Assab at the mouth of the Red Sea and used it as a base for expansion into Eritrea and Italian Somaliland. Not to be outdone, the French and British soon afterward established protectorates on parts of the Somali coast. Farther south two chartered East Africa companies, one German and one British, staked large claims reaching inland to the eastern borders of the Congo Free State. The French, who had an old but ineffectual claim to the island of Madagascar, finally annexed it in 1896. One of the few regions of Africa left unclaimed by a European power was the Coptic Christian kingdom of Ethiopia, also known as Abyssinia. In 1895 the Italians decided to annex it to their coastal territories. They began a slow and difficult march to the interior. Early in the following year the Italian army of twenty thousand men was annihilated by barefoot Ethiopian tribesmen at Adowa. That humiliating defeat ended temporarily Italian designs on the "king of kings."

In this fashion was the dark continent carved up and made to see the light. Before the outbreak of World War I only Ethiopia and Liberia, established by emancipated American Negroes in the 1830's, retained their independence. Both were nominally Christian. Annexation was one thing, however, effective settlement and development were quite another. The African colonies would have to wait a long time before receiving the fruits, if any, of European tutelage. The process of partition frequently brought the nations of Europe to the brink of war, but somehow the diplomats averted full-scale fighting, except in the special case of the Boer War. Perhaps it was the existence of this open frontier that enabled the expansive Europeans to work off their mutual antagonisms without resorting to arms. In any case, soon after this safety valve was sealed the European boiler exploded.

INTERPRETATIONS AND PERSPECTIVES

Asia and Africa were not the only areas subject to imperial exploitation, nor were the nations of Europe the only ones to engage in it. Once Japan had adopted Western technology, it pursued imperialistic policies not unlike those of Europe. In spite of strong domestic criticism, the United States embarked on a policy of colonialism before the end of the century. Besides the purchase of Alaska in 1867 and the acquisition by lease of the Panama Canal Zone in 1903, the United States participated with Britain, France, and Germany in the division of the islands of the Pacific, taking Hawaii and part of Samoa as its portion. In the war with Spain in 1898 the United States won the Philippines and Guam in the Pacific as well as Puerto Rico in the Caribbean.

Some of the British dominions were far more aggressively imperialistic than the mother country itself. The expansion of South Africa, for example, took place mostly through South African initiative and frequently against the wishes and explicit instructions of the government in London.

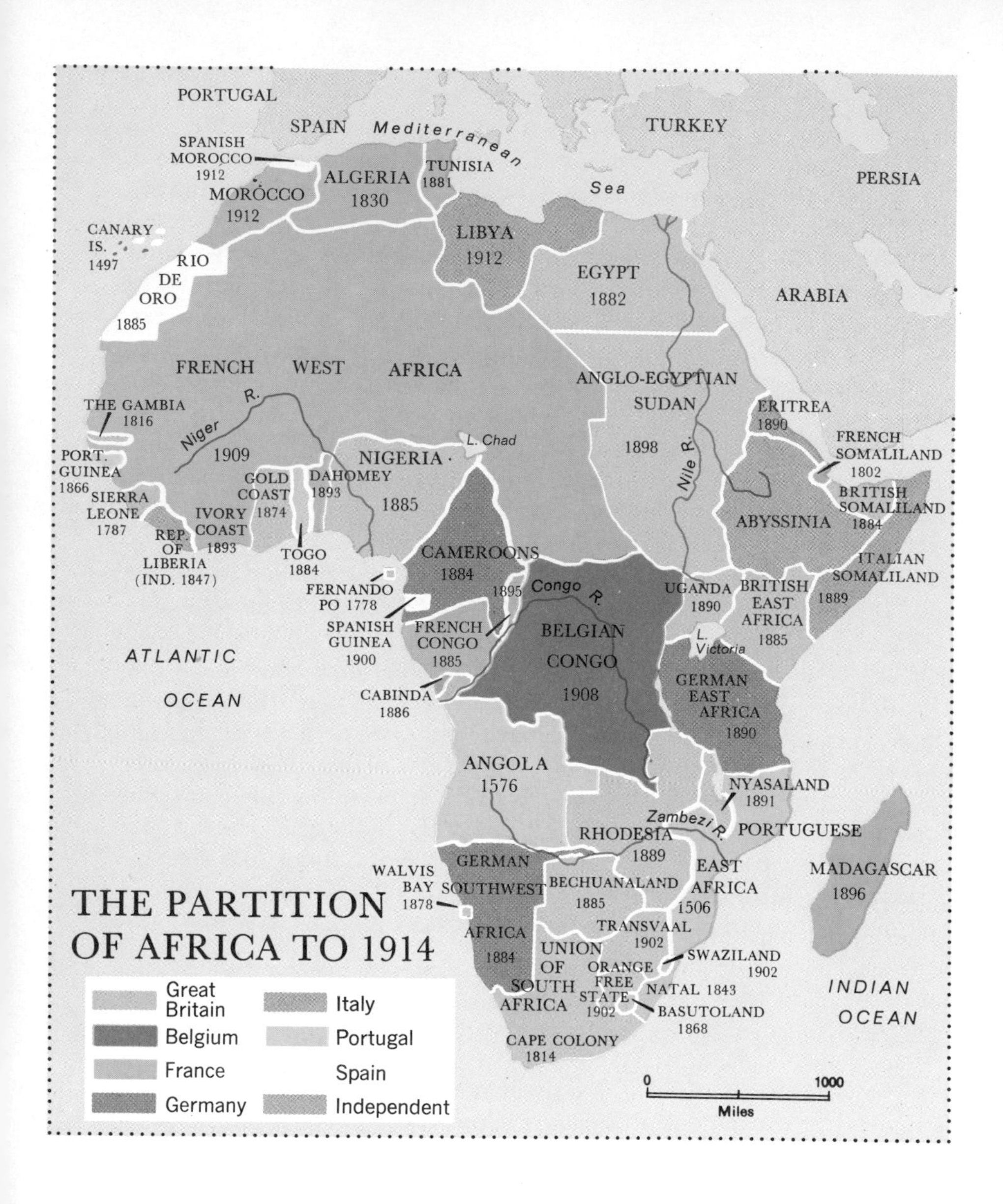
THE PARTITION OF AFRICA TO 1914
Great Britain
Belgium
France
Germany
Italy
Portugal
Spain
Independent
PORTUGAL
SPAIN
Mediterranean Sea
TURKEY
PERSIA
ARABIA
SPANISH MOROCCO 1912
MOROCCO 1912
ALGERIA 1830
TUNISIA 1881
LIBYA 1912
EGYPT 1882
CANARY IS. 1497
RIO DE ORO 1885
FRENCH WEST AFRICA
ANGLO-EGYPTIAN SUDAN 1898
ERITREA 1890
FRENCH SOMALILAND 1802
BRITISH SOMALILAND 1884
ABYSSINIA
ITALIAN SOMALILAND 1889
THE GAMBIA 1816
Niger R.
1909
PORT. GUINEA 1866
SIERRA LEONE 1787
REP. OF LIBERIA (IND. 1847)
IVORY COAST 1893
GOLD COAST 1874
TOGO 1884
DAHOMEY 1893
NIGERIA 1885
L. Chad
Nile R.
CAMEROONS 1884
FERNANDO PO 1778
SPANISH GUINEA 1900
FRENCH CONGO 1885
1895
Congo R.
BELGIAN CONGO 1908
UGANDA 1890
BRITISH EAST AFRICA 1885
L. Victoria
GERMAN EAST AFRICA 1890
ATLANTIC OCEAN
CABINDA 1886
ANGOLA 1576
NYASALAND 1891
Zambezi R.
RHODESIA 1889
PORTUGUESE EAST AFRICA 1506
MADAGASCAR 1896
WALVIS BAY 1878
GERMAN SOUTHWEST AFRICA 1884
BECHUANALAND 1885
TRANSVAAL 1902
UNION OF SOUTH AFRICA
ORANGE FREE STATE 1902
SWAZILAND 1902
NATAL 1843
BASUTOLAND 1868
CAPE COLONY 1814
INDIAN OCEAN
0
1000
Miles

The British annexation of southeastern New Guinea in 1884 (after the Dutch had claimed the western half and the Germans the northeast) was directly due to the agitation of the Queensland government in Australia.

A distinction is sometimes made between imperialism and colonialism. Thus, neither Russia nor Austria-Hungary had overseas colonies, but both were cleary empires in the sense that they ruled over alien peoples without the consent of the latter. The imperial powers did not as a rule establish colonies in China, yet China was clearly subject to imperial control. The countries of Latin America experienced no new attempts at conquest by outside powers, but it was frequently alleged that they constituted part of the informal empires of Britain and the United States as a result of economic dependence and financial control.

The causes of imperialism were many and complex. No single theory suffices to explain all cases. Nevertheless, it is worth reviewing some of the more important interpretations; whatever their validity, the interpretations themselves are a part of the intellectual history of the epoch.

THE HUMANITARIAN ARGUMENT

In the intellectual crosscurrents of the late nineteenth century confusion was bound to arise concerning the motives for imperial expansion. Although some proclaimed the expansion to be a necessity for the Western nations — for good or evil — others demanded the expansion on behalf of the colonial areas. Missionary activity, the desire to bring the comforts of Christianity to the "heathen races," and the belief of well-intentioned humanitarians that non-Europeans would benefit from Western legal institutions or technology, even if imposed by force, were advanced as reasons for dispatching expeditionary forces to distant lands. Rudyard Kipling (1865–1936), famed poet, wrote eloquently of "the white man's burden," and French apologists for imperialism spoke of their *mission civilisatrice*.

The evangelical zeal of both Catholic and Protestant missionaries is beyond dispute. For centuries before the nineteenth century they had carried their message far and wide to the most remote corners of the habitable world. In both Asia and Africa they usually preceded by many years the traders, diplomats, armies, and administrators. Normally they did not ask for military protection from their homelands, much less for territorial annexation. Theirs was a spiritual mission, quite unconnected with politics. When they were subjected to persecution, torture, and even death by the people they sought to convert — and this treatment was by no means rare — the demands for retaliation came most often from journalists, military men, and others, who had reasons of their own for desiring imperial conquest. In short, in the imperial game as it came to be played in the late nineteenth century, arguments based on religion were simply convenient excuses, and missionaries were pawns in the game.

Courtesy of The Historical Institute, The University of Tokyo

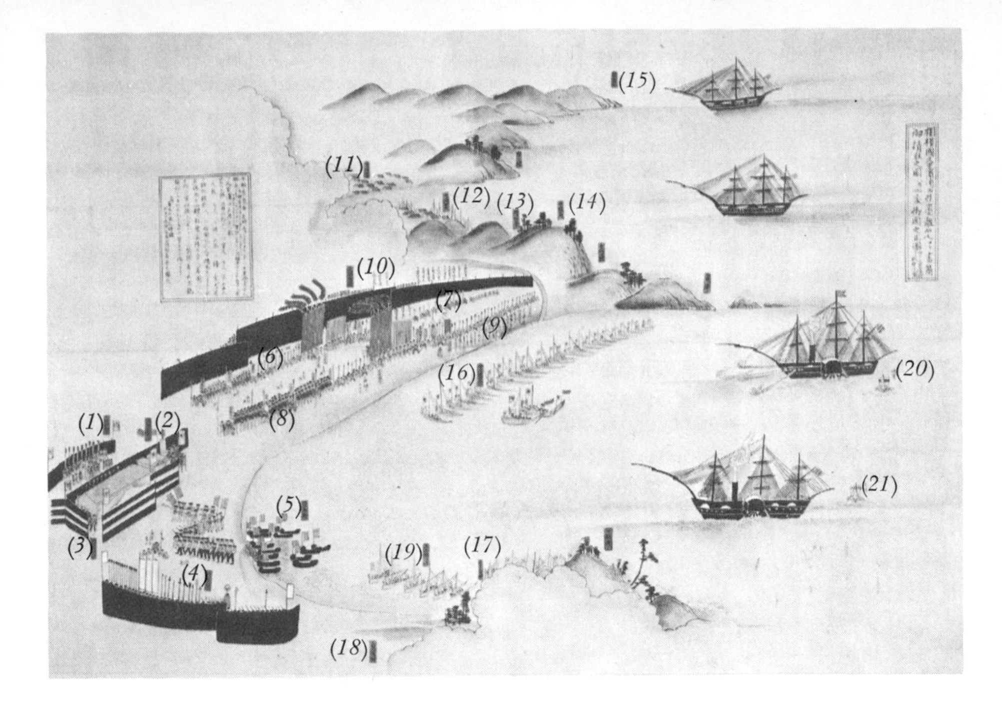

Scene of the Receipt of a Letter from the American (Commodore Perry) at Kurihama, Sagami, and a True Picture of the Four Clan Guard, Plus an Exposure from Kurihama Village

Two main vessels, steamer named Syusukuinna manned 350 and plain ship named Misushisufi manned 300. Strong vessel named fushikatto Furimouts manned 200 and the same named Saratoka m. 150 (k=g, f=p). The number of landing men at Kurihama: Geweer *group composed of 284 men; officers 7 men; flute players 15 men; drummers 7 men; flags 6 piece, gong 1 piece, dog 1 head; head gunners 2 men, directors 8 men; boats names 'batteira.' Fourteen boats brought these people to the land, the officers and directors bear on waists six-ch'd revolvers; all the guns mentioned above are equipped with* dondorof *tubes. In the 6th mo. 6th yr. Kaei, at the camp in Miyata, by order of the master, painted by Kyūkisai Unrai (send.)*

(1) *Additional force from Ogaki clan*
(2) *Camp of Gorr of Uraga*
(3) *Gur Kayama*
(4) *Kawagobe Clan Force*
(5) *boats named* batteira
(6) *gunners*
(7) *45 knights*
(8) *gunners*
(9) *60 knights*
(10) *Hikone Clan Force*
(11) *East Urga*
(12) *West Uraga*
(13) *Light House*
(14) *Hirame, Mtn.*
(15) *Kannon Saki*
(16) *Aizu Clan Force 1/10*
(17) *Sumiyoshi Shrine*
(18) *Kurihama Village*
(19) *Oshi Clan Force 1/10*
(20) *Uraga's*
(21) *Hikone's*

Courtesy of Henry T. Rockwell

The White (?) Man's Burden, cartoon from *Life,* March 16, 1899

"History shows me one way, and one way only, in which a high state of civilization has been produced, namely the struggle of race with race, and the survival of the physically and mentally fitter race. . . . This dependence of progress on the survival of the fitter race, terribly black as it may seem to some of you, gives the struggle for existence its redeeming features; it is the fiery crucible out of which comes the finer metal." Karl Pearson, NATIONAL LIFE FROM THE STANDPOINT OF SCIENCE. AN ADDRESS DELIVERED Nov. 19, 1900 (London, 1901).

In analyzing the broader argument of imperialism as a humanitarian movement, one can look at the results. It is true that some colonial areas benefited from the introduction of elementary law and order, of Western technology in the form of better medicine, of improved sanitary facilities, roads and railroads, and so on. Most of the improvements, however, were designed to benefit the colonial administration and to facilitate the economic or military exploitation of the colony on behalf of the imperial power. The benefits to the native populations were slight and indirect. After half a century or more of colonial development the average standard of living of the natives in most colonial areas was but little if at all above what it had been in the nineteenth century. This is telling evidence against the humanitarianism of imperialism, whatever the motives may have been.

THE ECONOMIC INTERPRETATION

One of the most popular explanations of modern imperialism concerns economic necessity. In fact, modern imperialism is often referred to as "economic imperialism," as if earlier forms of imperialism had no economic content. There is just enough empirical evidence in favor of these explanations to make them plausible.

One such explanation goes as follows: (1) competition in the capitalist world becomes more intense, resulting in the formation of large-scale enterprises and the elimination of small ones; (2) capital accumulates in the large enterprises more and more rapidly, and since the purchasing power of the masses is insufficient to purchase all the products of large-scale industry, the rate of profit declines; (3) as capital accumulates and the output of capitalist industries goes unsold, the capitalists resort to imperialism in order to gain political control over areas in which they can invest their surplus capital and sell their surplus products. Such is the essence of the Marxist theory of imperialism or, better, the Leninist theory, for Marx did not foresee the rapid development of imperialism even though he lived until 1883. Building on the foundation of Marxian theory and in some cases modifying it, Lenin published his theory in 1915 in the widely read pamphlet *Imperialism, the Highest Stage of Capitalism.*

Lenin was by no means the first person to advance an economic explanation of imperialism. He borrowed heavily from John A. Hobson, the liberal British critic of imperialism, who in turn adopted in revised form many of the arguments of the advocates of imperialism in capitalist countries. One such person was Captain A. T. Mahan, an American naval officer who strongly influenced Theodore Roosevelt, America's leading exponent of imperialism. Mahan's dictum was "Trade follows the flag." Still another capitalist advocate of imperialism was Jules Ferry, a French journalist and politician who twice became prime minister and was chiefly responsible for the largest colonial acquisitions of France. Interestingly, on both occasions his policy of colonial annexation cost him the premiership; but the French, like the British, found it difficult to withdraw once they had become committed to a particular conquest or annexation. It is equally interesting that Ferry did not utilize economic arguments in defending his actions before the French assembly; instead he stressed French prestige and military necessity. Only after he had permanently retired from office did he write books justifying his actions in which for the first time he emphasized the economic gains that France would supposedly realize from its colonial empire.

In many instances the advocates of imperialism were mere opportunists. Journalists sought to sell their books and articles; politicians sought election to office; military and naval officers sought larger appropriations of money for their armies and navies. They tried to achieve their ends by persuading the general public, as well as statesmen and bureaucrats, that imperialism would be good for the nation. The rise of new industrial nations and the massive imports of commodities from the Western Hemisphere and Australia had increased competitive pressures in both industry and agriculture. A severe depression beginning in 1873 inaugurated a long decline in general prices that lasted until 1896. These events precipitated the return to protective tariffs. Although tariffs went higher and higher in the last two decades of the century, they did not produce the desired results. Sales and profits increased for some industrialists and farmers, but decreased for others engaged in export industries. The masses — workers, salaried professionals, even the farmers themselves — paid the cost of this protection, which created social unrest and discontent and encouraged the growth of trade unions and socialist parties.

At this point the advocates of imperialism stepped in with their arguments for expansion. They argued that in addition to offering new markets and outlets for surplus capital, the colonies would provide new sources of raw materials and serve as outlets for the rapidly growing populations of the industrial nations. Many businessmen believed the arguments, and a few enriched themselves by taking advantage of privileged positions in the colonies. Others sanctioned imperialist adventures as a means of preventing unrest and possibly revolution by stirring up patriotic and nationalist sentiment and diverting attention from domestic political, social, and economic issues. It is therefore reasonably clear that belief in the necessity for economic expansion in colonial areas was important in motivating imperial policies. Whether or not that belief was justified is another question.

The argument that the colonies would serve as outlets for surplus population is easily seen to be fallacious. Most colonies were located in climates that Europeans found oppressive. Most emigrants preferred to

Table 1 *Trade with Empire as a Share of the Total Foreign Trade of European Colonial Powers, 1894–1913*

		Imports	*Exports*	*Total*
Great Britain	1894–1903	21.27%	30.42%	24.92%
	1904–1913	25.71%	34.75%	26.73%
France	1894–1903	9.86%	11.20%	10.49%
	1904–1913	10.58%	12.61%	11.53%
Germany	1894–1903	0.10%	0.35%	0.21%
	1904–1913	0.37%	0.62%	0.48%
Italy	1894–1903	0.04%	0.30%	0.16%
	1904–1913	0.21%	1.55%	0.75%

Source: Essays on Unbalanced Growth, Publications of the Institute of Social Studies, series maior, vol. X ('S-Gravenhage, 1962), p. 142.

go to independent countries, such as the United States and Argentina, or to the self-governing territories of the British Empire. It is true that colonies did in some cases furnish new sources of raw materials, but access to raw materials or to any purchasable commodity did not require political control. In fact, North and South America and the self-governing dominions of Australasia were the largest overseas suppliers of raw material for European industry.

The justification of colonies as markets for surplus manufactures was also fallacious. The colonies were neither needed for this purpose nor used for it after they were acquired. Prior to 1914 little more than 10 per cent of French exports went to French colonies. The colonies were too sparsely populated and too poor to serve as major markets. Moreover, as in the case of raw materials, political control was not required. India, "the brightest jewel in the British crown," was indeed a large market, for in spite of its poverty India purchased large quantities of European wares – but not from Britain alone. The Germans sold far more in India than in all their own colonies together. France sold more to India than to Algeria. Moreover, as important as India was for British manufacturers, the British sold far more to Australia, which had only a fraction of India's population. In spite of protective tariffs, the industrial, imperialist nations of Europe continued to trade predominantly with one another. The largest external market for German industry was Britain, and one of the largest markets for British industry was Germany. France was a major supplier and a major customer of both Britain and Germany. The United States was also a large customer and supplier of European countries.

Perhaps the most important argument for imperialism as an economic phenomenon concerned the investment of surplus capital, at least in

Marxist theory. Here again the facts do not substantiate the logic. Britain had the largest empire and the largest foreign investments (see p. 186); but over half of Britain's foreign investments were in independent countries, especially the United States, and in self-governing territories. The facts on France are even more surprising: less than 10 per cent of French foreign investments before 1914 went to French colonies. The French invested heavily in other European countries and in Latin America. Russia alone, itself an imperialist nation, took more than a fourth of French exported capital; and the French invested in Germany and Austria-Hungary, with whom they eventually went to war. German investments in German colonies were negligible. Some of the imperialist nations were actually net debtors; they included Russia, Italy, Spain, Portugal, and the United States.

Thus, the idea that imperialism was an economic necessity for the highly developed industrial nations is essentially fallacious, although it does contain some elements of truth and plausibility. The most crucial test for the validity of the economic argument is, did imperialism pay? And if so, to whom?

DID IMPERIALISM PAY?

This question has many aspects, and a complete answer would be very complex. Broadly, imperialism did not pay in a strictly pecuniary sense. With few exceptions, of which India was the most important, taxes collected in the colonies rarely sufficed to cover the costs of routine administration, much less those of conquest. It was argued, however, that the indirect benefits from increased trade made the venture worthwhile. Here the statistics are difficult to unravel and interpret. Colonial trade certainly did not bulk large in international trade; and in some cases, notably in France and Germany, the total value of trade with the colonies did not amount to as much as the expenditure incurred in taking and maintaining them.

It is indubitable that some individuals made enormous fortunes in colonial ventures – Cecil Rhodes is the outstanding example – and that many others earned a modest living; but the profits were by no means equally shared. Taxes had to be raised in the imperial nations to pay for the military and naval expeditions and garrisons and the officials who administered the colonies, as well as for whatever public works they constructed. Manpower had to be diverted from other uses to staff the armies, navies, and colonial services. Under the prevailing system of taxation in Europe, most of the tax money came from ordinary workers and farmers, who had no pecuniary interest, direct or indirect, in the colonies. In effect, income and wealth were redistributed by the process of taxation and expenditure; the masses paid the costs, the profits were garnered by a favored few. The ultimate costs, however, should be reckoned by the suffering and dislocation of the peoples subjected to Western imperialism, as well as the rivalries and frustrations generated in the race for colonial supremacy – rivalries that prepared Europe psychologically for war and themselves were factors leading to war. These costs are still being paid.

SOME FINAL REFLECTIONS

If neither the economic explanation, nor the belief in the validity of that explanation (which, it should be clear, are two different things), nor the humanitarian motive is sufficient to explain the burst of imperialism in the late nineteenth century, how can it be explained? Major responsibility must be assigned to sheer political opportunism, combined with growing aggressive nationalism. Disraeli's conversion to imperialism (he had been an anti-imperialist early in his career) was motivated principally by the need to find new issues with which to oppose the Liberal Gladstone. Bismarck encouraged French imperialism as a means of deflecting French campaigns for revenge on Germany, but at first rejected it for Germany itself. When at last he allowed himself to be persuaded, he did so to strengthen the bases of his own political support and deflect attention from the social question in Germany.

Power politics and military expediency also played an important role. Britain's imperial policy throughout the century was dictated primarily by the supposed necessity of protecting the Indian frontiers and lifeline. This explains the British conquest of Burma and Malaya, Baluchistan and Kashmir, as well as British involvement in the Near and Middle East. The occupation of Egypt, undertaken reluctantly by Gladstone with the promise of an early withdrawal, was deemed necessary to protect the Suez Canal. Other nations emulated the successful British, either in the hope of gaining similar advantages or simply for national prestige.

The intellectual climate of the late nineteenth century, strongly colored by Social Darwinism, likewise favored European expansion. Although Herbert Spencer, the foremost popularizer of Social Darwinism, was an outspoken anti-imperialist, others applied his arguments for the "survival of the fittest" to the imperial struggle. Theodore Roosevelt spoke grandly of "manifest destiny," and Kipling's phrase, "the lesser breeds without the law," reflected the typical European attitude toward the non-white races. The historical roots of European racism and ethnocentrism, however, reach far deeper than Darwinian biology. Christian missionary activity itself was an expression of old beliefs in European, or Western, moral and cultural superiority. Throughout their history – at least until the mid-twentieth century – Europeans and Christians have been expansionist and evangelical. In the final analysis, modern imperialism must be regarded as a psychological and cultural phenomenon as well as a political or economic one.

EUROPEAN CULTURE AND SOCIETY: THE END OF THE GOLDEN AGE
CHAPTER ELEVEN

Along with the economic, social, and political changes of the last decades of the nineteenth century, novel intellectual currents filtered through the European world. The new streams of thought resulted in part from growing industrialization, urbanization, and democratization; in part they were reactions to these processes. Above all they reflected the issues raised by the continuing progress of science. For some thinkers, reconsideration of Darwinian biology and mechanistic physics converted earlier optimistic ideas of universal progress into philosophies profoundly pessimistic in their conclusions and implications. A parallel and related development in imaginative literature and the arts clearly indicated disenchantment with conventional nineteenth-century standards and heralded the pessimistic, abstract, and neo-realistic tendencies of twentieth century art and literature. By 1914 these currents of thought had not yet created a new intellectual ethos for Western civilization, but they had made deep inroads in the old philosophic, moral, and aesthetic standards and presuppositions, indicating that the temper of twentieth-century civilization would be immeasurably different from that of the nineteenth.

FIN-DE-SIÈCLE LITERATURE AND ART

The reaction against realism in literature was most pronounced in poetry, which in fact had never undergone a realist phase. By 1885 the new movement in poetry had been christened "symbolism." It soon became clear that the new departures were not limited to poetry, or even to imaginative literature in general. Similar changes were taking place under a variety of labels in the fine arts of music, painting, and sculpture, as well as in philosophy and other fields of scholarship. In 1890 a Frenchman coined a new expression to cover all these diverse manifestations; he called them simply fin de siècle (end of century).

Alternating fashions in literature and art — from classicism to romanticism, from romanticism to realism to symbolism and neo-romanticism and so forth — are sometimes likened to the swings of a pendulum. A biological metaphor would be more appropriate: each movement originated in the womb of its predecessor, inherited many of the latter's features, and broke into open revolt only after gaining full self-consciousness. In the case of the fin-de-siècle movements the attainment of self-consciousness was fostered by new discoveries and inventions in science and technology, and new questionings of the role of intellect in mass society.

POETRY

Although the term symbolism had affinities with other branches of literature and art, it applied chiefly to poetry, and even more specifically to French poetry. Stéphane Mallarmé (1842–1898), the central figure, unlike many of his friends and contemporaries, lived an uneventful life as a teacher of English in French secondary schools. His entire poetic output consisted of less than two thousand lines, but his most famous poem, *L'Après-midi d'un faune,* has been called "the most skillful poem" and "one of the purest jewels" of the French language. Symbolist poetry was usually esoteric and oblique, not to say opaque, and almost always experimental, with great freedom of style. The symbols from which it got its name were not the standard symbols of historic literature but *ad hoc,* even private symbols. Although it abandoned the lyricism of romantic poetry, it made a great effort to convey musical images, as well as those of color, by means of words. The relationship was reciprocal among the artists of the time. The original edition of Mallarmé's *L'Après-midi d'un faune* was illustrated by the artist Édouard Manet, and in 1894 Claude Debussy composed a tone poem of the same name to serve as a prelude.

The symbolist movement has influenced almost all major poets, directly or indirectly, since the 1890's. Its influence was especially noticeable in the early work of the Irish poet William Butler Yeats (1865–1939), the Anglo-American T. S. Eliot (1888–1965), and the German Stefan George (1868–1933). With the triumph of symbolism many poets ceased to write primarily for the general public and wrote increasingly for those versed in literature itself.

DRAMA

Drama, which had reached a low ebb in the middle decades of the century, staged a remarkable survival. Symbolism influenced the theater, notably in the work of the Belgian Maurice Maeterlinck (1862–1949). The most important fin-de-siècle influence on the theater came from the Norwegian Henrik Ibsen (1828–1906). Ibsen was a bitter critic of contemporary bourgeois morality and hypocrisy, and partly for this reason his work was slow in gaining public recognition. Although starkly realistic in portrayal, his dramas went beyond conventional realism in the depth of their psychological probing and symbolic content, revealing their relationship with other novel intellectual currents. Other playwrights eventually followed Ibsen's lead. Among the notable examples of plays in a similar style are *Miss Julia* (1888) by the Swedish dramatist August Strindberg, *The Weavers* (1892) by Gerhart Hauptmann, and *The Cherry Orchard* (1904) by Anton Chekhov.

The leading English-language playwrights of the prewar generation were the Anglo-Irishmen George Bernard Shaw (1856–1950) and Oscar Wilde (1854–1900). In his earlier role as literary and music critic Shaw had been instrumental in winning British acceptance of Ibsen's dramas and Wagner's operas. In his plays he, too, dealt with important social and psychological problems, but both he and Wilde adopted a far more light-hearted manner than other leading dramatists, forcing their audiences to laugh at their own foibles.

FICTION

Realism and naturalism retained their sway much longer in fiction than in other branches of literature. Even after they began to yield to the influence of psychological and symbolist thought, novelists such as Thomas Hardy (1840–1928) and Joseph Conrad (1857–1924), as well as Zola, continued to make use of typically realistic settings. Occasionally novelists such as Anatole France (1844–1924) broke over into fantasy bordering on symbolism, as in *Penguin Island* and *The Revolt of the Angels.* After 1900 symbolism and new discoveries in psychology exerted a strong effect on novelists such as Romain Rolland (1866–1944), André Gide (1869–1951), and James Joyce (1882–1941). The stream-of-consciousness technique, pioneered in fiction by Joyce in *Ulysses* (1915), owed much to the new knowledge of psychology.

PAINTING

The vogue of realism in painting lasted but a short while. For exact portrayals of nature and life painters could not compete with the camera; for conveying moods and interpreting nature and life, the camera could not compete with painters. This discovery was made as early as the 1860's by Édouard Manet (1832–1883), the forerunner of a group of painters who came to be called impressionists. Although impressionism eventually spread to all countries, its fountainhead, like that of symbolism, was France. Its greatest names were Claude Monet (1840–1926), Edgar Degas (1834–1917), and Auguste Renoir (1841–1919). Making use of new scientific knowledge of light, color, and optics, the impressionists portrayed the impression that they received from their subjects, although their themes and temperaments were different. Thus their paintings had hazy outlines and blurs of color. In the use of light and color and the choice of subject matter the impressionists showed a kinship with the writers of naturalistic fiction as well as with the symbolist poets. The expatriate American painter Whistler, who had much in common with the impressionists, painted symphonies and nocturnes in color, while some of his contemporaries created poems in color.

Toward the end of the century Paul Cézanne (1839–1906) and Paul Gauguin (1848–1903), two talented French painters, sought to restore more exact form to painting while preserving the light and color of the impressionists. They were the leaders of the postimpressionist school, which had an enormous influence on twentieth-century painting. Although the Dutchman Vincent Van Gogh (1853–1890), a close friend of Cézanne, is sometimes grouped with the postimpressionists, he preferred to think of himself as an expressionist. He tried to put his own feelings, his own personality even, on the canvas in great blobs of color. At the beginning of the twentieth century a group of young artistic rebels who adopted and developed Van Gogh's techniques became known as *les fauves* (wild beasts) because of the exuberance of their paintings.

In the last decade of the century an artistic bombshell burst in Europe. It was the style called *art nouveau*. It pertained not only to painting but also to print making, design, typography, home furnishings and decorations, and even to architecture. Although its popularity lasted less than two decades, it opened up new vistas of almost unlimited horizons in painting as well as in other plastic arts, by breaking completely with the traditions of the past. In the first decade of the twentieth century abstract and nonrepresentational art had already carved out their niche, well before World War I shattered what was left of traditional art themes in Western civilization. The latest vogue in painting before the cataclysm of war was cubism, the forerunner of surrealism and other postwar styles of nonrepresentational art.

ARCHITECTURE, DECORATION, AND SCULPTURE

The nineteenth century was at best undistinguished for originality in architecture. Near the end of the century, however, new and distinctly original influences began to make themselves felt. Although they developed first from a concern for decoration, the ideal of nineteenth-century architecture, they evolved subtly but rapidly into a concern for simplicity of design and eventually into a belief in the harmony of form and function known as functionalism. Paradoxically, the central figure in the artistic movement that formed the bridge between past and future was reactionary in at least one respect, as was the movement itself. William Morris (1834–1896), a gifted artist and designer, revolted against the ugliness of English industrial cities and the lack of taste in domestic architecture and furnishings. Politically his revolt led him to socialism, but aesthetically he advocated a return to the simplicity of an earlier age, in which every craft was also an art. His simple yet intricately beautiful designs were the products of a reaction against the machine, but—ironically—they proved admirably suited for machine reproduction. The associated art nouveau, which reduced the overly decorated furniture and bric-a-brac of the Victorian era to flamboyant but elegantly simple lines, proved to be the opening wedge in the distinctive architectural styles of the twentieth century. To borrow a phrase subsequently made famous in another context, art nouveau and the reactionism of Morris were steps taken backward in order to go forward. The first really forward steps in architecture were taken by the Americans Louis Sullivan (1856–1924) and his protégé, the young Frank Lloyd Wright (1869–1959). In Europe the leading exponent of the new ideas in architecture was the German Walter Gropius (1883–1969).

At the end of the nineteenth century sculpture, like drama, experienced a noteworthy revival as a serious art form—in contrast to its use in monumental decoration. The man mainly responsible for it was Auguste Rodin (1840–1917), an independent artist who rarely accepted commissions but developed a revolutionary style that set him apart from the conventional sculptors who worked to order. Rodin's greatest work, "The Thinker," is one of the most renowned statues of all time. Another eminent sculptor of the period was Gustav Vigeland of Norway, who succeeded in capturing in stone, bronze, and even wrought iron the full range of human emotions from radiant joy to deepest despair. A large park in Oslo is devoted entirely to exhibiting his work.

MUSIC

Music, like poetry, did not experience a realist phase. On the contrary, the romantic movement in music continued to flourish in the works of Brahms, Lizst, and above all the dramatic operas of Wagner at the very time that realism was riding high in fiction and painting. After the death of Wagner in 1883 musical composition branched off in two directions. One continued in the romantic tradition and allied that tradition even more closely to the growing popular nationalism. It is best represented in the works of such nationalist composers as Tchaikovsky, Grieg, Smetana, Sibelius, and Dvořák. The other allied itself with symbolism and impressionism and produced such compositions as the tone poems of Debussy and Richard Strauss. In time the composers in this tradition deliberately broke with the poetic imagery of romantic and late romantic music and attempted to write pure or absolute music. Igor Stravinsky, Gustav Mahler, Béla Bartók, and Arnold Schönberg led in this development, which even before World War I had begun to make use of atonality, the twelve tone scale, and other strange innovations that became typical of serious compositions in the mid-twentieth century.

POSITIVISM AND ITS CRITICS

At the beginning of the final quarter of the nineteenth century the dominant philosophical system in Europe was positivism. (See p. 143.) Hippolyte Taine pithily summed up the general philosophical import of positivism in 1870: "All human facts, moral as well as physical, being bound up with causes and subject to laws, it follows that all works of man – art, religion, philosophy, literature, moral, political or social phenomena – are but the results of general causes that must be determined scientifically." By the end of the century this confident philosophy, complacently maintained by comfortable philosophers, had been almost completely eclipsed among serious and original thinkers. The reasons for its decline, though many, can be conveniently grouped in two broad categories. In the first place, new discoveries in science itself cast doubt on simple cause-effect relationships and undermined the basis of belief in a naive scientific or materialistic determinism. Second, the relative neglect and shallowness of the treatment of ethical and aesthetic problems, especially by such popularizing proponents of positivism as Herbert Spencer, aroused the moral indignation of a younger generation of social and intellectual rebels who identified positivism with the middle-class cult of crass material progress.

New developments in philosophic, scientific, and social thought accompanying the decline of positivism took two general directions, corresponding to the nature of the attacks on positivism. The first, the work of scientifically minded individuals in many fields of learning, did not reject positivism altogether but sought to build on and go beyond it. It continued to emphasize the use of rationality and logic while recognizing the existence of nonrational elements in human behavior and inexplicable phenomena in the universe. On the other hand, the fomenters of the revolt against positivism consisted mainly of literary philosophers, writers, and artists. They pointed out the role of intuition as a component of knowledge, laid great stress on the existence of primordial subconscious drives in human personality, and emphasized the importance of myths and mysticism in human history. Some went so far as to glorify the irrational qualities in man and to approve social action based on instinctual and anti-intellectual behavior. The dividing line between the two groups of critics of positivism was not always clear, but the first group fell, by and large, in the tradition of the thinkers of the Enlightenment, whereas the second belonged to the tradition of romanticism.

PHILOSOPHIES OF VIOLENCE

The Second Law of Thermodynamics, formulated by Kelvin in 1852, implies that eventually – in some millions of years – the sun will burn itself out and the solar system will freeze up like a mill pond on a cold day in January. Darwin's theory not only placed man among the animals but also by implication denied him immortality. These seemingly alarming conclusions did not immediately disturb those who accepted the scientific validity of the theories; instead, they rejoiced in the knowledge of physical certainty and congratulated themselves on being a part of such an advanced stage of evolutionary progress. Few troubled to examine the other aspects of their faith in progress, which was so vitally affected by the new discoveries of science. One who did was the German philosopher and litterateur Friedrich Nietzsche (1844–1900). Given to fits of irrationality that drove him permanently insane in 1888, Nietzsche was one of the important thinkers of the nineteenth century — all the more so in that his ideas inspired or were used to justify some of the most brutal outrages against humanity of the following century. Influenced by Schopenhauer as well as Darwin, Nietzsche regarded human life as a profound tragedy; at the same time he accepted the evolutionary process, which he interpreted as an imperative challenge to struggle and combat. He regarded traditional Christian morality as a "slave morality," incompatible with the great life struggle, the aim of which should be to produce a new race of supermen. "What is good? All that heightens in man the feeling of power, the desire for power, power itself. What is bad? All that comes from weakness. What is happiness? The feeling that our strength grows, that an obstacle is overcome. Not contentment, but more power; not universal peace, but war; not virtue, but forcefulness. The weak and ineffective must go under; that is the first principle of *our* love for humanity." Such ideas, wedded to then fashionable pseudoscientific racial theories, were used by demagogic orators to infect popular nationalism and convert it from a constructive to a destructive force.

One of the people influenced by Nietzsche was Georges Sorel (1847–1922), who combined his influence with that of Marx. Sorel created the doctrine of syndicalism (from *syndicat,* the French word for trade union), which became influential in the labor unions of all Latin countries, including those of South America. Accepting the Marxian notion of class war and Nietzsche's espousal of violence as an end in itself, Sorel advocated "direct action" by trade unions to achieve their goal of a socialist society: strikes, sabotage, riots, and any other form of violence. In Sorel's thought even more than in Nietzsche's there was an acceptance of the irrational as a legitimate motive of human conduct. It was the same message taught in their own way by the symbolist poets. It soon received a semblance of scientific backing in Freudian psychology.

THE LOGIC OF SCIENCE

Adhering to a naive materialism, convinced positivists regarded nature as the mechanical interaction of particles of matter having definite locations in space and time, and they accounted materialistically for purely mental phenomena such as consciousness, memory, empathy, and intuition. The Austrian physicist and philosopher Ernst Mach (1838–1916) reversed this emphasis. He remained a positivist in method but discarded completely the materialist view. According to Mach, men could know the "real," external world only by means of the sensations it produced on them, which were physical or mental phenomena. Carrying his reasoning one step further, Mach concluded that the world as we know it consisted exclusively of sensation, and the "real" world was an illusion. Known as "phenomenalism," this doctrine played an important role in the development of modern psychology.

The French mathematician and physicist Henri Poincaré (1854–1912) expressed similar views. According to him, scientific theories were accepted not because they were "true," for ultimate truth was not within the comprehension of mortals, but because they were "convenient," that is, they produced results. The German Hans Vaihinger (1852–1933) went even further than Poincaré. In *The Philosophy of "As If"* he maintained that such scientific concepts as lines, points, and atoms were pure fictions, but *useful* fictions in that they allowed valid predictions to be made. In other words, nature behaved as if it were composed of atoms, molecules, and so forth.

The culmination of this stream of thought came in the new philosophy of pragmatism, the lineal descendant and successor of positivism. The American philosopher and psychologist William James (1842–1910) called pragmatism "a new name for some old ways of thinking." With Poincaré the pragmatists denied that mortals could attain absolute certainty, absolute exactitude, or absolute universality. Instead of seeking ultimate truth, they were more interested in the meaning of ideas, concepts, and propositions, as seen in their consequences for individual behavior and social action. "A true proposition is one the acceptance of which leads to success, a false proposition is one which produces failure and frustration." Pragmatism thus introduced into philosophy a relativistic concept of truth analogous to Einstein's theory in physics.

The pragmatic emphasis on activity, consequences, and success was especially congenial to the American temperament, and pragmatism as a philosophy scored some of its greatest successes in the United States. An outstanding proponent was John Dewey (1859–1952), who developed a variety of pragmatism called instrumentalism or experimentalism. Pragmatism also exerted an important influence on philosophic, scientific, and literary thought in Europe that coincided with the sudden emergence of American influence in other more mundane matters, such as international politics and economic affairs, and may be taken to mark the end of America's provincialism and the beginning of its role as an independent shaper of the European world.

THE SCIENCE OF SOCIETY

Auguste Comte, founder of positivism, envisioned sociology as a comprehensive social science forming the capstone of his pyramid of knowledge. Karl Marx, founder of "scientific" socialism, regarded his subject matter alternatively as a "science of society." The social sciences did in fact emerge as distinct academic disciplines in the latter part of the nineteenth century, and all owed something to both Comte and Marx; but their actual emergence, as well as the specific forms they took, depended greatly on concrete historical developments and on the contemporary debates respecting philosophy and scientific method.

In earlier times the subject matter of the social sciences had been dealt with under moral and political philosophy, much as physics and chemistry were regarded as branches of natural philosophy. Economics, it is true, had broken away as political economy even before Comte and Marx; but it, too, went through a period of methodological strife after 1870 as successors of the German historical school of political economy opposed their empirical, historical, and "realistic" methodology against the essentially deductive methods of classical economics. The result was the establishment of economics on a new, more scientific basis and the creation of a new discipline: economic history.

Herbert Spencer and other Social Darwinists, such as William Graham Sumner in the United States, viewed sociology as a continuation of Darwinian biology, a study of the struggle for survival in society. Their approach to the subject was radically modified in the generation before World War I. In the United States, where rapid urbanization, the growth of big business, and the influx of new immigrants created novel social problems that gave rise to the Progressive movement in politics, and where pragmatic philosophy gained an early following, sociology attracted numbers of reformers who were more interested in the alleviation of social ills than in the dispassionate study of society. In continental Europe, however, differing academic traditions and the lively methodological debates in science and philosophy gave sociology a more scientific character.

Early social scientists faced three major methodological problems, all closely related. One was to divest their subject matter of value-charged and metaphysical notions, to give it a positive, empirical orientation by making it the study of actual social structures and processes. Another problem was that of objectivity: since individual social scientists were themselves members of society, belonging to specific races, nations, and social classes, how could they get "outside themselves" and free themselves from bias and preconceived ideas? Finally, since science proceeded by the use of reason, it assumed a rationality or underlying logical order in nature that was capable of being comprehended by reason, but increasingly the existence of irrational and nonrational elements in human personality and social behavior was becoming evident. Was it possible to study and understand by rational methods that which was itself not rational? The pioneers of social science did not fully succeed in solving these problems, nor have they yet been satisfactorily solved. But the prewar generation at least recognized and faced up to the problems. That was its greatest contribution to subsequent generations of social scientists.

Émile Durkheim (1858–1917), who established sociology as an academic discipline in France, was a positivist in that he regarded social phenomena as subject to scientific investigation, but he discarded the biological and organic analogies employed by the Social Darwinists. For him the study of society was an empirical task requiring painstaking observation, factual description, and inductive theorizing about such concrete social phenomena as the division of labor, suicide, and religious behavior. The Italian Vilfredo Pareto (1848–1923), trained as an engineer, achieved eminence as one of the first great mathematical economists, but he was equally prominent for his contributions to sociological theory. Pareto labeled the conscious products of the human mind "derivations"; they were highly transitory and changeable. The true unvarying determinants of human conduct, which he called "residues," were essentially nonrational and beyond human comprehension. Pareto is also known for his social philosophy, a theory of elites, which some regard as a precursor of fascism and other totalitarian systems. Max Weber (1864–1920), the greatest name in German sociology, attempted to bridge the gap between the study of natural phenomena and social phenomena by the process of critical yet sympathetic understanding called *Verstehen.* According to Weber, the social scientist could get "outside himself" by getting "inside" the social phenomena that he was studying. Weber is known especially for his studies of religion; his most widely read book is *The Protestant Ethic and the Spirit of Capitalism.*

Another way in which early social scientists attempted to achieve objectivity was by the study of contemporary primitive peoples, such as the Australian bushmen, Trobriand islanders, and Eskimos. Not only could they detach themselves from their own environments, but they also thought that the fundamental determinants of social behavior – analogous to Pareto's residues – could be discovered when uncluttered by the complexities of modern society. Archaeologists studied extinct civilizations such as the ancient Egyptian, Sumerian, and Mayan by means of the remnants of their material culture. The combination of ethnology, archaeology, and human biology produced the modern discipline of anthropology.

Political science is at once one of the oldest and newest of the social sciences. It resulted from the combination of political philosophy with detailed descriptive and analytic studies of the actual functioning of governments. Gaetano Mosca (1858–1941), who had long experience as a practical politician in Italy, was one of the founders of the new discipline. He came to the conclusion that politics and government were essentially the functions of small, self-selected, and self-perpetuating cliques or elites. Robert Michels (1876–1936), born of a German father and a French mother, had personal experience in the socialist parties of several countries before becoming an Italian citizen. He became disillusioned with the lack of democratic procedures even in social democratic parties and formulated the "iron law of oligarchy": in every organized social group effective power eventually devolves upon a small self-selected group. Michels, Mosca, and Pareto, who shared many views, are sometimes referred to as neo-Machiavellians. More idealistic views were held by Woodrow Wilson, one of the first political scientists in the United States, who was a professor and president of Princeton University before entering active politics.

The writing of history was also affected by the emergence of the social sciences and debates on scientific method. Historians in the positivist tradition tried to assimilate historical methods with those of the new social sciences; others in the idealist-romantic tradition denied that the methods of science were appropriate to the study of human phenomena. The Germans Wilhelm Dilthey and Ernst Troeltsch and the Italian Benedetto Croce argued that since man possesses a spirit, his history and culture have to be studied by methods entirely different from those used on the subjects of natural science. Their efforts to recapture the spirit of an age as expressed in its art, literature, and other products of culture showed an affinity with the symbolists in literature, on the one hand, and with the methods of Max Weber, on the other. All were reinforced by new discoveries in psychology.

THE DISCOVERY OF THE SUBCONSCIOUS

In 1899 Sigmund Freud (1856–1939), a Viennese physician, published a book entitled *The Interpretation of Dreams.* It became the foundation of modern psychoanalysis. Experimental psychology first developed out of physiology, notably through the work of Wilhelm Wundt and William James. Because of its physiological base, it is not surprising that early psychologists regarded their subject as a natural science. The phenomenon of consciousness was almost banished from the field in the work of the Russian Ivan Pavlov (1849–1936) on conditioned reflexes and in the so-called behavioral school of the United States. As a practicing physician, Freud found their approach of little value in dealing with the mental illnesses of his patients. He detected that human beings react not only to physical stimuli (as the behaviorists said) and to conscious motives (as the rationalists said), but also to purely mental stimuli of which they are unaware. The latter source of motivation Freud labeled

Brown Brothers

Sigmund Freud

"The unconscious is the larger circle which includes the smaller circle of the conscious; everything conscious has a preliminary unconscious stage, whereas the unconscious can stop at this stage, and yet claim to be considered a full psychic function. The unconscious is the true psychic reality; in its inner nature it is just as much unknown to us as the reality of the external world, and it is just as imperfectly communicated to us by the data of consciousness as is the external world by the reports of our sense-organs." Sigmund Freud. THE INTERPRETATION OF DREAMS, 3rd English edition, rev. (London, 1937).

the "subconscious." He maintained that the major part of subconscious mental activity derives from infantile experiences – in particular, the repression or sublimation of infantile eroticism and sexuality. In his view the animal instinct in humans fosters such sexuality, but the demands of civilization require that it be controlled. A "healthy" individual is one who manages to sublimate his sexual drives into socially approved activities. A mentally ill person has merely repressed, not sublimated, his primitive drives. Freud's method of treatment, called psychoanalysis, consisted in having the patient recall from his subconscious the events that had caused inner conflict or distress; the "cure" resulted from an "understanding" of these causes.

Even before Freud's main work Henri Bergson (1859–1941), a French philosopher, thought he had divined in dreams the key to the understanding of man's personality. Bergson distinguished between consciousness, a "superficial psychic life," and a life in the "depths of consciousness" in which "the deep-seated self" follows a logic of its own that is not comprehensible by mortal reason. Bergson called this "deep-seated self" the *élan vital* (vital spirit, intuition, instinct), which he regarded as the mainspring of human progress. For Bergson, reality was not a state of being but a process of becoming. He called the process "creative evolution."

The affinity of the ideas of Bergson and Freud to those of Nietzsche and Sorel – and even to Schopenhauer's concept of the "will" – are obvious. Such ideas were common property among the avant-garde intellectuals at the turn of the century. Bergson, a Nobel prize winner, and Freud, a man of science, gave them philosophical and scientific justification and thus heightened their currency. Bergson's concept of creative evolution inspired George Bernard Shaw's plays *Man and Superman* and *Back to Methuselah,* and Freudian psychology has made itself felt throughout modern literature. Bergson's influence waned sharply after World War I, but Freud's has continued to grow.

THE NEW REVOLUTION IN SCIENCE

The generation maturing at the turn of the century witnessed a number of discoveries in natural science that led to a new era in the interpretation of nature. Although the full significance of the discoveries did not become apparent until the twentieth century was well advanced, for the knowledgeable they overthrew earlier certainties about the essential simplicity of the physical universe and cast doubt on the associated belief in materialistic determinism.

The claim of science as a special and authoritative brand of knowledge accessible to humans through the powers of reason, which had been gathering force from the time of Galileo and Newton, reached a crescendo in the work of James Clerk Maxwell. (See p. 135.) The mechanical equivalence of heat and electricity had already been demonstrated. Maxwell's mathematical theorems purported to show that electricity, magnetism, and even light are essentially identical. Near the end of the century the discovery of electromagnetic or radio waves by Heinrich Hertz (1857–1894), in fulfillment of Maxwell's prediction, climaxed the triumph of classical physics. A few years later a renowned scientist remarked that the secrets of the universe had been unraveled: all that remained for the physicists of the twentieth century was to refine the measurements of phenomena discovered by the scientists of the nineteenth. Even before he spoke, however, new discoveries growing out of the work of Maxwell, Hertz, and others had begun to undermine the theoretical structure in which he exhibited so much confidence.

RADIOACTIVITY AND RELATIVITY

The atomic theory of matter, which had been basic to the achievements of nineteenth-century physical science, was the first element of the classical edifice to undergo modification. According to John Dalton, atoms, the smallest particles of matter, resemble tiny billiard balls; they are infinitesimally small but hard and solid. The combination of atoms into molecules implied that they possessed some form of attractive force, but the nature of the force was not fully understood. The study of electricity and magnetism revealed that particles of matter contain positive and negative charges, or forces of attraction and repulsion, but the charges were believed to be properties of different types of atoms rather than distinct phenomena. As knowledge progressed, Dalton's concept came to be recognized as unsatisfactory, and in 1892 the Dutch physicist Hendrik Lorentz posited the existence of electrons, tiny particles of electrically charged matter separate from but related to atoms. Lorentz's formulation proved to be incorrect, but it led to intensive study of the structure of the atom and abandonment of the billiard ball concept.

Experimental verification of the complex structure of the atom soon followed and demonstrated that atoms are not necessarily stable or indivisible. In 1895 the German physicist Wilhelm Roentgen discovered X-rays, and in the following year Antoine Becquerel, a Frenchman, observed the radiation of uranium. Shortly afterward the Franco-Polish couple Pierre and Marie Curie isolated and identified the radioactive elements radium and polonium. Further experimentation by the Englishman J. J. Thomson and his student Ernest Rutherford, a New Zealander, revealed that atoms are composed of still smaller particles and emit a variety of mysterious rays. The different combinations and arrangements of the smaller particles determine the chemical properties of the atoms. In 1919 Rutherford succeeded in transforming nitrogen into hydrogen by bombarding nitrogen gas with alpha particles from the element radium. The goal of the ancient alchemists – the transmutation of one element into another – had been achieved.

In 1887 Albert Michelson and E. W. Morley in America devised a new and greatly improved experiment for measuring the velocity of light. They discovered that it is a constant regardless of the velocity of its source. This experimentally determined fact had important theoretical implications in that it contradicted the laws of inertial motion and cast doubt on belief in the existence of a "luminiferous ether," which supposedly filled all space and was the medium by which the light of distant stars (as well as other objects) was transmitted to earth. In 1900 the German Max Planck discovered that radiation takes place not continuously but in discrete units or "quanta." According to classical physics all nature consists of two fundamental substances, matter and force (or energy), each with its own laws of conservation. Matter was thought to exist in discrete units or particles and to have weight; force was thought to operate continuously and to be weightless. The new quantum theory, developed principally by Planck, Albert Einstein, and the Danish physicist Niels Bohr, cast doubt on this entire intellectual edifice. Energy, it seemed, also exists in particles that have weight, or mass. Moreover mass or matter itself represents bundles of energy. Instead of two fundamental substances – matter and force – and two laws of conservation, the new theory posited a single substance – mass-energy – and a single law of conservation.

Einstein's special theory of relativity in 1905 and his general theory in 1915 incorporated these notions. The theory of relativity marked the greatest advance in man's understanding of the universe since Newton propounded his laws of gravitation. It succeeded in explaining all phenomena accounted for by the Newtonian system as well as some others that Newton's laws could not satisfactorily explain. It turned out, in fact, that the Newtonian laws represented a special limiting case of the general theory of relativity. The new theory passed its most crucial empirical test in 1919, when during a total eclipse of the sun scientists on both sides of the Atlantic Ocean observed the bending of light rays in the gravitational field of the sun, as predicted by Einstein.

Although it was incomprehensible in its details to all but a few highly trained specialists, the theory of relativity exercised an important intellectual influence on the Western world. In addition to replacing the classical dichotomy of matter and force by the singular entity mass-energy, the theory overturned the classical (and common-sense) dichotomy of absolute space and time. According to the theory of relativity, two events that are simultaneous for one observer may not be simultaneous for another. For example, with powerful telescopes we see now

Culver Pictures, Inc.

Albert Einstein

"Galileo and Newton made the universe Euclidian simply because reason dictated it so. But pure reason cannot do anything but invent systems of methodical arrangement. . . . It is clearly not these systems, not pure reason, which resolve the nature of the real. On the contrary, reality selects from among these possible orders or schemes the one which has more affinity with itself. This is what the theory of relativity means. The rationalist past of four centuries is confronted by the genius of Einstein, who inverts the time-honored relation which used to exist between reason and observation. Reason ceases to be an imperative standard and is converted into an arsenal of instruments; observation tests these and decides which is the most convenient to use." J. Ortega y Gasset, THE MODERN THEME (New York, 1933).

events in outer space that took place millions of years ago, such as the explosion of galaxies. The theory of relativity replaced three-dimensional space and one-dimensional time by a single four-dimensional space-time continuum. In conjunction with the quantum theory, it replaced the earlier belief in inexorable natural laws that determine all events according to cause and effect by a system of thought in which events take place in accordance with the laws of statistical probability—that is, in more or less random fashion. The concepts of cause and effect, certainty, and the absolute, which underlay so much nineteenth-century thought, no longer appeared either certain or absolute.

GENETICS AND EUGENICS

According to Darwin the explanation of biological evolution lay in small individual variations transmitted cumulatively from generation to generation by means of natural selection. Biological experiments in the last two decades of the nineteenth century seemed to show that small variations of the type assumed by Darwin were incapable of producing the effects attributed to them. The same experiments revealed that larger, discontinuous variations, called mutations, occur from time to time and that these traits, too, are transmissible by heredity. In 1900 the biological fraternity discovered, or rediscovered, in the annals of a scientific society in Moravia the results of scientific experiments of great significance. Gregor Mendel, an Augustinian monk who became abbot of his monastery but died in 1884 without achieving other distinctions, had been a contemporary of Darwin. Experimenting with common garden peas, he discovered what appeared to be fixed proportions in the characteristics of successive generations of hybrid plants. In these fixed proportions lay the secret of the transmission of hereditary characteristics, and thus of biological evolution. Mendel's experiments were re-

---

"The Bay of Marseille Seen from the 'Estaque,'"
by Paul Cezanne

"His conception of space is modern. . . . By dint of painting rocks and trees, and merging them closely into another, by dint of seeing them purely as solid figures, he finished by painting things at whose dimensions one cannot guess. One does not know whether one is looking at small rocks seen from very near, or big rocks seen from very far away; whether one is looking at shrubs an arm's length away or kilometres away. One devises some theory and the picture takes on certain characteristics; one devises another theory and the picture seems completely different. But after all, it is space that one sees in abstract pictures; the forms are near or far away, depending on what one imagines they could represent." Yvon Taillandier, P. CEZANNE, tr. Graham Snall (New York, 1961).

The Metropolitan Museum of Art.
Bequest of Mrs. H. O. Havemeyer, 1929. The H. O. Havemeyer Collection.

peated and confirmed with a variety of other plants and insects. The carriers of hereditary characteristics were identified as genes, submicroscopic elements present in the reproductive cells of all living beings. The combination of the genes of male and female parents determines the characteristics of the offspring. The study of the processes involved gave rise to the new science of genetics, the part of biology concerned with heredity.

Identification of the carriers of hereditary characteristics as discrete units, and the observation that biological change takes place by means of discontinuous jumps or mutations in place of the continuous variation of Darwinian evolution, introduced a quantum concept into biology that was analogous with the new view of atomic structure and radiation. In methods as well as concepts biology drew closer to physical science, producing the new hybrid disciplines of biochemistry and biophysics. Physical science already relied extensively on mathematical reasoning and made increasing use of the laws of statistical probability. Mendel was the first biologist to make significant use of mathematics in experiments. His successors in the science of genetics depended increasingly upon mathematics and statistical probability and made significant contributions to modern statistical theory as well as to biology.

Another new discipline stimulated by the progress of biology lay dangerously close to the uncertain border between science and pseudoscience. Eugenics was defined by Sir Francis Galton, its founder and a cousin of Darwin, as the study of the inherited characteristics of man and the application of that knowledge to the improvement of the human race. The more optimistic advocates of this new branch of knowledge believed that the physical and mental characteristics of the race could be improved by deliberate selective breeding in much the same way that agronomists and horticulturists produce new strains of livestock or fruit trees. William Bateson, a distinguished biologist, wrote in 1909: "The outcome of genetic research is to show that human society can, if it so please, control its composition more easily than was previously supposed possible. . . . Measures may be taken to eliminate strains regarded as unfit and undesirable elements in the population." Others took a more pessimistic view, pointing out that the declining birth rate of Europeans — of the upper income groups in particular — raised the possibility that the world would soon be overrun by "inferior" peoples. Even highly trained and qualified scientists encountered difficulties in maintaining scientific detachment and objectivity when they turned from their laboratories to the social implications of their findings. It is not surprising that less disciplined and more prejudiced minds made unwarranted and inappropriate use of the ideas of science. Social Darwinism and crude racialism continued to flourish long after their supposedly scientific bases had been shown to be incorrect or irrelevant.

TO THE ENDS OF THE EARTH: ARCTIC AND ANTARCTIC EXPLORATION

Not all of the scientific research of the period took place in laboratories and libraries. As in earlier days, men learned much about nature from direct contact with it. By the final quarter of the nineteenth century most of the earth's surface had been charted if not thoroughly explored. The principal exceptions were the polar regions.

Efforts to discover northwest and northeast passages from the Atlantic to the Pacific dated from the early years of the sixteenth century. Three hundred years later they were still unsuccessful. It became obvious that such routes, even if discovered, would have no commercial value, but man's natural curiosity and restless spirit drove him on to new efforts. In 1818 the British government offered a prize of £20,000 (almost $100,000) for the discovery of a northwest passage, and an additional £5,000 for the first person to reach 89° north latitude, or within seventy miles of the North Pole. (Henry VIII awarded John Cabot £10 for his discoveries!) In the course of the nineteenth century more than fifty major expeditions penetrated the Arctic seas, but none collected the rewards. Explorers from almost every country in Europe, the United States, and Canada participated in the voyages, financed sometimes by governments, more often by private resources. Many lost their lives or suffered cruelly from the harsh environment. Still they came – for glory, adventure, or scientific curiosity. They tried to reach the imaginary North Pole by ship, on foot with sledges over the Arctic ice packs, and eventually by balloon, dirigible, and airplane. Rarely were the financial returns commensurate with the efforts and hardships, but they added significantly to the store of geographical and other scientific knowledge.

As early as 1831 James Ross of Britain located the north magnetic pole, which lay in the Boothia peninsula of northern Canada some 1,200 miles south of the true pole. In 1878 and 1879 the *Vega,* commanded by A. E. Nordenskiold, a Swedish professor, steamed, sailed, and drifted from the Atlantic to the Pacific above Siberia – the northeast passage – reaching the Bering Sea after nine months' imprisonment in the pack ice. Not until 1906 did the Norwegian Roald Amundsen first succeed in forcing the northwest passage after four years of continuous battle with the elements in Arctic seas. Between 1893 and 1896 another Norwegian expedition under the command of Dr. Fridtjof Nansen carried out a remarkable feat. Utilizing a specially designed ship, the *Fram,* Nansen deliberately sailed into the pack ice north of central Siberia and allowed the polar drift to carry him within 400 miles of the pole. At that point Nansen and a single companion left the ship and tried to reach the pole over the ice with dog team and sledge. They achieved a record northern latitude but fell short of the pole by about 200 miles. They

Courtesy of Stephen J. Croad

managed to survive on the ice, on foot, for a full year until they were picked up by a relief ship in the Franz Josef archipelago (or Fridtjof Nansen Land). Nansen and his companion reached Tromsö, Norway, only a few days after the *Fram* had put in at the same port. The climax of Arctic exploration came in 1909, when the American Robert E. Peary, accompanied by a Negro, Matthew Henson, and four Eskimos, reached the pole on foot after a journey of more than 300 miles from their base ship.

Until the twentieth century the south polar region attracted much less interest than the north. Since ancient times rumors had persisted of a great Terra Australis Incognita or unknown southern continent. As late as the sixteenth century some maps showed it extending to tropical latitudes, but the Antarctic continent was not actually sighted until 1820. Only after many years was its continental nature definitely established. Several expeditions penetrated the south polar seas between 1820 and 1850, mainly in connection with the lucrative whale fisheries of the adjacent islands, but not until 1895 did human beings set foot on the polar continent itself. In the same year the Sixth International Geographical Congress meeting in London called attention to the importance of Antarctic exploration. Expeditions were launched almost yearly thereafter. As with Arctic exploration, explorers of many nations participated, financed by both government and private sources. National pride and personal glory proved the most important motivating forces, and a dramatic race for the honor of planting the first flag at the pole ensued. It was won by the Norwegian Amundsen, who had been deflected from a similar race for the north pole by the news of Peary's triumph. His party of five reached the south pole in December, 1911, after a harrowing seven-week dash across the glacial plateau. Just a month later a British party led by Captain R. F. Scott reached the same destination, but perished of starvation and exposure on the return journey. Such were the incentives and rewards of scientific exploration.

Red House

"Red House, which Philip Webb and Morris built, boasted no exquisite or palatial beauties, but a beauty and a homeliness all its own. Unlike other houses of that period, it was built entirely of red brick and roofed with red tiles. The building was L-shaped, two stories in height, standing amidst a veritable forest of apple and cherry trees, so closely to them, in fact, that in after years some of the apples actually fell inside the windows, disturbing many a restless sleeper on hot August nights." Lloyd Wendell Eshleman, A VICTORIAN REBEL; THE LIFE OF WILLIAM MORRIS (New York, 1940).

EUROPEAN SOCIETY AT THE END OF ITS GOLDEN AGE

Influential though they were, the artistic, literary, and scientific developments discussed above occupied the minds of only a small portion of the Western populace. For most people, untroubled by such complicated ideas, the last decade or so of the nineteenth century and the first few years of the twentieth century brought unprecedented material progress and intellectual complacency. The growth of wealth, the spread of literacy, the progress of democracy, the apparent obsolescence of warfare – all fitted well with the earlier optimistic predictions of Comte and Spencer, Hugo, Browning, and Walt Whitman.

CHANGING CONCEPTS OF SOCIAL CLASS

Rapid industrialization and urbanization, especially in northwestern Europe, brought about a major realignment of social classes. The traditional upper class, the landed aristocracy, found its importance greatly diminished by the large fortunes made in industry and commerce. The traditional middle class burgeoned to unprecedented proportions as its ranks were swelled by new professions and the growing class of salaried employees and executives. Historically the middle class had been identified with town dwellers to such an extent that middle class and bourgeoisie had become almost identical, but in an age when most of the population lived in cities, it was no longer realistic to identify the bourgeoisie exclusively with the middle class.

In place of the old designations based on the relationship of individuals to the land or the means of production, classes came to be defined chiefly according to income. There was still a close correlation between education, occupational status, and income. Those who worked primarily with their hands, whether in factories, workshops, or on farms, had the least education and lowest incomes. The middle classes included not only those who combined sedentary labor with the ownership of some property, such as small merchants and manufacturers, but also those whose investment in education or whose acquisition of special skills enabled them to earn a higher return from their labor. The expression upper class came to signify people of great wealth, whether inherited or earned, who could afford to live on the income from their property without being forced to work. Intellectuals and descendants of ancient titled families sometimes sneered at the social pretensions of the newly rich, but in Great Britain and other countries with monarchic institutions the device of newly created peerages made it possible to integrate into the upper classes people who had distinguished themselves in the art of making money as well as in other fields. In the United States no such devices were needed: wealth alone provided the key to social recognition.

Two changes that contributed to the increasing social mobility were the spread of public education and the growth of democracy. Between 1870 and 1900 almost every country in western Europe adopted or increased its facilities for public education. In most countries public education became compulsory (in principle, at least) for periods ranging from three to eight years. These were only small steps toward the goal of universally educated societies, but they were essential. They greatly increased the range of opportunities for young people. The spread of democracy created a new ladder of social mobility – professional politics – which together with business enterprise supplemented and partly replaced the old ladders of the army and the church.

POPULAR CULTURE AND RELIGION

Increased educational facilities produced a remarkable rise in literacy. During the 1860's in the countries of northwestern Europe between 50 and 60 per cent of the adult population was classed as literate. By 1900 approximately 90 per cent was so classified. The proportions were much less in southern and eastern Europe: about 66 per cent in Austria, 50 per cent in Italy and Hungary, 30 per cent in Spain and Portugal, and 20 per cent in Russia and the Balkans.

Literacy, however, means only the ability to read simple sentences and write one's name; it does not automatically create in one a desire for the world's great literature. The most popular living authors at the turn of the century were not Stéphane Mallarmé, the leader of the symbolists, or even Henry James or Thomas Hardy, much less Nietzsche or Sorel. They were such writers as Émile Zola, then at the height of his powers and a political figure as well; Rudyard Kipling, poet and novelist; Jules Verne and H. G. Wells, masters of the new art of science fiction; Arthur Conan Doyle, inventor of Sherlock Holmes and the detective novel; and the American adventure writer Jack London.

At a still lower level were the writers published in cheap magazines and newspapers. Between 1880 and 1900 the number of newspapers in Europe doubled from 6,000 to 12,000. By far the greater number were in the industrial countries of northwestern Europe. By 1900 several newspapers in the largest cities had daily circulations of more than a million copies, as compared with 50,000 for the London *Times* during the 1860's, the largest circulation of that period. Technical innovations in printing and publishing, such as typesetting machines, cheap paper made from wood pulp, and high-speed presses, as well as the larger market helped to reduce costs and increase the output of this branch of the information and entertainment industry. The 1890's witnessed still another innovation: "yellow" journalism or the featuring of lurid, scandalous, and often sensational stories in order to increase circulation and advertising revenue. Its pioneers were William Randolph Hearst in the United States, Alfred Harmsworth in Britain, and the Mosse family in Germany.

The most common forms of art enjoyed by the masses, apart from the frequently lurid sketches in newspapers and magazines, were cheap reproductions of religious paintings in the homes of the devout. Even substantial middle-class homes were more likely to contain stylized imitations of the old masters and mass-produced porcelain or plaster figurines than the works of contemporary painters and sculptors. A similar situation characterized music. Only people of refined musical taste or social pretention attended operas or concerts featuring the works of noted composers. Even operettas such as those of Gilbert and Sullivan were beyond the taste and pocketbook of the majority. Music entered their lives, if at all, only through the church, spontaneous singing of folk music and popular ballads, and the Sunday concerts of military bands in garrison cities.

The separation of art from everyday life worked in both directions. Many of the artists and writers who subsequently became famous led miserable if rather flamboyant lives. As rebels against conventional standards in life as well as art, they found themselves outcastes in society – their works unsold, their very existence ignored by the more conventional and successful practitioners who catered to the popular taste. As a result they developed a creed that went beyond the concept of "art for art's sake." It can best be summarized as "the supremacy of art over life." Not only was art an end in itself: it was the supreme end; nothing else mattered. This aesthetic view was shared even by relatively successful writers, such as the American expatriate Henry James and the eccentric and tragic Oscar Wilde.

Analogous developments took place in theology and religion. Theological disputes became increasingly recondite and concerned with the deeper issues of philosophy, whereas religion itself became increasingly democratic. Official Protestantism put more emphasis on good works, relatively less on personal piety. Catholics tended toward social Catholicism, and Pope Leo XIII, who did much to restore the prestige of the papacy after Pius IX, encouraged the study of science by Catholics. Protestant theologians inclined toward modernism, reconciling the teachings of the Bible with modern advances in science. Intellectuals within the churches inclined toward skepticism, but clergymen who had closer contact with the rank and file went in the opposite direction. In all countries where Protestantism flourished new splinter sects came into being and fundamentalism – belief in the literal interpretation of the Bible – opposed modernism both in the church and in everyday life. Closely related were the temperance movements, which opposed the use of alcoholic beverages in any form. They grew up in most countries with large Protestant populations and achieved their greatest successes in Scandinavia and in the adoption of the Eighteenth Amendment (prohibition) to the United States Constitution in 1919.

IDEOLOGY AND LIFE

The various literary, artistic, and philosophical currents of thought at the turn of the century inevitably attracted the ubiquitous suffix "-ism," but they did not qualify for the more technical name of ideology. The ideologies that constituted focal points for mass followings at the end of the century were the same that had grown to prominence in its beginning, namely, liberalism, socialism, and nationalism.

Liberalism had to its credit a remarkable series of triumphs. In Great Britain it was accepted with much the same unquestioning faith – and much the same backsliding in practice – as the Christian religion. Even members of the Conservative party accepted the fundamental principles of liberalism as an ideology while contesting with the Liberal party for control of the government. Although liberalism never attained the same degree of acceptance on the Continent as in Britain, it was largely responsible for the introduction of parliamentary government and other liberal institutions in one country after another. Even its bitterest opponents, such as the tsar of Russia and the sultan of Turkey, were forced to come to terms with it. Paradoxically, however, liberalism was a dying force in Europe by the beginning of the twentieth century. In large measure its weakness stemmed from the very extent of its success. In Britain and other democratic countries many of its ideals had already been achieved. Its proponents faced the dilemma of standing pat on its accomplishments and running the risk of being labeled old-fashioned or conservative, or of borrowing programs and slogans from more advanced or radical ideologies. In either case it meant the demise of classical liberalism.

Socialism had a much larger following in 1898 than in 1848, but it also suffered a kind of internal crisis. The failure of society to develop in accordance with the Marxist prediction deprived socialism of some of its messianic appeal. The desertion of some of its leaders to the heresy of revisionism appeared to be a fatal concession to bourgeois liberalism, dividing the movement just when the weakness of its opponents promised success.

The one ideology that continued to strengthen itself was nationalism, because it did not rival but fed upon other ideologies as a parasite. A conservative liberal or a liberal socialist was a contradiction in terms, but no one quibbled about a national liberal or a conservative nationalist. They were the names of recognized political parties in Germany. Even the various socialist parties organized themselves within the framework of national states, although they were nominally committed to international solidarity. Increasing literacy (minimal though it was) contributed to the growing force of nationalism. During periods of increased international political tension mass-circulation newspapers inflamed popular nationalism by magnifying even a minor dispute to the proportions of a *casus belli.* Nationalism received stimuli from other sources as well, and as public opinion became more and more important in the formation of public policy because of the spread of democracy, diplomats and politicians sometimes found themselves committed to courses of action contrary to their wishes. The nationalism that at the beginning of the nineteenth century had been a hopeful, liberal, constructive force had become a potential threat to the very objects of nationalism: the nation-states themselves. Yet such considerations carried no weight with the general public. To the generation of Europeans that reached maturity at the opening of the twentieth century the era seemed a prelude to infinite, universal progress. In reality, it was the end of the golden age for Europe.

THE TWENTIETH CENTURY: FROM WESTERN CIVILIZATION TO WORLD CIVILIZATION PART TWO

INTRODUCTION: FROM WESTERN CIVILIZATION TO WORLD CIVILIZATION

The world in the twentieth century is experiencing a process of millennial dimensions: the birth of a global civilization. What the mingling of classical and barbarian cultures in the European Dark Ages was for Western civilization, the mingling of Western and non-Western cultures is for the civilization of the future. As in the Dark Ages, the process is accompanied by violence and conflict. Just as Western civilization inherited characteristics from both its predecessors, so world civilization is taking on characteristics of both Western and non-Western cultures. Few of the participants, then or now, have been aware of the historic significance of their age; much less have they been able to predict the character of the emerging civilization. For all but a few, problems of personal and group survival in an uncertain but hostile environment discourage contemplation of the forces of historical change. A final resemblance is of particular interest for the last survivors of a uniquely Western civilization: just as the birth of Western civilization was preceded by the decadence, disintegration, and schism of classical civilization, so the birth of world civilization has been preceded by decadence, disintegration, and schism in the West.

THE DISINTEGRATION OF WESTERN CIVILIZATION

The distinguishing characteristics of Western civilization, especially as manifested in its final flowering in the nineteenth century, were a concern for freedom and rationality. In economic life these principles took the form of a rational, scientific technology and a worldwide organization of the economy based on free enterprise, free international trade, and free international migration. In political life they found expression in the proliferation of parliamentary institutions and the spread of democracy; in governments of laws, not of men; and in the guarantees of elementary civil and political liberties. They can be seen most clearly in the intellectual sphere in the almost unrestricted pursuit of science, the epitome of rationalism, and in the greater freedom of expression allowed artists and authors.

The triumph of rationality and freedom was not, of course, complete. The continuation of political absolutism in eastern Europe, the revival of economic restrictions and imperialism in the late nineteenth century, and the willingness of nations to resort to force in the settlement of international disputes reflected the least progressive aspects of the heritage of the past and accumulated a store of troubles for the future. New elements of irrationality and new restrictions on individual liberty crept in before the end of the century. But the most blatant defects in the character of Western civilization on the eve of its debacle resulted from the excesses of its virtues. Preoccupation with material goals and emphasis on pragmatic or realistic means together with a corresponding neglect of philosophic ends brought a near denial of the idealistic and humanitarian traditions of Western civilization. In a similar vein, excessive emphasis on individualism and liberty developed insensibly into crass egotism, the belief in the right of the individual to do as he pleased without regard for others, and the denial of the bonds of community and society. The development manifested itself in extreme versions of laissez faire economic policy and Social Darwinism, competition for empire and colonial exploitation, and the growth of militarism in Europe. The sudden, dramatic outbreak of World War I abruptly heralded the catastrophe of collapse; but the war itself was neither the beginning nor the end of the process of disintegration.

RIVAL PLANS FOR RECONSTRUCTION

When after two decades of continuing political, social, and economic crises it became apparent to all that a fundamental malaise afflicted Western civilization, blueprints for reconstruction proliferated in surprising numbers. Unfortunately most of them mistook the symptoms of disintegration for its causes, especially in the liberal plans for reconstruction. A further difficulty was that many of the schemes were mutually, even internally, contradictory.

As early as 1917 a scheme for total reconstruction based on an attempted fusion of Western rationality and Eastern despotism went into operation in Russia, which was itself an amalgam of Eastern and Western civilizations. Soon afterward, first in Italy, then in Germany and elsewhere in central Europe, new plans of reconstruction used rational means to achieve irrational ends and deny freedom. The dilatory and half-hearted attempts at reconstruction in western Europe and America allowed these denials of the basic values of Western civilization to gain headway.

THE FORGOTTEN TWO-THIRDS

The beneficiaries of Western civilization constituted a minority of the world's population. Most of them knew little and cared less about the rest of the world. Increasingly in modern times, however, non-Western cultures and civilizations have been affected by Western civilization. The contacts usually involved violence and coercion by the West, as well as more subtle forms of influence. The results were sometimes disastrous for the indigenous cultures, bringing them close to extinction. In all cases the West undermined the bases of traditional cultures and civilizations or modified their content. Frequently what non-Western peoples learned from the West through bitter experience reflected the worst, the most retrograde aspects of Western civilization. Insofar as they absorbed the progressive features, it was mainly in the sphere of material technology.

At the beginning of the twentieth century the power gap between the West and the rest of the world had never been wider or the extent of Western control greater. Both the disparity and the dominion seemed likely to grow indefinitely. Serious writers wrote about the eventual extinction of nonwhite races, while others wrote more vividly of the "Yellow Peril" and the necessity for prophylactic action. In 1914 it seemed unlikely that non-Western peoples would ever emancipate themselves from the tutelage of or bondage to the West. Yet fifty years later, although the disparity of material circumstances remained as great as ever, few non-Western peoples remained politically subservient to a Western nation. A comparison of membership in the League of Nations and the United Nations is revealing. In 1925, 48 of a total League membership of 55 were nations with a predominantly Western heritage (even without Germany, the Soviet Union, and the United States); 26 lay in Europe proper. In 1970, 74 of a total of 126 members of the United Nations were basically non-Western. If Latin America is excluded, only 31 nations within the European tradition belonged, and 10 of those were under Communist control.

This startling reversal resulted not from any increase in the physical strength of the rest of the world but solely from moral collapse and division within the West. World War I, which in spite of its name was essentially a civil war within Western civilization, inaugurated the process, although its consequences, a new global *Kulturkampf,* did not immediately become apparent. World War II, which more nearly lived up to its name even though it, too, began as a purely internal struggle within the West, delivered a hammer blow to Western pre-eminence. After the war Western material and technological superiority continued to increase, but the basic schism also increased, negating the claim of the West to moral leadership of the world as well as destroying its ability to lead. This was the paradox: as Western nations, divided into rival ideological camps, grew stronger, their own unique civilization became more diluted. The rising political power of non-Western nations reflected neither an increase in their material strength nor a reassertion of their traditional cultural traditions but the supersession of both Western and non-Western cultures by a new, global culture.

THE FIRST WORLD WAR
CHAPTER TWELVE

The end of the Franco-Prussian War left the newly founded German Empire the most powerful nation in Europe. France was not only defeated but isolated diplomatically. Although Great Britain was not indifferent to developments on the Continent, it was preoccupied with domestic reform and problems of empire. Russia, like Britain, devoted itself to domestic issues and its land empire in Asia. Austria-Hungary sought to unravel the problems of its dual monarchy; Italy, indebted to Prussia for the opportunity of acquiring Venetia and Rome, struggled for economic progress and social community to accompany its superficial political unity. The lesser states of Europe served only as pawns in the game of great power politics, and overseas the only nation that could pretend to great power status – the United States – was involved in the exploitation of its vast hinterland.

How different was the situation less than fifty years later at the end of World War I: Germany was prostrate, Austria-Hungary and the Ottoman Empire were dismembered; France was victorious, surrounded by its allies Britain, Italy, and the United States as well as several lesser nations. Russia, an erstwhile ally, was in the throes of revolution and civil war. Other allies and new powers on the international scene included Japan and the British dominions.

Developments on several fronts contributed to this startling reversal in international relations. The most important factor was the Franco-German rivalry. Other developments included the progressive collapse of the Ottoman Empire under constant Russian pressure and rising Balkan nationalism; the resulting Austro-Russian rivalry for dominance in the Balkans; the Russo-Japanese confrontation in eastern Asia and the rise of Japan as a great power; the German challenge to British naval supremacy and Britain's retreat from its "splendid isolation"; and American involvement in European power politics. The worldwide colonial rivalries influenced almost all aspects of international relations.

THE DIPLOMATIC PRELUDE, 1871–1914

The sentiment for revenge against Germany was high in France in the years following 1871. Although it abated or was deflected from time to time, the thought of Alsace-Lorraine under the German flag never let it die entirely. Frenchmen realized, however, that they could never again afford to go to war alone with Germany; they must have allies. The search for dependable allies was the constant preoccupation of the French foreign office. Bismarck – in Germany until 1890 only Bismarck's opinion mattered in foreign policy – having achieved his goal of German unification under Prussia, sought only to maintain the status quo. He realized that to do this he must prevent France from acquiring allies; the best way was to pre-empt all likely allies for Germany.

In effect, only five great powers existed in Europe in 1871; Italy was a dubious sixth. In order to ensure a balance of power in Germany's favor, Bismarck had to league at least two of them with Germany. "You forget," he once chided the Russian ambassador, "the importance of being a party of three on the European chessboard. . . . Nobody wishes to be in a minority. All politics reduce themselves to this formula: try to be *à trois* in a world governed by five powers." Such was Bismarck's dictum, and as long as he remained at the helm in Germany, he followed it with success.

BISMARCKIAN FOREIGN POLICY

Britain, France's traditional enemy, seemed safe enough from Germany's point of view as long as the British maintained their policy of nonalignment in European politics. This left Austria and Russia. Bismarck's greatest fear was a war on two fronts; at all costs he must prevent an alliance of France with either Austria or Russia. Although there appeared to be little likelihood of such an alliance in 1871, Bismarck took no chances. Foreseeing the possibility of Austro-Russian rivalry in the Balkans, he wanted to put himself in a position to mediate any possible dispute between them and thus to prevent one or the other from turning to France.

In 1872 Bismarck arranged for the three emperors – Franz Josef of Austria, Alexander II of Russia, and William I of Germany – to meet with their foreign ministers in Berlin. Under Bismarck's prodding both Austria and Russia agreed to try to maintain the status quo in the Balkans, at least temporarily. In the following year a series of bilateral military agreements among the three powers, by which each promised to aid the other in the event of an unprovoked attack on it, further strengthened their ties. Although the association of the three powers was not a formal alliance, it became known as the *Dreikaiserbund* (Three

Emperors' League). The association was further strengthened in the same year by a visit of King Victor Emmanuel of Italy to Vienna and Berlin to gain support in the event that France should try to restore Rome to the pope.

The Dreikaiserbund received its first test in 1875 and was found wanting. Clerical royalists had returned to power in France and, determined to pursue a policy of *revanche* (revenge), they began a campaign of rearmament and encouraged the German Roman Catholics in their Kulturkampf. (See p. 217.) Bismarck, hoping to frighten the French into backing down, inspired a press campaign in German newspapers hinting that war was again in sight. The French foreign minister at once declared to the other great powers that Germany was preparing a "preventive" war and must be restrained. Austria remained silent, winning Bismarck's gratitude, but Britain and Russia both protested to Berlin. They were not prepared to help France in an aggressive war on Germany, but neither were they willing to see German predominance strengthened further at French expense. Bismarck disavowed the whole episode, but he had discovered Germany's true friends.

The Congress of Berlin of 1878, which settled the Russo-Turkish War (see pp. 325–327), further strained Russo-German relations. Bismarck offered to serve as the "honest broker" in the settlement of the dispute, but Russia, nominal victor in the war, felt it gained less than Austria, which had not participated. Aware of Russian dissatisfaction, Bismarck decided to strengthen Germany's ties with Austria. In 1879 the two countries signed a treaty (the Dual Alliance), which remained in force until 1918. Its principal provision obligated either country to come to the aid of the other if attacked by Russia. Bismarck saw it as a purely defensive and precautionary alliance, but Austrian officials frequently regarded it as giving them a free hand to do what they liked in the Balkans without fear of Russian intervention.

The details of the Austro-German treaty remained secret, though the existence of such a treaty was well known. Fearing that it had a sinister implication for them, the Russians sought some assurance from Germany, preferably in the form of a treaty of mutual defense. The Russians also feared the possibility of a British fleet in the Black Sea as the result of their tense relations with Britain in the Middle East and elsewhere. Although Bismarck had temporarily deflected French *revanchisme* by encouraging the French conquest of Tunisia, he gladly accepted the opportunity of reestablishing friendly ties with Russia, but not precisely in the form requested. In 1881, after intensive persuasion on his part, he again brought Austria, Russia, and Germany together in a formal Dreikaiserbund. Whereas the earlier one had been no more than an informal understanding among the three monarchs, the new one was a formal commitment by the governments. In addition to guaranteeing to each at least the friendly neutrality of the others in the event of war with a fourth power, the treaty committed them to consultation and joint action if there were any changes in the status quo in the Ottoman Empire and the Balkans. Concluded originally for three years, the treaty was renewed for an additional three years in 1884.

Bismarck capped this achievement with yet another master stroke. The Italians, anxious for recognition as a great power, had planned to annex Tunisia, when France suddenly beat them to it. Humiliated and outraged, the Italians angrily turned to Bismarck for consolation; and in 1882 Austria, Germany, and Italy signed a treaty establishing the Triple Alliance, which endured until broken by Italy in 1915. In essence it guaranteed that Austria and Germany would support Italy if it were attacked by France, pledged Italy to support Germany under similar circumstances, and provided for Italian neutrality in the event of an Austro-Russian war.

The years 1882 to 1884 marked the high point in the success of Bismarck's policies. Soon after the formation of the Triple Alliance Britain occupied Egypt, much to the displeasure of France, and inaugurated twenty years of intense colonial rivalry between the two powers. As in the French occupation of Tunisia, Bismarck had secretly encouraged the British to take Egypt, but at the same time he secretly expressed his "sympathy" for France. This led to a temporary rapprochement with France, further strengthened by the Berlin Conference of 1884, called by Bismarck and Jules Ferry, in part to thwart British plans in Africa. Bismarck even boasted privately that he had reestablished Napoleon's Continental System with its center in Berlin.

The Franco-German entente did not last long. French nationalists and anti-imperialists engineered the fall of Ferry, while Bismarck came to terms with Britain on the colonies. Anti-German feeling reached a peak in France in 1886–87 during the meteoric rise of General Boulanger, but his even more rapid fall brought a reduction in temperatures and passions. Meanwhile the Three Emperors' League expired, and Russia refused to renew the treaty as a result of new disputes with Austria. Bismarck persuaded Russia to sign a secret three-year Russo-German Reinsurance Treaty guaranteeing the neutrality of one if the other became involved in war, except for an aggressive war by Russia against Austria or by Germany against France. Thus, in spite of increasing difficulties, Bismarck managed to keep France isolated and Russia in line.

THE FRANCO-RUSSIAN ALLIANCE

The headstrong young emperor William II peremptorily dismissed Bismarck on March 18, 1890. (See pp. 219–220.) On March 23 the German government decided against renewing the Reinsurance Treaty, due to expire on June 18. In a matter of days Bismarck's successors began to dismantle the structure that he had patiently built and maintained over twenty years.

The French quickly seized the opportunity presented by this unexpected turn of affairs. As early as 1886 private pressure groups in France and Russia had taken advantage of the anti-German feeling prevailing in both countries to urge a Franco-Russian alliance; but Russia, traditionally suspicious of and hostile to France – especially Republican France – had preferred to seek accommodation with Germany. Now there was nowhere else to turn. During a personal visit to Russia shortly after the expiration of the Reinsurance Treaty, William evaded the efforts of his kinsman the tsar to reach a new agreement. The Russians were further put off by obvious German moves to draw closer to Britain and by an early renewal of the Triple Alliance. In July, 1891, during a friendly visit by a French naval squadron to the Russian base of Kronstadt, the Emperor of All the Russias stood bare-headed while a marine band played the revolutionary anthem, the *Marseillaise*.

The French had hoped to obtain a definite treaty of alliance, but the Russians were still moving cautiously. The best the French could obtain in 1891 was an *entente cordiale* (cordial understanding) and an agreement for joint consultation in the event of any "threat to peace." The following year the chiefs of staff of the two armies agreed on a military convention which provided that each would come to the aid of the other if either were attacked by Germany, whether alone or in league with Austria or Italy. Significantly, the convention was to have "the same duration as the Triple Alliance." Although it was drawn up in 1892, political scandals and cabinet shake-ups in France delayed its ratification until the beginning of 1894.

These two agreements – the entente cordiale and the military convention – formed the basis of the Franco-Russian alliance. Their precise conditions remained secret, of course, and the two governments did not refer to them publicly until 1895; but during the twenty years after their ratification massive investments by Frenchmen in Russian government bonds and corporate securities demonstrated the popularity of the alliance with the French people. Frequent consultations and joint planning by the military authorities strengthened its fabric. The immediate effect of the alliance was to restore the balance of power to something like an equilibrium: neither France nor Germany, Austria nor Russia, had an obvious advantage over the other. For the future, however, Bismarck's nightmare came closer to reality: if war should come, Germany would be forced to fight on two fronts.

GERMAN NAVAL EXPANSION AND THE END OF BRITISH ISOLATION

As long as Britain pursued its policy of nonalignment with European powers, Bismarck was content to let Anglo-German relations coast. William II began his independent direction of foreign policy with earnest attempts to formulate an Anglo-German alliance, but at the end of a dozen years he succeeded only in driving Britain into the arms of France. Maladroit German diplomacy, such as William's ill-advised telegram to President Kruger of the South African Republic congratulating him for squelching the Jameson raid and hinting at promises of German support, served to alienate the British government and public. More fundamental forces also acted to produce an estrangement between the British and German nations.

The rapid growth of the German economy and its expansion into overseas markets adversely affected British economic interests. German businessmen were both efficient and aggressive and made deep inroads in traditional British markets. They even penetrated the British home market. In 1887 Parliament passed the Merchandise Marks Act, requiring foreign merchandise sold in Britain to be labeled with the name of the country of origin in order to discourage the German invasion. By the end of the century, however, British consumers had come to regard the stamp "Made in Germany" as a guarantee of quality rather than the reverse.

Because of the extension of Germany's overseas commerce as well as its debut as a colonial power, the German Admiralty had little trouble in 1898 in persuading the Reichstag to grant funds for a naval building program. In 1900 the program was enlarged, and German naval strategists developed the theory of the "risk fleet." They did not expect to surpass Britain as a naval power, but they reasoned that if their fleet and the next largest were together larger than the British, Britain would be unwilling to go to war against Germany in support of a third power. As early as 1889, however, the British navy had become alarmed by the growth of French and Russian sea power and had adopted the so-called two-power standard. This implied that Britain must have a fleet equal to the combined fleets of the next two largest navies. Thus the German decision touched off a naval armaments race that theoretically had no limit.

The British grew increasingly anxious over this development. It seemed as though the world was closing in on them. They had been at odds with France ever since the occupation of Egypt, and for a few months in 1898 they were on the brink of war over the Fashoda crisis. They had opposed Russian expansion in the Ottoman Empire, Persia, and East Asia. In 1902 they departed from their traditional policy of "splendid isolation" and concluded an alliance with Japan against Russia. Two years later, after almost a year of preliminary negotiations, they concluded a far-reaching agreement with France that provided for a complete settlement of all outstanding colonial disputes between the two powers. The Anglo-French entente of 1904 in no way committed the two nations to a military alliance, but subsequent conversations and negotiations resulted in a close understanding on many questions and placed

Courtesy of the Museum of Fine Arts, Boston

The European Balance, by Honoré Daumier

"History shows that the danger threatening the independence of this or that nation has generally arisen, at least in part, out of the momentary predominance of a neighboring State at once militarily powerful, economically efficient, and ambitious to extend its frontiers or spread its influence. . . . The only check on the abuse of political predominance derived from such a position has always consisted in the opposition of an equally formidable rival, or of a combination of several countries forming leagues of defense. The equilibrium established by such a grouping of forces is technically known as the balance of power, and it has become almost an historical truism to identify England's secular policy with the maintenance of this balance." Secret memorandum of Eyre Crowe of the British Foreign Office, Jan. 1, 1907, BRITISH DOCUMENTS ON THE ORIGINS OF THE WAR (London, 1928), Vol. III.

Britain under a "moral obligation" to come to the aid of France in the event of an unprovoked attack on it.

Although Britain still regarded Russia with grave distrust, the Russo-Japanese War revealed Russian weakness and put an end to the Russian danger in East Asia. Moreover, as a result of the British annexation of Cyprus in 1878 and its stronger position in Egypt, especially after the agreement with France, Britain had fewer fears of a Russian threat to Suez. Russia, for its part, was badly shaken by defeat and the revolution of 1905 and was anxious to resolve its differences with Britain. In 1907 the two countries reached agreement on spheres of influence in Persia and Afghanistan and settled other disputes. Although the agreement did not provide for positive military collaboration, it did make cooperation easier. With France serving as the pivot, the pincers were closing on Germany.

ITALIAN DUPLICITY

While this new and strange alignment of powers was emerging, Italy played a double-dealing game. It adhered to the Triple Alliance even though its traditional archenemy Austria was included, through fear of French retaliation for 1870 and in anger over the French seizure of Tunisia. In 1887 it joined Britain and Austria in a Mediterranean Agreement to thwart Russian designs on the Ottoman Empire. The other two signatories also undertook to support an Italian claim to Tripoli. In renewing the Triple Alliance in the same year, Germany agreed to far-reaching support of Italy in its North African rivalry with France. Ten years later Italy made a commercial treaty with France settling their long-drawn out tariff war, and in 1900 the two countries agreed to give one another a free hand in Tripoli and Morocco, respectively. In 1902 Italy went further and assured France that it would remain neutral if France became involved in war with a third power; it even asserted that this promise in no way violated its other "international obligations," although the promise flatly contradicted Italy's promises to Germany in the Triple Alliance, which was still in force. Italian duplicity reached a new peak in 1909 when Italy agreed to support Russian aims in the Dardanelles in exchange for Russian support of Italy's claim on Tripoli, in spite of Italy's obligations to Austria under the Agreements of 1887. Italy's behavior throughout this period can be explained in part by the amorality of its politicians. Equally important was the Italian desire for colonies, especially after the humiliations in Tunisia and Ethiopia; they were determined to avoid a similar reverse in Tripoli.

THE MOROCCAN CRISES

Tripoli and Morocco, the last two areas of Africa to come under European control, had far more significance for European diplomacy than their importance as colonial acquisitions would seem to warrant.

Morocco, a poverty-stricken, revolt-torn semidesert on the northwest corner of Africa, achieved importance mostly as a result of German intransigence and diplomatic blundering. Germany had no important interests in Morocco, economic or otherwise, whereas the French had common borders with Morocco in both Algeria and French West Africa. The frequent Moroccan tribal revolts occasionally spilled over into French territory. The French, therefore, made agreements with Italy, Spain, and Britain in the hope of establishing an eventual French protectorate over most of the country, with Spain having the northern tip. Germany, however, was determined to use Morocco to test the strength of the new Anglo-French Entente of 1904.

In the spring of 1905 William II visited Tangier and strongly indicated German support for Moroccan independence. His action created an uproar not only in Paris but also in London, where the government had already taken alarm at Germany's naval program. In January, 1906, an international conference including the United States and several smaller nations as well as the great powers met at Algeciras at the southern tip of Spain to deal with the Moroccan situation. In the showdown only Austria supported the German position – a clear indication of the new alignment of powers. The Act of Algeciras reaffirmed Moroccan "independence" but placed the police under French and Spanish tutelage and set up a state bank, in which France had a controlling interest, to deal with the country's disordered finances.

A new Moroccan crisis blew up in 1908 when French authorities forcibly seized three German deserters from the Foreign Legion who had taken refuge with a German consular official. The immediate issue was submitted to arbitration by the International Court in The Hague, but the more important result was a Franco-German agreement in 1909. Germany recognized France's "special political interests" in Morocco in return for French consideration of German economic interests.

The third and final Moroccan crisis occurred in 1911. As a result of anti-foreign demonstrations, the French occupied the city of Fez. The Germans, who had been dissatisfied with the operation of the agreement of 1909, dispatched the gunboat *Panther* to the coastal city of Agadir hoping to force a French withdrawal. Instead, the English rallied in support of the French. The result was that Germany gave France the free hand that it had so long been seeking in Morocco, in return for cession by the French of two strips of disputed territory in the Congo. In the following year France forced the sultan of Morocco to accept a French protectorate.

The true significance of the Moroccan crises for European power politics was that they converted the Anglo-French Entente of 1904 from a mere agreement to settle colonial disputes into an active military alliance. German strategy backfired completely, though not for the first nor the last time.

FROM THE EASTERN QUESTION TO THE BALKAN WARS

It is not easy to understand why the murder of an Austrian archduke in a remote village of southeastern Europe by a fanatical member of a secret society should have precipitated a global war, yet that is what happened. The secret-treaty network of alliances helps to account for the chain of events expanding the war after the first declaration, but it fails to explain why the great powers attached so much importance to this backward, poverty-stricken corner of Europe. All of them had, or thought they had, or came to have, interests in the Balkans. Had it not been for the progressive atrophy of the Ottoman Empire, these interests might not have arisen or might have remained latent; but as nature abhors a physical vacuum, so politicians abhor a political vacuum.

The Russian interest was most obvious and persistent. For more than a century a fundamental theme of Russian policy had been the drive to secure ice-free ports. Closely related to this was the Russian wish to control the Dardanelles and Bosphorus in order to permit the egress of Russian warships into the Mediterranean and to prevent the entry of hostile vessels into the Black Sea. Russian territorial claims in the Balkans were secondary, and complementary, to these two points. Even before the construction of the Suez Canal, Britain had resisted the Russian drive on the Balkans as a danger to communications with India; after the completion of Suez, Britain regarded control of the eastern Mediterranean as absolutely vital. It followed that the Dardanelles must be kept closed, or opened only with British permission.

After Austria-Hungary had been expelled from the leadership of central Europe in 1866, it looked to the Balkans for territorial aggrandizement to bolster its injured pride. Its diplomats occasionally manufactured slogans about controlling the mouths of the Danube or keeping open the route to Salonika, but their really vital interest in the Balkans was the purely negative one of keeping out the Russians. The French had long had important commercial relations with the Ottoman Empire, to which they added substantial foreign investments after the Crimean War. Although protection of their economic interests did not require territorial control, they naturally wanted a voice in deciding upon any changes in the status quo. Although German interests, symbolized by the Berlin-to-Bagdad railroad (rather, the Anatolian railroad, conceded to a German syndicate in 1888) were of recent date and as much political as economic, they were no less vigorous for that. Italy had no direct interests in the Ottoman Empire as such, but obsessed with the notion of obtaining Tripoli, it could not abstain from any activity that promised to weaken further the grip of the Turks.

Underneath this jumbled mosaic of conflicting great power interests lay the aspirations and ambitions of the people whose homes were in the Balkans: Albanians, Bulgarians, Greeks, Macedonians, Rumanians, various South Slavs (Serbs, Croats, Bosnians, Slovenes, Montenegrins)—and Turks. Although the inhabitants of the area were frequently regarded by the great powers as so many cattle, in the final analysis their actions and reactions provided the dynamic element in the entire Eastern Question.

THE RUSSO-TURKISH WAR AND THE CONGRESS OF BERLIN

In July, 1875, the inhabitants of Herzegovina and Bosnia rose in rebellion against their Turkish masters. Within a few months the revolt had spread to Macedonia and Bulgaria. In the following year Serbia and Montenegro declared war in sympathy with the rebels. In Constantinople, where the government had already defaulted on its foreign debt payments, a series of palace revolutions deposed two sultans in quick succession. It looked like the end of the Ottoman Empire. The powers hastily conferred but could reach no agreement on the disposition of the corpse of the "sick man of Europe."

Surprisingly, the sick man demonstrated unusual vitality, crushing the revolts with great brutality and driving the Serbs back into their homeland. The Serbs appealed to the powers for mediation. Under a threat from Russia the Turks agreed to an armistice and a conference of the great powers in Constantinople. Turkey outflanked Western demands for reform, however, by proclaiming a new constitution, which it promptly scrapped when the conference adjourned. Meanwhile, Russia had agreed with Austria to allow the latter a free hand in Bosnia and Herzegovina in return for a free hand for Russia in Rumania and Bulgaria, with independent Serbia as a buffer between them. In April, 1877, Russia declared war on Turkey.

The Serb, Montenegrin, Rumanian, and Bulgarian irregulars again went to war, joining with the Russians who were advancing south through the eastern Balkans. Again the Turks put up unexpectedly strong resistance, holding the Russians at the fortress of Plevna in Bulgaria for almost six months. At length the Russians broke through and in January, 1878, stumbled exhausted to the gates of Constantinople. Unable to do more and fearful of intervention by the other powers (Britain dispatched warships to Constantinople in February), the Russians hurriedly forced the Turks to sign the Treaty of San Stefano, which provided for a large autonomous state of Bulgaria under Russian protection.

As Russia feared and Turkey hoped, the other great powers would not accept the results of the Treaty of San Stefano. After preliminary bar-

gaining, representatives of the six great powers plus those of the Ottoman Empire met in Berlin at the invitation of Bismarck in the summer of 1878. The dispositions of the congress generally followed those of the Treaty of San Stefano except for the creation of Greater Bulgaria, which was divided into three parts: Bulgaria proper, north of the Balkan mountains, an autonomous principality within the Ottoman Empire;

Eastern Rumelia, south of the mountains (including the Black Sea coast), restored to the Turks but under a special administration; and Macedonia, returned outright to the Turks with promises of reform. Rumania achieved full independence and gained most of Dobrudja on the mouths of the Danube, but had to give up southern Bessarabia to Russia. Serbia and Montenegro also gained independence but within smaller boundaries than those provided at San Stefano. Austria occupied Bosnia and Herzegovina and stationed a garrison in the Sanjak (province) of Novi Bazar. Britain took over the administration of Cyprus, ensuring control of the Mediterranean approaches to Suez as well as to the Dardanelles. Apart from regaining Bessarabia, which it had lost in 1856, Russia obtained only a few towns in the Caucasus.

Hailed as a great peace-making achievement, the Congress of Berlin actually left most participants and beneficiaries less satisfied than before. It stifled the aspirations of Serbia, Bulgaria, and Greece. The Ottoman Empire lost most of its territory in Europe and was left with the remainder in a precarious, exposed condition, subject to both domestic agitation and foreign conquest. More ominous for the future of Europe, Russia, victorious in war, suffered humiliation in peace. Austria gained much at little cost, but incurred the hostility of the new Balkan states, whereas Russia earned their gratitude. Britain gained an important advantage, but it remained profoundly suspicious of the Russians. Finally, Bismarck, "the honest broker," incurred the enmity of the influential Russian nationalists and Pan-Slavists and found himself tied to Austrian ambitions in the Balkans.

BULGARIA AND SERBIA

The Bulgarians had the greatest reason of all to be dissatisfied with the Congress of Berlin. Their territory had been cut back to a fraction of its projected size, they still paid tribute to Constantinople, and their policies were decided in St. Petersburg. They received as their prince Alexander of Battenberg, a German who knew nothing of Bulgaria but was a favorite nephew of the Russian tsar. Nevertheless, when Eastern Rumelia revolted in 1885 and demanded annexation to Bulgaria, Alexander was forced to accept the leadership of the movement despite the protests of Russia, which in the meantime had turned against both him and the idea of a Greater Bulgaria. British pressure forced the sultan to recognize Alexander as governor of Eastern Rumelia and thereby accept the de facto union of the two provinces.

Although both Turkey and Russia had to accept the fait accompli of the enlargement of Bulgaria, the jealous Serbs, who regarded their country as "the Piedmont of the Balkans," did not. In 1885 Serbia declared war on Bulgaria with the aim of securing "compensation." Surprisingly, the Bulgarians defeated the Serbs so badly that the latter called on

Austria-Hungary, the oppressor of the South Slavs, for protection against their neighbor. Soon afterward the Bulgarians forced Alexander to abdicate and elected as his successor Prince Ferdinand of Saxe-Coburg. Since Ferdinand was even less acceptable to Russia than Alexander had come to be, Russia persuaded other nations to withhold recognition of his regime until 1896. Nevertheless, Ferdinand held on with the strong support of his adopted people.

Balkan politics, both domestic and international, appeared to many Western observers to have something of a comic opera aspect, despite the obvious suffering of the people. (George Bernard Shaw wrote a successful comedy based on the Serbo-Bulgarian war, *Arms and the Man,* which Oskar Straus converted into an even more successful muscial comedy, *The Chocolate Soldier.*) Serbians regarded Austria much as the Italians had in 1859, yet until 1903 the ruling dynasty of Serbia placed itself under Austrian protection. Russia had liberated Bulgaria from the Turks and treated it as a client state, yet the Bulgarians hated the Russians almost as much as they hated the Turks or the Serbs. In 1903 the Serbians overthrew the Obrenovich dynasty and recalled the Karageorgeviches, who had been banished some forty-five years previously. Thereafter Serbian hostility to Austria became more overt, while the Serbs looked increasingly to Russia as the protector of the South Slavs. Bulgaria, on the other hand, gradually grew closer to Austria in spite of improvement in its relations with Russia after 1896, and it eventually went to war against Russia as the ally not only of Austria and Germany, but also of Turkey.

THE POWDER KEG OF EUROPE

In 1908 the Young Turk revolution broke out within the Ottoman Empire. In the ensuing confusion Bulgaria declared its complete independence, and Austria-Hungary proclaimed the outright annexation of Bosnia and Herzegovina. Only the Turks objected to the former action, but the latter move aroused vigorous protests from Russia and Serbia as well as the Turks. The Russians demanded an international conference, and the Serbs were on the point of war with Austria. Both eventually backed down, but the episode left a further legacy of bitterness and distrust.

The next major disturbance in the Balkans resulted from the action of Italy, which in 1911 finally undertook its long-planned conquest of Tripoli. Unable to win a decisive victory, the Italians occupied the Dodecanese Islands off the coast of Turkey, and the war appeared to be heading for a stalemate. Taking advantage of the situation, Montenegro, Serbia, Bulgaria, and Greece patched up their mutual quarrels and in October, 1912, went to war with Turkey. The Balkan allies won a succession of victories and were on the point of overrunning Constantinople itself when the great powers intervened to save the remains of Turkey.

The Treaty of London on May 30, 1913, ended the first Balkan War. Turkey was obliged to give up the island of Crete and all but a small corner of its European territory. Since both Austria and Italy objected to the expansion of Serbia to the Adriatic, the new independent state of Albania was established.

The first Balkan War had just ended when the second erupted. Disappointed by the great powers in its claims on the spoils of war, Serbia demanded a larger share of Macedonia from Bulgaria. When the Bulgarians refused and launched a surprise attack, Serbia and Greece declared war on Bulgaria. They were shortly afterward joined by Rumania and Turkey. The second Balkan War lasted only a month, with Bulgaria quickly defeated under such heavy odds. By the Treaty of Bucharest on August 10, 1913, Rumania obtained southern Dobrudja; Greece and Serbia obtained the lion's share of Macedonia. In the separate Treaty of Constantinople on September 29 Turkey regained Adrianople.

The new nations of the Balkans had learned the lessons of *Realpolitik* only too well. No notions of enlightened self-interest, economic or otherwise, held back their expansionist tendencies. Their state finances were in deficit, their living standards were little above the subsistence level; still their leaders played the game of power politics with a reckless abandon that made even post-Bismarckian German diplomats shudder. Such was their exhilarating legacy of independence after more than four centuries of Turkish rule — plus the tutelage and example of the great powers.

THE WAR

The system of alliances erected by Bismarck was purely defensive. Its purpose was to prevent war, not provoke it. So, too, was the network of agreements worked out by France after 1890. Although many Frenchmen still harbored ideas of revenge on Germany, they feared the possibility of a German preventive war. In any case they would have been unable to persuade either Russia or Britain to go to war to restore Alsace-Lorraine. The system of alliances and ententes served its purpose up to a point. For more than forty years — the longest period in modern history — no major Western nation fought another despite the many rivalries and conflicts of interest. Nevertheless, it was in the nature of the alliance system that if war between two or more of the great powers should begin, no matter where it started or how trivial the cause, it would become a general war involving all.

SARAJEVO AND THE MARCH TO WAR

On June 28, 1914, a young Bosnian revolutionary shot and killed the Archduke Franz Ferdinand, heir to the Austro-Hungarian throne, and his wife in the course of the archduke's visit to Sarajevo, capital of the

Austrian province of Bosnia. Exactly one month later Austria declared war on Serbia. By the end of the following week general war had erupted.

Serbia, the focal point of Pan-Slavism in the Balkans, had long been a thorn in the flesh of Austria. Intent on creating a Greater Serbia incorporating all the Slavic peoples in the Balkans, the Serbian government made or tolerated anti-Austrian propaganda, gave haven to political refugees, and generally hampered Austrian efforts in the Balkans. The Austrian annexation of Bosnia and Herzegovina in 1908 particularly incensed the Serbs, who regarded the provinces as properly belonging to Greater Serbia. Austria's frustration of Serbia's plans to incorporate Albania at the end of the first Balkan War added fresh fuel to the fire of Serbian hatred. Austria long since would have squelched the Serbs if it had not been for the threat of Russian interference. Now the government resolved to do so in spite of the threat.

Franz Ferdinand was known to be more liberal than his aged uncle, the king-emperor. It was widely believed that on his accession to the throne he would give the Slavic inhabitants of the empire much greater autonomy, perhaps a position similar to that enjoyed by the Magyars, in a federal empire. Since that might postpone indefinitely the creation of a Greater Serbia, the Pan-Serbian secret society Union or Death, also known as the Black Hand, decided on his assassination.

The Austrians suspected the complicity of the Serbian government in the plot but could not prove it. During the month between the assassination and the declaration of war Austria conducted an intensive search for the proof that would forestall Russian intervention. Although they could not find the evidence, the Austrians decided to take over Serbia anyway. On July 23 they delivered an ultimatum to Serbia on the pretext of needing to carry on their search in Serbia itself. Had the Serbs accepted the ultimatum, it would have meant the end of Serbian independence. Acting on Russian advice, they replied in a conciliatory tone, indicating acquiescence on some of the Austrian points but evading the major issues.

Meanwhile the great powers had been engaged in frequent consultations. World public opinion was shocked by the assassination and viewed with favor Austrian efforts to punish the guilty parties; the French and Russians, however, suspected the Austrians of wishing to go further than mere punishment. The Russian government, in particular, had decided even before the episode at Sarajevo that its objectives could be achieved only as the result of a general war; hence, it was prepared for — even welcomed — a showdown in the Balkans. The German government also had reasons for allowing a showdown. Bethmann-Holweg, the chancellor, and many other Germans were obsessed by fears of Russian expansion and favored a preventive war. Convinced that a two-front war was inevitable and hoping that Britain would remain neutral, the German

General Staff had prepared a strategy as early as 1905, called the Schlieffen Plan, which demanded implementation before France and Russia became stronger. The German emperor, therefore, assured his confrere in Vienna of his support with the remark that he appreciated the necessity of "freeing your Serbian frontiers of their heavy pressure." The remark was interpreted by the Austrian government as the offer of a blank check from Germany. The French regarded it as simply another test of the strength of their alliances, similar to the Moroccan crises, and assured Russia of their support. Sir Edward Grey, the British foreign secretary, proposed an international conference, but Austria refused point-blank to submit "a question of national honor" to arbitration.

Immediately after the Austrian declaration of war on July 28, the German government pressured Austria into resuming direct negotiations with Russia while it tried to separate France from Russia and offered Britain a guarantee that it would not annex any part of France or Belgium in return for a British promise of neutrality. Neither France nor Britain would make a firm commitment, but Britain demanded that Germany respect the neutrality of Belgium, to which Germany would not commit itself. The Russian government, which had ordered a general mobilization of the army immediately on receipt of the news of the Austrian declaration, changed its order to limited mobilization against Austria when informed of the apparent German efforts to make peace. When the final Austro-Russian negotiations broke down, it again ordered general mobilization. The climax came on August 1. Almost simultaneously, Germany and France ordered general mobilization. That evening, having received no reply to a twelve-hour ultimatum to Russia to halt mobilization, Germany declared war on Russia.

The following day the German army had already moved into Luxembourg and requested permission of the Belgian government to cross Belgian territory. The Belgians refused, but the Germans invaded anyway, violating Belgian neutrality guaranteed by all the great powers by international treaty in 1839. On August 3 Germany declared war on France. The British cabinet was still struggling with its painful decision, but the invasion of Belgium settled the matter: on August 4 Britain declared war on Germany. By the end of the week all the great powers except Italy were involved, as well as Serbia, Montenegro, Luxembourg, and Belgium. Before the month was out, Japan declared war on Germany and Austria; and by the end of the year Turkey entered on the side of the latter two nations.

THE BALANCE OF FORCES

If it is the business of diplomats to prevent war, it is the business of generals to prepare for it. There is no question that in 1914 Germany was better prepared militarily than any other nation. The credit belonged principally to the German General Staff. The long tradition of Prussian militarism carried over into the German Empire, under whose peculiar constitution military leaders had enormous influence with only minor accountability to civilian authorities. When war broke out other nations required from one to three weeks to mobilize their forces; Germany was able to take the offensive immediately.

In a short war, which was all that anyone expected in August, 1914, Germany's modern industries, great production of coal and steel, dense, well-integrated rail network, and military preparedness would have given it the advantage. Its chief disadvantage, and Bismarck's nightmare, was the necessity of fighting on two fronts, even though its shorter supply lines and efficient transport system minimized that handicap in the short run. Moreover, Austria-Hungary, less modern and less efficient than Germany, bore the brunt of the fighting on the eastern front in the war's opening stages.

France had a smaller population, possessed fewer and smaller heavy industries, and lacked the military planning and preparedness of the Germans. Russia, in spite of a huge population, was backward both militarily and economically. As early as December, 1914, the Russian commander in chief informed his allies that he could no longer take the offensive for lack of military supplies. Russia's great distances and inadequate rail network hampered the movement of troops and supplies, while separation from its Western allies rendered negligible any hoped-for assistance from them. Although Britain controlled the sea lanes, it had only a small professional army and no system of compulsory military service. It could provide only marginal assistance to France at the war's outset.

Eventually Britain's sea power and overseas resources – including help from the self-governing dominions, who at once cast their lot with the mother country – proved decisive. In spite of a devastating German submarine campaign, the British fleet and merchant marine assured the supply of foodstuffs and war materials for the Western allies. The British naval blockade of the Central Powers (as Germany and its allies were called) imposed privations and hardships on the civilian population and military services alike and cut off supplies of many strategic materials, such as rubber, tin, and petroleum. Finally, the entry of the United States into the war at the very time that Russia was knocked out assured the Allied Powers of that superiority of men, machines, and materials essential to ultimate victory.

THE EARLY CAMPAIGNS

German strategy was based on a plan drawn up in 1905 by Count von Schlieffen, chief of the German General Staff from 1891 to 1906. It called for a defensive holding action against the Russians in the east while striving for an early defeat of France in the west. According to the military authorities, the capture of France would either keep Britain out of the war or prevent the landing of British troops. The Russians could then be dealt with easily.

On the western front the Schlieffen Plan envisaged another holding action on France's northeastern frontier, where heavily fortified and wooded hills were considered too dangerous to attack directly. The largest part of the army was to sweep through Holland, Belgium, and the level plain of northern France, cut off the Channel ports, and encircle Paris from the west. (That the plan called for the violation of Belgian neutrality showed the influence and independence of the German military authorities.) If any resistance then remained, it would be destroyed by a pincer movement hinged on the German fortress of Metz and closing in from both east and west.

The strategy nearly succeeded. The Germans began the invasion of Belgium on August 3, captured Brussels on August 20, and by the early days of September were within forty miles of Paris with a large area of northern France under their control. The French government hastily moved to Bordeaux. At that point, however, the Allied forces rallied and launched a strong counterattack along the Marne River northeast of Paris. The entire fleet of Paris taxis was pressed into service to carry soldiers to the front. After a week of heavy fighting (September 5–12) the German forces gradually retired to take a new stand on the Aisne River.

Apart from the strong resistance of the Allies on the Marne, several German tactical errors accounted for the failure of the Germans to carry out their original strategy. At the last minute before the war began, the German high command switched several divisions from the Belgian front to Lorraine to counter an expected French offensive. Instead of invading through Holland, they sent all their forces through the relatively narrow gap between the fortress of Liège and the Ardennes hills, incurring additional casualties and losing time in mopping up the Belgians. The unexpectedly early arrival of the British (between August 7 and 17) took the Germans by surprise. Instead of continuing on to the Channel coast to cut off new reinforcements, they headed directly for Paris but were pushed eastward by the defending French and British, making encirclement impossible. Perhaps most important, the German General Staff, believing the issue settled by the end of August, withdrew a number of divisions for use on the eastern front.

The Battle of the Marne marked the farthest German advance of the entire war. After the German retreat to the Aisne the two opposing armies settled in for months of exhausting, muddy, bloody trench warfare. The war of movement gave way to a war of position. In spite of numerous heavy attacks and counterattacks in which both sides suffered

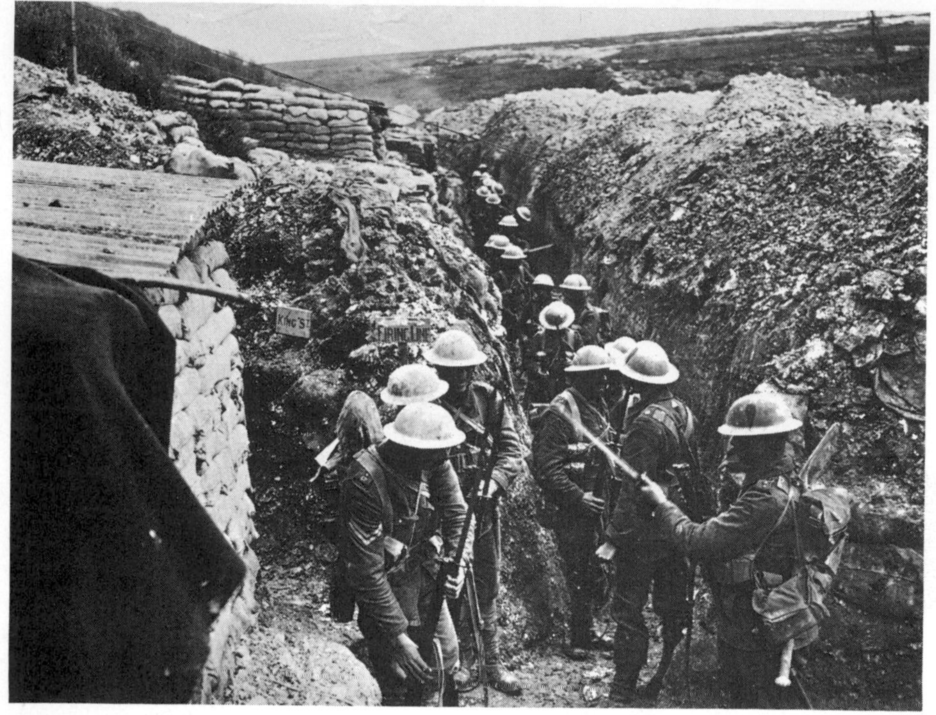

Courtesy of Imperial War Museum, London

Trench Warfare

> *"The trench lines ran continuously from the Alps to the sea, and there was no possibility of manoeuvre. . . . All the wars of the world could show nothing to compare with the continuous front which had now been established. Ramparts more than 350 miles long, ceaselessly guarded by millions of men, sustained by thousands of cannon, stretched from the Swiss frontier to the North Sea. . . . For the first time in recorded experience there were no flanks to turn. The turning movement, the oldest manoeuvre in war, became impossible. Neutral territory or salt water barred all further extensions of the Front, and the great armies lay glaring at each other at close quarters without any true idea of what to do next."*
>
> Winston S. Churchill, THE WORLD CRISIS, 1915 (London, 1923).

---

hundreds of thousands of casualties, the line of battle did not change by more than ten miles in the next three years.

The eastern front in the early months of the war was in reality two fronts. On the Austro-Russian frontier the Russians took the offensive and overran Austrian Galicia in the first six weeks before being stopped at the Carpathian Mountains. Russia invaded East Prussia and made an extensive advance before being turned back by a revitalized German army under generals Hindenburg and Ludendorff, whose forces killed and captured approximately 250,000 Russian soldiers. By the end of 1914 the Russians had fallen back almost to Warsaw. During the winter of 1914–15 the fighting on the eastern front was inconclusive. The Germans and Austrians mounted a new offensive in 1915, capturing nearly all of Poland. In 1916 the Russians took the offensive for the last time. They achieved limited successes against the Austrians in Galicia but failed in their ultimate objective. From that time forward the Russians were not only on the defensive but in a state of progressive military and political collapse. The revolution in the spring of 1917, although it did not remove Russia from the war, effectively ended any possibility that the Russians could make a positive contribution to the eventual Allied victory.

In the Balkans neither Austria nor Serbia was strong enough to penetrate far into the other's territory. After seesaw fighting in the fall and winter of 1914–15 their positions stabilized along the lines of the prewar frontier, while Austria devoted its main resources to the Russian front and Serbia recuperated. Meanwhile the diplomats from both sides tried to entice Greece, Bulgaria, and Rumania into the war with lavish promises of territorial acquisition. In September, 1915, Bulgaria was the first to succumb to the blandishments of the Central Powers. A combined offensive by the Bulgarians in the east and an Austro-German force in the north soon overran the entire peninsula north of Greece. Russia persuaded Rumania (which had been allied since 1883 with Austria and Germany) to enter on the side of the Allies in August, 1916. The timing was singularly unfortunate, for it was then that the Russian offensive collapsed. Within six months almost the whole of Rumania was in the hands of the Central Powers. Greece became the unhappy victim of a tug of war between rival foreign and domestic factions. The Allies could not budge Greece from its position of neutrality, but a French and British expeditionary force landed anyway at Salonika in a belated attempt to succor the Serbs. After months of internal strife amounting to civil war, in 1917 the Allies finally forced King Constantine to abdicate and installed a government that dutifully declared war on the Central Powers.

With the entry of Turkey on the side of the Central Powers in November, 1914 (in accordance with a secret treaty between Turkey and Germany, signed August 1), the area of conflict broadened. Although the Turkish offensives came to nothing, the British had to keep large numbers of troops in the Near East to protect the Suez Canal. Turkey closed the Dardanelles and Bosporus to Allied shipping, cutting off Western supplies to Russia except by the expensive and unsatisfactory routes to the Arctic ports and Vladivostok. The attempt of a British expeditionary force in 1915 to land at Gallipoli and capture Constantinople resulted

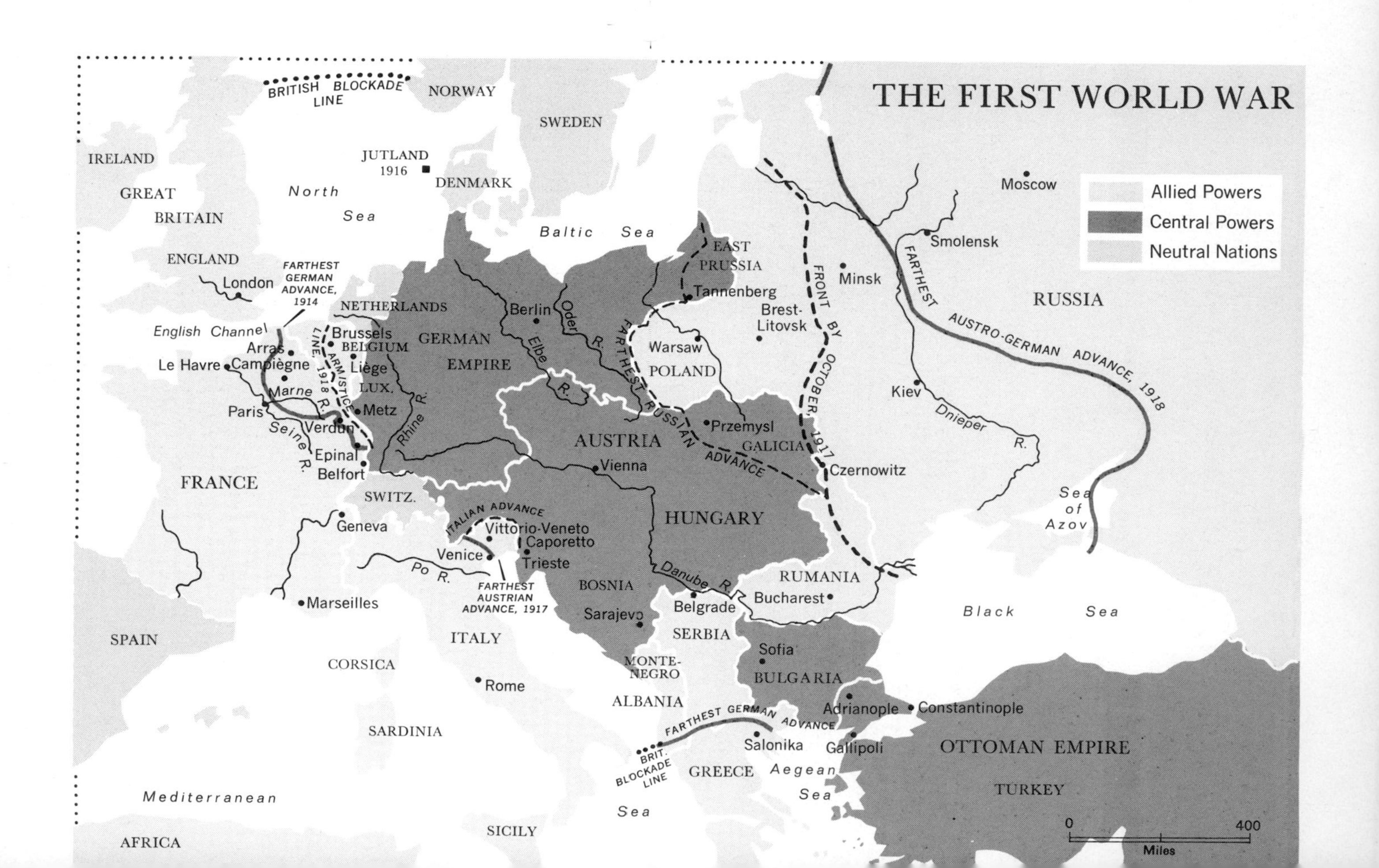
THE FIRST WORLD WAR
Allied Powers
Central Powers
Neutral Nations
BRITISH BLOCKADE LINE
NORWAY
SWEDEN
IRELAND
JUTLAND 1916
DENMARK
GREAT BRITAIN
North Sea
Baltic Sea
ENGLAND
London
FARTHEST GERMAN ADVANCE, 1914
NETHERLANDS
English Channel
Brussels
BELGIUM
Arras
Le Havre
Compiègne
Liège
ARMISTICE LINE, 1918
LUX.
Marne R.
Paris
Metz
Verdun
Seine R.
Epinal
Belfort
Rhine R.
GERMAN EMPIRE
Berlin
Elbe R.
Oder R.
EAST PRUSSIA
Tannenberg
Warsaw
POLAND
FARTHEST RUSSIAN ADVANCE
Brest-Litovsk
Minsk
FRONT BY OCTOBER, 1917
Moscow
Smolensk
FARTHEST AUSTRO-GERMAN ADVANCE, 1918
RUSSIA
Kiev
Dnieper R.
Przemysl
GALICIA
AUSTRIA
Vienna
Czernowitz
Sea of Azov
FRANCE
SWITZ.
Geneva
ITALIAN ADVANCE
Vittorio-Veneto
Caporetto
Venice
Trieste
Po R.
FARTHEST AUSTRIAN ADVANCE, 1917
HUNGARY
Danube R.
BOSNIA
RUMANIA
Bucharest
Belgrade
Black Sea
Marseilles
Sarajevo
SERBIA
SPAIN
ITALY
CORSICA
Sofia
MONTE-NEGRO
BULGARIA
Rome
ALBANIA
Adrianople
Constantinople
FARTHEST GERMAN ADVANCE
SARDINIA
Salonika
Gallipoli
OTTOMAN EMPIRE
BRIT. BLOCKADE LINE
GREECE
Aegean Sea
TURKEY
Mediterranean
Sea
SICILY
AFRICA
0
400
Miles

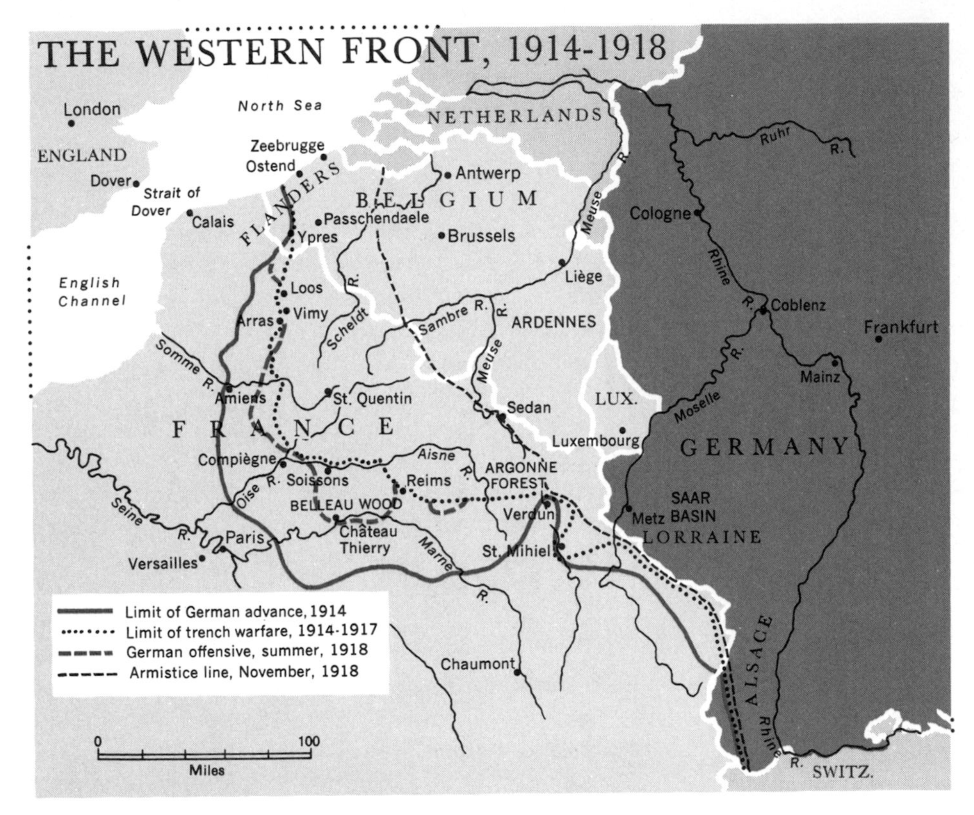

in failure. Not until 1917 did British forces in the Near East under General Allenby (supported by desert Arabs led by the romantic figure T. E. Lawrence) make substantial gains against the Turks.

The final theater of the war in Europe was in Italy. Having deserted its partners in the Triple Alliance in favor of an ambiguous neutrality, Italy pursued some hard bargaining throughout the winter of 1914–15 to see which side would offer most for its services. The Central Powers were handicapped in the bargaining by Austrian resentment of Italian perfidy and by extravagant Italian claims on Austrian territory. The Western allies had no compunctions in the matter, and in the secret Treaty of London on April 7, 1915, granted Italy lavish promises of territorial acquisition, some of which flatly contradicted other commitments of the Allies. It proved a poor bargain. After two years of repeated attacks along a very narrow front on the Austrian frontier northeast of Venice, the Italians had advanced only ten miles. After mopping up in Serbia and Rumania, the Germans sent six divisions in in 1917 to reinforce the Austrians on the Italian front. On the first day of the attack they regained all that the Italians had won in two years. At the end of a month the Italians had fallen back to the Piave River, where they held until the last weeks of the war, when the visible collapse of the Austro-Hungarian monarchy made it possible to advance into Austrian territory.

THE WAR AT SEA AND IN THE COLONIES

Since Germany's colonies had only skeleton military garrisons, they quickly fell to the Allies. Japan's main purpose in declaring war in August, 1914, was to secure Germany's Pacific islands and Chinese concessions for itself. Japanese naval forces quickly occupied the Marianas, the Marshalls, the Carolines, and Palau; a combined sea and land operation took over the Shantung peninsula of China. A New Zealand force occupied German Samoa, and the Australians took over the Bismarck Archipelago and German New Guinea. All these operations were secure by the beginning of November, 1914.

In Africa the German garrisons held out longer, although the actual fighting was rarely severe. Togoland capitulated to an Anglo-French force in August, 1914. Another combined Anglo-French attack drove the Germans out of the Cameroons during 1915. The Union of South Africa invaded German Southwest Africa at the beginning of 1915 and completed its conquest in six months. Only in German East Africa did the Germans put up a determined show of resistance. Their troops were still in the field at the time of the armistice in 1918, although most of the colony itself had fallen to British, South African, and Portuguese forces.

With few exceptions, the war at sea was singularly uninteresting. The highly touted and expensive German High Seas Fleet remained in port throughout the war except for a single inconclusive sortie. The British Grand Fleet was not much more venturesome, taking refuge on the west coast of Scotland, though its cruisers patrolled the North Sea on the lookout for submarines and occasional German raiders. The beginning of the war found a number of isolated German battle cruisers in foreign ports. They immediately put to sea and did some damage to Allied shipping and shore stations in the Pacific and Indian Oceans, but most were destroyed in the first few months of the war.

The one major naval engagement of the war, the Battle of Jutland, took place in 1916 in the Skagerrak between Denmark and Norway. The German fleet had timidly put to sea and was discovered by a British cruiser squadron. The Germans tried to retreat, but the main body of the British fleet came up behind and cut across its line. In the ensuing battle each fleet lost six capital ships, but the British losses were more important. Although the Germans had shown themselves superior in marksmanship and maneuver against a larger British force, they retreated to their own harbors, where they remained until the end of the war. The risk fleet took no more risks.

The most important development in naval warfare was the widespread utilization of submarines, especially by Germany. At the beginning of the war it was not clear what could be expected of these craft, but they soon proved to be exceedingly effective. In the early months German submarines sank several outmoded British warships. Soon they began to concentrate on merchant shipping and even passenger liners. In February, 1915, the Germans announced a submarine blockade of Britain. The sinking of the Cunard liner *Lusitania* on May 7, 1915, with a loss of 1,200 lives (including many Americans) outraged the Western world and brought the United States to the brink of war with Germany. Germany eventually agreed not to sink passenger ships in the future without warning and without provision for rescuing the passengers, but submarine attacks against ordinary merchant ships continued at an accelerated pace.

By the beginning of 1917 Germany had more than one hundred submarines and announced that it would no longer respect the rights of neutrals or provide for passengers. In April it sank 875,000 tons of Allied and neutral shipping. Germany's unrestricted submarine warfare was the major factor in bringing the United States into the war. The German military planners took account of this possibility but decided they would be able to drive Britain out of the war by cutting off its supplies of food and raw material before the United States could make an effective contribution. At the insistence of civilian authorities, however, the British navy finally began the practice of convoying merchant ships and improved its techniques of antisubmarine warfare. By the end of 1917 the worst of the submarine danger had passed. The Allies were destroying German submarines faster than they could be built and building new shipping tonnage faster than it could be sunk.

ENTER THE UNITED STATES, EXIT RUSSIA

The American declaration of war on Germany on April 6, 1917, was preceded by several attempts to seek a negotiated peace. At the beginning of 1916 President Wilson sent Colonel House, his confidential adviser, to Europe for consultations with leading Allied statesmen. Colonel House let it be known that the president was prepared to mediate a peace settlement; moreover, if the Allies accepted his offer but the Germans did not, the United States would probably go to war against Germany. The Allies were still confident of victory in the coming spring offensives, so nothing came of the offer. Toward the end of the same year Germany requested that the United States inform the Allies that it was prepared to consider a negotiated peace. Again the Allies rejected the offer. A part of the difficulty lay in the fact that neither side had clearly formulated or announced its war aims.

After Allied rejection of the German peace overture, the German government fell more than ever under the influence of the generals, especially Ludendorff. In January, 1917, the German war council decided on the policy of unrestricted submarine warfare. As soon as this news reached the United States, President Wilson severed diplomatic relations with Germany; still he did not take the country into war.

From the beginning many Americans had been sympathetic to the Germans. Many more – undoubtedly a majority at the beginning of the war – adopted the attitude that the war was none of America's business. Only a relatively small group, chiefly in the East, felt that America should join the Allies early in the war. Gradually their number grew as Allied propaganda had its effect (because the British controlled the transatlantic cables, America rarely received news directly from Germany). Others became converted because of the submarine campaign. Still others – influential bankers and financiers in particular – became converted because of the large American loans to the Allied Powers. When German submarines torpedoed several American vessels in February and March of 1917, majority opinion swung sharply to a desire for intervention.

America entered the war with a very small standing army and no system of military conscription. To recruit, train, and transport soldiers to France in substantial numbers required more than a year. Thus, although the navy went into action at once in convoy and antisubmarine duty, American soldiers did not make an appreciable contribution to the Allied cause on land until the summer of 1918.

Simultaneously events in Russia were drawing to a climax. Recurrent military defeats, increasing civilian hardships, and the autocratic and inefficient character of the government brought domestic unrest to a new peak. In March, 1917, a palace revolution overthrew the monarchy and installed a provisional government. (See p. 347.) Liberal and republican in character, the new government attempted to continue the war, but the breakdown of the internal administrative machinery was complete. The armies suffered new defeats, and conditions in the cities approached famine proportions. Soon after the March Revolution the Germans transported Lenin and other Bolshevik leaders to Stockholm, whence they made their way to St. Petersburg and organized the workers into an antigovernment party. In November the Bolsheviks overthrew the provisional government and at once began to negotiate for an armistice with Germany.

The Germans made extensive demands on the new regime, which even the Bolshevik government felt it could not accept. For almost three months the negotiations dragged on while the Bolsheviks attempted to consolidate their power and the Germans grew impatient. Meanwhile the old tsarist empire was breaking up into its constituent parts. The provisional government had already recognized the independence of Poland. While negotiations with Germany were taking place, Finland, Estonia, Latvia, the Ukraine, and Bessarabia all declared their independence of Russia. To prevent further defections and to rally their forces to fight the civil war that had broken out within Russia, the new Soviet government at last signed the Treaty of Brest Litovsk on March 3, 1918. Although the treaty compelled Russia to make extensive concessions to Germany and the new states, it remained a dead letter because of the German capitulation to the Allies eight months later. The final determination of the new Russian boundaries and the nature of the regime awaited the outcome of the civil war.

THE FINAL CAMPAIGNS

At the end of 1916 the Central Powers controlled the entire Balkan peninsula north of Greece. Greece was still technically neutral but was occupied by a small Allied expeditionary force. By knocking Russia out of the war in 1917, the Germans secured their eastern frontiers and could divert the released manpower to the deadlocked western front. It had become clear that the unrestricted submarine campaign could not alone drive Britain out of the war. General Ludendorff, who had become a virtual military dictator of Germany, decided on a last gigantic effort to achieve a decision in the west before the Americans could reach the front in large numbers. He launched his great offensive in March, 1918, with an unprecedented artillery barrage and the extensive use of poison gas. Favored by a persistent heavy fog, he broke the British lines in northwestern France, then launched a savage attack against the main French positions northeast of Paris. By the end of May he had driven to the Marne, within striking distance of Paris. Once again, as it had so many times before, the German strategy almost succeeded. On this occasion the offensive stalled because of the exhaustion of the German soldiers and the arrival in the nick of time of fresh American troops at the beginning of June. In the second Battle of the Marne (July 15 to August 7, 1918) the Allied forces definitely turned back the German threat. Thereafter the offensive lay with the Allies, and in view of the steady reinforcement of American troops the outcome was only a matter of time. The Germans now fought a defensive action to keep Allied soldiers off German soil until an armistice could be arranged.

From other fronts the Germans received nothing but bad news. Bulgaria capitulated on September 30 in the face of a massive Allied offensive launched from Albania and Greece. In the following month the Turks surrendered. At the beginning of November the Serbs re-entered Belgrade and began to invade Hungary. By this time the Austro-Hungarian monarchy had reached an advanced state of decomposition, with wholesale desertions from the army, riots and popular demonstrations in the cities, and risings of subject nationalities against their German and Magyar rulers. The Allies earlier had recognized the claims of the Czechs, Yugoslavs, and Poles to independent nationhood and allowed national brigades of their soldiers to fight along with Allied armies. At the end of October the Italians won a major victory at Vittorio Veneto and pushed on to occupy Trieste and Fiume. On November 3 the Austro-Hungarian government sued for peace.

On October 4 a new government took over in Germany. It was headed by Prince Max of Baden, a well-known liberal, and had the support of the Center, Progressive, and Socialist parties in the Reichstag, to which it agreed to be responsible. Immediately the new government appealed directly to President Wilson to arrange an armistice, basing its plea on Wilson's famous Fourteen Points. (See p. 344.) Wilson did not act on this request at once but began an exchange of notes to determine the exact terms of the proposed armistice. In the interim the political situation deteriorated seriously in Germany, with widespread rioting and street disorders. On November 3, having been ordered to sea for a last-ditch raid after spending the war bottled up in port, the sailors of the German navy mutinied. On November 7 a full-fledged revolution broke out in Munich, and on November 9 the government announced the abdication of William II. Although the emperor had not given his consent, he followed the advice of his military leaders and fled into exile in the Netherlands. On November 8 the German armistice commission met with Allied military leaders in France and worked out the details of the armistice. The harsh Allied terms fell little short of unconditional surrender, but the Germans had no alternative. On November 11, 1918, at 11 A.M., the armistice took effect. All was quiet on the western front.

SPECIAL FEATURES OF THE WAR

Before it became known in history books as the World War (later the First World War), the war of 1914–18 was known to millions of Europeans who experienced it as the Great War. In retrospect it seems a tragic prelude to the war of 1939–45, but for the generation who lived before 1939 its emotional and psychological as well as physical impact clearly justified the name. For concentrated destructiveness it surpassed anything in human history until the mass air raids and atomic bombings of World War II. Human casualties numbered about 10 million killed and twice that many seriously wounded. The direct money cost has been estimated at more than 180 billion dollars (contemporary purchasing power), and the indirect money cost (through property damage and so forth) at more than 150 billion dollars; but such figures have little meaning. The true costs — the broken lives, the shattered societies, the residues of frustration, bitterness, and hate that led to still further outrages on civilization — cannot be measured.

Apart from the magnitude of the war, it presented a number of special features that set it apart from all previous wars, even those of the Napoleonic era. Although the concept of total war did not emerge until World War II, its foundations were clearly laid in World War I. Never had entire populations been so directly engaged in or affected by a war effort. Almost all the continental countries had had some form of compulsory military service before the war; Britain introduced it in 1916, the United States in 1917. All combatant nations resorted to rationing strategic materials and many consumer goods; to requisitions, price controls, labor controls and allocation; and to many other forms of economic planning. All nations imposed either formal or informal censorships and in other ways curtailed ordinary human activities. Even Britain, the historic haven of individual liberties, adopted the Defense of the Realm Act, which in effect imposed martial law on the country.

In the half-century preceding the war industrial technology became increasingly scientific. As would be expected, so did military technology. A number of new and destructive weapons developed from the new science and the new industrial technology. The most effective was the submarine. More portentous for the future were the tank and military aircraft, although they played a secondary role in the war itself. Heavy artillery, which had been used in the past, experienced a spectacular advance in range, accuracy, and explosive force, as the shelling of Paris from forty or fifty miles away demonstrated. At the other extreme the machine gun greatly increased the effectiveness of small arms fire, especially on defense. These two devices, together with the tardy and incomplete development of the tank and the airplane, accounted for the immobility as well as the terrible destructiveness of the fighting on the western front. Trench warfare became a way of life for millions of young men on both sides and left terrible psychological as well as physical scars on many of those who survived.

Chemistry played a spectacular part with the development of toxic gases, but was no less important in the invention of ersatz or artificial commodities to replace natural commodities in short supply. The Germans took the lead in this area, both because of their superior chemical industries and education and because of their greater need. The nitrogen fixation process, invented by the German scientist Fritz Haber on the eve of the war, played a major role in maintaining German food production when the British blockade shut off the supply of Chilean nitrates for German agriculture. The wireless radio, another prewar invention with fruitful peacetime uses in the postwar period, played a limited role in military operations, especially at sea.

Propaganda was another war weapon which, though scarcely new, reached a new peak of development. Each nation sought to convince its own people as well as those of neutral nations that it was right, that the opponents were not only wrong, but committed all sorts of atrocities. They sought to undermine the morale of enemy soldiers and civilians by spreading false rumors about the course and conduct of the war. On the whole, because of their control of international cables, the Allied nations were favored in this psychological battle, especially in spreading their message to neutral nations overseas.

Closely related to propaganda were the statements of war aims by the various national leaders, which were intended to bolster the morale of their own people and to weaken the will to resist of the enemy. America was far and away the champion in this form of making war. For the first three years of the war both the Allied and the Central Powers limited their statements to protestations of innocence with respect to the origins of the war; for them it was simply a matter of survival and self-defense. For the Americans, however, it was a "war to end war" and "to make the world safe for democracy." (Fortunately for the latter slogan, the autocratic government of Russia was overthrown just before America entered the war.)

The most resounding and influential of all statements of war aims was embodied in President Wilson's Fourteen Points, delivered in an address to the Senate in January, 1918. Among other things, he called for frank and open diplomacy ("open covenants openly arrived at"), the readjustment of frontiers "along clearly recognizable lines of nationality," the right of all nations (including Russia) to "the freest opportunity for autonomous development," the limitation of armaments, and the creation of an international organization to settle disputes and guarantee peace. Although President Wilson was undoubtedly sincere in making the statement, it was never adopted by the United States as a formal statement of war aims, much less accepted by the Allies. Nevertheless, it was regarded as such by the Germans and by many Americans during the final months of the war and the first few months of peace. Indirectly and unintentionally, therefore, it was responsible for much of the misunderstanding, confusion, and acrimony that followed the war and disturbed the peace.

DISINTEGRATION AND COLLAPSE
CHAPTER THIRTEEN

The great crisis of Western civilization was a political, economic, social, and cultural crisis all in one. The first overt manifestation came with the breakdown in international relations culminating in the First World War, although the symptoms had been building for at least half a century and the aftereffects persist to the present day. The period of actual collapse lasted less than two decades, from 1914 to 1933.

The war disrupted normal social life and political relationships. It also resulted in a breakdown of the international economy and temporarily suspended the operation of free markets in most national economies. In Russia two successive revolutions, followed by a long and debilitating civil war, overturned the old order of society. Elsewhere in eastern and central Europe war-induced political collapse and social disorganization led to political demagoguery, organized banditry, mob violence, and mass hysteria. Instead of stabilizing the situation, the peace treaties concluding the war added new elements of tension.

Not realizing how extensively the foundations of society had been eroded, the people of western Europe and North America looked forward to a "return to normalcy." For them reconstruction meant primarily physical reconstruction and a return to the old way of life. Reconstruction, however, proved to be no simple matter. The difficulties experienced in all countries as a result of currency disorders and the first postwar depression in 1920–21 partially revealed the extent of the damage to the economic mechanism. Disastrous hyperinflations in Germany and elsewhere in central Europe provided further evidence and gave support to the critics of the peace treaties. By the beginning of 1925 the Western nations had succeeded in shoring up temporarily the economic mechanism and patching some of the more obvious rents in the social fabric. For a few years a precarious, almost frantic prosperity ensued. But the foundations had rotted, and the whole structure crashed in the worldwide depression from 1929 to 1933.

THE RUSSIAN REVOLUTION, 1917–1921

DISINTEGRATION, 1914–1917

The enthusiasm with which the Russian people greeted their country's entry into the First World War and their confidence in a quick victory soon disappeared when the old story of inept leadership at home and at the front led to crushing defeats and enormous casualties. The stupid and obstinate Tsar Nicholas relied increasingly for counsel on his hysterical wife and her adviser, the unordained monk Gregory Rasputin, an unwashed and illiterate Siberian peasant. Despite his openly immoral life, his bizarre behavior, and his blatant venality, Rasputin gained great power over the empress by his supposed ability to stop the hemophiliac bleeding of the youthful heir to the throne. In time she came to believe that God had sent him to guide Russia. When in 1915 the tsar left the capital to take personal command of the armies in the field, effective control of the government fell into the hands of the empress and Rasputin. Ministers came and went in confusing succession while corruption and inefficiency reached new heights. High aristocrats who feared for the survival of tsardom implored the tsar to dismiss Rasputin. When he refused, a small group of them assassinated the monk in December, 1916. Their act accomplished nothing, for Nicholas and his wife, resentful of the murder of their "Holy Friend," became ever more obstinate as the government approached complete paralysis.

The economic drain of the war, worsened by the mismanagement of the central government, brought severe stresses. Troop mobilization took manpower away from farming and industry: Russia raised an army of 15 million men. Much of the country's output went for military needs, while the imports of manufactured goods upon which Russia had depended heavily before 1914 dwindled. The costs of the war, the scarcity of goods, and the government's fiscal irresponsibility produced destructive inflation, so that by the beginning of 1917 the cost of living had risen approximately 700 per cent since 1914. During 1916 strikes and bread riots occurred with increasing frequency in the industrial centers of the empire.

THE FEBRUARY REVOLUTION

On February 23, 1917 – March 8 according to the Western calendar[1] – strikes and demonstrations broke out in Petrograd (the new name given to the capital to replace the German-sounding name of St. Peters-

[1] Imperial Russia used the old Julian calendar; the Soviet regime adopted the Gregorian calendar on January 31, 1918.

burg). At first no one expected that the disturbances would touch off a revolution, but the strike movement spread rapidly in succeeding days. Troops in Petrograd joined the demonstrators and gave them arms, while railroad workers prevented other troops from coming in to restore order. On March 12 and 13 leaders of the strikers and soldiers and representatives of socialist parties formed a Soviet (council) of Workers' and Soldiers' Deputies, as in the 1905 revolution, arrested the government's ministers, and took over control of the capital. On March 12 a committee of the Duma (parliament), which had previously been reluctant to join the developing revolution, decided to establish a provisional government. The new ministry headed by the liberal Prince George Lvov and dominated by members of the Constitutional Democratic party (Cadets) included only one socialist, Alexander Kerensky. On March 15 it obtained the tsar's abdication in favor of his brother Michael, who in turn abdicated the next day.

The long reign of the Romanovs had ended, terminated by a brief, leaderless, and nearly bloodless revolution. Many people both in Russia and abroad had long recognized the strong probability of the collapse of tsardom; but no one, not even the extreme radicals, had expected it to take place so quickly and easily.

THE PROVISIONAL GOVERNMENT

The new regime speedily introduced liberal political reforms, proclaimed freedom of speech, press, and religion, and announced plans for a far-reaching program of social reform and land distribution. It promised to summon a constitutional assembly to decide on Russia's permanent form of government. By vowing to continue the war against Germany it won recognition from the Western democracies, who held high hopes for it. In spite of its promising beginning, the provisional government lasted only eight months. Of the many factors that contributed to its early demise, two stand above the rest: its decision to continue the war, and its inability to establish control over the Petrograd Soviet of Workers' and Soldiers' Deputies.

The strength of the Petrograd Soviet lay in its close connection with the restless working class and its ability to marshal the masses for quick action. Until autumn of 1917 it was controlled by moderate socialists. They believed that Russia was not yet ready for socialism and were therefore willing to allow the provisional government to hold power until society had gone through the "bourgeois-democratic" stage of evolution. They supported the provisional government in the continuation of the war, claiming that now it was a democratic struggle against reactionary Germany and Austria. Soviets were formed elsewhere in the country, and in June hundreds of delegates met in Petrograd for the first All-Russian Congress of Soviets. Most of the representatives were

Socialist Revolutionaries (SR's) and Mensheviks. (See p. 237.) The Bolsheviks were very much in the minority.

The Bolsheviks had not been inactive, however. In April, 1917, V. I. Lenin, acknowledged leader of the Bolsheviks, returned from Swiss exile. The German government provided a special sealed train to take him across Germany to Stockholm, whence he reached Petrograd, in the hope that his agitation would disrupt the Russian war effort; but the Germans hardly expected that they would soon have to deal with him as head of the Russian government. Until Lenin's return the Bolsheviks could not decide whether to cooperate with the provisional government or not. Lenin had tried to direct policy by letter from Switzerland, but he had been unable to persuade the party to follow his advice. Once at the center of the revolution, he quickly assumed control. In his speeches and in a statement called the April Theses he announced his complete hostility to further cooperation with the provisional government. He declared that the revolution would soon pass through its bourgeois phase into a socialist dictatorship of the proletariat and insisted that "all power in the state from top to bottom, from the remotest village to the last street in the city of Petrograd, must belong to the soviets." He also urged Russia's immediate withdrawal from the war, capitalizing on the war weariness of the people and turning it into hostility to the provisional government.

The Bolsheviks had fewer than 30,000 members in February; by the end of April membership had increased to 76,000. The party's strength, however, lay not in numbers but in the ability and dedication of its members, in the appeal to the masses of its idyllic vision of a state run by the people, and in the skill and shrewdness of Lenin's leadership. He knew how to move quickly and surely in the uncertainties of the revolutionary situation, and unlike the leaders of other parties, whether bourgeois or socialist, he knew exactly in which direction he wanted the revolution to go.

Popular discontent arising from the continued hardships of the war compelled a series of cabinet reorganizations that brought more socialists into the provisional government. The general unrest erupted into civil violence in July when soldiers, sailors, and workers in Petrograd, inflamed by Bolshevik propaganda, attempted an insurrection. The Bolshevik Central Committee, the ruling body of the party, considered the rising premature and tried to curb it, but the government accused them of inspiring it. Loyal troops put down the insurrection, the government arrested several of the Bolshevik leaders claiming they were German agents, and forced the others into hiding. Lenin himself took refuge in Finland.

Soon after the July rising socialist pressure forced Prince Lvov to resign as head of the provisional government, and the moderate socialist

The Bettmann Archive

V. I. Lenin

"It was just 8:40 when a thundering wave of cheers announced the entrance of the presidium, with Lenin – great Lenin – among them. . . . Unimpressive, to be the idol of a mob, loved and revered as perhaps few leaders in history have been. A strange popular leader – a leader purely by virtue of intellect; colorless, humorless, uncompromising and detached, without picturesque idiosyncrasies – but with the power of explaining profound ideas in simple terms, of analysing a concrete situation. And combined with shrewdness, the greatest intellectual audacity. . . . Now Lenin, gripping the edge of the reading stand, letting his little winking eyes travel over the crowd as he stood there waiting, apparently oblivious to the long-rolling ovation, which lasted several minutes. When it finished, he said simply, 'We shall now proceed to construct the Socialist order!'"
John Reed, TEN DAYS THAT SHOOK THE WORLD (New York, 1919).

Alexander Kerensky became prime minister. Constitutional Democrats, army circles, and other nonsocialist groups then formed a right-wing opposition that looked upon General Kornilov, newly appointed commander in chief of the army, as its leader. The rivalry between the Kerensky and Kornilov factions culminated in Kornilov's withdrawing his allegiance from the provisional government in September and ordering his troops to march on Petrograd. Kerensky turned to the Bolsheviks for help in meeting the threat to his regime; he freed the Bolshevik leaders from jail, armed their followers, and encouraged Bolshevik agitators to spread propaganda among Kornilov's advancing troops. Demoralized by the Red propaganda, poor leadership, and inadequate supplies, Kornilov's soldiers refused to fight. The general was arrested and his mutiny collapsed.

Several weeks of confusion followed, with charges and countercharges from both Right and Left. After nearly a month Kerensky formed a five-man directory with himself at its head. Meanwhile the Bolsheviks had gained a majority in the soviets of Petrograd and Moscow as well as in most of the provincial soviets. Lenin, who was still hiding in Finland, decided that the time had come for his party to seize power. He returned secretly to Petrograd and urged his followers to ready themselves for armed insurrection.

THE OCTOBER REVOLUTION AND WAR COMMUNISM

During the night of October 24 (November 6 in the Western calendar) armed workers called Red Guards and sympathetic regular troops occupied the railroad stations, post offices, power stations, and other strategic points in Petrograd. At noon the next day they stormed the Winter Palace, the seat of government, and arrested members of the government. Kerensky himself had already fled. In less than one day the Bolsheviks took over both Petrograd and the Russian government. The next day Lenin formed a new government called the Council of Peoples' Commissars. The Bolsheviks had come to power.

The Bolsheviks quickly discovered that it was more difficult to retain power than to seize it. Nearly four years of bitter suffering, civil strife, and war followed the October Revolution. In their effort to survive and stay in power the Bolsheviks introduced a drastic regime called War Communism. It included nationalization of the urban economy, confiscation of land and its distribution among the peasants, and a new legal system. Its outstanding characteristic was the deliberate adoption by the government of a single-party dictatorship and of what Lenin called "an unsparing mass terror." In December, 1917, the government established a special secret police to combat "counterrevolutionaries." It was called the Cheka from the first letters of its Russian name. The Cheka was destined under different names to become a permanent and dreaded part of Soviet life.

In the elections to the long-awaited constitutional assembly the Socialist Revolutionaries won a large majority of the seats. The assembly met in January, 1918, but Lenin sent troops to dissolve it after one session, branding the Socialist Revolutionaries and other opponents of the Bolsheviks as counterrevolutionaries. The middle classes were persecuted from the start of the October Revolution, and it was not long before the workers and peasants also lost their freedom. Under the pressure of events and of their own ambitions for power, the men who had promised a society with freedom for all created a terrorist police state.

Russia suffered heavy territorial losses. The provisional government had recognized Poland's independence, and immediately after the October Revolution the new government acceded to Finland's demand for independence. In the next few months Lithuania, Estonia, and Latvia won independence in spite of Bolshevik opposition. The treaty of peace with Germany cost Russia much territory. The disintegration of the Russian army left the government powerless to resist German advances deep into Russia, and Lenin, who had initiated peace negotiations immediately upon seizing power, eventually had to accept the harsh German demands despite the opposition of many Bolshevik leaders. In March, 1918, the Russians signed the peace treaty of Brest Litovsk, in which they agreed to give up large parts of the Ukraine, White Russia, and Transcaucasia. Russia lost over 60 million people and 1.3 million square miles, including a large part of its industry and natural resources.

CIVIL WAR AND INTERVENTION

The enemies of the Bolshevik revolution ranged from radical Socialist Revolutionaries to extreme reactionaries who wanted to restore tsarist absolutism. The Socialist Revolutionaries revived their traditional policy of assassination, picking Bolshevik leaders as their victims this time, and in August, 1918, succeeded in severely wounding Lenin. The Bolsheviks met this threat with an official reign of terror that wiped out many of their political opponents and maintained their control of the central government, located after March, 1918, in Moscow.

The government found it far more difficult to combat the military anticommunist movements that erupted on the borders of Russia. A so-called White Army was formed in the Cossack lands of the south. Another was organized in eastern Russia and Siberia, augmented by forty thousand Czechs whom the Russians had captured during their war with Austria and who wanted to fight on the side of the Allies. Early in 1919 two other White armies were organized, one in the north and the other in the northwest.

In 1918 the government was beset by a new threat: Allied intervention. Russia's withdrawal from the war released great numbers of German troops for action on the western front and gave the Germans an opportunity to seize the large stocks of war material supplied to Russia by the Allies. To prevent this from happening and to gain whatever advantage they could from the seemingly certain disintegration of Russia, Allied nations ordered troops into northern and southern Russia and into Siberia. Only Japan, with 60,000 men, sent a large contingent. The United States sent about 8,500, Great Britain about 1,500, and France about 1,000; the other nations involved were represented by even smaller contingents. Although the Allied troops engaged in skirmishes with the Red Army, the major importance of the intervention lay in providing military supplies to the Whites and in blockading the Russian coasts. The Allies withdrew their troops in 1920, except for the Japanese, who remained in western Siberia until 1922 and in the Russian part of the island of Sakhalin until 1925. In the end the intervention accomplished nothing except to make the Russians suspicious of other powers and to embitter their relations with them for many years.

If the anticommunist forces had been as strong in the summer of 1918 as they ultimately became in 1919, the Bolshevik regime might have been overthrown. Their early weakness gave the Reds the opportunity to build up their own army under the inspired leadership of Leon Trotsky, a long-time revolutionary who became War Commissar in March, 1918. Until the end of 1919 victory seemed within the Whites' grasp. Then the tide turned. By the end of 1920 the Reds had triumphed and the civil war ended.

THE POLISH WAR AND NATIONAL SEPARATISM

The victory over the Whites did not bring an end to war. Early in 1920 the Poles, aided by Ukrainian nationalists and the southern White Army under General Wrangel, invaded the western Ukraine and White Russia, claiming that these territories belonged to Poland. The fortunes of battle went back and forth until French aid in the form of supplies and military advice won the upper hand for the Poles. Wearied of fighting, the Bolsheviks asked for peace in October, 1920. In the Treaty of Riga of March, 1921, they gave in to Polish demands for territories east of the Polish-Russian ethnic frontier (the so-called Curzon line, suggested in 1919 at the Versailles Peace Conference as the proper boundary between the two countries). More than 4 million Russians lived in these lands, a factor that disturbed Russo-Polish relations until World War II.

The Russians were also confronted with national independence movements in the Ukraine, Transcaucasia, and other frontier regions. In theory the Bolsheviks were committed to national self-determination for such peoples. When faced with concrete demands for independence, however, they proved as unwilling as their tsarist predecessors to free their subject nations and used troops and local Bolsheviks to reestablish Russian control. The status of the non-Russian nationalities remained unclear for two years after their reconquest. Then in 1922 Lenin decided to make Russia a federation, at least in name, against the advice of his specialist on nationality problems, the russified Georgian Josef Stalin. On December 30, 1922, the Union of Socialist Soviet Republics (U.S.S.R.) came into being. It was composed of the Russian Soviet Federated Socialist Republic (R.S.F.S.R.), including most of European Russia and Siberia, and the republics of the Ukraine, White Russia, and Transcaucasia. Later in the 1920's three central Asian republics were added. The federation was dominated by the R.S.F.S.R., the giant of the new organization. The other republics were allowed to retain a large measure of cultural autonomy, but political authority was exercised by Moscow, where the same small group of men controlled the machinery of both the Communist party and the government.

THE PEACE OF PARIS AND ITS AFTERMATH

While civil war raged in Russia, the diplomats of the victorious Allies gathered in Paris in January, 1919, to decide the fate of Germany and its defeated partners. Representatives of twenty-seven nations took part in the proceedings, although most major decisions were made by the Big Four: President Wilson; David Lloyd George, prime minister of Great Britain; Georges Clemenceau, premier of France; and Vittorio Orlando, prime minister of Italy. Since the Italian delegates boycotted the conference for a few weeks to protest the nonrecognition of some of their claims, many important decisions were made by the Big Three. Russia was not invited to the conference, and delegates from the defeated nations were called in only to accept the terms laid down to them. From the beginning, therefore, the conference took on the appearance of a cabal of the victors intended to parcel out the spoils of war.

The Allied leaders were by no means unanimous on the treatment to be accorded to the vanquished. With Clemenceau and the French people generally, the desire for revenge was uppermost; they demanded not only territorial compensation for the humiliation of 1870–71 but also reparations for the heavy costs of the war and security against further German aggression. The Italians demanded large territorial acquisitions at the expense of the now defunct Austro-Hungarian and Ottoman empires, basing their claim on the secret treaty of 1915. Although Lloyd George was personally disposed to moderation, he found himself hampered by the success of his own wartime propaganda in stirring up the British people to hatred of the Germans; as recently as December, 1918, his coalition government had won a general election with promises to punish German leaders and make Germany pay for the war. The claims of the lesser Allies had also to be heeded. Belgium demanded reparation for war damage. Japan had already seized Germany's Chinese and Pacific

EUROPE AFTER WORLD WAR I
NORWAY
Stockholm
FINLAND
L. Ladoga
Leningrad
North Sea
Baltic Sea
ESTONIA
GREAT
SWEDEN
Moscow
DENMARK
LATVIA
IRELAND
MEMEL
LITHUANIA
BRITAIN
N. SCHLESWIG
EAST PRUSSIA
Vilna
UNION OF SOVIET SOCIALIST REPUBLICS
London
Danzig
GERMANY
POLISH CORRIDOR
ATLANTIC OCEAN
NETH
Berlin
POLAND
Warsaw
BELGIUM
EUPEN
MALMEDY
UPPER SILESIA
Kiev
LUX.
Paris
Prague
SAAR
ALSACE LORRAINE
GALICIA
CZECHOSLOVAKIA
Vienna
FRANCE
SWITZ.
AUSTRIA
Budapest
BUKO-VINA
BESSARABIA
HUNGARY
TRANSYL-VANIA
Trieste
SLAVONIA
S. TYROL
CROATIA
BANAT
RUMANIA
PORTUGAL
Fiume
ISTRIA
Bucharest
SPAIN
Belgrade
Black Sea
Lisbon
ITALY
Madrid
CORSICA
YUGOSLAVIA
BULGARIA
Rome
Sofia
ALBANIA
Instanbul
SARDINIA
THRACE
TURKEY
GREECE
ANATOLIA
Mediterranean Sea
SICILY
Athens
AFRICA
CRETE
CYPRUS
Boundary of new nations
Demilitarized zone in the Rhineland
Area lost by Russia
Area lost by Germany
Area lost by Austria-Hungary
Area lost by Bulgaria

possessions. The successor states of the Austro-Hungarian Empire, who had been accorded de facto recognition by the Allies before the end of the war, began to squabble among themselves over disputed territory. The situation in Russia posed a grave threat to the stability of any attempted settlement in eastern Europe.

Only the United States made no territorial or financial claims on the defeated nations. President Wilson, the first American president to travel abroad during his term of office, received tumultuous popular ovations on his way to the conference. Wilson's personal popularity and the enthusiasm in Europe for the United States overshadowed temporarily the gulf between American and Allied war aims, but it did not alter the basic situation. Wilson's vision of the peace was based upon his Fourteen Points, above all on the provision for an international organization that would keep the peace. The Fourteen Points had been accepted by the Germans as the basis of the armistice, but neither Wilson nor the Germans reckoned sufficiently with the determination of the other Allies to press for a vindictive settlement. France and Britain had no great enthusiasm for Wilson's proposed "League of Nations" but used it as a bargaining counter to force concessions from Wilson on reparations and other matters of importance to them. The final form of the treaties, therefore, represented a series of compromises among the victors. The representatives of Germany and the other defeated nations had no option but to sign or face invasion and occupation.

The actual treaties received the names of the various suburbs of Paris in which they were signed. They were the Treaty of Versailles, with Germany (June 28, 1919); the Treaty of Saint-Germain, with Austria (September 10, 1919); the Treaty of Neuilly, with Bulgaria (November 27, 1919); the Treaty of the Trianon, with Hungary (June 4, 1920); and the Treaty of Sèvres, with Turkey (August 20, 1920).

THE TREATY OF VERSAILLES

The armistice of November 11, 1918, was dictated by the French military commander Marshal Foch and signed with only minor modifications by Matthias Erzberger, a German civilian and member of the new provisional government. It was designed to make it impossible for Germany to resume the war. It required the surrender of the entire German submarine fleet, most of the rest of the navy, 5,000 locomotives, 5,000 motor trucks, 150,000 freight cars, and large quantities of arms and munitions. It also provided for German evacuation and Allied occupation of the Rhineland and required that Germany renounce the treaties of Brest Litovsk and Bucharest. All these provisions of the armistice were incorporated in the Versailles Treaty, along with many others more severe.

The treaty deprived Germany of about one-tenth of its prewar territory and a corresponding proportion of its population. Alsace-Lorraine was

Photograph from UPI

The "Big Four" at Versailles, 1919. Left to right: Lloyd George, Vittorio Orlando, Georges Clemenceau, and Woodrow Wilson.

"Clemenceau (having seen with his own eyes the Palais de St. Cloud smoking across the flames of 1871) was, and with every justification, obsessed by the need of French security. Mr. Lloyd George . . . hoped to combine the vae victis *which the British Public expected, with the more reasonable pacification which his own instincts desired. And Signor Orlando, exponent of sacred egoism, sincerely strove to provide his unstable country with those spoils by which alone (so he imagined) the demon of socialism could be exorcised. . . . President Wilson disagreed with almost everything his colleagues suggested."* Harold Nicolson, PEACEMAKING, 1919 (Boston, 1933).

---

returned to France. France occupied the coal-rich Saar Valley, where it operated the coal mines for itself; the treaty provided for a plebiscite after fifteen years to determine the wishes of the inhabitants. Belgium received three small border communes. Wilson blocked a French proposal for a separate buffer state in the Rhineland, but he agreed to its demilitarization and occupation by the Allies for fifteen years. A plebiscite in Schleswig resulted in the northern part of that province returning to Denmark. In the east, Germany gave up Posen and West Prussia to the new state of Poland; West Prussia formed Poland's "corridor to the sea" and separated East Prussia from the rest of Germany. The German-speaking city of Danzig on the Baltic Sea became a free city within the Polish customs frontier. Poland also secured the most valuable part of Upper Silesia with its important mineral resources, although a plebiscite yielded a German majority for the province as a whole. Germany renounced claims on its former colonies, which had already been seized by the Allies.

The Allies sought to prevent future German aggression by rigid limitations on its war-making potential. In addition to Allied occupation of the Rhineland (with Germany bearing the costs) a belt thirty miles wide on the right (east) bank of the Rhine was demilitarized. The German army was to be limited to 100,000 men, and the General Staff was to be abolished. Germany might possess no tanks, no heavy artillery, no poison gas, no military aircraft, and no submarines. The navy was limited to six capital ships and a few supporting craft, and the naval base at Helgoland was razed. Finally, the emperor and the top military leaders were to be handed over for trial as "war criminals." Several of these provisions were never carried out effectively. The Dutch government refused to surrender the emperor, and charges were brought against only a few of the other leaders. In subsequent years the Germans found ways of circumventing the restrictions on their armed forces. The General Staff remained intact.

The Allies also imposed commercial restrictions on the Germans. They had to hand over all merchant ships of over 1,600 tons, half of those between 800 and 1,600 tons, and a quarter of the fishing fleet, as well as much coal and other raw materials. The German rivers were internationalized, and the Kiel canal was opened to the shipping of all nations. German property in Allied countries was confiscated and sold, and Germany's power to impose tariffs and other trade barriers was restricted.

The wisdom and expediency of these measures have often been debated. Many argued that they were not severe enough, especially Frenchmen. Others, the proponents of a "soft" peace, alleged that by so penalizing the Germans the peace treaty built up a store of bitterness and resentment that made a resumption of aggression inevitable. The validity of the arguments cannot be established, for the actual course of subsequent events was compatible with both. It is a fact that the treaty did not provide adequate means for enforcing all the penalties it imposed. In that sense it was unwise. Of far greater significance, however, were two additional provisions of the treaty.

WAR GUILT AND GERMAN REPARATIONS

Article 231 of the Treaty of Versailles read as follows: "The Allied and Associated Governments affirm and Germany accepts the responsibility of Germany and her allies for causing all the loss and damage to which the Allied and Associated Governments and their nationals have been subjected as a consequence of the war imposed upon them by the aggression of Germany and her allies." This statement was intended to justify Allied claims to German reparations, but at the same time it saddled Germany with the entire moral blame for the war, including the actions of its allies. In subsequent years it served to discredit the republic that accepted it and enabled the Germans to persuade themselves that the entire treaty lacked any moral force.

The question of reparations was itself a complex matter that excited angry passions on both sides. France and Britain demanded that Germany pay not only damages to civilians (reparations proper) but also the entire cost incurred by the Allied governments in prosecuting the war (an indemnity). Wilson made no claims for the United States and tried to dissuade the others from pressing theirs; but the American argument was not a strong one inasmuch as the United States insisted on repayment in full of the large loans it had made to the Allies to enable them to prosecute the war. A stronger but equally unheeded argument was put forward by the British economist John Maynard Keynes (1883–1946), who pointed out the literal impossibility of requiring Germany to pay the full costs of the war. According to him, even to force Germany to pay any sizable fraction would seriously derange the international economy and react adversely on the economic interests of the Allies themselves, as well as endanger the economic viability and political stability of Germany. His prediction proved to be all too accurate. The eventual compromise required Germany to pay as much as the Allies thought they could possibly extract, but in deference to Wilson the entire amount was called "reparations."

The method of assessing and collecting the reparations added further to German difficulties and exasperation. Since the Allied experts were unable to estimate the maximum bill before the treaty was signed, the treaty merely stated that the German government would be notified of the full amount it would have to pay "on or before May 1, 1921." In the meantime it would have to pay 5 billion dollars, against which offsets were allowed for confiscated German property and deliveries in kind. The sum ultimately imposed on April 27, 1921, was 33 billion dollars, an amount several times as large as Germany's total annual national income.

That German government that signed the onerous and humiliating *Diktat* of Versailles – as it was subsequently called in Germany, notably by Adolf Hitler – was not the government that fought the war. Immediately after the emperor's enforced abdication a new ministry formed by the Socialists, the Center party, and the Progressives (or Democrats, as they renamed themselves) proclaimed a republic and called for elections to a national assembly to draw up a new constitution. With the emperor in exile and the army in defeat, the chief opposition to the new republic came at first from the radical left wing of the old Social Democratic party, who now called themselves Spartacists. In January, 1919, they attempted a revolution of the Bolshevik type in Berlin. Although they were defeated by the provisional government with the aid of the remnants of the army, the revolt constituted a bad omen for the fledgling republic. In subsequent years the republic had to fend off domestic attacks from both Communists and the extreme Right as well as to struggle with the burdens laid on it by the Allies.

When the terms of the Treaty of Versailles became known, several ministers resigned rather than sign it. Their successors faced up to the inevitable, for Germany was in no position to resist. After futile attempts to have the war guilt clause removed, the government accepted the treaty rather than undergo indefinite occupation by Allied forces.

REDRAWING THE MAP OF EASTERN EUROPE

The minor treaties with Austria, Hungary, Bulgaria, and Turkey sought vainly to impress the seal of legitimacy on accomplished facts. The basic dispositions had already been made on the field of battle in the last weeks of the war, but continuing civil and international conflict kept the entire area of eastern Europe and the Near East in an unsettled state for several years after the conclusion of the treaties.

The breakup of the Austro-Hungarian Empire had been decided by the Congress of Oppressed Nationalities meeting at Rome in April, 1918, and by the action of various national councils of the subject nationalities. The emperor abdicated on November 11, 1918, and the proclamation of separate republics in Austria and Hungary soon followed. The Treaty of Saint-Germain ratified this situation but at the same time forced the new republic of Austria to pay reparations on behalf of the old empire. Austria recognized the independence of Czechoslovakia, Yugoslavia, Poland, and Hungary, and ceded the Trentino, South Tyrol, and Trieste to Italy. Formerly the center of an empire of 50 million, Austria was now a truncated state of less than 8 million whose economic viability was subject to great doubt. The Austrians themselves would have preferred to unite with Germany, but although this course was in accord with Wilson's principle of self-determination, it was specifically forbidden by both the Saint-Germain and the Versailles treaties.

Revolution, counterrevolution, and border wars delayed the separate treaty with Hungary until June 4, 1920. In March, 1919, a Communist revolt headed by Bela Kun overthrew the new republic and promptly went to war with Czechoslovakia and Rumania, who were destined under the peace treaty to receive large slices of Hungarian territory. The Rumanians were victorious. They overthrew the Communists and occupied Budapest from August, 1919, until February, 1920, when the great powers persuaded them to withdraw. In March, 1920, Admiral Nicholas Horthy proclaimed Hungary a monarchy with a vacant throne and named himself regent and chief of state. The counterrevolution in effect restored the old order. The Treaty of the Trianon, which in its territorial provisions merely confirmed decisions already made, sheared the historic kingdom of Hungary of almost three-fourths of its territory and two-thirds of its population. Yugoslavia took Croatia, Slavonia, and part of the Banat of Temesvar; Rumania took the rest of the Banat, Transylvania, and part of the Hungarian plain; Slovakia was joined to Bohemia in the new state of Czechoslovakia; and Austria received a portion of western Hungary near Vienna. All these cessions provoked constant irritation between Hungary and its neighbors over the next twenty years. To insure themselves against Hungarian attempts to regain lost territory, Czechoslovakia, Rumania, and Yugoslavia formed the so-called Little Entente.

The Treaty of Neuilly cut Bulgaria back to less than its 1913 territory. Bulgaria gave up its Aegean coastline to Greece and other small bits of territory to Rumania and Yugoslavia. Like Austria and Hungary, Bulgaria had to make reparations payments and suffer restrictions on its armed forces. Nevertheless, of all the former Central Powers Bulgaria received the mildest treatment.

In Turkey the situation was even more complicated and confused than in Hungary. During the war the Allies had made several secret treaties regarding the disposition of the old Ottoman Empire, envisioning among other things Russian occupation of Constantinople and Greek and Italian acquisitions on the mainland of Anatolia. After the Russian Revolution the Bolsheviks published these treaties to embarrass the Allies. President Wilson, who had not been a party to them, refused to recognize them as valid or binding. Nevertheless, the Greeks and Italians supported by other Allied forces made landings in Asia Minor. In August, 1920, the helpless government of the sultan was forced to sign the Treaty of Sèvres. By this treaty Turkey renounced all non-Turkish territory (principally the Arab states at the eastern end of the Mediterranean) and recognized the Greek and Italian claims on Anatolia.

Meanwhile, the Turkish Nationalist movement under the leadership of Mustapha Kemal (later called Kemal Atatürk – father of the Turks), who advocated a strictly Turkish nation following the modern Western model, had been gathering strength in inland centers since the end of the war. After the signing of the Treaty of Sèvres the Nationalist movement definitely broke with the government of the sultan and refused to recognize the treaty. Obtaining military supplies from Soviet Russia, Kemal's forces launched a counterattack against the Greeks and persuaded the Italians to withdraw. After routing the Greeks in 1922, they deposed the sultan and abolished the sultanate. In the following year Kemal's government signed the Treaty of Lausanne, which replaced the inoperative Treaty of Sèvres and became the definitive treaty of peace between Turkey and the Allies. Turkey abandoned all claims to non-Turkish territory but regained eastern Thrace, including the city of Adrianople. Greece retained most of the Aegean Islands, and Italy retained the Dodecanese, but both renounced claims on Anatolia, and Greece agreed to a large-scale compulsory exchange of populations. More than a million Greeks whose ancestors had lived in Asia Minor since ancient times were eventually repatriated to Greece, and a somewhat smaller number of Turks living in Greece took their places. Finally, Britain obtained formal possession of Cyprus, which it had occupied since 1878.

POSTWAR POLITICAL TURMOIL

The conclusion of the peace treaties did not mean the end of conflict in eastern Europe. Despite the pious pronouncements at Paris, it proved impossible to settle the boundaries "along clearly recognizable lines of nationality." In fact, the new frontiers left 3 million Germans inside the new state of Czechoslovakia, half a million both in Poland and Yugoslavia, and lesser numbers in the other countries. A million and a half Magyars lived under Rumanian control, 700,000 lived in Czechoslovakia, and 500,000 lived in Yugoslavia. Italy and Yugoslavia disputed the possession of Fiume and the Dalmatian coast until 1924, when Italy acquired Fiume in exchange for other coastal points. Yugoslavia was also torn by internal strife over the demands of the Croatians for a federal state in opposition to the Serbian desire for centralization. Italy and Greece resorted to warfare over the island of Corfu in 1923.

Greece, like most other Balkan countries, had its share of internal troubles. King Constantine, who had been deposed in 1917, was recalled in 1920 but deposed again in 1922. His son, George II, followed him into exile the following year. The Greeks proclaimed a republic in 1924, then recalled George in 1935. Meanwhile the country had been ruled by a succession of military juntas, one of which countenanced an invasion of Bulgaria in 1925. Bulgaria, for its part, engaged in border raids on Yugoslavia.

Austria and Hungary disputed the Burgenland, a small strip of land in historic Hungary only fifteen miles from Vienna and populated mainly by Germans. As a result of a plebiscite in 1921 most of it went to Austria. Because of its tense relations with its neighbors, Hungary's internal problems sometimes had international repercussions. On two occasions in 1921 ex-emperor Karl of Hapsburg returned to assume the royal dignity in Budapest, but on both occasions threats by Yugoslavia and Czechoslovakia to go to war forced the Hungarians to return him to exile. Hungary remained a monarchy without a king.

Poland proved to be one of the most troublesome countries of eastern Europe. It owed its resurrection in the first instance to rival attempts by Russians and Germans during the war to win Polish support with promises of independence. The Allies also promised independence, and the Treaty of Versailles fixed the western boundaries of the country, subject to slight subsequent alterations. A brief border war flared between Poland and Czechoslovakia in 1919–20 over the former Duchy of Teschen; Allied diplomats settled the matter by a division of the disputed area. In Upper Silesia the Poles refused to accept the results of a plebiscite in which the inhabitants voted overwhelmingly for reunion with Germany. A force of Polish irregulars occupied the area and with French support obtained a decision from the League of Nations granting the most important industrial areas to Poland.

The eastern boundary could not be settled in Paris owing to the absence of the Russians. British foreign minister Lord Curzon suggested a line drawn along the rather indistinct linguistic frontier that deprived the Poles of the city of Vilna. They occupied Vilna in defiance of the League of Nations and precipitated a long dispute with the new Baltic state of Lithuania. The Poles insisted on their historic boundaries of 1772, which included large areas of White Russia and the Ukraine and involved them in war with Russia. In 1921 the Polish borders were temporarily stabilized, but their long, exposed land frontiers populated by alien ethnic groups remained a constant temptation to the aggressive ambitions of resurgent Germany and Russia.

Russia for its part made a virtue of weakness while still in the midst of its own civil war. The Bolsheviks denounced imperialism and disclaimed any territorial ambitions beyond the historic frontiers of Russia proper. In 1920 they recognized the independence of Finland, Estonia, Latvia, and Lithuania. In 1921 they signed the Treaty of Riga with Poland and made treaties of friendship with Turkey, Persia (Iran), and Afghanistan. To Turkey and Persia they ceded small bits of disputed territory in the Caucasus area. In 1922, in the wake of an unsuccessful general European conference at Genoa, the two pariahs of Europe, Germany and the Soviet Union, concluded at Rapallo, Italy, a far-reaching agreement of friendship that contained provisions for mutual economic, technical, and military assistance. Although the Soviet-German understanding proved to be unstable, it enabled both countries to circumvent restrictions placed upon them by the victorious Western powers and cast a shadow of things to come.

THE GERMAN INFLATION

Germany's capacity to pay reparations depended ultimately on its ability to export more than it imported in order to gain the foreign currency or gold in which the payments had to be made. For a time it maintained a small surplus, but the other economic restrictions imposed by the treaty ensured that the surplus could never be large enough to meet the entire bill. Moreover, economic interests adversely affected by German competition persuaded Allied governments to raise new barriers against German exports, adding further to Germany's difficulties. In the late summer of 1922 the value of the German mark began to decline disastrously as a result of the heavy pressure of reparations payments. By the end of the year the pressure was so great that Germany ceased payments altogether.

French and Belgian troops promptly invaded the Ruhr in January, 1923, took over the coal mines and railroads, and attempted to force the German mine owners and workers to deliver coal. The Germans met the occupation with passive resistance: the miners, supported by both the mining companies and the government, refused to work. The government printed huge quantities of paper money to distribute as compensation payments to workers and employers, setting in motion a wave of uncontrolled inflation. The impasse lasted until the autumn of 1923, by which time the mark had depreciated to such an infinitesimal figure that it was worth less than the paper on which it was printed.

The adverse consequences of the inflation could not be confined to Germany. The French franc depreciated by one-fourth, and the international economy was confronted by a crisis much as Keynes had predicted. The French withdrew from the Ruhr, and a hastily convoked international commission under the chairmanship of Charles G. Dawes, an American investment banker, recommended a scaling down of annual reparations payments, the reorganization of the German Reichsbank, and a large international loan to Germany. Meanwhile a German financial expert, Hjalmar Schacht, initiated a plan to replace the depreciated and discredited German currency. As a result of these operations, especially the large loan to Germany (most of which was raised in the United States), the German economy revived and actually prospered with a continued inflow of American capital until the new and greater international economic crisis that lasted from 1929 to 1933.

The disastrous inflation left deep scars on German society. The unequal incidence of inflation on individuals resulted in drastic redistributions of income and wealth. While a few clever speculators gained enormous fortunes from the sudden and violent fluctuation of financial values, most citizens, especially the lower middle classes, saw their modest savings wiped out in a matter of months or even weeks. People whose money income was fixed (pensioners, bond holders, many salaried employees) suffered a sharp decline in their standard of living as a result of the lowered purchasing power of their fixed incomes. The inflation created personal hardship and social discontent, with many of those affected becoming converted to radical political programs of both the Right and the Left. Significantly, both Communists and Nationalists made large gains at the expense of the moderate democratic parties in the

Reichstag elections in the spring of 1924. In the following year retired Field Marshal von Hindenburg, candidate of the Rightist parties, became president, succeeding the Social Democrat Friedrich Ebert.

The Dawes Plan temporarily relieved but did not solve the problems created by reparations. In the summer of 1929 a new international commission headed by the American Owen D. Young reported a plan designed as a permanent solution. Before it could take effect the great crisis of 1929 again threw the international economy into a tailspin. As the financial crisis deepened President Hoover in 1931 proposed a one-year moratorium on all intergovernmental debts, including reparations and the inter-Allied war debts. In effect, the moratorium marked the end of reparations. Before normal financial relations could be resumed, Adolf Hitler came to power in Germany and proclaimed an end to "interest slavery."

ECONOMIC DISINTEGRATION AND COLLAPSE

Prior to 1914 the world economy had functioned freely and on the whole efficiently. In spite of some restrictions in the form of protective tariffs, private monopolies, and international cartels, the bulk of economic activity was regulated by free markets. The prices of commodities were determined not by governmental fiat but by supply and demand. A rise in the price of one commodity constituted a signal to the entire world that the commodity was in short supply in relation to demand, and the rise would accordingly stimulate an increase in production that tended to restore the price to equilibrium; conversely, a fall in price indicated an oversupply in relation to demand and was similarly self-adjusting. As a consequence, each area of the world tended to specialize in the production of goods for which it was best suited, taking into account its resources, the skills and education of its population, and other natural and acquired advantages.

Another feature of the prewar international economy was a general adherence to the gold standard. Most nations undertook to buy or sell their national currencies for a fixed weight of gold, which guaranteed stability of exchange rates (the rate at which one currency could be exchanged for another) and stimulated international trade and investment. These and other features made the world economy highly specialized and interdependent. Each nation depended on the others for goods that it did not produce and, in many cases, for capital as well. Such interdependence had the supreme advantage of greatly increasing productivity for the world as a whole, but it also had the disadvantage of making the economy extremely susceptible to outside shocks, of which war was the most damaging.

ECONOMIC CONSEQUENCES OF THE WAR

In addition to human casualties, direct war damage during World War I included the destruction of housing, industrial plants and equipment, livestock and farm equipment, transportation and communications facilities, and so forth. Most of the damage took place in northern France, Belgium, a small area of northeastern Italy, and the battlefields of eastern Europe. Ocean shipping also suffered greatly, primarily as a result of submarine warfare. The damage has been estimated at more than $150 billion, although such estimates are by their nature subject to wide margins of error. Not included are losses of production such as those occasioned by shortages of manpower and raw materials in industry or by overcropping and lack of fertilizer and draft animals in agriculture. In central and eastern Europe, which were cut off from economic relations with the rest of the world and further disrupted by the marching and countermarching of armies, the fall in agricultural output had reduced large areas to the point of mass starvation.

The war also occasioned indirect damage to the economic mechanism as a result of the disruption and dislocation of normal economic relations. Unlike the direct damage, the indirect damage did not cease with the war itself but continued to take its toll well into the postwar decade. In every belligerent nation the imposition of direct governmental controls on prices, production, and labor distorted the normal relationships of the economy, artificially stimulating some sectors and restricting others. The reestablishment of peacetime relationships after the removal of controls took place with difficulty. An immediate postwar boom in 1919–20, during which both consumers and producers sought to make up for wartime shortages, was followed in 1920–21 by a severe but relatively brief recession.

A more lasting dislocation resulted from the loss of foreign markets. During the war overseas nations undertook to manufacture for themselves or buy from other overseas nations goods that they had formerly purchased in Europe. Several Latin American and Asian nations established manufacturing industries which they protected after the war with high tariffs. The United States and Japan, which had already developed important manufactures before the war, expanded into overseas markets formerly regarded as the exclusive preserve of European manufacturers. Britain, highly dependent on overseas trade, was especially hard hit; Germany but slightly less so.

As had the loss of foreign markets, the loss of income from shipping and other services retarded the recovery of the European economy. Before the war Britain had by far the largest merchant fleet in the world; it carried goods not only to and from Britain, but also between foreign countries, thus adding substantially to Britain's overseas income. Britain emerged from the war with its fleet much diminished, while the United States had a greatly augmented merchant fleet and became a major competitor in international shipping for the first time since the American Civil War. Germany, which had to give up its merchant fleet in payment of reparations, also suffered. London and to a lesser extent other European financial centers likewise lost some of their income from banking, insurance, and other financial and commercial services, which had been transferred to New York and elsewhere (Switzerland, for example) during the war.

Before the war Britain, France, and Germany were the most important foreign investors. Since Britain and France in particular imported more than they exported, the income from foreign investments supplemented other invisible income (from banking and insurance, for instance) to close the gap left by the visible trade. Germany's investments in belligerent countries were confiscated during the war, and subsequently all were liquidated against reparations claims. Britain and France were both obliged to sell many of their investments to finance the purchase of urgently needed war materials. Other investments declined in value as a result of inflation and related currency difficulties. Still others suffered default or outright repudiation, notably the large French investments in Russia, which the Soviet government refused to recognize. Since Britain was the largest foreign investor as well as the most dependent on imported foodstuffs and raw materials, again it suffered most. The United States, on the other hand, converted itself from a net debtor into a net creditor as a result of its large loans to the Allies.

A fifth dislocation in both national and international economies resulted from inflation. The pressures of wartime finance forced all belligerents (and some nonbelligerents) except the United States off the gold standard. They all resorted to large-scale borrowing and the printing of paper money to finance the war. This caused prices to rise (which is the equivalent of a decline in the value of money), though they did not all rise in the same proportion. At the end of the war prices in the United States were on the average about 2.5 times as high as in 1914; in Britain, about 3 times; in France, about 5.5 times; in Germany, more than 15 times; and in Bulgaria, more than 20 times. The great disparity in prices and in the values of currency made the resumption of international trade difficult, and caused unfortunate social and political repercussions such as those in Germany.

ECONOMIC CONSEQUENCES OF THE PEACE

As though the wartime damage and dislocations were not enough, the peace settlement further exacerbated the difficulty of economic recovery and readjustment. The peacemakers did not intend this to happen (except in the treatment of Germany); they simply failed to take account of economic realities. Two major categories of economic difficulty resulted from the peace treaties: the growth of economic nationalism, and monetary and financial problems. In neither of them were the peace treaties solely to blame; yet in both the treaties added to the problems involved instead of attempting to solve them.

The prewar Austro-Hungarian Empire, however politically anachronistic, had performed a valuable economic function by providing a large free-trade area in the Danube basin. It encompassed manufacturing areas in Bohemia and the vicinity of Vienna and other large cities, as well as vast agricultural regions in the Hungarian and Slavic parts of the empire. The interchange of goods was mutually beneficial. The new nations that issued from the breakup of the empire were jealous of one another and fearful of great power domination. They therefore asserted their nationhood in the economic sphere by trying to become more or less self-sufficient in both agricultural and industrial production. Although complete self-sufficiency was a manifest impossibility because of their small size and generally backward economic condition, their efforts to achieve it hindered the economic recovery of the entire region and added to its instability. The height of absurdity came with the disruption of transportation. Before the war two large railroad companies had served the entire empire. Immediately after the war when borders were subject to dispute and border fighting continued, each country simply refused to allow the railroad locomotives and cars in its territory to leave. For a time trade came to an almost complete standstill. Eventually international agreements overcame such extremes of economic nationalism, but other types of restriction remained: in addition to protective tariffs, new devices in the form of physical quotas and discriminatory treatment of foreign merchandise.

Economic nationalism was not restricted to the new nations that emerged from the breakup of empires. During its civil war Russia simply disappeared from the international economy. When it re-emerged under the Soviet regime, its economic relations were conducted in a manner completely different from any previously experienced. The state became the sole buyer and seller in international trade. It bought and sold only what its political rulers regarded as strategically necessary or expedient.

In the West, countries that formerly had been highly dependent on international trade resorted to a variety of restrictions including protective tariffs and also more drastic curtailments on trade, such as import quotas and absolute prohibitions. At the same time they sought to stimulate their own exports by granting export subsidies or setting the foreign exchange value of their currencies at artificially low rates. Among the major European nations France was one of the worst offenders, but it was by no means alone. Great Britain, before the war the great champion of free international trade, had imposed tariffs during the war as a measure of war finance. They remained after the war, and in the 1920's new industries producing for the domestic market grew up beneath the umbrella of tariff protection. The United States, which already had relatively high tariffs before the war, raised them to unprecedented levels thereafter. The Emergency Tariff Act of 1921 placed an absolute embargo on imports of German dyestuffs. (The dyestuff industry had not even existed in the United States before the war; it began with the confiscation of German patent rights during the war.) The Fordney-McCumber Tariff Act of 1922 contained the highest rates in American tariff history, but even those were surpassed by the Smoot-Hawley Tariff of 1930.

The adverse economic consequences of this neomercantilism, as such policies were called, did not stop with the immediate application of the laws in question. Each new measure of restriction provoked retaliation by other nations whose interests were affected. Whereas total world trade had more than doubled in the two decades before the war, it rarely achieved the prewar level in the two decades that followed. During the same period the foreign trade of European countries, which had also doubled in the two prewar decades, equaled the prewar figure in but a single year – 1929. In 1932 and 1933 it was lower than it had been at the end of the nineteenth century. Such exaggerated economic nationalism delayed the return to normal economic intercourse between nations and contributed to the heightening of tension in international politics.

The monetary and financial disorders occasioned by the war and gravely aggravated by the peace treaties led eventually to a complete breakdown of the international economy. The problem of reparations was at the heart of these disorders, but the "reparations tangle" was in reality a complex problem involving the question of inter-Allied war debts and the whole mechanism of international finance. The insistence of Allied statesmen, especially Americans, in treating each question in isolation instead of recognizing their relationships was a major factor in the subsequent debacle.

Until the United States entered the war, Britain was the chief financier of the Allied war effort. By 1917 it had loaned almost 4 billion dollars to its allies. France had loaned 500 million, roughly equal to its borrowings from Britain. Over half of all these loans had gone to Russia and were repudiated by the Soviet regime at the end of the war. When the United States entered the war, it took over the role of financier from Britain, whose financial resources were almost exhausted. By the end of the war inter-Allied debts had reached almost 20 billion dollars, about one-half of which had been loaned by the United States government. Among the European allies the loans had been loans in name only;

actually they treated them as direct subsidies and expected to cancel the indebtedness at the end of the war. They naturally regarded the American loans in the same light, all the more in that the United States had been a latecomer to the war, had contributed less in both manpower and materials, and had suffered negligible war damage. The United States, however, regarded the loans as commercial propositions. Although it agreed after the war to lower the rate of interest and lengthen the period of repayment, it insisted on repayment of the principal in full.

The failure to link the question of war debts with that of reparations revealed the full extent of misunderstanding of the basic problem. The United States wanted the Allies to renounce reparations altogether, or at least hold them to a minimum, but at the same time insisted on repayment of the war debts. The French wanted the United States to cancel the war debts but insisted on collecting reparations. The British suggested the cancellation of both, but the Americans stubbornly refused to recognize any relationship between the two. The American attitude was summed up in a remark subsequently made by President Coolidge: "They hired the money, didn't they?"

In fact, given the weakened economies of the European countries and the precarious state of the international economy, France, Britain, and the other allies could repay the United States' loans only if they received an equivalent amount in the form of reparations. Germany and the other defeated powers could in fact pay reparations only if they exported far more than they imported, or if they in turn received unilateral transfers of funds from an outside power. The crisis of 1923 revealed the inadequacy of the arrangements. The system was temporarily saved by the Dawes Plan of 1924 with its provision of a large international loan, chiefly from the United States, to allow Germany to get on its feet and resume reparations payments. It was followed by a further flow of American capital to Germany in the form of private loans to German municipalities and business corporations, who borrowed extensively in the United States and used the proceeds for modernization. In the process the German government obtained the foreign exchange it needed to pay reparations.

For the five years from 1924 to 1929 it seemed that "normalcy" had returned. Reconstruction of physical damage had been largely achieved; the most urgent and immediate postwar problems had been solved; and under the newly formed League of Nations and the "spirit of Locarno" (see pp. 380–381) a new era in international relations apparently had dawned. Most countries, especially the United States, Germany, and France, experienced a period of prosperity. Yet the basis of the prosperity was fragile indeed, depending on the continued voluntary flow of funds from America to Germany.

THE GREAT DEPRESSION

Unlike Europe, the United States emerged from the war stronger than ever. In economic terms alone, it had converted itself from a net debtor to a net creditor, had won new markets from European producers both at home and abroad, and had established a highly favorable balance of trade. With its mass markets, growing population, and rapid technological advance it seemed to have found the key to perpetual prosperity. Although it experienced a sharp depression in 1920–21, the drop proved to be brief, and for almost a decade its growing economy felt only minor fluctuations. Social critics who insisted on revealing the disgraceful conditions in both urban and rural slums, or who pointed out that the new prosperity was shared most unequally between the urban middle classes on the one hand and factory workers and farmers on the other, were dismissed by the former as cranks who did not share the American dream. For them the "new era" had arrived.

In the summer of 1928 American banks and investors began to cut down their purchase of German bonds in order to invest their funds through the New York stock market, which accordingly began a spectacular rise. During the speculative boom of the "great bull market" many individuals with modest incomes were tempted to purchase stock on credit. By the late summer of 1929 European economies were already feeling the strain of the cessation of American investments abroad, but since stock prices were at an all-time high, American investors and officials paid scant heed. With European financial institutions strained to the utmost in the attempt to continue international payments, and with American credit resources locked up in stock market speculation, any small quiver in the financial system could set off a chain reaction that might bring down the whole system.

On October 24, 1929 – Black Thursday in American financial history – a wave of panic selling on the stock exchange caused stock prices to plummet and eliminated millions of dollars of fictitious paper values. By mid-November the index of stock prices stood at half the peak it had reached before the crash. Banks called in loans, forcing still more investors to throw their stocks on the market at whatever prices they would bring. Americans who had invested in Europe ceased to make new investments and sold existing assets there in order to repatriate the funds. Throughout 1930 the withdrawal of capital from Europe continued, placing an intolerable strain on the entire financial system. In May, 1931, the Austrian Creditanstalt, one of the largest and most important banks in central Europe, suspended payments. The panic spread from bank to bank, industry to industry, country to country. Millions of workers in all countries were thrown out of work, adding further to the deflationary cycle.

Table 1 *Economic Collapse, 1929–1932*

	1929	*1932*
United States		
Index of industrial production (1923–1925 = 100)	119	64
Unemployed (in 1,000's)	1,864	13,182
General wholesale price index (1910–1914 = 100)	139	95
Foreign trade[1] (millions of dollars)	9,783	2,967
United Kingdom		
Index of industrial production (1924 = 100)	110.6	84.9
Unemployed (in 1,000's)	994	2,273
General wholesale price index (1913 = 100)	141.1	94.1
Foreign trade[1] (millions of dollars)	8,956	3,555
Germany		
Index of industrial production (1928 = 100)	101	60
Unemployed (in 1,000's)	1,679	5,575
General wholesale price index (1913 = 100)	137.2	96.5
Foreign trade[1] (millions of dollars)	6,415	2,471
France		
Index of industrial production (1913 = 100)	127	96
Unemployed (in 1,000's)	9.7	305
General wholesale price index (1901–1910 = 100)	143	94
Foreign trade[1] (millions of dollars)	4,247	1,945

[1] Imports plus exports.

Sources: E. Varga, *Mirovye Ekonomicheskie Krizisy 1848–1935* (Moscow, 1937), I, part II, tables 41, 42, 43, 44 for index of industrial production and general wholesale price index; International Labor Office, *Year-Book of Labor Statistics, 1935–36* (Geneva, 1936), table 1, for unemployment statistics; W. S. and E. S. Woytinsky, *World Commerce and Governments* (New York, 1955), pp. 48, 50 for foreign trade statistics.

President Hoover, forced by circumstances to recognize the interdependence of the international economy, called for a one-year moratorium on all intergovernmental payments in the summer of 1931, but it was too late to stem the panic. In September Great Britain, which had returned to the gold standard with great difficulty in 1925, was again forced off, followed by many others. After a severe American banking crisis that included thousands of failures and led to the decree of a four-day "bank holiday" as an emergency measure by Franklin Roosevelt, the new president, the United States also abandoned the gold standard in the spring of 1933. The international monetary chaos was complete.

CRISIS OF THE SPIRIT

The twentieth century began in an atmosphere of optimism. Pessimists were in a minority and spoke in muted voices. For the multitude the age was one of universal progress. In the European world living standards were improving more rapidly than ever, democracy was spreading at an unprecedented rate, and large-scale war seemed a thing of the past. World War I, followed by economic collapse and the rise of totalitarian political systems, brought radical changes in outlook. As early as 1918 Oswald Spengler, a German philosopher of history, published his influential book *The Decline of the West,* in which he asserted that Western civilization was dying. For many the titles of two of T. S. Eliot's poems, *The Waste Land* (1922) and *The Hollow Men* (1925), symbolized the spirit of the times. The latter concludes with the mockingly bitter lines

> This is the way the world ends
> Not with a bang but a whimper.

By the 1930's the dominant mood was one of stark pessimism.

A noted literary critic of the 1890's referred to fin-de-siècle literature as a "decadent movement." Decadent or not, it proved to be the germ of much creative literature of the next century, and especially of the grim interwar decades. The stylistic features of fin-de-siècle literature and art – symbolism and free verse in poetry, stream of consciousness in fiction, greater abstraction and nonobjectivism in painting and sculpture – were increasingly exploited and subjected to further experimentation and innovation. Cubism and futurism, the last of the pre-World War I fads in art, were succeeded by dadaism and surrealism. They had in common subjects drawn from dreams and the subconscious mind and methods of execution that seemed to lack conscious design. The dadaists were deliberately absurd in their revolt against prevailing taste, morality, and behavior. One of them wrote of their creations, "These pictures are Realities in themselves, without meaning or cerebral intention. We rejected everything that was copy or description, and allowed the Elementary and Spontaneous to react in full freedom." The fad of dadaism soon passed, but surrealism, which took itself more seriously, continued to influence young artists for many years. The most renowned artists of the first half of the twentieth century belonged to no single school, although they greatly influenced surrealism and similar movements. Among them were Marc Chagall, Vasily Kandinsky, Paul Klee, and the most famous of all, Pablo Picasso.

The new departure in music dated from the publication in 1911 of Arnold Schönberg's *Theory of Harmony*. Schönberg abandoned traditional scales in favor of the twelve-tone scale. Igor Stravinsky and Paul

Hindemith achieved similar effects with atonality and polytonality. The world premiere of Stravinsky's *Sacre du Printemps* in Paris in 1913 ended in a riot that had to be quelled by police; the composer escaped from the angry crowd through a window backstage. One of the early advocates of futurism in music wrote: "The art of combining musical sounds reached its peak at the end of the nineteenth century. In the music of the future the sounds of our mechanical civilization – its machinery and crowded cities – will be subtly combined into an art of noises."

In spite of the mood of disillusion and despair that darkened the interwar years, the need for postwar reconstruction and continued urbanization stimulated the development of new architectural forms. One of the most creative centers of architectural thought and design was the school called the Bauhaus, founded in Germany by Walter Gropius in 1919. In the Bauhaus Gropius brought together not only architects but also interior decorators, furniture designers, and even painters; Kandinsky and Klee were two of its teachers. The style of architecture that Gropius favored was functionalism. Le Corbusier (the pseudonym of the Franco-Swiss Charles-Edouard Jenneret), at one time associated with Gropius and one of the leading exponents of the new architecture, defined a house as "a machine for living in." The triumph of the Nazis, traditionalists in art and architecture, halted the innovations in Germany, but indirectly led to their spread elsewhere as many famous architects, Gropius himself among them, fled abroad.

The stupidity of war, the wastefulness of economic depression, and the divergence between the ideals and realities of Western culture gave rise to a literature of social protest. H. G. Wells wrote novels frankly intended as tracts for social reform. Marcel Proust, perhaps the outstanding French novelist of the first half of the twentieth century, pictured society in a state of dissolution as a result of inner moral corruption in outwardly respectable people. Aldous Huxley revolted against the stifling conformity fostered by the modern industrial system; his most famous novel, *Brave New World* (1932), is a bitter satire of that system. American writers such as Sinclair Lewis, John Steinbeck, John Dos Passos, and Ernest Hemingway depicted the futility of war, criticized the existence of poverty in the midst of plenty, and satirized the hypocritical complacency of America's middle classes. Another American author, Pearl Buck, became the third American to win a Nobel Prize for literature (after Lewis and Eugene O'Neill) for her sensitive, dramatic story of ordinary peasants caught up in the Chinese civil war, *The Good Earth* (1932). Two of the most influential novels of the period were the posthumously published works of a driven man, Franz Kafka; in both *The Trial* (1925) and *The Castle* (1926) a semi-anonymous anti-hero finds himself involved in a living nightmare in which his efforts to understand lead only to further bewilderment and eventual destruction. "Kafkaesque" became a synonym for the predicament of modern man, and his novels gained a prophetic reputation after the revelation of Nazi torture chambers and Russian purge trials.

Freudian thought exerted an enormous influence on literature in the interwar period and afterward. D. H. Lawrence was one of the earliest authors consciously affected by Freud, but after World War I very few writers could avoid his influence altogether. The greater frequency of sexual themes and symbols and the more graphic description of sexual episodes, even by writers otherwise ignorant of the significance of Freudian psychology, testified to his influence. Although writers of the stature of Thomas Mann, one of Germany's greatest novelists, did not emphasize sexual matters, they acknowledged the importance of Freud's elucidation of the role of subconscious motives and irrational drives in human nature. Freud's influence was also heavy on Eugene O'Neill, possibly the most powerful dramatist in any language in the interwar period. One of his closest rivals for that distinction was the Italian Luigi Pirandello whose play *Six Characters in Search of an Author* seemed to symbolize the confusion and aimlessness of the interwar years.

LIBERAL ATTEMPTS AT RECONSTRUCTION CHAPTER FOURTEEN

The twentieth-century inheritors of nineteenth-century liberalism little realized the extent of the damage the war caused society. They regarded the war as a great catastrophe, but failed to perceive either its origins in the nineteenth century or its full implications for the future. For them it was one of the unfortunate accidents of history, the responsibility of a relatively small number of willful, malicious men – militarists and autocratic rulers. At most, it was evidence that the liberal reforms of the nineteenth century had not proceeded far enough in eliminating archaic survivals from the past. Accordingly, their program for postwar reconstruction was appealingly simple and straightforward, involving above all the extension of liberal principles to all areas of life. It implied further democratic reforms in countries that already had representative governments (women received the vote for the first time in Britain, Germany, the United States, and several smaller democracies in the decade following the war); the establishment of compact nation-states with parliamentary governments in areas of eastern Europe previously dominated by autocratic, multinational empires; and on the international plane the creation of an organization by means of which the independent nation-states, without surrendering their sovereignty, might work in concert for the maintenance of peace and social progress.

President Wilson typified this view of the world and its problems. His Fourteen Points gave the most concise statement of the liberals' war aims and the liberal program for reconstruction. Although the actual settlement did not accord with Wilson's points in every detail, it did so in its main outlines. That it did not produce the desired results – this became increasingly evident throughout the interwar period – caused spreading dismay among liberal theorists and policy makers. Shaken, but still clinging to the notion that their analysis of the problem had been basically correct, they were reduced to emergency expedients in dealing with the mounting crises. It is not surprising, therefore, that after events had falsified their earlier diagnosis, their subsequent attempts at reconstruction should have been hesitant, confused, and contradictory.

THE LEAGUE OF NATIONS AND COLLECTIVE SECURITY

Wilson regarded the League of Nations as the most vital part of postwar rehabilitation. In order to secure the adhesion of France and Britain he compromised his principles on many other points, notably the question of reparations, in the belief that the League itself would be able to rectify any defects or inequities in the treaties. He emphasized this feature in his opening address to the peace conference on January 25, 1919. "Settlements may be temporary, but the actions of the nations in the interests of peace and justice must be permanent. We can set up permanent processes. We may not be able to set up permanent decisions." Ironically, it was Wilson's insistence that the Covenant of the League be inserted as an integral part of each of the peace treaties that hampered the use of the League as an instrument of revision and conciliation, for it was thereafter identified by victors and vanquished alike with the settlement itself.

The League in no way constituted a superstate or world government. It was not even a federation of nations but merely a voluntary association. The framers of the Covenant, among whom Wilson was foremost, made it quite clear that the League did not infringe the sovereignty of any nation. It had no independent powers of coercion, and members might withdraw simply by giving notice. The League thus represented a return to the old idea of the concert of Europe on an extended and more formal basis. Even the provision for mutual aid to prevent or punish aggression – the famous concept of collective security – did not mark a new departure, for in that respect the Covenant resembled a multilateral defense treaty depending upon the good faith of the signatories to make its decisions effective, as was the case in all such treaties. The League was simply an application of nineteenth-century liberal political theory to international relations. Although in the beginning it was widely regarded as the foundation of a new world order, it was in effect only the capstone of the old. Unperceived by the architects, the true foundations had been shaken beyond repair.

In accordance with the provisions of the treaties, the League formally came into existence on January 10, 1920, although its first meeting did not take place until the following autumn. It began with forty-one charter members, growing to fifty by 1924. More significant than the quantity of members was the importance of some of the nonmembers.

Both Germany and Russia were excluded, outcasts from the society of nations. No less important, the United States, whose elected leader was the father of the League, refused to join. Under the United States Constitution ratification of treaties and international agreements required the concurrence of at least two-thirds of the Senate. In the elections of 1918 the Republicans had gained control of both houses of Congress; in effect, Wilson had lost a vote of confidence just before leaving for the peace conference. Although the Senate contained several of Wilson's personal enemies, they opposed him not just for personal reasons or for the sake of opposition, but because a strong current of opinion in the country at large advocated a return to America's historic policy of diplomatic isolation and noninterference in European affairs. The League was, of course, primarily a European body. After long and bitter debates the Senate refused to ratify the Treaty of Versailles in March, 1920. Although the vote was actually against the League, it had the incidental effect of leaving the United States technically at war with Germany; this situation was not remedied until 1921.

ORGANIZATION

The League consisted of two principal deliberative bodies; the Council and the Assembly. The latter included the entire membership on the basis of one nation, one vote. With few exceptions, all major decisions had to receive unanimous approval in the Assembly in order to take effect. The most important exception prevented members who were party to a dispute from voting on that question. The Council acted as a sort of steering committee for the Assembly, deciding (also by the rule of unanimity) what matters might be discussed in the larger body. The initial draft of the Covenant provided for five permanent members of the Council (the United States, Britain, France, Italy, and Japan) and four rotating members elected by the Assembly. When the United States refused to join, the number of permanent members was reduced to four. The rotating membership was raised to six in 1922 and nine in 1926. Of the four permanent members of the Council, Japan and Italy withdrew from the League in 1933 and 1937, respectively, after being charged with aggression, and subsequently went to war against the others. Of all the great powers only Britain and France – neither of whom had been enthusiastic about the League at its beginning – belonged throughout the interwar period. This fact lent some substance to the charges that the real effect of the League, if not its original purpose, was simply to preserve the advantages that France and Britain had gained by the treaties.

In addition to the Council and Assembly the League maintained a permanent secretariat at its headquarters in Geneva and sponsored a number of specialized agencies. Among the more important of the latter were the Permanent Court of International Justice, set up in The Hague

Photoworld

Meeting of the Council of the League of Nations

"Ah, gentlemen, the cynics, the detractors of the League of Nations, those who take pleasure daily in putting its solidity in doubt and who periodically announce its disappearance, what are they thinking if they attend this session? Is it not a moving spectacle, especially edifying and comforting, that, only a few years after the most frightful war in history, with the battlefields almost still damp with blood, the same nations that fought one another so bitterly are here assembled peacefully and mutually affirm their common desire to collaborate in the work of universal peace." Aristide Briand, speech on the admission of Germany to the League of Nations, September 10, 1926, from Aristide Briand, DISCOURS ET ÉCRITS DE POLITIQUE ÉTRANGÈRE, ed. Achille Elisha (Paris, 1965).

---

in 1922, and the International Labor Office with headquarters in Geneva. The International Court supplemented but did not replace an earlier Court of Arbitration, which had been set up by an international conference at The Hague in 1900; it rendered legal decisions (as distinct from arbitration awards) on disputes between nations involving international law, but only if requested to do so by all parties to the dispute. The ILO sought to achieve improved working conditions and uniform labor standards in all countries. Both of these semi-independent agencies survived World War II and the League itself.

FUNCTIONS

The primary function of the League was to provide the machinery for the settlement of international disputes without recourse to war. It also performed a number of lesser services, some well, some less well, which often escaped public attention. They included the elaboration of codes for the protection of women and children, the suppression of the slave trade and illicit traffic in drugs, and activities to protect public health and prevent disease. In the field of international administration the League's civil servants conducted plebiscites in disputed territories and provided a professional staff to administer the Saarland and the city of Danzig, both of which were placed under League control.

The former German colonies and the ex-dominions of the sultan in the Near East were also placed nominally under League control. The League did not attempt to administer them directly but turned them over as "mandated territories" to the powers that were already in effective occupation. The only obligations assumed by the mandatory powers were to abide by a few vague and pious rules set forth in the Covenant and to render an annual report to the Permanent Mandates Commission. In fact, mandated territories soon became indistinguishable from ordinary colonies. The Covenant did, nevertheless, distinguish between mandated territories on the basis of the degree of their development in the direction of self-government, granting some greater local autonomy than others. Thus the Arab countries at the eastern end of the Mediterranean became Class A mandates, divided between the French and British; those of central Africa became Class B mandates; and the former German Southwest Africa, which went to the Union of South Africa, and the Pacific islands became Class C mandates.

Recognizing the problems created by the boundaries in eastern Europe, the League Council created a permanent committee on national minorities. Theoretically all League members agreed to observe certain uniform standards concerning ethnic or national minorities within their territory. The committee could hear complaints from minorities who alleged violation of the standards, and it could publish reports on them, but it had no power to take direct action against an offending member, for minorities constituted "internal problems" and to interfere would be a violation of national sovereignty. Such action was no part of the League's program.

ACHIEVEMENTS AND FAILURE

Members of the League undertook, in the words of the Covenant, "to promote international cooperation and to achieve international peace and security: by the acceptance of obligations not to resort to war, by the prescription of open, just and honorable relations among nations, by the firm establishment of the understandings of international law as the actual rule of conduct among Governments, and by maintenance of justice and a scrupulous respect for all treaty obligations in the dealings of organized peoples with one another." Of the methods provided for the settlement of disputes, the most commonly used were arbitration, judicial settlement by the International Court, and reports by the Council itself. Utilization of the first two required the consent of the parties to the dispute; that of the last required a unanimous vote in the Council. All were difficult to achieve. Once a settlement was made, however, if a member (or even a nonmember) failed to abide by it, all the others might impose "sanctions" ranging in severity from a formal reprimand to a declaration of war. The crux of the matter was that effective enforcement depended upon both the willingness and the ability of the various states to take the indicated action; the League itself, as a separate organization, was powerless to impose sanctions.

In its early years the League scored some small successes in the settlement of disputes between Sweden and Finland (1921), Poland and Germany (1922), and a few others. In the same years, however, it failed to settle the bitter quarrel between Poland and Lithuania over the city of Vilna. Moreover, Mussolini refused to submit his disputes with Greece and Yugoslavia to League jurisdiction, and such major issues as French occupation of the Ruhr were not even raised in formal League discussion, which strengthened the view that the League was in reality a league of the large states against the small, of the victors against the vanquished.

After the settlement of the Ruhr crisis, the stabilization of the German monetary system, and the temporary return of prosperity, the tensions in international relations eased somewhat. In 1925 at the Swiss resort city of Locarno the foreign ministers of Britain, France, Germany, and several smaller states met to conclude a number of important agreements. Among other things they provided for an undertaking by Britain to guarantee the Franco-German and Belgian-German borders against aggression from either side, and a similar undertaking by France (Britain demurring) with respect to Germany's borders with Poland and Czechoslovakia. It was also agreed informally that Germany should be admitted to the League, an event that took place in 1926. Although the agreements contained a number of grave defects which subsequently became apparent, the mood of friendship and conciliation they engendered became known as "the spirit of Locarno." This balmy spirit prevailed so long as prosperity lasted and the men who created it remained in office; that is, about four years.

The Locarno spirit owed much to the personal characteristics of the foreign ministers of Germany, France, and Britain: Gustav Stresemann, the apostle of "fulfillment" of German treaty obligations; Aristide Briand, an old socialist and apostle of peace; and Austen Chamberlain,

Courtesy of *The Columbus* (Ohio) *Dispatch*

The Highest Point Ever Reached in Europe
cartoon by Ireland in The Columbus Dispatch

"The representatives of the German, Belgian, British, French, Italian, Polish and Czechoslovak Governments, who have met at Locarno, from the 5th to the 16th October, 1925, in order to seek by common agreement means for preserving their respective nations from the scourge of war and for providing for the peaceful settlement of disputes of every nature which might eventually arise between them, have given their approval to the draft treaties and conventions which respectively affect them and which, framed in the course of the present conference, are mutually interdependent." Final Protocol of the Locarno Conference, reprinted in W. H. Cook and E. P. Stickney, eds., READINGS IN EUROPEAN INTERNATIONAL RELATIONS (New York, 1931).

---

an urbane Englishman. In 1928, as a result of communications between Briand and American secretary of state Frank B. Kellogg, sixty-five nations signed the Pact of Paris or Kellogg-Briand Pact, which committed them to the "renunciation of war as an instrument of national policy." The pact was regarded as especially significant in that it included not only France and Germany but also the United States and the Soviet

Union, neither of whom were members of the League. The euphoria of the moment (which earned Briand the Nobel Peace Prize) obscured the fact that all nations already had made equivalent pronouncements and undertakings and that the pact provided absolutely no means for enforcement.

Such easing of tensions as took place in the late 1920's was not brought about directly by the League but rather by old-fashioned methods of diplomacy. Nevertheless, the League continued with its work, primarily in the cause of disarmament. Early in the 1920's Britain, the United States, and Japan made several agreements outside the League proper for the limitation of naval armaments, but overall disarmament proved more difficult and elusive. In spite of many meetings and conferences both in and outside the League, the nations were as far apart in 1933, when they gave up the attempt altogether, as they had been in 1923.

The Locarno era ended abruptly in 1929 when both Chamberlain and Briand lost office and Stresemann died, all within six months of one another and of the Wall Street crash. Although hopes remained that peace might be preserved, the outlook grew darker and darker. In 1933 the Japanese announced their withdrawal from the League over the Manchurian question. (See p. 434.) In the same fateful year Adolf Hitler became master of Germany and soon withdrew it from the League. Although Soviet Russia then rushed to gain international respectability by applying for membership, and was accepted, the League was weaker than before. The Italian rebuff to the League in 1935 and the failure of its members to take effective action (see p. 435) spelled its doom as either a peace-making or peace-keeping body. It staggered on a few years more, and in its weakness did what it had not dared to do in earlier and balmier days when it might have helped; it expelled a member, the Soviet Union, in 1939 for an attack on Finland. That proved to be its dying gesture; World War II had already begun.

THE WEIMAR REPUBLIC IN GERMANY

Of all liberal attempts at reconstruction, none began more hopefully nor ended more pathetically than the German republic. On paper — that is, in its constitution — it appeared to be one of the most advanced democratic nations of the times, but almost from the beginning it encountered die-hard opposition from both ends of the political spectrum. Its founders carried the onus of having accepted the Versailles treaty with the war guilt clause. It was overwhelmed by the worldwide depression, which struck Germany with greater severity than almost any other nation. Furthermore it failed to carry out any fundamental economic or social reforms. It did not break up the General Staff (as the Versailles treaty had demanded) or the Junker estates of eastern Germany, which were the economic base of the Prussian military caste. Finally, it did not attempt to break the power of big business in either economic or political life; in fact, it encouraged the formation of monopolies and cartels.

The republic got off to a bad start. The provisional government declared an immediate end to martial law and the reestablishment of traditional civil liberties and set about preparing for an election for a constituent assembly. Before the election could take place the Spartacist uprising in Berlin showed that the forces of democracy would be opposed on the Left as well as the Right. The government called on elements of the old imperial army to suppress the revolt and executed its leaders without trial, both of which were bad precedents for a new democracy. At the same time it went ahead with plans for the election, the freest and most democratic in Germany's history.

The election gave the Social Democrats 163 of a total of 423 delegates to the assembly. They were the largest party but fell far short of an absolute majority. The Catholic Center party and the Democrats, the two other moderate groups, had as many delegates combined, while the Nationalists and other right-wing groups and the left-wing Independent Socialists had many fewer. The three moderate parties formed a coalition both to govern the country and to frame a new constitution. The assembly elected Friedrich Ebert first president of the German republic, with Philipp Scheidemann, also a Social Democrat, serving as chancellor.

At the beginning of February, 1919, the constituent assembly convened in Weimar, the city of Goethe and Schiller, in order to avoid intimidation by the army and the mobs of Berlin, still in a state of anarchy. Although the seat of government remained in Berlin, and the assembly itself moved there after a few months, the short-lived democracy to which it gave birth will forever be known as the Weimar Republic.

THE STRUCTURE OF GOVERNMENT

The constitution borrowed freely from American, British, French, and Swiss precedent and practice, but all of these democratic shoots were grafted onto a solidly Germanic trunk. Although the republic was federal in form, the states were clearly subservient to the central government, which had greater power in principle if not in fact than it had under the Second Reich. There were also fewer component states than in the Second Reich as a result of amalgamation. The president, elected for a seven-year term, was similar to an elective constitutional monarch, as in contemporary France, rather than being an active head of government, as in the United States. He did, however, possess certain important emergency powers. The actual business of governing was confided to a chancellor and cabinet of ministers responsible to the legislature.

The legislature, bicameral in form, was unicameral in effect, as clearly indicated in the constitution itself. The Reichstag (the name lingered, even in a republic) voted all legislation and determined the fate of ministries. The Reichsrat, the second chamber, was composed of delegates from the state governments and had only a suspensory veto on legislation and no authority over ministries.

Although Social Democrats dominated the moderate coalition in the beginning, they were not strong enough to give the constitution a socialist character. The few references in it to economic organization specifically guaranteed "freedom of trade and industry," freedom of contract, and the right of private property. As a predominantly political document, the constitution incorporated the most advanced features of contemporary liberal political theory, including "universal, equal, direct and secret suffrage by all men and women over twenty years of age," proportional representation, a provision for referenda, and a broad range of civil rights and liberties. Ironically, Article 48 of the constitution provided that "if public safety and order . . . are materially disturbed or endangered," the president might suspend the constitution and "take the necessary measures to restore public safety and order . . . if necessary . . . by force of arms." The purpose of this article was to prevent either a communist or a monarchist *putsch* (coup d'état) against the republic, either of which appeared quite possible in the spring of 1919. In fact it was used in 1933 by Adolf Hitler, after he had acquired power by legal means, to dispose of the republic itself.

THREATS TO THE REPUBLIC

The republic was under constant pressure throughout its short life. Although it suppressed the Spartacist uprising in Berlin, further communist putsches were attempted in Berlin and other cities in subsequent months. A Soviet-style republic held Bavaria for a time in the spring of 1919, and the following year another revolt very nearly succeeded in the Ruhr. After the Treaty of Rapallo with the Soviet Union in 1922 the threat of Communist revolution subsided, but right-wing threats remained.

The government's use of free corps or volunteer armies of ex-servicemen to put down the Spartacist rising, together with its extremely broad interpretation of the constitutional provision for freedom of association, gave rise to the phenomenon of private armies, of which the Nazi Brownshirts or storm troopers became notorious. Lawlessness was rife and took such extreme forms as frequent assassinations of political leaders. Two of the outstanding leaders of the moderate coalition – Matthias Erzberger (who signed the armistice agreement of 1918) and Walter Rathenau – were assassinated within a year of one another in 1921 and 1922 by right-wing conspirators. The most serious of the attempted reactionary revolts was the Kapp putsch of 1920. Organized by Wolfgang Kapp, a minor politician, with the assistance of Generals von

Lüttwitz and Ludendorff, returning soldiers from the Baltic provinces who were destined to be demobilized by Allied command took Berlin, proclaimed the fall of the Weimar government, and installed Kapp as chancellor. The legal government escaped to the country and, in view of the passivity and outright sympathy for the revolt of many professional army officers, called for a general strike of workers. The strike proved effective, and the leaders of the putsch fled in fear and confusion within a week, but the experience revealed the reactionary spirit and doubtful loyalty of the officer corps.

If the Kapp putsch demonstrated the unreliability of the military, still dominated by East Elbian Junkers, it also showed that most workers were loyal to the democratic republic before the great inflation. The inflation constituted one of the two great watersheds of the Weimar republic. The other was the depression of 1929 to 1933, which brought the republic to an end. Although the almost miraculous economic recovery and prosperity that followed the inflation temporarily covered over the wounds it left in the body politic and social, they festered all the more for being hidden. Reactionary and nationalist sentiment, strong before the inflation, had been confined to social classes that were temporarily discredited by the war, including the officer corps itself and other Junker aristocrats. The war guilt clause of the Versailles treaty had been a bitter pill, but most Germans had swallowed it even though the Scheidemann cabinet resigned rather than sign it, and the great German sociologist Max Weber predicted, "We shall all be nationalists in ten years." The inflation, together with the accompanying French action in the Ruhr, cut the ground from under the moderates and overturned the political allegiances of the various social classes. The group that suffered most was the lower middle class of shopkeepers, clerks, and white-collar workers, who later formed the backbone of Nazi supporters. Both skilled and manual workers also suffered, and after being disillusioned by the weakness of socialism and democracy, they divided into hostile camps. The majority became increasingly enticed by communist blueprints of a workers' state, but many others worked off their frustrations and found emotional release in Nazi rituals and discipline and anti-Semitic demonstrations.

STRESEMANN, LOCARNO, AND "FULFILLMENT"

In the first elections to the Reichstag in June, 1920, the Social Democrats lost their dominant position, and after 1923 they participated in no further cabinets until 1928. The People's party, a resurrection of the old National Liberals dominated by big business interests, took their place in the moderate coalition, which thus moved a step to the Right. In the elections of 1924 Communists and Nationalists both gained at the expense of the moderate parties, and in 1925 a new cabinet included a

Photoworld

Unemployed Line Up for Free Soup

"The situation deteriorated in 1930 more rapidly in Germany than in England or the United States. . . . Total industrial production shrank, relatively, as much or more than it did in this country. . . . The total number of unemployed was about 3 millions during the first ten months and rose to nearly 4.4 in December. There cannot be any doubt that . . . extra-economic factors . . . had much to do with this. Superimposing themselves on what would in any case have been a depression, they intensified it greatly." J. A. Schumpeter, BUSINESS CYCLES (New York, 1939), Vol. II.

Nationalist for the first time, marking yet another step to the Right. In the presidential election soon afterward, Field Marshal von Hindenburg, the Nationalist candidate, won with a mere plurality – not a majority – as a result of Communist inroads on the moderate vote.

Meanwhile both the domestic economic picture and the international diplomatic scene had changed radically for the better, if only temporarily. The inflation had come and gone, leaving a wreckage of broken hopes, homes, and dreams, but also clearing the decks of debt and leaving the enterprises and individuals who had survived it wide-open opportunities for economic expansion and prosperity under the new regime of international loans. Large new vertical and horizontal combinations took shape, such as the I. G. Farbenindustrie (chemicals, dyestuffs, pharmaceuticals), and the Vereinigte Stahlwerke A. G. (steel, armaments, engineering). The rationalization movement, which sought both technical modernization and the elimination of unwanted competition through merger and amalgamation, made rapid headway.

The most significant development on the political and diplomatic front was the advent of Gustav Stresemann, a businessman and former ardent nationalist, who emerged as leader of the People's party. Stresemann served as chancellor for four months in 1923, long enough to preside over the liquidation of the inflationary upheaval and to inaugurate the new, stabilized currency. Although he lost the chancellorship thereafter, he remained as foreign minister in every succeeding cabinet until his death in 1929. His efforts at Locarno and afterward were dictated by the hard-headed businessman's respect for realities; they gained him a Nobel Peace Prize and won Germany's entry into the League of Nations as a member of the Council in 1926. His principles did not prevent him from renewing the Rapallo treaty of friendship and neutrality with the Soviet Union, also in 1926, under which the German army gained valuable experience with new developments in military technology in exchange for industrial and technical aid to Russia.

The gains for democracy, whatever they may have been, proved fleeting. Stresemann's death coincided with the onset of the great depression. The middle-class government, deathly afraid of a repetition of the collapse of the mark of 1923, pursued a deflationary policy in the midst of the worst deflation the world had experienced in over a hundred years. By the beginning of 1932 the number of unemployed in Germany had reached 6 million — more than one-fourth of the labor force. Conditions were ripe for the Nazi revolution.

ADOLF HITLER AND THE DEATH THROES OF THE REPUBLIC

Adolf Hitler, son of a minor Austrian civil servant, showed signs of paranoia from early childhood. He rebelled against his strict, narrow-minded father, and after the latter's death took advantage of his over-indulgent mother. In the last years before the First World War he made a precarious living as a third-rate artist in Vienna, where his failures and frustrations crystallized into a bitter, burning anti-Semitism. Shortly before the war he drifted across the border into southern Germany, and after its outbreak he enlisted in the Bavarian army, where during four years of service he rose to the rank of corporal. War service provided an emotional release for his twisted yearnings, and he became an intense pan-German nationalist. He was in a military hospital recovering from gas poisoning when the armistice was signed; the effect of the event appears to have produced a kind of emotional crisis that strengthened his fanaticism and released his libido. After demobilization he returned to Munich, where in the turbulence and confusion of the first postwar year he became an informer for the army, checking up on communist sympathizers in the wake of the short-lived Bavarian Soviet Republic.

In this connection he first acquired knowledge of the German Workers' party, one of the hundreds of little political groups formed in the early months of the German republic. Although the name was suspect, he soon discovered that its small membership consisted principally of fanatical nationalists like himself. He joined the party in September, 1919, became a member of its executive committee, and the following year altered its name to the National Socialist German Workers' party (*National Sozialistische Deutsche Arbeiter Partei* or NSDAP), whose members received the nickname, at first derisive, of Nazis.

For several years the party remained small and ineffectual, although Hitler gained a local reputation for spellbinding demagogic oratory. In 1923 it achieved temporary national prominence when with the assistance of General Ludendorff it sought to overthrow the Bavarian state government in the Munich beer-hall putsch. This was one of the lesser of many such attempts by disaffected groups. The government easily put down the putsch and sentenced Hitler to five years in prison. As it had after the Kapp putsch, the government let Ludendorff off in deference to his services to the old Reich; such were the ambivalent feelings of Germans toward monarchy and democracy. Hitler was pardoned after only a year, during which time he had dictated to his faithful henchman Rudolf Hess, imprisoned with him, the book *Mein Kampf (*My Struggle), subsequently known as the bible of the Nazi party. Originally entitled "Four and a Half Years' Struggle against Lying, Stupidity, and Cowardice," it is a rambling, confused account of Hitler's early life and political activities to the time of his imprisonment, as well as a turgid exposition of his hates, prejudices, and visions of a Germany dominated by himself. Except for its seemingly prophetic passages and the insight it gives into its author's psychology, it is not worth reading today.

The Nazis remained insignificant throughout the Locarno period, but they hung on somehow. The depression provided them with their great opportunity. Unemployed workers joined the brown-shirted storm troopers, for which they received a pittance plus indoctrination in loyalty to their leaders and hate for "the others," whomever they might be: communists or capitalists, Jews or the beneficiaries of the Diktat of Versailles. In the election of September, 1930, the party's representation in the Reichstag jumped from twelve to more than one hundred. The Communists also increased to seventy-seven, while all the moderate parties except the Social Democrats lost heavily. During the next two and a half years parliamentary government ceased to function. Unable to form stable majorities out of the shifting coalitions of the Reichstag, successive chancellors resorted to ruling by decree under Article 48 of the constitution, with the consent of Hindenburg, while in the streets armed clashes between Nazi Brownshirts and Communists became increasingly frequent and destructive.

A new election in July, 1932, sent the Nazi representation up to 230, giving them the largest party in the Reichstag. After several futile attempts to form a stable government without the Nazis or to enlist their support for other parties, which Hitler refused except on his own terms, President Hindenburg named Hitler chancellor on January 30, 1933. Hitler immediately called for another election on March 5, using the combined powers of the government and his storm troopers to stir up popular support for the Nazis and to intimidate his opponents. Five days before the election a fire broke out in the Reichstag. Although the real arsonists (who may have been Nazis) were never apprehended, Hitler accused the Communists and used his emergency powers under Article 48 to outlaw the Communist party. In spite of this tactic the Communists won 81 seats, while the Nazis obtained 288. The Nazis still did not have a majority in the Reichstag, but with the aid of their Nationalist allies, the expulsion of the Communists, and the intimidation of the moderates, Hitler forced through the Reichstag on March 23 the crucial Enabling Act, which gave him emergency dictatorial powers for a period of four years. Thus he accomplished the Nazi revolution and put an end to Germany's liberal attempt at reconstruction.

THE DEMOCRACIES OF WESTERN EUROPE

Although victorious in war, Britain, France, and Belgium faced many of the same problems in peacetime as did their defeated enemy. They succeeded with difficulty in retaining their traditional attachment to political and civil liberty and parliamentary forms of government, but they were no more successful than Weimar Germany in solving the economic and social problems issuing from the collapse of Western civilization. Even the smaller Western democracies that had remained neutral in the great conflict – Switzerland, the Netherlands, and the Scandinavian countries – found themselves involved in the general collapse and disintegration. Traditional remedies availed little. Only in Scandinavia did the people and their political leaders respond creatively to the crisis and bring forth solutions both novel and effective.

BRITAIN, IMPOVERISHED EMPIRE

Economic problems loomed large in postwar Britain. Even before the war Britain's unusually great dependence on international trade and overcommitment to lines of industry that were rapidly becoming obsolete had guaranteed that the British would face a difficult period of adaptation to the twentieth century. During the war they lost foreign markets, foreign investments, a large part of their mercantile marine, and other sources of overseas income. Yet they depended as much as ever on imports of food and raw materials, and they found themselves with even greater worldwide responsibilities as the strongest of the victors in Europe and as the administrator of new territories overseas. Export they must, yet factories and mines lay idle while unemployment mounted. In 1921 more than 1 million men — about one-seventh of the industrial labor force — had no work; even in the relatively prosperous years of the 1920's the rate of unemployment rarely fell below 10 per cent, and in the worst years of the depression it mounted to 25 per cent or more.

The government's measures to deal with its economic problems were timid, unimaginative, and ineffective. Its only solution for unemployment was the dole, a system of relief payments that was entirely inadequate to support the families of the unemployed while placing a heavy burden on an already overstrained budget. For the rest, government economic policy consisted mainly in paring expenditures to the bone, thus depriving the nation of urgently needed expansion and modernization of its schools, hospitals, highways, and other public works. The single forthright initiative taken by the government in the economic sphere resulted in disaster. In 1925 the chancellor of the exchequer, Winston Churchill, who had earlier shifted his allegiance from the Liberal to the Conservative party, resolved to return Britain to the gold standard at the prewar gold parity. Because of the inflation that had occurred since 1914, this measure necessitated a substantial fall in prices, which while it restored the prewar purchasing power of fixed money incomes also produced a fall in wages averaging about 10 per cent. It also brought about a redistribution of income in favor of the rentier classes, adding to the discontent of the workers who were already suffering from unemployment and short time, or reduced working hours.

The coal industry was one of the most severely affected by the loss of foreign markets and higher costs. Coal miners were among the most radical of British workers; they had already staged several major strikes in the early postwar years. When faced with a wage cut as a result of the government's policy, the miners went out on strike on May 1, 1926, and persuaded many other trade unions to join them in what was intended to be a general strike. About 40 per cent of British trade union members joined in, mainly those in public utilities and similar industries, but the strike lasted only ten days and ended in a defeat for the unions. Middle-class volunteers manned essential services, and the trade union leaders gave up rather than risk civil war in the face of the government's strong and successful opposition. Brief as it was, the general strike left a bitter legacy of class division and hatred, which made concerted national action against both domestic and international problems even more difficult.

Lloyd George's handling of the wartime coalition government, which remained in office until 1922, resulted in disaster for his own Liberal party. The Labour party then emerged as the second largest party and replaced the Liberals as His Majesty's Loyal Opposition. For a few months in 1924 it actually formed a government, but this turned out to be a misfortune instead of an opportunity. Without an absolute majority in the House of Commons, it could not have carried out a program of reform even if it had had one – which it did not. A similar situation occurred in 1929, when it formed another minority government just on the eve of the depression. As the crisis deepened Prime Minister J. Ramsay MacDonald could offer no program but the conventional middle-class solution of budgetary retrenchment. His inadequacy cost him the support of his own party. MacDonald thereupon reformed his cabinet in 1931 as a coalition dominated by Conservatives. His own party expelled him and went into opposition once more, where it remained until World War II. Thus ended all attempts at socialist reform until 1945.

While domestic difficulties mounted Britain still had to fend for and contend with its empire, enlarged by the acquisition of the former German colonies and the mandated territories of Palestine, Transjordan, and Iraq. The sun still shown on the British Empire, but a hint of things to come shot forth like a shower of sparks from Ireland, "John Bull's other island." The Home Rule Bill of 1914, which was to have taken effect after the war, never did so. In April, 1916, the Sinn Fein (We ourselves) party of Irish Nationalists launched the Easter Rebellion, relying on German assistance which never arrived. Although the British easily suppressed the rebellion, the anti-British agitation continued and again broke out into general warfare in 1919–20. Suppression proved more difficult this time, despite the greater ferocity of the British counteroffensive. In 1920 the British Parliament passed a new home rule law, but the Sinn Fein refused to accept it, insisting on complete independence. After long negotiations the British in 1921 signed an agreement providing for dominion status for southern Ireland as the Irish Free State. Although a majority of the Irish accepted the solution, a militant minority of Irish republicans refused to do so and initiated a guerrilla civil war against their own Irish government.

One of the most militant leaders of the Irish Republicans was Eamon de Valera, born in New York of a Spanish father and an Irish mother. Sentenced to death for his part in the Easter Rebellion, he was reprieved because of his American nationality and in 1917 became the leader of the Sinn Fein movement. He broke with the majority of his party and refused to recognize the treaty of 1921, but in 1926 after imprisonment and release by his own former comrades he entered the politics of the Irish Free State on a more normal basis. In 1932 he became chief of the Irish government, a post that he occupied continuously until 1948 (and again from 1951 to 1954 and from 1957 to 1959), during which time he completely severed southern Ireland's ties with Britain, reorganizing it as the Irish Republic or Eire. The six northern counties in the Protestant province of Ulster had accepted special status in the United Kingdom of Great Britain and Northern Ireland under the act of 1920.

Although the self-governing dominions of Canada, Australia, New Zealand, and South Africa loyally joined Britain in the war, they showed increasing signs of restiveness with their position in the empire in the postwar period. In 1926 an imperial conference declared Great Britain and the dominions to be "autonomous communities within the British Empire, equal in status, in no way subordinate to one another in any aspect of their domestic or external affairs, though united by a common allegiance to the crown." In 1931 Parliament passed the Statute of Westminster, giving the force of law to that declaration and creating the British Commonwealth of Nations.

Other portions of the empire had to wait longer for independence. Britain formerly renounced its protectorate over Egypt in 1922 but maintained an army of occupation and advisers in Egypt until after World War II, with the result that it was continually embroiled in difficulties and disputes there. In India the British introduced a strictly limited degree of self-government in 1919 and extended it slightly in 1935. Not satisfied, the Indians under the moral leadership of Mohandas K. (Mahatma) Gandhi began a campaign of passive (nonviolent) resistance to British rule, which culminated in independence after World War II.

In Britain a long, slow, and incomplete recovery from the depression got under way in 1934. With a single notable exception, the nation's attention gradually shifted to foreign affairs in the march toward World War II. The exception was an interlude devoted to the royal family, more than ever an object of public concern and affection since the monarch had ceased to rule. George V died at the beginning of 1936 after a twenty-six-year reign, in which he set the style for modern constitutional monarchs. His son and successor Edward VIII was a bachelor, but rumor soon linked his name with that of Mrs. Wallis Warfield Simpson, an American whose second marriage was headed for the divorce courts. Edward indicated his intention of marrying Mrs. Simpson, but the government of the day, presided over by Stanley Baldwin, raised a constitutional issue and refused to proceed with the coronation ceremony. In December, 1936, Edward abdicated, having reigned uncrowned for less than a year, and assumed the title Duke of Windsor; he married Mrs. Simpson the following year. He was succeeded by his younger brother, who carried on the tradition set by their father. For the two years from the Silver Jubilee of George V in 1935 to the coronation of George VI in 1937 British newspapers devoted more space to the royal family than to either economic or foreign affairs. It was symptomatic of a concern for propriety at the expense of action.

FRANCE, THE FRIGHTENED VICTOR

No Western nation suffered more from the war than France. Most of the fighting on the western front had taken place in its richest area. More than half of France's prewar industrial production, including 60 per cent of its steel and 70 per cent of its coal, had been located in the war-devastated area, which was also among the most important agricultural regions. Most appalling was the loss of life: 1.5 million Frenchmen – one-half of the prewar male population of military age – had been killed, with half as many more permanently disabled. It is not surprising, therefore, that France demanded that Germany pay for the war, nor that Frenchmen sought security above all. Unhappily, whatever the justice or equity of the French demands, they could not easily be reconciled with the realities of the world situation. Attempts to attain them in spite of all difficulties contributed to weakening France still more.

Counting on German reparations to pay the cost, the French government undertook at once an extensive program of physical reconstruction of the war-damaged areas, which had the incidental effect of stimulating the economy to new production records. When German reparations failed to materialize in the expected amount, the ramshackle methods used to finance the reconstruction took their toll. The problem was compounded by the expensive and ineffective occupation of the Ruhr. The franc depreciated more in the first seven years of peace than during the war. Realizing at last that "the Boche" could not be made to pay, a coalition cabinet headed by Raymond Poincaré and containing six former premiers stabilized the franc in 1926 at about one-fifth of its prewar value by drastic economies and stiff increases in taxation. This solution was more satisfactory than either of the more extreme solutions utilized by Germany and Britain, but it alienated both the rentier class, which lost about four-fifths of its purchasing power in the inflation, and the working classes, which bore most of the burden of increased taxation. Thus, as in Germany, the inflation contributed to the growth of extremism on both Right and Left.

On the Left the Socialist party congress in 1920 voted by a three-to-one margin to join the Third International, directed from Moscow, and renamed itself the French Communist party. The minority led by Léon Blum walked out; they retained the name Socialist but gave up all else – the party newspaper, organizational apparatus, and most of the membership. The future of the non-Communist Left looked bleak indeed, but the astute leadership of Blum, plus the incompetence of the Communist party leaders and constant meddling from Moscow, revived the Socialist party in a most remarkable way. By 1932 the Socialists outnumbered the

Communists in the Chamber of Deputies by 100 to 10, and in 1936 Léon Blum became French premier as the head of the largest party in the Chamber.

On the extreme Right several shrill but small groups preached doctrines similar to facism. The most important was an organization called Action Française, led by the vitriolic writer Charles Maurras. It was rabidly nationalist and frankly reactionary, appealing for a return to the monarchy and clerical domination of the state. Although at first supported by the Catholic Church, it was repudiated by the Vatican in 1926 and its popular influence declined rapidly. Its intellectual influence lingered on, however, and flowered again in the Vichy regime during World War II.

In spite of the growth of radical and extremist movements, political control of France remained firmly in the hands of the moderate parties. The multiplicity of parties in the French Chamber of Deputies, already notable before the war, became even more striking with the adoption of proportional representation in 1919. More than thirty parties were represented, resulting in a succession of shifting coalitions and cabinet upsets. The moderate parties fell into two main groups; the right-center *Bloc National,* to which Clemenceau belonged and which was subsequently dominated by Poincaré and Briand; and the left-center *Cartel des Gauches,* dominated by Édouard Herriot, leader of the so-called Radical Socialist party (which was neither radical nor socialist).

French political parties united on only one objective: the desire to preserve French hegemony on the Continent. They hoped to accomplish it through the League with the aid of the United States and Britain. The United States Senate, however, not only refused to join the League but killed a tripartite treaty by which the United States and Britain would have guaranteed France assistance if attacked by Germany. Britain thereupon regarded its responsibilities under the treaty as abrogated. Britain also differed with France on reparations. This desertion by their allies, as Frenchmen regarded it, accounted for much of the stridency and go-it-alone attitude of France's foreign policy in the early 1920's, culminating in the occupation of the Ruhr. That fiasco tempered French intransigence so much that France did not again resort to unilateral action even when it might have been effective, as during the German remilitarization of the Rhineland in 1936. (See p. 437.) Instead, it speeded construction of the Maginot line, a vast network of interconnecting fortresses along the Franco-German border, and built a paper wall of treaties around Germany with Poland and Little Entente powers of Czechoslovakia, Rumania, and Yugoslavia. Realizing the weakness of these allies, Briand came to terms with Germany itself in the Locarno agreements. In 1935, after Hitler had announced German rearmament in defiance of Versailles, France even negotiated an alliance with Soviet Russia, which had been anathema to most Frenchmen ever since Lenin had repudiated the debts of the tsarist government. That treaty was no more effective than the others in protecting France from a resurgent Germany.

Meanwhile the depression struck, later in France than elsewhere and perhaps less severely, but also longer lasting. The trough did not come till 1935 or 1936, and France was still floundering when war broke out in 1939. As it had in other countries, the depression spawned social protest and a new crop of extremist organizations. For a time in the winter of 1933–34 many Frenchmen expected a reactionary or fascist coup d'état, and open rioting broke out in February, 1934, ominously reminiscent of the Berlin street fighting in 1932. The political storm blew over, however, and the next political turning for France was to the Left.

To combat fascist tendencies, the Socialists overcame their dislike of the Communists and brought them together with the Radicals in a Popular Front. This step was made easier by the recent Franco-Soviet alliance. In the elections of 1936 the Socialists emerged as the largest party, the Radicals second, and the Communists made a surprising leap from ten to seventy-two seats in the Chamber of Deputies. Léon Blum became the Popular Front prime minister. Although held back by its Radical allies from outright socialization, the government enacted a number of reform measures, especially in the field of labor, including a legal forty-hour work week, compulsory arbitration of labor disputes, and paid vacations. As mild as these reform measures were, they aroused the hostility of the conservatives, and after the first blush of enthusiasm for reform had passed, Blum had to give way as prime minister in 1937 to a Radical colleague. In 1938 the Popular Front broke up after only two years as foreign affairs increasingly dominated the political scene. In France as in Britain liberalism proved too weak, too timid, too lacking in imagination to tackle the task of reconstruction of society as a whole.

THE SMALLER DEMOCRACIES

Even more than before World War I the fate of the smaller nations of Europe lay beyond their control, intimately associated with international affairs and the policies of the great powers. As a result two major features of the interwar period, the depression and the diplomatic trials and failures that eventually led to World War II, overshadowed the purely domestic histories of the smaller democracies. Only the Scandinavian countries managed to shield themselves from some of the ravages of the depression, and only Sweden and Switzerland remained neutral during the Second World War.

The problems of Belgium, the only one of the small nations of western Europe to be involved in the first war, resembled those of France. The response to those problems also resembled the French; that is, the Belgians followed strictly orthodox economic and financial policies in coping with successive crises until 1936, when the government of the day followed the French Popular Front in introducing very mild social and economic reforms. In foreign policy Belgium tied itself more closely to France, even participating in the occupation of the Ruhr. In 1936, however, in the face of growing German strength and obvious French weakness, the Belgians sought vainly to save themselves by denouncing their military alliance with France and reverting to their traditional neutrality. In internal affairs Belgium was troubled, as were all democratic countries in the 1930's, by the growth of domestic totalitarian movements. Calling themselves Rexists, the Belgian fascists reached the peak of their strength in 1936 when they won twenty-one seats in parliament; but by 1939 their influence had been reduced to insignificance. A more serious social conflict for Belgium was the old hostility between the French-speaking Walloons and the Flemish. A law in 1922 made both Flemish and French the official languages, as a concession to the Flemings, but after 1932 French was used only in the Walloon provinces, with Flemish the only official language in Flanders. The capital, Brussels, remained officially bilingual. In spite of such concessions, riots and other forms of conflict continued to mark the relations between the two ethnic groups.

The Netherlands, traditionally a free trade nation and heavily dependent on international commerce, suffered from both the depression and growing economic nationalism. The Dutch took the initiative in attempts to keep trade free with Belgium and Luxembourg, ultimately resulting in the Benelux customs union after World War II. They also played a prominent role in negotiating the Oslo Convention of 1932, intended to facilitate trade among the Low Countries and those of Scandinavia. A Dutch National Socialist party modeled on the German caused grave concern from 1934 to 1936, but as with the Rexists in Belgium, its strength had been spent by 1938.

Switzerland's overweening national interest throughout the interwar period lay, as always, in maintaining its historic neutrality. Its location and scenery made it a favorite spot for international conferences and the headquarters of international organizations (the International Red Cross was established at Geneva in 1864, the International Postal Union at Bern in 1874). This also had its drawbacks, however. After the diplomats in Paris chose Geneva as the seat of the League of Nations in 1919, it was a full year before the Swiss responded to the honor with a decision to enter the League, and then only after receiving assurances that they would not be called upon to go to war in support of League decisions. The national referendum by which the Swiss decided the issue gave the League a margin of only four to three. Significantly, Switzerland was the only independent nation that later chose to remain outside the United

Nations. The Swiss tried to avoid antagonizing Italy and Germany, although they refused to extend diplomatic recognition to the Soviet Union until after World War II. At the same time, by means of their unique system of universal military service and strong border fortifications they let it be known that they would not be willing victims of aggression.

By 1938 the only outpost of democracy in eastern Europe was Czechoslovakia. In spite of the absence of any tradition of self-government, the presence of hostile nations on all sides, and the existence of strong religious and ethnic divisions within the country itself, the literate and industrious Czechs had managed to establish and preserve parliamentary government as well as an elementary respect for basic civil and political liberties. Much of the credit belonged to Thomas Masaryk, who served as president from the creation of the provisional government in 1918 until 1935, and to his successor Eduard Beneš. Czechs, Slovaks, and Ruthenians made up the greater part of the population of the Czechoslovak state, but owing to decisions made in the peace conference, it also included several minority nationalities. The largest and most important of the minorities were the Germans, numbering more than 3 million, who lived principally in the Sudeten Mountains that ringed the western end of the long, lizard-shaped country. Although their inclusion in the new state was clearly a violation of Wilson's principle of nationality, it was justified by the diplomats – and acquiesced to by Wilson – on the grounds that the mountains provided the Czechs with their only natural defense against Germany. In any event, the Sudeten Germans provided fertile soil for the growth of irredentist agitation after the advent of National Socialism in Germany. The activities of the Nazi-inspired *Sudetendeutsche Partei* of Konrad Henlein prepared the way for German dismemberment and absorption, which was carried out with the acquiescence of both France and Britain after the historic Munich conference of September, 1938. (See pp. 438–440.) Thus was democracy extinguished in eastern Europe. It has yet to be revived.

In the Scandinavian countries, on the other hand, democracy flourished as never before. One of the most heartening triumphs for democracy was the emergence of Finland, after more than a century of tsarist rule, as a democratic nation between the rival threats of local communist and fascist movements supported by the Soviet Union and Nazi Germany, respectively. All the Scandinavian countries had been fortunate in escaping the ravages of war. They were less fortunate in the depression, but owing to such relatively enlightened international cooperation as provided for in the Oslo Convention and to bold, imaginative antidepression policies, they suffered far less than most. Sweden was the most successful. Its political spectrum broke down into Conservatives, Agrarians, Liberals, and Socialists. The Socialists dominated the govern-

Brown Brothers

Dr. Thomas Masaryk

"We restored our State in the name of democratic freedom, and we shall only be able to preserve it through freedom increasingly protected. In home affairs as in foreign, democracy must be our aim. . . . Our position is not solely that our State must be democratic; it cannot be undemocratic. . . . In the past our democratic aims were negative, a negation of Austrian absolutism. Now they must be positive. What we took as our ideal must become reality — and it will not be easy." Dr. Thomas Garrigue Masaryk, THE MAKING OF A STATE, ed. Henry Wickham Steed (London, 1927).

ment for most of the interwar period, but almost always in coalition with at least one of the other parties. Partly for this reason but partly from temperament, their socialism was of a pragmatic, not dogmatic, variety. In the 1920's they enacted a wide range of progressive labor and social welfare legislation, and in the 1930's they encouraged cooperatives and municipal governments to undertake large-scale housing programs. As a result Sweden had the lowest rate of unemployment in western Europe and boasted the best-housed population and most attractive cities in the world. Norway, Denmark, and Finland had similar political line-ups and followed similar policies; but their economies, less evenly balanced than Sweden's, left them more exposed to the fluctuations of international markets.

THE UNITED STATES: NEW ERA AND NEW DEAL

In spite of the relatively brief and limited American involvement in World War I, the war introduced a number of significant changes into the tone and tempo of American life. Mobilization of the economy resulted in basic changes in the economic organization that persisted long after the last American doughboy had returned from Europe. The war hastened the process of social change and gave it new directions. Politically the war induced a revulsion against American involvement in European and world affairs. In the presidential election of 1920 Warren G. Harding, the Republican nominee, campaigned successfully on a platform calling for a "return to normalcy."

"NORMALCY" IN AMERICA

The most readily observed changes in American life occurred in the realm of fashions, manners, and social intercourse. With one exception, all these changes reinforced and accentuated the tendency toward greater personal freedom and informality. The single exception resulted in part from the wartime controls prohibiting the use of food products for making distilled beverages, in part from the popular belief that most breweries and distilleries were owned by Germans, and in part from the absence of large numbers of young men in Europe. All these factors facilitated the adoption in 1919 of the Eighteenth Amendment to the Constitution, banning the manufacture or sale of intoxicating beverages. Prohibition ensured that all hard drinking of the New Era would be strictly illegal, contributed directly to widespread disrespect for legal and moral standards, and made it possible for criminal elements engaged in illegal liquor traffic to exercise powerful political influence.

By providing new sources of income and employment the war hastened the emancipation of women, culminating in the adoption of the Nineteenth Amendment regarding women's suffrage in 1920. Woman's new role, together with increased urbanization, the faster pace of life made possible by the automobile and radio, and the prosperity of the 1920's, accounted for much of the tone of social life in the postwar decade. Jazz came to be regarded as a respectable popular art form, night clubs and movies replaced vaudeville and the traveling medicine show as popular entertainment, and Hollywood became a new symbol of American life. Americans, it seemed to the rest of the world, sought diversion and merriment as avidly and earnestly as they sought wealth. There may have been a connection between the two.

In more serious matters, the postwar decade witnessed a reversal of America's historic policy of free immigration. Organized labor (many of whose leaders were immigrants or sons of immigrants) campaigned for restriction in the mistaken belief that they could thereby obtain higher wages; misconceptions of Darwinian biological theory and popular notions of Social Darwinism convinced many Americans that the new immigrants were somehow undesirable; and the war itself made Americans more conscious of foreigners. The Immigration Act of 1921 limited the number of immigrants from each country annually to 3 per cent of the foreign-born persons of its nationality residing in the United States according to the census of 1910. A new law in 1924 further limited the numbers and discriminated against immigrants from southern and eastern Europe by restricting the annual quotas to 2 per cent of foreign nationals according to the census of 1890. It also provided for total exclusion of Japanese immigrants, thereby violating an unofficial agreement of the United States with Japan.

Political life was more completely dominated by big business than at any time since the end of the nineteenth century. One of President Coolidge's aphorisms, "The business of America is business," summed up the popular view. In the popular mythology small business was as important as big business, but this notion was belied by the statistics of corporate concentration and the influence in politics of a relatively small number of key industries. The petroleum industry, once the whipping boy of American politics (the Standard Oil Company had been broken up by court order as recently as 1911), wielded enormous behind-the-scenes influence and typified the new international outlook of big business. Primarily as a result of the oil industry's concern over the fate of oil fields in the Near East, the Harding administration reversed its policy of noninterference in European affairs and sent an observer to the Lausanne conference of 1923. The oil industry also involved the United States in bitter disputes with its neighbor Mexico. The famous Teapot Dome episode of 1924, the greatest political scandal of the 1920's, resulted from oil company bribes to the secretary of the interior, Albert Fall. Shrewder men discovered a more effective way of securing favorable government treatment than bribery. Andrew Mellon, head of a vast empire that included coal, steel, aluminum, and sulphur as well as oil, served as secretary of the treasury throughout the 1920's and was responsible, among other things, for the generous depletion allowances in the tax liability of oil producers and owners of other mineral resources.

The political influence of big business reflected changes in the structure and organization of American industry. Although the changes were inherent in the technological progress of the preceding fifty years, the wartime organization of the economy hastened them along. Underlying the organizational changes was a philosophy of both government and industry that held that government participation in the economy was desirable when its purpose was to assist and encourage private enterprise, but intolerable when it aimed at regulation and control. One of the leading exponents of this view was Herbert Hoover, a brilliant mining engineer with wide international contacts and experience who served as wartime food administrator, then as director of American famine relief in Europe. He became secretary of commerce under Presidents Harding and Coolidge and used the office effectively to promote greater rationalization and integration of the economy and to coordinate the activities of American business in foreign markets. Largely because of his success in that field the American people elected Hoover to the presidency in 1928.

Taking office at the peak of the boom, Hoover spoke for the many businessmen and business-oriented government officials who thought that they had discovered the key to perpetual prosperity. Great was their dismay when less than a year later the bottom dropped out of the stock market to signal the beginning of the worst depression in American history. The stock market crash was not identical with the depression, nor even the cause of it; but it was both symptomatic and symbolic. The people who lost money — in many cases borrowed money — in the Wall Street collapse had been the beneficiaries of the new prosperity: independent businessmen, corporation executives, professional men, and middle-class housewives, as well as wealthy rentiers. The depression, however, was by no means confined to them. The greatest suffering affected the millions of unemployed factory workers and the hundreds of thousands of farmers who lost their farms through debt foreclosure or were evicted for inability to pay their rentals. For the farmers, the depression had begun several years before, as farm prices fell steadily through the 1920's from their inflated wartime peaks. Factory workers, too, had failed to share in the prosperity of the twenties, for real wages rose hardly at all. Had the exponents of the new business system looked at the trend of real wages or at farm prices instead of corporate profits and stock prices before 1929, their optimistic forecasts might have been more guarded.

ROOSEVELT AND THE NEW DEAL

When Franklin Roosevelt took office as thirty-second president of the United States on a cold, blustery day in March, 1933, the nation lay in the grip of its worst crisis since the Civil War. With more than 15 million unemployed – almost 50 per cent of the industrial labor force – industry had virtually shut down and the banking system was on the verge of complete collapse. Nor was the crisis solely economic. An army of about 15,000 unemployed veterans marched on Washington in 1932, only to be dispersed by the regular army. In rural areas farmers sometimes took the law into their own hands to prevent the foreclosure of mortgages; and violence ruled in city streets. Membership in the American Communist party reached an all-time peak, and protofascist groups sprang up across the land. It was uncertain whether or not the United States would go the way of Italy and Germany.

In his campaign speeches Roosevelt had called for a "new deal" for America. In the famous hundred days that followed his inauguration a willing Congress did his bidding, turning out new legislation at an unprecedented rate. In fact, for the four years of his first term the volume of legislation surpassed that of any previous administration. It dealt mainly with economic recovery and social reform in the areas of agriculture, banking, the monetary system, the securities markets, labor, social security, health, housing, transportation, communications, natural resources – in fact, every aspect of the American economy and society.

Perhaps the most characteristic enactment of the entire period was the National Industrial Recovery Act. It created a National Recovery Administration to supervise the preparation of "codes of fair competition" for each industry by representatives of the industry itself. Although hailed at the time as a new departure in economic policy, it turned out to be very like the trade association movement that Hoover had promoted as secretary of commerce (without the element of coercion). It was even more like the wartime economic administration; a number of high government officials had, in fact, served in the wartime mobilization of the economy (including Roosevelt himself, as assistant secretary of the navy). The NRA also bore striking similarities to the fascist system of industrial organization in Italy, though without the brutality and police-state methods of the latter. In essence, it was a system of private economic planning ("industrial self-government"), with government supervision to protect the public interest and guarantee the right of labor to organize and bargain collectively.

In 1935 the Supreme Court declared the NRA unconstitutional. In other areas in which the Court struck down his initial legislation Roosevelt achieved his goals by new laws, but with respect to industry he altered his stand and initiated a campaign of "trust busting" (itself subsequently reversed with the approach of World War II). The industrial recovery had been disappointing, and in 1937 the economy suffered a new recession without having achieved full employment. The United States returned to war in 1941 with more than 6 million still unemployed. Although many of the New Deal reforms were valuable in themselves and continue to make a vital contribution to American life, the New Deal system as a whole was no more successful as an answer to the problems that beset Western civilization than contemporary programs in Europe.

THE NEW DEAL AND FOREIGN POLICY

The foreign relations of the New Deal were even more contradictory and confusing than its domestic policy. Roosevelt began by breaking up an international monetary conference called for the summer of 1933 in London in an attempt to secure agreement on international currency problems. In the following year Congress reiterated its condemnation of countries in default on intergovernmental indebtedness, but at the same time it passed the Reciprocal Trade Agreements Act which gave the president wide authority to reduce tariffs by agreement. In strictly political foreign relations Roosevelt respected the country's ingrained isolationist bias toward Europe but took the initiative in formulating a "good neighbor policy" for Latin America. Both the government and the country publicly deplored Japanese aggression in China (see pp. 434–435) but were not prepared to take positive action to deter it. As the war clouds gathered in Europe the president openly expressed his sympathies for the democracies, but he was so far from persuading the country of the desirability of intervention that in September, 1939, he officially proclaimed American neutrality in the "European" war.

AUTHORITARIAN ATTEMPTS AT RECONSTRUCTION
CHAPTER FIFTEEN

Liberal attempts at reconstruction were characterized by piecemeal, ad hoc measures to patch up the old order, to improve its virtues, and to eliminate its defects. Most authoritarian attempts aimed at a total reconstruction of society along radically different lines. The emphasis on the totality of the effort, extending to the means as well as the ends, resulted in the invention of a new word to describe such societies: totalitarian.

Totalitarianism covers all attempts at social organization in which all the resources of the society are devoted – by coercion if necessary – to the realization of one all-embracing goal. It applies to the conventional political Left, or communism, as well as to movements on the political Right, which go under a variety of names. In a sense it applies even to the organization of the war effort of the United States and the other Western allies in World War II, in which the single goal was total victory, implying total mobilization of the society for total war. The crucial difference is that the totalitarian effort of democratic nations was intended from the beginning to be temporary, ending with the achievement of victory, whereas in the totalitarian nations proper it is regarded as the permanent state of society.

Several other terms closely identified with totalitarianism need preliminary definition to avoid confusion. The most important is dictatorship, which refers simply to the authoritarian rule of a single individual or political party. Dictatorship is an ancient form of government, and historically it has been one of the most common. Although dictatorship is an essential ingredient of modern totalitarianism, it is only one ingredient of a concept that is much broader and more inclusive.

Another closely related word, sometimes regarded as synonymous with totalitarian dictatorship, is fascism. Originally applied to the doctrines of the Fascisti, a political party organized in 1919 by Benito Mussolini to take control of the government of Italy, it derives from the Italian *fascio,* meaning group or bundle, which in turn derives from the Latin *fasces,* a bundle of sticks or rods with an ax projecting from them used as a symbol of authority in ancient Rome. By extension, fascism came to be applied to any right-wing totalitarian movement.

Nazism refers more specifically to the totalitarian movement headed by Adolf Hitler in Germany. It derives from the German pronunciation of the first two syllables of National Sozialistische Deutsche Arbeiter Partei (NSDAP), the National Socialist German Workers' party (Arbeiter was subsequently dropped). This party took as its symbol the swastika, in ancient times a symbol of welfare or well-being but since the 1930's a symbol of hatred and cruelty because of its association with the Nazis. Other authoritarian movements took other names (the Falange in Spain, for example) and other symbols (the rising sun of the Japanese Empire or the hammer and sickle of Russian Communism), but all had common elements that set them off clearly from movements deriving from the liberal tradition of the nineteenth century. There were also important differences among authoritarian movements, especially between Communism on the extreme Left and the various authoritarian movements on the Right.

COMMUNISM IN RUSSIA, 1921–1938

Communism constituted the most comprehensive and systematic of all the attempts to reconstruct society in the period between the wars. To say that it was systematic, however, does not imply that its realization involved the implementation of a preconceived plan. The foremost aim of the Bolshevik leaders in 1917 was to seize power and after that to maintain themselves in power. They had formulated their other aims in only the most general way. The eventual form of the Soviet state and society evolved by a process of trial and error, pragmatic compromise, and internal rivalry and dispute over more than fifteen years.

THE STRUCTURE OF GOVERNMENT

Several constitutional changes have occurred in the history of the Soviet Union. The brief description here is based upon the most important common features of the constitutions of 1923 and 1936. Superficially the government of the Soviet Union (the Union of Soviet Socialist Republics) resembles that of certain Western democracies. It is a federation of nominally independent republics, of which the Russian Socialist Federal Soviet Republic is by far the most important.[1] It is democratic

[1] The number of constituent republics within the Soviet Union has fluctuated with internal political changes and external conquest. Just prior to World War II there were eleven: the Russian S.F.S.R., the Ukrainian S.S.R., the Byelorussian S.S.R., the Armenian S.S.R., the Georgian S.S.R., the Azerbaijan S.S.R., the Uzbek S.S.R., the Turkmen S.S.R., the Tadjik S.S.R., the Kazakh S.S.R., and the Kirghiz S.S.R. After the war several new republics were created in the conquered areas in the west.

THE U.S.S.R. IN 1939
ARCTIC OCEAN
NORWAY
SWEDEN
FINLAND
Baltic Sea
ESTONIA
LATVIA
LITHUANIA
POLAND
Barents Sea
Murmansk
KOLA PENINSULA
L. Ladoga
Leningrad
Archangel
Minsk
Gorkii
BELORUSSIAN S.S.R.
Moscow
Kiev
UKRAINIAN S.S.R.
Odessa
Don R.
Volga R.
Kazan
Rostov
Stalingrad
Black Sea
RUSSIAN
SOVIET
FEDERATED
SOCIALIST
REPUBLIC
SIBERIA
Sverdlovsk
Cheliabinsk
Tobolsk
Omsk
Ob R.
Novosibirsk
Yenisei R.
Lena R.
Kolyma R.
Iakutsk
KAMCHATKA
Sea of Okhotsk
SAKHALIN
Amur R.
Khabarovsk
Vladivostok
Sea of Japan
JAPAN
KOREA
MANCHURIA
CHINA
TANNU-TUVA
Irkutsk
L. Baikal
Ulan Bator
MONGOLIAN PEOPLE'S REPUBLIC
GEORGIAN S.S.R.
Tiflis
Erevan
ARMENIAN S.S.R.
AZER-BAIJAN S.S.R.
Baku
Caspian Sea
KAZAKH S.S.R.
Aral Sea
L. Balkhash
TURKMEN S.S.R.
UZBEK S.S.R.
Ashkhabad
Tashkent
Frunze
Alma-Ata
KIRGIZ S.S.R.
Stalinabad
TADZHIK S.S.R.
IRAN
Boundaries of Soviet Republics
Capital cities of Soviet Republics
0
1000
Miles

and parliamentary in form, with almost universal suffrage and a pyramidal structure of parliamentary institutions from the village councils at the base to the bicameral All-Union Congress of Soviets – later called the Supreme Soviet – at the apex. The Supreme Soviet rarely meets, however, and only to ratify the decisions of the real rulers of the country, who hold positions of power within still smaller bodies. Among the smaller bodies are the Presidium or central executive committee of the Supreme Soviet, whose president is nominal chief of state of the Soviet Union; and the Council of People's Commissars – later called the Council of Ministers – whose chairman functions as the prime minister. In addition, there are many administrative bodies.

Paralleling the formal organization of the government is the real ruling organ of the state, the Communist Party of the Soviet Union, as the Bolsheviks renamed themselves in 1918. It, too, has local, regional, national, and federal or all-union units of organization. The apex of the party organization is the All-Union Congress, corresponding to the Supreme Soviet, but as in the government, the most important decisions are made in smaller groups: the Central Committee of the All-Union Congress, corresponding to the Presidium; and the Politburo (Political Bureau), corresponding to the Council of Ministers. In practice, there is a large degree of overlap in the membership of the Central Committee and Politburo and their corresponding organs in the formal government structure. The most powerful position in the Soviet state is that of secretary of the Central Committee of the party, which Stalin held from 1922 until his death in 1953. Both Stalin and his successors have frequently held the office of chairman of the Council of Ministers (or premier) as well.

The Communist party is the only legal political party in the Soviet Union. It nominates all candidates for elective office. Although it may on occasion nominate a person who is not a member of the party, all nominees are carefully screened for their loyalty, not merely to the Soviet Union but also to the ruling clique within the party. As the "vanguard of the revolution," the party was and remains an elite group, constituting before World War II no more than 2 or 3 per cent of the adult population. Although the numbers fluctuated somewhat as the result of numerous purges as well as new additions, the membership in 1940 was about 3 million.

No account of the structure of Soviet government would be complete without mention of the secret police. Under different names at different periods (Cheka, OGPU, NKVD) the police – both secret and not-so-secret – have been of fundamental importance in enforcing both civic and party discipline, in engaging in espionage against enemies of the regime and of the ruling clique within the party, and in disposing of disaffected persons by legal or illegal means. Had it not been for the secret police, the government of the Soviet Union would be vastly different today; it is quite likely, in fact, that there would be no Soviet Union at all.

THE "NEW ECONOMIC POLICY"

When the Bolsheviks seized power in 1917 they had no immediate, concrete plans for taking over or operating the economy. Their immediate objective was to secure political control, and they expected to deal with economic questions after their control had been firmly established. Their first important measure in the economic field was a decree to legitimize and hasten the peasants' expropriation of the land, livestock, and equipment of the tsarist landowners. The Bolsheviks soon discovered, however, that they could not depend upon capitalist owners and managers of industrial enterprises, banks, etc., to continue producing for them. They were thus forced into a policy of hasty, widespread, and unplanned nationalization or confiscation. This so-called policy of War Communism lasted from 1918 to 1921. Although the new regime succeeded in winning the civil war and repulsing foreign intervention, the damage and dislocations of the wartime upheavals (before as well as after the revolution) and the lack of skilled technicians and managers resulted in a disastrous drop in production. By the end of 1920 over-all industrial production had fallen to about one-fifth of its prewar level.

Bolshevik agricultural policy produced no better results. Agricultural output fell to about half its prewar level. Worse than that, the peasants whose land seizures the Bolsheviks had legitimized refused to deliver grain and other products at the artificially low prices set by the government, preferring to consume it themselves, hoard it, or sell it illegally at inflated prices. As early as August, 1918, the government sent detachments of armed industrial workers into the countryside to force the peasants to sell their grain at the legally fixed price or, if the peasants refused, to confiscate it.

Faced with economic paralysis and the possibility of peasant revolts on a scale larger than any of the tsarist period, Lenin in the spring of 1921 decided on a radical reversal of the policy of War Communism. Called the New Economic Policy (NEP), it was a compromise with the capitalist principles of production based on private property and exchange in free markets. Lenin called it "a step backward in order to go forward." The new policy had three major features. (1) A special tax in kind on agricultural produce was substituted for compulsory requisitions; peasants were allowed to sell their surpluses at free market prices. (2) Internal free trade and free markets were reintroduced: small-scale industries (employing fewer than twenty workers) were returned to private ownership and allowed to produce for the market; some existing enterprises were leased to foreign entrepreneurs, and special concessions were granted to others to introduce new industries. (3) The so-called commanding heights of the economy remained under state ownership and operation; they included all large-scale industries, transport and communications, finance and banking, and foreign trade. Other features of the NEP period included a vigorous program of electrification of the country, the establishment of technical schools for the training of engineers and industrial managers, and the creation of a more systematic organization of planning and coordination for the state-owned and operated sectors of the economy.

The results of the New Economic Policy were much as Lenin had predicted. Despite some further difficulties with the peasants, output increased in both the agricultural and nonagricultural sectors. By 1926 or 1927 the prewar levels of output had been substantially regained. Meanwhile, crises of a different nature were taking place within the Communist party.

INTERNAL RIVALRIES

In May, 1922, Lenin suffered the first of three paralytic strokes. Although he returned to his office briefly in the autumn of 1922, he never completely regained his strength. He weakened steadily during 1923 and died on January 21, 1924. Prior to his illness Lenin had gained complete supremacy within the party. So great was his prestige that no other party official dared challenge him directly; even after his death any official who could plausibly argue that he was carrying out Lenin's wishes found strong support from the party faithful. In spite of his great position of strength, Lenin refrained from explicitly designating his successor. In fact, in a unique political will, read before the assembled Central Committee of the party shortly after his death, he pointed out both the strengths and the faults of all his close associates and possible successors.

The most popular figure in the party after Lenin was Leon Trotsky. As war commissar (minister of war), he had been the "organizer of victory" over the White armies during the civil war. He was also a gifted orator and had a large following both within and outside the Communist party. As a potential successor to Lenin, however, he suffered from his late conversion to the Bolshevik cause, having followed an independent policy within the party until the October Revolution. He was therefore suspect to the Old Bolsheviks, who also may have been jealous of his oratorical abilities and popularity.

Another possible successor of Lenin was Joseph Stalin, although he was not seriously considered as such in the years immediately following Lenin's illness and death. Stalin was one of the oldest of the Old Bolsheviks. He had been a faithful adherent of Lenin since the party split of 1903, and he had dutifully performed a variety of tasks within the party ever since. Just a month prior to Lenin's first stroke he had become general secretary of the Central Committee, a position he used effectively to build up his own strength within the party. In spite of his allegiance to Lenin, the latter's will accused him of "rudeness" and lack of scruples and warned the party against an overconcentration of power in his hands. Stalin managed to gloss over these criticisms, as well as other slights by Lenin, but he was not yet strong enough to take over unquestioned leadership. He had to rely on his political shrewdness to put together a network of shifting alliances with more prominent party members in order to dispose of his great rival, Trotsky.

Among the other leaders of the party at the time were Grigorii Zinoviev, chairman of the Leningrad Soviet and president of the Comintern (see p. 415); Leo Kamenev, chairman of the Moscow Soviet; Nikolai Bukharin, whom Lenin called the party's "greatest theorist"; Mikhail Tomsky, leader of the trade unions; and Aleksei Rykov, who succeeded Lenin as chairman of the Council of People's Commissars. Prior to Lenin's death Zinoviev, Kamenev, and Stalin had formed a sort of informal triumvirate with the purpose of isolating and eventually deposing Trotsky. They succeeded, partly because of Trotsky's own egotism and his penchant for making tactless statements about his colleagues. In January, 1925, the Central Committee removed Trotsky from the War Commissariat; in 1926 he was removed from the Politburo; and in the following year he was dismissed from the party. Soon afterward he was banished to Turkestan, then allowed to go into exile. After several years of wandering he eventually settled in Mexico, where he continued to try to organize opposition to Stalin within the party. For this reason Stalin engineered his assassination in 1940.

The internal party struggles arose not merely from clashes of personalities but also from fundamental issues of foreign and domestic policy. Whereas Trotsky advocated world revolution, Stalin's motto became "socialism in one country," namely, the Soviet Union. Trotsky's power had scarcely been broken before Stalin began to maneuver his erstwhile associates Zinoviev and Kamenev into the ranks of the "Left Deviationists," as he called them, for their criticisms of the NEP. He formed an alliance with Bukharin, Rykov, and Tomsky, all of whom were advocates of the NEP, and drove his former fellow triumvirs into disgrace. Then Stalin immediately turned on his new associates for their "Rightist Opposition" – that is, advocating too strongly the merits of the NEP! Stalin maintained that since prewar levels of production had been regained, it was imperative to move on to a new stage in the development of socialism by means of comprehensive economic planning. Stalin launched his attack on Bukharin and his associates in 1928; by 1930, when Stalin's henchman V. M. Molotov succeeded Rykov as chairman of the Council of People's Commissars, Stalin's control over the party and the country was almost complete.

SOVIET ECONOMIC PLANNING

Stalin had already initiated the most ambitious attempt in modern times to regiment an entire society. The basis of the attempt was comprehensive economic planning. So drastic and sweeping were the measures and their consequences for the Soviet people that the inauguration of the first five-year plan in 1928 has been referred to as the "second Bolshevik revolution."

The purpose of the five-year plans was not just to achieve socialism. Stalin and the other Soviet leaders, who had long since given up the hope of a worldwide communist revolution, decided that it was necessary for the survival of their regime in the face of a hostile world to industrialize the country and make it both self-sufficient and powerful. Economic planning was also a convenient device for increasing their control over the lives of their subjects, stifling dissatisfaction, and preventing attempts to overthrow the regime. Consequently the initiation of the five-year plans marks the real beginning of Soviet totalitarianism.

The decision to undertake comprehensive economic planning had several implications. Perhaps the most important was an all-out drive for industrialization, especially in heavy industries. Addressing a group of industrial managers in 1931, Stalin declared, "We are fifty to a hundred years behind the advanced countries. We must cover that distance in ten years. Either we do this or they will crush us." Nearly as important was the collectivization of agriculture, necessary for two reasons: first, in order to obtain the labor and other resources for industrialization; second, to break the peasants of their traditionalist orientation and convert them into an agricultural proletariat dependent upon the state for access to the means of production and livelihood. Finally, since collectivization and forced-draft industrialization involved heavy sacrifices in consumption and the free choice of occupations, they had to be undertaken against the wishes of the people. Economic planning thus involved the use of coercion and, on occasion, violence.

All resources of the Soviet government were directly or indirectly utilized in the effort. On the purely technical plane the State Planning Commission (Gosplan) was the over-all planning agency with the responsibility for formulating plans, setting output goals, and sending directives to various subsidiary agencies. The Gosplan was paralleled at regional and local levels by planning bureaus for areas and for special industries. Industries were organized in what the Russians called trusts, cartels, and syndicates, words with a familiar capitalist ring; in essence, what the Soviets did was to adapt the organizational devices of large-scale, concentrated capitalist industry to planning in a socialist country.

The trade unions were called upon to assist in the industrialization of the country. In totalitarian countries trade unions and other labor or-

Sovfoto

Leaders of the Communist Party and the Soviet Government on the Experimental Field of the Tractor and Automobile Scientific Research Institute, by K. I. Finogenov

"The fundamental task of the five-year plan was to convert the U.S.S.R. from an agrarian and weak country, dependent upon the caprices of the capitalist countries, into an independent and powerful country, fully self-reliant and independent of the caprices of world capitalism. . . .

"What dictated this fundamental task of the five-year plan; what were the grounds for it? The necessity of putting an end to the technical and economic backwardness of the Soviet Union, which doomed it to an unenviable existence; the necessity of creating in the country the prerequisites that would enable it not only to overtake but in time to outstrip, technically and economically, the advanced capitalist countries." Stalin to the Joint Plenum of the Communist Party, January 7, 1933, reprinted in J. V. STALIN, WORKS (Moscow, 1955), Vol. XIII.

---

ganizations perform functions very different from those of trade unions in North America and western Europe. In place of representing workers and protecting their interests, they preserve labor discipline, prevent strikes and sabotage, encourage productivity, and in other ways facilitate the attainment of state objectives. The ideal of "workers' control" of industry, held by Tomsky and other trade union leaders before the final triumph of Stalin, had no place under the five-year plans.

The collectivization of agriculture presented the Soviet government with one of its most difficult and persistent problems. During the NEP the peasants had been left almost entirely to their own devices. In addition to bringing output back to prewar levels in a relatively brief period, a few of them, called kulaks (village usurers) by the Communists, had become fairly prosperous. Almost all the peasants had strengthened their traditional attachment to their own plots of soil and livestock.

The government had two devices for collectivization: state farms and collective (cooperative) farms. It preferred the state farm. In it the state owned all the land, livestock, and equipment and appointed a professional manager; the peasants who worked it constituted a pure agricultural proletariat. Not surprisingly, the peasants resisted this kind of regimentation, in many instances burning their crops and slaughtering their livestock in order to prevent them from falling into the hands of the government. In the face of such determined resistance even Stalin backed off, though not until many peasants (especially the kulaks) had been killed outright or shipped off to prison or exile in Siberia and the far north. As a compromise with the peasants, the government allowed them to form collective farms, on which most of the land was tilled in common but with each household retaining small plots for its own use and even for the sale of its surplus on the free market. The state supplied technical advice and machinery to the collective farms from state-owned Machine-Tractor Stations, which could also be used for inspection, propaganda, and control.

The objectives of the first five-year plan were officially declared to have been achieved after only four and one-quarter years. In fact, the plan was far from a complete success. Although output in some lines of industry had grown prodigiously, most industries failed to make their quotas, which had been set at unrealistically high figures. In agriculture about 60 per cent of the peasants had been collectivized, but agricultural output had actually fallen and the number of livestock had declined to between one-half and two-thirds of the 1928 figure. The costs of the five-year plan were enormous, especially the human costs. In the collectivization of agriculture alone more than 5 million people lost their lives through starvation or execution.

In 1933 the government inaugurated a second five-year plan. The emphasis was supposed to be on consumer goods, but in fact the country continued to devote an extraordinary proportion of its resources to capital goods and military equipment. In spite of great increases in industrial production, which put the Soviet Union in the second or third rank in many lines of industry and even in the first rank in a few, the country remained predominantly agrarian, and agriculture was its weakest sector. A third five-year plan, launched in 1938, was interrupted by the German invasion in 1941.

ASPECTS OF SOVIET SOCIETY AND CULTURE

Although the Soviet population remained primarily rural at the outbreak of World War II, urban growth had made rapid gains with industrialization. In 1926 more than 80 per cent of the population lived in rural areas, almost as large a percentage as during the last years of the tsarist regime. A dozen years later the figure was less than 70 per cent. The bulk of the growth was concentrated in the largest cities. Moscow and Leningrad both doubled in population between 1926 and 1939. In the latter year there were twenty-eight cities with more than a quarter of a million people, as against only nine in 1926.

Most Russians were devoutly religious, a characteristic of a peasant society. Prior to World War I the Eastern Orthodox Church had been the state religion of the Russian Empire. There were also sizable groups of Moslems, Jews, and people of other religions among the 180 or so separate ethnic groups. Most leaders of the Communist party, however, were militant atheists and regarded traditional religion as an obstacle to be destroyed in achieving the new society. At first they proceeded cautiously; Lenin did not want to jeopardize his major goals over what, for him, was a trivial matter. After Stalin took over totalitarian control the campaign against the church stepped up, but even Stalin did not try to abolish it altogether. He worked through weak and willing tools within the church hierarchy itself to ensure that it did not seek to undermine his rule.

The Communists faced a similar problem in dealing with writers, artists, and other intellectuals. Under the old regime many of them had belonged to disaffected or radical groups and welcomed the revolution as a liberating movement. In the first years the new regime followed an ambivalent policy, striving to woo the intellectuals both within and outside Russia by means of honors, promises, and propaganda, but at the same time trying to coax, persuade, and at times coerce them into bridling their intellectual freedom in the interests of the party and the state. Stalin had no compunctions about artistic or intellectual freedom; for him the only test of a good writer, artist, or musician was whether or not he followed the party line. His own artistic tastes were rather primitive, betraying his peasant upbringing. He had no use for the modernism characteristic of the art, literature, and music of the 1920's. By strictly enforcing his own canons of taste, he stifled the development of many promising artists and writers.

The Soviet leaders realized that in order to build an industrial society they had to have trained scientists, technicians, and managers. At the time of the revolution over half the Russian people were illiterate. A system of universal education was established — compulsory to age twelve — that gave ample opportunity for advanced training to those who were intellectually and ideologically fitted. It reduced illiteracy to less than 20 per cent by 1939. At the same time the educational system was used for ideological indoctrination; the leaders had little hope of converting the majority of the prerevolutionary generation to a wholehearted acceptance of socialism, but they expected to attain their goals with the new generations. For this reason they also set up youth organizations (Little Octobrists, Pioneers, Young Communists) as training grounds for future members of the Communist party.

The use of secret police, informers, brutality, and terrorism continued to be characteristic of the regime. Indeed, after the consolidation of Stalin's power they came to be its hallmark. Between 1934 and 1938 the "great purge" of the Communist party occurred, the causes and convolutions of which remain a mystery to the outside world to this day. More than 8 million people were arrested; many were executed, but the majority were merely deported to forced labor camps or left to languish in prison. The chief targets were the Old Bolsheviks of the former Right and Left opposition, although all of them had recanted their errors, sometimes more than once. All surviving members of the 1921 Politburo except Stalin were executed. In many instances Stalin's own henchmen were tried, or executed without trial – including the chief of the secret police who had been responsible for rounding up the Old Bolsheviks. The purge extended far down into the ranks of the Communist party and even into the mass of ordinary citizens, who had no idea of why they were arrested. One of the most mystifying elements was the series of mock trials at which prominent leaders of the party, the government, and the army confessed to political crimes they could not possibly have committed.

SOVIET FOREIGN POLICY

In the main, Soviet foreign policy followed the shifts in domestic policy. During the period of War Communism, when the Western Allies were lending assistance to the White armies and the Bolsheviks expected a proletarian revolution in the West momentarily, they did what little they could to effectuate it. Their principal instrument was the Third, or Communist, International (Comintern), which was supposed to be an international organization of working-class leaders similar to the First and Second Internationals. In fact, it was a collection of Communist conspirators organized, subsidized, and dominated by the Communist party of the Soviet Union. The Comintern continued to work for the overthrow of so-called bourgeois governments even after the Soviet Union had officially established friendly relations with them.

After the advent of the NEP the official Soviet policy toward the West changed to one of conciliation. Although the Soviet government refused to recognize the debts of the tsarist regime, it sought by other means to establish normal diplomatic relations with Western nations. When invited to the Genoa conference of 1922, it responded with alacrity. Although the conference failed to produce any notable results, it led to the Rapallo agreements between the Soviet Union and Germany. (See p. 386.) The Soviet Union also signed the Kellogg-Briand Peace Pact.

After the triumph of Stalin and the inauguration of the first five-year plan the Soviet Union relapsed into a sort of isolationism in international affairs. The major exception was its contradictory role toward Germany. On the one hand, it continued economic and military collaboration with the Weimar Republic in the spirit of Rapallo; on the other, it occasionally collaborated with the Nazis by means of the Comintern and the German Communist party in order to overthrow the republic. Stalin apparently expected that the seizure of power by the Nazis would unite the German people behind the Communist party. He realized his mistake too late. Not until 1934 did he definitely break off relations with the Nazis and begin to favor a popular front, an alliance with the socialists, in France, to which he had previously been hostile. After the withdrawal of Germany the Soviet Union was finally admitted to the League of Nations, but by that time the international situation had deteriorated too far for it to make any difference. After a brief intervention in the Spanish Civil War against the forces of Germany and Italy (see pp. 435–436), the Soviet Union withdrew once more from the world arena. When it re-emerged in 1939, it did so in a totally different guise.

FASCISM IN ITALY, 1922–1938

Postwar Italy proved a fertile breeding ground for diseases of the body politic. Although allied with the victors, Italy's contribution to the victory had been negligible. The refusal of the men of Versailles to give Italy a larger share of the spoils of war galled the more fervid nationalists among the Italians, of whom there were many. One of the most picturesque, the poet Gabriele D'Annunzio, gave vent to his feelings by leading a band of volunteer legionnaires against the Adriatic port of Fiume, which had been assigned to Yugoslavia. He seized and occupied it for several months in 1919–20 in defiance of both international opinion and his own government. The government demonstrated its own weakness by its unwillingness or inability to deal summarily with such open defiance of its authority.

The prewar coalitions of so-called Liberal splinter groups had been shaky enough; in the infinitely more trying times after the war they were beset on both Right and Left by rival political parties with few scruples and less respect for the existing system. Over all lay the pall of economic chaos. Poverty, endemic in Italy, had been made much worse by the economic dislocations of the war and the postwar depression. Italy suffered simultaneously from a heavy burden of debt and taxation, a yawning government deficit that produced rampant inflation, severe unemployment, and dire shortages of basic foodstuffs and essential raw materials for industry. The workers responded to these economic and political conditions by staging strikes and sabotaging factories; the employers resorted to lockouts of striking or unruly workers; the unemployed indulged in street riots and mob violence; the peasants seized large estates and destroyed property; and the deputies in parliament castigated one another's shortcomings — past, present, and future. The government did nothing.

MUSSOLINI AND THE ORIGINS OF FASCISM

Benito Mussolini (1883–1945), the future *Duce* (leader) of Italy, was the son of an anticlerical blacksmith. Dismissed from a Catholic seminary for allegedly putting a knife in one of his fellow seminarians, he led a gypsy existence for a number of years, skipping the country to avoid military service and then getting expelled from both Switzerland and Austria. Along the way he picked up a smattering of socialist doctrine and supported himself as a trade union organizer and radical journalist. He gained a certain amount of notoriety by opposing Italy's conquest of Libya and spent a few months in jail for the manner in which he expressed his opinion. In 1912, after his release, he became editor of the *Avanti* (Forward) of Milan, the leading socialist newspaper in Italy. Mussolini broke with his socialist comrades on the question of Italian intervention in World War I. They upheld international socialist solidarity and pacifism, while he became an ardent nationalist, using the curiously perverted Marxist argument that Italy, as a "proletarian" nation, must attack "capitalist" Austria. He became so carried away by his patriotism that he actually enlisted in the army, where he rose to the rank of corporal.

Clearly, Mussolini was neither a conventional socialist nor a conventional nationalist. Consistency was not one of his characteristics. As he later said of his doctrines, "The spirit of Fascism is will and action, not intellect." Yet he was not without ability: he was persuasive as both a journalist and an orator, had the shrewdness of a peasant, and above all had ambition, though at times his boldness was interspersed with indecision bordering on cowardice.

After the war Mussolini toyed with the notion of trying to regain his position within the socialist movement in order to make himself master of Italy, much as Lenin had done in Russia. His former comrades would have nothing to do with him. He therefore devoted himself to organizing an anti-socialist group called the *Fascio di combattimento*. Most of his followers were ex-soldiers and unemployed youths, but he also obtained financial support from wealthy industrialists who found his strong-arm bands useful for breaking strikes and intimidating workers. Mussolini dressed them in black shirts and subjected them to military discipline, with elaborate rituals and frequent parades. He had no specific positive program, but the conditions of the time favored his anti-Communist stand. The left wing of the Socialist party split off in 1920, becoming the Italian Communist party with strong Russian connections through the Comintern. Thereafter Mussolini's movement attracted wide support from frightened property owners, devout Catholics, and others terrified by the prospect of a Soviet Italy. Within a few years his Fascist party had 300,000 members, and in the election of 1921 it seated thirty-five members in the Chamber of Deputies.

THE MARCH ON ROME

Economic unrest and social disorder continued to mount until the late summer of 1922, when the Socialists declared a general strike. Preparations for the strike were badly made and it proved an immediate failure; nevertheless, it gave the Fascists a welcome opportunity to flex their muscles by attacking strikers, Socialist party headquarters, newspapers, and even Socialist-controlled city governments. When the national government did not interfere to prevent the Fascists from taking over the city governments by force, it consigned itself to oblivion. In October, 1922, the Fascists held a triumphant party congress in Naples, and Mussolini boasted to his uniformed followers that "the government will be given to us or we shall march on Rome." Preparations for the march were made, although Mussolini himself did not participate directly. Meanwhile, the Liberal prime minister demanded permission from King Victor Emmanuel III to declare martial law in order to deal with the situation. The king refused, and the cabinet resigned. The country was thus without a government in this crucial moment. The king, who had already been in contact with Fascist politicians, named Mussolini prime minister. Although he had resorted to threats and violence, Mussolini's accession to power was, in a technical sense, perfectly legal.

THE ORGANIZATION OF THE FASCIST STATE AND PARTY

Mussolini's first action as prime minister was to demand and obtain from the cowed parliament a year's grant of dictatorial power. During this year he placed his followers in strategic spots throughout the government, brought the army into line, and enacted a new electoral law. After another campaign of terror and violence, the Fascists in a rigged election in April, 1924, obtained an overwhelming majority in the Chamber of Deputies. By the end of the year their domination of Italy was complete.

Brown Brothers

Mussolini and Hitler Review Troops

"I always enjoy meeting the Duce. He's a great personality. . . . Don't suppose that events in Italy had no influence on us. The brown shirt would probably not have existed without the black shirt. The march on Rome, in 1922, was one of the turning points of history. The mere fact that anything of the sort could be attempted, and could succeed, gave us an impetus. A few weeks after the march on Rome, I was received by the Minister Schweyer. That would never have happened otherwise." Hitler, July 21, 1941, in HITLER'S SECRET CONVERSATIONS, 1941–1944 (New York, 1953).

The Fascists still had no notable, positive program except the will to power. Mussolini was content to retain the forms of monarchy while Victor Emmanuel receded into the background as a barely visible figurehead. A series of constitutional changes reduced the parliament to a rubber stamp for the Fascist party; all other parties were outlawed. The Fascists exercised tight censorship of the press and controlled the other mass media directly. A secret police organization kept check on the activities of actual and potential enemies of the regime, while squads of Blackshirts, now full-fledged instruments of the state, awed the populace.

Membership in the party, which in its early days had attracted mainly roughnecks and hoodlums, became a position of prestige and power, attracting ambitious politicians, businessmen who wished favors from the state, and even remnants of the old aristocracy. Except for individuals who could be immediately useful to him, Mussolini prescribed a long period of apprenticeship and limited membership to about 5 per cent of the total adult population. In 1932 the party rolls carried the names of approximately 1,250,000 people, organized in a hierarchy of about 10,000 local and regional units. Presiding over all was the Fascist Grand Council, composed of about twenty of the most important leaders and dominated by Mussolini. The Grand Council was in effect a sort of supergovernment in that it named all candidates for political office, supervised regular government officials in the performance of their duties, and dictated the general policies of both government and party.

FASCIST IDEOLOGY AND THE CORPORATE STATE

In order to bolster the ideological underpinnings of his regime Mussolini employed the philosopher Giovanni Gentile, a former student of Benedetto Croce, to provide a rationalization of Fascism which was then widely publicized as Mussolini's own philosophy. What emerged was an amorphous blend of ideas from a variety of sources, including Hegel, Croce, Nietzsche, Sorel, Pareto, and other idealist and antirational writers. Fascism glorified the use of force, upheld war as the noblest human activity, denounced liberalism, democracy, socialism, and individualism, treated material well-being with disdain, and regarded human inequalities as not only inevitable but desirable. Above all, it deified the state as the supreme embodiment of the human spirit: "For us Fascists, the State is not merely a guardian, preoccupied solely with the duty of assuring the personal safety of the citizens; nor is it an organization with purely material aims, such as to guarantee a certain level of well-being and peaceful conditions of life. . . . The State, as conceived of and as created by Fascism, is a spiritual and moral fact in itself. . . . The State is not only a living reality of the present, it is also linked with the past and above all the future, and thus transcending the brief limits of individual life, it represents the immanent spirit of the nation." The government employed compulsory military service, Fascist youth groups, and similar devices in the largely unsuccessful attempt to inculcate these ideas into the populace.

As an attempted total reconstruction of society, Fascism had to have a distinctive form of economic organization. Mussolini developed the corporate state, one of the most publicized and least successful innovations of the Fascist regime. In principle, the corporate state was the antithesis of both capitalism and socialism. Although it permitted private ownership of property, the interests of both owners and workers were to be subordinated to the higher interests of society as a whole, as represented by the state. To accomplish this, all industries in the country were organized into twelve corporations — corresponding to an American trade association rather than to a business corporation. Workers, proprietors, and the state were represented, with party functionaries holding the important administrative posts. All previously existing labor unions were suppressed. The functions of the corporations included the regulation of prices, wages, and working conditions and the provision of social insurance. Later elaborations provided for the replacement of the Chamber of Deputies with a Chamber of Corporations. In practice, insofar as the corporations functioned at all, they acted mainly as capitalistic trade associations with the aim of increasing the income of businessmen and party administrators at the expense of laborers and consumers. Other aspects of Fascist economic policy were no more successful. In spite of a large public works and armaments program, Italy suffered severely from the depression; even the argument that "Mussolini made the trains run on time," sometimes used by American apologists for Fascism, was false.

THE LATERAN TREATY

One of the most successful of Mussolini's policies concerned his relations with the Catholic Church. Since the Italian occupation of Rome in 1870 no reigning pope had set foot outside Vatican City, a small enclave within the city of Rome, or received the ruler of Italy. The Lateran Treaty of 1929, named for the church in which it was signed, ended the long dispute between the Church and the Italian state and bestowed the pope's implicit moral approval on Mussolini's regime. In return for a promise by the pope not to interfere in politics and to obtain government approval of the appointment of bishops (who also had to swear loyalty to the state), Mussolini granted Pius XI recognition as sovereign over the "temporal domain" of Vatican City, promised financial support, and allowed the Church a large measure of control over education. Mussolini thereby not only disposed of a troublesome domestic political issue but also gained the approval of many Catholics and others outside Italy.

NAZISM IN GERMANY, 1933–1938

Although the election in Germany in March, 1933, was carried out under the coercive influence of the Nazi storm troopers in an atmosphere of near hysteria after the burning of the Reichstag, it did not result in a clear victory for the Nazis. More than half the electorate voted against the National Socialist party. With the aid of some fifty conservative Nationalists in the Reichstag, however, Hitler was able to form a new government. In spite of the tenuousness of his victory, he moved quickly to consolidate his power and eliminate the opposition.

THE CONSOLIDATION OF NAZI POWER

Immediately after the election Hitler arrested the leaders of the Communist party and expelled the Communist members from the Reichstag, using the Reichstag fire as the excuse. With the opposition thus reduced he introduced in the Reichstag the so-called Enabling Act to give the cabinet full legislative and budgetary powers for four years, allowing it to govern without check either from the Reichstag or the president. On March 23, 1933, with its temporary meeting place surrounded by storm troopers, the Reichstag considered the bill. Only the leader of the Social Democratic party spoke in opposition; only the Social Democrats voted against it. The bill passed by a vote of 441 to 84. The Reichstag had abdicated its power to Hitler.

The pace of Nazi ascension accelerated. Hitler reorganized the civil service, dismissing more than a quarter of its officials, especially those in the higher posts, and replaced them with his own trusted lieutenants. Hermann Goering – a World War I flying hero, president of the Reichstag, and one of Hitler's most trusted henchmen – took charge of the nation's police forces and at once organized a special secret police division, the Gestapo, with almost unlimited powers. Hitler ousted the elected officials of state and local government units and replaced them with men of his own choosing, usually local *Gauleiters* (district leaders) of the Nazi party. The judiciary and the universities were similarly reorganized and screened for loyalty, or at least obedience, to the Nazis. In January, 1934, Hitler completed the process of centralization by abolishing in form as well as in fact all local government divisions; for the first time in history Germany became a completely unified, centralized state.

Hitler tidied up the political scene by abolishing all other political parties. After the Communists had been outlawed, the turn of the Social Democrats came in June, 1933. Other parties were allowed to dissolve themselves voluntarily. On July 14, 1933, Hitler declared the Nazis the only legal party. The Nazis also moved against other voluntary organizations, subjecting them to party discipline or forcing them out of existence. On May Day, 1933, traditionally a labor holiday, the government declared a national holiday and cooperated with trade union leaders in staging a giant celebration. The following morning the trade union leaders returned to their offices to find them raided, their records confiscated, and themselves under arrest.

To facilitate the education of the German people in Nazi aims and ideology, the government took complete control of the radio. It already controlled the postal, telephone, and telegraph services, and did not hesitate to use them for espionage and surveillance. It established a heavy censorship of the press, cinema, and theater. Public meetings were forbidden, except those organized by the Nazis, and even the churches were subjected to surveillance. Joseph Goebbels, the Nazi minister for propaganda, organized huge mass meetings and other programs to inculcate positive loyalty to the regime. As in Italy and the Soviet Union, special youth groups indoctrinated children and young people in Nazi ideology and trained them to spy on others, including their parents, for signs of disloyalty to the regime.

Hitler sought to consolidate popular support for his regime by providing a scapegoat, "somebody to hate," in the persecution of whom the masses could work off the frustrations accumulated in ordinary life. An ideal vehicle for his purpose was the latent anti-Semitism of many Germans, which was amply attested by the popularity of *völkisch,* romantic, and racist literature from the nineteenth century. In *Mein Kampf* Hitler had fulminated against the Jews as the manipulators of both communism and "usurious capitalism." On April 1, 1933, the day the Enabling Act took effect legally, he unleashed an orgy of persecution against them. Persons of the Jewish faith or with Jewish ancestry were dismissed from the government and prohibited from practicing such professions as law and medicine. The police tolerated and even abetted the destruction of Jewish property and the physical molestation of Jewish shopkeepers and industrialists by organized gangs of roughnecks. In later years an even more terrible fate awaited the survivors of these pogroms.

Within less than a year after coming to power Hitler had succeeded in making himself almost complete master of the nation. Only two potential sources of opposition remained: the army and dissident elements within his own Nazi party. The way in which he used these two groups to neutralize one another and to ensure his own supremacy was indicative of his unscrupulous cunning and will to power. Many within the party felt that the Nazi revolution had not gone far enough and that the leaders were coming to terms with the old power structure and calling a halt to the revolution. They wanted more power and plunder for themselves. The ringleader of these radicals was Ernst Roehm, chief of staff of the storm troopers, whose desire was to become commander of all the armed forces of the nation.

The army, for its part, had generally remained aloof from the political maneuvering preceding and following Hitler's advent to power. The officer corps had survived intact both wartime defeat and the pacifism of the Weimar Republic; its members regarded themselves as the trustees and ultimate defenders of the nation's honor and traditions. Although

Photoworld

Adolf Hitler on the First Anniversary of His Government

"The Fuehrer combines in himself all of the sovereign authority of the state; all public authority in the state . . . comes from the authority of the Fuehrer. We must speak not of 'state authority' but of 'Fuehrer-authority' if we wish to designate properly the political authority in the Reich. For it is not the state as an impersonal entity that holds political authority, but this is entrusted to the Fuehrer as the executor of the collective will of the Volk. *The authority of the Fuehrer is complete and total . . . extends to all areas of the life of the* Volk *. . . is not limited by spheres of privilege or individual rights, but is free and independent, exclusive and unlimited. However, it is not tyrannical and it is not arbitrary, but carries its obligations within itself. It comes from the* Volk, *it is on behalf of the* Volk, *and it derives its justification from the* Volk. *It is free of all external ties because in its innermost being it is inextricably tied to the fate, the welfare, the mission, and the honor of the* Volk." Ernst R. Huber, VERFASSUNGSRECHT DES GROSSDEUTSCHEN REICHES (Hamburg, 1939).

they looked upon Hitler and his cronies with contempt as upstarts, they made no effort to prevent the Nazi seizure and consolidation of power so long as their own status was not challenged – and Hitler was careful to avoid that.

Roehm's aggressiveness, therefore, presented Hitler with a dilemma: he must either disavow a substantial element within his own party, or risk antagonizing the army, the only power in the nation that was strong enough to topple him. Events moved toward a showdown in the early summer of 1934. With the connivance of Goering and Heinrich Himmler, who were rivals and personal enemies of Roehm, Hitler secretly arranged for the sudden seizure and murder of Roehm and hundreds of his associates and sympathizers in the famous Blood Purge of June 30, 1934. As an excuse for this betrayal of his own supporters Hitler cited an alleged conspiracy to overthrow his government, but the conspiracy was mainly if not wholly of his own making. In any case, he not only silenced the potential opposition within the party but also won the approval of the General Staff. When the aged President Hindenburg died the following August, Hitler assumed the office of *Fuehrer und Reichskanzler* (leader and imperial chancellor) and received a personal oath of loyalty from the entire army. From that time forward he wielded absolute power in Germany.

NAZI IDEOLOGY

The Nazi seizure of power was facilitated by several more or less fortuitous occurrences – German defeat in World War I, the humiliations of the Versailles treaty, the disastrous economic and social consequences of the hyperinflation and the great depression, and the special features of the Weimar constitution – but the Nazis gained strength as a mass movement by appealing to certain intellectual and emotional tendencies long present in German history. Hitler's genius as a politician consisted in uniting his appeal to deep-seated ideological tendencies with an efficient organization, discipline, and a maniacal will to power. The temper of the German people in the interwar decades that allowed him to succeed has been called a "flight from reality." Hitler himself was one of its foremost examples.

Nazi ideology drew heavily on the romanticism of the early nineteenth century, on the racism of such writers as H. S. Chamberlain, and on the antirationalism and nihilism of some late nineteenth- and early twentieth-century philosophers. Like the romantics, the Nazis drew inspiration from legends of the heroic past of the Germanic people, clouded in the mists of obscurity but shining brightly in their purity and nobility. After 1933 the Bayreuth festival of Wagnerian opera became an official Nazi rite. The basic tenet of Nazi ideology was belief in the moral supremacy of the Aryan race, whom the Nazis identified with the Teutonic ancestors of the German Volk. According to Hitler, the whole of history was a cosmic struggle by this "master race" to dominate various "inferior" races, such as the Slavs, the Latins, and especially the Jews. The belief, whether real or feigned, that they were merely the executors of some grand design of Fate or Providence provided the Nazis with a convenient rationalization for their persecution of the Jews, for systematic terrorism, and for the grossest kind of barbaric, inhuman actions. Nazi racist policies attained their ultimate manifestation during World War II when thousands upon thousands of men, women, and children were executed in gas chambers and by firing squads for no other crime than that of being "non-Aryan."

The Nazi notion of a "master race" fitted well with Nietzsche's concept of a "superman" who was not bound by ordinary conventions of law and morality. So, too, did their emphasis on eternal struggle, violence, and power for its own sake. In some respects, however, the Nazis were quite conventional, even old-fashioned. Their viewpoint on the role of women in society was summed up in the slogan *Kinder, Kirche, Küche* (children, church, and kitchen). To indoctrinate the nation in their ideology, they made extensive use of mass rallies, great political spectacles with torchlight parades, military displays, and other devices that subordinated the individual personality to the "collective will." Their objective was to impress the populace with the Nazi notion of the individual's highest duty: service to the state.

NAZI ECONOMIC POLICY

The Nazis came to power in the midst of the greatest economic depression of modern times; indeed, the distress produced by that depression was one of the major factors that catapulted them to power. To counteract the depression Hitler introduced a gigantic public works program that melded gradually into a rearmament program. As a result Germany was the first nation to recover from the depression. In the process it developed the first modern highway system (the famed autobahns) and greatly strengthened and expanded its industries, which gave Germany a decided advantage over its enemies in the early years of World War II. From 6 million unemployed in 1933 the German economy reached the point in 1939 of having more jobs than workers to fill them.

In place of the voluntary trade unions, which were destroyed in 1933, the Nazis established compulsory membership in the National Labor Front under the leadership of Robert Ley. They abolished collective bargaining between workers and employers, substituting boards of labor trustees with full power to determine wages, hours, and conditions of work. Industrialists were persuaded to cooperate with the new industrial regime by the promise of an end to labor problems if they did and the threat of confiscation and imprisonment if they did not. Unlike the totalitarian regime in Russia, the Nazis did not resort to wholesale nationalization of the economy (although confiscated Jewish enterprises were frequently turned over to party members); they relied on persuasion and controls to achieve their objectives.

One of the principal economic objectives of the Nazis was to make the German economy completely self-sufficient in the event of war. They recalled the crippling effects of the Allied blockade in World War I and wished to be immune to such difficulties in the future. They directed their scientists to develop new *ersatz* or synthetic commodities, both consumer goods and military supplies, which could be manufactured from raw materials available in Germany. The policy of *Autarkie* (self-sufficiency) determined the character of German trade relations with other nations. Dr. Hjalmar Schacht, Hitler's economic adviser, devised numerous intricate new financial and monetary controls to prevent the flight of capital from Germany. He also negotiated trade agreements with Germany's neighbors in eastern Europe and the Balkans providing for the direct barter of German manufactured goods for raw materials and foodstuffs. Very few German goods were in fact shipped, but the policy successfully tied eastern Europe into the German war economy.

HITLER'S FOREIGN POLICY

In his propaganda campaign before achieving power Hitler had repeatedly hammered the theme of the immorality and injustice of the Diktat of Versailles. Soon after taking office he used the depression as an excuse to proclaim "an end of reparations," and in the autumn of 1933 he utilized the disarmament conference, then in session at Geneva under the sponsorship of the League of Nations, to discredit the Versailles treaty. Hitler demanded peremptorily that all other major nations reduce their armaments to the level imposed on Germany by the treaty. When the demand was refused, as Hitler had anticipated, he withdrew Germany from the League. This successful defiance of the League and of international opinion not only strengthened Hitler within Germany but also encouraged him in his aggressive foreign policy.

OTHER AUTHORITARIAN REGIMES

According to Woodrow Wilson, World War I had been fought to make the world safe for democracy. As factual description, such a statement was patently false; but in the first flush of Allied victory many people were carried away by Wilson's high-sounding phrases and idealism and actually believed that democracy would be universal. Disillusionment soon set in. By 1933, when the Weimar Republic succumbed to Hitler's Nazis, democracy was everywhere in retreat before the forces of authoritarianism. In Europe seventeen of the twenty-seven nations had one or another form of authoritarian government.

AUSTRIA

The Austrian republic, a "head without a body" after the dissolution of the Hapsburg monarchy, was now composed almost entirely of German-speaking citizens. Beset by currency disorders and widespread unemployment, it struggled desperately merely to exist. The country was sharply divided between two bitterly antagonistic political parties: the conservative Christian (Catholic) Socialists, who controlled the government but had their main strength outside Vienna, and the radical, Marxist-oriented Social Democrats, who controlled the municipal government of the capital. This division was further complicated by the rise of an Austrian Nazi party that took its orders from Hitler. To combat the Nazi menace after Hitler's accession to power, Austrian chancellor Engelbert Dollfuss created his own brand of fascism, a Christian Corporate State, and destroyed the Social Democrats as an organized body by armed force. In 1934 the Austrian Nazis attempted a coup d'état and assassinated Dollfuss, but the intervention of Mussolini and France prevented Hitler from taking advantage of the situation to absorb Austria. Kurt von Schuschnigg succeeded Dollfuss as chancellor and continued his policies; but with the Social Democrats out of the way the will to resist Hitler found few strong adherents in Austria, and Hitler had only to bide his time for a favorable moment to incorporate Austria into the German Fatherland.

EASTERN EUROPE

Except for Czechoslovakia and Finland, which hung onto democratic forms by the barest margin, eastern Europe capitulated entirely to authoritarian regimes. The Poles, whose nation had been resurrected in republican form at the end of the war, found it as difficult to agree among themselves as they had a century and a half before. To put an end to the wrangling of the political parties, Marshal Joseph Pilsudski staged a coup d'état in 1926 and established a military dictatorship. A similar development took place in Rumania in 1930 when King Carol II, who had been barred from the throne, deposed his infant son and assumed dictatorial powers. Hungary never tasted the fruits of democracy. After its short-lived Communist government at the end of the war, the old Magyar aristocracy regained power, and Admiral Nicholas Horthy governed in dictatorial fashion as regent for a nonexistent king. Yugoslavia was torn by continuing struggles among the various ethnic groups that composed the new nation. The struggles culminated in 1928 with the assassination of the opposition leaders in parliament. Shortly afterward King Alexander dissolved parliament, suspended the constitution, and governed as dictator. Alexander himself was assassinated on a trip to France in 1934, but the regency that governed in the name of his young son Peter II continued his policies. Greece and Bulgaria, both of which were nominally constitutional monarchies, experienced continual conflicts between dictatorial kings and reactionary military cliques. Albania and the new Baltic republics of Lithuania, Latavia, and Estonia also succumbed to dictatorial governments after brief experiments with democracy.

THE IBERIAN PENINSULA

Having avoided involvement in World War I, Spain escaped many of the dilemmas and problems that beset other European countries. Nevertheless, Spain was a poor and backward country, unprogressive politically as well as economically. It had never enjoyed democratic government, and during the premiership of Miguel Primo de Rivera from 1923 to 1930 the government became frankly dictatorial. Unrest mounted throughout the country. To save himself, King Alfonso XIII forced Primo de Rivera to resign; when that did not quell the discontent, the king himself fled to exile in the following year. Proclamation of a republic followed this bloodless revolution, and the democratic forces within Spain set out to create a progressive, enlightened commonwealth against the trend of the times.

Unhappily for Spain, neither its internal resources nor the external environment favored the experiment. The mass of the population, poverty stricken and illiterate, lacked both the experience and the ability—perhaps even the desire—for self-government. The government itself was a loose and refractory coalition of middle-class liberals, radical democrats, socialists, and even anarchists. In addition to its internal divisions, it soon encountered determined opposition from the conservative and reactionary elements who still controlled the bulk of the wealth of the country: the Church, the great landowners, and most of the higher army officers. In 1936 General Francisco Franco led a revolt against the government. The bloody, destructive civil war that followed invited foreign intervention and became a major milestone on the road to World War II. For Spain it resulted in the triumph of General Franco, who reorganized the Falange party, created by Primo de Rivera, on the model of Mussolini's Fascists and Hitler's Nazis, and proceeded to establish a reactionary authoritarianism that outlasted by far its models.

Portugal, like its neighbor, was a poor, benighted country. In spite of the revolution of 1911, which established a republican form of government, the country remained a prey to social strife and political unrest. In 1926 a military coup overthrew the elected government, and in 1932 Dr. Antonio Salazar, finance minister since 1928, became prime minister and in effect dictator. In the following year he introduced a new constitution which resembled in many respects that of Fascist Italy. Salazar retained his power for more than thirty-five years, outlasting even Stalin and setting a new record in modern times for one-man rule.

MILITARISM IN JAPAN

Authoritarian movements also arose in countries outside of Europe. They did not make much headway or constitute a serious menace to existing forms of government in the United States or the British dominions, but in Latin America, where democracy had never been effectively established, some form of dictatorship, however diluted, was the general rule. Most of Africa and much of Asia were ruled in the 1930's by the democratic countries of western Europe, though the method of rule was anything but democratic, with the result that democracy in those areas suffered a taint of hypocrisy which time has not yet erased. The independent or semi-independent countries of the Near East, the Middle East, and the Far East (East Asia, as it has come to be called) had no liberal or democratic traditions and continued to be ruled in the tradition of Oriental despotisms.

The one non-Western nation that had succeeded in adapting itself to Western ways followed the trend toward totalitarian dictatorship. During the 1920's Japan made progress in the extension of democratic practices and followed a policy of international cooperation in spite of the objections of Japanese militarists. The great depression cut short this peaceful evolution. Japan had a population of 65 million – half that of the United States – in an area smaller than the state of California. It was heavily dependent upon international trade, both for markets for its exports and for imports of food stuffs and raw materials. The shrinkage of international trade during the depression gave the militarists and other ultranationalists, including the great industrial dynasties, their opportunity to seize power. In 1931 they carried out the conquest of Manchuria despite the feeble protest of the League of Nations (see p. 434), and on the basis of this success they consolidated their domestic political power. The Japanese emperor, Hirohito, who had been a constitutional monarch, became a mere figurehead for the militarists and imperialists who used his prestige and attributes of divinity as a rallying point for ultranationalist sentiment. Making full use of the special advantages of Japanese tradition, they converted their nation to a brand of totalitarianism even more fanatical than those of Italy, Germany, and Russia.

THE COMMON ELEMENTS

In spite of differences, totalitarian and other dictatorial regimes possess many elements in common. The most obvious is the very fact of totalitarianism itself; that is, the subordination of all individual interests and objectives to one supreme goal. This feature is in marked contrast to the pluralism or multiplicity of recognized individual interests and objectives that characterizes liberal societies. The subordination of the individual implies the existence of only one political party to give voice to the prevailing official doctrine. Criticism and dissent are not tolerated. In a totalitarian country the very notion of a loyal opposition is a contradiction; any opposition to the regime or to official dogma is by definition disloyal.

For loyalty or disloyalty to exist there must be an object of loyalty. In the 1930's the focus of totalitarian loyalty was the national state. In fact, totalitarianism is sometimes referred to as "integral nationalism," an exaggerated, all-encompassing nationalism. Even in the Soviet Union, which is sometimes regarded as the fountainhead of international revolution, nationalism plays a large role. Nationalism, however, is not enough. The goals of the nation are determined by the party, and those of the party by its leader, whether he be *Il Duce, Der Führer,* or the People's Commissar. All power springs from the top. Such is the essence of totalitarian dictatorship.

The forms of dictatorship are many and varied. Consciously or unconsciously dictators follow the dictum of Machiavelli that tyranny is most easily achieved under familiar names. Thus, the Soviet Union takes the form of a federated republic; Fascist Italy was nominally a constitutional monarchy; and Nazi Germany at first took the guise of a republic, then in a strange anomaly became an empire without an emperor.

There are normally three stages in establishing a dictatorship. First is the stage of preparation, in which ideology is important as a device for attracting followers. The specific content of the ideology is of less significance than its mere existence. It should contain both positive inducements — a promise of reward — and poles of negative attraction — "somebody to hate." Even more important than ideology is the organization, the party. To achieve power and eliminate all other parties, the party must be extremely well disciplined. The second stage is investiture. It may or may not be achieved by legal means. In Soviet Russia and Spain it came about by means of revolution, but in Italy, Germany, and Japan it was achieved initially by legal processes. The third and in many respects the most crucial stage is consolidation. It involves the systematic elimination of all rival parties as well as all dissidence within the party. In Russia the former was achieved during the civil war, and the latter was effected by a long succession of intrigues ending with the great purge trials of the 1930's. Since in Italy and Germany the dictators had come to power in the first place by legal means, they were able to utilize the legal instruments of the state to eliminate the opposition, but they, too, were forced to resort to purges to purify their parties.

Once a dictatorship has established itself, it must strive by constant vigilance to maintain itself. For this it has many instruments. To discourage overt hostility to the regime, it utilizes force, violence, and terrorism: the armed forces, paramilitary forces, regular police, secret police, spies, and informers, to say nothing of prisons, concentration camps, torture, and death. To indicate positive loyalty, still other devices must be called into play — and it is in this area that modern totalitarian regimes have distinguished themselves from old-fashioned tyrannies. Propaganda is a major weapon. The use of propaganda for political purposes is by no means new, but modern mass communications and psychology make it infinitely more powerful and important than ever before. Closely related to propaganda are compulsory membership in patriotic organizations and the use of indoctrination and education for thought control. Censorship is resorted to as a matter of course in totalitarian societies, as are the teaching of special ideological subjects in schools and universities, political supervision of academic institutions, and loyalty oaths for both students and teachers. Academic freedom, like other freedoms, is a meaningless expression in such societies.

Dictatorships are established by force and maintained by force. The rulers must keep their subjects in a constant state of tension and anxiety to divert their attention from daily hardships and to provide a justification for the use of police-state methods. Fear can sometimes be aroused by alleging a threat of internal subversion. Even more effective is the pretense of an external threat to the nation, so that patriotism can be utilized to reinforce whatever loyalty the subjects may feel for the regime. Life in such a society becomes a constant state of war or preparation for war and is subject to the discipline of the barracks.

Finally, since dictatorships are created by force and maintained by force, they also perish by force. Napoleon, who is sometimes regarded as the first modern dictator, reputedly remarked that although bayonets were useful for many purposes, they could not be used as stools. Such is a dictator's paraphrase of the biblical injunction that those who live by the sword shall die by the sword.

THE SECOND WORLD WAR
CHAPTER SIXTEEN

The demoralization of the democracies in the wake of economic collapse and the failure of their liberal attempts at reconstruction enabled the dictatorships not only to consolidate their power internally but also to engage in external aggression. Repeatedly in the 1930's Japan, Italy, and Germany flouted international opinion, disregarded the League of Nations, and broke their treaty obligations. It seemed that the United States had permanently turned its back on the rest of the world in a retreat to isolation, and the feeble, half-hearted efforts of France and Britain to halt the aggressors merely annoyed the latter and stimulated them to further aggression. If, as Winston Churchill said, the Second World War was an "unnecessary" war in the sense that a vigorous and determined collective effort to halt aggression at any time prior to 1938 would have prevented it, thereafter the war became necessary for the survival of democracy.

In spite of the clear portents in the months and years preceding, the outbreak of the war in September, 1939, found the democracies tragically unprepared militarily, economically, and psychologically. The dictatorships, on the other hand, had for several years been engaged in a deliberate military and economic build-up, and the confidence engendered by their recent triumphs gave them a substantial psychological advantage. In the early years of the war Nazi Germany in particular went from success to spectacular success. After a series of disastrous defeats, Britain rallied in 1940 to fight off almost single-handedly a threatened invasion, while the United States gradually bestirred itself. In 1941 the aggressors made two fatal mistakes. Hitler suddenly and unexpectedly turned on the Soviet Union, his former partner-in-conquest, forcing it into an alliance with the Western powers; and with equal unexpectedness Japan attacked the United States, galvanizing American efforts in what at last became a common cause. For almost two more years the issue remained in doubt, but when the Allies finally mobilized their overwhelming resources, they gradually forced the Axis Powers back into their homelands. The war ended in Europe in May, 1945, with the complete and unconditional surrender of Germany, and in the Pacific in September with a similar surrender by Japan.

THE ORIGINS OF TOTALITARIAN AGGRESSION

Germany, Italy, and Japan, together with their satellites, eventually became allied as the Axis Powers, so-called from the Italo-German treaty of October, 1936, which established the Rome-Berlin "axis." Prior to 1936 each had pursued its aggressions independently and to some extent in opposition to one another.

JAPANESE EXPANSION IN ASIA AND THE PACIFIC

Japanese participation in World War I had been motivated principally by the desire of the Japanese to take over German possessions in the Pacific and German concessions in China. In this goal they were successful. They also utilized the Russian revolution to extend their interests in Manchuria, under the nominal suzerainty of China, by taking control of the South Manchurian Railway. In September, 1931, the Japanese troops guarding the railroad occupied Manchuria by force and shortly afterward set up a puppet regime, renaming the country Manchukuo. China appealed to the League of Nations for protection against the violation of its sovereignty; but France and Britain, in the midst of great economic difficulties, were reluctant to antagonize Japan, and the League proved powerless to act. A special commission took more than a year to produce a report, during which time the Japanese consolidated their position in Manchuria. Although the commission's report was critical of Japan, it recognized Japan's "special interest" in the area and recommended an "autonomous" government under Japanese tutelage. Even this solution did not satisfy the Japanese, who withdrew from the League in 1933 and defied its injunctions with impunity. Thus the first major test of the League's ability to prevent aggression tended to discredit it and encouraged other attempts to defy its authority.

Japan continued its pressure on China with the intention of forcing the Chinese into a position of subordination in what the Japanese rulers began to refer to as a "New Order" in Asia — a euphemism for a greatly enlarged Japanese Empire. The Chinese, much to the surprise of world opinion, overcame their internal divisions and under the leadership of a rejuvenated government put up a determined resistance. Despairing of gaining their objective without resort to force, the Japanese in 1937 provoked a military "incident" and began an all-out though still undeclared war on China. Japanese superiority in organization and equipment enabled them to capture the major cities and control the entire seacoast of China, but the Chinese fought on desperately and retreated slowly inland, refusing to surrender. The struggle had reached a stalemate when the outbreak of war in Europe gave the Japanese further opportunities for expansion elsewhere in Asia.

THE CONQUEST OF ETHIOPIA

Italy's Mussolini, eager for a foreign policy triumph and encouraged by the failure of the League to intervene effectively in the Manchurian dispute, resolved upon the conquest of Ethiopia, the one remaining independent native state in Africa. Ethiopia had galled the pride of nationalist Italians ever since the Ethiopians defeated an Italian army in 1896. In December, 1934, soldiers in Italian Somaliland provoked a border dispute as a pretext for an invasion. Frantic diplomatic negotiations ensued, but differences between France and Britain as to whether the Italians or the Germans constituted the greater menace prevented effective cooperation. Hoping to secure Italian support against the remilitarization of Germany, France in effect gave Italy a free hand. Britain concentrated a naval force in the Mediterranean, but lacking French support and adequate air power, it refrained from direct or provocative action. In September, 1935, Italian troops crossed the Ethiopian frontier and began the conquest of the country.

The League of Nations, which was in session at the time, immediately declared Italy the aggressor and voted sanctions in the form of a boycott of Italian exports and an embargo on exports to Italy. The embargo did not include petroleum; moreover, several nations that had just declared Italy an aggressor and voted for the sanctions refused to enforce them. Unwilling to risk an armed conflict, the British did not close the Suez Canal to Italian ships, although it was the only practical way for Italy to transfer troops and supplies to the battlefront. Utilizing modern weapons, including aircraft and poison gas, the Italians soon overcame the barefooted Ethiopian tribesmen and occupied the country. The actions of the League had no other effect than to antagonize Mussolini and push him closer to Hitler. In a vain attempt to prevent a rapprochement between Italy and Germany and to keep Italy in the League, the League formally voted to withdraw the sanctions against Italy, in effect recognizing the Italian conquest. The action completely discredited the League in the eyes of both friends and foes.

INTERVENTION AND NONINTERVENTION IN SPAIN

The furor over the Ethiopian crisis had barely subsided when civil war broke out in Spain. The Republican government, which had recently formed a Popular Front similar to that in France, immediately appealed to France and Britain for assistance; but those two countries, hoping to localize the conflict, called for an international agreement against intervention and banned the shipment of war materials to either side. Although Germany and Italy participated in the committee on non-intervention, they also supplied men ("volunteers"), munitions, and equipment to General Franco's insurgents. In the early part of the war the Soviet Union sent military advisers to assist the Loyalist forces, as well as driblets of equipment by means of merchant vessels, but distance and the difficulties of communication prohibited any large-scale aid to the Republican government. The United States maintained its now traditional posture of isolation and neutrality, but many idealistic young Americans, as well as antifascists from other lands, joined an International Brigade to fight for what they regarded as the cause of freedom and democracy. In this respect as well as in the sphere of military technology the Spanish civil war seemed to be a sort of rehearsal for World War II. The major German contribution took the form of dive bombers and other mechanized equipment, which proved to be the decisive factor in the triumph of the insurgent forces and gave the German General Staff valuable experience in the new techniques of warfare.

In spite of their disadvantages in trained manpower and modern equipment and supplies, the forces loyal to the Republican government fought on doggedly for almost three years. The struggle destroyed cities, ravaged the countryside, and left Spain both physically and morally exhausted. It took almost a million lives, including executions and civilian deaths from bombing and starvation, out of a population of approximately 25 million. In its international aspect it gave the forces of aggression further cause for self-congratulation and further sullied and demoralized the democracies.

THE ASCENDANCY OF NAZI GERMANY

Hitler's repudiation of the League of Nations within nine months of his accession to power clearly indicated the future trend of Nazi foreign policy. Although he received a minor setback in 1934 when Mussolini opposed his designs on Austria, it proved to be temporary. In January, 1935, the inhabitants of the Saarland on the border between France and Germany voted overwhelmingly for reunion with Germany in a plebiscite provided for by the Versailles treaty. On the strength of this triumph Hitler shortly afterward denounced the clauses of the treaty pertaining to the limitation on German armaments and reintroduced universal military service in Germany. Thoroughly alarmed, France convoked representatives of Britain and Mussolini's Italy at a conference in Stresa, Italy, and secured a condemnation of Germany by the League. The League, however, had no means of forcing German adherence, and Hitler cleverly divided his opponents by agreeing to a limitation on naval armaments with Britain. This agreement strained Franco-British relations, prevented effective cooperation in the Ethiopian crisis, and led France to seek an alliance with Soviet Russia. In the following year Hitler took advantage of Italy's involvement in the Ethiopian war with its international repercussions to denounce the Locarno agreements of 1925 and to remilitarize the Rhineland. France protested, but momentarily isolated diplomatically and embroiled in a domestic political crisis, it took no effective action.

Thus far only Mussolini had effectively opposed any of Hitler's moves in the international arena. After his African adventure, however, Mussolini himself began to feel the need for a friend on the international stage. The fact that both Germany and Italy were revisionist nations (in the sense that both wanted to revise the territorial provisions of the Treaty of Versailles), the similarity in their forms of government, and their common collaboration with the Spanish insurgents drew the two totalitarian dictatorships together. Only the Austrian question separated them. To remove this obstacle, Hitler in 1936 concluded a pact with the Austrian government wherein he promised to respect Austrian sovereignty; for its part, Austria agreed on the advice of Mussolini to conduct itself "as a German nation." With the path thus cleared, Hitler and Mussolini reached an accord in October, 1936, which resulted in the formation of the Rome-Berlin "axis." The following month Germany and Japan signed an "Anti-Comintern" treaty, ostensibly directed against the spread of international communism, to which Italy adhered in the following year. The Axis Powers of World War II had initiated their fateful alliance.

Hitler's early opinion of Mussolini had been one of exaggerated respect, whereas Mussolini had regarded Hitler as something of an upstart. Their opinions underwent a subtle transformation in the two years following the Italo-German accord. Hitler greatly impressed Mussolini with German efficiency and industrial and military power during an elaborately staged state visit in 1937, while Hitler cynically took the measure of his Italian ally. Hitler continued to go forward with his rearmament program in Germany and further established his ascendancy over both the army and the foreign office by replacing career officers in the highest positions by men who were personally loyal to him, such as Joachim von Ribbentrop as foreign minister.

THE ANNEXATION OF AUSTRIA

Hitler's first attempt at foreign aggrandizement had been directed against Austria in 1934. It was a natural, even a predictable move: Hitler was himself a native of Austria, and on the first page of *Mein Kampf* he had stated his belief in the desirability of uniting all German-speaking peoples in a "Greater Germany." His own weakness and Mussolini's opposition had stymied the first attempt, but the situation had changed greatly since then. Italy and Germany were now bound by a treaty of friendship and cooperation, and Italy was heavily involved in Mediterranean affairs. As for France and Britain, the only other powers able to interpose effective opposition, they had already shown their weaknesses.

In February, 1938, Hitler peremptorily summoned the Austrian Chancellor Kurt von Schuschnigg to his mountain retreat at Berchtesgaden in the Bavarian Alps. He stormed and ranted that the Austrian government was violating the agreement of 1936 by suppressing and persecuting the Austrian National Socialist party. Without giving Schuschnigg an opportunity to reply, Hitler demanded that all imprisoned Nazis in Austria be pardoned, that Nazis be allowed to engage in political activity, and that some of them be admitted to the Austrian cabinet. Hitler specifically demanded that Arthur Seyss-Inquart, the Austrian Nazi leader, be made minister of the interior with full control of the police. He added that neither France nor Britain, nor even Italy, would intervene on behalf of Austria, that Germany was invincible, and that he, Hitler, had become "perhaps the greatest German in history." Schuschnigg, who had traveled to Germany with but a single attendant, weakly agreed; but after returning to Austria, he sought to circumvent Hitler by calling for a national plebiscite. When Hitler learned of it, he went into one of his characteristic rages and immediately ordered the closure of the Austrian frontier and the mobilization of German troops along the border. At the same time he sent a personal messenger to Mussolini with a letter of explanation and reassurance. Greatly to his relief, Mussolini raised no objections – it was possibly the last time until the end of the war that Hitler entertained any doubts of his own infallibility – and Hitler put his plan in motion. With Goering giving the orders by telephone from Berlin, Seyss-Inquart forced Schuschnigg's resignation and seized power for himself. He then called on Germany to send in its army to preserve "law and order." On Saturday, March 12, 1938, German troops marched into Austria; the following day Hitler laid a wreath on the tomb of his parents in the little town of Braunau. The wayward son had returned.

On March 14 in Vienna Hitler formally proclaimed the *Anschluss* (union) of Austria and Germany. To legitimize his victory, he called for a plebiscite and new elections to the Reichstag. Under Nazi supervision, which was accompanied by unusually severe persecution of the Jews and other potential enemies of the regime, the Austrians responded with a 99.75 per cent favorable vote.

THE MUNICH CRISIS AND CZECHOSLOVAKIA

The ease with which Hitler achieved his objective in Austria tempted him to further conquests. Czechoslovakia was the next logical victim.

Hitler had come to hate the Czechs during his early days in Vienna. The multinational state, an artificial creation of the Treaty of St. Germain, projected into Germany like a drumstick in the mouth of a ravenous man. Its western fringes contained more than 3 million German-speaking citizens — the *Sudetendeutsch*. Aided by the local affiliate of the Nazi party led by Konrad Henlein, Hitler utilized the German minority to agitate first for self-determination for themselves and then, more boldly, for unification with the Third Reich. As in Austria, Hitler made full use of the slogans of Wilson during World War I. He prepared for an invasion in May, 1938; but an unexpectedly strong stand by France, which had defensive treaties with both Czechoslovakia and the Soviet Union, deterred him.

French belligerence did not last long. Deeply divided on domestic political and social questions as well as militarily weak, France was subject to a strong current of pessimism. This was known equally well to Hitler and to the French government. Hitler intensified his pressure on the Czechs, even stating his general intentions publicly at a Nazi party congress. Britain, for its part, was not only militarily unprepared but strongly influenced by pacifism. Many Britons, convinced of the mistakes of the Versailles treaty, sympathized with German desires to revise it and insisted on "peace at any price." British prime minister Neville Chamberlain, half-brother of the earlier British foreign minister Austen Chamberlain, shared their view, apparently believing that Hitler was no less sincere than Stresemann. In August, 1938, he sent his representative, Lord Runciman, to Prague to persuade the Czech leaders to conciliate Hitler. In September Chamberlain personally made three flying trips to Germany, an unprecedented action for a British prime minister, to confer with the German leader. On the final trip he was joined by Édouard Daladier, premier of France, and Hitler's ally Mussolini. On September 29–30 in Munich these four, acting without representatives of either Czechoslovakia or Russia, with whom both France and Czechoslovakia had alliances, agreed to the partition of Czechoslovakia. Chamberlain returned to Britain to the cheers of the multitude and with the slogan "Peace in our time." Subsequently, "Munich" and "appeasement" became almost synonymous with shortsightedness and cowardice.

The Munich agreement only provided for the cession of the Sudetenland to Germany. Although it was all that Hitler had demanded both in public and with Chamberlain, he secretly harbored the desire to eliminate Czecho-Slovakia (as it was spelled after Munich) altogether. He therefore encouraged both Poland and Hungary in their desires to chip off portions of the truncated country, and he supported the Slovaks and Ruthenians in their demands for autonomy from the Czechs. With the help of such internal disturbances it proved a simple matter in March, 1939, for Hitler to swallow completely the remains of Bohemia and

Photograph from UPI

Delegates at Munich, 1938. Left to right: Neville Chamberlain, Édouard Daladier, Adolf Hitler, Benito Mussolini

"[*The people*] *should know that we have sustained a defeat without a war . . . ; they should know that we have passed an awful milestone in our history . . . and that the terrible words have for the time being been pronounced against the Western democracies: 'Thou art weighed in the balance and found wanting.' And do not suppose this is the end. This is only the beginning of the reckoning. This is only the first sip, the first foretaste of a bitter cup which will be proffered to us year by year unless, by a supreme recovery of moral health and martial vigor, we arise again and take our stand for freedom as in the olden time.*"
Speech by W. S. Churchill in the House of Commons, October 5, 1938, in W. S. Churchill, BLOOD, SWEAT, AND TEARS (New York, 1941).

Moravia, the homeland of the Czechs, and to make Slovakia a "protectorate" of Greater Germany. Hungary absorbed Ruthenia and thereby gained a common frontier with Poland. These actions caught the democracies completely by surprise, for many had believed Hitler when he stated that the reunion of the *Sudetendeutsch* with Germany fulfilled his final international objective. Although this perfidy was carried out in circumstances that rendered the democracies powerless to act, it strengthened the hands of those in the West like Winston Churchill who had come to regard war with Hitler as inevitable.

BLITZKRIEG, 1939–1941

In one of his first actions in the field of foreign affairs Hitler had concluded a ten-year nonaggression pact with Poland in January, 1934. In the wake of the Munich agreement he encouraged the Poles in their demands on Czechoslovakia. Six months later, however, Hitler created a crisis in Polish-German relations by demanding cession of the Free City of Danzig to Germany and rights of extraterritoriality for Germans in the so-called Polish Corridor, the strip of Poland bordering the Baltic Sea, which separated East Prussia from the rest of Germany. The crisis was not entirely unexpected, for apart from historic Polish-German hatreds the Germans had never reconciled themselves to their loss of territory to resurrected Poland after World War I, and German Nazis in Danzig had been agitating for reunion with Germany for several years. Even before the rise of Hitler, Poland had sought to insure itself by concluding alliances and agreements with France, Rumania, Yugoslavia, and Czechoslovakia, as well as with another historic enemy of Polish independence – Russia. The Czechoslovakian debacle showed the worthlessness of the existing agreements and initiated a diplomatic scramble to preserve the existing situation in eastern Europe. Britain and France at once pledged assistance to Poland in the event of attack and began to negotiate with the Soviet Union for a common front against the Axis Powers.

In the 1920's, when both the Soviet Union and Germany were outcasts among the family of nations, they had engaged in clandestine cooperation. After the rise of Hitler with his blatant anti-communist program and pronouncements the Russians had sought alignments with the West. They entered the League of Nations, encouraged communists in France and elsewhere to enter Popular Fronts, and concluded alliances with France and Czechoslovakia directed against a renewal of German aggression. The weakness and vacillation of the Western powers in the face of repeated crises gave the Russians little confidence in their ability to withstand Hitler, however. Before Munich the Russians had publicly declared their willingness to support Czechoslovakia against Germany, but in spite of the joint Franco-Russian guarantee to the Czechs they were not even consulted during the Munich crisis. Although Chamberlain had called on Hitler three times in person, the British sent only a civil servant to negotiate in Moscow in the spring of 1939. The Russians therefore remained profoundly suspicious of the Western powers and took steps of their own to ensure their western borders by negotiating secretly with Hitler. On August 23, 1939, in a historic reversal of both Nazi and Soviet policy, Germany and the Soviet Union concluded a nonaggression pact that prepared the way for a new partition of Poland.

In spite of frantic diplomatic activity and last-minute appeals by President Roosevelt, Germany attacked Poland without a formal declaration of war on September 1, 1939. Fast-moving motorized columns streaked across the Polish plain, converging on Warsaw from East Prussia, Silesia, and Slovakia. In the air the new German *Luftwaffe* quickly knocked out the inadequate Polish air force, and German dive bombers added a new dimension of terror and destructiveness to warfare by mass bombardments of hapless civilians. The Germans called their new military techniques *Blitzkrieg* (lightning war). It proved devastatingly effective, breaking the backbone of Polish resistance in a matter of days. France and Britain formally declared war against Germany on September 3, but they were in no position to render immediate material aid to Poland.

SOVIET AGGRESSION

The rapidity of the German advance startled the Russians no less than the Western powers. A secret protocol to their treaty with Germany provided for a sharing of the spoils in eastern Europe. To make sure that they would obtain their share they launched a sudden invasion of Poland from the east on September 17, and two days later they joined up with the advancing German columns at Brest Litovsk, the scene of a previous historic German-Soviet encounter. On this occasion they met as cobelligerents. Before the month was out German and Russian troops completely subdued Poland and divided the country between them.

In the crisis leading up to the invasion of Poland the Baltic countries of Lithuania, Latvia, and Estonia had all signed treaties with Germany under thinly veiled threats of coercion. They now found themselves almost completely surrounded by the Soviet Union, except for the Baltic sea front and a short Lithuanian-Prussian border. Under similar threats from Russia they signed far-reaching agreements that made them virtual protectorates of the Soviet Union. In the following year they became component republics of the Union of Soviet Socialist Republics.

The Soviet Union made similar demands on Finland which the Finns rejected. On November 30, 1939, three Soviet armies invaded Finland to begin the Winter War. The Finns fought bravely and inflicted heavy losses on the numerically superior Russians, but in the absence of external aid the eventual outcome was never in doubt. In March, 1940, the Finns sued for peace. They ceded the Karelian Isthmus, an important naval base, several islands, and other pieces of territory to the Soviet Union, but they retained their autonomy. The heroic defense of their homeland by the Finns, though it ended in military defeat, constituted the only source of encouragement to the foes of aggression in a long year of disappointment and disaster.

NEW NAZI SURPRISES

Throughout the fall and winter of 1939–40 action on the western front had been minimal. The French dug in behind their supposedly impregnable Maginot Line, expecting World War II to be a replay of World War I, while German forces mopped up in Poland and then redeployed to the west. The British concentrated on building up their armaments and imposed a naval blockade on Germany. Cynical Western journalists, especially in the neutral United States, dubbed the war in the west a "Phony War" and a *Sitzkrieg*. Some faint-hearted souls even hoped that Germany and the Soviet Union would become embroiled with one another and give France and Britain an opportunity to withdraw. Hitler soon disabused them of the notion.

Before dawn on the morning of April 9, 1940, German armored columns crossed the border of Denmark, with which Germany had signed a nonaggression pact less than a year before, and German airborne troops parachuted down throughout the country. At the same time Germany launched an air and sea invasion against Norway. Caught defenseless and completely by surprise, the Danes surrendered to German occupation without formal resistance. The Norwegians, equally surprised but having more opportunity to organize resistance, fought fiercely for a time. A small Anglo-French expeditionary force was hurriedly sent to their assistance, only to withdraw with heavy casualties after two weeks. The conquest of Norway required less than a month. King Haakon VII and his government escaped to London in British naval vessels and remained a "government in exile" throughout the war. In both Denmark and Norway the German success was facilitated by local Nazi sympathizers. The name of one of them, Vidkun Quisling, who subsequently became head of the Germans' puppet regime in Norway, became synonymous with traitor.

Hitler's victorious legions gave the Allies no time to recover from their shock. On May 10 the *Wehrmacht* and the *Luftwaffe* struck simultaneously in the neutral Netherlands, Belgium, and Luxembourg with no more warning than before. A massive air attack using incendiary bombs practically wiped out the city of Rotterdam, inflicting enormous civilian casualties. The Dutch opened the dikes and flooded their low-lying country, but even that recourse could not slow the airborne conquerors. On May 14 the small Dutch army capitulated. The government and royal family followed the Norwegian precedent and fled to London.

The Belgians held out longer, supported by the French and a small British expeditionary force, until in a lightening drive across northern France to the Channel coast the Germans separated them from the main body of the French army. Short of supplies and faced with overwhelming odds, King Leopold ordered his troops to lay down their arms on May 26. The remaining French and British troops, along with some Belgians who refused to surrender, fell back on Dunkirk where they were trapped with their backs to the sea. Harassed by constant air attack and long-range bombardment, hundreds of British vessels — warships, fishing boats, even pleasure craft manned by civilian volunteers — miraculously evacuated more than 300,000 men (including 100,000 French and Belgians) from the Dunkirk beaches in the early days of June. The cost was enormous: more than 30,000 casualties and prisoners, and abandonment to the Germans of nearly all equipment and munitions.

THE FALL OF FRANCE

Dominated by the strategic thinking of World War I, the French high command had taken psychological as well as physical refuge behind the Maginot Line. In spite of the precedent of a German invasion through neutral Belgium in 1914, they had constructed only a light line of fortifications along the Belgian frontier. The German air force and armored divisions were greatly superior to the French in both quantity and quality. The French were therefore almost totally unprepared for the kind of warfare forced upon them by Hitler's *Panzer* (armored) divisions. The shock of realizing the extent of their unpreparedness shattered the morale of the French army and society — from the high command to the lowliest recruit, from cabinet ministers to kitchen help. The only notable resistance offered by the French army was a tank attack near Abbéville, brilliantly executed against overwhelming odds by a major general named Charles de Gaulle. The French received a further jolt on June 10 when Mussolini unexpectedly declared war and launched an invasion of southern France. Paris fell without a battle on June 14. The government fled to Bordeaux amid recrimination and dispute as to whether to fight on or to sue for peace. On June 16 Marshal Henri-Philippe Pétain, the "hero of Verdun" in World War I, replaced Paul Reynaud as premier and immediately requested an armistice.

The truce terms, dictated by Hitler personally at Compiègne in the same railroad carriage that had been the scene of the armistice of 1918, forced France to disband its armed forces, surrender all military equipment and munitions (including the navy), and submit to German occupation of more than half of its territory. The government of octogenarian Marshal Pétain moved to the health resort of Vichy in unoccupied France, where it became known as the Vichy regime. The dazed and frightened parliament voted dictatorial powers to Pétain, who formally abolished the Third Republic and set up an authoritarian government with himself as chief of state and Pierre Laval as prime minister.

Not all Frenchmen paid allegiance to the Vichy government. Thousands fled to North Africa, Britain, and elsewhere. Among them was Charles de Gaulle, who had been one of the few to recognize and decry the obsolescence of French military policy in the 1930's. He secured recognition from the British government as head of the French National Committee of Liberation (popularly known as the Free French or Fighting French). He organized the remnants of the French army in Britain (and later in North Africa) as an adjunct of the Allied forces and made stirring radio broadcasts from London to his countrymen in France. Many Frenchmen who remained in their homes and jobs joined the *Maquis* and other underground organizations of French patriots, and engaged in espionage and sabotage against the Germans.

THE BATTLE OF BRITAIN

Immediately after the German invasion of the Low Countries Winston Churchill replaced Neville Chamberlain as prime minister of a National (all-party) government in Great Britain. Churchill had been an articulate but little-heeded critic of both Hitler and British appeasement in the 1930's. His oratorical abilities now played a crucial role in stimulating British morale and weaning the United States from its isolationist mentality. With the fall of France Britain became the only active belligerent against the Axis Powers in Europe, although it was supported by the British dominions, which had all made common cause with Britain in 1939.

In September, 1940, Germany, Italy, and Japan (which was still at war with China) concluded a new and more far-reaching military and economic alliance. Hitler turned his attention to crushing his last rival in Western Europe. In order to do so, it would be necessary to invade Britain, but a cross-channel invasion required mastery of the air. The Battle of Britain was first and foremost an aerial battle. The *Luftwaffe* mounted massive attacks by both fighters and bombers in order to destroy British airpower, industrial capacity, and civilian morale. The losses inflicted were enormous. Thousands of civilians died in mass bombings, accentuated by the use of incendiary bombs. The automotive center of Coventry was reduced to rubble, as were large portions of many other industrial and port cities, including London. But the Royal Air Force, strengthened by contingents of volunteers from many lands and aided by a newly developed radar network, held its own and exacted an exhorbitant cost from the attackers. In the three months of most intense aerial warfare (from the beginning of August to the end of October, 1940) the RAF destroyed almost 2,500 enemy aircraft while losing less than 1,000 of its own. Churchill's eulogy is their most lasting monument: "Never in the field of human conflict was so much owed by so many to so few."

While Britain stood almost alone in actual combat, the United States extended increasing material aid. In response to a direct appeal from Churchill after Dunkirk the American War Department shipped large quantities of military supplies to Britain. In September, 1940, President Roosevelt exchanged fifty overage American destroyers for long-term leases on British military and naval bases in the Western Hemisphere. In March, 1941, he persuaded Congress to enact the Lend-Lease Bill, by which the United States supplied vast amounts of foodstuffs and military equipment to beleaguered Britain. The United States Navy also took an active part in antisubmarine patrols and convoy duty in the North Atlantic.

Had the Germans actually launched an invasion of Britain in the autumn of 1940, it is conceivable that they might have succeeded, even though Churchill promised that "we shall fight on the beaches . . . on the landing grounds . . . in the fields, and in the streets . . . we shall never surrender." Apparently the German high command overestimated the British reserves of supplies, equipment, and trained manpower, which were then at an all-time low. The General Staff was reluctant to undertake a cross-channel invasion, and it seems clear in retrospect that Hitler himself, who had overruled the timidity of his generals and admirals before, never really wanted or expected to invade Britain. He waited a month after the fall of France before unleashing his great air attacks in the expectation that Britain itself would ask for a truce, and he gave the preparatory orders for an invasion only after the British had declined to respond to a conciliatory speech he made in the Reichstag. In any event, the *Luftwaffe* never achieved the aerial superiority regarded as necessary even by Hitler, and with the approach of winter the Germans gradually abandoned their plans for an invasion of Britain in favor of further expansion in the east.

AFRICA AND THE BALKANS

Meanwhile Hitler's ally involved him in costly and annoying diversions in the south. Mussolini had piously proclaimed Italy's neutrality during the invasion of Poland and watched with envy Hitler's spectacular successes in Scandinavia and the Low Countries. Even crumbling France had held his armies at bay after having been defeated in the north. Hitler added to his humiliation by refusing to let Italian troops occupy the south of France and take over the French empire in Africa. To salve his wounded pride, Mussolini took advantage of Britain's preoccupation with the defense of its homeland to launch attacks from Ethiopia and Libya against British possessions in Africa. In October, 1940, he sprung an invasion of Greece from the Albanian protectorate which he had acquired almost unnoticed in the alarums of the spring of 1939.

At first his aggressive intentions succeeded. British forces evacuated British Somaliland and retreated in both Egypt and central Africa, and the Greeks recoiled in the face of his surprise attack. Within a few months, however, the situation reversed itself. In December British and Imperial forces under General Wavell counterattacked with spectacular success in Africa, and at the same time Greek units, supported by the scanty British garrison in Egypt, repulsed the Italians and invaded Albania.

Hitler, whom Mussolini had neither consulted nor forewarned, fumed and raged, but in order to protect the German flank he came to Mussolini's rescue. He had already imposed his will upon the governments of Hungary, Bulgaria, and Rumania in the fall of 1940, forcing Rumania to give up territory to the other two. In the spring of 1941 the Germans overran Yugoslavia and unleashed a massive ground and air attack on Greece, which succumbed in a matter of weeks. The British troops in Greece retreated first to Crete, then fled from an airborne invasion of that island to Cyprus and Egypt. Simultaneously German troops under the command of General Erwin Rommel, who had entered Africa by way of Italy, forced the British North African army back on Egypt. The Germans once more demonstrated their superior organization and tactics, but the dispersion of their forces prevented them from driving on to total victory in any single area.

THE INVASION OF RUSSIA

Notwithstanding his cynical pact of August, 1939, with the Soviet Union, Hitler never abandoned his plans for an eventual attack on Russia. His contempt for Slavic peoples was second only to his hatred of the Jews. His sudden onslaughts against Norway, Denmark, and the Low Countries and his rapid victory in France had been intended primarily to protect Germany from an attack from the west while it carried out its aggressive intentions in the east. He hoped and expected that Britain would sue for peace after the fall of France, and he undertook the Battle of Britain with reluctance. Even while that battle was at its height in the fall of 1940, he gave the order to prepare an invasion of Russia.

Hitler originally contemplated the invasion of Russia for the spring of 1941 in order that German airpower and mechanized equipment could be used to best advantage during a long summer campaign. The problems created by Mussolini's failures in the Balkans and North Africa forced a postponement of the invasion. Hitler's own failure to persuade General Franco to enter the war deprived him of the opportunity to take Gibraltar and nullify British power in the Mediterranean. Overruling his military advisers, who advised a decisive contest in the Mediterranean and North Africa, Hitler went forward with his long-nourished dream for the conquest of Russia.

Although taken by surprise in the matter of timing, the Soviet Union was not entirely unprepared for this act of perfidy. Its own adherence to the pact with Germany had taken place in full recognition of Hitler's ultimate intentions. It had fortified itself in the summer of 1940 by taking over the Baltic republics; subsequently it took over Bessarabia and northern Bukovina from Rumania. Hitler's occupation of the Balkans and a treaty with Finland giving German troops the right of access to that country had strengthened Stalin's suspicions. Militarily, however, the Soviet armies were no match for German power. The German invasion, supported by Rumanians, Hungarians, and Finns, began on June 22, 1941, across the entire length of the western frontier of the Soviet Union. Following the tactics that had proved so successful in the two previous years, the invaders quickly rolled back the Russian defenders.

Sovfoto

The Battle of Stalingrad

"The soldiers of the Red Army have sealed this German Army group within an unbreakable ring. All hopes of the rescue of your troops by a German offensive from the south or southwest have proved vain. The German units hastening to your assistance were defeated by the Red Army. . . .

"The German air transport fleet, which brought you a starvation ration of food, munitions and fuel, has been compelled . . . repeatedly to withdraw to airfields more distant from the encircled troops.

". . . The situation of your troops is desperate. They are suffering from hunger, sickness and cold. The cruel Russian winter has scarcely yet begun. Hard frosts, cold winds and blizzards still lie ahead." From the Russian demand for surrender, January 8, 1943, reprinted in D. Flower and J. Reeves, eds., THE WAR 1939–1945 (London, 1960).

History never repeats itself exactly; yet the parallels between Napoleon's invasion of Russia and that of Hitler are striking. Hitler, like Napoleon, invaded Russia after attempts to bring Britain to its knees had failed. Like Napoleon, Hitler had allies among several of the smaller states of Europe, whose rulers hated and despised the Russians but feared Hitler even more. In 1941–42, as in 1812, the invaders were better equipped and disciplined than the defending armies but did not take sufficiently into account the vast distances, the bitter winters, and the dogged resistance of the Russian people — civilians as well as soldiers. Finally, the crowning parallel was that the Russian invasions of both Napoleon and Hitler marked the peak of their power after several years of almost unbroken success: the checks and eventual defeats that they suffered in Russia proved the preludes to a sudden drastic shrinkage and then collapse of their respective empires.

Before the invasion Hitler confidently expected to conquer Russia in the course of the summer. He might well have done so had the invasion begun on schedule. As it was, the German armies completely encircled Leningrad, drove to the outskirts of Moscow, and occupied most of southern Russia before the onset of winter temporarily halted the German offensive. The winter punished the German troops severely and gave the Russians a much-needed respite to reorganize their defenses and begin receiving supplies from Britain and the United States, whose material contributions to the Allies increased enormously after it became directly involved in the war in December, 1941. The German offensive resumed in the summer of 1942, and although it failed to take either Leningrad or Moscow, it made further substantial gains in southern Russia, pushing deep into the Caucasus in an attempt to gain the Caspian oil fields. By September the invaders had penetrated to Stalingrad, a strategic point on the Volga River.

Stalingrad marked the high point of the German invasion. By that time the invading armies had greatly overextended both their supply lines and their battle lines. German industrial production suffered from increasingly heavy Allied aerial bombardment, and troops had to be diverted to meet Allied invasions in the Mediterranean area, while Russian equipment and munitions increased in both quantity and quality as a result of American aid. Again the winter set in. After a fierce battle that raged for four months, the Germans finally abandoned the attack on Stalingrad at the beginning of 1943 and began a long, slow, costly retreat. By mid-April the Russians had regained all the territory conquered by the Germans in their 1942 offensive. The war continued on Russian soil for more than a year, until August, 1944, but the invaders were gradually driven backward into their homeland. Hitler's bid for mastery of the Eurasian heartland had failed.

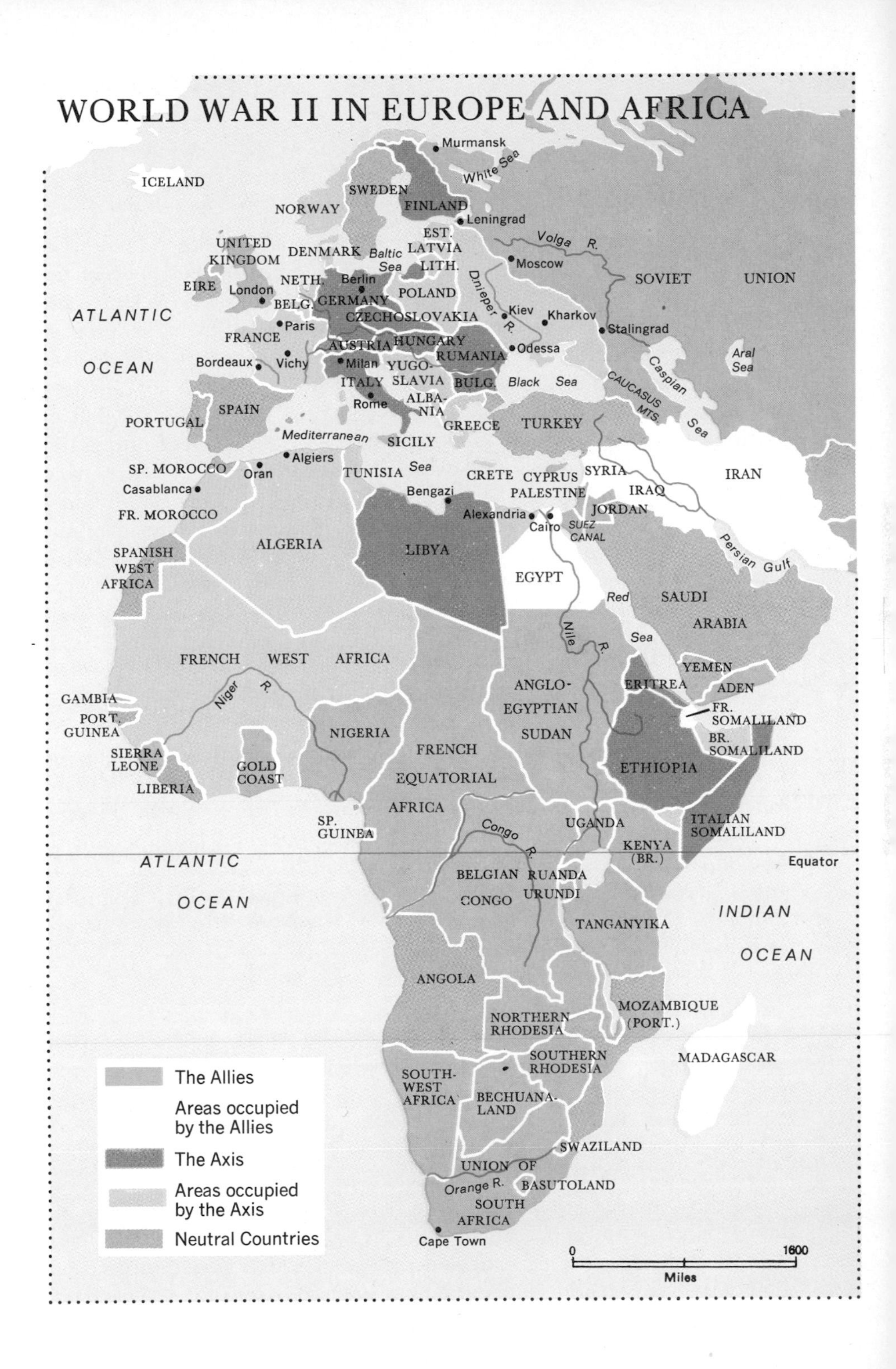
WORLD WAR II IN EUROPE AND AFRICA
Murmansk
White Sea
ICELAND
SWEDEN
NORWAY
FINLAND
Leningrad
EST.
LATVIA
LITH.
UNITED KINGDOM
DENMARK
Baltic Sea
Volga R.
Moscow
EIRE
London
NETH.
Berlin
BELG.
GERMANY
POLAND
Dnieper R.
SOVIET UNION
ATLANTIC OCEAN
Paris
CZECHOSLOVAKIA
Kiev
Kharkov
Stalingrad
FRANCE
AUSTRIA
HUNGARY
RUMANIA
Odessa
Bordeaux
Vichy
Milan
YUGO-SLAVIA
Aral Sea
Caspian Sea
ITALY
BULG.
Black Sea
CAUCASUS MTS.
SPAIN
Rome
ALBA-NIA
PORTUGAL
GREECE
TURKEY
Mediterranean Sea
SICILY
Algiers
SP. MOROCCO
Oran
TUNISIA
CRETE
CYPRUS
SYRIA
IRAN
Casablanca
Bengazi
PALESTINE
IRAQ
FR. MOROCCO
Alexandria
JORDAN
Cairo
SUEZ CANAL
SPANISH WEST AFRICA
ALGERIA
LIBYA
Persian Gulf
EGYPT
Red Sea
SAUDI ARABIA
Nile R.
FRENCH WEST AFRICA
YEMEN
ANGLO-EGYPTIAN SUDAN
ERITREA
ADEN
GAMBIA
Niger R.
FR. SOMALILAND
PORT. GUINEA
NIGERIA
BR. SOMALILAND
FRENCH EQUATORIAL AFRICA
SIERRA LEONE
GOLD COAST
ETHIOPIA
LIBERIA
SP. GUINEA
Congo R.
UGANDA
ITALIAN SOMALILAND
KENYA (BR.)
Equator
ATLANTIC OCEAN
BELGIAN CONGO
RUANDA URUNDI
INDIAN OCEAN
TANGANYIKA
ANGOLA
NORTHERN RHODESIA
MOZAMBIQUE (PORT.)
MADAGASCAR
SOUTHERN RHODESIA
SOUTH-WEST AFRICA
BECHUANA-LAND
SWAZILAND
UNION OF SOUTH AFRICA
Orange R.
BASUTOLAND
Cape Town
The Allies
Areas occupied by the Allies
The Axis
Areas occupied by the Axis
Neutral Countries
0
1600
Miles

PEARL HARBOR AND THE WAR IN THE PACIFIC

Japan took advantage of the war in Europe to enhance its power in Asia. Germany and Italy, who had no vital interests of their own in the Orient, sought to draw Japan into a closer alliance in order to embarrass France and Britain, who did have extensive interests there. Hoping to avoid harassment from the rear, the Soviet Union agreed to a settlement of outstanding differences with Japan concerning East Asian territory and even signed a treaty of neutrality in April, 1941. After the fall of France, Japan and Germany pressured the Vichy government into granting Japan a virtual protectorate over French Indochina. Hoping to avoid open hostilities with Japan, Britain withdrew its forces from China and halted the flow of supplies to the Chinese Nationalist armies over the Burma road. Japan began to speak boldly of a "Greater East Asian Co-prosperity Sphere," a more ambitious version of its "New Order."

In the United States President Roosevelt and other opponents of Axis aggression had been working to prepare the American public, still strongly isolationist in sentiment, for the possibility of eventual intervention in the war. The government relaxed its neutrality laws so as to favor the provision of war equipment to the Allies, strengthened its military and political ties with Latin American countries, built up its own army and navy (notably by introducing the first peacetime draft in American history), and issued various warnings to the Axis Powers. Throughout 1941 tension between the United States and Japan mounted. The Japanese, increasingly under the influence of militaristic leadership, regarded the United States as the only obstacle to their complete domination of the Orient. In the fall of 1941 they resorted to desperate measures to remove that obstacle.

THE JAPANESE OFFENSIVE

Early on the Sunday morning of December 7, 1941, Japanese carrier-based aircraft, operating thousands of miles from their home islands, made a daring strike against the main United States naval base in the Pacific at Pearl Harbor, Hawaii. Taken completely by surprise in spite of the recent build-up in diplomatic tension, the main body of the fleet lay at anchor in the harbor with boilers cold and only skeleton crews on actual duty. In the ensuing confusion the United States suffered more than 5,000 casualties and lost five battleships, three cruisers, and numbers of lesser craft, as well as 177 airplanes, most of which were destroyed on the ground. Other ships and military installations suffered serious damage. It was the worst military disaster to befall the United States in its history.

Photograph from U.S. Navy

U.S.S. *Shaw* Exploding During the
Japanese Raid on Pearl Harbor

"Yesterday, December 7, 1941 — a date which will live in infamy — the United States of America was suddenly and deliberately attacked by the naval and air forces of the Empire of Japan.

"The United States was at peace with that Nation, and at the solicitation of Japan, was still in conversation with its Government and its Emperor looking toward the maintenance of peace in the Pacific. Indeed, one hour after Japanese air squadrons had commenced bombing in Oahu, the Japanese Ambassador to the United States and his colleague delivered to the Secretary of State a formal reply to a recent American message. While this reply stated that it seemed useless to continue the existing diplomatic negotiations, it contained no threat or hint of war or armed attack." Address of President Roosevelt to the Congress, December 8, 1941, U.S. Department of State, PEACE AND WAR: UNITED STATES FOREIGN POLICY, 1931–1941 (Washington, 1943).

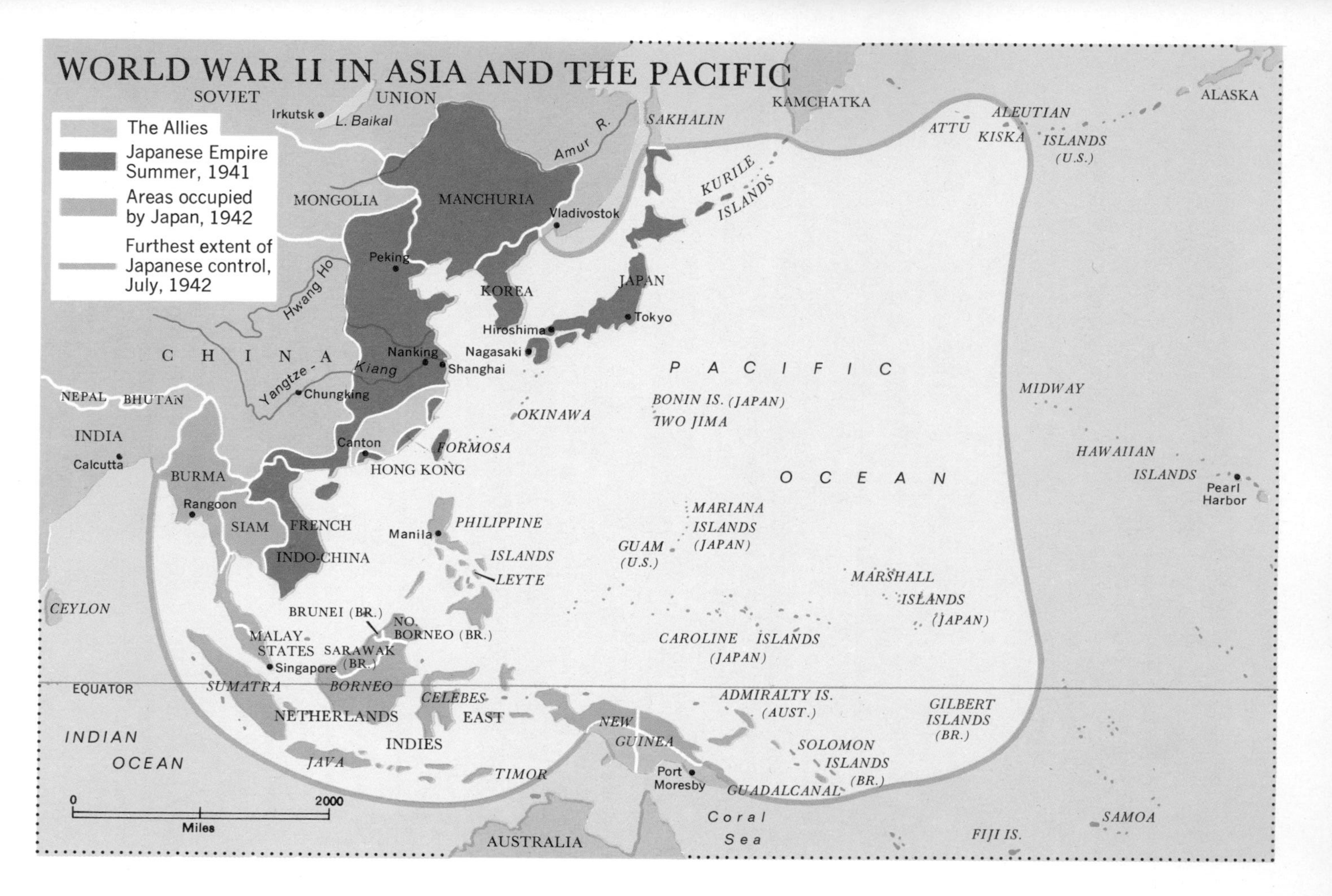
WORLD WAR II IN ASIA AND THE PACIFIC
The Allies
Japanese Empire Summer, 1941
Areas occupied by Japan, 1942
Furthest extent of Japanese control, July, 1942
SOVIET UNION
Irkutsk
L. Baikal
MONGOLIA
MANCHURIA
Amur R.
Vladivostok
SAKHALIN
KAMCHATKA
KURILE ISLANDS
ATTU
KISKA
ALEUTIAN ISLANDS (U.S.)
ALASKA
Peking
KOREA
JAPAN
Tokyo
Hiroshima
Nagasaki
Hwang Ho
C H I N A
Yangtze - Kiang
Nanking
Shanghai
Chungking
NEPAL
BHUTAN
INDIA
Calcutta
Canton
HONG KONG
FORMOSA
OKINAWA
BONIN IS. (JAPAN)
IWO JIMA
P A C I F I C
O C E A N
MIDWAY
HAWAIIAN ISLANDS
Pearl Harbor
BURMA
Rangoon
SIAM
FRENCH INDO-CHINA
Manila
PHILIPPINE ISLANDS
LEYTE
GUAM (U.S.)
MARIANA ISLANDS (JAPAN)
MARSHALL ISLANDS (JAPAN)
CEYLON
BRUNEI (BR.)
NO. BORNEO (BR.)
MALAY STATES
SARAWAK (BR.)
Singapore
CAROLINE ISLANDS (JAPAN)
EQUATOR
SUMATRA
BORNEO
CELEBES
NETHERLANDS EAST INDIES
ADMIRALTY IS. (AUST.)
GILBERT ISLANDS (BR.)
INDIAN OCEAN
JAVA
TIMOR
NEW GUINEA
Port Moresby
SOLOMON ISLANDS (BR.)
GUADALCANAL
0
2000
Miles
AUSTRALIA
Coral Sea
FIJI IS.
SAMOA

Immediately following their success at Pearl Harbor Japanese forces struck other United States military installations in the Pacific. Guam capitulated within a week, Wake Island within two weeks. Early in January, Japanese forces captured Manila and the United States naval base at Cavite in the Philippines. The remaining American and Philippine forces entrenched themselves on the Bataan peninsula and the island of Corregidor in the entrance to Manila Bay. General Douglas MacArthur, the American commander in the Philippines, escaped to Australia on the command of President Roosevelt. After a valiant defense the remaining American forces under General Jonathan Wainwright finally capitulated in May, 1942.

Meanwhile the Japanese pursued their prime target: control of the sources of oil, rubber, tin, and other strategic supplies in Southeast Asia and Indonesia. Great Britain declared war on Japan immediately after the United States, and the Japanese responded by sinking two British battleships that had been dispatched to reinforce the major British base at Singapore. Japan concluded an alliance with Thailand and persuaded it to declare war on Britain and the United States. Operating from its newly acquired bases in Indochina, Japan captured Hongkong and launched invasions of Burma, the Malay peninsula, and Indonesia. Singapore, which was heavily fortified on its seaside but all but defenseless by land, fell to the Japanese from the rear in mid-February. At the end of the month the Japanese won an overwhelming naval victory over combined Allied naval forces in the Battle of Java Sea and forthwith occupied the Dutch East Indies. The British evacuated an untenable position in Rangoon, and Japan quickly overran and occupied Burma.

In less than six months after the attack on Pearl Harbor Japan had achieved mastery over all of Southeast Asia and the Southwest Pacific as far as New Guinea. The way lay open for the conquest of Australia – or so it seemed. On May 7 Allied air and naval forces intercepted a large Japanese fleet, including troopships, steaming southward through the Coral Sea and sank more than 100,000 tons of Japanese shipping. That defeat convinced the Japanese that they would have to complete what they had begun at Pearl Harbor but had failed to carry through: the destruction of United States naval power. They assembled a large armada and headed once more for Hawaii, while sending a decoy force to make landings in the Aleutian Islands. The United States had succeeded in breaking the Japanese radio code and did not fall for the decoy. It concentrated the remnants of its naval and air forces and intercepted the Japanese near Midway Island. There in early June a tremendous air and naval battle raged for four days. The United States suffered many losses, but the Japanese losses were heavier still, forcing them to withdraw and relieving the pressure on the United States Pacific defenses.

THE ALLIED COUNTEROFFENSIVE

The early Japanese successes were facilitated by careful planning, the element of surprise, and the unpreparedness of the United States, which had not fully recovered from the great depression of the 1930's. The very enormity of the Japanese gains, however, required time for assimilation and organization, and strained Japanese manpower and resources to the utmost. The Battle of Midway marked the high tide of Japanese conquest and power. Thereafter their losses in both manpower and materiel accumulated more rapidly than military conscription and industry could replace them. In the United States, by contrast, the shock of Pearl Harbor settled the lingering dispute over isolation or intervention, unified the American people behind the war effort, and brought the full range of American industrial capacity and manpower into battle on the side of the Allies. While retaining private ownership and operation of industry for the most part, the American government initiated a far-reaching system of organization and control which resulted in an ever-increasing flow of airplanes, tanks, ships, munitions, and other war materials for the supply not only of the American army, navy, and air force but of its allies as well.

Allied forces had stemmed the Japanese advance in the great naval battles of Midway and the Coral Sea, but the danger was by no means ended. In August, 1942, United States forces invaded the Solomon Islands in order to protect communications with Australia, and after months of heavy fighting they finally dislodged the enemy. For the next year sporadic fighting took place in New Guinea and the adjacent islands, but neither side launched a major campaign. The Allies had agreed to concentrate their major efforts on winning the war in Europe first, and the Japanese were still engaged in consolidating their earlier gains and replacing their losses. In the summer of 1943 the Allies began a systematic campaign of "island hopping"; that is, instead of attempting to retake every Japanese-held island in the Pacific, they selected their targets strategically to knock out the major Japanese bases and cut the enemy's supply lines, leaving the remainder to "wither on the vine." Their strategy succeeded so well that within a year American forces had conquered the Mariana Islands, from which huge United States Air Force bombers could bomb the Japanese home islands. It marked the beginning of the end of the war in the Pacific.

THE GRAND ALLIANCE

Although American policy had been staunchly isolationist in the 1930's and many influential individuals and groups remained so until the tragedy of Pearl Harbor, it became increasingly clear to perceptive observers that the entry of the United States into the war on the side of Britain was only a matter of time. As early as November, 1939, Congress amended the Neutrality Act of 1937 to permit the export of arms and munitions to belligerents on a "cash and carry" basis; the act manifestly favored Britain and France, who had both foreign currency reserves and control of the oceans. Immediately after the fall of France the United States greatly stepped up its defense expenditures, began construction of a "two ocean navy" and a greatly enlarged air force, and initiated compulsory military service. The "destroyers for bases" deal of September, 1940, and the Lend-Lease Act of March, 1941, as well as the activities of the United States Navy in tracking German submarines and convoying merchant vessels, brought the United States closer to the status of an active belligerent. Well before the Japanese attack on Pearl Harbor the United States was, in effect, engaged in undeclared naval warfare with Germany.

ROOSEVELT AND CHURCHILL

In August, 1941, President Roosevelt and Prime Minister Churchill held a dramatic meeting on board a warship off the coast of Newfoundland to discuss problems of global strategy and logistics. At the conclusion of the meeting they issued a statement known as the Atlantic Charter. This document, the germ of the United Nations Charter, was an attempt to formulate war aims (even though the United States was still technically at peace) in such a way as to lay the basis for an enduring peace, and at the same time to influence public opinion in favor of an Anglo-American alliance. In the Charter the signatories declared that they had no territorial ambitions, promised that after the return of peace boundaries would be drawn and governments established in accordance with the principles of national self-determination, recognized the importance of "the fullest collaboration between all nations in the economic field," and re-emphasized the concept of the "Four Freedoms" that Roosevelt had earlier enunciated: freedom of speech and of worship, freedom from want and from fear. In many ways the Atlantic Charter resembled Wilson's Fourteen Points, but in spite of the unfortunate parallel fifteen governments – nine of them in exile – endorsed the Atlantic Charter within a few weeks.

Among the subjects discussed at this first conference between Roosevelt and Churchill was military aid to Russia, recently attacked by Nazi Germany. Britain and Russia had already agreed upon a mutual aid treaty, and after the United States formally entered the war the Soviet Union became one of the chief beneficiaries of Lend-Lease aid. In 1942 Churchill made trips to both Washington and Moscow to promote collaboration among the three major Allies, and in 1943 an even more important series of conferences took place between Roosevelt and Churchill:

in Casablanca, French West Africa (January), attended by General de Gaulle; in Quebec (August), attended by representatives of the British commonwealths; in Cairo, Egypt (November–December), attended by Chiang Kai-shek; and in Tehran, Iran (December–January, 1944), attended by Stalin. The last conference served as a prelude to the still more important conferences between the heads of the three major Allies at Yalta in February, 1945, and at Potsdam, Germany, in July, 1945.

NORTH AFRICA AND ITALY

Meanwhile the Allies had taken the offensive. In November, 1942, an Anglo-American amphibious force under General Dwight D. Eisenhower made landings in French Morocco and Algeria. After token resistance the representatives of Vichy France in North Africa capitulated and made common cause with the Allies. The German and Italian troops in North Africa were caught between the invaders and British and Imperial forces in Egypt. Fierce fighting ensued, but by the end of May, 1943, Axis forces had been eliminated and the Allies controlled the entire North African coast, freeing the Mediterranean for Allied shipping and exposing Italy to invasion.

The Allies invaded Sicily in July, 1943, and effected its conquest in less than six weeks. Meanwhile, dissident elements in Italy with the active assistance of the king had overthrown Mussolini and begun negotiations for an armistice with the Allies. A provisional government under Marshal Pietro Badoglio, conqueror of Ethiopia, surrendered on September 3, one day after Allied landings in southern Italy. German troops had already taken over the defense of Italy, however; they rescued Mussolini and installed him as puppet ruler of an Italian Fascist Republic with its capital in Milan. Fighting in southern Italy during the winter of 1943–44 was unusually severe and costly for the Allies. They did not take Rome until June, 1944, and did not expel the Germans from Italy until the final defeat of Germany in 1945. After the collapse of the Nazi-Fascist regime in Italy, Italian partisans (underground fighters) seized Mussolini as he was trying to escape to Switzerland with his mistress, assassinated both without trial, and hanged their corpses by the ankles in Milan. Such was the inglorious end of one totalitarian dictator.

THE LIBERATION OF FRANCE

Stalin had long been agitating for a second front in Europe. The relatively unsuccessful Italian campaign did not satisfy him. Allied military leaders also recognized that the ultimate battles would have to be fought in Germany itself. At length on D-Day, June 6, 1944, after a long build-up of air, sea, and ground forces in England, a huge Allied amphibious force under General Eisenhower, supreme Allied commander, landed on the Normandy peninsula of France. It was the most massive and, from a technical point of view, the most elaborately organized military campaign in history. For months Allied bombers had insistently pounded German cities, industrial establishments, troop concentrations, and communications centers. On D-Day great armadas of naval vessels joined the bombers in destroying the German defenses. Huge concrete piers and docks were floated across the channel from England to facilitate the landing of troops, who came in by airplane and parachute, amphibious ship, and troopship. The Germans put up a strong defense, but having lost mastery of the air their defeat was not in doubt. By the beginning of August Normandy was secured for the Allies, and on August 15 a second invasion in southern France added to the German debacle. Members of the French underground rose in Paris on August 24, and by the beginning of September the Germans had been effectively routed from France. A new provisional government under the leadership of General de Gaulle took charge.

THE COLLAPSE OF GERMANY

The Allies quickly followed up their success in France by liberating Belgium and beginning the invasion of Germany. Simultaneously Russian forces in the east cracked the spine of German resistance and began to roll back German armies across the broad plains of Poland. Nevertheless, in spite of enormous losses of manpower and crippling aerial bombardments, the German defense stiffened as it retreated into German territory. In December, 1944, the Germans launched a desperate counteroffensive against the Western Allies in Belgium and very nearly succeeded in breaking the Allied lines in the Battle of the Bulge. In the east the Germans fought off the Russians within thirty miles of Berlin for almost ten weeks. But the overwhelming might of the combined Allies eventually broke the German defense like a mighty nutcracker. At the end of April American and Russian troops joined forces on the Elbe River, and on April 30, 1945, Adolf Hitler, entrenched in an underground fortress in Berlin but unwilling to surrender, committed suicide in company with his mistress and a few faithful retainers. Thus ended the days of glory of the Thousand Year Reich.

THE JAPANESE SURRENDER

In the Pacific theater the war against Japan moved swiftly to a climax. In October, 1944, American forces invaded the Philippine Islands and with the help of Philippine underground fighters quickly drove out the Japanese. In the Battle of the Philippine Sea the Japanese navy lost forty ships and more than four hundred airplanes. It withdrew to its home waters and thereafter no longer seriously challenged American naval superiority. Nevertheless, the Japanese continued to resist desperately; the conquest of the strategic islands of Iwo Jima and Okinawa in the spring of 1945 cost many thousands of American casualties, and specially trained and indoctrinated *kamikaze* pilots flew suicide missions, ramming their explosive-packed planes directly into American warships in a futile attempt to turn the tide. The helplessness of the Japanese navy, the conquest of island airbases within a few hundred miles of Japan, and the surrender of Germany, depriving Japan of its last ally and releasing hundreds of American bombers for operation in the Pacific, led to increasingly frequent and damaging attacks on Japan itself. During the summer of 1945 the United States Air Force unleashed an aerial offensive against Japan greater even than the Allied bombardments of Germany.

The culmination of the offensive came on August 6, 1945, when an American bomber dropped the first operationally effective atomic bomb on the city of Hiroshima, with results both spectacular and disastrous. A single bomb flattened half of the large industrial city, killed over seventy thousand people, and maimed many thousands for life – perhaps for generations. Three days later the Americans dropped a second atomic bomb on the city of Nagasaki, with similar lethal effects.

The Soviet Union hastened to declare war on Japan on August 8 and began a massive invasion of Manchuria. Stalin had agreed at the Yalta Conference earlier in the year to bring the Soviet Union into the war against Japan within three months of the end of the war in Europe but had hoped to gain further political advantage, expecting that the invasion of Japan would be a long and costly operation. Faced by this new coalition and realizing their helplessness against further atomic attacks, the Japanese agreed to an "unconditional surrender" on August 14, 1945. (Japanese officials requested a single condition, which the Allies accepted: maintenance of the hereditary position of the emperor as nominal head of the government.) On September 2, 1945, General Douglas MacArthur accepted on behalf of the Allies the formal surrender of the Japanese authorities on board the U.S.S. *Missouri* in Tokyo Bay, bringing the Second World War to its end.

SPECIAL FEATURES OF THE WAR

The Second World War was by far the most massive and destructive of all wars in history. In some respects it represented merely an extension and intensification of features that had manifested themselves in World War I, such as increasing reliance on science as the basis of military technology, the extraordinary degree of regimentation and planning of the economy and society, and the refined and sophisticated use of propaganda both at home and abroad. In other respects it differed markedly from all previous wars.

Truly a global war, it involved directly or indirectly the populations of every continent and almost every country in the world. Unlike its predecessor, which had been primarily a war of position, it was a war of movement — on land, in the air, and at sea. Aerial warfare, an incidental feature of World War I, became a critical element in the Second World War. Naval operations, especially the use of carrier-based aircraft, became far more important. Science-based technology accounted for many of the special new weapons, both offensive and defensive, ranging from radar to rocket bombs, jet-propelled aircraft, and the atomic bomb. The economic and especially the industrial capacities of the belligerents acquired new importance. Mere numbers counted for less than ever before, even though size was still a factor in assessing the relative power of the opposing sides. In the final analysis the production line became as important as the firing line: the ultimate secret weapon of the victors was the enormous productive capacity of the American economy.

THE AFTERMATH OF WAR
CHAPTER SEVENTEEN

At the end of the war Europe lay prostrate, almost paralyzed. All belligerent countries except Britain and the Soviet Union had suffered military defeat and enemy occupation. Large areas of the Soviet Union had been effectively occupied by the Germans and fought over foot by foot, twice or even more often. Although Britain had not been occupied (except by Americans), it suffered severe damage from aerial bombardment of its densely populated cities and from acute shortages of food and other necessities. Only the few European neutrals escaped direct damage, but even they suffered from many war-induced shortages.

Wartime casualties in Europe, exclusive of the Soviet Union, have been estimated at more than 15 million deaths: over 6 million soldiers and more than 8 million civilians, including 4.5 to perhaps 6 million murdered Jews. Military and civilian casualties in the Soviet Union may have added another 10 million deaths. These estimates do not include the millions more who were wounded or who suffered from near-starvation and disease. Whole populations were uprooted and displaced, first by the policies of Nazi Germany, then by the surge of warring armies and the flight of refugees. Political boundaries were almost obliterated by the tides of battle and the armies of occupation. Martial law and provisional regimes replaced normal political authorities.

The economy came to a near standstill. Warfare destroyed or damaged railroads, highways, bridges, and port facilities, gutted buildings and factories, collapsed and flooded mines, and leveled cities. Fields remained uncultivated for want of manpower; or if planted, in many instances they were ravaged by battle before the harvest. In the first year after the cessation of hostilities farm production lagged substantially behind that of the prewar years, not only because of the shortage of labor but also because yields had fallen drastically with the shortages of fertilizer and equipment.

Both land and aerial warfare took their toll of housing. In Germany approximately 10 million dwelling units – about 40 per cent of the prewar total – were either destroyed or rendered unfit for habitation. France lost between 20 and 25 per cent of its dwellings. In Rotterdam the whole center of the city was leveled, and many other cities suffered almost as much. Millions of buildings that escaped total destruction were severely damaged, and even those not directly affected by hostilities had deteriorated from inadequate maintenance during the war years.

Factories, which had been among the prime targets of aerial bombardment, survived surprisingly well. Although many were damaged, only about 10 per cent were knocked out completely. More serious was the poor condition of their equipment and especially the shortages of raw materials. In the industrial heartland of continental Europe – that is, in Germany, northern France, and Belgium – production fell by more than half.

A major reason for the shortages and dislocations in both industry and agriculture was the damaged transportation system. Of all sectors of the economy it suffered the greatest physical damage. Every bridge over the Loire and Seine rivers, which separate northern and southern France, and all but one bridge over the Rhine in Germany, were destroyed. Other railroad bridges, junctions, and dock and port facilities were hard hit. The stock of locomotives and other railroad equipment fell to less than half the prewar level in France, Germany, and some other areas. The destroyed bridges and other debris clogged rivers and canals, hindering navigation. Highways suffered similarly. Civilian automobile and motor truck production all but ceased during the war, while a large part of the existing stock of motor vehicles either was destroyed or deteriorated.

Besides direct damage and dislocations the war left other serious economic problems. The currencies of all countries, even neutral ones, had been greatly overissued, resulting in rampant but uneven price inflation. Attempts to impose direct price controls led to evasions and black markets, further intensifying shortages of goods. Germany reverted to an almost pure barter economy when the population deserted the legal currency and substituted such items as cigarettes, coffee, and chocolate as media of exchange.

Before the war Europe imported more than it exported, foodstuffs and raw materials in particular, and paid for the difference with the earnings of its foreign investments and shipping and financial services. After the war, with merchant marines destroyed, foreign investments liquidated, financial markets in disarray, and overseas markets for European manufacturers captured by American, Canadian, and newly arisen firms in formerly undeveloped countries, Europe faced a bleak prospect merely to supply its population with basic needs. Millions faced the threat of death from starvation, disease, and the lack of adequate clothing and shelter immediately after the war. Victor and vanquished were alike in their misery. The urgent need was for emergency relief and reconstruction.

EMERGENCY RELIEF AND RECONSTRUCTION

Relief came through two main channels, much of it originating in America. As the Allied armies advanced across western Europe in the winter and spring of 1944–45, they distributed emergency rations and medical supplies to the stricken civilian population, enemy as well as liberated. Because the Allies had committed themselves to a policy of unconditional surrender, after the cessation of hostilities they had to assume the burden of policing defeated Germany, which included the continuation of emergency rations for the helpless civilian population.

Even more impressive than the Allied military help was the emergency aid administered through UNRRA, the United Nations Relief and Rehabilitation Administration. A collective international agency, it performed its major tasks from 1944 through 1947. In 1945–46 it spent more than 1 billion dollars and distributed more than 20 million tons of food, clothing, blankets, and medical supplies. Most of it went to the liberated and former enemy countries of eastern Europe and to China. The United States bore about two-thirds of the cost, other United Nations members the remainder. After 1947 the work of UNRRA was continued by the International Refugee Organization, the World Health Organization, and other specialized agencies of the United Nations, as well as by voluntary and official national agencies.

EXHAUSTED VICTORS

One of the most urgent tasks facing the peoples of Europe after the satisfaction of their survival requirements was the restoration of normal law, order, and public administration. In Germany and its satellites Allied military governments assumed these functions pending peace settlements. Most of the countries that had been victims of Nazi aggression had formed governments in exile in London during the war. These governments returned to their homelands in the wake of the Allied armies and soon resumed their normal functions.

Their return, however, did not imply a mere "return to normalcy," the chimera of the 1920's. Memories of the economic distress of the 1930's lingered through the ordeal of war, and no one wanted a repetition of either experience, which almost all agreed were in some way related. On the Continent the leadership of the underground opposition to Nazi Germany played a large role in postwar politics, and the comradeship of those movements, in which Socialists and Communists had figured prominently, did much to overcome prewar class antagonisms and bring new men to positions of power. The wartime collaboration of the Soviet Union and the Western democracies facilitated the formation of popular front governments in which Communists collaborated with reformist political parties, such as Socialists and Christian (or Catholic) Democrats. In Britain the participation of the Labour party in Churchill's wartime coalition cabinet gave its leaders great prestige and influence. Finally, the very magnitude of the task of reconstruction indicated a much larger role for the state in economic and social life than had been characteristic in the prewar period.

In all countries the consequence of these various tendencies was widespread public demand for political, social, and economic reforms. The response to the demands took the form of nationalization of key sectors of the economy, such as transportation, power production, and parts of the banking structure; extension of social security and social services, including retirement pensions, family allowances, free or subsidized medical care, and improved educational opportunities; and assumption by governments of greater responsibilities for maintaining satisfactory levels of economic performance. Even the United States passed the Employment Act of 1946, which created the President's Council of Economic Advisers and pledged the federal government to maintain a high level of employment.

THE FOURTH REPUBLIC IN FRANCE

France had a government in exile headed by General de Gaulle, but he was not an elected representative of the French people. In spite of difficult personal relationships, Churchill and Roosevelt granted him half-hearted recognition and after the Normandy invasion allowed him to form a provisional government, which included representatives of the underground resistance to Nazi Germany. The provisional government set about at once to restore the damaged French economy. It nationalized the railroads, coal mines, gas and electricity companies, the armaments industry, the Bank of France, and a number of the largest commercial banks and insurance companies. Under Jean Monnet it instituted a novel form of economic planning that relied more on persuasion than on coercion. The provisional government also reorganized the army to participate in the final assault on and occupation of Germany, and it brought to trial as traitors the principal officials of the Vichy regime. Both Marshal Pétain and Pierre Laval received death sentences, but that of the former was commuted to life imprisonment in recognition of his earlier services to his country.

In October, 1945, de Gaulle called for the election of a National Constituent Assembly to draw up a new constitution for France. The Communist party polled the largest number of votes — almost a third. The Socialists and a new Christian Democratic party, the MRP (Popular

Republican Movement), also seated large groups of deputies. That leaders of all these parties had figured prominently in the resistance movement had an important bearing on their electoral success. The traditional center parties saw their representation cut drastically, and the prewar Right was eliminated almost entirely.

The new assembly elected de Gaulle provisional president of the republic in deference to his prestige, but it refused to follow his wishes in designing the new constitution. He favored a constitution providing for a strong executive. Opposition on this issue and harassment on others led de Gaulle to resign the presidency in January, 1946, and to campaign publicly for rejection of the draft constitution. Caught between Communists on the left and Gaullists on the right, the Socialists and Popular Republicans were maneuvered by the old center parties into supporting a bicameral legislature with a figurehead president and a prime minister and cabinet subject to the whims of the National Assembly. The Fourth Republic, therefore, bore a striking resemblance to the Third. The French electorate rejected the first draft constitution in a referendum in May, 1946, but in October it adopted a slightly revised version by a vote of about 9 million to 8 million – with almost 8 million abstentions. The Fourth Republic thus got off to a bad beginning and soon exhibited all the faults and weaknesses of its predecessor. It survived for only a dozen years.

SOCIALISM IN BRITAIN

In one of the most stunning electoral upsets in British history the voters in June, 1945, chose the Labour party and Clement Attlee over the Conservatives and Winston Churchill. Churchill, first elected to the House of Commons in 1900, had entered politics as a Conservative, deserted to the Liberals in 1903, then rejoined the Conservatives in 1924. During the 1930's he held aloof from all parties until the outbreak of war. As prime minister in the wartime coalition government he had given the most important posts concerning domestic matters to members of the Labour party. In the election Labour capitalized on its wartime record of "fair shares" and campaigned on a platform calling for the nationalization of several key industries and the broad extension of social services.

True to their campaign promises, the Labourites nationalized the railroads, the motor transport industry, the coal mines, the electricity industry, the Bank of England, and the steel industry. They instituted a comprehensive "cradle to the grave" social insurance system and a National Health Service providing free medical care. Unfortunately for Britain, however, not all of its economic difficulties could be solved by domestic reform. Britain was even more dependent than other European countries on international trade. Before the war it had imported two-thirds of its food supply and almost as large a proportion of the raw materials for industry. It had paid for much of the imports with earnings from its merchant marine, banks, insurance companies, and foreign investments. During the war it had been forced to liquidate its foreign investments; much of its merchant shipping had been sunk; and the bulk of international financial transactions had shifted from London to New York. Its manufacturing industries had emerged from the war with obsolete, damaged, or deteriorated equipment, while their overseas markets had been captured by other producers. To enable the country to live within its income, the Labour government found itself obliged to adopt a strict austerity program of high taxation, rationing of all essential commodities, and rigid controls on imports, foreign exchange, and foreign travel. The unpopularity of these measures, together with the failure of the socialized sector of the economy to perform as well as had been hoped, cost the Labour party much of its electoral support. It retained its majority in the House of Commons by a narrow margin in 1950, but it lost to Churchill and the Conservatives in a new election the following year.

THE SOVIET UNION

Russia suffered the greatest damage in an absolute sense of any nation engaged in the war, with 10 million killed and 25 million left homeless. Large areas of the most fertile agricultural land and some of the most heavily industrial regions had been devastated. The situation was not improved in 1946, the first full peacetime year, when drought caused widespread crop failures and desperate food shortages.

In spite of the sufferings of the Russian people, the Soviet Union emerged as one of the two super powers of the postwar world. Its vast territory, the largest in the world, and its population, the greatest of any European nation, as well as the tight control exercised by the government over the people, allowed it to play this role. To restore the devastated economy and boost output to new high levels, the government launched the fourth five-year plan in 1946. As previous plans had done, it emphasized heavy industry and military production, giving particular attention to atomic energy, which indicated that the Soviet leaders intended to maintain and strengthen their position in world affairs. The new plan made extensive use of physical reparations and tribute from the former Axis countries and Russia's new satellites.

Stalin, more powerful than ever, instituted a number of changes in the high offices of both government and the economy in the immediate postwar years. A constitutional revision in 1946 replaced the Council of People's Commissars by a Council of Ministers, in which Stalin assumed the position of chairman or prime minister. The ministries charged with supervision and control of industry and agriculture experienced drastic purges of personnel on grounds of incompetence and dishonesty. Other high officials of government and party were dismissed on similar grounds, although there is reason to believe that Stalin's real motive was distrust of their personal loyalty to him.

Stalin continued to insist upon complete ideological conformity. In 1948 the Central Committee of the Communist party accused such leading composers as Shostakovich, Prokofiev, and Khachaturian of betraying "bourgeois" influences in their music and obtained from them confessions of "guilt" and promises of reform. Shortly afterward the biologist T. D. Lysenko, who occupied a leading position in the Academy of Sciences, denounced classical or Mendelian genetics in favor of a theory harking back to the time of Lamarck, which stressed the inheritance of acquired characteristics. Scientists who refused to accept the party line on this subject were demoted and sent to remote outposts and even jailed. Because the insistence on conformity was carried to such lengths, Russia's intellectual and cultural life in the last years of Stalin's rule showed few signs of originality or creativity.

OTHER ALLIED NATIONS

The United States emerged from the war stronger both relatively and absolutely than when it had entered. To a lesser extent, so also did Canada, the other Commonwealth nations, and several countries of Latin America. Spared from direct war damage, their industries and agriculture benefited from the high wartime demand, which permitted full utilization of capacity, technological modernization, and expansion. The United States possessed the world's largest air force, navy, and merchant marine. Many American economists and government officials feared a severe depression after the war, but after the removal of price controls and rationing, which had held prices at artificially low levels during the war, the pent-up consumer demand for war-scarce commodities created a postwar inflation that doubled prices by 1948. In spite of the hardships that the inflation brought to people living on fixed incomes, it kept the wheels of industry turning and enabled the United States to extend needed economic aid for the rebuilding of Europe and other war-devastated and poverty-stricken lands.

DEFEATED ENEMIES

At the same time that they undertook the reconstruction and reconversion of their own shattered countries, the victorious Allies in Europe and North America had to face the problem of making peace with their former enemies. Most statesmen were well aware of the failures of the peace settlement after World War I and were determined not to repeat the mistakes of the Versailles treaty. They succeeded remarkably well in this objective. New difficulties arose in the form of disagreements among the victors, however, rendering the resulting settlements both tentative and fragile.

THE BIG THREE

Relations between Russia and the western Allies were clouded by what each regarded as the perfidious behavior of the other in the critical years from 1938 to 1940, as well as by still older animosities. Although Churchill had promised aid to Russia immediately after the Nazi attack in 1941 and the United States had granted Lend-Lease assistance even before it became formally involved in the war, Stalin had refused to travel far from his homeland to attend the earlier conferences of the wartime leaders. In part to overcome his suspicions, Roosevelt and Churchill agreed to meet with him on nearby neutral territory in Tehran in the winter of 1943–44. Their discussions focused mainly on the plans for a second front in Europe, although the Big Three also took up the question of a possible postwar international organization – the United Nations.

A year later with the end of the war in Europe in sight the Big Three met again at Yalta in the Russian Crimea. Three topics dominated the discussions: (1) final plans for the defeat and disposition of Germany and eastern Europe; (2) the date and agenda for a conference to establish the United Nations; and (3) participation of the Soviet Union in the war on Japan. With respect to the first, the Allies agreed not to try for an immediate settlement after the German surrender but to occupy Germany jointly until a final peace treaty could be decided. They agreed that a conference to draw up the charter of the United Nations should be convened in San Francisco on April 25, 1945 – by chance, on the same day that Russian and American troops met at the Elbe. The third topic was in many ways the most difficult. Although work on the atomic bomb was well advanced, it had not yet been tested, and there was no certainty that it would be successful. Roosevelt and Churchill were therefore anxious that the Soviet Union should join the war on Japan at the earliest possible moment in order to avoid, if possible, a long and costly invasion. To persuade Stalin, they made several concessions that subsequently caused dispute and bitterness between Russia and the West, as well as in American domestic politics.

The Big Three met once again in July, 1945, at Potsdam, Germany, in the wake of the German defeat. President Roosevelt had died shortly after his return from Yalta and had been succeeded by Harry S Truman. Midway through the Potsdam Conference the results of the British election called for Clement Attlee to replace Churchill. Stalin was thus the only one of the original Big Three to participate in the final deliberations. Few formal decisions were actually made at the conference, though in the long run its actions achieved a permanence not intended by its delegates. The decision to have a four-power occupation of Germany and to postpone a final settlement was reaffirmed and made more precise. A council of foreign ministers was charged with the responsibility for preparing peace treaties with Italy, Austria, Hungary, Bulgaria, Rumania, and Finland. In return for ceding a large part of its prewar territory to the Soviet Union, the Polish provisional government was granted "temporary administration" over most of East Prussia and that part of Germany east of the Oder and Neisse rivers. Finally, in return for a promise to enter the war on Japan at the earliest practical moment, the Soviet Union obtained a promise of substantial advantages in East Asia. In both the decisions arrived at and the matters left undecided the Potsdam Conference built up a store of troubles for the future of East-West relations.

THE PARTITION OF GERMANY

The initial decision for joint occupation of Germany was not meant as a permanent division of the country but was merely for temporary convenience. As events unfolded, the disagreements between Russia and the Western Allies led the latter to give greater and greater measures of autonomy to the Germans in their zones of occupation. The Soviet authorities responded with similar nominal concessions in the eastern zone, though they maintained firm control through their puppets and the presence of Soviet troops. The ultimate result was the division of Germany into two separate states: the German Federal Republic (West Germany) and the German Democratic Republic (East Germany).

The Soviet zone of occupation extended from the Oder-Neisse line in the east to the Elbe in the west. British troops occupied the northwest sector of the country, including the mouth of the Elbe and the lower Rhine. The United States took southern Germany as its zone, and France received two strips of territory adjacent to its borders. Although Berlin was deep inside the Soviet Zone, it, too, was divided into four sectors. In the absence of a German government the Allied Control Council served as the nominal supreme authority, although in fact each occupying power administered its zone independently.

The Potsdam Conference had condoned the dismantling of German armaments and other heavy industries, reparations to the victors and the victims of Nazi aggression, strict limitations on German productive capacity, and a vigorous program of denazification, including the trial of Nazi leaders as war criminals. In fact, only the last aim was realized as originally intended. In November, 1945, an Interallied Tribunal began the trials of twenty-two of the most important Nazi leaders at Nürnberg, the site of many Nazi party rallies. After almost a year in trial the tribunal acquitted three defendants and convicted the remainder with

sentences ranging from ten years imprisonment to death. Lesser officials were also brought to trial. The United States conducted the last of its war crimes trials in 1949, then turned its responsibilities over to the new West German government, which continued to bring former Nazis to trial.

The Soviet authorities dismantled many German factories in their zone and carried them to Russia as reparations. After a brief attempt by the Western powers to collect physical reparations and to break up large industrial combines in their zones, they realized that the German economy would have to be kept intact not only to support the German people but also to assist in the economic recovery of western Europe. They reversed their policy and, instead of limiting German production, took steps to facilitate it. One means of doing this was to provide for economic reunification, a process initiated with the creation of Bizonia, a union of the American and British zones of occupation at the end of 1946, to which the French zone was subsequently added. Just as the Zollverein served as the precursor of the German Empire, the economic unification of the western zones of occupation delineated the future German Federal Republic, which was officially proclaimed in May, 1949. Not to be outdone, the Soviet authorities soon afterward set up the so-called German Democratic Republic. Thus, without a peace treaty ever having been signed or even seriously discussed, the rivalry of the former Allies resulted in the creation of two nominally independent Germanies from the rubble of a former common enemy.

THE RESTORATION OF ITALY

Italy occupied an ambiguous position in the immediate postwar period. Although it had been one of the original Axis aggressors, it was allowed to change sides after the overthrow of Mussolini. No separate peace treaty was signed, however, and it was treated as one of the defeated nations after 1945. Victor Emmanuel III had sought to preserve the monarchy for his dynasty by deserting Mussolini after the Allied invasion of 1943, then by abdicating in favor of his son Umberto in May, 1946. His efforts proved in vain, for the Italians in the next month voted in favor of a republic. Although the Italians were allowed the formality of maintaining an independent government, final authority was wielded by an Allied military government until the ratification of the peace treaty in 1947.

The treaty required Italy to give up its colonial empire, to cede the Dodecanese Islands to Greece, and to give Venezia Giulia to Yugoslavia. Trieste and its hinterland became a free territory under United Nations supervision until 1955, when an agreement between Italy and Yugoslavia gave Trieste itself to Italy and the surrounding territory to Yugoslavia. Italy had to pay reparations of $360 million, of which $100 million went to the Soviet Union and most of the remainder to Yugoslavia and France.

After resuming control of their own affairs in 1947, the Italians faced many difficult problems, including widespread poverty and unemployment, inflation, and government instability. The political spectrum in Italy was broader than that of most countries, ranging from monarchists and neo-Fascists on the right to the largest Communist party in western Europe on the left. To add to its troubles, the Italian Socialist party split into two factions, one a Marxist group usually allied with the Communists, the other favoring democratic socialism and aligned with moderate reformist parties. The most important of the moderate reform parties was the Christian Democratic party headed by Alcide de Gasperi. From 1947 until his retirement in 1953 he succeeded in maintaining a fluctuating but manageable coalition of center and left-center parties.

THE REHABILITATION OF JAPAN

As with Germany, the Allies did not quickly seek a peace treaty with Japan. They wished to maintain control for a considerable period in order to re-educate the Japanese and to establish democratic political institutions. For this purpose General Douglas MacArthur, Allied commander in the Pacific, became the supreme authority in Japan. The Japanese had to give up their colonial empire as part of the unconditional surrender, but MacArthur retained the existing governmental structure to facilitate the execution of his orders. In quick succession he abolished the trappings of Japan's militarist and imperialist past, including the compulsory state religion, leaving Shintoism as one of several competing sects; restored civil liberties; introduced universal suffrage; revised the educational curriculum; and encouraged the formation of labor unions. At MacArthur's instigation Emperor Hirohito in a New Year's message on January 1, 1946, disavowed the divinity attributed to him by the Shinto religion. An international military tribunal undertook the trial of Japan's wartime leaders and eventually sentenced General Hideki Tojo and six others to death. In 1947 MacArthur promulgated a new constitution for Japan, providing for a bicameral legislature, a responsible cabinet, a substantial degree of local self-government, and a broad range of civil rights and liberties.

The Japanese accepted these imposed reforms with alacrity. Vigorous democratic political activity developed quickly, and MacArthur came to occupy a position of prestige in Japanese opinion second only to that of the emperor. Japan's main problems were economic: how to maintain its large, dense population after the loss of its colonial empire and under the restrictions placed by Allied regulations on its industrial production and foreign trade. For a time the United States subsidized the Japanese while simultaneously insisting on the enforcement of the restrictive regulations. The definitive solution to Japanese economic problems came with the outbreak of the Korean War in 1950. Japan served as the staging area for American troops and benefited from an economic boom. The new alignment of powers on the international scene led the United States to press for a lenient peace settlement. In 1951 the United States and forty-seven other nations signed a treaty with Japan restoring the latter's sovereign powers. The Soviet Union and other Communist countries refused to recognize the treaty and did not end their formal state of war with Japan until 1956.

THE FATE OF EASTERN EUROPE

Although the Allies found it inexpedient at first and subsequently impossible to agree on the terms of a peace treaty with Germany, they did succeed in signing treaties with Germany's satellites and in agreeing on the treatment of the victims of Nazi aggression in eastern Europe. The general terms of the east European settlement had been foreshadowed in wartime conferences, notably the one at Yalta. They had envisaged a preponderant role for the Soviet Union, although Stalin had promised to allow free elections and "broadly representative governments" – a promise that proved to be meaningless. After a year and a half of postwar negotiations among the foreign ministers of the Big Three and other Allied nations, at which representatives of the defeated nations had the opportunity to plead their cases, treaties were signed in Paris with Rumania, Hungary, Bulgaria, and Finland, as well as Italy, in February, 1947.

THE LIBERATED NATIONS

The resurrection of Czechoslovakia and Albania was taken for granted. Since those countries had never been at war with the Allies – had, in fact, been among the first victims of Axis aggression – there was no problem in restoring their independence. The manner in which they were liberated, however, guaranteed that they would be within the Russian sphere of influence. Albanian partisans under Communist leadership took over the country in the wake of the retreating Axis forces, and the government that they formed received official diplomatic recognition in November, 1945. In January, 1946, a constituent assembly proclaimed the People's Republic of Albania.

Czechoslovakia was liberated by Soviet troops, and Eduard Beneš returned as president of the provisional government. In a relatively free election in May, 1946, the Communists polled a third of the votes and seated the largest delegation in the new constituent assembly. Klement Gottwald, the Communist leader, became prime minister, but the assembly unanimously re-elected Beneš as president. The country continued under a coalition government, with Beneš hoping to make Czechoslovakia a bridge between Russia and the West, until the Communists seized power in February, 1948.

During the war Churchill and Stalin, without consulting Roosevelt, agreed to exercise equal spheres of influence in Yugoslavia after the war. In fact, Yugoslav partisans led by Marshal Tito liberated the country with very little help from Russia and negligible aid from Britain, thus allowing the country a measure of independence. Elections in November, 1945, gave Tito's Communist-dominated National Liberation Front

Brown Brothers

Marshal Tito

"We study and take as an example the Soviet system, but we are developing Socialism in our country in somewhat different forms. In the present period under the specific conditions which exist in our country, in consideration of the international conditions which were created after the war of liberation, we are attempting to apply the best forms of work in the realization of Socialism. We do not do this in order to prove that our road is better than that taken by the Soviet Union, that we are inventing something new, but because this is forced upon us by our daily life." Letter from the Central Committee of the Communist Party of Yugoslavia to the Central Committee of the Communist Party of the Soviet Union, April 13, 1948, in Robert Bass and Elizabeth Marbury, THE SOVIET-YUGOSLAV CONTROVERSY, 1948–58: A DOCUMENTARY RECORD (New York, 1959).

a substantial majority in the new constituent assembly, which promptly overthrew the monarchy and proclaimed a Federal People's Republic. On paper the new constitution closely resembled that of the Soviet Union, and Tito governed the country in a manner similar to that of Stalin in Russia. He refused to accept dictation from the Soviet Union, however, and in 1948 publicly broke with the latter and its other Communist satellites.

The determination of Poland's postwar boundaries and form of government constituted one of the thorniest problems of peacemaking. In the closing phases of the war there had been two Polish provisional governments: the government in exile in London and the Soviet-sponsored Committee of National Liberation in the Russian-occupied part of Poland. At Russian insistence and with Western acquiescence the two groups merged to form a Provisional Government of National Unity, with a promise of early "free and unfettered elections." The coalition lasted until 1947, when the Communists ousted their partners and assumed complete control.

The territorial settlement agreed on provisionally at Potsdam in effect moved Poland three hundred miles to the west. The language of the agreement had provided only that Poland should have "temporary administration" of the area east of the Oder-Neisse line, or about one-fifth the area of prewar Germany, but the Poles with Soviet support regarded the settlement as definitive compensation for their cessions to the Soviet Union, which constituted almost half of prewar Poland. They forthwith expelled the millions of Germans who resided in the area to make room for other millions of Poles streaming in from the Russian-occupied zone. The enormous transfers of population, together with similar transfers in other parts of eastern Europe, including the movement of Germans from the Sudetenland, returned the ethnic boundaries to something resembling "the *status quo ante* 1200 A.D.," in the words of Arnold J. Toynbee.

THE SATELLITE STATES

The peace treaties with Rumania, Bulgaria, and Hungary – Germany's east European satellites – contained territorial provisions that fell into a well-established historical pattern. Rumania regained Transylvania from Hungary, but it had to return Bessarabia and Northern Bukovina to the Soviet Union and Southern Dobrudja to Bulgaria. Hungary lost the most, for it gained nothing and had to cede a small area to Czechoslovakia. All three defeated nations had to pay reparations: $300 million for Hungary and Rumania and $70 million for Bulgaria, the bulk of which went to Russia. Under the protection of Soviet troops the Moscow-trained Communists in their popular front governments had few difficulties in disposing of their Liberal, Socialist, and Agrarian collaborators and soon established people's democracies in the Soviet pattern. Finland lost some territory to Russia and had to pay $300 million in reparations, but it escaped the fate of other popular front governments on Russia's borders and maintained a precarious neutrality.

The peace treaties had nothing to say about the disappearance of the Baltic countries of Latvia, Lithuania, and Estonia. Part of the tsarist empire before 1917, they had been incorporated by the Soviet Union in 1939–40, then overrun by Germany in 1941. Reoccupied by the Red Army in 1944–45, they were quietly annexed to the Soviet Union as so-called autonomous republics. That they were not mentioned in the peace negotiations implied recognition that they again formed parts of the new Russian empire.

Austria was treated as a liberated territory rather than as a willing accomplice of Germany, but a treaty was necessary to formalize its independence. Until a treaty could be signed, it was subjected to four-power occupation. As in the case of Germany, its capital, Vienna, was located inside the Russian zone and was jointly occupied. Free elections held in 1945 resulted in a negligible vote for the Communists and sizable votes for the Catholic People's party and the Social Democrats, who formed a coalition government. The coalition enjoyed substantial domestic autonomy but remained subject to the Allied Control Commission. In numerous conferences the Soviet Union blocked the final signature of an Austrian treaty on one pretext after another until 1955 while drawing large reparations in the form of petroleum and machinery. The treaty of 1955 restored Austrian sovereignty, pledged it to perpetual neutrality guaranteed by the great powers, and forbade reunion with Germany.

THE UNITED NATIONS

The failure of the League of Nations to prevent World War II disillusioned many persons who had expected much from international organization and cooperation. For many others the experience seemed to call for a stronger, broader-based organization to preserve the peace. From the union of this belief and the wartime cooperation of the Allied Powers the United Nations was born.

The Atlantic Charter, agreed upon by Roosevelt and Churchill in the summer of 1941, contained the germ of the union. In December, 1941, soon after the Japanese attack on Pearl Harbor, Churchill visited Washington, and on January 1, 1942, the representatives of twenty-six nations, including the Soviet Union, proclaimed adherence to the principles of the Atlantic Charter. Roosevelt began to refer to the Allies as "the United Nations." Wartime discussions between the leaders and representatives of the Allies anticipated continued international cooperation after the war; and on April 25, 1945, a conference including representatives of fifty-one nations convened in San Francisco to draft a charter for the permanent structure of the United Nations. The resulting organization resembled the League in many respects, but it also differed in several important particulars.

ORGANIZATION

The principal resemblances occur in the formal structure of the two organizations. Like the League, the United Nations is a voluntary association of sovereign nations. As did the League, it consists of two main deliberative bodies: the General Assembly and the Security Council. The General Assembly includes all member nations on the basis of one nation, one vote. Unlike the League, it can decide most questions by majority vote. The Security Council, however, charged specifically with the maintenance of world peace, requires unanimity of at least its five permanent members except on procedural questions. These members are the United States, Great Britain, the Union of Socialist Soviet Republics, France, and China (China was named to the Security Council chiefly because of the insistence of the American delegates; the fall of the Nationalist government to the Communists in 1949 created grave problems for the entire organization). The Security Council also contains ten rotating members elected for two-year terms.

Like the League, the United Nations operates under the administrative direction of a permanent Secretariat and maintains a number of specialized bodies. Among the most important of these are the International Court of Justice, successor to the Permanent Court of International Justice established in The Hague, and the Economic and Social Council, which has several regional commissions. There are also numerous agencies related to the United Nations such as UNESCO (United Nations Educational, Scientific, and Cultural Organization), the World Health Organization (WHO), the International Labor Organization (ILO), the International Monetary Fund, and the World Bank.

The General Assembly annually elects a president, but the office is largely honorific. The first president was Paul Henri Spaak, a devoted internationalist from Belgium. In subsequent years presidents have frequently come from former colonial nations. A more permanent and important position is that of secretary general, the main administrative officer of the organization. As the chief international civil servant, the secretary general is supposed to be above both party factionalism and nationalism. Although formally separated from policy-making decisions, the secretary general is in a position to wield great influence because of his constant preoccupation with all affairs of the United Nations. The first person to hold the post was Trygve Lie of Norway. He resigned in 1953 after years of criticism and abuse by the Soviet Union. His successor was Dag Hammarskjöld from neutral Sweden, who was killed in a plane crash in 1961 while trying to bring peace to the strife-torn Congo. U

Thant, a former General Assembly president from Burma, succeeded Hammarskjöld. The Security Council, originally deemed the most powerful element in the United Nations, has no permanent officers. Each representative serves as chairman for a month at a time under a system of continual rotation.

The location of the headquarters of the United Nations posed a problem. Switzerland, disillusioned with the League, refused to join the United Nations. After lengthy investigations and debate the General Assembly accepted a gift of land on Manhattan's East Side from John D. Rockefeller, Jr., and built a large modern skyscraper and other buildings of advanced design to house its large staff. Although it is located physically within the United States, the United Nations is not within its legal jurisdiction. Delegates and staff members enjoy the same privileges that are accorded to diplomats in Washington.

FUNCTIONS

The primary purpose of the United Nations, as of the League, is to preserve international peace. Unlike the League, the United Nations has provided special peace-keeping military forces for selected world trouble spots, such as Palestine, Cyprus, and the Congo. It has no permanent or regular forces of its own but utilizes mixed contingents drawn from various members, usually the smaller and traditionally neutral nations, such as Sweden and Eire. Technically, all the troops engaged in these activities are under the banner of the United Nations.

The United Nations' record as a peace keeper has been spotty. Although no wars between the great powers have occurred during its existence, it cannot take major credit for this fortunate circumstance. Other factors, such as the general fear of the awesome destructiveness of an atomic or thermonuclear war, have been greater deterrents. The intervention of the United Nations in the Korean War resulted from the prompt action of President Truman and the temporary absence of the Soviet Union from the Security Council. The United Nations has had only limited success in preventing or halting even the minor wars between neighboring countries that have wracked the newly emerging (or re-emerging) nations, such as the Palestinian War of 1948–49 and the dispute between India and Pakistan over Kashmir. The prompt cessation of the 1956 invasion of Egypt by Israel with French and British support was due to threats and persuasion by the United States and the Soviet Union rather than to any action by the United Nations. The brevity of the Arab-Israeli war of 1967 resulted from the rapid success of the Israelis in achieving their limited objectives. The United Nations has not even attempted to intervene in certain potentially major disputes, such as those between China and India and between China and Russia.

There are several reasons for the relatively poor showing of the United

Nations as a peace keeper. One is that it has no independent source of revenue and is dependent upon the voluntary support of its member nations to finance its activities. Even more important, its charter forbids it to interfere in the internal affairs of sovereign nations. Several important wars, including the Algerian war for independence from France, the struggle of Egypt and Saudi Arabia in the Yemen, and above all the series of wars in Southeast Asia, have passed under the guise of domestic revolts and revolutions and have thus escaped the active involvement of the United Nations. The most important reason for the United Nations' inadequacy is the split that early developed between the Soviet Union and its satellites on the one hand, and the Western Allies on the other, which has tended to paralyze United Nations action in all disputes involving the great powers, such as the Berlin blockade of 1948. Nevertheless, by providing a regular, permanent forum in which all nations can express their views on important issues, and by furnishing facilities for immediate consultation and conciliation, the United Nations has made important indirect contributions to world peace.

DIVIDED ALLIES

In the rosy afterglow of Allied victory over the Axis Powers many people hoped and expected that the wartime cooperation of the great powers would continue in the postwar period and ensure the peaceful reconstruction and rehabilitation of a shattered world. In this spirit they hailed the charter of the United Nations. Others, less sanguine and possibly more realistic, predicted that the very achievement of the wartime goal – the defeat of their common enemies – would remove the incentive to cooperate and result in the reassertion of mutually antagonistic policies by Russia and its Western Allies. Without doubt, influential persons in both the Soviet Union and the nations of the West neither expected nor wanted continued cooperation. Some American military leaders even advocated a "preventive war" against the Soviet Union while the United States still had a monopoly of atomic weapons. Fortunately for the world, saner counsels prevailed within the highest echelons of government.

THE THREAT OF ATOMIC WARFARE

Control of atomic energy was one of the most vexing political problems of the postwar era, domestically as well as internationally. American military authorities wanted to retain exclusive jurisdiction over the production and disposition of fissionable material. After lengthy public discussions and congressional debates the Congress in 1946 enacted legislation to create an Atomic Energy Commission under civilian control, along with a watchdog Joint Congressional Committee on Atomic Energy. At about the same time the United Nations created its own Atomic Energy Commission to discuss ways and means of developing peaceful uses of atomic energy and preventing its use for aggressive or belligerent purposes. The United States government proposed to turn over both its fissionable material and its scientific formulas to the United Nations on condition that other nations should open themselves to inspection to prevent clandestine production of atomic weapons, but the delegates of the Soviet Union and its satellites argued that the control of atomic energy should be considered in the context of proposals for general disarmament. The United States objected, and the Soviet Union killed discussion of the American proposal in 1947 with a veto in the Security Council. One of the reasons for Russian intransigence on this issue became clear in 1949 when the Soviet Union exploded its own atomic bomb.

THE TRUMAN DOCTRINE AND INCREASING TENSIONS, 1946–1947

President Roosevelt apparently believed that he would be able to win Stalin over to a policy of continued cooperation after the war. After Roosevelt's death President Truman and his advisers, frustrated by Russian attitudes on such matters as atomic energy and the German question, adopted a more cautious attitude. In the words of Secretary of State James F. Byrnes in September, 1946, dealing with the Russians required "patience and firmness." Six months later American policy veered around to one of "containment" of the expansionist attempts of the Soviet Union and international communism.

In 1946 Greece, which had been liberated and occupied by the British in the closing months of the war, became the scene of a civil war between the restored royalist government and guerrillas supplied by Communist-dominated governments in Bulgaria, Albania, and Yugoslavia. Early in 1947 the British, hard pressed by domestic difficulties as well as by worldwide commitments, served notice of their intention to withdraw their occupation forces. The following March President Truman requested that Congress authorize a program of far-reaching military and economic aid to Greece and Turkey and, by implication, to other nations threatened by communist subversion. This policy became known as the Truman Doctrine. Shortly afterward General George Marshall, who had become secretary of state, called on all European nations, including the Soviet Union and its satellites, to unite in a program of economic recovery with American assistance.

The leaders of international communism had been quietly tightening their grip on the nations of eastern Europe while continuing their policy of collaboration with popular front governments in western Europe. In accordance with classical Marxist doctrine, they believed that a final catastrophic economic collapse would overtake the capitalist nations in the postwar period and that they would succeed to positions of power either by legitimate means or by internal subversion. They discovered to their disappointment that instead of collapsing, the countries of western Europe were becoming stronger. In the spring of 1947, in a desperate attempt to paralyze and possibly overthrow the governments, Communist-dominated labor unions in France and several other countries resorted to strikes and fomented civil disorders. The democratic elements within the governments responded with stern measures. In France and Italy they expelled their Communist colleagues from the government in May; Belgium, the only other country of western Europe with Communist cabinet ministers, had taken the same step two months earlier. These actions marked the end of popular front collaboration in western Europe. In retaliation, the Communist-dominated governments of Bulgaria, Rumania, Hungary, and Poland, with the support of the Soviet armies of occupation, systematically purged all non-Communists from their governments in the summer of 1947.

THE MARSHALL PLAN AND THE "COUP DE PRAGUE"

In July, 1947, in response to Secretary of State Marshall's invitation, representatives of sixteen European nations met in Paris to draw up a joint request to the United States for financial aid to assist in their economic recovery. The following spring the United States Congress passed the Foreign Assistance Act, establishing the European Recovery Program or Marshall Plan, and authorized an initial sum of $5.3 billion to be distributed as loans and grants by the newly created Economic Cooperation Administration (ECA). The recipient nations formed the Organization for European Economic Cooperation (OEEC) to administer the aid in Europe and pledged themselves to a long-term program of mutual assistance and cooperation.

Under the law creating the ECA, recipients of American aid had to put up in their own currencies a sum of money equivalent to the amount received from the United States. These "counterpart funds" were then expended along with the original aid money according to plans drawn up by the OEEC and approved by the ECA. In the four years of its existence the ECA supervised the expenditure of more than $11 billion in American aid. Most of it went for "social overhead capital," such as improvements to railroads, highways, port facilities, and installations for power production, although some also took the form of loans to privately owned or nationalized industries to aid in the rehabilitation of mines and factories and to provide fertilizer and modern equipment for farms. The most populous nations received the largest share of the aid, with the largest absolute amounts going to France, Great Britain, Italy, and West Germany (admitted to the OEEC in 1949). All European nations outside the Soviet sphere of influence except Spain and the neutrals eventually participated in the European Recovery Program.

The Soviet Union and most of its satellites immediately branded the Marshall Plan a new instrument of "capitalist imperialism" and declined to attend the meeting that led to the OEEC. Czechoslovakia and Finland, however, the two countries in the Soviet sphere that still had democratic regimes, sought to participate until they were called to account by the Soviet Union. In the fall of 1947 representatives of Communist parties throughout the world met in Warsaw at the behest of the Soviet Union to establish the Communist Information Bureau (Cominform). In effect, it was a resurrection of the Comintern that had been dissolved in 1943. The purpose of the organization was to coordinate the activities of the various national Communist parties and to make them more amenable to control from Moscow.

In February, 1948, in a still more daring and brutal show of force than the purges of the summer of 1947, the Communists in Czechoslovakia expelled the democratic members of the government, murdered or brought about the suicide of Jan Masaryk, the internationally respected foreign minister, and forced the resignation of President Beneš, who died soon afterward. Called the *coup de Prague,* this action caused widespread revulsion in the West and rendered still more unlikely the possibility of further cooperation between the Soviet Union and its former allies. Largely as a result of events in Czechoslovakia, the Western Allies decided to go ahead with the economic and political reconstruction of West Germany.

THE BERLIN BLOCKADE

In June, 1948, the Western powers carried out a reform of the German currency as a measure to stimulate economic recovery. In retaliation, the Soviet authorities immediately instituted a blockade of West Berlin by closing off all rail and highway transportation from West Germany. The Soviet Union hoped to force a withdrawal of Western forces from Berlin, or at least to secure concessions on disputed points; instead, the Western Allies responded promptly with a large-scale air life of strategic supplies. In a tremendous operation lasting more than a year the United States Air Force and the RAF flew almost 300,000 flights into Berlin, transporting at its peak more than 8,000 tons of supplies daily. The air lift supplied not only Western troops but also the 3 million inhabitants of West Berlin.

In May, 1949, the Russians finally lifted the blockade. The outcome was a substantial victory for the Western powers, greatly strengthening their prestige among the Germans in particular. During the blockade the Allies worked out a plan for the transference of political authority in West Germany to a German government operating under the surveil-

Photoworld

Gatow Airport During Berlin Airlift

"I was down at Tempelhof airfield that first morning to see the planes arrive. They were wartime twin-engined C-47 transports — 'Gooney Birds,' the pilots called them with affectionate contempt. Old, tired, and patched, the planes had been hastily collected from military airfields in the Western zones of Germany and rushed into the Berlin service. Many veterans still wore their camouflage paint from North Africa. Each plane had brought in two and a half tons of flour in a two-hour flight from Frankfurt. . . .

"The airlift was a reality by the first week in July, acquiring strength with every succeeding day. That first month, we brought in fifty thousand tons of food for civil consumption, a fraction of what we were to achieve when the lift got into its stride, but enough to convince the Russians that we meant business and to prove to the Germans that, if they stood by us, we could feed them." General Frank Howley, BERLIN COMMAND (New York, 1950).

---

lance of an Allied High Commission. In 1949, shortly after the Russians lifted the blockade, the new German Federal Republic came into existence.

NATO AND COMECON

In the atmosphere engendered by the Marshall Plan the nations of western Europe undertook a number of other ventures entailing greater international cooperation. France and Britain had already signed a treaty of alliance in February, 1947, and in October Belgium, the Netherlands, and Luxembourg ratified an agreement for the Benelux customs union. In March, 1948, these five nations signed the Treaty of Brussels, providing for joint consultation and cooperation in economic, social, and military affairs. In the following year they were joined by Denmark, Norway, Sweden, Ireland, and Italy in the Council of Europe, with headquarters at Strasbourg, France. The Council consisted of a Consultative Assembly with representatives elected by the parliaments of the participating nations and an executive committee of foreign ministers. Its functions were mainly consultative and advisory. To be binding, decisions of the committee of ministers had to be unanimous. Many persons hoped that from this organization a United States of Europe would grow. Greece, Turkey, Iceland, Austria, Switzerland and West Germany were subsequently admitted, as well as Cyprus and Malta.

Simultaneously with the establishment of the Council of Europe most of its member nations plus Portugal signed a treaty with the United States and Canada (April 4, 1949) creating the North Atlantic Treaty Organization (NATO). The signatories pledged themselves to mutual assistance in the event of armed aggression against any one of them, and they undertook far-reaching military collaboration under the direction of the North Atlantic Council. In the following year West Germany was admitted to the Council of Europe, and plans were made for the inclusion of West German forces in a unified European command.

Between the promulgation of the Truman Doctrine in the spring of 1947 and the formation of NATO in the spring of 1949 the international communist movement suffered continual setbacks in its attempt to gain power in western Europe. The Soviet rulers and their puppets abroad reacted to the situation by severe measures to increase their control over eastern Europe and by new, more overt attempts to embarrass or overthrow the governments of western Europe. In January, 1949, following the initial success of the European Recovery Program, the Soviet Union created the Council for Mutual Economic Assistance (COMECON) in an attempt to mold the economies of eastern Europe into a more cohesive union. Thus the division of Europe into two rival ideological camps became more pronounced and apparently more nearly permanent than ever.

As early as March, 1946, Winston Churchill, speaking at Westminster College in Fulton, Missouri, under the approving eye of Harry S Truman, coined the phrase "an iron curtain" for the borders of the Russian sphere of influence, extending from Stettin on the Baltic to Trieste on the Adriatic. By 1949 the phrase was common parlance in the Western world, and a still newer phrase, "the Cold War," to define the East-West struggle, had entered Western vocabularies. In little more than a year the Cold War became uncomfortably warm.

Photograph from UPI

President Truman Presents Winston Churchill to Westminster College Audience, Fulton, Missouri

"From Stettin in the Baltic to Trieste in the Adriatic, an iron curtain has descended across the Continent. Behind that line lie all the capitals of the ancient states of Central and Eastern Europe. . . . These famous cities and the populations around them lie in what I must call the Soviet sphere, and all are subject . . . to a very high and, in many cases, increasing measure of control from Moscow. . . .

"From what I have seen of our Russian friends and Allies during the war, I am convinced that there is nothing they admire so much as strength, and there is nothing for which they have less respect than for weakness, especially military weakness. . . . If the Western Democracies . . . become divided or falter in their duty and if these all-important years are allowed to slip away then indeed catastrophe may overwhelm us all." Speech of Churchill at Fulton, Missouri, March 5, 1946, reprinted in W. S. Churchill, THE SINEWS OF PEACE (Boston, 1949).

THE KOREAN WAR

The dramatic events taking place in Europe in the years following the war deflected the attention of Americans as well as Europeans from the no less dramatic and important events in Asia. After the government of Chiang Kai-shek had taken its place in the United Nations as a permanent member of the Security Council, a Chinese Communist revolution drove it into exile on the island of Formosa (Taiwan). In Korea after the defeat of Japan American and Soviet armies occupied the country jointly. Their zones were separated only by the thirty-eighth parallel of latitude. Efforts to unite the country under a single regime failed, and in 1948 Soviet and American authorities organized separate regimes in their respective zones of occupation and shortly afterward withdrew their armed forces. Difficulties soon arose between the Communist-dominated North Korean government and the somewhat autocratic regime of President Syngman Rhee in South Korea. On June 25, 1950, a well-equipped force of North Koreans launched an all-out attack on South Korea and soon overran Seoul, the nation's capital.

The United Nations, at the urging of the United States during a temporary boycott of the Security Council by the Soviet Union, branded North Korea an aggressor and demanded the withdrawal of North Korean troops, but to no avail. President Truman, with United Nations approval, quickly ordered American troops based in Japan to the defense of South Korea and called on other nations to do likewise. Before the United Nations forces could effectively organize themselves, the North Korean forces had driven them almost off the peninsula. After a determined holding action on the Pusan beachhead the United Nations forces under the command of General Douglas MacArthur launched a strong counterattack, and in two months they had driven the North Koreans almost to the border of China. At this point, at the end of November, 1950, large forces of so-called volunteers from Communist China intervened on the side of North Korea, and by the end of the year they had driven the United Nations armies back to the vicinity of the thirty-eighth parallel. There the fighting settled down to a long-drawn-out period of trench and seige warfare. After months of fruitless negotiations a truce was finally arrived at in 1953.

The Soviet Union did not participate directly in the Korean War, but North Korean and Chinese Communist armaments were almost all of Russian manufacture. Neither did the Soviet Union take any part in the truce negotiations. These facts further divided the Soviet Union from its former allies. Moreover, the intervention of the Chinese Communists signaled another important turn in world history: henceforth the struggle of Communists and anti-Communists would no longer be confined to Europe. It had become global in extent.

THE END OF WESTERN HEGEMONY CHAPTER EIGHTEEN

In the four centuries and more between the voyages of Columbus and the outbreak of World War I the nations of European culture had come to dominate directly or indirectly virtually the whole of the inhabited world. The First World War resulted in some changes in the identity of the ruling powers with the breakup of the German and Ottoman empires. It also caused some changes in the legal forms of control when former colonies became mandates or trust territories under nominal League of Nations supervision. In many respects, however, the interwar years witnessed the apogee of European imperialism and colonialism, for under the impress of exaggerated political and economic nationalism the imperial powers sought to assimilate and integrate the economies of their colonial possessions with their own.

The Second World War dealt a death blow to European imperialism. The Philippines, the Dutch East Indies, French Indochina, and British Burma and Malaya fell under the temporary control of Japan. Elsewhere in Asia and Africa the defeat of France, Belgium, and Italy and the preoccupation of the British with the war effort left their colonial dependencies largely on their own. Some dependencies proclaimed their independencies at once; others witnessed the rise of independence parties that agitated against continued colonial rule. The wartime slogans of the Western Allies themselves, calling for liberty and democracy throughout the world, strengthened the appeal of the independence movements by highlighting the contrast between Western ideals and the realities of colonialism; they also undermined the willingness of the peoples of western Europe to tax themselves in order to dominate others. In the immediate postwar years the imperial powers regained control temporarily in most of their former colonies, but their own war-induced weaknesses, the growing strength of native independence movements, and the ambivalent position of the United States led to a gradual abandonment of imperialist controls. In a few cases colonial areas fought successful wars of independence against their former masters. Increasingly the imperial powers relinquished dominion voluntarily, if reluctantly, rather than experience the costs and hazards of war. By providing a forum for the expression of the sentiments of independent non-Western nations the United Nations likewise hastened the end of Western imperialism.

NEW NATIONALISMS

One of the many elements of Western culture that was absorbed, albeit imperfectly, by colonial peoples during their long years of tutelage was the idea of nationalism. Both African tribalism and pre-Western imperialism in Asia had been fundamentally nonnationalistic. The growth of nationalism amongst non-Western peoples was abetted by the example of the imperialist nations themselves and by the common experience of subordination to uniform colonial laws and controls. Frequently the nationalism of colonial peoples had no tangible basis other than the more or less arbitrary political divisions imposed by the imperial powers, although in some cases it was reinforced by common religions and languages.

ARAB NATIONALISM

Although the majority of the inhabitants of western Asia and North Africa speak the same Arabic language and pay allegiance to the same Moslem faith, the new nations that have come into being in these areas reflect the political divisions initially imposed by the Ottoman Empire for administrative convenience and subsequently maintained by the Western powers when they assumed control in the nineteenth and twentieth centuries.

After the fall of France in 1941 Lebanon and Syria declared independence, but the British and Free French occupied them to forestall German penetration. At the end of the war France attempted to reassert control, but because of widespread local opposition Britain and the United States persuaded France to recognize Syrian and Lebanese independence. Britain granted independence to Iraq in 1930 but maintained control of its military and foreign policy by treaty agreements. During the war British troops again occupied the country, where they remained until 1947. Britain granted independence to Transjordan in 1946, which soon renamed itself the Kingdom of Jordan. In both Iraq and Jordan, Britain tried to maintain influence by means of subsidies, military assistance, and technical advice, but both countries pursued policies that made them increasingly independent of Britain. In 1958 a revolution overthrew the ruling dynasty in Iraq and replaced it with a strongly nationalistic republic.

In Egypt Britain maintained control of military affairs and foreign policy after formally terminating its protectorate in 1922. During the war Egypt served as the main base of Allied military operations in Africa and western Asia. Nationalist agitation continued after the war, and in 1952 a military junta led by General Mohammed Naguib overthrew the British puppet King Farouk. The following year Naguib proclaimed a republic. Naguib in turn gave way to the still more strongly nationalistic Colonel Gamal Abdel Nasser. In 1955 Nasser's government forced the withdrawal of the last British troops, and in 1956 it nationalized the Suez Canal.

In 1945 the governments of Egypt, Iraq, Lebanon, Saudi Arabia, Syria, Jordan, and Yemen formed the Arab League in an attempt to speak with one voice for their thirty-five million Arabic-speaking subjects and their two hundred million coreligionists of the Islamic world. Libya, Sudan, Tunisia, Kuwait, Algeria, and Morocco joined the league soon after gaining independence. Cultural affinities of language and religion, however, could not overcome the nationalistic legacy of postimperial political divisions. On the political spectrum the members of the league ranged from strongly socialist republics to the absolute monarchy of Saudi Arabia. In 1958, after one of Syria's perennial military coups d'état, Syria joined Egypt in the United Arab Republic. Nasser hoped to expand the U.A.R. to include the entire Arab world; but he obtained no new recruits, and three years later after another coup Syria withdrew. In 1962 Egypt supported a revolution against the imam (ruler) of Yemen and came into conflict with royalist Saudi Arabia, which supported the imam. Similar differences prevented effective cooperation in military and economic affairs. The one subject on which all Arab nations agreed — although even there they could not achieve unanimity of action — was opposition to the new state of Israel.

THE REBIRTH OF ISRAEL

The world's Jews had been a homeless, persecuted minority since the Diaspora (dispersion) of Roman times. During the Dreyfus affair in France — a nation that had previously been regarded as the most urbane and tolerant of all — Theodor Herzl (1860–1904), an Austrian journalist of Jewish faith, had projected the idea that the Jews should have a "national homeland." A movement called Zionism developed in support of his idea. By no means did all Jews support Zionism, nor did all of those who became Zionists intend to move to the "national homeland" if one could be found. In 1917 in a move calculated to win Jewish support for British war aims Arthur Balfour, the British foreign secretary, pledged British government cooperation for the settlement of Jews in Palestine, their biblical home. At that time Palestine was nominally a province of the Ottoman Empire, inhabited chiefly by Arabs. Jews constituted less than one-tenth of the population, and they lagged far behind European Jews in wealth and culture. Nevertheless, when Britain gained Palestine as a League of Nations mandate after World War I, it facilitated the efforts of wealthy, philanthropic Jews in Europe and America to purchase land in Palestine as a haven for Jewish refugees. The refugees flooded in, especially after the accession of Hitler to power in Germany, in spite of the bitter opposition of Palestinian and other Arabs, who resorted to riots, terrorist activity, and boycotts of Jewish and British merchandise. By the outbreak of World War II the Jews amounted to one-fourth of the population in Palestine.

Interwar efforts to establish self-government in Palestine foundered on the undying hostility between Jews and Arabs. The British were forced to rule by executive decree and frequently by martial law. The postwar influx of Jewish refugees from central and eastern Europe, entering illegally in many instances, exacerbated not only the political problem but also the economic problem of how to support the thousands of new inhabitants in what was essentially a barren, crowded land. The United Nations had no better success than the British in finding a solution to Jewish-Arab conflicts, and in 1948 the hard-pressed British withdrew their forces and terminated the mandate, leaving Jews and Arabs to their own devices. The Jews at once proclaimed the state of Israel and made Chaim Weizmann, an internationally known chemist, president and David Ben-Gurion premier.

Open warfare immediately broke out between Jews and Arabs. The Jews, at first on the defensive, soon gained the upper hand as a result of superior organization and equipment. In 1949 a United Nations mediation commission arranged a fragile truce, which led to the de facto division of Palestine into a Jewish national state (with a substantial Arab minority) and the incorporation of the remainder of the country into the Kingdom of Jordan. Israel made good use of the accumulated skills and knowledge of its European settlers and, aided generously by European and American Zionist philanthropists, soon outstripped its Arab neighbors in wealth and industry. This intensified Arab hatred and did nothing to alleviate the latent antagonism between the European and Islamic worlds.

THE MODERNIZATION OF IRAN

The ancient kingdom of Persia, officially renamed Iran in 1935, became increasingly involved in European diplomacy, especially after the discovery of oil by European concessionaires in 1908. During World War II the country was jointly occupied by American, British, and Russian forces. After the war the Russians attempted to organize a separatist movement in the northern province of Azerbaijan, but the Iranians defeated the movement after intervention by the United Nations. In 1951 the strongly nationalist Mohammed Mossadegh became premier and sought to exterminate British influence, chiefly by nationalizing the Anglo-Iranian Oil Company. Mossadegh was overthrown and imprisoned in 1953, but the oil concessions were nationalized. In subsequent years Mohammed Reza Pahlavi, a shah (king) who ruled as a benevolent dictator, introduced a number of legal, economic, and social reforms with a view to modernizing his country.

INDIA AND PAKISTAN

Nationalist sentiment had been growing in Britain's vast Indian empire since the Sepoy Rebellion of 1857. Nationalism had many obstacles to overcome in India, however. With two major religions, each with numerous sects, several mutually unintelligible languages, and a variety of forms of government in the many provinces, India's millions had only common opposition to British rule to unite them. Eventually India's nationalism polarized around the two principal religious faiths, Hinduism and Islam, which were more antagonistic toward one another than toward Britain.

The first self-conscious organ of Indian nationalism was the Indian National Congress (a political party, not a legislative body), created in 1885. Because of its agitation Britain introduced a strictly limited degree of self-government in 1909. During World War I India remained loyal to Britain, but demands for self-government and independence increased. In 1919 the British Parliament enacted the Government of India Act, conferring a larger measure of self-government, but even this measure failed to satisfy most Indian nationalists. About that time a remarkable person arose to become the leader and symbol of Indian opposition to British rule.

Mohandas K. Gandhi (1869–1948), popularly called Mahatma (great-souled), a London-educated lawyer of aristocratic Indian birth, sought to revive both the spiritual and political greatness of ancient India. Although he might have lived a life of luxury, he identified with the common people of India, dressed simply (a loin cloth was his usual costume), ate simply in strict accordance with Hindu dietary laws, and fasted often. His most notable contribution to the techniques of political agitation was the doctrine of civil disobedience and passive resistance. He used it so effectively that the British imprisoned him on several occasions, but they always discovered to their dismay that his martyr-like incarceration caused them more trouble than his freedom. During the Second World War Gandhi adopted a pacifist position with respect to the war while continuing his campaign of passive resistance to the British.

Other nationalist leaders, including Gandhi's close friend Jawaharlal Nehru, felt that more would be gained for India's cause by supporting the British war effort. Britain had already offered to grant India domes-

Photoworld

Nehru and Lord Mountbatten, July, 1947

"After a generation of intense struggle with a great and powerful nation, we achieved success and perhaps the most significant part of that achievement for which credit is due to both parties was the manner of it. History hardly affords a parallel to the solution of such a conflict in a peaceful way followed by friendly and co-operative relations.

"It is astonishing how rapidly the bitterness and ill-will between the two nations have faded away giving place to co-operation and we in India have decided of our own free will to continue this co-operation as an independent nation." Address of Pandit Nehru at Columbia University, October 18, 1949, BEFORE AND AFTER INDEPENDENCE . . . SPEECHES DELIVERED BY JAWAHARLAL NEHRU (New Delhi, 1950).

---

tic autonomy with dominion status, but Gandhi and Nehru would settle for nothing less than complete independence. After the war Britain's Labour government finally agreed to their demands. At this point civil war broke out between Moslems and Hindus.

As independence drew near, it became clear that India would be dominated by the Hindu majority. In the 1930's the Moslem League under

Mohammed Ali Jinnah, its fiery leader, had begun to demand a separate Moslem state. Although Gandhi had earlier opposed partition, the clashes between Moslems and Hindus on the eve of independence persuaded him to accept it. When Britain at last withdrew from India on August 15, 1947, after almost two centuries of dominion, not one but two independent nations emerged: the Union of India and the Islamic state of Pakistan (Land of the Pure). Both retained dominion status within the Commonwealth.

Neither independence nor partition solved India's pressing problems. Both new nations were badly overpopulated and desperately poor. Pakistan was divided into two widely separated parts: West Pakistan (with the nation's capital, Karachi), which stretched on both sides of the Indus River, and East Pakistan across India on the Ganges River. In spite of partition and massive exchanges of population, both nations contained sizable minorities of the opposite faith. The most serious problem involved Kashmir, a mountainous province in the northwest, which both nations claimed and neither would relinquish. Efforts of the United Nations to mediate the dispute came to naught.

Nehru became the first prime minister of India, a post that he retained until his death in 1964. In 1948 a Hindu extremist assassinated Gandhi for his part in the partition. Nehru set the nation on a course of moderate, democratic socialism, and in 1949 he converted it into a federal republic while still retaining its ties with the Commonwealth. Pakistan followed suit a few years later. Ceylon, which had been governed as a part of India, did not participate in the internal Indian struggle for power, but it obtained a large measure of self-government in 1946. In 1948 it gained dominion status and full self-government.

BURMA AND MALAYSIA

Burma was another nation created in the mold of colonial rule. Burmese unity had been a tenuous thing prior to the British conquest, but resentment against colonial government provided a common focus for Burmese nationalism. Britain promised dominion status for Burma near the end of World War II, but the Burmese preferred complete independence. In 1948 they proclaimed a federal republic, the Union of Burma, free of all ties to the Commonwealth. As with India and Pakistan, independence not only failed to solve the nation's problems but added many new ones. Separatist movements developed in a number of the component states, and Communist agitation alienated large segments of the population from the central government.

After most other former British colonies in Asia had gained complete independence, either within or outside the Commonwealth, the Federation of Malaya remained dependent on Britain while gaining more self-government. For several years after the war Communist forces kept up a guerrilla war against British rule and the established local governments. In 1963 the former crown colonies of Singapore, Sarawak, and North Borneo joined the other Malayan states in the Federation of Malaysia, a fully self-governing dominion within the Commonwealth of Nations; but in 1965 Singapore withdrew.

THE REPUBLIC OF INDONESIA

The peoples of Java, Sumatra, Borneo, and the hundreds of other islands comprising the Dutch East Indies had long resented Dutch rule, but they did not succeed in establishing a cohesive independence movement until the Japanese occupation during World War II. Immediately after the withdrawal of the Japanese the Indonesian People's party under the leadership of Sukarno (like many Indonesians, he had only one name) proclaimed the independence of the Republic of Indonesia. The Dutch refused to recognize the new government and with the aid of the British defeated the Indonesian People's Army, but then agreed to the creation of a United States of Indonesia as an equal partner with the Netherlands under the Dutch crown. Both sides soon found fault with the agreement, and repeated violations of the truce occurred. In 1949, under pressure from both the United Nations and the United States, the Dutch agreed to full independence for Indonesia, which was admitted to the United Nations the following year.

The problems facing the new nation were formidable. It had a population of more than 70 million scattered over 3,000 islands within an area of hundreds of thousands of square miles. Population densities on some of the islands were among the highest in the world, while other islands consisted almost entirely of uninhabited tropical jungle. The Islamic Buddhist, Hindu, and Christian faiths intermingled, not always peacefully. Levels of living were among the lowest in the world. Dissident groups within the islands staged revolts against the central government, which sought to impose its authority as brutally as the Dutch had done in the colonial era. Instead of attacking its economic, political, and social problems directly, Sukarno, who governed in dictatorial fashion, indulged in the most pernicious excesses of nationalism, nationalizing all Dutch property in 1955, forcing the Dutch from West Irian (Dutch New Guinea) in 1962, and objecting to the creation of the Federation of Malaysia in 1963. In 1965 Indonesia became the first member to withdraw from the United Nations, in protest over the seating of Malaysia on the Security Council, and later that year the pro-Chinese Communist party with the tacit agreement of Sukarno tried to take complete control of the country. The army under General Suharto smashed the attempted coup, stripped Sukarno of his powers, and put the nation back on a friendlier course with the West. In 1966 Indonesia resumed membership in the United Nations.

INDOCHINA

Before World War II the French had granted only the barest nominal concessions of self-government to their possessions in Southeast Asia. During the war and the Japanese occupation the nationalist movement made considerable headway, but the new government of the Fourth Republic showed no signs of willingness to grant independence. Instead it organized its former colonies as partially self-governing "Associated States within the French Union." Fighting broke out in 1946 between the French and the strongly nationalist Viet Minh organization in Annam, the largest of the former French colonies. The independence movement received support from the Soviet Union and later from Communist China. In spite of military aid from the United States, the French suffered defeat at the hands of the Viet Minh in 1954, and accepted partition between North Vietnam, under Communist control, and South Vietnam. The truce agreement provided for a plebiscite to determine the form of government for the entire country, but in 1955 Ngo Dinh Diem, the pro-Western premier of the interim government of South Vietnam, proclaimed the southern zone a republic and made himself president. The plebiscite was never held. In the end France granted independence to all its former Asian colonies, including Laos and Cambodia.

THE PHILIPPINES

In 1935 the Philippines, America's greatest colonial possession in the Asian Pacific area, obtained commonwealth status providing a substantial measure of self-government, and was promised eventual independence. World War II delayed the achievement of independence until July 4, 1946, when the Republic of the Philippines was formally established. Like all former colonial possessions, the Philippines faced difficult economic problems in adjusting to world markets. It also had to deal with the Communist-inspired guerrilla warfare of the Hukbalahap or Huks. The Huks finally called off their civil war in 1954, but the Philippines still faced the problems of dire poverty, backward social arrangements, and a burgeoning population.

THE CHINESE REVOLUTIONS

China underwent two revolutions in the space of a generation. The first, the Nationalist revolution, was incomplete at best. It never succeeded in unifying the country or in throwing off foreign domination. The second, the Communist revolution, not only overthrew the Nationalist government and established dominion over the whole of mainland China but also engaged in imperialist adventures of its own.

THE NATIONALIST REVOLUTION

Although the revolution of 1912 (see pp. 264–265) was apparently successful in that it overthrew the decadent Manchu dynasty, it fell prey to internal divisions. The first president of the Republic of China, a former official of the Manchu Empire, soon sought to restore the monarchy and to make himself emperor. He was defeated by the Kuomintang (National Peoples' party) of Dr. Sun Yat-sen, but rival warlords, military leaders who refused to recognize the sovereignty of the central government, ruled their individual provinces in dictatorial fashion.

China remained subject to foreign imperialism in the form of territorial concessions, financial controls and indemnities stemming from the Boxer Rebellion, and the rights of extraterritoriality for foreign citizens; which exempted them from the jurisdiction of Chinese courts. In 1915 the Japanese presented a humiliating set of "Twenty-One Demands," which made China a virtual protectorate of Japan. Partly in the hope of escaping from its ignominious position, China declared war on Germany in 1917, but it was allowed to contribute only labor battalions. The Versailles treaty disappointed Chinese nationalists in that it transferred Germany's concessions in China to Japan instead of returning them to China. China retaliated by refusing to sign the treaty and instituted an ineffective boycott against Japanese merchandise.

Failing to secure support for his movement in the capitals of Western nations, Dr. Sun turned to the Soviet Union for assistance in the drive for independence and unity. After Dr. Sun's death in 1925, General Chiang Kai-shek, who had received military training in both Japan and the Soviet Union, became de facto head of the Kuomintang. With the support of Russian technicians and advisers he launched a successful military campaign against the warlords in the north. As soon as he had achieved victory in 1927, Chiang broke with his Communist supporters. He established a single-party government with himself as president and, in effect, dictator. The organic law which served as a constitution made no provision for an elective legislature. Dr. Sun's goal of nationalism had apparently been achieved, but democracy was postponed, and socialism was abandoned altogether. Chiang's alliance with native Chinese capitalists, symbolized by his marriage in 1927 to a daughter of the wealthy Soong family, played a prominent role in succeeding developments.

The renewal of Japanese aggression in 1931 and its intensification in 1937 brought an unaccustomed unity to Chinese policy. Even the Chinese Communists, whom Chiang had disavowed and persecuted, supported him in his resistance to the Japanese. The Soviet Union began to supply him with military equipment as early as 1937, while the United States and other Western powers were still trying to effect a reconciliation with Japan.

THE CHINESE IN WORLD WAR II

Japan's undeclared war on China merged gradually into the greater conflict of World War II. The Kuomintang forces, poorly equipped and supplied, retreated to the west and established a capital at Chungking in the mountainous province of Szechwan. There they were cut off from communication with the Western powers by sea and received only a tiny driblet of supplies via the long and difficult Burma Road. After the Japanese attack on Pearl Harbor the United States and Britain granted direct military and financial aid to the Chungking government and sent the American General Joseph Stilwell as Allied commander of the China-Burma theater. Although the Allied forces, now including those of the Kuomintang, did not win any notable victories in China, they did keep large numbers of Japanese troops tied down on the mainland, and thus facilitated Allied victories in the Pacific. The suffering of the Chinese people was enormous. Already one of the poorest peoples in the world before the war, suffering frequent famines and natural disasters such as floods, they now had the added horrors of aerial bombardment of overcrowded, defenseless cities, the disruption of agriculture by military operations, and a drastic hyperinflation brought on by unlimited issues of paper money. The war prevented the Kuomintang government from carrying out its promised reforms, and the corruption, venality, and inefficiency of many of its officials turned the Chinese people against it even though they supported the war against Japan.

THE COMMUNIST REVOLUTION

During the war the Chinese Communists cooperated with Chiang in his resistance to the Japanese but maintained an independent army in northern China, supplied and equipped by the Soviet Union. As Japanese power on the mainland collapsed in the closing months of the war, both the Nationalists and the Communists rushed in to fill the vacuum, and as a consequence came into armed conflict with one another. Shortly after the end of the war President Truman sent General George C. Marshall to effect a conciliation between Communists and Nationalists. Although he once arranged a brief truce, his mission met with repeated frustrations because of the irreconcilable attitudes of reactionaries in the Kuomintang and radicals among the Communists. Marshall at length gave up the mission, reporting that "sincere efforts to achieve settlement have been frustrated time and again by extremist elements of both sides."

Nevertheless, the United States continued its military and financial aid to the Nationalist government, which came to depend upon it as almost its only support. The aid was badly used, and the government fell more and more into the hands of reactionary and corrupt elements.

Sovfoto

Chairman Mao Tse-Tung

"The contradiction between imperialism and the Chinese nation and the contradiction between feudalism and the great masses of the people are the basic contradictions in modern Chinese society. Of course, there are others, such as the contradiction between the bourgeoisie and the proletariat and the contradictions within the reactionary ruling classes themselves. But the contradiction between imperialism and the Chinese nation is the principal one. These contradictions and their identification must inevitably result in the incessant growth of revolutionary movements. The great revolutions in modern and contemporary China have emerged and grown on the basis of these basic contradictions." From "The Chinese Revolution and the Chinese Communist Party," December 1939, in SELECTED WORKS (Peking, 1965), Vol. II.

The inflation continued to unprecedented heights, and some Nationalist officials actually sold American arms and munitions to their Communist enemies for personal profit. The Communists, meanwhile, had won large numbers of supporters among the war-weary peasants. The Nationalists steadily lost ground to the Communists in 1948, and in the following year their retreat turned into a rout. On October 1, 1949, the Communists under Mao Tse-tung and Chou En-lai formally proclaimed the People's Republic of China with the capital in Peking. Chiang Kai-shek and his remaining supporters in the Kuomintang completed their evacuation to Formosa (Taiwan), which had been returned to China by Japan, and abandoned the mainland to Communist control.

CHINESE COMMUNIST IMPERIALISM

According to classical Marxist doctrine, China was even less prepared for communism than Russia had been in 1917. The Communists nevertheless began a wholesale reorganization of Chinese society, nationalizing factories and organizing peasant villages into rural communes. Although they achieved some success in increasing the production of steel and other heavy industrial products, their agricultural progress failed to keep pace with the rapid increase of population in the overpopulated country.

In spite of severe economic problems, the government did not hesitate to engage in political and military action beyond its frontiers. In 1950, just a year after its formal establishment, it sent legions of so-called volunteers to oppose the United Nations in Korea. The following year it scored a bloodless coup by taking control of Tibet and gaining a common frontier with India. This circumstance brought on sporadic armed clashes with India, a strong protagonist of neutralism in the struggle between communism and the Western democracies. China replaced the Soviet Union as the chief supporter of Communist revolutionary movements throughout Southeast Asia. As Soviet foreign policy began to swing back toward "peaceful coexistence" with the West, Chinese insistence on an ultimate war of annihilation led to increasing tensions and an eventual rupture between the two most powerful partners in the Communist bloc. Communist China's greatest technological and political triumph came in 1964, when it exploded an atomic bomb. Thus, in the space of half a century China had changed from a helpless decaying nation subject to imperialist exploitation to an aggressive, expansionist nation with imperialist intentions of its own.

THE EMERGENCE OF INDEPENDENT AFRICA

The political map of Africa at the end of World War II differed little from that of the interwar years. The great imperial powers of the past still ruled almost all the continent. British colonies included most of east central Africa – the Rhodesias, Nyasaland, Tanganyika, Kenya, and Uganda – and important areas in West Africa, such as Nigeria and the Gold Coast. Although Egypt was nominally independent, it remained subject to British military control, and Britain and Egypt exercised joint authority in the Sudan. The Union of South Africa, a member of the British Commonwealth governed by a white minority of European culture, ruled not only its own territory but some adjacent areas as well. The French Empire included most of West Africa, the North African littoral from Tunisia to Morocco, large parts of Central Africa, and the island of Madagascar. Belgium retained the huge Belgian Congo. Portugal controlled Angola, Mozambique, and a few smaller possessions. Spain retained its few colonial territories on the west coast. Superficially, the momentous events of the two previous decades appeared to have had little effect on Africa. Underneath the surface, however, powerful currents of change had been set in motion that in the next two decades completely altered the face of the continent.

A few changes that took place immediately after the war were indicative of the shape of things to come, but they were either so slight or so expected that they left the world unprepared for the magnitude of subsequent changes. Italy lost its African empire, of course. Ethiopia regained independence and formed a federation with Eritrea. Libya came under United Nations supervision with a promise of eventual independence. Italy retained temporary administration over the former Italian Somaliland, but with independence promised by 1960.

The French Empire underwent some changes. The constitution of the Fourth Republic, adopted in 1946, changed the status of the former colonies to that of "overseas territories and departments" within a "French Union," gave their inhabitants full rights of citizenship, and provided for representation in the French parliament, although not in proportion to population. On paper this represented a substantial improvement in the position of their subjects, and the new regime introduced a number of ameliorations in the fields of health, education, and economic affairs; actually, the realities of political control changed little. The British government also liberalized educational facilities for Africans and allowed them to enter the lower ranks of the civil service. The Belgians, however, continued their policy of paternalism in the Congo, and the Portuguese resisted all symptoms of change.

INDEPENDENCE FOR NORTH AFRICA

The former Italian colony of Libya became the first African nation to gain independence after the war. The United Nations made the decision as early as 1949, and the new state came into existence at the end of 1951 as a constitutional monarchy. With its sparse population, paucity of natural resources, and backward economy, the future of the new nation was far from promising, but Western subsidies, some of which took the form of payments by the United States Air Force for air base facilities, helped it to survive until the discovery of petroleum deposits strengthened its economic base. Although it retained ties with the Western powers, to whom it owed its independence (the Soviet Union had opposed and refused to recognize it until 1955), Libya also adhered to the Arab League. In 1969 a military coup ousted King Idris and installed an Arab Socialist regime.

Egypt, after gaining its independence, expressed a determination to retain control of the Sudan. The British, however, took measures to introduce self-government in the Sudan before their withdrawal. In a plebiscite in 1955 the Sudanese voted heavily in favor of independence under a republican form of government. The Sudan thus became the second new African nation to secure independence in the postwar period.

In contrast to the relative ease with which Libya and the Sudan obtained independence, the former French colony and protectorates of Algeria, Tunisia, and Morocco engaged in long, difficult, and costly struggles. Tunisia and Morocco had retained their traditional forms of government, which functioned under the direction of French authorities. Algeria, on the other hand, where the French had been established for more than one hundred years and which had more than a million inhabitants of European ancestry (about one-tenth of the population), was treated as part of France for some purposes. Strong nationalist and pan-Arab movements developed in all three countries after the war. The French government responded with nominal concessions to greater autonomy for Tunisia and Morocco but attempted to integrate Algeria more firmly with France. Neither policy worked. The nationalist parties in Tunisia and Morocco demanded complete independence, and in 1956, rather than engage in another war like that in Vietnam, the French granted them "independence within interdependence." Under this arrangement the former protectorates retained privileged positions in the French market and obtained economic aid in return for allowing French military bases on their territory. Both countries subsequently moved steadily in the direction of complete independence. In 1957 the Neo-Destour party in Tunisia overthrew the Bey of Tunis, a figurehead monarch, and proclaimed a republic under the presidency of Habib Bourguiba, strongest leader of the nationalist movement. In Morocco the former sultan became king, took a more active role in the movement for independence, and emerged as the actual as well as the nominal ruler of the country. After independence the governments of both Tunisia and Morocco engaged in vigorous efforts to modernize their countries and on the international scene tried to follow a policy of friendship but nonalignment with both East and West.

The success of the independence movements in Tunisia and Morocco stiffened the determination of some Frenchmen — notably the Algerian

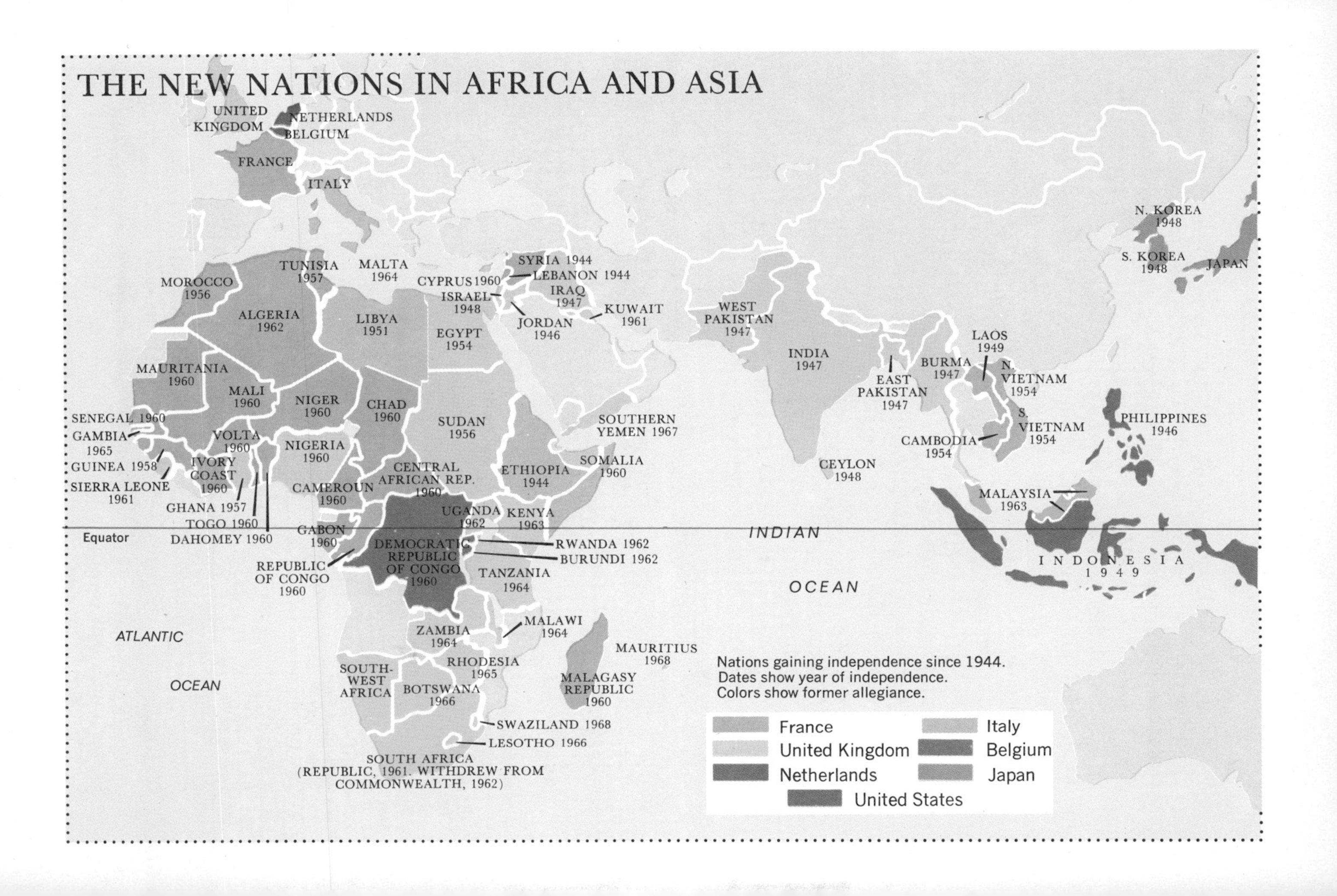
THE NEW NATIONS IN AFRICA AND ASIA
UNITED KINGDOM
NETHERLANDS
BELGIUM
FRANCE
ITALY
MOROCCO 1956
TUNISIA 1957
MALTA 1964
ALGERIA 1962
LIBYA 1951
EGYPT 1954
CYPRUS 1960
ISRAEL 1948
SYRIA 1944
LEBANON 1944
IRAQ 1947
JORDAN 1946
KUWAIT 1961
WEST PAKISTAN 1947
INDIA 1947
EAST PAKISTAN 1947
BURMA 1947
LAOS 1949
N. VIETNAM 1954
S. VIETNAM 1954
CAMBODIA 1954
CEYLON 1948
MALAYSIA 1963
PHILIPPINES 1946
N. KOREA 1948
S. KOREA 1948
JAPAN
INDONESIA 1949
MAURITANIA 1960
MALI 1960
NIGER 1960
CHAD 1960
SUDAN 1956
SENEGAL 1960
GAMBIA 1965
GUINEA 1958
SIERRA LEONE 1961
VOLTA 1960
IVORY COAST 1960
GHANA 1957
TOGO 1960
DAHOMEY 1960
NIGERIA 1960
CAMEROUN 1960
CENTRAL AFRICAN REP. 1960
ETHIOPIA 1944
SOMALIA 1960
SOUTHERN YEMEN 1967
UGANDA 1962
KENYA 1963
GABON 1960
REPUBLIC OF CONGO 1960
DEMOCRATIC REPUBLIC OF CONGO 1960
RWANDA 1962
BURUNDI 1962
TANZANIA 1964
MALAWI 1964
ZAMBIA 1964
RHODESIA 1965
SOUTH-WEST AFRICA
BOTSWANA 1966
MAURITIUS 1968
MALAGASY REPUBLIC 1960
SWAZILAND 1968
LESOTHO 1966
SOUTH AFRICA (REPUBLIC, 1961. WITHDREW FROM COMMONWEALTH, 1962)
Equator
ATLANTIC OCEAN
INDIAN OCEAN
Nations gaining independence since 1944.
Dates show year of independence.
Colors show former allegiance.
France
United Kingdom
Netherlands
Italy
Belgium
Japan
United States

colons (European settlers in Algeria) and high army officers — to resist any notion of independence for Algeria. They were opposed by the National Liberation Front (FLN) which in 1954 began an intensive guerrilla war, frequently marked by acts of terrorism against both the European civilian population of Algeria and the natives who collaborated with the French authorities. Unable to locate and destroy the top leadership of the movement, who often took refuge in other Arab countries, the French Army responded with terrorist activities of its own. The government in Paris followed confusing and sometimes contradictory policies, neither giving the army full support nor exercising firm control over it. In May, 1958, faced with the threat of an army revolt and coup d'état, the government of the Fourth Republic abdicated its powers to General de Gaulle. (See p. 1040.) De Gaulle returned to power with the support of the army and the Algerian settlers, who expected him to keep Algeria French. At first de Gaulle seemed intent on doing so, but after further years of bloodshed and fruitless attempts to reach an understanding with the Algerian leaders for autonomy within the French Community, he agreed in 1962 to grant Algeria full independence. This decision was followed by the wholesale evacuation of European *colons* to France. The new government under Ahmed Ben Bella followed a strongly nationalist line, but at the same time flirted with the Chinese Communists, who sought to increase their influence in Africa. In 1965 a military coup overthrew Ben Bella and the new leaders took a neutralist stance.

REACTION IN SOUTH AFRICA

The population of the Union of South Africa at the end of the war was approximately 12 million, of whom more than three-fourths were Negroes. The population also included sizable numbers of Asians (mainly from India) and "colored" persons (mulattos). Inhabitants of European descent constituted less than a fifth of the population, and of those the Afrikaners (Dutch-speaking) outnumbered the English-speaking peoples by about three to two. The Europeans controlled the government and most of the wealth of the country. In spite of some pro-German sentiment among the Afrikaners during the war, Jan Christian Smuts, South Africa's great statesman who had fought against the British in the Boer War, kept the nation in the war on the side of the British. In 1948, however, Smuts's United party lost an election to the Afrikaner Nationalist party under Daniel Malan.

The new government revealed its attitude in international affairs by refusing to convert its League of Nations' mandate over Southwest Africa into a trusteeship under United Nations supervision, and in 1949 it annexed the area in express defiance of the United Nations. Of even greater significance for the future was the government's policy of *apartheid* or strict segregation of the races. The government enacted a series of stringent laws depriving Negroes of elementary civil liberties and property rights; when the South African Supreme Court ruled some of the laws unconstitutional, the parliament passed a new law declaring itself to be the highest court on constitutional questions. The government's repressive policies resulted in domestic opposition and foreign criticism, especially from the new nations of Africa and Asia. In 1961 in a gesture of defiance to Great Britain the government reconstituted itself as a republic. The following year the Republic of South Africa withdrew from the Commonwealth. Meanwhile it intensified its oppression of the nonwhite population of the country, provoking them to strikes, riots, and the formation of underground and exiled revolutionary organizations.

THE EMANCIPATION OF BLACK AFRICA

In the early 1950's most observers expected that a generation or more would be required for the Negro peoples of Central and West Africa to obtain independence; yet within a decade more than a score of new nations had arisen from the former British, French, and Belgian colonial empires. The strength of native independence movements accounted for this striking development only in part. Equally important, domestic difficulties of the imperial powers made them unwilling to bear the high cost – economic, political, and moral – of continuing to rule alien peoples against their will. Once the process of emancipation had begun, it continued like a chain reaction, with each new day of independence hastening the next.

After the war the British government realized that it would have to do a better job of preparing its African wards for self-government if it was to avoid costly colonial wars and a total loss of the economic benefits of empire. It began by establishing more schools, creating universities, and opening the civil service to Africans. In 1951 the Gold Coast and Nigeria obtained constitutions granting them a measure of local autonomy. The British intended that, perhaps after several decades, they should acquire still greater rights of self-determination. In the Gold Coast, however, Kwame Nkrumah, a remarkable political leader, demanded immediate independence for his people and showed determination to win it even from his prison cell. Rather than risk a full-fledged revolt, the British agreed to most of Nkrumah's demands, and in 1957 the state of Ghana (so called from the medieval African empire of that name) emerged as the first black nation in the British Commonwealth. Ghana also became a member of the United Nations. With this precedent before it, Nigeria achieved independence in 1960 and other former British possessions in West Africa did the same in subsequent years.

Paradoxically, the first British colonies in Africa to achieve full in-

Photograph from UPI

Kwame Nkrumah

"My . . . two recurrent themes. The first is freedom of the individual. The second is political independence, not just for Ghana or for West Africa, but for all Africa. I do not know how anyone can refuse to acknowledge the right of men to be free." Kwame Nkrumah, I SPEAK OF FREEDOM (London, 1961).

---

dependence were among the least advanced economically and politically. Because they were populated almost entirely by black Africans, there was no problem of white minorities. In East Africa and the Rhodesias, however, British settlers had acquired vast tracts of property and enjoyed substantial local self-government. Deprived of political rights and economic opportunity, the Africans constituted sullen, rebellious majorities who sometimes resorted to violence, such as the Mau Mau terrorism in Kenya during the 1950's. By 1965 Britain had granted independence to all its African colonies except Rhodesia. The exception resulted from the refusal of Rhodesia's white population to accord equality of status to their black fellow citizens, who greatly outnumbered the whites. In 1965 the white-dominated government of Premier Ian Smith made a unilateral declaration of independence — the first such occurrence in the British Empire since 1776. Britain attempted to apply economic sanctions to force Rhodesia to change its policy, but with some assistance from the Republic of South Africa Rhodesia successfully resisted the sanctions. Several years of negotiations between Britain and Rhodesia produced no results, but Britain was unwilling to employ military force, as advocated by some black African nations.

When promulgating the constitution of the Fifth Republic in 1958, France's de Gaulle offered the French colonies, except Algeria, the option of immediate independence or the position of autonomous states within the new French Community (a replacement for the defunct French Union) with the right to secede at any time. Although this remarkably liberal offer was occasioned in part by de Gaulle's recognition that it would probably be impossible to hold the colonies against their will, it nevertheless stands in marked contrast to the stubborn unrealism and blunders that had previously characterized French colonial policy. Of their fifteen colonies in black Africa (including Madagascar), only Guinea, under the leadership of Sekou Touré, chose independence. The others organized their own governments but allowed France to retain control of defense and foreign policy in return for economic and technical assistance. In 1960 a further constitutional change granted them full independence while permitting them to continue to enjoy special economic rights and privileges.

The sudden achievement of freedom by France's colonies stirred the formerly placid subjects of Belgium to rioting, pillage, and demands for similar treatment. The Belgians had made no provision for self-government in the Congo, much less for independence. The disturbance took them by surprise, but they promised in January, 1959, that a plan for independence would be worked out speedily. A year elapsed, but no plan materialized; political and social unrest mounted in the Congo, with new outbreaks of violence. Early in 1960 the Belgian government suddenly decreed that the Congo was to become independent on June 30. Elections were hastily arranged, a constitution was drawn up, and the largely illiterate Congolese, none of whom had ever voted before, were called upon to choose a complete set of government officials. When the day of independence arrived, many of them expected their standard of living to be magically transformed to the level enjoyed by their affluent former masters. In their disappointment they again resorted to pillage and wanton destruction. The Congolese army proved unable to maintain order and sometimes even contributed to the looting and violence. Rival political groups fell to attacking one another, and the mineral-rich province of Katanga tried to secede from the new nation. The central government called for assistance from the United Nations to restore order, but rebellion and wild outbursts of violence continued to occur sporadically.

THE REMNANTS AND LEGACY OF COLONIALISM

By the mid-1960's the former European colonial powers, with the exception of Portugal, had granted independence to almost all their African dependencies. South Africa faced the problem of enforcing its policy of apartheid without inflaming its victims to the point of open revolt or attracting the intervention of their African brethren. Portugal scornfully rejected all suggestions that it prepare its colonies for eventual liberation. In spite of these remnants of colonialism, the magnitude of the changes that had taken place in less than twenty years constituted one of the outstanding and most hopeful occurrences of the postwar period. The dark continent had found a place in the sun.

Although colonialism was dying if not dead, it left a rueful legacy. With few exceptions, and those confined to the areas of European settlement, African nations were desperately poor. In three-quarters of a century of colonialism the nations of Europe had extracted vast fortunes in minerals and other commodities but shared little of their wealth with the Africans. Only belatedly had some of the colonial powers made any effort to educate the Africans or to prepare them for a responsible role in government. When retribution came in the form of riots, civil wars, and terrorism accompanying the struggles for independence, it fell on the innocent and the guilty alike — and there were more of the former than of the latter.

In spite of their unhappy experiences at the hands of the democratic nations who had ruled them, most of the new African nations made at least a pretense of following democratic forms, and some made a valiant effort to achieve true democracy. As in some other parts of the world, however, the social and economic bases for stable, viable democracies did not exist. Because of this as well as the lingering irritant of the remnants of colonialism, Africa would long remain a continent in turmoil.

LATIN AMERICA IN FERMENT

Before World War II the Spanish- and Portuguese-speaking nations of the Western Hemisphere resembled in many respects the African and Asian colonies of Europe, although they were not subject to foreign political dominion. Most were very poor, with accompanying low levels of literacy, widespread unemployment or underemployment, and a high incidence of malnutrition and disease. In spite of their general poverty, great extremes of wealth existed between the relatively small landowning class and the masses. Their economies depended primarily on agriculture, much of it the subsistence variety with backward technology and low productivity. The few modern sectors were frequently owned by foreigners and produced mainly for export. Their extreme dependence on exports of one or a few primary products – coffee in Brazil, sugar in Cuba, meat, wheat, and hides in Argentina, copper and nitrates in Chile, tin in Bolivia – rendered them highly vulnerable to international economic fluctuations. All these factors contributed to social unrest and political instability. They had been particularly hard hit by the great depression of the 1930's, and this gave rise to a variety of political extremist movements of both Right and Left.

During and immediately after the war most Latin American nations benefited from strong demands and consequent high prices for their major exports. Some of them – notably Argentina, Brazil, Chile, and Mexico – took advantage of the wartime shortage of manufactured goods to begin new industries producing for their domestic markets. These embryonic industrial revolutions ran into difficulties in the 1950's with the recovery of the European and Japanese economies and the unfavorable price movements for their export products. They also suffered from the continuing wide gap between the very rich and very poor, which deprived them of mass purchasing power for the products of industry. The inefficiency of the governments allowed galloping inflations that contributed to dislocation, misery, and social unrest.

THE MEXICAN REVOLUTION

Mexico became the first Latin American nation to experience a social revolution. After the brief experiment with democracy under Juarez (see p. 166), Mexico relapsed into the long dictatorship of Porfirio Díaz (1876–1911). In 1911 a broadly-based revolutionary movement overthrew Díaz, but the revolutionary leaders soon became engaged in factional strife. A state of near anarchy ensued, complicated by armed intervention by the United States in 1914, 1916, and 1917. Paradoxically, the intervention helped to unify the revolutionary movement and to give it a strong nationalist and anti-imperialist character. In 1917 the Mexican Congress adopted a new constitution with many progressive social provisions, such as universal suffrage, agrarian reform, minimum wages and an eight-hour day for urban workers, and restrictions on the power and property of both the church and foreign property owners. The constitution of 1917 continued as the basis of Mexican government, but for almost three decades Mexico hovered on the verge of a relapse into dictatorship or anarchy. In 1946 Miguel Alemán became the first civilian to occupy the office of president, and since that time democracy and social reform, accompanied by rapid economic development, have continued to grow, giving Mexico one of the most stable and progressive governments in Latin America.

DICTATORSHIPS OF THE RIGHT

The military elite played a prominent political role in most Latin American countries. In the smaller, more unstable countries military juntas made and unmade presidents and prime ministers without benefit of elections; sometimes they held sham elections in which the outcome was never in doubt. One of the hardiest Latin American dictators was General Rafael Trujillo of the Dominican Republic, who wielded unchallenged authority in his small island domain from 1930 to 1962. He ruled the country as a personal fief and even renamed the capital city Ciudad Trujillo. Although petty despots in other countries had less time to entrench themselves, they often followed similar policies. Fulgencio Batista ruled Cuba as either president or president-maker from 1940 until he was overthrown by revolution in 1959.

Even the larger, more stable, and generally more democratic countries had their periods of dictatorial rule. In 1930 a depression-bred revolt in normally calm Brazil brought Getulio Vargas to the presidency. By a series of constitutional changes Vargas gradually tightened his control on the office and introduced a number of fascist economic and political organizations. When World War II broke out, however, he followed the lead of the United States, and Brazil became one of the first Latin American nations to declare war on the Axis Powers. In 1945 a combination of his opponents, including some of his former supporters, forced Vargas to resign, but he was elected again in 1950 and served until 1954. He was again confronted with demands for his resignation, and he committed suicide.

Argentina, another country with a better-than-average record for democracy and stability and with one of the best balanced, most prosperous economies in Latin America, contained a number of influential Axis sympathizers. It remained neutral until the very last weeks of World War II, when it made a token declaration of war against the Axis Powers. In 1946 the Argentinians elected Colonel Juan D. Perón president. Perón had a record of collaboration with Nazi Germany and soon showed his totalitarian bent with police state methods, including strict censorship of the press, regimentation of the economy, and the use of force against his opponents. Although re-elected for a six-year term in 1951, Perón succumbed to a junta of his former fellow officers in 1955 and went into exile in Europe. For the next decade Argentina was governed by a succession of weak presidents, but in 1966 a military coup overthrew the constitutional president and replaced him with a general. Both Vargas and

Perón relied heavily on the political support of organized labor, which further confused the conventional distinction between Left and Right in Latin America.

DICTATORSHIPS OF THE LEFT

Communists and other left-wing radicals found fertile ground for cultivation in the miserable living and working conditions of the lower classes in Latin America. At times they commanded substantial popular followings, but they rarely achieved the seats of power. In most countries Communist parties were outlawed, and their leaders had to resort to subversive activities. In a few cases, however, left-leaning governments did come to power. In both Bolivia and Guatemala revolutionary left-wing regimes gained power temporarily in the postwar period. In British Guiana the Communist-supported government of prime minister Cheddi Jagan, a native of India, frequently conflicted with both the large Negro population and the British Colonial Office until it was turned out in the election of 1964. The new government achieved full independence in 1966. Brazil's President João Goulart (1961–1964) seemed to be leading his country in the direction of Communist control until he was toppled by a military coup in April, 1964.

The only thoroughly Communist government to install itself in the Western Hemisphere was that of Fidel Castro in Cuba. Castro was one of many idealistic young Cubans who resented the corrupt and reactionary Batista regime. For more than two years before 1959 he led a romantic guerrilla war against the government in the mountainous Oriente Province of Cuba. In spite of military aid from the United States in the form of modern weapons and equipment, Batista's regime was unable to suppress the movement, which had the sympathy and active support of the peasants in the area. In the latter months of 1958 Castro's July 26 Movement gathered increasing popular support, while Batista's discredited regime visibly crumbled. Batista fled in December, and on January 8, 1959, Castro made a triumphal entry into Havana. At that time Castro was committed to a program of far-reaching social and economic reform but had not formally proclaimed allegiance to either Marxist principles or the Communist party. A series of diplomatic blunders by the United States, combined with pressure from some of his closest advisers, persuaded Castro to turn to communism and to an alliance with the Soviet Union.

HEMISPHERIC COOPERATION AND CONFLICT

The nations of Latin America have traditionally regarded the United States with a mixture of fear, envy, and respect. In the early years of the twentieth century American intervention in the internal affairs of Mexico and the Caribbean nations gave rise to impassioned anti-Ameri-

Wide World Photos

Fidel Castro

"I believe that we have arrived at a decisive moment in our history: tryanny is overthrown, and joy is immense everywhere. Nevertheless, there is much still to be done. . . . The first duty of every revolutionary is to speak the truth. To deceive the people, to delude them with false illusions would result in the worst consequences. That is why I say that we must be on guard against exaggerated optimism." From a speech on January 8, 1959, by Fidel Castro.

canism, but successive administrations since that of Herbert Hoover have striven to erase the impression that the United States was one of the imperialist nations. These efforts have taken the form of Roosevelt's Good Neighbor policy of the 1930's, wartime cooperation for the defense of the hemisphere, economic aid under the Truman and Eisenhower administrations, and the Alliance for Progress inaugurated by the Kennedy administration. The United States also encouraged the formation of hemispheric organizations, such as the Pan American Union, an information bureau dating from 1889, and the Organization of American States (OAS), created in 1948. Nevertheless, heavy handed American policies such as support for a projected invasion of Cuba in 1961 and direct armed intervention in the Dominican Republic in 1965 tinted the American image with hypocrisy in the eyes of many Latin Americans.

After decades of mutual bickering the nations of Latin America exhibited tendencies of a greater willingness to cooperate with one another in the postwar years. The small countries of Central America created a single customs union as the possible precursor of a more extensive economic union, and the Latin American Free Trade Association (LAFTA) promised to establish a single market for the entire continent, although its actual accomplishments were small. These efforts were manifestly intended to promote economic development as a means of reducing Latin America's dependence on the more advanced industrial nations and ending forever the stigma of colonialism.

THE WEST AND THE REST

The end of Western hegemony over the rest of the world marks a turning point in world history no less momentous than that brought about by the voyages of Columbus and Vasco da Gama at the end of the fifteenth century. Just as they inaugurated the era of Western predominance in the development of civilization, so the assertion of independence and the right of self-determination by peoples outside the Western tradition, or only marginally related to it, signals the advent of a truly global civilization. Whether or not the global civilization of the future will represent an improvement over its predecessors remains to be seen. One thing is certain: a great responsibility lies upon the principal carriers of the Western tradition, still the most powerful nations on earth, to preserve world peace and create a framework within which the civilization of the future can evolve.

THE STRUGGLE FOR A NEW WORLD ORDER
CHAPTER NINETEEN

By 1949 the worst ravages of the war in Europe had been repaired, and most of the sources of political confusion had been dissipated. The Soviet blockade of Berlin climaxed the growing tensions between the former Allies and radically altered the character of East-West relations. Instead of dealing with Germany as a defeated enemy, the Soviet Union and the Western Allies began to assist the economic and political recovery of their respective zones of occupation and to integrate them into their own regional power blocs. The Soviet bloc and the reconstructed Atlantic alliance settled down to what leaders of both sides expected to be a protracted rivalry for economic and military superiority and political domination. With the threat of atomic or nuclear destruction ever present, the welfare of mankind urgently required a new and more stable framework for international relations, but the national interests of the principal protagonists also demanded that they remain strong enough to resist potential aggression. In these circumstances the struggle for a new world order began.

RECOVERY AND REINTEGRATION IN WESTERN EUROPE

The economies of Western Europe had substantially recovered their prewar levels of production even before the Marshall Plan took full effect. The years just before the war, however, had been years of depression and stagnation. The levels of production of 1929 were not achieved until 1950 or 1952. In effect, the European economies had stagnated for an entire generation. In addition to having forfeited their potential increment of growth, they operated with obsolete equipment, lagged behind the United States in technological progress, and still suffered the handicaps of prewar and war-time restrictions and barriers to trade. Clearly, the economic health of Europe required more than mere recovery of prewar levels of production.

The Marshall Plan allowed the nations of Western Europe to maintain essential imports, especially foodstuffs and capital equipment, until they could achieve economic independence. Concurrently the OEEC conditioned statesmen and businessmen alike to new techniques of cooperation in the international sphere, laying the groundwork for further, more comprehensive programs of cooperation and integration. The results of the Marshall Plan were spectacular. In the three years from the end of 1947 to the end of 1950 physical output in the OEEC nations registered a 25 per cent increase. After the Korean War broke out, and with the regeneration of Western Europe's economy assured, the United States shifted the emphasis of foreign aid from economic to military assistance, renaming the Economic Cooperation Administration the Mutual Security Agency.

THE ECONOMIC MIRACLE

The rapid postwar economic growth of Western Europe continued throughout the 1950's and 1960's, making it the longest period of economic progress uninterrupted by slumps or depressions since the origins of the modern industrial system. By 1962 the total output of goods and services of the OEEC countries was double that of 1948 and the prewar years, and it was expected to double again by 1975. So remarkable was this performance – and so unexpected as late as 1952 – that it was described as an "economic miracle." The expression was first used with reference to West Germany, but it soon came to be applied to Western Europe generally. France and Italy in particular, two countries that had lagged behind the leaders in adopting modern industrial technology, had growth rates in the postwar era as high as that of Germany. Great Britain, on the other hand, fell behind, with a growth rate only about one-half that of Western Europe as a whole. The United States also grew more slowly than Western Europe, although at a very satisfactory rate in comparison with its record in the interwar years. Nevertheless, because of the high level of per capita income achieved by the British before the war and their smaller amount of war damage, they still had one of the highest standards of living in Europe. For the same reason per capita income in the United States remained far higher than that in Europe.

Unprecedented though it was, there was really nothing miraculous about Western Europe's economic resurgence. Many factors contributed, a few of which had primary importance. American aid played a crucial role in sparking the recovery. Thereafter Europeans kept it going with high levels of saving and investment. At times the competition between consumption and investment spending caused severe inflationary pressures, but none were so disastrous as the hyperinflations after World War I. Much of the investment went into equipment for new products and processes. During the depression years and the war a backlog of technological innovations had built up which only awaited capital and skilled manpower to be employed. Thus, technological modernization both accompanied and was an important contributory factor to the so-called economic miracle.

Another major factor was the attitude and role of governments. They participated in economic life both directly and indirectly on a much larger scale than previously. They nationalized some basic industries, drew up economic plans, and provided a wide range of social services. Nevertheless, private enterprise was responsible for by far the largest part of economic activity. On the average, between one-fourth and one-third of the national income in Western Europe originated in the government sector. Though this proportion was much greater than it had been before the war, it was less than half the contribution of the private sectors of the economy. The economic systems of postwar Western Europe were equally far from the stereotyped old style capitalism of the nineteenth century and from the doctrinaire socialized economies of Eastern Europe. In the mixed or welfare state economies that became characteristic of the Western democracies, government assumed the tasks of providing over-all stability, a climate favorable to growth, and minimal protection for the economically weak and underprivileged, but it left the main task of producing the goods and services desired by the population to private enterprise. The postwar governments of Western Europe also took the initiative in dismantling the barriers to international economic cooperation and competition erected by their predecessors.

THE DRIVE FOR UNIFICATION

The dream of a united Europe is as old as Europe itself. Charlemagne's Holy Roman Empire closely approximated the boundaries of the present-day European Economic Community plus Switzerland and Austria. Napoleon's French Empire and its satellites in the Continental System encompassed almost all of continental Europe. The concert of Europe, which grew out of the Vienna Congress of 1815, represented an attempt to coordinate policy at the highest level of government. The League of Nations was a concert of the European victors in World War I. Hitler very nearly succeeded in creating a *Festung Europa* under Nazi domination. All such efforts failed, however, owing to the inability of the would-be unifiers to maintain a monopoly of coercive power and the unwillingness of the members to submit voluntarily to their authority. In earlier times the difficulties of communication contributed to the fractionation of Europe. Then the idea of nationalism became so deeply entrenched in European thought, especially after the French Revolution,

Table 1 *The Economic Recovery of Western Europe, 1948–65*

	Index of general industrial production (1958 = 100)		*Steel production (1,000's of metric tons)*		*Production of electrical energy (in million kilo-watt hours)*		*Manufacture of passenger cars and trucks (in 1,000's)*		*Foreign trade (imports plus exports; mil-lions of dollars)*	
	1948	*1965*	*1948*	*1965*	*1948*	*1965*	*1948*	*1965*	*1948*	*1965*
France	54	138	7,236	19,604	28,851	101,442	198.4	1,616.1	5,453	20,390
West Germany	27	157	6,790	36,821	32,836	168,762	59.6	2,971.4	2,270	35,374
Italy	44	176	2,125	12,660	22,694	79,228	59.4	1,175.5	2,616	14,535
United Kingdom	74	132	15,116	27,439	48,036	196,027	508.1	2,344.4	14,367	28,881
Belgium	78	148	3,920	9,169	8,236	21,706	–	–	3,736	12,758
Netherlands	53	163	334	3,138	5,577	25,010	–	–	2,895	13,865

Source: United Nations, *Statistical Yearbook,* 1966 (New York, 1967).

that sovereignty — that is, supreme authority or dominion — and nationhood became almost synonymous in the minds of Europeans. Prior to World War II modern nation-states zealously opposed all proposals or attempts to infringe upon or in any way diminish their sovereignty.

It is important to bear in mind the distinction between international and supranational organizations. International organizations depend upon the voluntary cooperation of their members and have no direct power of coercion. Supranational organizations require their members to surrender at least a portion of sovereignty and can compel compliance with their mandates. Both the League of Nations and the United Nations are examples of international organizations. Within Europe the OEEC and most other postwar organizations of nations have been international rather than supranational. Continued successful cooperation may lead eventually to a pooling of sovereignties, which is the hope of the proponents of European unity. Proposals for some kind of supranational organization in Europe have become increasingly frequent since 1945 and have issued from ever more influential sources.

The proposals spring from two separate but related motives — political and economic. The political motive, manifested somewhat tenuously in the Council of Europe, is rooted in the belief that only through supranational organization can the threat of war between European powers be permanently eradicated. Some proponents of European political unity further believe that the compact nation-state of the past is now outmoded; if the nations of Europe are to resume their role in world affairs, they must be able to speak with one voice and have at their command resources and manpower comparable with those of superpowers such as the United States and the Soviet Union. The economic motive rests upon the argument that larger markets will promote greater specialization and increased competition, thus higher productivity and standards of living. The two motives merge in agreeing that economic strength is the basis of political and military power and that a fully integrated European economy would render intra-European wars less likely, if not impossible. Because of the deeply entrenched idea of national sovereignty, most of the practical proposals for a supranational organization have envisaged economic unification as a preliminary to political unification.

BENELUX

The Benelux Customs Union, which provided for the free movement of goods within Belgium, the Netherlands, and Luxembourg and for a common external tariff, grew out of the realization that under modern conditions of production and distribution the economies of the separate states were too small to permit them to enjoy the full benefits of mass production. Belgium and Luxembourg had, in fact, joined in an economic union as early as 1921, and the governments-in-exile of Belgium and the Netherlands had agreed in principle on the customs union during the war. Formal ratification of the treaty came in 1947. Statesmen of these countries have been the warmest advocates of a European common market and have continued to work for a closer economic integration of their own countries independently of broader European developments.

THE SCHUMAN PLAN

The OEEC and its subsidiary organizations such as the European Payments Union (EPU) resulted from American initiative and provided only for cooperation, not full integration. In 1950 French foreign minister Robert Schuman proposed the integration of the French and West German coal and steel industries and invited other nations to participate. Schuman's motives were as much political as economic. Coal and steel lay at the heart of modern industry – the armaments industries in particular – and all signs pointed to a revival of German industry. Schuman was desirous of propitiating German industrialists and at the same time keeping German industry under control or at least under surveillance. Anxious to be admitted to the new concert of Europe, West Germany responded with alacrity, as did the Benelux nations and Italy, afraid of being left behind if they did not participate. Great Britain, with nationalized steel and coal industries at the time, replied more cautiously and in the end did not participate. The treaty creating the European Coal and Steel Community (ECSC) was signed in 1951 and took effect early in 1952. The treaty provided for the elimination between signatory nations of tariffs and quotas on trade in iron ore, coal, coke, and steel, as well as a common external tariff on imports from other nations. To supervise its operations several bodies of a supranational character were established: a High Authority with executive powers, a Council of Ministers, a Common Assembly, a Court of Justice, and a Consultative Committee. The community was authorized to levy a tax on the output of enterprises within its province in order to finance its operations.

EUROPEAN DEFENSE COMMUNITY

Soon after the signing of the treaty creating the Coal and Steel Community the same nations attempted another giant step forward on the road to integration with a treaty for a European Defense Community. Developments such as the Korean War, the formation of the NATO alliance, and the rapid economic recovery of West Germany had demonstrated the importance of including German contingents in a Western European military force, but proposals to do this naturally aroused the suspicion and hostility of the nations that had recently been the victims of German aggression. One proposal to overcome their fears suggested including the German contingents in a unified military command. The EDC treaty made provisions accordingly, but after prolonged debates the French National Assembly finally rejected the treaty outright in August, 1954. This setback to the movement for unification demonstrated once again the difficulty of securing agreement on proposals for the limitation of national sovereignty. Other ways were found for Germany to make a contribution to the military defense of Western Europe. Meanwhile proponents of European unity resorted to more cautious tactics, once again in the area of economics.

THE COMMON MARKET AND EURATOM

In 1957 the participants in the Schuman Plan signed two more treaties in Rome, creating the European Atomic Energy Community (EURATOM) for the development of peaceful uses of atomic energy and, most important, the European Economic Community (EEC) or Common Market. The Common Market treaty provided for the gradual elimination of import duties and quantitative restrictions on all trade between member nations and the substitution of a common external tariff over a transitional period of twelve to fifteen years. Members of the community pledged themselves to implement common policies respecting transportation, agriculture, social insurance, and a number of other critical areas of economic policy and to permit the free movement of persons and capital within the boundaries of the community. One of the most important provisions of the treaty was that it could not be renounced unilaterally and that after a certain stage in the transitional period further decisions could be made by a qualified majority vote rather than by unanimous action. Both the Common Market and EURATOM treaties created high commissions to oversee their operations and merged other supranational bodies (councils of ministers, common assemblies, courts of justice, and consultative committees) with those of the ECSC. The Common Market treaty took effect on January 1, 1958, and within a few years it confounded the pessimists by shortening instead of lengthening the transitional period. In 1965 the high commissions of the three communities were merged, providing a more effective agency for eventual political unification. On July 1, 1968, all tariffs between member nations were completely eliminated, several years earlier than the date originally foreseen.

BRITAIN BETWEEN EFTA AND EEC

In the preliminaries to the treaties of Rome invitations were extended to other nations to join the Common Market. Britain objected to the surrender of sovereignty implied in the treaties and attempted to persuade the OEEC nations to create a free trade area instead. After signature of the Common Market treaty Britain, the Scandinavian nations, Switzerland, Austria, and Portugal joined in the European Free Trade Association (EFTA), the so-called outer seven, in opposition to the inner six of the Common Market. The EFTA treaty only provided for the elimination of tariffs on industrial products among the signatory nations. It did not extend to agricultural products, it did not provide for a common external tariff, and it could be abrogated by any member at any time. It was thus a much weaker union than that of the Common Market.

In 1961 Britain signified its willingness to enter the Common Market if certain conditions could be met. If effected, this move would have entailed the membership of most of the EFTA partners also. Lengthy negotiations over the terms of entry ensued, but in January, 1963, President de Gaulle of France in effect vetoed Britain's membership, an action he repeated in 1967 and 1969. After de Gaulle's retirement, however, the French government took a more moderate attitude on the question of British membership, which the other Common Market countries favored.

THE ATLANTIC ALLIANCE

Another development of the postwar era that was no less striking than the rapid economic progress and political cooperation of Western Europe was the acceptance by the United States of global responsibilities – a startling reversal of the isolationism of the interwar years. The two developments were intimately related. The Marshall Plan not only assisted the recovery of Europe but also sparked the cooperation that eventuated in the Common Market and other international and supranational ventures. The United States continued its policies of cooperation with and assistance to other nations of the so-called free world. It took a prominent part in the formation of the Organization of American States in 1948, the North Atlantic Treaty Organization in 1949, and the regional military alliances for Southeast Asia (SEATO) and the Middle East (the Bagdad Pact). It came to the assistance of Greece and Turkey in 1947 and of South Korea in 1950; it sent military advisory missions to Vietnam and several other world trouble spots. Hardly a day passed without producing newspaper headlines telling of American involvement in some remote or not-so-remote corner of the globe. In most instances United States policy makers justified their actions as a means of "containing communism" or "opposing Soviet aggression," although humanitarianism also lay behind American aid to underdeveloped nations. A brief review of some aspects of the domestic history of the United States since 1945 will help give an understanding of America's involvement in international affairs.

THE UNITED STATES IN THE POSTWAR ERA

One notable feature of recent American history has been the continuity of basic policy through Democratic and Republican administrations. Harry S Truman, a Democrat, succeeded Roosevelt at the latter's death on the eve of victory over Germany and won an upset victory over Thomas E. Dewey in 1948, serving almost two full terms. Truman followed Roosevelt's major policies in both foreign and domestic affairs. Surprisingly, Dwight D. Eisenhower, former supreme commander of the Allied forces and the first Republican president in two decades, continued such fundamental features of American policy as military and economic aid to nations outside the Soviet bloc (including Fascist Spain and Communist Yugoslavia) and the extension of social security and other welfare state activities. John F. Kennedy, the first Catholic president and the youngest man ever elected to the presidency, won a closely contested race against Republican Vice President Richard Nixon in 1960. Kennedy studded his administration with intellectuals from the academic world and emphasized "new frontiers" to challenge the imagination and ingenuity of Americans, but in actual practice he did not depart radically from established policies. After his tragic assassination in 1963, Vice President Lyndon B. Johnson, a veteran legislator and able politician, generally followed and expanded the policies laid down by his predecessors. That these policies commended themselves to the American people received striking confirmation in 1964 in the overwhelming victory of Johnson over the conservative Senator Barry Goldwater, who offered the electorate the most clear-cut choice of programs in many years. Johnson's escalation of the war in Vietnam cost him so much support among the liberals in his own party, however, that he withdrew from the election of 1968, which Richard Nixon won by a narrow margin over Vice President Hubert Humphrey, who inherited the legacy of the Johnson administration.

Certain domestic problems had an important bearing on the image of the United States abroad and on its capacity for world leadership. One that commanded widespread attention abroad was the struggle for legal equality by American Negroes, known as the civil rights movement. Citizens of other lands, especially in Asia, Africa, and South America, viewed with interest the apparent divergence between American ideals and reality and the efforts made to repair it. In 1954 the Supreme Court issued a historic decision banning legalized segregation in public schools and followed it with several other decisions aimed at eliminating from all aspects of life segregation based on race or color. The decisions met with strong resistance in parts of the American South. At length Negroes took matters into their own hands, organizing massive campaigns reminiscent of the passive resistance movement inspired by Gandhi in India. In 1964 Congress passed a strong civil rights law. In the same year the Reverend Martin Luther King, one of the Negro leaders, became the second American Negro to win the Nobel Peace Prize for his part in organizing the movement. (Ralph Bunche had been the first for his role as United Nations mediator in the Arab-Israeli war of 1948–49.) King's assassination by a white racist in 1968 fueled the fires of a far more militant and violent campaign against white society that had begun winning converts among Negro youth as early as 1965.

A similar issue, of great interest abroad, concerned questions of patriotism, loyalty, and the role of dissent in a democratic society. The issue commanded greatest attention in the early 1950's when Senator Joseph McCarthy of Wisconsin made widely publicized but undocumented charges of disloyalty against government officials, university professors, and others. Playing on widespread fears of a Communist conspiracy and internal subversion, McCarthy and other demagogues wreaked havoc with the lives of innocent persons and brought the nation near to mass hysteria. McCarthy himself received a formal vote of censure from the Senate in 1954, which relegated him to obscurity even before his death in 1957; but the mischief he caused lived after him, notably in the attitude and behavior of young people.

The college students of the late 1940's, including many veterans of World War II continuing their education with federal assistance under the G.I. Bill, had maintained some of the idealism that had characterized young people in the 1930's and the war years. During the 1950's, however, under the baleful influence of McCarthyism and the general atmosphere of apprehension, college students and other youths imitated their elders and adopted an attitude of cautious noninvolvement in controversial questions that led them to be dubbed "the silent generation" and "the beat generation." The true beatniks, also called hippies in the 1960's, who wished to demonstrate indifference to social conventions but feared to participate in social controversy, resorted to wearing outlandish clothing, invented a special variety of slang, and made frequent public exhibitions of their unconventional morality, including widespread use of marijuana and more powerful drugs. In the 1960's much of youth regained its more normal activist mentality, as evidenced, on the one hand, by the notable participation of both white and Negro young people in the civil rights movement and, on the other, by their somewhat unaccustomed role of leadership in various conservative and reactionary movements. Such activism reached a peak in the protests against American policy toward Vietnam and in the related youthful revolts against the alleged hypocrisy of adult American society. The protests were directed at the universities in particular, and in a few instances threatened to disrupt the educational process completely.

NATO

The North Atlantic Treaty Organization, created in 1949, further demonstrated the willingness and determination of the United States to assume leadership of the non-Communist world in order to prevent the spread of Communist-controlled governments. The original members of the organization were the United States and Canada, Britain, France, the Benelux countries, Denmark, Norway, Iceland, Italy, and Portugal. Greece and Turkey adhered in 1951; West Germany became a member in 1955. The treaty creating the organization declared that "an armed attack against one or more" members of the organization "shall be considered an attack against them all." Coming after the *coup de Prague* and the Berlin blockade, the treaty meant in effect that the nations of Western Europe were determined to resist armed aggression by the Soviet Union and that the United States stood ready to assist them in this determination. The treaty provided for a ministerial body, the North Atlantic Council, to direct operations and for a unified military command. General Eisenhower, who had commanded the Allied invasion of Europe in World War II, was called back from retirement to serve as the first Supreme Commander, Allied Powers, Europe, from 1950 until his resignation to run for the presidency of the United States in 1952.

THE REHABILITATION OF WEST GERMANY

The economic miracle of West Germany has been frequently commented upon, but its economic recovery was no more miraculous than the creation of a genuinely democratic state in a nation long subject to authoritarian monarchy and dictatorship. The process began as early as 1946 when, in accordance with the Potsdam agreements, the Germans elected officials for new state (*Länder*) governments. In 1948 Britain, France, and the United States allowed a parliamentary council of the states within their zones of occupation to meet in the ancient university city of Bonn in the Rhineland. The council drew up a basic law which took effect the following year and continued to serve the German Federal Republic as a constitution. It was modeled on the constitution of the Weimar Republic, modified to remove such obvious defects as the emergency powers of the president. Much of the success of West Germany in regaining international prestige resulted from the political sagacity and skill of Konrad Adenauer, its first chancellor, who served from 1949 until his retirement in 1963 at the age of eighty-seven. Adenauer headed the Christian Democratic Union (CDU), the largest political party in West Germany, though it did not always command an absolute majority in the Bundestag (lower house of parliament). As a result, the CDU frequently formed coalitions with the Free Democratic party and smaller groups. The main opposition came from the Socialist party

(SPD) until 1966, when the SPD joined the CDU in a so-called grand coalition. In a turnabout after the election of 1969, the SPD formed a coalition with the Free Democrats.

West Berlin occupied an anomalous position that occasioned several international crises. Located well inside East Germany, it was not technically a part of the German Federal Republic. Nevertheless, the two entities maintained close relations, and Willy Brandt, the Socialist mayor of West Berlin, became foreign minister of the German Federal Republic in the coalition government of 1966, and chancellor in 1969. In spite of its tremendous concentration of population (over 3.5 million in 1970), its enormous wartime damage, and the difficulties imposed by its location, West Berlin enjoyed a booming prosperity and one of the highest standards of living in Europe. Expenditures of the Allied occupation forces and subsidies from West Germany helped. Another reason for the rapid growth and prosperity of West Berlin, particularly in the 1950's, was the enormous influx of refugees from East Germany. To put a stop to this embarrassment and the drain of skilled manpower, the East German authorities in 1961 built a high wall between East and West Berlin, making the separation more than merely symbolic.

The German Federal Republic faced many difficult problems in its early years, but it surmounted most of them successfully. At first the flood of refugees from East Germany and other Soviet-dominated areas, totaling more than 12.5 million persons, posed a serious problem because of the shortages of housing and jobs; as recovery persisted, they proved a blessing in disguise. Their skills and energies contributed to the rebuilding of West Germany and alleviated a severe labor shortage. Other major problems involved West Germany's relations with the Soviet bloc and the Western allies, the question of rearmament, and the even more ticklish question of reunification. With respect to the first two, Adenauer followed a policy of friendship and cooperation with the West, which resulted in the restoration of German sovereignty in 1955. This led in turn to the beginnings of rearmament under the auspices of NATO and to tacit recognition by the Soviet Union despite the lack of a formal peace treaty. Adenauer repeatedly postponed serious consideration of the reunification of East and West Germany without ever disavowing the possibility of eventual reunion. The continuing integration of West Germany in the Common Market and the North Atlantic Alliance has rendered reunification ever more unlikely, but as long as East and West Germany remain divided, the situation will present a strong temptation to ambitious demagogues.

"THE REPUBLIC IS DEAD; VIVE LA RÉPUBLIQUE!"

France under the Fourth Republic compiled an ambivalent record. Superficially all was chaos and instability. The constitution deliberately provided for a figurehead president and a cabinet dependent upon the National Assembly. The latter split into a number of volatile parties, no one of which could command a majority. The Communist party, usually the largest single party with about a fourth of the deputies, was the only one to maintain strict party discipline. The center parties formed coalition governments, sometimes with Socialist support or at least acquiescence, but their lack of party discipline resulted in their frequent overthrow. The average life of cabinets under the Fourth Republic was even shorter than under the Third. In other respects postwar France seemed to be tottering on the brink of a volcano. The labor movement, like the political parties, splintered into various rival groups, with the Communists commanding the largest membership. Strikes, often politically motivated, were more frequent than in almost any other country. Inflation remained a persistent problem. France's colonial empire engaged in a series of revolts and civil wars, nearly all of which went badly for France and drained it of manpower and wealth.

In spite of this apparently dismal record, the nation made substantial progress in several respects, proving that even in the twentieth century governments are not the sole determinants of a nation's welfare. After a century of slow, almost stagnant population growth, the birth rate rose at the end of the war and remained at a level comparable to that of other Western nations. As the age distribution shifted toward younger people, their greater vitality was reflected in the nation at large. After some transitional difficulties in the early postwar years, the French economy staged a spectacular revival and transformation. Industrial production rose 55 per cent between 1952 and 1958 – a greater percentage than in any other Western nation. Agricultural production increased substantially while the labor force employed in agriculture declined by half; by 1958 France was the only nation in Western Europe that was self-sufficient in agricultural production, and even had a surplus for export. Because of its modernized economy France enjoyed one of the highest standards of living of any of the former belligerents of Europe in World War II.

France took the initiative in many of the ventures in international cooperation. In spite of frequent cabinet shuffles, government personnel changed relatively little. Robert Schuman and Georges Bidault, both members of the same party, between them held the portfolio of foreign affairs throughout most of the life of the Fourth Republic. The French civil service, highly educated, competent, and relatively permanent, provided an important element of stability and continuity underneath the troubled surface.

The downfall of the Fourth Republic resulted from its failure to solve the problem of Algeria. Faced with the threat of an army coup d'état in May, 1958, the government called on General de Gaulle, who for some years had been writing his memoirs in semiretirement, to take over as prime minister. De Gaulle refused except on condition that he be granted almost dictatorial powers, including the power to remake the constitution. After some days of anxious negotiation the president and parliamentarians accepted most of de Gaulle's terms, and on June 1 he took over the reins of government. He went to work at once to revamp the constitution. In September the electorate, thoroughly wearied of the Fourth Republic, approved the constitution of the Fifth Republic in a popular referendum by a vote of four to one.

The new constitution greatly strengthened the presidency at the expense of parliament. The president appoints all ministers, including the prime minister, and personally presides over the cabinet or Council of Ministers. Through his ministers he proposes legislation, and if the National Assembly passes a vote of censure on the government, he may dissolve it and call for new elections. He may take proposals for constitutional amendments and other major questions directly to the people in a popular referendum, and in case of emergency he may govern by decree. The parliament, consisting of a National Assembly elected by universal suffrage in single-member constituencies and a Senate elected indirectly, has strictly limited powers. It may initiate legislation as well as approve or disapprove what is proposed by the government, but it no longer has the power, as under the Fourth Republic, to provoke ministerial crises of indeterminate length. The new constitution also provided for a number of administrative and judicial reforms aimed at modernizing and streamlining the governmental apparatus.

De Gaulle was elected first president of the Fifth Republic for a seven-year term by an overwhelming vote in December, 1958, and took office (in succession to himself as last premier of the Fourth Republic) the following January. Somewhat surprisingly he continued most of the policies of the discredited Fourth Republic, but with greater firmness and éclat. Assisted by a monetary reform at the beginning of 1960, the economy continued its upward march. De Gaulle respected France's commitments in the treaties creating the Common Market and other international obligations, and he brought about greater cooperation with Germany through his personal friendship with Chancellor Adenauer. He did, however, veto Britain's membership in the Common Market, and in general he favored a "Europe of fatherlands" rather than a United States of Europe. For this reason he persisted in making France the fourth nuclear power when the United States refused to share its atomic secrets, and acted independently of NATO in other respects. In 1966 he actually withdrew France from NATO's military command, and forced the latter to transfer its headquarters from France to Belgium. The most decisive and meaningful accomplishment of his regime was the liquidation of France's colonial empire, including Algeria. In the process he brought the army to heel and purged its top echelons of potential leaders of military juntas. In 1965 de Gaulle was re-elected for a new seven-year term. In the spring of 1968 a series of popular demonstrations that began as a student revolt in a university on the outskirts of Paris threatened to boil over into social revolution; and later that year a severe financial crisis threatened the value of the franc. De Gaulle stood fast on both occasions, but resigned the presidency the following year, as he had done in 1946, over a relatively minor issue. In the election of June, 1969, Georges Pompidou, a former Gaullist prime minister who had fallen from the general's favor, was elected president of France.

OTHER POLITICAL DEVELOPMENTS

In Great Britain a Conservative government was elected in 1951. It denationalized the steel industry and reopened the motor transport industry to private enterprise, but it did not interfere with the other nationalized industries and it maintained the social reforms of the Labour party with only minor modifications. The venerable Churchill resigned as prime minister in 1955 at the age of eighty-one but retained his seat in the House of Commons until 1964, the year before his death. Anthony Eden, who succeeded Churchill as prime minister, led the party to victory in the election of 1955 but was forced to resign in the aftermath of the Suez crisis of 1956. (See p. 544.) Harold Macmillan, also a Conservative, served as prime minister from 1957 until 1963, having again won over the Labour party in the election of 1959. Labour at last won an election by a narrow margin in 1964, and Harold Wilson became prime minister.

After the death of Alcide de Gasperi in 1953, Italy was governed by a succession of unstable coalitions built around the Christian Democrats, who remained the largest single party. The Communists maintained their strength undiminished, commanding between 20 and 25 per cent of the vote in parliamentary elections; but the possibility of a Communist take-over, which appeared very strong in the immediate postwar years, receded as the alliance between the Communists and the left-wing Socialists crumbled. A brief revival of monarchist and neofascist activity in the 1950's amounted to little. In the early 1960's the center coalition created an "opening to the left," climaxed by the election of a Socialist as president, but the left-center coalition was no more durable than its predecessors. Italy's major problems have been economic and social – in particular, the continued great contrast between the backward, agrarian south and the industrially progressive north. Superficial political instability has not prevented Italy any more than France from making rapid economic gains, but it still has far to go to catch up with its more prosperous neighbors. Italy's coalition governments have steadfastly supported the Common Market, NATO, and other instruments of international cooperation and unification.

© Bruno Barbey Magnum

French Students During Paris Riots

"The March 22nd movement constitutes a tiny minority in the [French Student Association]. . . . We realized how sterile verbal differences were in relation to the possibilities of common action. . . . During the famous night of March 22, we tried to define the framework in which it would be possible for all of the 'sects' to participate in a single political activity: the challenge to the university." French student leader on Radio Luxembourg, May 17, 1968.

EUROPE IN 1970

Members of the Free Trade Association

Members of the European Economic Community (Common Market)

The Communist Bloc

Members of the North Atlantic Treaty Organization (N.A.T.O.)

Members of the Warsaw Pact

0 500
Miles

ICELAND
NORWAY
Bergen
Oslo
SWEI
SCOTLAND
Glasgow
Edinburgh
UNITED KINGDOM
OF GREAT BRITAIN
AND NO. IRELAND
EIRE
Belfast
Dublin
Cork
Manchester
WALES
ENGLAND
London
North Sea
DENMARK
Copenhagen
Mal
Hamburg
Amsterdam
NETHERLANDS
Bremen
EAST
Elbe R.
Berlin
Potsdam
GERMANY
Dresd
Brussels
BELGIUM
WEST
Cologne
Bonn
LUX.
GERMANY
Prague
CZE
Le Havre
Rouen
Paris
Seine R.
Nuremberg
Strasbourg
Rhine R.
Munich
Vie
Salzburg
AUSTRIA
ATLANTIC
OCEAN
Loire R.
FRANCE
Bay of Biscay
Bordeaux
Geneva
Berne
SWITZ.
Lyon
Garonne R.
Rhône R.
Toulouse
Milan
Venice
Zagreb
Trieste
Turin
Po R.
Genoa
Marseille
ANDORRA
Florence
Oporto
PORTUGAL
SPAIN
Ebro R.
Lisbon
Tagus R.
Madrid
Barcelona
CORSICA
ITALY
Rome
Guadalquivir R.
Seville
SARDINIA
Naples
Strait of Gibraltar
Palermo
SICILY
AFRICA
Mediterranean

*ALBANIA aligned with Communist China

*FINLAND aligned with Soviet Union by treaty

*YUGOSLAVIA Communist but independent of the Soviet Union

White Sea
Archangel
N. Dvina R.
U. S. S. R.
Tobolsk
Perm
Chelyabinsk
Gulf of Bothnia
FINLAND*
L. Onega
L. Ladoga
Helsinki
Gulf of Finland
Leningrad
Tallinn
Stockholm
ESTONIAN S.S.R.
RUSSIAN SOVIET FEDERATED
SOCIALIST REPUBLIC
Kazan
Magnitogorsk
LATVIAN S.S.R.
Riga
Moscow
LITHUANIAN S.S.R.
Dvina R.
Smolensk
Kaliningrad
Vilna
Minsk
Gdansk
BELORUSSIAN S.S.R.
Ural R.
Don R.
KAZAKH S.S.R.
Warsaw
Volgograd
Kharkov
Kiev
Volga R.
Vistula R.
Lvov
UKRAINIAN S.S.R.
Donetsk
Krivoi Rog
Rostov
Zhdanov
Dnieper R.
MOLDAVIAN S.S.R.
Budapest
Sea of Azov
Caspian Sea
Cluj
Odessa
CRIMEA
Yalta
RUMANIA
GEORGIAN S.S.R.
AZER-BAIJAN S.S.R.
Baku
Belgrade
Bucharest
Black Sea
Sarajevo
Danube R.
ARMENIAN S.S.R.
Erevan
BULGARIA
Sofia
Istanbul
IRAN
Ankara
Salonika
TURKEY
GREECE
Tigris R.
Izmir
Adana
Aleppo
Athens
Euphrates R.
Baghdad
Nicosia
SYRIA
CYPRUS
IRAQ
Sea
CRETE
LEBANON

Greece and Turkey, although subject to mutual suspicion and jealousy over the fate of the island of Cyprus and other questions, were united in their fear of Soviet aggression and support of the Western alliance. Both joined NATO in 1951, and ten years later they became "associates" of the European Economic Community. Greece became a cause of anxiety within the alliance in 1967 when a military junta overthrew the legitimate government, established a dictatorship, and subsequently expelled the king. Spain and Portugal were gradually assimilated in the Western alliance in spite of their dictatorial forms of government. Portugal, in fact, participated as a charter member of NATO and in 1957 became associated with Britain and other nations in the European Free Trade Association. Spain was treated as an outcast among nations by both East and West after the war, but it gained formal recognition from the United States in 1953 and two years later under American sponsorship was admitted to the United Nations. Spain's participation in the military alliance depended upon its bilateral relationship with the United States, which maintained air bases in Spain. In 1959, however, the OEEC admitted it to membership in return for a promise to stabilize its economy and to permit a liberalization of its international exchanges. The harsher features of Spain's political system were moderated somewhat in anticipation of the replacement of General Franco, its elderly dictator, who in 1969 indicated Juan Carlos de Borbon, grandson of Alfonso XIII, as his eventual successor as head of state. All of the Mediterranean countries remained desperately poor, although each one made some progress in modernizing its economy after centuries of stagnation.

The Nordic countries differed in their approaches to international cooperation. All participated in the OEEC; Denmark, Norway, and Sweden also joined the Free Trade Association. Denmark, Norway, and Iceland became charter members of NATO, but Sweden held aloof, concerned for its traditional neutrality. Treading a fine line in the shadow of the Soviet Union, Finland could not afford wholesale cooperation with the West in either the political or the economic spheres, but it drew closer to the Scandinavian countries with trade and cultural agreements. Austria and Switzerland continued their policies of political and military neutrality but joined the Free Trade Association and indicated their willingness to become associated with the Common Market, though not as full members.

COMMUNISM AFTER STALIN

A new era opened for the Communist world when Joseph Stalin died in March, 1953. In the Soviet Union the Stalinist system of government, based upon fear and terrorist repression and marked by the imprisonment or execution of real or imagined opponents, evolved in the direction of more humane, if still harsh, methods of rule. Within the Soviet bloc of nations a gradual movement away from a monolithic character and toward greater diversity developed as each nation worked out its own variations of Communist ideology and institutions. The Soviet Union suffered reverses in dealing with other Communist nations, above all with Yugoslavia and China, as well as in its relations with the Western powers. Finally, the economic recovery of the Soviet bloc was far slower than that of the Western nations. There was no economic miracle on the other side of the iron curtain.

POLITICAL STRUGGLES WITHIN THE RUSSIAN COMMUNIST PARTY

After Stalin's death leading political and army figures bargained for power among themselves until a triumvirate emerged. Georgi Malenkov, chairman of the Council of Ministers, held the leading position, with Lavrenti Beria, chief of the secret police, and V. M. Molotov, expert in foreign affairs, as his chief coadjutors. The new collective leadership was soon torn by internal dissension. In the struggle Beria lost. In July, 1953, he was arrested as an "enemy of the people" and secretly executed together with a number of his supporters. After Beria's death a little-known party figure named Nikita Khrushchev, who after Stalin's death had become first secretary of the Communist party, became a member of the triumvirate. Under Malenkov's leadership the government introduced a new emphasis on consumer goods and attempted to reorganize agricultural production. Malenkov's program failed, and in February, 1954, he was forced to resign as premier, although he remained in the Politburo for a time. Nikolai Bulganin became premier and nominal head of government, but it soon became obvious that Khrushchev was the dominant figure.

At the Twentieth Communist Party Congress in February, 1956, Khrushchev gave a long speech in which he denounced Stalin as a ruthless, morbid, almost insane tyrant who had ordered the execution of countless innocent people, whose egotism had led him to make mistakes for which all Russia suffered, who had caused the government to lose touch with the people, who had established the "cult of personality" to glorify himself. Khrushchev carefully pointed out, however, that Stalin's despotism represented an aberration from an essentially correct policy and claimed that the new collective leadership had returned to proper Leninist principles of government. Supposedly secret, Khrushchev's speech was allowed to leak out to the public. It caused much confusion and ferment among the peoples of the Communist countries and did serious damage to the cause of communism by its confirmation of the evils of Stalin's regime. The government began an official program of "de-Stalinization" that included the removal of Stalin's pictures and statues from public

Sovfoto

Molotov, Stalin, and Andreyev

"Stalin acted not through persuasion, explanation, and patient co-operation with people, but by imposing his concepts and demanding absolute submission to his opinion. Whoever opposed this concept or tried to prove his viewpoint, and the correctness of his position — was doomed to removal from the leading collective and to subsequent moral and physical annihilation. . . . Arbitrary behavior by one person encouraged and permitted arbitrariness in others. Mass arrests and deportations of many thousands of people, execution without trial and without normal investigation created conditions of insecurity, fear, and even desperation. . . .

"The cult of the individual acquired such monstrous size chiefly because Stalin himself, using all conceivable methods, supported the glorification of his own person. . . . Was it without Stalin's knowledge that many of the largest enterprises and towns were named after him? Was it without his knowledge that Stalin monuments were erected in the whole country?"

Speech of Khrushchev to the 20th Congress of the Communist Party, U.S.S.R., February 25, 1956.

places, changes in the names of towns and schools that had been named for him, and the removal of his body from the famed Lenin Tomb in Moscow's Red Square. Changes bringing about a more relaxed social and political atmosphere were introduced, such as reforms in court procedure to provide more protection for accused persons, the release of thousands of political prisoners, and improvements in wages and pensions.

Risings in several of the satellite states and economic difficulties at home intensified the power struggle in the Kremlin. Khrushchev was blamed for these troubles and for weakening the regime by his disavowal of Stalin. In mid-1957 a bitter fight broke out in the innermost councils of the party aimed at forcing Khrushchev to resign. He managed to ride out the storm and forced his opponents from their high posts, branding them an "anti-party" group. In the spring of 1958 Bulganin, who had gone against Khrushchev, resigned as premier and Khrushchev took over his office. Officially he was both head of the party and leader of the government. The era of collective leadership seemed to have ended.

Khrushchev's difficulties were far from over, however. For a few years, it is true, he appeared to wield power almost as absolute as Stalin's and was on the verge of establishing a new cult of personality. But reverses in international affairs, economic difficulties at home, and the growth of diversity and discontent in countries of the Soviet bloc compelled him to adopt a defensive tone in some of his addresses. He publicly stated that owing to his advancing years – he became seventy in 1964 – he could not expect to remain in office much longer. He showed no willingness, however, to transfer any of his power to others. In October, 1964, that decision was made for him when without warning the government announced that he had been relieved of his duties for reasons of "age and deteriorating health." Leonid Brezhnev and Aleksi Kosygin were named to succeed him as head of the party and premier, respectively. Khrushchev had been overthrown by a revolt of men within the Kremlin who were dissatisfied with his leadership.

SOVIET INDUSTRY AND AGRICULTURE

Soviet industry continued to increase its output of heavy goods but still fell far short of the intention expressed by Soviet leaders to overtake and surpass the production of the United States. In 1955 the government announced the fulfillment of the goals of the fifth five-year plan, instituted in 1950, although high officials complained of widespread inefficiency, and Premier Bulganin stated publicly that one-third of Soviet industrial enterprises failed to meet their production targets. The production of consumer goods, always given a low priority in Soviet planning, continued to lag, so that the citizens were plagued by shortages and inferior goods.

Soviet agriculture remained in a condition of almost unrelieved crisis throughout the postwar period, despite massive efforts by the government to increase productivity. The collective farm system did not offer enough incentive for the peasants. Instead, they concentrated their energies on the small private plots of up to one-half hectare (1.2 acres) that they were allowed to cultivate, part of whose produce they could sell on the market. These plots formed little more than 3 per cent of Russia's cultivated land, but they produced as much as one-fifth of the country's milk and one-third of its meat. In 1954 Khrushchev, who had long been interested in agriculture, started a "virgin lands" project to bring great stretches of arid land in Soviet Asia into cultivation. The next year he launched a drive to increase the production of corn, and in 1957 he announced a campaign to overtake the United States by 1961 in the production of milk, butter, and meat per person. None of these programs came anywhere near their stated goal. Despite threats of dire punishment and wholesale dismissals of agricultural officials, Khrushchev and his planners could not overcome poor soil, bad weather, bureaucratic mismanagement, fertilizer shortages, and above all the peasants' lack of enthusiasm. Food shortages continued to characterize Soviet life, to the embarrassment and discomfort of the regime. In 1963 the situation became so bad that the government was compelled to buy for gold over 10 million tons of grain from Canada and Australia.

"THE THAW"

In 1955 Ilya Ehrenburg, a well-known Soviet author, published a story called "The Thaw." The title was widely believed to refer to the changes that had been taking place in Russia since Stalin's death, and it became the symbolic name for the new era that began in 1953. The Soviet Union remained a totalitarian state, but the dread of the secret police, of purges, and of forced labor camps that had haunted Soviet life during Stalin's rule lessened. The government relied more on persuasion than on coercion to gain popular support. Selected Russians were allowed to travel and even study abroad, and foreign visitors were welcomed. A lively cultural exchange developed between the Soviet Union and the non-Communist world. Writers and other intellectuals were allowed greater freedom of expression. They were constantly reminded, however, that if they criticized aspects of Soviet life, they had to point out that those and all other shortcomings of Soviet society were being successfully overcome by the Communist party, or else they could expect some form of censure or punishment. The world became aware of this harsh fact in 1957 when *Dr. Zhivago,* a novel by Boris Pasternak, sixty-seven-year-old

Soviet novelist and poet, appeared in translation in several Western countries but could not be published in Russia. Although the novel was imbued with a deep love of Russia and its people, it questioned certain values of Soviet society. Pasternak was denounced as an enemy of socialism and forced to decline the Nobel Prize for literature offered him in 1958. He had to plead with Khrushchev to be allowed to remain in his beloved Russia. After four decades the Soviet rulers were still so uncertain of their hold over the people that they feared a single voice of dissent.

THE SOVIET BLOC

When Stalin died in 1953 the Soviet bloc in Europe presented the appearance of monolithic unity. It included Albania, Bulgaria, Rumania, Hungary, Czechoslovakia, Poland, and East Germany. (China and North Korea also formed a part of the Communist world, but they stood on a somewhat different footing.) Each of the satellites was more or less a small-scale replica of the Soviet Union, and all danced to the same tune – called in Moscow. Nevertheless, divisive tendencies hid behind the façade of unity. When Yugoslavia had earlier broken away from the Soviet bloc, although remaining a Communist nation, numbers of people in the other satellites would have liked to have done the same. Almost every Communist party had included some "national Communists" who wanted their nation to follow independent policies, but after Tito's defection the Stalinists – those who faithfully followed the Moscow line – had dismissed them from positions of leadership with the assistance of Soviet troops and police and in some cases had imprisoned or executed them. Soon after Stalin's death a wave of restiveness swept over the satellite states. In Czechoslovakia strikes and other demonstrations reached such proportions that Soviet tanks had to be called in to quell them, and in June, 1953, a full-fledged revolt broke out in East Germany, requiring several days of bloody fighting to be repressed.

In an effort to hold the bloc together without such an overt use of force the Soviet Union developed its own versions of NATO and the Common Market. In May, 1955, shortly after West Germany had been admitted to NATO, the Soviet Union and its satellites signed the East European Mutual Assistance Treaty, commonly called the Warsaw Pact, a twenty-year agreement of friendship, military assistance, and collaboration in international affairs. At the same time Russia reinvigorated the East European Council of Mutual Economic Assistance, founded in 1949 as a counter to the Marshall Plan but inactive for some years. Known as COMECON, it was ostensibly intended to coordinate the economic development of the Communist countries and promote a more efficient division of production among them; actually, however, Russia hoped to use it to make the satellites economically dependent on the Soviet Union.

DE-STALINIZATION AND THE HUNGARIAN REVOLT

After Khrushchev's speech to the Twentieth Party Congress de-Stalinization began to take effect in the satellites as well as the Soviet Union. Many political prisoners and victims of earlier purges were released from prison — or honored posthumously — and a slight relaxation of police controls became evident. Liberalization did not proceed fast enough or far enough to suit most people, however, and a new wave of unrest rippled across Eastern Europe. In the summer of 1956 riots in Poznan, Poland, became so serious that the Soviet authorities had to use force to suppress them. They then decided to rehabilitate Wladyslaw Gomulka, a former party leader who had been imprisoned for Titoism in 1948, and make him a member of the government. Gomulka refused to join the government unless the Russians agreed to recall the Soviet marshal who served as Poland's minister of defense and to permit other reforms. In October the Russians consented. Gomulka calmed the people and obtained for Poland an unprecedented degree of freedom within the Soviet bloc. He even succeeded in getting aid from the United States.

Encouraged by the success of the Poles, the Hungarians also pressed for more and faster reforms. Imre Nagy, a "national Communist" who had earlier been dismissed from the party, was restored and on October 24, 1956, became prime minister. He promised widespread reforms, including free elections, and persuaded the Soviet authorities to withdraw their troops from Hungary. On October 31 the last Soviet troops left Budapest; meanwhile, however, the Soviet army had been massing on Hungary's northeast border, and detachments began to pour into the country and surround every large city and important military and industrial installation. Nagy announced that Hungary was withdrawing from the Warsaw Pact and requested that the United Nations guarantee the perpetual neutrality of Hungary on the same basis as Austria. Too late: on November 4 at 4 A.M. Soviet tanks and bombers began a synchronized attack, inflicting destruction at least as horrible as that of World War II. For ten days Hungarian workers and students fought heroically against overwhelming odds with weapons furnished by their own soldiers. Even after the Russians and a new puppet government under Janos Kadar regained control, many continued guerrilla activity in the hills, while more than 150,000 escaped across the open border to Austria and eventually sought refuge in the West. The Western powers expressed sympathy for the rebels but did nothing to aid them, in part because of the paralysis caused by the Suez crisis. (See p. 544.) The Hungarian revolt showed plainly that even a de-Stalinized Russia was not prepared to give up its Communist empire.

Photograph from Keystone Press

Revolutionaries in Budapest

" 'We wanted freedom and not a good comfortable life,' an eighteen-year-old girl student told the [United Nations] Committee. 'Even though we might lack bread and other necessities of life, we wanted freedom. We, the young people, were particularly hampered because we were brought up amidst lies. We continually had to lie. We could not have a healthy idea because everything was choked in us. We wanted freedom of thought. . . .'

"It seemed to the Committee that this young student's words expressed as concisely as any the ideal which made possible a great uprising. The motives which brought together so many sections of the population were essentially simple. It seemed no accident that such clear expression should be given to them by a student not as part of a set speech, but simply and spontaneously, in answer to an unexpected question." Foreign Office, THE HUNGARIAN UPRISING. AN ABRIDGEMENT OF THE REPORT OF THE UNITED NATIONS SPECIAL COMMITTEE ON THE PROBLEM OF HUNGARY (London, 1957).

RELATIONS WITH YUGOSLAVIA AND CHINA

The unity of the Communist world had first been breached in 1948 when Yugoslavia, under the leadership of Marshal Tito, broke with the Soviet Union. Stalin's successors made peaceful overtures to Tito, and by 1956 the two governments had become officially reconciled, with Russia agreeing that Yugoslavia had the right to determine its "own road to socialism." In succeeding years relations between the two countries fluctuated between friendship and cold formality. The Yugoslavs carefully retained their position of nonalignment, refusing to link themselves either to the Soviet bloc or to the West. This policy of neutrality, skillfully directed by Tito, placed Yugoslavia in the advantageous position of being courted with economic and military assistance by both the Soviet Union and the United States.

The next great rift occurred between China and the Soviet Union. The latter had provided Red China with a steady stream of economic aid, arms, advisers, and technicians. In 1955 Russia agreed to furnish China with equipment and experts for developing atomic power for industrial purposes and to train Chinese students in atomic physics. The leaders of the two countries vied in praise of one another and promises of eternal amity. The Chinese even included a statement of friendship with the Soviet Union in the preamble of the constitution adopted in 1954. As early as 1956, however, Chinese leaders made it clear that although they appreciated Soviet aid, they did not intend to be subordinate to Russia. By 1959 greater strains had appeared in Sino-Soviet relations, caused mainly by Chinese suspicion of Khrushchev's efforts to establish peaceful relations with the West. Fearful of a rapproachement between Russia and the United States, the Chinese began to praise Stalin for his unceasing enmity to the "imperialist" powers, violently attacked the United States as the arch-imperialist, and indirectly criticized Khrushchev's policy by condemning what they called "right-wing revisionism." They found supporters for their position in other Communist parties, notably that in Albania, the smallest and poorest state of the Soviet bloc. Russia, unwilling to assail China directly, turned on Albania. It withdrew its aid and technicians, forced Albania out of COMECON, and in 1962 broke off diplomatic relations. Albania turned to China for aid and protection. Relations soon deteriorated to the point where the Chinese and Russian leaders publicly denounced one another and resorted to other forms of harassment. The situation was complicated by the outbreak of the "great cultural revolution" in China, apparently the result of an internal power struggle within the Chinese Communist party from which Mao Tse-tung again emerged victorious. In 1969 Russian and Chinese soldiers actually fought one another in limited clashes along the Chinese-Siberian border.

ANOTHER OCCUPATION OF CZECHOSLOVAKIA

Meanwhile Russia's European satellites continued to agitate for greater independence and freedom. In 1965 Rumania adopted a new constitution that proclaimed it a Socialist rather than a People's Republic. The following year it threatened to withdraw from COMECON and the Warsaw Pact, but was restrained by Russian counterthreats.

Wide World Photos

Revolutionaries in Prague

"The boy [an 18-year-old machine tool worker] said 'None of us are afraid of the Russians. This is our country.' A young worker from Slovakia who also was present last night said that the Russians did not dare disperse the students because this would give the lie to their assertions that they were here as liberators. The youths of Prague have many other ways, besides defying curfews, to express their contempt for the Russians." NEW YORK TIMES, August 26, 1968.

The movement for genuinely democratic socialism went furthest in Czechoslovakia. In January, 1968, the Czech Communist party under Alexander Dubcek dismissed the old-guard Stalinist leaders and instituted a far-reaching program of reforms that included a greater reliance on free markets in place of government-dictated prices, the relaxation of press censorship, and a considerable measure of personal freedom. The rulers in the Kremlin, annoyed by criticism of the Soviet Union in the Czech press and fearful that Czech attitudes and policies might spread to other countries in the Soviet bloc, held several conferences with Czech leaders to try to persuade them to return to orthodox Communist policies, but without success. At length, in August, 1968, the Soviet army and air force – with token contingents from Poland, Hungary, and East Germany – invaded Czechoslovakia and established martial law. Efforts to set up a puppet government at first failed in the face of the near-unanimous support given by the Czech people to their leaders. Young people taunted the Russian soldiers, and in a few instances engaged in violent demonstrations against them; but for the most part the Czechs accepted the occupation with passive resistance, hoping that international opinion would oblige the Russians to withdraw and permit a resumption of the program of liberalization. When this hope failed to materialize, a few passionate patriots resorted to dramatic actions, such as self-immolation, to demonstrate their opposition to the Russian occupation. In April, 1969, the Russians succeeded in forcing the Czech Communist Party to replaced Dubcek with Gustav Husak, a Slovak more amenable to Russian wishes. Once again, as in East Germany in 1953 and in Poland and Hungary in 1956, events proved that Russia's Communist empire could be held together only by force.

BIRTH PANGS OF WORLD CIVILIZATION

Although the emergence of world civilization in the second half of the twentieth century was facilitated by organizations such as the United Nations, new ideas of national and racial equality and justice, and the accelerating revolution in communications, it frequently threatened to abort in global conflict based on old ideas of power politics, national sovereignty, and religious or racial superiority. The history of international relations after about 1950 can be characterized by two main themes: the East-West split between the powerful industrial nations of the world, chiefly European; and the struggle of the emerging nations of Asia, Africa, and Latin America for political recognition and economic progress. Each of these struggles, in turn, was complicated by internal fissures within the protagonist groups.

The Soviet Union, leader of world communism, experienced increasing difficulty in keeping its minions in line – notably Red China, which came to play an independent role as the major power in Asia and challenged the Soviet Union for the leadership of the Communist movements in Africa and Latin America. Similarly, the United States, the heart and core of the Atlantic alliance (which also included Japan as a sort of associate member), was unable to secure the unswerving allegiance of its nominal allies – especially de Gaulle's France, which pursued a course not unlike that of Mao's China in the Soviet bloc. Finally, the emerging nations were tempted – and divided accordingly – by the blandishments of both great power blocs and their rival forms of government and economy.

KOREA TO VIETNAM: THE STRUGGLE IN THE EAST

The Korean War settled down to a desultory though destructive stalemate in 1951 during the protracted negotiations for a truce. When it was finally concluded in June, 1953, the armistice merely restored the status quo ante bellum. The cost in human suffering and material destruction had been enormous, considering the war's limited scope, yet the outcome left the situation in Korea fundamentally unchanged. What had changed was the balance of forces in Asia.

China emerged as an independent power on the world stage. Although it remained for a time in the Soviet orbit, it became the dynamic nucleus of Communist advance in Asia and the Pacific. It compensated for its poverty and industrial backwardness by sheer size and numbers and the ideological commitment of its rulers. At enormous cost to their subjects the rulers engaged in a gigantic effort, a "great leap forward," to industrialize their nation as the Soviet Union had done between the wars. The industrialization program broke down when Chinese agriculture failed to produce enough food to support the burgeoning population, and a great famine ensued, the traditional nemesis of Chinese despots. Even this did not deter the Chinese Communist leaders from their aggressive course.

They gave aid and encouragement to Communist-led movements throughout Southeast Asia. The Viet Minh expelled the French and set up a Communist-dominated government in North Vietnam. In Malaysia, Burma, Laos, Cambodia, and especially South Vietnam, Communist China supported local efforts to undermine or overthrow established governments. It supported Indonesia in that country's aggressive designs on Malaysia and in its decision early in 1965 to withdraw from the United Nations. Even India, a fervent advocate of neutralism in the struggle between East and West, fell victim to the aggressive tendencies of Chinese communism in a series of border conflicts provoked by China in 1962 and afterward.

The most overt, vicious, and costly struggle developed in South Vietnam. After the partition of Vietnam in 1954 the Communist-led

Viet Cong, an underground organization opposed to the Western-oriented government of South Vietnam, engaged in subversion and guerrilla warfare with the encouragement and assistance of North Vietnam and, ultimately, Communist China and the Soviet Union. The United States supplied military advisors and assistance to South Vietnam, but corruption in the government of the latter, bitter disputes between the country's Buddhist majority and Roman Catholic minority, and a series of coups d'état weakened the people's will and ability to resist. In 1964 the United States initiated a major military build-up, committed American forces to large-scale ground combat, and shortly after began to bomb military and industrial targets in North Vietnam to force that nation to cease its aid to the Viet Cong. While stepping up its military operations the United States announced its willingness to engage in "unconditional negotiations" for peace, but not until 1968, with many conditions imposed by all concerned, did negotiations actually get underway. Meanwhile the unpopularity of the war made it a major political issue in the United States, and it was largely responsible for President Johnson's decision not to seek re-election in 1968.

THE EXPLOSIVE NEAR EAST

Farther west but in an area of the world still regarded by people of European heritage as part of the "mysterious East," troubles of a somewhat different nature threatened the peace of the world. In 1956 the young state of Israel, surrounded by bitterly hostile Arab neighbors, learned of a projected holy war to destroy it. Taking advantage of its superior organization and intelligence network and hoping to capitalize on world preoccupation with the Hungarian revolt and American preoccupation with the presidential campaign, the Israelis in October launched a surprise attack against Egyptian forces in the Sinai Desert. Britain, angry with Nasser for having nationalized the Suez Canal in violation of Egypt's treaty obligations, and France, angry because of Egyptian assistance to the Algerian rebels, joined forces to launch a combined air attack against Egypt. The Israelis scored a spectacular success against greatly superior Egyptian forces, but Nasser appealed to the United Nations.

Both the United States and the Soviet Union demanded a cease-fire and withdrawal of all forces, and the General Assembly by an overwhelming vote branded the Israeli action as aggression. Faced with hostile criticism within their own countries as well as with adverse world opinion, the British and French governments withdrew. United Nations security forces moved into the Sinai Desert to serve as a buffer between Egypt and Israel. Israel gained its immediate objective, the destruction of Egypt's potential attacking force, but as a consequence Egypt closed the Suez Canal to ships coming from or destined for Israel's ports. In spite of the humiliation of defeat by Israel, Egypt gained prestige among its Arab neighbors by having successfully appealed to the United Nations against France and Britain. The French and British intervention irritated their relations with the United States and allowed the Soviet Union to offset the damage to its reputation from events in Hungary by appearing before the nations of Asia and Africa as their champion against the imperialist powers of old.

Neutral soldiers under the flag of the United Nations served as a buffer between Egypt and Israel along the Sinai-Negev border for more than ten years. Meanwhile Arab terrorists operating from Syria and Jordan continued to harass Israel, and border incidents were frequent. In May, 1967, President Nasser of Egypt, stung by taunts from fellow Arab rulers that he was hiding behind the U.N., demanded the withdrawal of United Nations troops. Secretary-General U Thant acceded reluctantly. Almost immediately Egyptian troops occupied the Gaza Strip and the heights overlooking the Strait of Tiran, through which shipping bound for the Israeli port of Elath had to pass. Shortly afterward Nasser declared the strait closed to Israeli shipping. Frantic activity at United Nations headquarters produced no tangible results, and both Israeli and Arab leaders issued increasingly bellicose statements. On June 5, 1967, after a round of artillery attacks from Jordan and Syria, Israel unleashed a stunning air attack that destroyed on the ground virtually the entire air forces of its three belligerent Arab neighbors. Concurrently Israeli ground forces sliced the Egyptian army in ribbons and occupied the whole of the Sinai peninsula, Jordanian territory on the west bank of the Jordan river (including the Old City of Jerusalem), and the Golan Heights in Syria.

The Security Council called for a cease fire on June 6, which both Arabs and Israelis accepted on June 10. The resulting truce remained extremely fragile, however. The Arab nations refused to enter into direct negotiations with Israel and declared that they would maintain a state of war as long as Israel occupied Arab territory. The Israelis, on the other hand, declared that they would not evacuate the conquered territory until the Arabs agreed to a peace settlement and recognized the right of Israel to exist. The United Nations again showed its powerlessness to achieve a peaceful settlement. Border incidents became almost daily occurrences, and the Israelis responded to Arab terrorist raids with devastating retaliation.

On the world stage the Five Days' War further polarized the East-West split. The Arab nations broke off diplomatic relations with the United States and Great Britain with the unfounded charge that their warplanes had aided the Israeli attack. The Soviet Union, for its part, severed diplomatic relations with Israel and promptly began to re-supply the Arab states with planes, tanks, rockets, and other military hardware, and military advisors as well. De Gaulle's France tried to adopt a neutral stance, but after Israeli forces attacked the Beirut (Lebanon) airport in retaliation for another terrorist attack, de Gaulle personally forbade the further sale or delivery of French military equipment (especially airplanes) to Israel, and confiscated funds that Israel had already paid to French manufacturers. The situation remained tenser than ever, as any new outbreak of hostilities might easily involve both the Soviet Union and the United States.

Another Near Eastern trouble spot was the island of Cyprus. Occupied by Britain since 1878, the island ceased to be of strategic importance after the withdrawal of British forces from Suez in 1955. The Greek-speaking majority of the island's population had long agitated for *enosis* (union) with Greece. Britain, fearing reprisals against the Turkish-speaking minority, arranged for the island to assume independence in 1959 under an arrangement prohibiting union with Greece. The Greek Cypriots accepted the arrangement, but in 1963 they renewed terrorist attacks on their Turkish compatriots. United Nations forces intervened to keep the peace, but the resulting tensions between Greece and Turkey threatened to undermine the unity of the NATO alliance in the eastern Mediterranean.

THE AFRO-ASIAN BLOC

The growing number of newly independent states with mutual economic problems and political grievances led them to attempt to concert their efforts in the world arena. In 1955 a meeting in Bandung, Indonesia, attracted delegates from twenty-nine nations of Asia and Africa. In 1957 the Asian-African People's Solidarity Conference at Cairo was attended by representatives of forty countries, including the Soviet Union. Such meetings produced unanimous votes on resolutions condemning colonialism and racism and favoring disarmament and economic assistance, but the interests of the members were too heterogeneous and sometimes too conflicting to enable them to take concrete positive action. Even in the United Nations, where they tended to vote as a bloc on issues concerned with colonialism or similar matters, they could rarely achieve unanimity on other questions.

As Africa moved rapidly toward independence, its political leaders sought to speak with one voice by forming the Conference of Independent African States, subsequently transformed into the Organization of African Unity. Representatives of only eight nations attended the first meeting in Accra, Ghana, in 1958; six years later its membership had grown to more than thirty-five. Increasing world recognition came to Africans when Chief Albert Lutuli, a leader of South Africa's persecuted Negroes, won a Nobel Peace Prize. In 1964 Sir Alex Quaison-Sackey of Ghana became the first black African to be elected president of the General Assembly of the United Nations.

Conflicting interests also divided the former colonial countries. Some of them succumbed to one-party governments, frequently influenced by Russian or Chinese Communists. Others remained loyal to the liberal parliamentary institutions inherited from their former colonial masters, in spite of great difficulties. Some, such as the Congo and Nigeria, fell victim to internal anarchy and civil war because of the feuds of rival tribes. At a meeting of African political leaders in Cairo in 1964 Premier Moise Tshombe of the Congo was forcibly detained by Egyptian police and prevented from attending because of his use of white mercenaries in fighting rebellious tribesmen. In 1967, after his government was overthrown by a coup d'état, he was kidnapped and held prisoner by the Algerian government, where he died under mysterious circumstances in 1969. The rivalry of interests in Africa, both among and within the countries, posed a threat to world peace by tempting outsiders — Communists or others — to exploit them in their own interests.

CUBAN CRISES

Other threats to world peace arose from the success of the Cuban revolution and the conversion of Fidel Castro to communism. In April, 1961, the new Kennedy administration, acting on plans devised by the Central Intelligence Agency under the Eisenhower administration, carried out an attempted invasion of Cuba, in which Cuban exiles supported by American sea and air forces were to regain control of the island. The invasion attempt resulted in a ludicrous fiasco, damaging the reputation of the United States throughout the world and giving the Soviet Union the opportunity to pose as Cuba's protector by threatening atomic war in the event of a renewal of the invasion effort. A year and a half later another Cuban crisis again brought the world to the brink of atomic war. Russian technicians and military advisers began installing rocket-launching bases in Cuba with Castro's consent and probably at his insistence. The United States detected the installations in aerial photographs, and President Kennedy in a dramatic television appearance warned the Soviet Union to withdraw its missiles or face the consequences of an American missile attack. For several days the world waited in suspense, but the Soviet leaders, unprepared to risk war over Cuba, withdrew their missiles and technicians.

SUMMITS AND SHADOWS

Khrushchev's ten-year rule as dictator produced many alternations in the Soviet Union's relations with the West. At times Khrushchev acted with all the ruthlessness of Stalin, as in the suppression of the Hungarian revolt and his bellicose pronouncements on the Suez and Cuban crises. More often he posed as a jovial rival, speaking eloquently of "peaceful coexistence" and friendly competition to raise the world's living standards. The two faces of Khrushchev received extraordinary exposure in two successive "meetings at the summit" or gatherings of the heads of state of the Big Four (the United States, Russia, Britain, and France) and several lesser powers. The first meeting took place in Geneva in 1955. The main item on the agenda was discussion of the reunification of Germany. No binding decisions were reached, but the atmosphere of the conference was so congenial that Khrushchev followed it up with a visit to the United States, where he visited with Iowa farmers and enjoyed the attractions of Southern California as well as conferring with President Eisenhower. The next summit conference, scheduled for 1960 in Geneva, ended in confusion and dismay. Khrushchev took advantage of the recent shooting down of a United States reconnaissance aircraft over Russia and the capture of its pilot to denounce the United States "espionage," and the conference broke up without even discussing the agenda. In 1961 President Kennedy confronted Khrushchev in Vienna, and in 1967 President Johnson and Premier Kosygin met in Glassboro, New Jersey, in the wake of the Arab-Israeli war; but none of these meetings resulted in the permanent settlement of differences between the two superpowers.

The threat of atomic warfare continued to hang over the world like a symbolic mushroom cloud. In 1952 the United States announced that its scientists had perfected a far more powerful hydrogen bomb, and stories leaked out about other deadly atomic weapons. Britain, France, and eventually Communist China succeeded in creating atomic and hydrogen bombs, and new fears were aroused that in time all nations would have atomic arsenals, increasing the likelihood of atomic war as the result of mischance or the action of an irresponsible leader in any one of a hundred or more nations. To reduce the possibility of an atomic accident triggering an all-out war, the American and Russian leaders agreed to establish a direct radio-telephone connection, the "hot line," from Washington to Moscow. Meanwhile discussions and negotiations to remove the possibility of a nuclear holocaust continued fitfully. In 1963, after many deadlocks and disappointments, the Soviet Union, the United States, and the United Kingdom signed a treaty banning atomic or nuclear testing and explosions in the atmosphere, underwater, or in outer space. Although it was a step toward reducing the threat of radioactive poisoning of the atmosphere, the treaty left intact the already formidable atomic arsenals of the two great powers, and it did not prohibit atomic testing underground. Even more ominous, both France and Communist China refused to sign the treaty. In 1968 the United States, the Soviet Union, and the United Kingdom agreed on a nuclear non-proliferation treaty (ratified by the United States Senate in 1969) to which many non-nuclear nations adhered; but again France and China, as well as several other nations, stood aloof. The world still lives in the shadow of the mushroom cloud.

TENDENCIES OF TWENTIETH-CENTURY CIVILIZATION
CHAPTER TWENTY

SCIENCE, TECHNOLOGY, AND INDUSTRY

A list of the distinguishing features of twentieth-century civilization might include such factors as its increasingly global dimensions, the greater role of science, and man's enhanced ability to master his environment. One feature, however, pervades all others and seems to provide the key to understanding the distinctive character and special historical import of the twentieth century: the accelerated pace of change. In earlier ages the mark of success of human societies was their ability to adapt to their environments. In the modern world the mark of success is the ability to manipulate the environment and adapt it to the needs of society. The fundamental means of manipulation and adaptation is technology – more specifically, technology based on modern science. A major reason for the more rapid pace of social change in recent times is the marked acceleration of scientific and technological progress.

It sometimes appears that science and technology have pursued an independent course unaffected by the political, social, and economic dislocations to which they have contributed. It is no doubt true that both possess an internal dynamic whereby each scientific discovery, each new technological triumph, contributes to still further progress; it is also true that both the rate and direction of scientific and technological progress are profoundly influenced by political, social, and economic factors. Many new developments in the basic sciences of chemistry and biology have been stimulated by their commercial applications in agriculture, industry, and medicine. The requirements of war and national rivalry have led governments to devote huge resources to scientific research and development for military purposes. Military crash programs have resulted in the development of radar and other electronic communications devices, in the successful harnessing of atomic energy. and in experiments leading to the launching of space rockets and artificial satellites. Medical research has also been stimulated by military needs as well as by a heightened social consciousness of the possibility and desirability of mitigating human suffering. Whether or not scientific progress would have been as rapid in the absence of military demands and the political circumstances behind those demands is a moot question. Certainly it would have taken a different direction. Fortunately for mankind, however, even the most deadly developments of military technology have proved adaptable to constructive peacetime purposes.

THE ACCELERATION OF SCIENTIFIC PROGRESS

The recent history of transportation and communications provides a graphic example of the acceleration of scientific and technological progress. At the beginning of the nineteenth century the speed of travel had not changed appreciably since the Hellenistic era. By the beginning of the twentieth century men could travel at velocities of up to eighty miles per hour by means of the steam locomotive. The development of automobiles, airplanes, and space rockets dwarfed even that achievement in speed and also in range and flexibility. Until the invention of the electric telegraph, communication over appreciable distances was limited to the speed of human messengers. The telephone, radio, and television added immeasurably to the convenience, flexibility, and reliability of long-distance communication. Almost instantaneous communication with most inhabited portions of the world became commonplace. Each successive improvement in the means of transportation and communication depended increasingly on the application of basic science.

The ability of science and technology to grow rapidly depends upon a host of accessory developments, some of them stemming from the progress of science itself. A major example is the electronic computer, which performs thousands of complicated calculations in a fraction of a second. The first mechanical calculating machine beyond the simple abacus was invented in the 1830's and was powered by steam. By the beginning of the twentieth century a few rudimentary mechanical devices were employed, chiefly for commercial purposes, but the age of the electronic computer did not dawn until after World War II. Its progress since then has rivaled the rapidity with which it operates. Without it many other scientific advances, such as the exploration of outer space, would have been impossible.

Another requisite for scientific and technical advance is a sizable pool of educated manpower — or brainpower. At the beginning of the twentieth century more than half the population of the Western nations possessed at least rudimentary literacy. By mid-century almost all the

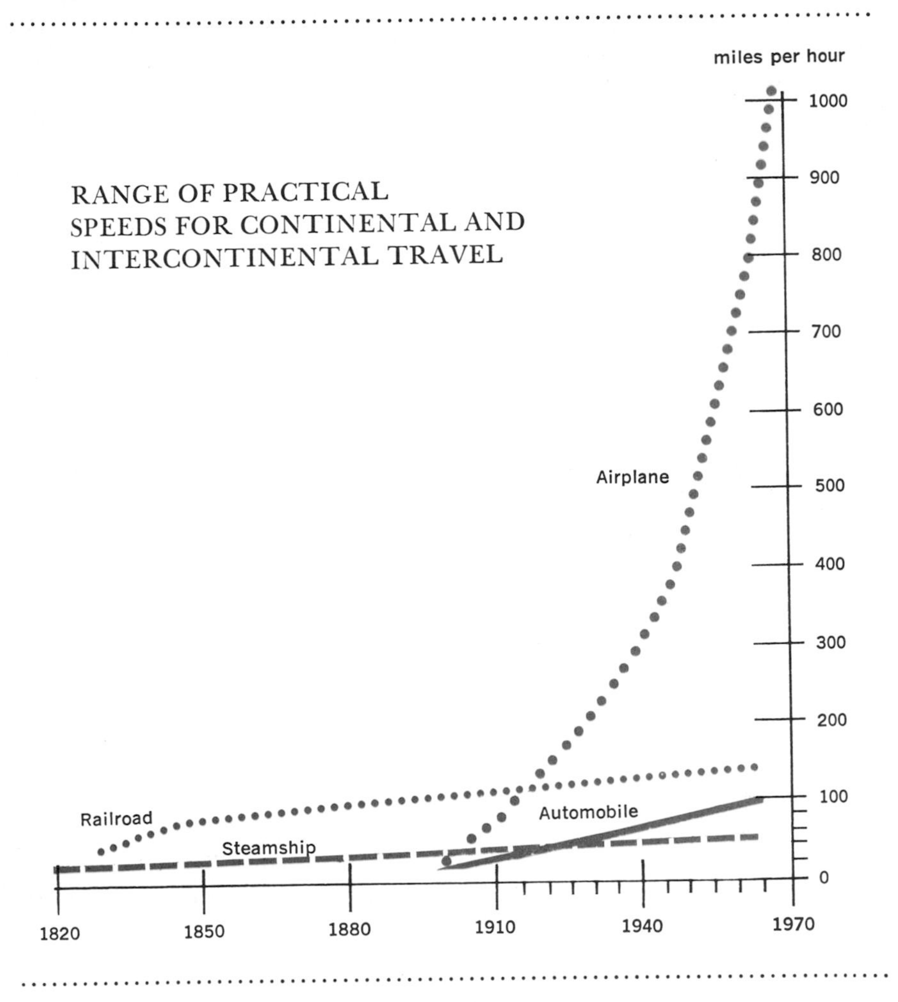

educable population had attained literacy, and the average number of years of schooling ranged from six to ten. The ability of individuals to participate fully and effectively in the new scientific-technological matrix of civilization, whether as scientists and technicians or in its commercial and bureaucratic superstructures, increasingly required advanced study at the college or university level and beyond.

There is little doubt that science generally is a paying proposition, but scientific research is also expensive and rarely can scientists or scientific institutions garner the pecuniary benefits directly. Subsidies for scientific research have increased enormously in the twentieth century, especially in recent decades. The largest sums come from governments, followed by private philanthropies and the industrial and commercial concerns that exploit the discoveries of science. There is a tendency for the rich nations to become richer in relation to the poor ones because they can afford the large initial expenditures required for basic research.

The widening technical gap between the developed and underdeveloped parts of the world is reflected in differences in educational levels as well as in differences in income. In many parts of Asia, Africa, and Latin America literacy rates in the mid-twentieth century averaged much less than 50 per cent — as low as 10 per cent in some nations. The proportion of university-trained people was much lower.

The demands of science affect the nature of education as well as the number of the educated. Russian scientific achievements, symbolized by the rapid development of atomic bombs and even more by the first space flight of Sputnik I in 1957, shocked the United States and other Western nations into recognizing inadequacies in their educational systems. Curricular reforms that had previously been proposed by some educators benefited from public support at a strategic moment and affected the teaching of science and mathematics and of other subjects as well, including history.

THE CONQUEST OF DISEASE

Although notable progress in medical science was made in the last half of the nineteenth century by Pasteur, Koch, Lister, and others, the general level of medical practice at the beginning of the twentieth century even in Western nations was still quite low. It is questionable whether doctors cured more patients than they killed. Tuberculosis, influenza, and pneumonia were major causes of death; such childhood diseases as measles, mumps, and diptheria were potent killers.

One reason for the low level of medical practice was the poor state of medical education. Practical medicine was still an art, lacking a scientific basis. Bacteriology, microbiology, and biochemistry, which provided the basis for the subsequent scientific practice of medicine, were still in their infancy. The Rockefeller Foundation and other philanthropic organizations led the way in the areas of medical research, education, public health, and preventive medicine. In the nineteenth century local governments in advanced countries assumed the responsibility for providing water and maintaining other sanitary facilities in large cities, but governmental activities in the area of health and medicine were narrowly restricted until the private organizations, including church-supported missionaries, demonstrated the possibility of effective action. The most spectacular successes were recorded in the prevention or control of hookworm, malaria, and yellow fever. Although they were among the most lethal and widespread of all diseases at the beginning of the century, by mid-century hookworm and yellow fever had been all but eradicated and the incidence of malaria had been greatly reduced. The successes of the private philanthropic organizations led to the establishment of public health services as integral parts of government in almost all nations, climaxed in 1948 by the creation of the World Health Organization under the auspices of the United Nations.

Laboratory scientists made progress in isolating and identifying the causes and carriers of many diseases and in developing immunization techniques. Within a few decades vaccines were developed for typhoid fever, typhus, tetanus, yellow fever, and cholera. In the 1950's, after a well-financed and highly publicized program against poliomyelitis spanning more than three decades, Dr. Jonas Salk and Dr. Albert Sabin succeeded in creating effective vaccines which came within reach of eradicating the disease within a few years. Their success was facilitated by the earlier discovery that polio and several other diseases, including influenza and the common cold, are caused by viruses, microorganisms smaller than bacteria. Research by biochemists discovered and identified vitamins and other food elements essential to growth and to disease prevention.

Although some of the most spectacular advances in medical science took place in the new field of preventive medicine, equally important discoveries were made in curative medicine. Early in the century new drugs were developed for the treatment of syphilis and diabetes. In the 1930's and 1940's a large family of sulfa drugs, derivatives of sulfanilamide, was developed with applications for many bacterial diseases. In 1940 medical researchers successfully applied penicillin, the first of many antibiotic drugs. Surgery, one of the oldest medical specialties, developed techniques for delicate operations on the brain, heart, and other vital organs, including transplantation of organs, that previously had been regarded as impossible. Psychiatry, the medical specialty dealing with diseases of the mind, absorbed much from the teachings of Sigmund Freud and became a flourishing branch of medical practice. Many of the traditional killing diseases have been brought under control, and the emphasis in medical research has shifted to diseases whose incidence is greatest in the later years of life — cancer and heart disease in particular.

NEW MODES OF PRODUCTION

The productivity of human labor, rapidly advanced by the application of scientific technology beginning in the nineteenth century, continued at an accelerated pace in the twentieth. Output per worker in agriculture — still the major source of supply for the majority of the world's foodstuffs and raw materials — has been increased greatly in Western nations by scientific techniques of fertilization, seed selection, and stock breeding, and by the use of mechanical power. Much progress has also been made in growing food in the seas, and important experiments now under way will sooner or later result in artificial photosynthesis, greatly increasing potential supplies of foodstuffs for the world's expanding population.

The rise in power production is even more remarkable. World power production increased more than forty-fold between 1900 and 1970. Most of the increase took place in areas of European culture and in forms that had been in their infancy at the beginning of the century. For example, the generation of electrical energy increased more than one hundred times. Petroleum and natural gas, which at the beginning of the century accounted for only a small fraction of the total energy consumption, have surpassed coal as a source of energy, approaching 50 per cent of the world's energy output. The growing importance of electricity and petroleum products has brought numerous social and economic changes. Electric energy is far cleaner, more efficient, and more flexible than most other forms of energy. It can be transmitted hundreds of miles at a fraction of the cost of transporting coal or petroleum. It can be used in massive concentrations to smelt metals or in tiny motors to operate delicate instruments, as well as to provide light. Its application to domestic appliances has helped to revolutionize patterns of family life, the status of women, and the employment of domestic servants.

The internal combustion engine, the most important consumer of petroleum, was an invention of the nineteenth century, but it produced a revolution only when applied to two of the most characteristic technological devices of the twentieth century; the automobile and the airplane. A few automobiles were built in the last years of the nineteenth century, but not until Henry Ford introduced the principle of mass production with a moving assembly line in 1907 did the automobile become more than a rich man's toy. Ford's techniques of production were soon imitated by other manufacturers in the United States and Europe, and the automobile industry became one of the largest employers of any manufacturing industry, as well as providing unprecedented opportunities for personal mobility. The techniques of assembly line production were adopted in other industries, including the aircraft industry in World War II. Social critics complained that they reduced workers to automatons, but the critics overlooked the additional fact that the assembly line saved labor and therefore resulted in higher wages and fewer working hours.

The scientific basis of modern industry resulted in hundreds of new products and materials. Beginning with the invention of rayon in 1898, dozens of artificial or synthetic textile fibers have been created. In relatively recent years plastic materials made from chemicals have replaced the more conventional wood, metals, earthenware, and paper in thousands of uses ranging from lightweight containers to high-speed drilling machines. The increasing use of electrical and mechanical power, the invention of hundreds of new labor-saving techniques, and the development of automatic instruments of control have brought about a revolution in the conditions of life and work more far-reaching than the classic industrial revolution in Britain. In an extreme instance, a single worker can oversee the operations of a huge petroleum refinery. These new developments in industry have created a role for human labor vastly different from anything previously experienced. Sheer strength counts for less than ever before; intelligence and training for far more. The cascading improvements in technology have made millions of unskilled laborers redundant, creating technological unemployment; but they also created a new demand for special skills and knowledge with remuneration proportional, not to the number of hours worked or human energy expended, but to the specialized talent of the employee.

THE RELEASE OF NUCLEAR ENERGY

No field of science has experienced more rapid or extensive changes in both pure and applied aspects than physics. The gradual understanding of the complex structure of the atom, beginning with the discovery of X-rays and the radioactive properties of certain elements, opened great theoretical possibilities. The work of Albert Einstein and others indicated that tremendous sources of energy lie locked within the atom. Beginning in the 1930's, huge cyclotrons and other atom smashers were used to transform the atoms of one element into those of another. In the process scientists discovered that they could create new elements heavier than those that occur in nature. Some of them, such as plutonium, were found to be especially susceptible to chain reactions that could generate enormous quantities of energy. In December, 1942, at the University of Chicago a group of physicists under the direction of the exiled Italian scientist Enrico Fermi set off the first controlled chain reaction of atomic energy. In July, 1945, another group led by J. Robert Oppenheimer exploded an experimental bomb on the proving grounds of Los Alamos, New Mexico. The following month the bombs dropped on Hiroshima and Nagasaki inaugurated a new age of terror.

Governments have responded to the possibilities for the peaceful use of atomic energy with markedly less alacrity than to its military potentialities. Some progress has been made, nevertheless. Medical science has found a number of important uses for radioactivity and associated phenomena. The most promising use for atomic energy is in the generation of electrical power. Several generating stations are at work in various parts of the world, and it is predicted that by the end of the century between one-third and one-half of the world's electricity will be generated by atomic energy. Other projects made possible by atomic energy include digging a new isthmian canal in Central America, reversing the flow of a river in Siberia, and changing the climate of the Libyan desert by means of a canal from the Mediterranean to a newly created artificial sea.

Astronaut Edwin "Buzz" Aldrin on the Moon, July 20, 1969

"That's one small step for a man, one giant leap for mankind." Astronaut Neil Armstrong's comment as he became the first man to step on the moon.

THE EXPLORATION OF SPACE

As recently as the 1940's manned flight in space was chiefly a subject for science fiction. While comic strips portrayed scantily clad men and women of the twenty-fifth century flying through space with rockets strapped to their shoulders, learned men made calculations that purported to prove that no vehicle could ever attain the velocity required to leave the earth's gravitational field. During World War II scientists gained much valuable experience as a result of their work with jet engines and military rockets, but few people expected that it would be possible for men to survive in outer space even if they could reach it. New developments such as more powerful rocket engines, electronic signaling and control devices, and computers for rapid calculation of trajectories concurred to make space flight a real possibility. On October 4, 1957, scientists in the Soviet Union put a capsule into orbit around the earth. The Space Age had begun.

Further progress took place rapidly, largely stimulated by national rivalry. A second orbiting Russian rocket followed a month later, and early in 1958 the United States placed a capsule in orbit. Within a few years both nations rocketed men into space and successfully retrieved them. Unmanned satellites were put into more or less permanent orbits to relay scientific information back to earth by means of radio and television, and other rockets were sent to the moon, Venus, and Mars with similar aims. In December, 1968, the United States put a space crew in orbit around the moon, but outdid even that feat the following year. On July 20, 1969, astronauts Neil Armstrong and Edwin Aldrin, supported by astronaut Michael Collins and a crew of thousands of scientists and technicians on earth, became the first men to set foot on the moon. Truly, mankind had created a new age. One measure of the difference between that new age and all previous eras of human achievement lay in the manner in which the event was publicized. When Columbus discovered the New World (which he mistook for the Indies), the event was witnessed only by the actual participants, and it was months, even years, before the news reached a large public. The first step of man on the moon, in contrast, was witnessed by hundreds of millions all over the earth by means of television relays — the largest audience, in fact, ever to witness a single event.

NASA

While astronauts explored the nearby fringes of outer space, astronomers and astrophysicists continued their probes of the outermost reaches of space in the hope of discovering the secrets of the universe. Aided by powerful new reflector and radio telescopes, they made startling discoveries, but the secret of the origin and nature of the universe continued to elude them. As recently as 1930 they discovered Pluto, the outermost planet of the solar system. In 1965 astronomers using the huge 200-inch telescope on Mount Palomar in California discovered a group of quasars (for "quasi-stellar radio sources") more than 8 billion light years distant – excitingly close to the 13 billion years which some astronomers thought represented the age of the universe. Further discoveries of this kind may help settle the question of the origin of the universe: whether it originated in a "big bang" at some definite point in space and time billions of years ago, or whether it is infinite and eternal, as other astrophysicists maintain.

SOCIAL TRENDS

The spectacular growth of science and of a science-based technology is reflected in almost equally spectacular social changes. New industries have arisen on the basis of new technologies, creating new skills, new patterns of work and leisure, new standards of behavior – and new social problems. Among the most potent social foces are the advances in biological and medical science, which brought about a population explosion.

THE POPULATION EXPLOSION

In the two and one-half centuries between 1650 and 1900 the world's population increased threefold, rising from approximately 500,000,000

No. 160b (Improvisation 28), 1912, by Vasily Kandinsky

"The freer the abstract form, the purer and more primitive is its appeal. In a composition, therefore, where the material side may be more or less superfluous, it can be accordingly more or less omitted and replaced by non-objective forms or through abstractions of de-materialized objects. In any case of translation into the abstract or the employment of non-objective forms, the artist's sole judge, guide, and principal consideration should be his feeling. Finally, the more abstractions the artist employs the more at home will he feel in the realm of the non-objective. Likewise the observer, led by artistic attainment to better knowledge of the language of the abstracted, finally, becomes fully conversant." Kandinsky, ON THE SPIRITUAL IN ART (New York, 1946).

Courtesy of The Solomon R. Guggenheim Museum Collection

to about 1,500,000,000. In the next two generations, from 1900 to 1960, the population doubled, attaining approximately 3 billion. At presently projected rates of increase the number of persons is expected to double again, surpassing 6 billion, by the end of the century. Such staggering rates of increase are without precedent in the history of the world.

Table 1 *World Population, 1930–1967*

	Population in millions (estimated)		*Annual rate of increase (per cent)*	*Population per sq. km.*
	1930	*1967*	*1960–1963*	*1963*
Africa	164	328	2.5	10
North America	134	220	1.5	10
Latin America	108	259	2.9	11
East Asia	591	877	1.5	71
South Asia	529	1030	2.4	58
Europe (without USSR)	355	452	0.9	89
USSR	179	236	1.7	10
Oceania	10	18	2.3	2
World	2070	3420	1.9	23

Source: United Nations, *Demographic Yearbook, 1967* (New York, 1968).

In earlier eras rises in population usually resulted from temporary increases in birth rates or equally temporary decreases in death rates. The dominant factor in population growth in the past century has been the apparently permanent decline in death rates. In large areas of the world famine has been eliminated as a cause of death, and the incidence of disease, especially in the early years of life, has been greatly reduced. In Ceylon the widespread use of DDT for mosquito (malaria) control

Ronchamp, by Le Corbusier

"Although the church, in its union of cavern with thrusting force, is an appropriate embodiment of the Virgin to whom it is dedicated . . . it is most of all an image of modern man, full of memories, with an ironic view of himself, no longer believing that he occupies the center of the world by right. He is under pressure in the interior of Ronchamp, which does not swell outward from him but presses in upon him. . . . he can only act, or gesture; and that act, like . . . the upward lifting prow of Ronchamp on its hilltop, has no defined boundary and is open-ended toward the ultimate reaches of space." Vincent Scully, Jr., MODERN ARCHITECTURE (New York, 1961)

Shostal

resulted in a halving of the death rate between 1945 and 1960. With the birth rate almost unchanged, the resulting increase in population was little short of fantastic. The Japanese death rate fell by one-half in an even shorter period, from 1947 to 1955, but the birth rate also declined significantly.

The unequal incidence of changes in birth and death rates has resulted in changes in the relative geographic distribution of population. Voluntary limitation of births by means of contraception and other birth control measures began to reduce birth rates in Europe in the nineteenth century, but birth rates have remained high in many other areas of the world. In 1900 about 40 per cent of the world's people lived in Asia; by 1960 the proportion had grown to 50 per cent; and by the year 2000 an estimated 60 per cent of the world's population will be Asian. By that time at the present rates of increase there will be more people in China alone than there were in all the world in 1900.

Such alarming rates of population growth create pressing new problems — economic, social, political, and even moral. Any positive rate of population growth, if long continued, must eventually produce an unacceptably large population, in which the majority will live in misery and die of starvation, disease, or war. An equilibrium of births and deaths is essential if mankind is not to be overtaken by such Malthusian horrors.

NEW STYLES OF LIVING

The civilization of the twentieth century proved to be an increasingly urban culture, in underdeveloped no less than in developed areas. The changes in agriculture together with the rapid growth of population directed increasing streams of people into the cities. The swelling size of cities created pressures for new social services, including mass rapid transit. Tramways or streetcars, subway trains, and eventually automobiles worked a revolution in the design of cities. To accommodate the automobile, large areas of valuable land were taken for interurban express highways, urban expressways, and parking facilities. The relative importance of central cities declined, creating slums and breeding delinquency, crime, and alienation, whereas outlying suburbs mushroomed as new recruits to the ever-growing middle class sought to escape the disadvantages of city living while retaining its conveniences.

The great productivity made possible by modern technology created wealth in amounts and forms undreamed of by earlier generations. It also resulted in its more equitable distribution, especially in the industrial nations of the West. Greater economic equality fostered greater social equality by increasing social mobility and blurring the lines between social classes. In many instances workers in modern industries, though functionally members of the working class, enjoyed a standard of living that would have aroused the envy of the middle classes of an earlier generation. Socially the middle class expanded at both ends of the spectrum, encompassing a larger and larger proportion of the population, leaving only a small archaic upper class at one end and a somewhat larger but contracting group of unfortunates at the other.

Poverty by no means disappeared even in the wealthiest societies, but besides afflicting a smaller proportion of the population, it changed its forms. In earlier times and in poorer societies poverty was regarded as the more or less permanent state of the masses, both urban and rural. In the twentieth century in technologically progressive nations it afflicted certain rather well-defined groups. These include chiefly those who, for whatever reason, failed to secure a rudimentary education, older workers rendered obsolete by technological change, and persons isolated either by geographical barriers or by various kinds of discriminatory practices.

THE USES OF LEISURE

For those who benefited most from material progress the new technology opened a new era of comfort and convenience and also posed new moral and social problems. As income increased, the demand for leisure also increased. At the beginning of the twentieth century a sixty-hour work week was common in most employments. By mid-century the forty-hour week was standard, and in some occupations hours were even fewer. As leisure time increased, the question of how to use it became more pressing. The solutions of earlier, less complicated times—churches, voluntary social organizations, village or neighborhood taverns—no longer sufficed. Large new industries grew up for the sole purpose of providing entertainment and diversion on a commercial basis. The cinema and radio spurted to prominence in the interwar years; television placed them both in partial eclipse after World War II. Professional sporting events, assiduously promoted by profit-minded entrepreneurs, gained in popularity. Moralists and philosophers frequently deplored the stultifying effects of such uses of leisure, together with the opportunities they created for the unscrupulous manipulation of mass sentiment for pecuniary or political advantage. That these diversions did not satisfy completely the desire for the constructive use of leisure time was demonstrated by the increasing popularity of facilities for adult education, both private and public, and new efforts to overcome the work-leisure dichotomy. Some of the efforts took the form of do-it-yourself movements in which individuals who put in six or eight hours in a factory or office as specialized parts of huge impersonal organizations reverted at the end of the day to simple craftsmen, working in gardens or building and repairing their own furniture, boats, and even homes.

The challenge of leisure time affected young people in particular. Instead of being forced to earn their way from the age of ten or twelve, as in the past, child labor laws, compulsory school attendance, and changing social customs kept them out of permanent gainful employment until ever higher ages. For most of those fortunate or ambitious enough to pursue higher education the increased leisure presented few problems, but for many it created problems both for themselves and for society. With the natural energy and exuberance of youth liberated from the necessity of continual labor and not provided with alternative constructive social outlets, they sometimes turned to such antisocial activities as delinquency and vandalism, or to social and political agitation and revolution.

MANNERS AND MORALS

The status of women altered greatly in the first half of the twentieth century. In 1902 Australia became the first nation to grant women the right to vote. Elsewhere the woman's suffrage movement made little headway before World War I. In many nations, including some otherwise advanced in the arts of civilization, the law regarded women as little more than chattels in the hands of their fathers or husbands. World War I with its large demand for female labor to replace men called to arms acted as a powerful stimulus to the movement for female emancipation. Women secured the right to vote on equal terms with men in the United States in 1920, in Great Britain in 1928, and in several other nations in the same or following decades. In Latin nations female suffrage had to wait until after World War II; and in Switzerland, often praised as the world's oldest democracy, women still cannot vote.

The success of the woman's suffrage movement owed much to the increasing economic independence of women. Domestic service declined with increasing opportunities for higher-paying jobs in industry and commerce, while such household labor-saving devices as washing machines and vacuum cleaners lightened the burden of domestic chores. Paralleling women's political and economic progress was their greater social freedom. The number of divorces rose from less than 5 per cent of the total number of marriages in Western Europe (less than 1 per cent in Great Britain) at the beginning of the century to more than 10 per cent after World War II; in the United States approximately one marriage in four ended in divorce in the postwar period. The higher divorce rates both symbolized and contributed to greater sexual freedom, which was also facilitated by the invention of simple and inexpensive contraceptive devices.

Urbanization and the emancipation of women altered the character of family life. Falling birth rates reduced the average size of families. Whereas in rural environments children could begin to earn their keep as early as the age of six by helping in various farm operations, under the conditions of modern urban societies they remained financial burdens on the family until they attained adulthood. Residence, workplace, and school were often widely separated, adding to the dichotomy between work and leisure. Instead of working together or in close proximity throughout the day, modern families frequently came together only at bedtime – if then. (This change affected the middle classes primarily; working-class families were often separated in this way from the beginning of the nineteenth century.) Although children and young people remained economically dependent upon their parents longer, they, like women, gained more social freedom, manifested in greater informality in clothing and in relations between the sexes.

THE "AMERICANIZATION" OF SOCIETY

Before the First World War educated Europeans regarded Americans as country cousins – brash, uncultured, lacking in social refinement. The increasing influence of the United States in world affairs, notably in the two world wars and after 1945, required some modification of that view, especially when American methods and fashions began to be imitated in Europe. Many of the social changes of the twentieth century appeared first in the United States before spreading gradually to Europe. Most Europeans favor the importation of American technology, which they believe to be the foundation of American wealth and power, but many deplore what they feel is the growing influence of American social customs and patterns of behavior. Much of what they deplore is not in fact specifically American but the result of modern technology and the affluence it produces. The Americanization of society is in reality merely the operation upon society of fundamental technological and economic change.

THE ARTS IN TWENTIETH-CENTURY CIVILIZATION

The rapid pace of change observable in science, technology, and social mores had its counterpart in literature and the arts. Technological progress affected modes of artistic expression, and changes in themes and styles created an intellectual revolution as far-reaching as the theory of relativity in physics or the impact of Freud on psychology. Technological change made its most profound impression on music and drama. The invention of the cinema, phonograph, radio, and television created audiences of millions for forms of artistic expression that had earlier been limited to a select few.

SERIOUS ART VERSUS POPULAR ART

The growth of income and leisure time, the expansion of the middle class, and above all the proliferation of modern mass communications media made commercial exploitation of the fine arts possible. Music was most profoundly affected. In earlier times music had not been subjected to market forces. Folk music sprang spontaneously from the people; serious music was usually subsidized by the church, public authorities, or wealthy patrons. The commercialization of music offered composers and performing musicians an unaccustomed degree of economic independence and even affluence, but in some respects it was disastrous for the general level of musical taste. Tunesmiths whose creations made the hit parade and shaggy-headed, musically illiterate singers who tapped the teenage market became celebrities, while serious new compositions still subsidized by the universities, private philanthropies, and governments, became increasingly esoteric and remote. The influence of commercialization and the mass media was not, however, wholly bad. It enabled some forms of folk music, notably jazz, to acquire the status of serious art. More important, it permitted millions without access to operas or symphony concerts to become familiar with and enjoy the masterworks of music by means of electronic reproduction.

The cinema, radio, and television revolutionized the dramatic arts. The stage suffered a relative decline in popularity, although the intellectual influence of a few playwrights made itself felt far beyond the world of the theater. The new media — the cinema in particular — created new possibilities for the dramatic arts but also imposed new limitations on them. The extreme commercialization or state control to which they were subjected in most countries resulted in a generally low level of quality. Innovation was more apparent in technical aspects of production than in artistic conception. Many writers and producers deliberately sacrificed edification for cheap entertainment. A few, however, such as Ingmar Bergman of Sweden, exploited the artistic possibilities of the new media imaginatively and produced great modern dramas.

Commercialization similarly influenced painting, sculpture, and the graphic arts. The demand for illustrators and commercial artists, especially in the new profession of advertising, guaranteed large returns to technically proficient artists, but it produced no masterpieces of the human spirit. Serious artists who did not cater to the public taste — indeed, in many instances they seemed determined to outrage the public — nevertheless found themselves lionized by avant garde intellectuals. Private collectors, many of whom viewed their art purchases as investments, vied with one another in seeking to discover promising young artists whose creations might grace the museums of the future. Thousands of individuals found in amateur art a satisfying use for leisure time and relief from the tensions and frustrations of the workaday world. Probably not since the eighteenth century did art and artists hold such a prominent place in society as in the second half of the twentieth century. Whether the average quality of artistic production merited that status is a question beyond objective evaluation.

THEMES AND TENDENCIES

The main tendencies of twentieth-century art, music, and literature had already been indicated before the First World War. (See pp. 284–288.) In spite of great diversity, the various modern art forms shared certain common characteristics that clearly distinguished them from the art of earlier centuries. They exhibited a greater degree of abstraction, notably in painting and sculpture, greater freedom of expression in both themes and manner of execution, and a pronounced reaction against earlier aesthetic standards of order, harmony, and unity. The tone of many modern works was irrational, even antirational, and was frequently combined with a strong current of pessimism. Modern art reflected the rootlessness of modern urban culture, the rapidity of social change, the disillusion produced by modern warfare, and the challenge to traditional beliefs posed by the discoveries of science.

Abstract and nonobjective subjects dominated painting even more completely after World War II than in the interwar period. In the earlier period nonobjective artists were frequently the objects of ridicule and achieved recognition only with great difficulty, but the tables were turned after the war; then it was the representational artist who had to prove the relevance of his subject. Even the later works of Picasso, Matisse, and Chagall, who were still active in the postwar period and whose works occasionally contained recognizable objects, seemed almost conventional in comparison with the blobs and swatches of color (or black and white lines) of the dominant school of abstract expressionism. One artist, Josef Albers, devoted his whole life to painting "Homage to the Square" consisting of nothing but superimposed squares of various colors. The American Jackson Pollock was the pioneer of the school of action painting, which had many followers in Europe in the 1950's. Pollock literally threw himself into his work, dripping and dribbling paint on a canvas stretched out on the floor and working from all directions. Pollock commented on his technique, "When I am *in* my painting, I'm not aware of what I'm doing. It is only after a sort of 'get acquainted' period that I see what I've been about." Such tendencies led almost inevitably to the pop art and op art of the 1960's. More serious European and American artists studied and adopted motifs and styles from Oriental and African art, thus testifying to the universality of art in the twentieth century. African and other primitive art forms were especially influential in sculpture.

ARCHITECTURE AND MODERN DESIGN

Architecture, which for so long had been essentially imitative, became one of the most creative art forms of the twentieth century. Like modern art, it was bedeviled by false starts and encountered strong opposition on aesthetic and other grounds, but it eventually developed a distinctive twentieth-century style. Technological advance in the form of new materials and techniques of construction created new opportunities for architects and engineers. Concurrently, new ideas concerning the purpose and nature of architecture replaced the notions of the nineteenth century. The American Frank Lloyd Wright and his master Louis Sullivan had already broken new ground before World War I, and Wright's influence continued to grow throughout the century. A leading exponent of the so-called international style of architecture was Ludwig Mies van der Rohe, a disciple of Walter Gropius who came to the United States in 1937. He won fame primarily as a designer of large modern office buildings. Le Corbusier, who designed the new capital of India at Chandigarh, and Otto Niemeyer, a Brazilian of German extraction who designed the strikingly modern new capital of Brazil, also won many new converts to modern architecture. Finnish architects were among the most daring innovators, and the Japanese proved themselves expert, as usual, at combining the modern international style with their own traditions.

The chief characteristic of modern architecture is its functionalism. It makes extensive use of glass, reinforced and precast concrete, and new materials like aluminum. Many of its earlier structures appeared massive and ungainly, but gradually architects refined their designs to produce the impression of light and airy space. The architectural revolution primarily affected cities, which, under intense pressure for efficient land use, grew upward as well as outward.

Interior decoration and furniture design underwent a similar transformation. Scandinavian designers took the lead in this development, in which the key word was functionalism. In place of the overstuffed, heavy decorations of the Victorian era, modern furnishings have abstract, simple lines.

THE LIFE OF THE MIND IN THE TWENTIETH CENTURY

The twentieth century witnessed the greatest increase in both population and in standards of material well-being of any equivalent period in human history. Yet this same period has been referred to as an "era of violence" and an "age of crisis." Is there a contradiction here?

The student of history should learn — as perhaps he has learned from this text — that every historical epoch has episodes of heroism and great achievement along with episodes of failure and despair, just as every human life has moments of both triumph and tragedy. The common man of the European world, whether peasant, carpenter, or clerk, has experienced the advantages of modern civilization: the higher living standards, greater longevity, mass education, and mass entertainment by radio, television, and similar media. Even the inhabitants of the non-

European world have participated at least marginally in the march of progress. Yet the verdict of thinking men on the progress of the twentieth-century civilization is one of guarded hopefulness at best, deep despair at worst.

IMAGINATIVE LITERATURE

Poets, dramatists, and novelists, have been called the consciences of humanity. It should not be surprising, therefore, that after the brutality of totalitarian regimes, the horrors of World War II, the fear of the atomic bomb, and the tensions of the cold war, a principal theme of imaginative literature should have been man's inhumanity to man or, in the words of a famous novel, "the human condition." Although some serious authors continued to deal with the problems of the inner man or the individual personality (perhaps mankind writ small?), the majority turned its attention to mankind in general. William Faulkner, one of America's greatest novelists who received the Nobel Prize for literature in 1949, stated the problem for many: "There are no longer problems of the spirit; there is only the question, *when will I be blown up?*" But Faulkner, an optimist in spite of himself, went on to say that men had been dominated by fear for so long that "by now we can even bear it."

Similar sentiments were expressed by France's existentialist novelist-poet-playwright-philosopher, Jean-Paul Sartre, who attracted a large following in the immediate postwar years. Another French novelist, also claimed by the existentialists, whose stories dealing with ordinary individuals may well outlast those of Sartre, was Albert Camus; his message was that life is what it is, but it must go on. A British novelist and essayist, George Orwell, who had been tempted by communism in his youth, dealt more directly with contemporary political questions. In *Animal Farm* (1945) he satirized the class structure of Soviet society ("all animals are equal, but some animals are more equal than others"); in *Nineteen Eighty Four* (1948) he evoked a Kafkaesque state of permanent warfare and totalitarianism that infected all regions of the earth.

In the second half of the twentieth century the theater continued to exert a primary influence on social thought in spite of the financial difficulties it encountered as a result of its competition with the cinema and television. Paradoxically, the competition itself insured its survival, since its most successful plays almost inevitably became the basis for even more successful screenplays. The German Marxist, Berthold Brecht, was one of the most fertile sources of inspiration, even though his productions were forbidden in both Nazi Germany and the German Federal Republic. Other dramatists in the Brechtian vein were Peter Weiss, whose *Persecution and Murder of Jean Paul Marat as Staged by the Inmates of the Asylum of Charenton under the Direction of the Marquis de Sade* achieved international success, and Rolf Hochhuth, who in

The Deputy blamed the papal legate in Germany, subsequently Pius XII, for failing to try to stop the Nazi persecution of the Jews. In Britain a group of "angry young men," mostly of working-class background, revolutionized the theater and had a notable impact on fiction as well. In the United States Tennessee Williams, Arthur Miller, and Edward Albee achieved international acclaim for their dramas of personal maladjustment. One of the leading dramatists writing in the French language was the Irishman Samuel Beckett, whose existentialist drama *Waiting for Godot* was one of the first experiments in what has been called the "theater of the absurd."

Poetry suffered an eclipse in the clouded, uncertain decades after Hiroshima, in spite of the gesture by young President John F. Kennedy in asking the venerable Robert Frost to read from his poems at the 1961 inauguration. The ebullient Welshman, Dylan Thomas, who died prematurely in 1953, made a valiant effort to restore lyricism to poetry. The contributions of non-Europeans to world literature began to receive recognition after World War II. In 1945 Gabriela Mistral, of Chile, became the first Latin American to receive a Nobel Prize for literature. Her left-leaning countryman, Pablo Neruda, also received international recognition for his verse. In 1968 a Japanese author, Yasunari Yawabata, became the first Oriental to receive a Nobel Prize for literature. The Anglo-Indian, Rabindranath Tagore, had received a Nobel Prize as early as 1913, but the Nobel Prize commission was slow to bestow its accolades on writers in non-European languages.

PHILOSOPHY IN AN AGE OF CRISIS

The philosophical outlook of any age usually reflects issues of vital concern to the public, especially in periods of political and social upheaval or crisis. In the twentieth century academic or professional philosophers, nominally engaged in the abstract pursuit of truth, beauty, and goodness, could not avoid dealing with the concrete issues of practical life. Moral and ethical questions fused with political, social, and economic problems. Even logic, the most abstract branch of philosophy, felt the impact of change in the external world. In addition to political and social turmoil, the new discoveries in science forced a reconsideration of accepted philosophical positions. Freudian psychology and the theory of relativity had already shaken the foundations of the rationalist, materialist philosophies of the nineteenth century. In 1927 the German physicist Werner Heisenberg added to the difficulties of those who still sought simple cause-effect relationships with his announcement of the principle of uncertainty, according to which it is impossible to determine simultaneously the position and velocity of a subatomic particle. It seemed that the world of nature was no more orderly or predictable than the world of man.

Two new philosophical movements grew up in response to the problems of the twentieth century. Logical positivism (later called logical empiricism to disassociate it from the positivism of the nineteenth century) was a radical form of empiricism that denied meaning to any proposition that was not subject to rigorous empirical verification. The logical positivists declared the whole of metaphysics and most of ethics and aesthetics to be meaningless. Their denial of meaning to large parts of human experience represented one form of the philosophy of despair.

The other form of the philosophy of despair was existentialism, which had certain affinities with logical positivism but reached fundamentally different conclusions. Existentialists did not possess a single coherent logical structure for their philosophy, but all agreed that man gains a knowledge of reality not by detached reason or reflection but by immediate experience, with the emphasis on the inner personal character of experience. Existentialism was thus fundamentally antirational, even anti-intellectual in some of its manifestations. It was symptomatic of the revolt against reason that characterized the first half of the twentieth century. The existentialists claimed as forerunners Nietzsche and the nineteenth-century Danish theologian Sören Kierkegaard. Among their outstanding exponents — who, however, did not in any sense form a school — in addition to Sartre, were Martin Heidegger of Germany, Nikolai Berdyaev, a Russian exile, and José Ortega y Gasset of Spain.

Not all philosophers reached such pessimistic conclusions. The rationalist, analytical philosophy of Bertrand Russell and the pragmatists occupied a middle ground between the extreme skepticism of the logical positivists, on the one hand, and the despair of the existentialists, on the other. The rationalism of St. Thomas Aquinas experienced a modern revival in the movement known as neo-Thomism. Étienne Gilson and Jacques Maritain, both French Catholic laymen, did much to restore metaphysics as a respectable branch of philosophy.

THEOLOGY AND THE CHURCHES

The new philosophical movements had important implications for theology. The logical positivists thought they had banished theology as a serious intellectual subject, but existentialism proved quite adaptable to theological ends, even though many of its exponents were avowed atheists. Kierkegaard, its putative founder, was a Protestant theologian; and Paul Tillich, also a Protestant theologian, proved to be one of its more lucid expositors. According to Tillich, Christ was the prototype of existential man who solved the dilemma of existence by obedience to God. Not all Protestant churches accept existentialism, however. Karl Barth, a Swiss and perhaps the most noted Protestant theologian of the twentieth century, preached a pessimistic neofundamentalism. According to Barth, God cannot be apprehended by reason or attained by human endeavor; men are miserable sinful creatures wholly at His mercy. Roman Catholicism eschewed modernism in philosophy but benefited from the revival of Thomist philosophy, which facilitated the reconciliation of Church dogma with modern science.

Organizational developments within the churches were at least as important as theological movements. At the beginning of the century the Roman Catholic Church was embroiled in difficulties with several countries over church-state relations. As the most international – or supranational – of Christian churches, it also found itself in a particularly difficult position during both World Wars. The pope made fitful attempts to play the role of peacemaker but without success. All denominations suffered from increasing urbanization and the anonymity of large cities. Church membership continued to grow, but it is doubtful that the number of active communicants kept pace with the growth of population. To counteract the demoralizing influence of cities, the churches instituted social action programs specifically aimed at urban workers, but their efforts were only moderately successful.

One of the most important developments in religious organization was the ecumenical movement. Several Protestant sects that had earlier splintered rejoined one another, and negotiations took place for the eventual merging of several of the larger denominations. In 1948 the World Council of Churches brought together representatives of the Anglican, Orthodox, and most Protestant churches in an organization to promote interfaith and international cooperation. The Roman Catholic Church at first held aloof from the ecumenical movement, but under Popes John XXIII (1958–1963) and his successor Paul VI it instituted a number of significant reforms. It invited other denominations to send observers to the Second Ecumenical Council of the Vatican (1962–1965), hailed as one of the most important gatherings of Roman Catholic prelates since the Council of Trent in the sixteenth century. The council streamlined the organization of the Roman Catholic Church, made it more democratic, and allowed the introduction of the language of the people into the liturgy in place of the traditional Latin. On the important subject of birth control, however, Pope Paul overruled the recommendation of his own commission to restudy the subject and reaffirmed the Church's traditional opposition to artificial contraception, thereby setting off a storm of opposition within the Church and criticism from outside.

SOCIAL AND POLITICAL THOUGHT

Most of the social sciences were still in their infancy at the beginning of the twentieth century. The most authoritative pronouncements on social questions came from statesmen, theologians, philosophers, journalists, and businessmen. Universities then began to give specialized professional training in the various social science disciplines. At first the training followed the pattern already established in history, philosophy, and other humanistic disciplines, but gradually it took on a more scientific character, including an emphasis on precise measurement, the testing of hypotheses, and the use of mathematics. Until the 1930's professional and social scientists found employment chiefly as university professors. After the brilliant career of John Maynard Keynes (1883–1946) and the so-called Keynesian Revolution, economists were increasingly called on to serve in government and business. During and after World War II extra-academic employment opened up for other social scientists in a variety of occupations. In the second half of the twentieth century the most authoritative pronouncements on social questions still came from statesmen (usually ghost-written by professional advisers) and occasionally from journalists and businessmen, but the theologians and philosophers were replaced by professional social scientists – although the general public sometimes had difficulty in distinguishing the categories.

The functions of government, with its manifold interferences in the lives of individuals, grew enormously in the twentieth century in democratic nations as well as in authoritarian ones. The twentieth century generally acknowledged that governments must accept responsibilities today that in the nineteenth century were left to private individuals. In this respect the nineteenth century appears to be an aberration; the twentieth is more in line with the practice of earlier centuries, but with the difference that in the past governments were looked upon as the masters of men, whereas now they are proclaimed on both sides of the Iron Curtain as their servants. For democratic nations this growth in the participation of government in everyday life posed several dilemmas. In view of the complexities of the modern world and the findings of social science concerning the role of irrationality in human behavior, is it really possible for men to govern themselves? Some political scientists maintain that the democratic process is a delusion, that in fact all key decisions are made by a relatively small group of individuals, not all of whom are visible to the public or subject to democratic control. Voters, they say, are manipulated by the techniques of social psychology and mass communications and are given only the illusion of choice. Even less cynical students of society are obliged to recognize that modern social science has eroded the foundations of the contract theory of government, just as the events of the twentieth century brought about the decline of classical liberalism. One of the most excruciating dilemmas of twentieth century democratic thought is the role of the individual in mass society. Is it possible to preserve individual liberty and freedom from the tyranny of mass conformity as well as from the tyranny of omnipotent government?

In the fifteenth and sixteenth centuries the greater power and resources of such nation-states as France, Spain, and England rendered the small medieval city-states obsolete. In the twentieth century the power and resources of such superstates as the United States, the Soviet Union, and potentially China and a possible "United States of Europe" have rendered the traditional nation-state obsolescent. The decline of the nation-states does not necessarily mean that they will cease to exist, for the ideology of nationalism is still so strong that the twentieth century has witnessed the proliferation of dozens of new nations. It does suggest, however, that new forms of international or supranational organization will have to be devised to overcome the limitations of existing national boundaries and to obtain the political, economic, and military advantages of superstates. A number of regional organizations, such as the European Economic Community, the Organization of African Unity, and the Organization of American States, are potential embryos of new superstates.

In a sense even the superstates are already obsolescent, because the development of weaponry since World War II has given the two existing superstates the ability to inflict irreparable damage on each other in the event of war, regardless of which struck first. For the time being this massive retaliatory power serves as a deterrent to all-out war, but as new superstates arise, the situation will not remain stable. World government is a conceivable alternative, although in the eighth decade of the twentieth century there are few visible signs that it is imminent. Nevertheless, any reasonably informed person can infer that the system of international relations that resulted from the breakdown of the nineteenth-century balance-of-power concept is transitory at best — calamitous at worst.

EPILOGUE: THE EMERGENCE OF WORLD CIVILIZATION

Although serious historians resist, with good reason, the temptation to prophesy the future, it is a part of their responsibility to identify the features of the past that have helped to shape the present and which, by implication, will also affect the future. In the final third of the twentieth century it is possible to identify at least some of the basic features of the world civilization that has begun to emerge during the last half-century.

To say that Western civilization is being superseded does not imply that Western nations or Western society will cease to exist. Not only will Western nations continue to exist, but many elements of their civilization will be incorporated in the new. For the peoples of the rest of the world the outstanding feature of Western civilization has been its technology; this is what destroyed their own civilizations, and this is what they have been able to absorb from the West. The technological basis of the civilization of the future will grow out of the technology of the West. Whether non-Western peoples will also be able to take over and absorb the rational spirit that underlay the development of that technology – indeed, whether the lineal heirs of the West will be able to retain that spirit – is questionable. Equally in doubt is the ability of the generations to come, Western and non-Western alike, to retain the belief in freedom, rooted in respect for the individual human personality, which has been one of the basic values of Western civilization. Although many non-Western nations have superficially adopted the political forms of the West it is still too soon to know if those forms, and the values they embody, will take root and grow.

The influence of non-Western traditions on global civilization lies chiefly in the field of nonmaterial culture. Oriental and African art forms have already had a significant influence on Western art, and it is likely that the art of the future will blend both traditions even more thoroughly as well as bring forth completely new themes and forms of expression. Oriental religions have influenced religious thought and expression in the contemporary West. Indeed, the two predominant religious traditions of the West, Judaism and Christianity, themselves originated in the Orient.

The creation of a new civilization is not a matter of decades or even generations. In the case of Western civilization fully five centuries elapsed after the collapse of classical civilization before the distinctive traditions of its successor became firmly established. Nor is civilization a static concept, as the history of the Western world in the last thousand years makes abundantly clear. Thus, time will be an essential ingredient in the emergence of a global civilization. It may be that modern technology, especially the technology of communications, which has speeded up every aspect of modern life, will also hasten the process of cultural assimilation and amalgamation. Yet modern technology, together with the social tensions and political strains that inevitably accompany cultural change, also poses a serious threat to the future of terrestrial civilization. The outcome cannot be predicted, but barring a nuclear holocaust that would reduce all the works of man to heaps of radioactive ashes, historians of the future will look back to the twentieth century for the origins of world civilization.

Chronology

Date	*Europe and Europe Overseas*	*Western Europe*	*Central Europe*	*Borderlands Europe*	*Arts, Letters, and Science*
1816	wars for Latin American liberation				
1817		English Coercion Acts	Wartburg Festival		
1818	Congress of Aix-la-Chapelle				Hegel at University of Berlin
1819		Peterloo massacre	Carlsbad Decrees		
1820	Congress of Troppau	French "Ultras" Spanish and Portuguese revolutions	Italian revolutions (1820–21)		
1821	Congress of Laibach			Greeks revolt against Turks	
1823	Monroe Doctrine promulgated				
1824		Charles X (1824–30)			Ranke's *Zur Kritik*
1825	Latin American independence achieved			Decembrist Revolution Nicholas I (1825–55)	Stephenson's locomotive
1829		Catholic emancipation in Britain		Treaty of Adrianople	
1830	French occupy Algeria	July Monarchy Belgian independence	Italian revolutions (1830–32)	Polish revolution	Berlioz's "Symphonie Fantastique"
1831				Mohamed Ali's Syrian coup	Hugo's *Notre Dame de Paris*
1832		British Parliamentary Reform Act	Metternich's Six Acts Young Italy		
1833	Abolition of slavery in British empire	Carlist War in Spain		Official Nationality in Russia	

1834		Owen's Grand National Union	Zollverein		
1835		municipal reform in Britain			
1837	Durham Report (Canada)	Victoria (1837–1901)			
1838	regular trans-Atlantic steam service established	Chartism			Blanc's *Organization of Labor*
1839	Opium War (1839–42)				Stendhal's *Charterhouse of Parma*
1840	Union Act unites Canada first settlement of New Zealand			"Tanzimat" reform begins	
1841					List's *National System*
1846		British Corn Law Repeal	Pope Pius IX (Pio Nono) (1846–78)		
1847		Second French Republic			
1848	Year of Revolution				Mill's *Political Economy* Marx's *Communist Manifesto*
1849	Year of Reaction				
1850	Australia becomes self-governing Taiping Rebellion (1850–64)		Olmütz Humiliation		Courbet and realism in painting
1851		Amalgamated Society of Engineers		Christian shrine dispute in Holy Land	Crystal Palace Exhibition, London
1852		Napoleon III's Second Empire	Bach System Cavour (1852–61)		Comte's *Positivist Catechism*
1853	Crimean War				Gobineau's *Inequality of Human Races*
1854	Commodore Perry opens Japan				

Date	*Europe and Europe Overseas*	*Western Europe*	*Central Europe*	*Borderlands Europe*	*Arts, Letters, and Science*
1855				Alexander II (1855–81)	Spencer's *Principles of Psychology*
1856	Paris Peace Conference				
1857	Sepoy Mutiny in India				Flaubert's *Madame Bovary* invention of Bessemer steel process
1858	French occupy Saigon		Meeting at Plombieres		
1859			War of Italian Unification		Darwin's *Origin of Species*
1860		Napoleon III's "Liberal Empire"	Treaty of Turin		
1861	American Civil War (1861–65)		William I (1861–88) Kingdom of Italy proclaimed	emancipation of Russian serfs	
1862			Bismarck (1862–90)		Turgenev's *Fathers and Sons*
1863	Maximilian becomes emperor of Mexico			Polish rebellion	Renan's *Life of Jesus*
1864	Syllabus of Errors	First Communist International	Danish War	Zemstvos reforms in Russia	
1865					Tolstoi's *War and Peace*
1866			Seven Weeks' War Italy annexes Venetia		Dostoevski's *Crime and Punishment*
1867	Canadian Confederation	British Reform Act	North German Confederation Dual Monarchy		Marx's *Capital*
1868	Meiji Restoration Japan (1868–1912)	Gladstone vs. Disreali Spanish Revolution			
1869	Suez Canal opened Vatican Council				

1870		Franco-Prussian War Third French Republic	German Empire Italy annexes Rome		
1871		Paris Commune	Kulturkampf (1871–83) Second Reich (1871–1918)		
1872		British secret ballot act			
1873					Maxwell's *Electricity and Magnetism*
1874		Spanish Bourbons restored Disraeli (1874–80)		Russian army reform	
1875		Organic Laws	German Social Democratic Party		
1876	Belgian Congo Company incorporated			Turkish rebellion	
1877	Russo-Turkish War (1877–78)				
1878	Congress of Berlin	British Trades Union Congress	Bismarck outlaws Social Democratic Party		
1879			Dual Alliance (1879–1918) liberalization begins in Austrian Empire		
1880		workmen's compensation (Britain)			Zola's *Roman Experimental*
1881	Alliance of Three Emperors (1881–87) French in Tunis			Alexander III (1881–94)	
1882	Triple Alliance British occupy Egypt				
1883	German colonial expansion				

Date	*Europe and Europe Overseas*	*Western Europe*	*Central Europe*	*Borderlands Europe*	*Arts, Letters, and Science*
1884	Berlin Conference	British Third Reform Act			Spencer's *Man Versus the State*
1885	Spanish in Rio de Oro British in Nigeria			Anti-Semitic pogroms in Russia	"Fin de Siecle" begins
1886					Hertz demonstrates electromagnetic waves
1887	Reinsurance Treaty				Michelson and Morley experiment
1888		Boulanger challenge in France	Kaiser William II (1888–1918)		Strindberg's *Miss Julia*
1889		Second Communist International			
1890	Leo XIII's "Rerum Novarum"				
1891			German Social Democratic revolutionary platform	Trans-Siberian railway begun	
1892	Franco-Russian Alliance			Witte's industrialization	Lorentz posits electrons
1893		defeat of Gladstone's Irish home rule			
1894	Berlin Conference	Dreyfus Case in France (1894–1906)		Nicholas II (1894–1917)	Durkheim's *Rules of Sociological Method*
1895		French General Confederation of Labor			Roentgen discovers X-Rays
1896	Jameson Raid Italians defeated in Ethiopia				
1897	Germans occupy Kiao-Chow				
1898	Spanish-American War Fashoda Crisis				

1899	Boer War Open Door Policy for China				Freud's *Interpretation of Dreams*
1900	Boxer Rebellion (1900–01)		Geman fleet expansion		Planck posits quantum theory
1902	British-Japanese Alliance	British Labor Party founded			Pareto's *Social Systems*
1903	Belgian Congo scandal			Bolshevik-Menshivik split	
1904	Russo-Japanese War Anglo-French Entente		Italian general strike		Chekhov's *Cherry Orchard*
1905	First Morroccan Crisis	separation of church and state in France	Schlieffen strategy drafted	Russian Revolution	Einstein's special theory of relativity
1906		British Liberal reform era (1906–11)		Duma	
1907	Anglo-Russian entente				
1908	Second Moroccan Crisis		Austria annexes Bosnia and Herzegovina "Giolittism" in Italy	Revolt of the Young Turks	
1909		Lloyd George's social reforms			Peary reaches North Pole
1911	*Panther* Crisis Italy occupies Tripoli Third Moroccan Crisis	British Parliament Bill		assassination of Stolypin	
1912	Sun Yat-Sen's revolution in China	Italian electoral reform	Socialist election victory in Germany	First Balkan War (1912–13)	
1913		defeat of Home Rule for Ireland		Second Balkan War	Stravinsky's "Sacre du Printemps"
1914	World War I (1914–19)		Ancona riots, Italy	assassination of Austrian heir in Sarajevo	Gide's *Caves du Vatican*
1915	stalemate on Western Front				Einstein's general theory of relativity

Date	Europe and Europe Overseas	Western Europe	Central Europe	Borderlands Europe	Arts, Letters, and Science
1916	battle of Verdun battle of Somme battle of Jutland battle of Trentino	Lloyd George's cabinet		murder of Rasputin	Lenin's *Imperialism* Joyce's *Ulysses*
1917	U.S. enters war, Russia exits	Clemenceau (1917–20)	German electoral reform Orlando (1917–19)	Russian Revolutions Lenin (1917–24)	
1918	armistice		Rome Congress of Oppressed Nationalities	Treaty of Brest-Litovsk	Spengler's *Decline of the West*
1919	Peace of Paris (Treaty of Versailles)		Fascist party formed Weimar Republic Nazis founded	White War allied intervention	
1920	League of Nations established		Czechoslovakian constitution	victory of the Red armies	Gropius founds Bauhaus
1921		Irish independence		NEP	
1922	Genoa Conference		destructive inflation in Germany Mussolini (1922–45) Mussolini's "March on Rome"	USSR created Kemel Ataturk's revolt	
1923			occupation of the Rhur Munich *putsch*	Stalin (1923–53)	
1924	Dawes Plan for reparations	first British Labor government			
1925	Locarno Conference		Hindenburg elected German president		
1926	Germany admitted to League	British general strike		Pilsudski's coup in Poland	Klee founds Blue Four movement
1928	Kellogg-Briand Peace Pact			First Five Year Plan	

1929	Great Depression begins		Lateran Treaties	destruction of the kulaks	
1930	London Naval Conference				Gasset's *Revolt of the Masses*
1931	Japan invades Manchuria	Spanish Republic Statute of Westminister			
1932			Nazi election success		
1933	Japan and Germany leave League		Nazi coup Hitler (1933–45)	U.S. recognizes Soviet Russia	
1934	Russia joins League	Stavisky riots in France	Nazi blood purge	Russian Great Purge begins	
1935	Italy invades Ethiopia	Popular Front formed in France	Saar Plebescite Nazi laws vs. Jews	Franco-Russian Alliance	
1936	Germany occupies Rhineland	Spanish Civil War abdication of Edward VIII	Berlin-Rome Axis	new Russian constitution	
1937		fall of Blum's government			
1938	Anschluss Munich Agreements			Arab-Jewish strife in Palestine	
1939	World War II (1939–45)		Germany annexes Czechoslovakia	German-Russian Pact Russo-Finnish War (1939–40)	
1940	Fall of France Battle of Britain	Churchill (1940–45)			penicillin applied
1941	Germany invades Russia Japan attacks Pearl Harbor			siege of Leningrad	
1942	battle of Midway			siege of Stalingrad	Fermi's nuclear reaction
1943	North African campaign		overthrow of Mussolini		

Date	*Europe and Europe Overseas*	*Western Europe*	*Central Europe*	*Borderlands Europe*	*Arts, Letters, and Science*
1944	D-Day and the Russian drive west				
1945	United Nations formed	British Labor government (1945–51)	occupation of Germany		Atomic bomb dropped
1946	Truman Doctrine Churchill's "Iron Curtain" speech	Fourth French Republic	Italian republic proclaimed Nürnberg Trials of war criminals	Fourth Five Year Plan	
1947	Marshall Plan Benelux established	Communist strikes in France and Italy		Cominform established	
1948	Berlin blockade and airlift	Britain gives India independence	Communist coup in Czechoslovakia	Tito breaks with Soviet Russia Israeli-Arab conflict	World Health Organization established
1949	NATO established Chinese Communists victorious		German Federal Republic (West Germany) established	COMECON	
1950	Korean War (1950–53)				
1951	beginning of African independence	Conservatives form British government			
1952		Elizabeth II (1952–)			
1953			East Germans riot vs. Russia		
1954	French defeated in Indo-China			Khrushchev (1954–64)	
1955	Bandung Afro-Asian Conference First Summit Conference		Austrian and German peace treaties	Warsaw Pact	Ehrenburg's "The Thaw"
1956	Suez War		Hungarian Revolution	Twentieth Soviet Party Conference	

1957		Common Market European Free Trade Association			Pasternak's *Dr. Zhivago* Sputnik I
1958		De Gaulle forms Fifth French Republic	Pope John XXIII (1958–63)		
1959				Russian-Chinese tension Cyprus independent	
1960	U-2 incident Second Summit cancelled	De Gaulle's economic reforms			
1961			Berlin Wall erected Vatican Council (1962–65)		
1962	Chinese threaten India		Pope Paul VI (1963–)	Russian-Chinese split	
1963	Nuclear disarmament treaty	De Gaulle vetoes Britain's entrance into Common Market			
1964	U.S. begins buildup in Vietnam				
1965					discovery of quasars
1967		Spanish student disturbances		Israeli-Arab "Six Day" War	
1968	Paris peace talks begin	Paris student riots	Russian repression of Czechoslovakian liberalization		
1969		De Gaulle resigns			United States lands men on moon

A Reading List

This reading list is designed to provide the interested student with suggestions for further reading and the titles of books with which he can begin research for course papers and independent work. With these purposes in mind we have restricted our recommendations to books in English. Most of the works listed contain bibliographical information that will provide the student with detailed assistance in further reading or research in the subject that interests him.

An asterisk before the title indicates that the book is available in a paperback edition.

BIBLIOGRAPHIES

The titles and authors of important works in every field of historical research, often with valuable critical comments, are contained in G. M. Dutcher and others, *A Guide to Historical Literature* (1931) and *The American Historical Association's Guide to Historical Literature* (1961). The annual *International Bibliography of the Historical Sciences* should also be consulted. There are many specialized bibliographies. Their titles can be found in T. Besterman, *A World Bibliography of Bibliographies* (4 vols., 1955–56), and C. M. Winchell, *Guide to Reference Books* (7th ed., 1951).

In 1957 the Service Center for Teachers of History of the American Historical Association began the publication of a series of pamphlets, each written by a specialist, that present concise summaries of publications reflecting recent research and new interpretations in a particular field of history. Historical periodicals, such as the *American Historical Review,* the *Journal of Modern History, Speculum,* and many others, contain book reviews and lists of new books and recently published articles.

REFERENCE WORKS

Useful reference works include W. L. Langer, ed., *An Encyclopedia of World History* (4th ed., 1968), a detailed collection of important events and dates from the beginning of recorded history; *The Columbia Encyclopedia* (3rd ed., 1963), the best of the one-volume encyclopedias. W. R. Shepherd, *Historical Atlas* (new ed., 1965) and R. R. Palmer, ed., *Atlas of World History* (1957) are helpful aids, as is *Lippincott's Pronouncing Gazetteer* (1962). Most important nations have their own multi-volume biographical dictionaries; in English the major ones are the *Dictionary of National Biography* (1885–1960) for Great Britain and the *Dictionary of American Biography* (1928–36).

The *Encyclopaedia Britannica* is still the most useful of the general encyclopedias; regrettably, its quality has declined in recent years. The *Encyclopedia of the Social Sciences* (1930–35) is still useful, but the new *International Encyclopedia of the Social Sciences* (1968) is more up to date. The *New Catholic Encyclopaedia,* the *Jewish Encyclopedia,* the *Encyclopedia of Philosophy* (1967) and the *Encyclopaedia of Islam* are among the most valuable of the specialized encyclopedias.

GENERAL HISTORIES

Historians have often joined together to write comprehensive histories that are published either as collaborative volumes, with each chapter written by a different author, or as individual volumes each by a single author. These works are of an uneven quality. The best known of the collaborative works in English are *The Cambridge Ancient History* (8 vols., 1923–39), *The Cambridge Mediaeval History* (8 vols., 1911–36), *The Cambridge Modern History* (13 vols., 1902–12), *The New Cambridge Modern History* (1957–), and *The Cambridge Economic History of Europe* (1941–). The last two are still incomplete. W. L. Langer is editing a series called *The Rise of Modern Europe,* in which each volume is written by a single historian. Nearly all of the projected twenty volumes have appeared. Many of them are listed in the following pages. E. Eyre, ed., *European Civilization, Its Origin and Development* (7 vols., 1934–39), is an often overlooked but useful collaborative work.

There are many general histories, in both single and multi-volume form, of the countries and of the institutions, ideas, economic life, and culture discussed in this book. A number of them are mentioned in the reading lists for the individual chapters. A useful beginning guide to general histories with excellent critical comments is provided in M. Faisler, *Key to the Past* (3rd ed., 1965), a publication of the Service Center for Teachers of History.

ROMANTICISM AND REACTION CHAPTER ONE

THE VIENNA SETTLEMENT AND THE CONCERT OF EUROPE

* F. B. Artz, *Reaction and Revolution, 1814–1832* (1934, 1950). A broad general survey of all aspects of the period; Rise of Modern Europe Series.

C. J. Bartlett, *Castlereagh* (1967). A biography of the man as well as a study of his policies.

* G. Ferrero, *The Reconstruction of Europe: Talleyrand and the Congress of Vienna, 1814–1815* (1941). An authoritative work by an Italian scholar.

H. A. Kissinger, *A World Restored: Metternich, Castlereagh and the Problems of Peace, 1812–1822* (1957). A study by a political scientist.

A. A. Lobanov-Rostovsky, *Russia and Europe, 1789–1825* (1947). Contains an account of Alexander I and his relations with the western powers.

G. de Bertier de Sauvigny, *France and the European Alliance, 1816–1821* (1958). A masterly study of the reintegration of France in the Concert of Europe.

* L. C. B. Seaman, *From Vienna to Versailles* (1955). A lively diplomatic history especially useful for the Congress system and its sequels.

C. K. Webster, *The Congress of Vienna, 1814–1815* (1934, 1963). A brief, classic treatment by one of the wisest of modern historians. Originally written as background material for the plenipotentiaries at the Peace of Paris, 1919.

ROMANTICISM IN LITERATURE AND THE ARTS

* J. Barzun, *Berlioz and the Romantic Century* (2 vols., 1950). A detailed account of the most representative composer of the romantic period.

———, *Romanticism and the Modern Ego* (1943). Assesses the significance of romanticism for our own times.

* M. Berger, ed., *Madame de Staël on Politics, Literature and National Character* (1964). Selected writings of one of the central figures of the romantic movement.

K. Clark, *The Gothic Revival* (2nd ed., 1950). Shows the Neo-Gothic influence in England.

A. Einstein, *Music in the Romantic Era* (1947). A general survey by one of the leading historians of music.

J. C. Herold, *Mistress to an Age* (1958). A readable, fascinating biography of Madame de Staël.

T. H. von Laue, *Leopold Ranke, the Formative Years* (1950). A critique of the founder of "scientific" history.

* E. Newton, *Romantic Rebellion* (1962). A fresh treatment of romantic art.

ROMANTICISM IN PHILOSOPHY, POLITICS, AND RELIGION

C. C. Brinton, *English Political Thought in the Nineteenth Century* (2nd ed., 1949). Supersedes his earlier *Political Ideas of the English Romanticists* (1926).

* G. W. F. Hegel (R. S. Hartman, ed. and transl.), *Reason in History. A General Introduction to the Philosophy of History* (1962). Selections from the pen of the German idealist philosopher.

H. Kohn, *The Mind of Germany* (1960). An intellectual history of modern Germany concentrating on the romantic, liberal, and nationalist tendencies.

H. Marcuse, *Reason and Revolution: Hegel and the Rise of Social Theory* (1954). A study in the relationships of ideas and politics by an influential modern philosopher.

C. S. Phillips, *The Church in France, 1789–1848* (1929). A sympathetic account of the revival of the power of the Catholic Church.

H. S. Reiss, *The Political Thought of the German Romantics* (1955).

R. Soltau, *French Political Thought of the Nineteenth Century* (1931). Contains chapters on the writers of the romantic era.

J. L. Talmon, *Political Messianism: The Romantic Phase* (1960). A provocative interpretation of the origins of modern totalitarian movements.

P. Viereck, *Conservatism Revisited: the Revolt against Revolt, 1815–1949* (1949). Contains a sympathetic account of Metternich and his conservative contemporaries.

E. L. Woodward, *Three Studies in European Conservatism* (1929). An incisive analysis of Metternich, Guizot, and the Catholic Church.

RESTORATION POLITICS

A. Cecil, *Metternich, 1773–1859: A Study of His Period and Personality* (3rd ed., 1947). By a leading British biographer.

* E. Halevy, *England in 1815* (2nd ed., 1949). Vol. I of the celebrated French author's *History of the English People in the Nineteenth Century.*

N. E. Hudson, *Ultra-royalism and the French Restoration* (1936). A detailed study of French conservatism.

* A. J. May, *The Age of Metternich, 1814–1848* (1933). A useful brief introduction.

* L. Namier, *Vanished Supremacies* (1958). Selected essays on Talleyrand, Metternich, and related subjects by one of the most distinguished modern historians.

M. Raeff, *Michael Speransky, Statesman of Imperial Russia, 1772–1839* (1957). Biography of one of the chief ministers of Alexander I and Nicholas I.

D. Read, *Peterloo: The Massacre and Its Background* (1958).

W. Simon, *The Future of the Prussian Reform Movement, 1807–1819* (1955). Details the resurgence of conservatism.

L. I. Strankhovsky, *Alexander I of Russia* (1947).

R. J. White, *Waterloo to Peterloo* (1957).

THE RISING TIDE OF REVOLUTION CHAPTER TWO

REVOLUTIONARY CURRENTS: LIBERALISM AND NATIONALISM

G. Barany, *Stephen Széchenу and the Awakening of Hungarian Nationalism, 1791–1841* (1968). Outstanding study of Hungary's political, social, and economic evolution in the early nineteenth century.

* L. T. Hobhouse, *Liberalism* (1911). An early classic on English liberalism.

* H. Kohn, *The Idea of Nationalism: A Study in its Origins and Background* (1944). Traces the early development of nationalism. See also his *Mind of Germany* (1960).

L. Krieger, *The German Idea of Freedom* (1957). Discusses the dilemma of German intellectuals concerning liberalism and nationalism.

H. J. Laski, *The Rise of Liberalism* (1936, 1948). A provocative interpretation by a distinguished British socialist.

K. R. Minogue, *Nationalism* (1967). A stimulating brief treatment of nationalism as a political ideology.

* G. de Ruggiero, *The History of European Liberalism* (1927). A standard account by an Italian liberal.

* B. C. Shafer, *Nationalism: Myth and Reality* (1955). A clear, modern statement.

REVOLUTION AND SELF-GOVERNMENT IN THE AMERICAS

J. B. Brebner, *North Atlantic Triangle* (1945). A charmingly written account of the relationships of the United States, Canada, and Great Britain.

J. L. Morison, *British Supremacy and Canadian Self-government, 1839–54* (1919). Old but valuable.

* D. Perkins, *Hands Off! A History of the Monroe Doctrine* (rev. ed., 1963). The authoritative work on its subject.

F. Thistlethwaite, *The Anglo-American Connection in the Early Nineteenth Century* (1959). Also appears as * *America and the Atlantic Community, 1790–1850.* Lucid, elegant interpretation.

* A. de Tocqueville, *Democracy in America* (1835). There are numerous editions of this classic.

J. B. Trend, *Bolivar and the Independence of Spanish America* (1948). A good introduction.

F. J. Turner, *The United States, 1830–1850* (1935). By the author of *The Frontier in American History* (1920).

C. K. Webster, *Britain and the Independence of Latin America, 1812–1830* (1944). A standard work.

A. P. Whittaker, *The United States and the Independence of Latin America* (1941). An authoritative study.

ROMANTIC REVOLUTION, 1820–1829

R. Carr. *Spain, 1808–1939* (1966). The most recent general history; the early chapters deal with Ferdinand VII and the revolution.

G. T. Romani, *The Neopolitan Revolution of 1820–1821* (1950).

R. H. Thomas, *Liberalism, Nationalism and the German Intellectuals, 1822–1847* (1952).

C. M. Woodhouse, *The Greek War of Independence* (1952). A short but well-written account.

M. Zetlin, *The Decembrists* (1958). The most recent study of the "first Russian revolution."

LIBERAL REVOLUTION, 1830–1834

G. L. Dickinson, *Revolution and Reaction in Modern France* (1892, 1927). A pioneering work, still worth reading. Covers the period from 1789 to 1871.

E. E. Y. Hales, *Mazzini and the Secret Societies* (1956). A sympathetic, fascinating account of the dean of Italian revolutionaries.

* E. J. Hobsbawm, *The Age of Revolution: Europe, 1789–1848* (1962). A general survey from the viewpoint of a western Marxist, with chapters on the revolutions of 1830.

E. Holt, *The Carlist Wars in Spain* (1967). Well-written popular account.

R. F. Leslie, *Polish Politics and the Revolution of November 1830* (1956).

H. van der Linden, *Belgium: The Making of a Nation* (1920).

J. Plamenatz, *The Revolutionary Movement in France, 1815–1871* (1952). To be compared with Dickinson.

PARLIAMENTARY REFORM IN GREAT BRITAIN

B. Blackburn, *Noble Lord: The Seventh Earl of Shaftesbury* (1949). A biographical study of an aristocratic reformer.

A. Briggs, *The Age of Improvement* (1959). An interesting, well-rounded modern view of English life and society in the first half of the nineteenth century, with good treatment of the Great Reform.

G. D. H. Cole, *The Life of William Cobbett* (1924). A readable biography of one of the most colorful figures of the age.

N. Gash, *Politics in the Age of Peel* (1953). A detailed study of the techniques of parliamentary representation.

* E. Halevy, *The Triumph of Reform, 1830–1841* (2nd ed., 1950).

G. M. Trevelyan, *Lord Grey of the Reform Bill* (2nd ed., 1929). Standard work by a master of British history.

G. Wallas, *The Life of Francis Place, 1771–1854* (new ed., 1925). The standard biography of the leader of the London Workingmen's Association.

THE REVOLUTION IN ECONOMIC LIFE CHAPTER THREE

THE RISE OF MODERN INDUSTRY

* T. S. Ashton, *The Industrial Revolution, 1760–1830* (1948, 1962). A brief, balanced, lucid introduction by a leading authority. Excellent bibliography of specialized studies.

J. H. Clapham, *An Economic History of Modern Britain,* vol. I [1820–1850] (2nd ed., 1930). Compendious; the standard reference.

* P. Deane, *The First Industrial Revolution* (1965). A survey based on the most recent scholarly studies.

P. Deane and W. A. Cole, *British Economic Growth, 1688–1950* (1962). Recent and authoritative; analytical rather than narrative.

* R. M. Hartwell, *The Causes of the Industrial Revolution in England* (1967). An informed selection of recent scholarly articles. Debates in Economic History Series.

* E. L. Jones, *Agriculture and Economic Growth in England, 1650–1815* (1967). Companion to the previous volume.

* E. E. Lampard, *Industrial Revolution: Interpretations and Perspectives* (1957). An exceedingly brief but highly illuminating survey. AHA Service Center Series.

* P. Mantoux, *The Industrial Revolution in the Eighteenth Century* (1906, 1937). The pioneering work in the field, embodying prodigious research and great erudition. Still basic to a sound understanding of the phenomenon.

* W. W. Rostow, *The Stages of Economic Growth* (1961). A stimulating but controversial interpretation of the process of economic growth.

A. P. Usher, *A History of Mechanical Inventions* (1929, 1954). Unsurpassed for profundity of scholarship and insight.

EARLY INDUSTRIALISM IN EUROPE AND AMERICA

R. Cameron, *France and the Economic Development of Europe, 1800–1914* (1961, abridged ed., *1966). The migration of French capital, entrepreneurs, and engineers; also legal and institutional influences.

* J. H. Clapham, *The Economic Development of France and Germany, 1815–1914* (1920, 1936). A standard survey, but badly out of date.

A. L. Dunham, *The Industrial Revolution in France, 1815–1848* (1955). A detailed, slightly old-fashioned treatment.

* C. M. Green, *Eli Whitney and the Birth of American Technology* (1956). A solid account of the origins of American industrial supremacy.

H. J. Habakkuk, *American and British Technology in the 19th Century* (1962). A scholarly attempt to explain the causes of American industrial supremacy.

W. O. Henderson, *Britain and Industrial Europe, 1750–1870* (1954). The migration of British entrepreneurs and technicians.

D. C. North, *The Economic Growth of the United States, 1790–1860* (1961). Presents a stimulating, controversial thesis on the causes of American growth.

SOCIAL ASPECTS OF EARLY INDUSTRIALISM

D. Bythell, *The Handloom Weavers* (1969). An authoritative study of the most publicized "victims" of the Industrial Revolution.

F. Engels, *The Condition of the Working Classes in England in 1844* (1st German ed., 1845). A Marxist classic.

J. L. and B. Hammond, *The Rise of Modern Industry* (1925, 1939). A general account of the industrial revolution, with emphasis on its alleged ill effects. Compare von Hayek.

* F. A. von Hayek, ed., *Capitalism and the Historians* (1954). A spirited attack on the alleged "left wing bias" of historians dealing with the industrial revolution.

N. J. Smelser, *Social Change in the Industrial Revolution* (1960). By a sociologist.

E. P. Thompson, *The Making of the English Working Class* (1964). A detailed study by a leftist of the emergence of the English proletariat between 1790 and 1830.

A. F. Weber, *The Growth of Cities in the Nineteenth Century* (1899, 1964). A classic.

ECONOMIC LIBERALISM, LAISSEZ-FAIRE, AND FREE TRADE

D. G. Barnes, *A History of the English Corn Laws* (1930). Still the standard work.

* H. Girvetz, *From Wealth to Welfare: The Evolution of Liberalism* (1963). Points out the changing meaning of the concept of liberalism in the twentieth century.

W. D. Grampp, *The Manchester School of Economics* (1960). A concise, scholarly account.

F. A. Haight, *A History of French Commercial Policies* (1941). Good chapters on the nineteenth century.

* R. Heilbroner, *The Worldly Philosophers* (1952). A readable, popular, and sound review of the ideas of the great economists.

W. O. Henderson, *The Zollverein* (1939, 1959). The standard account in English.

F. List, *The National System of Political Economy* (1844). An influential book in both Europe and America.

* C. Woodham-Smith, *The Great Hunger: Ireland, 1845–1849* (1962). A vivid, well-written history of the Irish famine.

REVOLUTION AT FLOODTIDE CHAPTER FOUR

CONTRASTING LIBERALISMS IN THE WEST

Louis Blanc, *The History of Ten Years, 1830–1840* (2 vols., 1844–45).

* J. F. C. Harrison, ed., *Society and Politics in England, 1780–1960* (1965). A selection of significant contemporary source materials with editorial comments.

* E. Halevy, *The Growth of Philosophic Radicalism* (rev. ed., 1949). A brilliant analysis of the doctrines of radical reform in England.

D. Johnson, *Guizot: Aspects of French History 1787–1874* (1963). A fresh evaluation of one of the major figures of the July Monarchy.

S. Mellon, *The Political Uses of History* (1958). An analysis of Guizot, Thiers, and other historians of the French Restoration period.

E. L. Woodward, *The Age of Reform, 1815–1870* (1938). Oxford History of England.

G. Wright, *France in Modern Times* (1960). Brilliant chapters on the July Monarchy and the revolution.

THE GROWTH OF SOCIAL PROTEST

* E. H. Carr, *Studies in Revolution* (1950). Essays on Socialist theorists and activists.

G. D. H. Cole, *Socialist Thought: The Forerunners, 1789–1850* (1953). Engagingly written by a master of the subject.

J. F. C. Harrison, *The Quest for a New Moral World* (1969). Robert Owen and the Owenites in Europe and America.

M. Hovell, *The Chartist Movement* (1918, 1925). An old but reliable account.

G. G. Iggers, *The Cult of Authority* (1958). A critical view of the Saint-Simonians.

F. E. Manuel, *The New World of Henri Saint-Simon* (1956). A sympathetic yet critical analysis.

* K. Marx and F. Engels, *The Communist Manifesto* (numerous eds.). Should be read by all educated persons.

R. Owen, *The Life of Robert Owen, by Himself* (1858). A delightful and informative if somewhat partisan autobiography.

E. Wilson, *To the Finland Station* (1953). An interesting study of socialism, utopianism, and Marxism by a master stylist.

THE REVOLUTION OF 1848 IN FRANCE

F. Fejto, ed., *The Opening of an Era: 1848* (1948). A reassessment of the revolutions on the occasion of their centenary.

A. de Lamartine, *History of the French Revolution of 1848* (transl., 1891). By a participant.

D. C. McKay, *The National Workshops* (1933). A well told story of an ill-fated experiment.

R. Postgate, *Story of a Year: 1848* (1955). A somewhat lighthearted view of the revolutions as seen from England.

* P. Robertson, *The Revolutions of 1848* (1952). An entertaining and scholarly comparative study of all the revolutionary movements of 1848.

F. A. Simpson, *The Rise of Louis Napoleon* (3rd ed., 1950). Traces the career of the future emperor from youth through the Second Republic.

OTHER REVOLUTIONARY MOVEMENTS

J. Blum, *Noble Landowners and Agriculture in Austria, 1815–1848* (1948). The background of the Austrian peasant emancipation.

T. S. Hamerow, *Restoration, Revolution, Reaction: Economics and Politics in Germany, 1815–1871* (1958). Centers on the revolutionary years.

B. King, *A History of Italian Unity* (2 vols., 1923). A standard work. Vol. I carries the story through 1849.

* Sir L. B. Namier, *1848: The Revolution of the Intellectuals* (1946). An attack upon German liberals, especially those in the Frankfurt Assembly.

R. Olden, *The History of Liberty in Germany* (1946). Covers the entire period 1807 to 1933.

R. J. Rath, *The Viennese Revolution of 1848* (1957). An able study.

C. Sproxton, *Palmerston and the Hungarian Revolution* (1919). A detailed, older study of England's foreign policy.

A. J. P. Taylor, *The Italian Problem in European Diplomacy* (1934).

THE REALIST REACTION CHAPTER FIVE

EBB TIDE OF REVOLUTION, 1848–1851

* R. C. Binkley, *Realism and Nationalism 1852–1871* (1935). A good general account of all aspects of the period; Rise of Modern Europe Series.

* K. Marx, *The Eighteenth Brumaire of Louis Napoleon* (several eds.). Marx on the coup d'état of 1851.

A. Schwarzenberg, *Prince Felix zu Schwarzenberg, Prime Minister of Austria 1848–1852* (1947). A somewhat partisan study of the man who turned back the Austrian revolutionaries.

F. A. Simpson, *Louis Napoleon and the Recovery of France, 1848–1856* (3rd ed., 1951). Readable and reliable.

REALISM IN LITERATURE AND THE ARTS

G. M. C. Brandes, *Main Currents in Nineteenth Century Literature* (6 vols., 1901–1905). Dated but still useful.

H. R. Hitchcock, *Architecture: Nineteenth and Twentieth Centuries* (1958). A very good survey.

M. Raynal, *The Nineteenth Century: Goya to Gauguin* (1951) and *History of Modern Painting* (3 vols., 1949–50). Thorough coverage, excellent illustrations.

J. C. Sloane, *French Painting Between the Past and Present: Artists, Critics and Traditions from 1848 to 1870* (1951).

THE PROGRESS OF SCIENCE

A. Einstein and L. Infield, *The Evolution of Physics* (1938). A brief, semi-popular account of the major theoretical developments from Newton to the twentieth century.
J. C. Greene, *The Death of Adam: Evolution and Its Impact on Western Thought* (1959). A wide-ranging, closely reasoned study, with superb illustrations.
G. Himmelfarb, *Darwin and the Darwinian Revolution* (1959).
J. T. Merz, *A History of European Thought in the Nineteenth Century* (4 vols., 1896–1914). An indispensable reference work for the history of science.
W. P. D. Wightman, *The Growth of Scientific Ideas* (1951). A good general survey.

THE WARFARE OF SCIENCE WITH THEOLOGY

* C. C. Gillespie, *Genesis and Geology* (1951). Discusses the relation of science to religious belief in England from 1790 to 1850.
E. E. Y. Hales, *Pio Nono, a Study in European Politics and Religion in the Nineteenth Century* (1954).
W. Irvine, *Apes, Angels, and Victorians* (1955). Amusing.
A. D. White, *A History of the Warfare of Science and Theology* (several eds., 1896). A classic.

MATERIALISM AND POSITIVISM

* W. Bagehot, *Physics and Politics* (numerous eds., 1873, 1956).
* ——— (N. S. Stevas, ed.), *Walter Bagehot's Historical and Political Essays* (1959). A selection from the writings of one of the leading social and political analysts of the period.
* J. Barzun, *Darwin, Marx, Wagner* (1941). An attempt to show the similarities of three outwardly dissimilar individuals.
M. R. Davie, ed., *Sumner Today* (1940). A series of essays by William Graham Sumner, a leading Social Darwinist.
* G. P. Gooch, *History and Historians in the Nineteenth Century* (2nd ed., 1952). Critical essays by a master historian.
* R. Hofstadter, *Social Darwinism in American Thought* (1955). A well written study.
Z. A. Jordan, *The Evolution of Dialectical Materialism* (1967). Heavy reading, but highly illuminating.
W. M. Simon, *European Positivism in the Nineteenth Century* (1963). Deals with the theoretical aspects.
H. Spencer, *Man Versus the State;* also numerous other books by this outstanding exponent of Social Darwinism.

THE POLITICS OF POWER, 1852–1871 CHAPTER SIX

NAPOLEON III AND THE SECOND FRENCH EMPIRE

T. A. B. Corley, *Democratic Despot: A Life of Napoleon III* (1961). Highlights the contradictory features of the man.

D. Pinkney, *Napoleon III and the Rebuilding of Paris* (1958). A sound scholarly study of an important but neglected topic.

J. S. Schapiro, *Liberalism and the Challenge of Fascism: Social Forces in England and France, 1815–1870* (1949). A stimulating work that assigns to Napoleon III the role of precursor of fascism.

J. M. Thompson, *Louis Napoleon and The Second Empire* (1954). Well written, sympathetic.

* R. L. Williams, *Gaslight and Shadow: The World of Napoleon III, 1851–1870* (1957). Favorable to Napoleon III.

* C. Woodham-Smith, *The Reason Why: An Exposé of the Charge of the Light Brigade* (1953). A fascinating account of the Crimean War, exposing the incompetence and inefficiency of the British Army.

T. Zeldin, *The Political System of Napoleon III* (1958). Makes the emperor resemble a modern politician more than an absolute monarch.

THE RISORGIMENTO AND ITALIAN UNITY

K. R. Greenfield, *Economics and Liberalism in the Risorgimento: A Study of Nationalism in Lombardy, 1814–1848* (1934, 1964). A pioneering study, recently republished.

R. Grew, *A Sterner Plan for Italian Unity: The Italian National Society and the Risorgimento* (1963). An authoritative recent treatment.

D. Mack Smith, *Garibaldi* (1956). The best biography in English.

A. J. Whyte, *The Political Life and Letters of Cavour, 1848–1861* (1930). A standard biography.

FOUNDATIONS OF GERMAN UNITY

C. W. Clark, *Franz Joseph and Bismarck: The Diplomacy of Austria Before the War of 1866* (1934).

W. E. Mosse, *The European Powers and the German Question* (1958). Comprehensive and well balanced.

O. Pflanze, *Bismarck and the Development of Germany: The Period of Unification, 1815–1871* (1963). A major recent study.

A. J. P. Taylor, *The Struggle for Mastery in Europe, 1848–1918* (1954). Diplomatic history revolving about Prussia-Germany.

THE CLASH OF POWER IN NORTH AMERICA

* D. W. Brogan, *Abraham Lincoln* (1963). A sensitive brief biography and judgment on an age by a noted British historian.

D. G. Creighton, *Dominion of the North, a History of Canada* (1944).

H. M. Hyde, *Maximilian of Mexico* (1948). A good story.

J. G. Randall, *Civil War and Reconstruction* (2nd ed., 1961). A good history of this controversial period in American historiography.

THE WATERSHED OF 1867–1871

M. Howard, *The Franco-Prussian War* (1961). Mainly military history.
R. H. Lord, *The Origins of the War of 1870* (1924). An older, standard account.
L. D. Steefel, *Bismarck, the Hohenzollern Candidacy, and the Origins of the Franco-German War of 1870* (1962).

THE SPREAD OF MODERN INDUSTRY CHAPTER SEVEN

TECHNOLOGICAL BASES OF THE NEW INDUSTRIALISM

T. K. Derry and T. I. Williams, *A Short History of Technology* (1961). An excellent one-volume work on technology.
L. F. Haber, *The Chemical Industry in the Nineteenth Century* (1958). Comprehensive, intelligible.
L. Mumford, *Technics and Civilization* (1933). A modern classic.
N. G. B. Pounds and W. N. Parker, *Coal and Steel in Western Europe* (1957). Covers the period from the mid-eighteenth to the mid-twentieth century; by a geographer and an economic historian.
C. Singer *et al., A History of Technology* (vols. 4 and 5, 1958, 1960). Primarily for reference.

BUSINESS ORGANIZATION AND THE WORLD MARKET SYSTEM

A. K. Cairncross, *Home and Foreign Investment, 1870–1913* (1953). A careful, detailed analysis.
H. Feis, *Europe, The World's Banker, 1870–1914* (1930). A basic work.
A. H. Imlah, *Economic Elements in the Pax Britannica, 1815–1914* (1958). Somewhat technical, but rewarding.
L. H. Jenks, *The Migration of British Capital to 1875* (1927). Sprightly and scholarly.
S. B. Saul, *Studies in British Overseas Trade 1870–1914* (1960).
B. Thomas, *Migration and Economic Growth* (1954). An analysis of British investment in and migration to America.

NATIONAL ECONOMIC STYLES

J. H. Clapham, *An Economic History of Modern Britain* (vols. 2 and 3, 1932–38).
S. B. Clough, *France: A History of National Economics, 1789–1939* (1939). Concentrates on economic policy.
* T. C. Cochran and W. Miller, *The Age of Enterprise: A Social History of Industrial America* (1942, 1961). A stimulating book.
* M. L. Hansen, *The Immigrant in American History* (1940). A landmark in its field.

C. P. Kindleberger, *Economic Growth in France and Britain, 1851–1950* (1963). Analytical rather than narrative and interestingly written.

G. Stolper *et al., The German Economy, 1870 to the Present* (1967). Best treatment in English.

T. Veblen, *Imperial Germany and the Industrial Revolution* (1919, 1939). Outdated facts but valuable interpretation.

ORGANIZED LABOR AND THE REVIVAL OF SOCIALISM

I. Berlin, *Karl Marx: His Life and Environment* (1948). Short but reliable.

E. Burns, *A Handbook of Marxism* (1935). A good introduction.

G. D. H. Cole, *Socialist Thought: Marxism and Anarchism, 1850–1880* (1954). Fundamental.

D. Footman, *Ferdinand Lassalle: Romantic Revolutionary* (1946). An interesting portrait of an early Socialist.

P. Gay, *The Dilemma of Democratic Socialism* (1952). A brilliant account of Bernstein's revisionism.

H. Goldberg, *The Life of Jean Jaurès* (1962). A monumental biography of the great French Socialist.

* P. Kropotkin, *Memoirs of a Revolutionist* (1896). Autobiography of an aristocratic Russian anarchist.

C. Landauer, *European Socialism* (2 vols., 1959). A comprehensive general study.

* G. Lichtheim, *Marxism: An Historical and Critical Study* (1961). Recent authoritative analysis.

V. R. Lorwin, *The French Labor Movement* (1954). Its historical chapters are unsurpassed in any language.

H. Pelling, *A History of British Trade Unionism* (1963). The most authoritative recent treatment.

DEMOCRATIC REFORM AND SOCIAL STRIFE, 1871–1914 CHAPTER EIGHT

THE TRIUMPH OF DEMOCRACY IN BRITAIN

J. C. Beckett, *A Short History of Ireland* (1952).

* A. Briggs, *Victorian People* (1955). Sketches of personalities of the period 1851 to 1867.

M. Cowling, *1867: Disraeli, Gladstone and Revolution; The Passing of the Second Reform Bill* (1967). Extremely detailed.

* E. Halevy, *Imperialism and the Rise of Labour, 1859–1905* (2nd ed., 1952). Vol. V of *History of the English People in the Nineteenth Century.*

* ———, *The Rule of Democracy, 1905–1914* (2nd ed., 1952). Vol. VI of *History of the English People in the Nineteenth Century.*

H. Pelling, *The Origins of the Labour Party* (1954). Authoritative.

* E. Wingfield-Stratford, *Those Earnest Victorians* (1930). Well written and entertaining.

* G. M. Young, *Victorian England: Portrait of an Age* (1954). A stimulating sketch of the period.

THE THIRD FRENCH REPUBLIC

G. Chapman, *The Dreyfus Case* (1955). A modern re-evaluation.

A. Horne, *The Fall of Paris* (1966). An exciting account of the siege of Paris and the Commune.

* K. Marx, *Class Struggles in France* (1872 and subsequent eds.). Marx's view of the Commune.

J. A. Scott, *Republican Ideas and the Liberal Tradition in France, 1870–1914* (1951).

P. Spencer, *The Politics of Belief in Nineteenth Century France* (1954). Deals with the role of the church.

* D. Thomson, *Democracy in France since 1870* (1946, 1964). An admirable synthesis.

THE SECOND GERMAN REICH

* G. A. Craig, *From Bismarck to Adenauer: Aspects of German Statecraft* (1958, 1964). Perceptive essays on statesmen and their problems.

* E. Eyck, *Bismarck and the German Empire* (1950). A short study by a noted liberal German historian.

A. Gerschenkron, *Bread and Democracy in Germany* (1943). A stimulating interpretation of German economic and political development.

V. L. Lidthe, *The Outlawed Party: Social Democracy in Germany 1878–1890* (1966). The best study in English of this critical period in the history of the party.

J. A. Nichols, *Germany after Bismarck* (1959).

THE LESSER STATES OF WESTERN EUROPE

E. Bonjour, H. S. Offler, and G. R. Potter, *A Short History of Modern Switzerland* (1952). Especially good on the nineteenth century.

R. Carr, *Spain, 1808–1939* (1966). Authoritative.

C. Seton-Watson, *Italy from Liberalism to Fascism, 1870–1925* (1967). A detailed sympathetic treatment of all aspects of Italian life, with emphasis on political history.

D. Verney, *Parliamentary Reform in Sweden, 1866–1921* (1957). Swedish democratic evolution was unusually calm.

THREE ARCHAIC EMPIRES CHAPTER NINE

RUSSIA IN THE NINETEENTH CENTURY

* J. Blum, *Lord and Peasant in Russia—from the 9th to the 19th century* (1961). The final chapters deal with the emancipation of the serfs.

* H. Kohn, ed., *The Mind of Modern Russia: Historical and Political Thought of Russia's Great Age* (1954). Selections from the great writers of the nineteenth century.

* W. E. Mosse, *Alexander II and the Modernization of Russia* (1962).

M. B. Petrovich, *The Emergence of Russian Pan-Slavism, 1856–1870* (1956). The definitive work in English.

W. Pinter, *Russian Economic Policy under Nicholas I* (1967). Analyzes the part played by governmental economic policy in the decline of Russia.

N. V. Riasanovsky, *A History of Russia* (1963). The best general account in English.

G. T. Robinson, *Rural Russia under the Old Regime* (1932, 1949). A survey of the changes brought about by the emancipation of the serfs.

* M. Rywkin, *Russia in Central Asia* (1964).

* H. Seton-Watson, *The Russian Empire, 1801–1917* (1967). Supersedes the author's *Decline of Imperial Russia, 1855–1914* (1952). An authoritative, readable history.

* A. Yarmolinsky, *Road to Revolution, A Century of Russian Radicalism* (1957, 1962).

AUSTRIA: THE MULTINATIONAL EMPIRE

* O. Jaszi, *The Dissolution of the Habsburg Monarchy* (1929). An older work, still valuable especially for its treatment of Hungary.

R. Kann, *The Multinational Empire: Nationalism and National Reform in the Hapsburg Monarchy, 1840–1918* (2 vols., 1950). A comprehensive study of the eroding forces of nationalism.

H. Kohn, *Pan-Slavism: Its History and Ideology* (1953).

C. A. Macartney, *The Hapsburg Empire, 1790–1918* (1969). The best survey.

A. J. P. Taylor, *The Habsburg Monarchy, 1809–1918* (2nd ed., 1948). A brief and well written study.

THE OTTOMAN EMPIRE

R. H. Davison, *Reform in the Ottoman Empire, 1856–1876* (1963). A thorough recent scholarly study.

J. Haslip, *The Sultan: The Life of Abdul Hamid II* (1958). An unusual kind of biography.

* W. Miller, *The Ottoman Empire and its Successors, 1801–1934* (1948). The standard work in English.

* L. S. Stavrianos, *The Balkans, 1815–1914* (1962). A valuable general survey of a troubled area.

THE REVIVAL OF WESTERN IMPERIALISM CHAPTER TEN

THE SECOND BRITISH EMPIRE

A. L. Burt. *The Evolution of the British Empire and Commonwealth from the American Revolution* (1956). A standard text.

E. Holt, *The Boer War* (1958). A recent general account.

F. G. Hutchins, *The Illusion of Permanence: British Imperialism in India* (1967). Lucidly and elegantly written.

P. Knaplund, *The British Empire, 1815–1939* (1941). An authoritative survey from the British viewpoint.

S. Sen, *Eighteen Fifty-seven* (1957). A centennial history of the Sepoy Mutiny by an Indian historian.

A. P. Thornton, *The Imperial Idea and Its Enemies: A Study in British Power*

(1959). The rise and decline of the British belief in the "white man's burden."
B. Williams, *Botha, Smuts, and South Africa* (1948). Boers who became firm supporters of the British Empire.

THE OPENING OF ASIA

J. F. Cady, *The Roots of French Imperialism in Eastern Asia* (1954). Background of the Vietnam question.
T. F. Power, Jr., *Jules Ferry and the Renaissance of French Imperialism* (1944). Much broader than the title indicates.
J. Pratt, *The Expansion of Europe in the Far East* (1947). Good general account.
G. B. Sanson, *The Western World and Japan* (1950). A concise history by a leading authority.
Ssy-yu Teng and J. K. Fairbank, *China's Response to the West: A Documentary Survey, 1839–1923* (1954, 1963). A comprehensive survey using contemporary sources.

THE PARTITION OF AFRICA

P. Curtin, *The Image of Africa* (1964). British ideas about Africa from 1780 to 1850.
D. Forde and P. M. Kaberry, *West African Kingdoms in the Nineteenth Century* (1967). Reveals the diversity and complexity of indigenous African political and social life.
J. T. Gallager and R. I. Robinson, *Africa and the Victorians* (1961). A stimulating original interpretation of British strategy and tactics in Africa.
L. H. Gann and Peter Duignan, *Burden of Empire* (1967). A rebuttal of the argument that economic factors were of major importance in the colonization of Africa; traces the story to the epoch of de-colonization.
D. S. Landes, *Bankers and Pashas: International Finance and Economic Imperialism in Egypt* (1958). Reads like a novel.
H. I. Priestly, *France Overseas: A Study of Modern Imperialism* (1938). A detailed study of French imperialism from 1815 to 1930.
R. L. Tignor, *Modernization and British Colonial Rule in Egypt, 1882–1914* (1966). By a modern social scientist.

INTERPRETATIONS AND PERSPECTIVES

J. H. Hobson, *Imperialism: A Study* (1902). A pioneering study that attacked the traditional English idea of imperialism.
* V. I. Lenin, *Imperialism, the Highest Stage of Capitalism* (1916, 1939). The fundamental statement of the Marxist-Leninist theory of imperialism.
* A. T. Mahan, *The Influence of Seapower upon History* (numerous eds., 1893). A highly influential book in its day.
J. A. Schumpeter, *Imperialism and Social Classes* (1919, 1951). A refutation of the economic interpretation of imperialism.
E. Staley, *War and the Private Investor: A Study in the Relations of International Politics and International Investment* (1935). Shows the influence of government policies on foreign investment.
E. M. Winslow, *The Pattern of Imperialism* (1948). A study of the motives and interests of the imperial powers.

EUROPEAN CULTURE AND SOCIETY: THE END OF THE GOLDEN AGE CHAPTER ELEVEN

* C. J. H. Hayes, *A Generation of Materialism, 1871–1900* (1941). A general study of all aspects of the life of the times, including literature, art, social thought, and politics; Rise of Modern Europe Series.

The best way to appreciate the literature of the period is to read some of the books mentioned in the text. Illustrated histories of art are numerous.

FIN-DE-SIÈCLE LITERATURE AND ART

S. Giedion, *Mechanization Takes Command* (1948). Shows the influence of industrialization upon art.
A. Hauser, *The Social History of Art* (1952). The influence of art on society and vice versa.
* E. Neff, *The Poetry of History: The Contribution of Literature and Literary Scholarship to the Writing of History Since Voltaire* (1947).
N. Pevsner, *Pioneers of the Modern Movement from William Morris to Walter Gropius* (1936). A classic study of architecture and design by a noted authority.
H. A. Reyburn, *Nietzsche: The Story of a Human Philosopher* (1948).
M. Rheims, *The Age of Art Nouveau* (1967). Excellent illustrations.
* E. Wilson, *Axel's Castle, A Study in the Imaginative Literature of 1850–1930* (1931). A masterpiece of literary history.

POSITIVISM AND ITS CRITICS

H. Alpert, *Emile Durkheim and His Sociology* (1939). One of the best studies of the influential French sociologist.
S. Hughes, *Consciousness and Society: The Reorientation of European Social Thought, 1890–1920* (1958). A study of the influence of new ideas on man's view of society.
E. Jones, *Sigmund Freud* (1 vol. ed., 1961). An abridgment of the massive "authorized" biography.
* R. B. Perry, *The Thought and Character of William James* (1935, 1948). An abridged edition of this major work is available in paperback.
P. Rieff, *Freud: The Mind of the Moralist* (1959). A penetrating critique of one of the most influential personalities of modern times.
H. Vaihinger, *The Philosophy of "As If"* (transl., 1927). English translation of an important work in the philosophy of science.

THE NEW REVOLUTION IN SCIENCE

C. T. Chase, *The Evolution of Modern Physics* (1947).
* L. Infield, *Albert Einstein: His Work and Its Influence on Our World* (1950). A good introduction for the layman.
J. Mirsky, *To the North: The Story of Arctic Exploration* (1934, 1948).
W. Sullivan, *Quest for a Continent* (1957). A history of Antarctic exploration from the 1820's to the International Geophysical Year.

EUROPEAN SOCIETY AT THE END OF ITS GOLDEN AGE

G. Dangerfield, *The Strange Death of Liberal England* (1936). An examination of social and political changes in the decade preceding World War I.

* H. F. May, *End of American Innocence: A Study of the First Years of Our Time, 1912–1917* (1959).

J. H. Nichols, *A History of Christianity, 1650–1950* (1956). An authoritative modern work of scholarship with special attention to developments since about 1870.

J. G. J. Pulzer, *The Rise of Political Anti-Semitism in Germany and Austria* (1964).

* W. Rauschenbusch, *Christianity and the Social Crisis* (1907, 1963). A document of the times by the founder of American "social Christianity."

P. N. Stearns, *European Society in Upheaval: Social History since 1800* (1967). Also recommended for the earlier period.

THE FIRST WORLD WAR CHAPTER TWELVE

THE DIPLOMATIC PRELUDE, 1871–1914

H. E. Barnes, *The Genesis of the World War: An Introduction to the Problem of War Guilt* (1926). Of special interest because of the author's revisionist approach.

E. Brandenburg, *From Bismarck to World War: A History of German Foreign Policy, 1870–1914* (1927). A German view of the origins of World War I.

* W. L. Langer, *European Alliances and Alignments, 1871–1890* (1931, 1950).

* ———, *The Diplomacy of Imperialism, 1890–1902* (2 vols., 1935). These volumes and the above constitute the definitive diplomatic history of their period.

N. Mansergh, *The Coming of the First World War* (1949). An authoritative study of the breakdown of the balance of power concept.

G. Monger, *The End of Isolation: British Foreign Policy, 1900–1907* (1963).

R. J. Sontag, *European Diplomatic History, 1871–1932* (1933). A standard text.

J. A. Thayer, *Italy and the Great War: Politics and Culture, 1870–1915* (1964). A penetrating recent study.

FROM THE EASTERN QUESTION TO THE BALKAN WARS

E. M. Earle, *Turkey, the Great Powers, and the Bagdad Railroad* (1923). A study of Western involvement in the Near East.

E. C. Helmreich, *The Diplomacy of the Balkan Wars, 1912–1913* (1938). Dry, factual, but reliable.

W. N. Medlicott, *The Congress of Berlin and After* (1938, 1963). The authoritative work on the Near Eastern settlement of 1878 to 1880.

J. Remak, *Sarajevo, The Story of a Political Murder* (1959). A gripping account of this explosive event.

C. Sforza, *Fifty Years of War and Diplomacy in the Balkans* (1941). By an Italian diplomat.

THE WAR

* H. Baldwin, *World War I* (1962). A brief, clear survey by a leading military analyst.

E. M. Coffman, *The War to End All Wars* (1968). American participation in the war.

J. Cameron, *1914* (1959). Recreates the atmosphere of the times.

F. Chambers, *The War Behind the War, 1914–1918* (1939). The home front in various countries.

* C. Falls, *The Great War, 1914–1918* (1959). Somewhat more detailed than Baldwin.

G. D. Feldman, *Army, Industry and Labor in Germany, 1914–1918* (1966). The home front in Germany.

A. Horne, *The Price of Glory: Verdun, 1916* (1963). The story of one of the costliest battles of the war.

A. Marwick, *The Deluge* (1965). A scholarly study of British society during World War I.

* A. Moorehead, *Gallipoli* (1958). The story of the disastrous British campaign to take the Dardanelles.

J. M. Read, *Atrocity Propaganda* (1941). A study of a crude form of psychological warfare.

G. Ritter, *The Schlieffen Plan* (transl., 1958). By a German historian.

H. R. Rudin, *Armistice, 1918* (1944). A standard account.

E. Taylor, *The Fall of the Dynasties* (1963). A popularized political history of the war and the years immediately preceding.

* B. Tuchman, *The Guns of August* (1962). Opening weeks of the war; reads like a novel.

R. M. Watt, *Dare Call It Treason* (1963). Mutinies in the French army in 1917, news of which was long suppressed.

DISINTEGRATION AND COLLAPSE CHAPTER THIRTEEN

THE RUSSIAN REVOLUTION, 1917–1921

E. H. Carr, *The Bolshevik Revolution, 1917–1923* (1950–56). Vols. I–III of *A History of Soviet Russia,* the most comprehensive and detailed account in English.

I. Deutscher, *The Prophet Armed: Trotsky, 1879–1921* (1958). A sympathetic biography.

L. Fischer, *Lenin* (1964). The best biography.

C. Hill, *Lenin and the Russian Revolution* (1947). Good, brief introduction.

G. F. Kennan, *The Decision to Intervene* (1958). American involvement in the Russian Revolution.

* A. Moorehead, *The Russian Revolution* (1958). A well written, popular account, not entirely reliable.

* J. Reed, *Ten Days that Shook the World* (1919, 1960). Eyewitness account of the Bolshevik seizure of power by an American journalist.

L. Schapiro, *The Origins of the Communist Autocracy: Political Opposition in the Soviet State, 1917–1922* (1955).

L. Trotsky, *The History of the Russian Revolution* (2 vols., 1932, 1937). Trotsky was the Bolshevik War Commissar.

A. B. Ulam, *The Bolsheviks* (1965). An important study of the origins of Russian communism.

J. W. Wheeler-Bennett, *The Forgotten Peace: Brest-Litovsk, March, 1918* (1939). The negotiations between the Bolsheviks and the Germans.

* B. D. Wolfe, *Three Who Made a Revolution: A Biographical History* (1948, 1964). An exciting story of Lenin, Trotsky, and Stalin.

THE PEACE OF PARIS AND ITS AFTERMATH

T. A. Bailey, *Wilson and the Peacemakers* (1947). The U.S. role in the peace conference.

P. Birdsall, *Versailles Twenty Years After* (1941). An evaluation of two decades of controversy over the peace settlement.

T. Jones, *Lloyd George* (1951). A sound biography.

F. S. Marston, *The Peace Conference of 1919* (1944). A brief guide to the conference.

I. Morrow, *The Peace Settlement in the German-Polish Borderlands* (1936). An especially important area.

ECONOMIC DISINTEGRATION AND COLLAPSE

A. L. Bowley, *Some Economic Consequences of the Great War* (1930). Written by an economist in the midst of the depression.

P. Einzig, *The World Economic Crisis, 1929–1931* (1931). The author was a financial journalist.

J. M. Keynes, *The Economic Consequences of the Peace* (1920). A most influential book.

E. Mantoux, *The Carthaginian Peace—or The Economic Consequences of Mr. Keynes* (1946). A sharp attack on the Keynesian thesis that the Treaty of Versailles was too harsh on Germany by a young Frenchman who died in World War II.

H. G. Moulton, and L. Pasvolsky, *War Debts and World Prosperity* (1932). The economists' view.

CRISIS OF THE SPIRIT

Just for fun, try J. Dos Passos's *U.S.A.*, E. Hemingway's *Farewell to Arms,* J. Steinbeck's *Grapes of Wrath,* A. Huxley's *Brave New World,* or A. Gide's *The Immoralist.*

LIBERAL ATTEMPTS AT RECONSTRUCTION CHAPTER FOURTEEN

THE LEAGUE OF NATIONS AND COLLECTIVE SECURITY

E. H. Carr, *International Relations between the Two World Wars, 1919–1939* (rev. ed., 1948). A good survey of international affairs.

R. Dell, *The Geneva Racket, 1920–1939* (1941). A cynical view of the League.

R. H. Ferrell, *Peace in Their Time* (1952). A study of the origins of the Kellogg-Briand peace pact.

F. B. Walters, *A History of the League of Nations* (2 vols., 1952). A detailed study of the League.
A. Zimmern, *The League of Nations and the Rule of Law* (1936).

THE WEIMAR REPUBLIC IN GERMANY

K. Epstein, *Matthias Erzberger and the Dilemma of German Democracy* (1959). A sensitive, penetrating study.
E. Eyck, *A History of the Weimar Republic* (2 vols., transl., 1963). An authoritative study by a liberal German historian.
G. Freund, *Unholy Alliance* (1957). Germany's relations with the Soviet Union.
H. J. Gordon, *The Reichswehr and the German Republic, 1919–1926* (1957). The German army under the Weimar Republic.
* S. W. Halperin, *Germany Tried Democracy: A Political History of the Reich from 1918 to 1933* (1946). A well balanced scholarly history.
J. Plamenatz, *German Marxism and Russian Communism* (1954).
G. Scheele, *The Weimar Republic: Overture to the Third Reich* (1947).
* H. A. Turner, *Stresemann and the Politics of the Weimar Republic* (1963). A reappraisal of the role of the German statesman in domestic politics.

THE DEMOCRACIES OF WESTERN EUROPE

M. W. Childs, *Sweden, the Middle Way* (1947). Neither unbridled capitalism nor dogmatic socialism.
* R. Graves and A. Hodges, *The Long Weekend: A Social History of Great Britain, 1918–1939* (1940). A well written, somewhat satirical social history.
J. M. Keynes, *The End of Laissez-Faire* (1927). Brilliant essays by the noted economist. His *Essays in Persuasion* and *Essays in Biography* are also well worth reading.
* E. J. Knapton, *France since Versailles* (1952). A short, clear survey.
* L. C. B. Seaman, *Post-Victorian Britain, 1902–1951* (1966). A pithy reinterpretation of the first half of the twentieth century in Britain.
W. R. Sharp, *The Government of the French Republic* (1938). A valiant attempt to unravel the tangled skein of the Third Republic.
* D. Thomson, *England in the Twentieth Century, 1914–1963* (1964). An excellent brief survey.
S. H. Thomson, *Czechoslovakia in European History* (1943, 1953).
A. Werth, *The Twilight of France, 1933–1940* (1942). Highly recommended.

THE UNITED STATES: NEW ERA AND NEW DEAL

* F. L. Allen, *Only Yesterday* (1957) and *Since Yesterday* (1958). Lively social histories of conditions in the U.S. during the 1920's and 1930's.
D. Brogan, *The Era of Franklin D. Roosevelt* (1951). A perceptive account by a distinguished British historian.
* J. K. Galbraith, *The Great Crash* (1955). An exciting account of the stock market collapse of 1929.
* W. Leuchtenburg, *Franklin D. Roosevelt and the New Deal, 1932–1940* (1963).
* J. A. Schumpeter, *Capitalism, Socialism, and Democracy* (1942, 1952). A wise

and penetrating analysis by a distinguished social scientist; applies to western Europe as well as the U.S.

* A. Sinclair, *Era of Excess: A Social History of the Prohibition Movement* (1962).
* E. Wilson, *American Earthquake: A Documentary of the Jazz Age, the Great Depression and the New Deal* (1958). Social history by a noted literary critic.

AUTHORITARIAN ATTEMPTS AT RECONSTRUCTION CHAPTER FIFTEEN

COMMUNISM IN RUSSIA, 1921–1938

* R. N. Carew Hunt, *The Theory and Practice of Communism* (1951). The international Communist movement.

E. H. Carr, *The Interregnum, 1923–1924,* and *Socialism in One Country, 1924–1926.* Vols. IV–VI of the monumental *A History of Soviet Russia.*

* I. Deutscher, ed., *The Age of Permanent Revolution: A Trotsky Anthology* (1964). A selection from the writings of Stalin's archrival.
* ———, *Stalin: A Political Biography* (1948).

L. Fischer, *The Life and Death of Stalin* (1953).

S. N. Harper and R. Thompson, *The Government of the Soviet Union* (1949). Its structure and functions.

G. F. Kennan, *Russia and the West under Lenin and Stalin* (1961). A perceptive analysis of Soviet foreign relations.

R. Pipes, *The Formation of the Soviet Union* (1954). A useful account of the minorities in Russia from 1917 to 1923.

H. Schwartz, *Russia's Soviet Economy* (1950, 1954). A good introduction.

* H. Seton-Watson, *From Lenin to Khrushchev: The History of World Communism* (1953, 1960).

FASCISM IN ITALY, 1922–1938

D. A. Binchy, *Church and State in Fascist Italy* (1941). A Catholic historian discusses the historical problem of church-state relations.

G. A. Borgese, *Goliath: The March of Fascism* (1937). By an antifascist.

C. F. Delzell, *Mussolini's Enemies: The Italian Anti-fascist Resistance* (1961). An able study of the Italian underground.

I. Kirkpatrick, *Mussolini: Study of a Demagogue* (1964). By far the best biography.

G. Megaro, *Mussolini in the Making* (1938). An excellent study of Mussolini's early life.

G. Salvemini, *Under the Axe of Fascism* (1936). A sound treatment of Italian fascism by a distinguished antifascist.

C. T. Schmidt, *The Corporate State in Action: Italy under Fascism* (1939).

NAZISM IN GERMANY, 1933–1938

* A. Bullock, *Hitler: A Study in Tyranny* (rev. ed., 1962). The best biography of Hitler.

* K. Jaspers, *The Question of German Guilt* (transl., 1961). An existentialist psychologist probes the question of public responsibility for Nazi atrocities.
* G. Lewy, *The Catholic Church in Nazi Germany* (1964).
F. Lilge, *The Abuse of Learning: The Failure of the German University* (1948). Shows the take-over of the German universities by the Nazis.
* H. Mau and H. Krausnick, *German History 1933–1945* (transl., 1958). A study by two young German historians.
* F. Meinecke, *The German Catastrophe: Reflections and Recollections* (1946, 1950). Personal reminiscences of a great German historian.
* G. L. Mosse, *The Crisis of German Ideology: Intellectual Origins of the Third Reich* (1964). An incisive analysis of the ideological background of National Socialism.
D. Schoenbaum, *Hitler's Social Revolution: Class and Status in Nazi Germany, 1933–1939* (1967). A penetrating study by a brilliant young historian.
* W. L. Shirer, *The Rise and Fall of the Third Reich* (1960). An account by an American journalist.
L. L. Snyder, *German Nationalism: The Tragedy of a People* (1952).
H. R. Trevor-Roper, *The Last Days of Hitler* (1947). A dramatic account of the end of National Socialism.
J. W. Wheeler-Bennett, *The Nemesis of Power: The German Army in Politics, 1918–1945* (1953). An indispensable analysis.

OTHER AUTHORITARIAN REGIMES

R. Benedict, *The Chrysanthemum and the Sword* (1946). The rise of militarism in Japan.
* G. Brenan, *The Spanish Labyrinth: An Account of the Social and Political Background of the Civil War* (1943). One of the best works of the events leading up to the Civil War.
D. M. Brown, *Nationalism in Japan* (1955).
C. A. Gulick, *Austria from Habsburg to Hitler* (2 vols., 1948). A detailed, comprehensive history.
M. MacDonald, *The Republic of Austria, 1918–1934: A Study in the Failure of Democratic Government* (1946).
H. Seton-Watson, *Eastern Europe between the Wars, 1918–1941* (1946). The best general account.
* H. Thomas, *The Spanish Civil War* (1961). The best history of the war.
G. O. Totten III, *The Social Democratic Movement in Prewar Japan* (1966). Covers many aspects of the period from 1925 to 1940.

THE COMMON ELEMENTS

A. Cobban, *Dictatorship: Its History and Theory* (1939).
* E. Fromm, *Escape from Freedom* (1941). A psychiatrist probes the reasons for submission to dictatorship.
D. Spearman, *Modern Dictatorship* (1939). A comparative survey.

THE SECOND WORLD WAR CHAPTER SIXTEEN

THE ORIGINS OF TOTALITARIAN AGGRESSION

G. W. Baer, *The Coming of the Italian-Ethiopian War* (1967). Detailed scholarly work.

G. Brook-Shepherd, *Anschluss: The Rape of Austria* (1963). A good recent study.

* W. Churchill, *The Gathering Storm* (1948). Vol. I of Churchill's *History of the Second World War;* highly personal.

F. Gilbert and G. A. Craig, eds., *The Diplomats, 1919–1939* (1953). Penetrating studies of the principal diplomats of the era.

W. L. Langer and S. E. Gleason, *The Challenge to Isolation, 1937–1940* (1952) and *The Undeclared War, 1940–1941* (1953). A detailed history of the U.S. role leading up to 1941.

D. J. Lu, *From the Marco Polo Bridge to Pearl Harbor: Japan's Entry into World War II* (1961). A military-diplomatic history of Japanese aggression.

* L. B. Namier, *Diplomatic Prelude, 1938–1939* (1948). Perceptive essays on the origins of the war.

* A. J. P. Taylor, *The Origins of the Second World War* (1961, 1963). A revisionist view; highly controversial.

* J. W. Wheeler-Bennett, *Munich: Prologue to Tragedy* (1948, 1963). An outstanding contribution.

BLITZKRIEG, 1939–1941

H. F. Armstrong, *Chronology of Failure* (1940). An on-the-spot discussion of the collapse of France in 1940.

R. Aron, *The Vichy Regime* (1950). A critical history by a noted French author.

M. Bloch, *Strange Defeat* (1949). A distinguished French historian's perceptive study of France's surrender to Germany. (Bloch was executed by the Germans in 1944 for underground activities.)

B. Collier, *The Second World War: A Military History* (1967). Deals mainly with general fighting.

* C. Falls, *The Second World War* (2nd ed., 1950). A sound military history.

A. S. Milward, *The German Economy at War* (1965).

G. L. Weinberg, *Germany and the Soviet Union, 1939–1941* (1954). The diplomatic history of a strange alliance.

A. Werth, *The Year of Stalingrad* (1947). An interesting journalistic account.

D. Young, *Rommel: The Desert Fox* (1950). An absorbing story of the commanding German general in North Africa.

PEARL HARBOR AND THE WAR IN THE PACIFIC

R. J. C. Butow, *Japan's Decision to Surrender* (1961). The end of the war in the Pacific.

* D. Congdon, ed., *Combat: The War with Japan* (1962). A popular account of the war in the Pacific.

J. Creswell, *Sea Warfare, 1939–1945* (1967). Covers all naval operations.

S. E. Morison, *The Two-Ocean War: A Short History of the United States Navy in the Second World War* (1963). A one-volume abridgment of the multi-volume history of U.S. naval operations, by one of the most distinguished American historians.

THE GRAND ALLIANCE

* W. Churchill, *Closing the Ring* (1951). Churchill's own account of the invasion of Europe.
* D. D. Eisenhower, *Crusade in Europe* (1949). By the Supreme Allied Commander.
* T. R. Fehrenbach, *The Battle of Anzio* (1962). A crucial battle of the invasion of Italy.

H. Feis, *Churchill, Roosevelt, Stalin* (1957). An interesting account of the relations between these three war leaders. See also Feis's other accounts of the diplomatic history of the war.

* C. Ryan, *The Longest Day* (1959). June 6, 1944, the Normandy invasion.
* C. Wilmont, *The Struggle for Europe* (1952). A critical account of American policy by an Australian scholar.

AFTERMATH OF WAR CHAPTER SEVENTEEN

EXHAUSTED VICTORS

R. A. Brady, *Crisis in Britain: Plans and Achievements of the Labour Government* (1950). An economist's account of the difficulties encountered by Britain's first Socialist government.

M. Einaudi *et al., Communism in Western Europe* (1951). A study of French and Italian Communists.

S. Hoffmann *et al., In Search of France* (1962). An interdisciplinary approach to a fascinating problem.

H. Luethy, *France Against Herself* (1954). An unusually lucid and penetrating analysis of French society, economy, and politics.

B. Ward, *The West at Bay* (1948). A trenchant and perceptive analysis of the situation of the former Great Powers of Europe in the aftermath of war.

F. Williams, *Socialist Britain* (1949).

P. M. Williams, *Politics in Postwar France* (1954). A sensible yet stimulating interpretation of the problems of the Fourth Republic.

G. Wright, *The Reshaping of French Democracy* (1948). A study of constitution making in postwar France.

DEFEATED ENEMIES

G. C. Allen, *Japan's Economic Recovery* (1958). By an economist well versed in Japanese affairs.

G. A. Almond, ed., *The Struggle for Democracy in Germany* (1949). Aspects of denazification, the occupation, and the founding of the Federal Republic.

E. Davidson, *The Death and Life of Germany* (1959). A study of the American occupation.

H. Feis, *Between War and Peace: The Potsdam Conference* (1960). An outstanding account of the first critical postwar meeting of the Big Three.

M. Grindrod, *The Rebuilding of Italy, 1945–1955* (1955). An interesting account of postwar reconstruction, economic and political.

K. Kawai, *Japan's American Interlude* (1960). A study of the postwar occupation.

R. Opie *et al., The Search for a Peace Settlement* (1951). A research study sponsored by the Brookings Institution.

F. W. Pick, *Peacemaking in Perspective: From Potsdam to Paris* (1950). An account of the negotiations leading up to the peace treaties of 1947.

E. O. Reischauer, *The United States and Japan* (rev. ed., 1957). By far the best introduction to American relations with Japan since the war.

THE FATE OF EASTERN EUROPE

H. F. Armstrong, *Tito and Goliath* (1951). Yugoslavia's defiance of the Soviet Union.

D. J. Dallin, *The New Soviet Empire* (1951). A distinctly anti-Soviet point of view.

J. Korbel, *The Communist Subversion of Czechoslovakia 1938–1948* (1964). The background of the *coup de Prague.*

J. P. Nettl, *The Eastern Zone and Soviet Policy in Germany, 1945–1950* (1951). The standard work on the subject.

H. Seton-Watson, *The East-European Revolution* (1950, 1956). The best account of the Communist take-over in Eastern Europe.

E. Wiskemann, *Germany's Eastern Neighbours* (1955).

R. L. Wolff, *The Balkans in Our Time* (1956). A detailed account of the Balkans before and after World War II.

THE UNITED NATIONS AND DIVIDED ALLIES

* H. W. Gatzke, *The Present in Perspective: A Look at the World since 1945* (1957, 1965). A general survey of the postwar period, especially useful for its perspective on the Cold War and international relations.

G. F. Kennan, *Realities of American Foreign Policy* (1954).

———, *Russia, the Atom, and the West* (1958). Two distinguished contributions by one of America's foremost scholar-diplomats.

J. Lukacs, *A History of the Cold War* (1961).

R. Leckie, *Conflict: The History of the Korean War 1950–1953* (1962).

* H. G. Nicholas, *The United Nations as a Political Institution* (1953).

R. B. Russell, *A History of the United Nations Charter* (1958). The ideas and compromises that made the charter, from the Atlantic Charter to the San Francisco conference.

THE END OF WESTERN HEGEMONY CHAPTER EIGHTEEN

NEW NATIONALISMS

C. Dubois, *Social Forces in Southeast Asia* (1959). A good introduction.

R. N. Frye, *Iran* (1953). A brief general introduction to the modernization of a nation.

* J. D. Legge, *Indonesia* (1964). Modern Nations in Historical Perspective Series.

H. Z. Nuseibeh, *The Ideas of Arab Nationalism* (1956). By an Arab nationalist.

J. Romein, *The Asian Century: A History of Modern Nationalism in Asia* (1956, transl., 1962). A good general introduction to Asian nationalism.

* H. M. Sachar, *The Course of Modern Jewish History* (1958). Useful for understanding the historical background of the modern state of Israel.

H. Tinker, *Experiment with Freedom: India and Pakistan, 1947* (1967). Brief, synoptic account of the background of independence.

M. Zinkin, *Asia and the West* (1953). An interpretative study of the social and economic problems of Asian countries.

THE CHINESE REVOLUTIONS

O. E. Clubb, *Twentieth Century China* (1964). A general survey of the period since the first Chinese revolution of 1911.

J. K. Fairbank, *The United States and China* (1958). An authoritative account of American relations with China, including American involvement in the civil war and the stalemate with Communist China.

E. Hahn, *Chiang Kai-shek: An Unauthorized Biography* (1955). A perceptive human account by a skilled writer.

H. R. Isaacs, *The Tragedy of the Chinese Revolution* (1961).

* K. S. Latourette, *China* (1964). A brief general survey by a distinguished historian. Modern Nations in Historical Perspective Series.

B. Schwartz, *Chinese Communism and the Rise of Mao* (1951). An authoritative study of the leader of the Chinese Communists.

* R. Walker, *China Under Communism: The First Five Years* (1955). A severe critique of Chinese Communism.

THE EMERGENCE OF INDEPENDENT AFRICA

* R. M. Brace, *Morocco, Algeria, Tunisia* (1964). Modern Nations in Historical Perspective Series.

K. A. Busia, *Africa in Search of Democracy* (1967). By a noted Ghanian politician.

G. M. Carter, *The Politics of Inequality: South Africa since 1948* (1958). An analysis of racial tensions in South Africa.

* R. Emerson, *From Empire to Nation* (1960). A history of the crumbling of colonialism in both Asia and Africa.

R. Oliver and J. D. Fage, *A Short History of Africa* (1962). The emphasis is on the background of the independence movement.

C. E. Welch, Jr., *Dream of Unity: Pan-Africanism and Political Unity in West Africa* (1966). Only a dream.

LATIN AMERICA IN FERMENT

T. Draper, *Castro's Revolution: Myths and Realities* (1962).

A. O. Hirschman, *Journeys Toward Progress* (1963). Vivid, sympathetic accounts of Latin American efforts to achieve economic development.

H. L. Mathews, ed., *The United States and Latin America* (1963).

T. Szulc, *The Winds of Revolution: Latin America Today and Tomorrow* (1963). An unusually perceptive analysis by a skilled journalist.

THE STRUGGLE FOR A NEW WORLD ORDER CHAPTER NINETEEN

RECOVERY AND REINTEGRATION IN WESTERN EUROPE

W. Diebold, Jr., *The Schuman Plan: A Study in Economic Cooperation* (1959). Detailed, comprehensive, and scholarly.

E. B. Haas, *The Uniting of Europe* (1958). A scholarly study of political, social, and economic forces.

* G. Lichtheim, *The New Europe Today—and Tomorrow* (1963). A good brief introduction by an incisive analyst and writer.

* K. Martin, *Britain in the Sixties: The Crown and the Establishment* (1964). Social commentary and critique by an "angry young man."

H. C. Wallich, *Mainsprings of the German Revival* (1955). The "economic miracle" in Germany.

P. M. Williams and M. Harrison, *De Gaulle's Republic* (1960). A penetrating, somewhat critical evaluation of the Fifth Republic.

* J. W. Wuorinen, *Scandinavia* (1964). Modern Nations in Historical Perspective Series.

THE ATLANTIC ALLIANCE

H. Borton, *Japan Between East and West* (1957). Cultural, political, and economic tensions.

* E. Goldman, *The Crucial Decade—And After: America, 1945–1960* (1960). A close scrutiny of the postwar United States and its role in world affairs.

* A. Grosser, *The Federal Republic of Germany: A Concise History* (1964).

* H. A. Kissinger, *Nuclear Weapons and American Foreign Policy* (1957). A controversial analysis of the bases of U.S. foreign policy by a political scientist of the "realistic" school, adviser to President Nixon.

Royal Institute of International Affairs, *Atlantic Alliance: NATO's Role in the Free World* (1952). A report explaining the aims, organization, and accomplishments of NATO.

COMMUNISM AFTER STALIN

A. Brumberg, ed., *Russia under Khrushchev* (1962). Essays on selected aspects of Soviet life.

* E. Crankshaw, *The New Cold War: Moscow vs. Peking* (1963). An analysis of the ideological split within the Communist bloc.

* M. Djilas, *The New Class: An Analysis of the Communist System* (1957). A critique of communism by a former Yugoslav Communist leader.

* S. Fischer-Galati, ed., *Eastern Europe in the Sixties* (1963). A country-by-country survey by experts.

* D. Granick, *The Red Executive: A Study of the Organization Man in Russian Industry* (1960). Excellent book on a little known subject.

R. Kolkowicz, *The Soviet Military and the Communist Party* (1967). Civil-military relations under communism.

C. A. Linden, *Khrushchev and the Soviet Leadership, 1957–1964* (1966). Highly informative.

* Z. K. Brzezinsky, *The Soviet Bloc: Unity and Conflict* (1963). A study of the relations between Russia and the satellite states.

BIRTH PANGS OF WORLD CIVILIZATION

* V. M. Dean, *The Nature of the Non-Western World* (1957). A useful introduction.

B. B. Fall, *The Two Viet-Nams* (1963). The split between North and South and its consequences for peace in Southeast Asia.

W. R. Fischel, *Vietnam: Anatomy of a Conflict* (1968). A collection of conflicting analyses and opinions on the war in Vietnam.

E. Fischer, *The Passing of the European Age: A Study of the Transfer of Western Civilization and Its Renewal in Other Continents* (1948). The subtitle indicates its scope.

A. L. George, *The Chinese Army in Action: The Korean War and its Aftermath* (1967). Based on interviews with captured Chinese soldiers.

* R. L. Heilbroner, *The Great Ascent: The Struggle for Economic Development in Our Time* (1963). An able, lucid explanation for the layman.

F. S. C. Northrop, *The Meeting of East and West* (1946). Cultural contrasts and similarities explored by a modern philosopher.

* H. Seton-Watson, *Neither War Nor Peace: The Struggle for Power in the Postwar World* (1960). One of the best accounts of the troubled state of international relations; wise and reflective.

A. J. Toynbee, *The World and the West* (1953). Reflections of one of the best known historians of civilization.

TENDENCIES OF TWENTIETH-CENTURY CIVILIZATION CHAPTER TWENTY

SCIENCE, TECHNOLOGY, AND INDUSTRY

* R. Aron, *The Century of Total War* (1954). Analysis of the political and economic forces at work and their relations to science and technology.

* B. Barber, *Science and the Social Order* (1952). Examines the relationship between science and society.

P. M. S. Blackett, *Atomic Weapons and East-West Relations* (1956). An English scientist discusses the impact of nuclear weapons.

* J. Bronowski, *Science and Human Values* (1956). An informed discussion by a noted scientist.

V. Bush, *Modern Arms and Free Men: A Discussion of the Role of Science in Preserving Democracy* (1948). The author was President Truman's science adviser and played an important role in developing the atomic bomb.

* Sir A. Eddington, *The Expanding Universe* (1958). A popular exposition of the significance of recent discoveries in astronomy.

W. Esslinger, *Politics and Science* (1955).

* P. de Kruif, *The Microbe Hunters* (1926, 1939). A popular account of the progress of the biological and medical sciences in the first third of the twentieth century.

SOCIAL TRENDS

* T. C. Cochran, *The American Business System: A Historical Perspective, 1900–1955* (1956). Many of the changes in American business are being felt in Europe as well.

J. K. Galbraith, *The New Industrial State* (1967). How the "technostructure" is transforming society.

* C. B. Hoover, *The Economy, Liberty, and the State* (1959). A fine discussion of the relations between the economic system and fundamental human freedoms, with examples from recent history.

* V. O. Packard, *The Status Seekers* (1959). An examination of the class structure of American society, which has some parallels in Europe.

* D. Riesman, *The Lonely Crowd* (1947, 1953). A social-psychological interpretation of the individual in mass society.

A. Shonfield, *Modern Capitalism* (1965). A balanced survey of the changes in the economic system in Europe and America since the 1930's.

* W. H. Whyte, *The Organization Man* (1957). A study of the organizational compulsion in modern society and its effect on individual personality.

* C. Vann Woodward, *The Strange Career of Jim Crow* (rev. ed., 1957). The history of discrimination against Negroes in the United States.

THE ARTS IN TWENTIETH-CENTURY CIVILIZATION

A. H. Barr, *What Is Modern Painting?* (rev. ed., 1956). A useful introduction.

R. Brustein, *The Theater of Revolt* (1964). Modern tendencies in the theater by a noted critic.

T. M. Finney, *A History of Music* (1947).

K. London, *The Seven Soviet Arts* (1937). A critical survey of the arts under Stalin.

N. Lynton, *The Modern World* (1965). Landmarks of the World's Art Series.

C. Mauriac, *The New Literature* (1959). Essays on modern French authors.

* J. M. Richards, *An Introduction to Modern Architecture* (1951).

R. Richman, ed., *The Arts at Midcentury* (1954). Essays examining the status of the fine arts in Europe and the United States.

A. Webern, *The Path to the New Music* (1963). By a leading modern composer and theorist.

THE LIFE OF THE MIND IN THE TWENTIETH CENTURY

* J. Barzun, *The House of Intellect* (1959). A careful explanation and appraisal of the role of scholarship, education, and the higher culture.

R. Harper, *Existentialism: A Theory of Man* (1949). An introduction for the layman.

H. S. Hughes, *An Essay for Our Times* (1950). A thoughtful discussion of international politics and the future of man.

R. Niebuhr, *The Structure of Nations and Empires* (1959). A famous theologian's view of the problems of international politics.

* M. Polanyi, *Science, Faith, and Society* (1964). An essay on their relationships by a modern philosopher.

* K. R. Popper, *The Open Society and Its Enemies* (1950). A spirited, scholarly defense of pluralistic social systems.

D. D. Rune, ed., *Twentieth Century Philosophy* (1942). A series of stimulating essays on the main philosophical ideas of the twentieth century.

B. Russell, *The Autobiography of Bertrand Russell* (1967). It is different.

C. P. Snow, *The Two Cultures and a Second Look* (2nd ed., 1964). An examination of the sciences and the humanities and the lack of communication between them.

K. W. Thompson, *Political Realism and the Crisis of World Politics* (1960). A searching examination of the bases of world peace.

Try reading recent works of fiction, drama, and poetry by such authors as A. Camus, J. P. Sartre, W. Faulkner, B. Pasternak, D. Thomas, and B. Brecht.

Index

EUROPE IN 1970
Members of the European Free Trade Association
Members of the European Economic Community (Common Market)
The Communist Bloc
Members of the North Atlantic Treaty Organization (N.A.T.O.)
Members of the Warsaw Pact
0
500
Miles
ICELAND
NORWA
Bergen
Oslo
SCOTLAND
UNITED KINGDOM OF GREAT BRITAIN AND NO. IRELAND
Glasgow
Edinburgh
Belfast
EIRE
Dublin
Cork
Manchester
WALES
ENGLAND
London
North Sea
DENMARK
Copenhagen
Malm
Hamburg
Weser R.
Elbe
Bremen
Ber
Potsdar
EAST GERMANY
Amsterdam
NETHERLANDS
Brussels
BELGIUM
LUX.
WEST GERMANY
Cologne
Bonn
Prag
CZEC
Nuremberg
Munich
Salzbu
AUSTR
ATLANTIC OCEAN
Le Havre
Rouen
Paris
Seine R.
Loire R.
Strasbourg
Rhine R.
FRANCE
Bay of Biscay
Berne
SWITZ.
Geneva
Lyon
Rhône R.
Bordeaux
Garonne R.
Toulouse
ANDORRA
Marseille
Milan
Venice
Turin
Po R.
Triest
Genoa
Florence
ITALY
Rome
Naples
CORSICA
SARDINIA
Tyrrhenian Sea
Palermo
SICILY
Oporto
PORTUGAL
Lisbon
Tagus R.
Madrid
Ebro R.
SPAIN
Barcelona
Seville
Guadalquivir R.
BALEARIC IS.
Strait of Gibraltar
* ALBANIA aligned with Communist China
* FINLAND aligned with Soviet Union by treaty
* YUGOSLAVIA Communist but independent of the Soviet Union

Murmansk
KOLA PENINSULA
Pechora R.
White Sea
Archangel
WEDEN
FINLAND
Gulf of Bothnia
L. Onega
Perm
L. Ladoga
RUSSIAN SOVIET FEDERATED
Helsinki
Leningrad
Gulf of Finland
Stockholm
Tallinn
Kazan
ESTONIAN S.S.R.
L. Peipus
SOCIALIST REPUBLIC
LATVIAN S.S.R.
Riga
Moscow
Dvina R.
Baltic Sea
LITHUANIAN S.S.R.
U. S. S. R.
Smolensk
Vilna
Kaliningrad
Minsk
Gdansk
BELORUSSIAN S.S.R.
KAZAKH S
Vistula R.
Warsaw
Volga R.
Wroclaw
Don R.
Volgograd
POLAND
Kiev
Kharkov
UKRAINIAN S.S.R.
Lvov
Dnieper R.
Donetsk
OVAKIA
Krivoi Rog
Rostov
Zhdanov
Casp
MOLDAVIAN S.S.R.
enna
Budapest
Sea of Azov
HUNGARY
Cluj
Odessa
CRIMEA
greb
RUMANIA
Yalta
Belgrade
GEORGIAN S.S.R.
Bucharest
YUGOSLAVIA
Black Sea
ARMENIAN
Sarajevo
Danube R.
Erevan
BULGARIA
Sofia
Istanbul
Tirana
ALBANIA
Salonika
Ankara
GREECE
TURKEY
Aegean Sea
Izmir
Adana
Athens
Aleppo
SYRIA
Euphrates
Tigris
Nicosia
CRETE
CYPRUS
IRAQ
LEBANON